D1171617

THE PRACTICE OF MARKETING

THE PRACTICE OF

MARKETING

Kenneth E. Runyon
Northern Arizona University

Charles E. Merrill Publishing Company
A Bell & Howell Company
Columbus Toronto London Sydney

Published by
Charles E. Merrill Publishing Company
A Bell & Howell Company
Columbus, Ohio 43216

This book was set in Korinna.
Photo Acquisitions Editor: Cynthia Donaldson
Text Design: Ann Mirels
Production Editor: Clare Wulker
Cover: Poster by Lev Moross

International Standard Book Number: 0-615-09886-6

Library of Congress Catalog Card Number: 81-84165

1 2 3 4 5 6 7 8 9 10 — 87 86 85 84 83 82

Printed in the United States of America

This book is dedicated to students of marketing, and to their professors who help prepare them for their business careers.

PREFACE

This book is intended as a text for a first course in marketing. It is the outgrowth of twenty years of experience in marketing management and twelve years' experience in teaching marketing in a university setting.

The book has been designed to introduce the student to the concepts and terminology that are a necessary part of a business school education. At the same time, the formal material has been leavened with examples and experiences from the real world of business. Thus, each chapter begins with two or three business examples pertinent to the material to be covered in the chapter. Other business examples are liberally sprinkled throughout the text in order to help students relate the concepts that are discussed to the practice of marketing as it is employed by business.

Of course, no one can learn how to market products and services by simply reading and studying a marketing text. One learns to analyze marketing data, to develop marketing strategies, and to formulate marketing plans by actually performing these operations—by learning from one's successes and failures. However, a marketing text can provide a valuable foundation of knowledge and understanding that will facilitate the learning process after entrance into the business field. I entered the field of marketing directly from an academic background in psychology. I knew nothing about business or the practice of marketing at the time that I was hired by a major advertising agency. Many of the mistakes that I made could have been avoided had I studied marketing in college.

This book has been organized in such a way as to facilitate the development of an understanding of the marketing process. It is divided into four parts, progressing from the general to the specific.

Part 1—The Nature of Marketing—provides the setting for the practice of marketing in the United States. The first chapter, The Business of Marketing, briefly, examines the economic system within which marketing occurs, emphasizing the competitive nature of this system and the necessity for business profits. It then defines the role of marketing in the business firm, considers the business firm in terms of its resources, discusses the controllable marketing activities, and the organization of the firm for the practice of marketing.

Succeeding chapters deal with the uncontrollable environmental variables that influence marketing plans and activities, discuss the concept of markets and marketing strategy, and provide a detailed outline and discussion of the marketing plan—the control document through which various marketing activities are coordinated.

Part 2—The Tools of Marketing—provides some helpful techniques for organizing and analyzing marketing data, discusses demographic trends, examines industrial markets, provides insights into the understanding of consumer behavior, introduces students to marketing research and test marketing, and discusses forecasting and its role in the marketing process.

Part 3—Marketing Communications and the Elements of Marketing—emphasizes the role of communications in a mass consumption society and recognizes that the elements of marketing—the product, brand names and packaging, pricing, channels of distribution, physical distribution, personal selling, advertising, sales promotion, and product publicity—are a part of the total communications process. And they are. If there is one thing that I learned in marketing products for some of the nation's leading companies it is that *all* of the foregoing marketing elements must be thought of and treated as channels of communication with intermediate customers and the ultimate consumer.

Finally, Part 4—Special Topics in Marketing—deals with areas that are growing in importance in today's world—International Marketing, Corporate Planning, and Business and Society.

Since marketing is an extremely broad and complex subject, it is not possible to cover all of its areas in detail in an introductory text. It follows that one must carefully choose what to include and the depth of treatment to be given to the subjects covered. I have made these choices on the basis of my experience with both the business world and with students. My intent has been to provide a balanced coverage that will serve the needs of both marketing majors and other business students who will take no further marketing courses.

As an aid to the learning process, each chapter ends with a set of review questions, a set of discussion questions, and a problem or case that may be used by instructors at their discretion. Further teaching aids are provided in the *Instructor's Manual.*

In the preparation of this book, I am indebted to many organizations and to many people—debts that can only be acknowledged, never repaid. I am indebted to the client organizations with which I have worked. I am indebted to the products I have marketed—both the successes and the failures. I am indebted to the Gardner Advertising Company and its people who taught me what marketing was all about. I am indebted to my colleagues at Northern Arizona University—Professors Corby, Grape, Straw, and Williams—whose patience and suggestions made the writing of this possible. I am particularly indebted to Terrence O'Brien of Kansas State University, Richard Berger of Fairleigh-Dickinson University, and Richard Hill of the University of Illinois at Urbana-Champaign who reviewed the manuscript and contributed many valuable suggestions.

Kenneth E. Runyon

CONTENTS

Marketing at work.
(Photo by Paul Conklin)

PART 1

THE NATURE OF MARKETING

Marketing, simply understood, is buying and selling. But, the practice of marketing in a modern, industrialized society is much more complex than this simple understanding implies. Marketing involves business firms, products, packages, distribution, advertising, personal selling, sales promotion, and a basic philosophy for conducting a business. In order to understand marketing, and to practice it well, marketing must be understood from the standpoint of the individual firm and the environment in which it operates.

Chapter 1 deals briefly with the economic system and with the role of the business firms which produce goods and services required by society. Each firm uses the elements of marketing in different ways, depending upon the nature of the industry, the size of the firm, and its philosophy of business. Yet, despite these differences, all firms are subject to certain internal constraints and problems, some of which will be identified and examined.

Chapter 2 deals with the uncontrollable factors of the external environment to which the practice of marketing must adapt if it is to be successful. The factors include cultural variables, demographics, levels of economic activity, technology, legal constraints, and consumerism. Since the primary focus of this text is marketing in the United States, we will deal with these variables within the context of the U.S. economy. In a later chapter, we will briefly examine some of the problems and challenges of international marketing.

Chapter 3 deals with markets and marketing strategy. Here, the concept of a market will be clarified, and the strategies of product differentiation and market segmentation developed.

In Chapter 4, we will turn our attention to the marketing plan and its role in the marketing of individual products. We will discuss the need for planning, the functions of the marketing plan, and dwell to a considerable extent on the structure and content of the marketing plan itself. This chapter will not only provide an understanding of the importance of the marketing plan for individual products, but will provide a detailed guide to its preparation.

In sum, these first four chapters will provide a framework for the rest of the text which will deal in greater detail with the various elements of marketing.

The Business of Marketing

- *The marketing economy.*
- *The role of profit in business.*
- *The importance of marketing and innovation in the conduct of a business.*
- *The marketing concept.*
- *The resources of the business firm.*
- *Controllable marketing activities.*
- *Organization and conflict in the business firm.*

MARKETING EXAMPLES

Most students taking a first course in marketing have only a vague idea of what marketing is all about, and precisely what it involves. Yet, all aspects of our daily lives are influenced by marketing activities, even though we may not think of it in these terms. Consider the following examples.

BRAND NAMES

Although the specific brands mentioned in the following narrative may vary, the pattern is much the same for many of us. After working all day we drive home in our Ford *Fairmont,* which is powered by Exxon gasoline and lubricated by *Penzoil,* and pass a dozen billboards advertising a variety of products. During the course of the day we may have sat at a *Shaw-Walker* desk, used a *Scripto* pencil or pen, read memoranda reproduced on a *Xerox,* made telephone calls on the *Bell* system, and used a *Dictaphone* for dictating letters to be typed on an *IBM* typewriter.

In the evening we may watch a *Sony* television set while drinking *Coca Cola* and eating *Planters* peanuts. During the course of the evening we are bombarded with commercials for *7-Up, Toyota, Dodge, Kellogg,* and *Oscar Mayer.* Nearby, children may be playing with *Fisher-Price* toys or teenagers may be listening to a *Panosonic* stereo. Before turning in for the night we have a glass of *Borden* milk or a dish of *Sealtest* ice cream, and toss a *Milkbone* dog bisquit to the dog. After brushing with *Crest* toothpaste, we set our *GE* alarm clocks, and fall blissfully to sleep on our *Perfect Sleeper* mattress and *Springmaid* sheets.

Each of the brands mentioned above is a product of marketing, and each makes our life a little easier or a little more pleasant.

MEDIA

The United States has the most fully developed commercial media network in the world. Some 1,600 daily newspapers have a total circulation of approximately 115 million; another 10,000 semiweekly,

weekly, biweekly, monthly, and bimonthly newspapers serve suburban communities, small towns, and rural areas. In addition, the nation boasts over 3,600 business and professional publications, and some 1,200 consumer and farm magazines. Over 1,000 local television stations serve some 75 million households, and 4,300 AM and 2,200 FM radio stations broadcast daily to over 400 million radio sets.

These media provide news, sports, drama, literature, music, and other forms of entertainment. And, they are all supported by marketing.

THE ECONOMY

In 1980, the gross national product of the United States approximated $2,200 billion. About 2.1 percent of this total (some $56.7 billion) was spent on advertising. The strength of the U.S. economy, and the standard of living that it has made possible for U.S. citizens, have been fueled by the marketing activities of over 14 million individual business firms.

These three examples emphasize the importance of marketing in most of our lives. Marketing provides us with products, jobs, transportation, news, and entertainment. None of us are immune to the effects of marketing, and some 40 percent of the U.S. labor force is directly engaged in marketing activities.

Many students, when they enter business, will be directly involved in some aspect of marketing. Others, while not directly involved, will interact on a day-to-day basis with those who are. As a consequence, a knowledge of what marketing is, and an understanding of basic marketing concepts, may well be a valuable asset in their business careers.

Marketing, as a concept and as a business practice, is much more complex than many of us imagine. In order to understand marketing well, we must view it from both a *macro* and a *micro* perspective.

MACROMARKETING

Macromarketing refers to the economic system that characterizes a society. All nations have an economic system. Such a system is necessary to facilitate the exchange of goods, to provide income for a nation's population, to maintain national strength, and to provide for human needs. Not all nations have the same kind of economic system, however, even though the purposes that an economic system serve are the same in all instances. Differences in economic systems arise because of fundamentally different beliefs about how the economic needs of a society can best be met.

Underlying all economic systems is the basic problem of *distributive justice.* Simply stated, distributive justice refers to the ways in which an organized society distributes its benefits and burdens among its members. Distributive justice is a perplexing national problem for three reasons:

- Individual members of society differ in their willingness and/or ability to contribute to society's welfare.
- The aggregate needs of a society (sometimes referred to as "wants") are infinite.
- The resources necessary to meet these needs are limited.

The task of devising an equitable basis for distributing limited resources within a society where members have infinite needs and make differential contributions to society's welfare is a thankless and dismal task. For this reason, economics is sometimes referred to as the "dismal science." Before examining possible economic solutions to the problem of distributive justice, let's look at the three dimensions of this problem more carefully.

Differential Contributions by Society's Members

Although all people may be born equal in terms of human dignity, they are not equal in terms of human ability. Some are more intelligent than others; some more creative. Others have greater physical strength and agility. Still others have greater artistic or musical talent. In addition to these innate differences, people differ in the extent to which they are willing or able to develop their natural capacities. Two individuals, with comparable innate capacities, may develop these capacities differently. One, through a combination of fortuitous circumstances, ambition, and hard work, becomes a brillant physician. The other, for a variety of reasons, may become barely literate and be confined to the performance of menial tasks. Obviously, the value of the contributions that these individuals can make to society's welfare will differ.

How should these two individuals be rewarded by society? Equally? Differently? If differently, what should be the magnitude of the difference? This is one of the problems of distributive justice.

Aggregate Needs Are Infinite

Each individual in society has a variety of needs and, in the aggregate, these needs are infinite. We have needs for food, clothing, shelter, protection, education, medical care, status, recognition, and prestige—to mention only a few of our generic needs. Many, if not all of these necessities require economic resources for their satisfaction. If economic resources were unlimited, there would be no problem, at least in the economic sense. Unfortunately, economic resources are not unlimited. They are finite. Thus, decisions have to be made about which needs will be met, and how fully they should be satisfied. These are problems of distributive justice.

Limited Resources

Historically blessed with a relative abundance of natural resources and productive capacity, some nations have met the needs of their populations better than others. Nonetheless, inadequate supplies of food, clothing, and shelter on a worldwide basis have been a scourge of mankind throughout recorded history. Even relatively affluent societies have been unable to abolish poverty.

Shortages exist, not only in raw materials, but also in productive capacity, skilled personnel, transportation, and capital fund formation. The Club of Rome, in a pessimistic survey of world resources, published a dreary forecast of future supplies of raw materials.[1] Robert Heilbroner, an eminent economic philosopher, has painted a bleak picture of worldwide shortages of energy, raw materials, and food.[2] Recently, lack of available supplies of petroleum-based fuels has created a worldwide energy crisis which has disrupted industrial growth, increased the cost of transportation, played havoc with the balance of payments among nations, and threatened the world monetary system. Continued population growth has placed increasing burdens upon existing resources, the arms race has diverted productive capacity away from more constructive uses, and wars have savaged agricultural capacity in many parts of the world. Today, widespread famine is a grim reality in many parts of the world; the World Bank has estimated that 700 million people are seriously malnourished and that hunger is directly and indirectly implicated in millions of deaths each year.[3]

Within these perspectives, the problems of the world appear unsolvable, and may well be. Yet, within the world community, individual societies still must face the pragmatic problem of how they shall order their internal economic affairs, and how they will allocate their resources. For individuals, this translates into such practical questions as:

Who will own a home?

Who will have a car?

Who will have an education?

Who will receive medical care?

Who will have a refrigerator?

Who will eat steak?

What salaries will be paid for different jobs?

These are some of the questions with which distributive justice must deal.

As nations answer these questions reasonably well, they survive and prosper. As they answer them poorly, they are torn by internal dissent and civil strife, and may fall prey to more successful and politically aggressive neighbors.

TYPES OF ECONOMIC SYSTEMS

Every society, if it is to survive, must find some way of reconciling the disparity between supply and demand, between limited resources and unlimited needs. Generally, there are two polar approaches which nations have taken in ordering their economic affairs—*planned economies* and *free economies.* Planned economies and free economies differ in three major dimensions:

- The ownership of productive capacity.
- The extent to which the government allocates resources and provides for the welfare of its citizens through government-sponsored programs to equalize income.
- The extent to which the political affairs of the society are rooted in relatively free, democratic processes, or dominated by an authoritarian political system.

No economy is either totally free or totally planned. And, mixed economies vary substantially in the degree of government influence present.

1. The Club of Rome, *The Limits of Growth* (New York: Universe Books, 1972).

2. Robert Heilbroner, *An Inquiry into the Human Prospect* (New York: W. W. Norton and Co., 1974).

3. *World Hunger and Malnutrition: Improving the U.S. Response,* A Report to the President by the World Hunger Working Group (Washington, DC: U.S. Government Printing Office, Stock Number 041-002-00013-1), p. 9.

Further, some economies are in a state of transition. A case in point is the United Kingdom. Under the leadership of the Labor party that dominated United Kingdom governance since World War II, Great Britain moved substantially in the direction of a planned economy. However, with the election of a Tory government led by Prime Minister Margaret Thatcher in 1979, the British began showing signs of moving in the direction of a free economy.

Planned Economies

Superficially, a planned economy appears to be the simplest, most rational way of resolving the conflict between supply and demand. Someone in society—a central committee or government—identifies goals beneficial to society as a whole and then allocates resources to achieve those goals during a specified period of time. As new societal needs arise, resources may be used to meet them. Salaries and wages are controlled by the government either through taxes or decree. The government uses prices to regulate demand, and the entire system emerges as a straightforward, intellectual process emphasizing efficiency and rational planning.

Unfortunately, the planned economy is not as simple as it sounds. Failure to identify consumer needs properly, conflicts in priorities among planners, inability to coordinate and control the execution of the plan, and the rigidity of the entire process turn an apparently rational process of allocation into an exercise in frustration, bureaucratic bungling, and corruption. Products that consumers want are underproduced, and planned economies are plagued with chronic shortages. Products that are overproduced or rejected by consumers because of shoddy workmanship pile up in useless inventories, and the promise of efficiency is sabotaged by wasted resources and unwanted merchandise.[4]

Free Economies

Free economies, often referred to as *marketing economies,* differ from planned economies in that they appear to operate without conscious planning. No central committee or government agency determines the needs of society and allocates its resources. This is not to say that planning does not exist. Rather, planning is done primarily at the level of the individual business firm, within broad constraints established by the government.

Adam Smith first described the marketing system in the *Wealth of Nations,* published in 1776. He described an economic system that recognized *self-interest* as the primary motivation underlying human behavior, and devised a way to harness this powerful motivational force in the service of society. The basic assumption underlying a marketing economy is that members of society are best able to determine their own needs, and should be left free to pursue their own self-interest without government interference. Supply and demand are regulated by the price mechanism. That is, products are produced that consumers are willing to pay for, and consumers pay for those products they want. The consumers' "votes," measured in dollars of purchasing power, determine resource allocation automatically. Producers are free to make whatever products they choose in the quantities they are willing to produce. The only restriction on producers' actions is their ability to induce consumers to purchase their products. If the producer sells all or most of what is produced at a price that is greater than the costs, there will be a profit. Producers unable to sell the total production at a satisfactory price, will suffer a loss and, in extreme cases, be forced out of business. Failure in one business does not preclude shifting to another, provided the capital required to start the new enterprise is available. And, producers are free to raise capital by all legal means.

The entire thrust of the marketing economy is based on four concepts:

Freedom of choice. Consumers are free to spend their incomes for those goods and services that meet their particular needs.

Freedom to produce. Producers are free to enter any business they choose, provided they can raise the capital assets to do so.

4. For a discussion of some of the problems of a planned economy, see Hedrick Smith, *The Russians* (New York: Quadrangle/The New York Times Book Co., 1976).

Freedom of competition. Each producer is free to compete with other producers for the consumers' spending power. With success in this competition comes prosperity and growth. Failure means displacement or being forced out of business. In short, producers are free to succeed and free to fail.

Freedom from government. The government remains aloof from the business enterprise. Government's primary function in the business realm is to provide an equitable system for adjudicating contractual disagreements that may arise during the normal course of business.

Smith characterized the operation of the marketing system as the "invisible hand." As each individual pursues self interest, the *invisible hand of competition* obtains maximum benefits for individuals as well as for society as a whole.

As is the case with planned societies, the marketing system did not function as smoothly as its promise implied. Competition is not perfect. Some business organizations are more effective than others, and monopolies and oligopolies developed. Some entrepreneurs, through fraud and greed, victimized both consumers and society by producing seriously contaminated and patently harmful items. Product misrepresentation was rampant. Government regulation was required to curb abuses, and to enable the system to operate as it was intended.

Today, the basic concept of the marketing system has survived as the driving force in many industrialized countries, particularly in the United States and, to a lesser extent, in South America, Western Europe, and parts of Asia. Not without fault, the marketing system has proved itself a remarkable instrument for increasing national wealth, raising living standards, creating opportunity for individuals, and providing an almost endless array of goods and services from which consumers may choose.

The Economy of the United States

The United States is a leading exponent of the marketing system. Freedom of choice for the consumer, freedom to produce for the manufacturer, and freedom to compete are all basic ingredients in the U.S. economy. Competition among producers exists as a national policy of the U.S. government, and federal legislation has been enacted to discourage monopolies and unfair competition. The government has also intervened to protect consumers from harmful products, mislabeling, fraud, and deceit. Acting to prohibit irresponsible exploitation of the environment and of workers, the government has encouraged the growth of labor unions to protect workers' rights.

Many believe that the government has sometimes violated good judgment in these areas and, by doing so, impaired the nation's economic health. These criticisms of government intervention in business reached a peak in the late 1970s; the national elections of 1980 were interpreted by many as a rebuke to the government for interference in the nation's economic affairs.

Fundamentally, however, competition is a way of life for the U.S. producer. Within the constraints of federal and state legislation, each manufacturer and seller must compete with others for the consumers' bounty. Competition exists in all areas; in many it is intense. The success of a business enterprise depends upon its ability to persuade consumers to purchase its products; and consumers are only persuaded by products that meet their needs.

MICROMARKETING

Micromarketing is concerned with the operation of individual business firms as they function within the constraints and under the economic philosophy of the macromarketing system. *The focus of this text is on micromarketing—the activities of individual business firms as they compete for the purchasing power of consumers within the framework of a free or marketing economy.*

Individual business firms are the basic building blocks of a marketing economy; operation of various firms makes the system function. In the remainder of this chapter, we will examine the size and structure of U.S. business, the role of profit, marketing and innovation, resources of the firm, organization of the firm, and conflict within the firm.

TABLE 1–1: Ownership of U.S. Business Firms
SOURCE: *Statistical Abstracts of the United States: 1979* Table 915.

Ownership	1965 Thousands	1965 Percent	1970 Thousands	1970 Percent	1975 Thousands	1975 Percent
Proprietorships	9,078	79.5%	9,400	78.3%	10,332	77.8%
Partnerships	914	8.0	936	7.8	1,073	7.7
Corporations	1,424	12.5	1,665	13.9	2,024	14.5
Total	11,416	100.0%	12,001	100.0%	13,429	100.0%

TABLE 1–2: Annual Receipts of U.S. Business Firms in 1974
SOURCE: *Statistical Abstracts of the United States: 1979* Table 917.

Size group	Number in Thousands	Percent	Receipts in Billions	Percent
Under $25,000	9,142	65.8%	$54.2	1.6%
$25,000–$49,999	1,506	10.8	52.4	1.6
$50,000–$99,999	1,228	8.8	85.3	2.6
$100,000–$499,999	1,512	10.9	315.2	9.5
$500,000–$999,999	241	1.7	162.7	4.9
$1,000,000 +	273	2.0	2,650.5	79.8
Total	13,902	100.0%	$3,320.3	100.0%

TABLE 1–3: U.S. Firms and Receipts Classified by Industry in 1975
SOURCE: *Statistical Abstracts of the United States: 1979* Table 916.

Industry	Number in Thousands	Percent	Receipts in Billions	Percent
Agriculture, forestry, and fishing	3,546	25.4%	$ 108.5	3.0%
Mining	86	0.6	71.2	2.0
Construction	1,144	8.2	186.7	5.2
Manufacturing	468	3.3	1,273.8	35.3
Transportation and public utilities	453	3.2	247.2	6.8
Wholesale and retail trade	3,001	21.5	1,145.0	31.8
Finance, insurance and real estate	1,590	11.4	360.3	10.0
Service	3,669	26.3	211.9	5.9
Not allocatable to individual industries	21	0.1	1.0	–
Total	13,978	100.0%	$3,605.6	100.0%

THE SIZE AND STRUCTURE OF U.S. BUSINESS

Approximately 14 million firms do business in the United States. In 1979 the largest seller was Exxon, with sales of $79.1 billion, assets of $49.5 billion, and 169,000 employees. The smallest? Who knows? A corner delicatessen, or a local cabinet shop, or a Tasty-Freeze doing a few thousand dollars of business a year, owned and operated by a proprietor whose children work there after school and on weekends.

Statistical Abstracts defines a business firm as *a business organization under a single management which may include one or more plants or outlets.* Thus, a giant retailer, such as Sears, Roebuck and Company is a single business firm as is a "mom & pop" grocery outlet. Exxon, with receipts of $79.1 billion is a single business firm, as is a small, independent gasoline station whose owner barely makes ends meet.

Tables 1–1, 1–2, and 1–3 summarize some of the characteristics of the U.S. business community. Examination of these tables indicates that business firms may differ in a variety of ways: in the type of ownership, in size, and in the industries in which they compete. Note that the volume of business is heavily concentrated in a relatively small number of firms: 2 percent of the business firms account for 79.8 percent of business receipts, whereas 65.8 percent of the firms account for only 1.6 percent of receipts.[5]

Despite these differences, however, all firms have one thing in common: They all require profits to support their operations.

THE ROLE OF PROFIT

Earlier, we noted that self-interest is a driving force in a marketing economy. Although self-interest may manifest itself in a variety of forms in a business enterprise—power, recognition, and status to mention a few—*monetary profit* is the indispensible condition for privately-owned businesses. Ultimately, profit is the rationale for business and, in order to survive, a business must make a profit. This does not mean that a real world business seeks to maximize profit. Indeed, the concept of profit maximization is too ambiguous a concept to be applied to the operation of a real world business.[6]

Practically, profit serves three—and only three—functions in a business enterprise:

- Profit rewards investors for their investments in the firm, normally in the form of dividends or capital gains for stockholders or owners.
- Profit is a source of future capital, either through retained earnings or by establishing a record of profitable operation that facilitates obtaining future funds through stock offerings, loans from financial institutions, or bond offerings.
- Profit is an unequivocal measure of operational efficiency, serving as a common basis of comparison that can be applied to companies, to divisions, and to products.

As a consequence, although profit is an essential component of business, most firms seek a satisfactory profit, not profit maximization. That is, firms' managers seek that level of profits demanded by stockholders or owners, or that level perceived to be required for business needs. In any case, profits are a form of self-interest that sustains private investment and keeps business firms solvent.

In order to make a profit, however, a firm must create customers because only through

5. This data, compiled in *Statistical Abstracts of the United States: 1979,* was derived from U.S. Internal Revenue Service preliminary reports: *Statistics of Income, Business Income Tax Returns,* and *Statistics of Income, Corporation Income Tax.* Note that although this represents the most recent information compiled by the U.S. Government in this form, it is based on information for 1974 and 1975. As a consequence, the number of firms shown is probably somewhat less than the actual number existing today. Further, because of the high inflation rate during the latter half of the 1970s, business receipts are considerably understated in comparison to current business receipts. Nonetheless, the relationships between the size of firms and the receipts they generate are probably substantially correct, even for today's economy.

6. Profit maximization is a normative, economic concept applicable only to a closed system in which all costs, prices, and outcomes are known. It also requires perfectly objective decision makers. These conditions do not prevail in the real world of business. Nonetheless, the term "profit maximization" is widely, if incorrectly, applied to business operations to mean "making as much as possible," either in the short or long term. For discussions of profit maximization, see: James G. March and Herbert A. Simon, *Organizations* (New York: John Wiley & Sons, 1958), pp. 140–141; Herbert A. Simon, "Theories of Decision Making in Economics and Behavioral Sciences," *American Economic Review,* Vol. 19 (June, 1959): 262–65; Joel Dean, *Managerial Economics* (Englewood Cliffs, NJ: Prentice Hall, Inc., 1951), p. 28; and Peter F. Drucker, *Management* (New York: Harper & Row, Publishers, 1974), pp. 59–61.

We've come a long way since the general store. (Photo courtesy of Safeway Stores, Inc.)

customers does a firm derive the income that makes profit possible.

MARKETING AND INNOVATION

Regardless of its size, ownership, or the industry segment which it serves, the purpose of a business firm is to create customers. This has led Peter Drucker, a highly respected management consultant and business writer, to identify *marketing* and *innovation* as the basic functions of a business. According to Drucker: "Because its purpose is to create a customer, the business enterprise has two—and only these two—basic functions: marketing and innovation. Marketing and innovation produce results; all the rest are costs."[7]

Manufacturing, finance, accounting, personnel, data processing, and a variety of other business activities are, indeed, costs because they are simply the support systems for a firm's marketing efforts.

7. Peter Drucker, *Management* (New York: Harper & Row, Publishers, 1974), p. 61–62.

This does not mean, however, that these activities are nonessential. On the contrary, one cannot run a large, complex business without them. *Manufacturing* produces the products that are marketed. *Finance* provides the funds necessary for capital investment and often for short-term cash flow. *Accounting* develops records and information necessary for determining profit and for allocating and controlling expenses. *Personnel* is the source of competent people and equitable compensation plans. And *data processing* is an invaluable tool for storing and analyzing large quantities of data for all parts of a business organization. *But, there is no income and no profit until a sale is made, and sales are a fundamental part of marketing.*

Marketing

All business firms are involved in marketing. They may do it well, or they may do it badly, but they can't avoid marketing if they wish to stay in business. It is simply not true that, if you build a better mousetrap, the world will beat a path to your door. Many people have built better mousetraps, some truly fascinating devices, and gone broke in the

FIGURE 1–1: *Internal Communications*

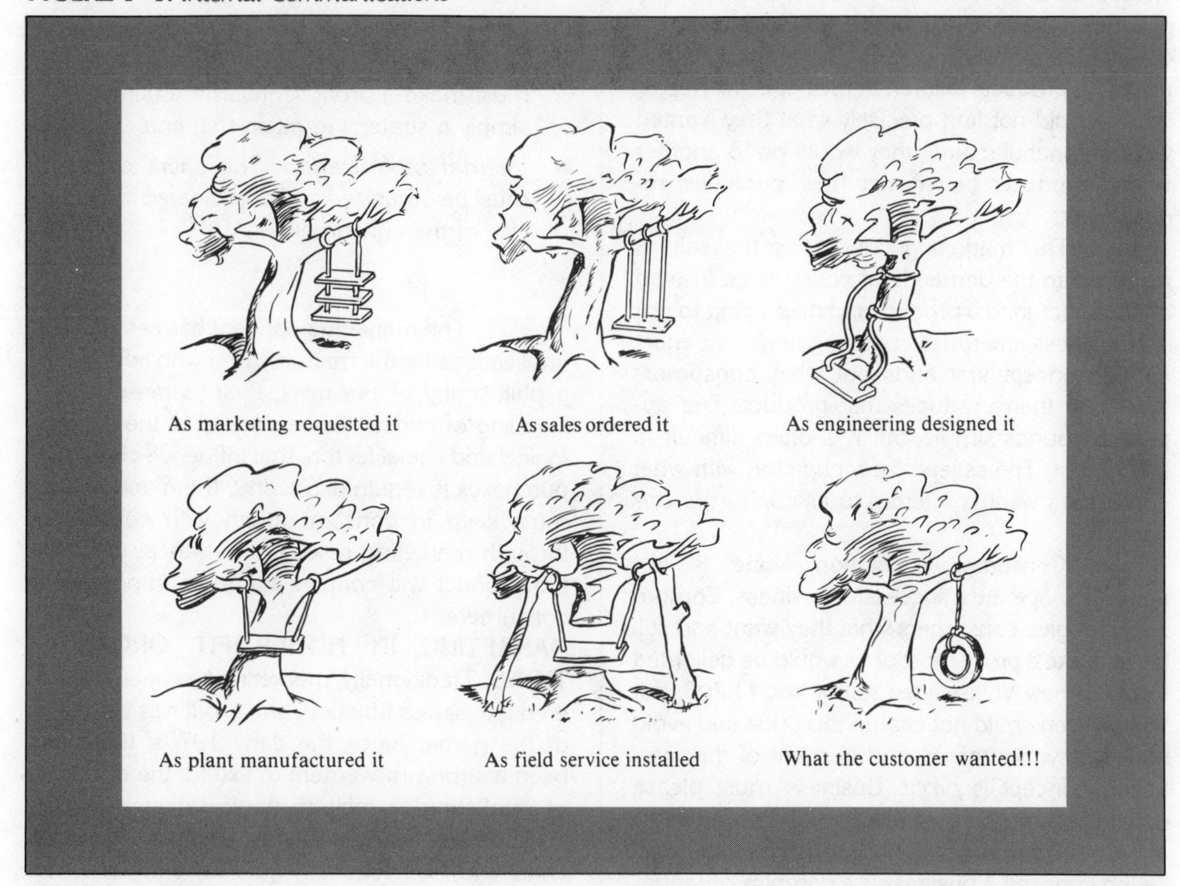

process. In order to be salable, a product must not only serve some useful function, but also be designed, packaged, and priced so that consumers will want to buy it. Even this is not enough. Consumers must be told about the product, and it must be available for them to purchase with at least a reasonable amount of convenience.

Marketing has been defined in many ways. One definition that has been recommended by the American Marketing Association's Committee on Definitions is *Marketing is the performance of business activities that direct the flow of goods and services from producer to consumer or user.*[8]

8. *Marketing Definitions,* compiled by Ralph S. Alexander and the Committee on Definitions of the American Marketing Association (Chicago: American Marketing Association, 1960), p. 15.

In order to make this marketing definition meaningful in terms of the individual business firm, however, it must be related to the marketing concept.

THE MARKETING CONCEPT. The marketing concept is the central theory of marketing which has emerged as the response of business to changes in the economic environment. During its history, the United States economy has grown from an undeveloped to a highly developed one, and the nation from an agricultural society with few manufacturing facilities to an industrial society that produces an almost infinite variety of manufactured goods in a constant stream. The growth of manufacturing facilities, along with the development of an extensive system of distribution, became so great that consumers could demand choice and variety in the things they purchased. Businessmen found they could no longer produce a product, distribute it, and high pressure consumers into buying it. Consumers began demanding products tailored to their specific needs. If they could not find precisely what they wanted with one manufacturer, they would go to another whose products better met their particular requirements.

The marketing concept is the seller's response to the demands of consumers. Instead of manufacturing a product and then trying to sell it, a business enterprise operating under the marketing concept first finds out what consumers want and then produces that product. The approach sounds simple, but it is often difficult to implement. The sellers' preoccupation with what consumers want is referred to as *consumer orientation.*

Consumer orientation alone is not enough to operate a successful business. Companies can give consumers what they want and still fail to make a profit. Most of us would be delighted to buy a new Volkswagen Rabbit for $1,200, but Volkswagen could not charge this price and avoid bankruptcy. So, the second element of the marketing concept is *profit.* Business must please consumers, but it must also make a profit.

There is still a third element in the marketing concept: A business is a complex organization, requiring communication and coordination within the enterprise. Decisions at one level or in one division of a business operation may be cancelled out unconsciously or intentionally by activities at another level or in another sector. The product designed with the consumer in mind may be sabotaged by a cost-conscious production department. The effort of a salesperson to build warm customer relations may be erased by the thoughtless decision of a credit manager. To avoid such errors, a consumer orientation must permeate the entire enterprise, and the company must be organized for the service of consumers. Lack of such coordination may lead to the humorous situation depicted in Figure 1–1.

To summarize, the marketing concept is made up of three parts:

- *Consumer orientation.* The products of the firm must be created with consumer needs in mind.
- *Profit.* In serving the consumer, the enterprise must make a profit. Consumer orientation is simply a strategy to attain that end.
- *Internal organization.* The entire company must be organized and coordinated in the service of the consumer.

The marketing concept has certain clear implications for the manufacturer who adopts it as a philosophy of business. *First,* a basic understanding of consumer needs and of the psychological and social factors that influence consumer purchases is required. *Second,* the manufacturer must keep in constant touch with consumers through marketing research so that, at all times, the product will contain attributes important to consumers.

MARKETING IN NONPROFIT ORGANIZATIONS. Traditionally, marketing has been considered a business function, and profit was the name of the game. Since the early 1970s, there has been a strong movement to extend the definition of marketing to include nonbusiness organizations as well—organizations such as churches, charitable institutions, government, and so forth.[9]

Those who support this extended definition of marketing argue that many marketing activities can be used in support of causes and organizations for which economic profit is not a major objective. Of course, they can. Many of the tools of marketing—objective and systematic thinking, identification of target groups for persuasion, paid communications (advertising), and so forth can be applied to many other areas of human activity.

Critics of this point of view, while agreeing that many marketing activities can be applied to nonprofit organizations and causes, insist that marketing is more than a "bundle of techniques"; it also involves a body of theory, a system of eth-

9. Philip Kotler and Sidney J. Levy, "Broadening the Concept of Marketing," *Journal of Marketing* (Jan. 1969): 1–15.

FIGURE 1–2: *Resources, Constraints, and Major Lines of Influence in a Business Firm*

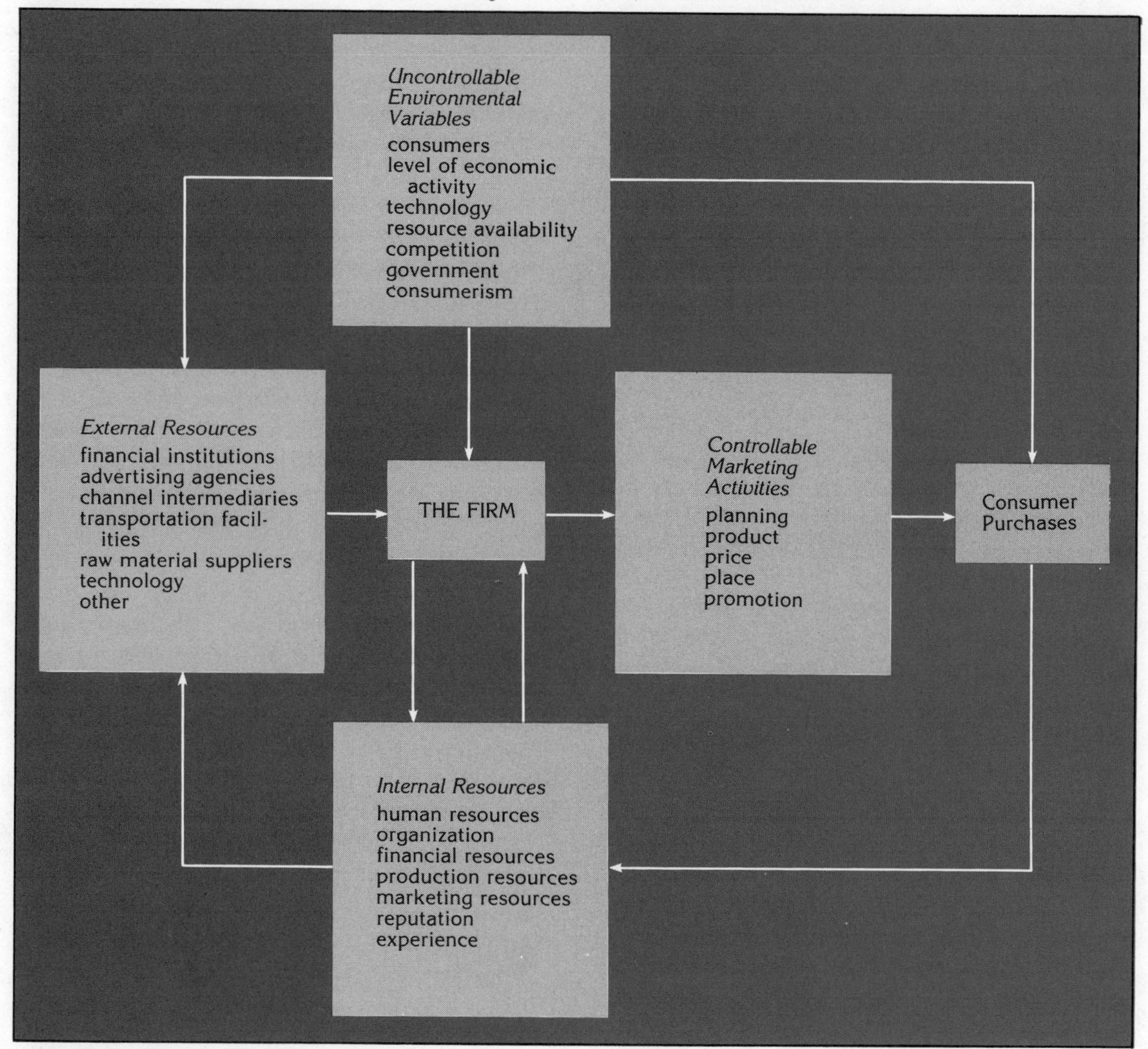

ics, and an economic philosophy that may not be applicable to charitable foundations, churches, politics, and other nonprofit endeavors.

While recognizing that marketing may have application in nonbusiness areas, this text will be devoted to marketing in a business context under the assumption that most students are interested in the traditional applications of marketing. Those who are interested in nonbusiness marketing are referred to *Marketing for Nonprofit Organizations* by Philip Kotler.

Innovation

Innovation is the second key function of a business firm. Innovation may be defined as *the introduction of some new thing or method.* Innovation enables a firm to develop products and services more appealing to consumers than those offered by their competitors. Innovation also enables organizations to reduce costs, devise useful analytical techniques, organize data in new and meaningful ways, improve employee relations, and increase productivity.

In a competitive environment, innovation is often the key to survival, and innovative firms are the ones that tend to dominate industries. Yet, innovation is also the Achilles' heel of most business firms because most firms are not highly innovative. The entire field of business is filled with people who are excellent at copying what others have done, but not very good at doing things in new and interesting ways. When a new, innovative product appears on the market and is successful, competitors flock to copy the product and flood the market with imitations. When an innovative and effective television commercial appears, the airways are shortly filled with imitators. And, when a new marketing research or analytical technique becomes public, everyone jumps on the bandwagon. This means that innovation for a successful firm is not a one-time thing, but a continuous process that provides a constant challenge to a firm's ingenuity.

Since the performance of a firm in a marketing economy is intimately bound up in marketing and innovation, the firm's resources should support these functions.

RESOURCES OF THE FIRM

Regardless of size, or industry, or ownership, all firms have resources. Sometimes the resources are inadequate for the task at hand. Sometimes they are poorly used. Nonetheless, the way in which a firm uses its resources is often critical to its survival.

Figure 1–2 is a graphic representation of a firm's resources, constraints, and major lines of influence. Among the constraints are the uncontrollable environmental forces which will be discussed in Chapter 2. Let's focus our attention on the other major boxes in the diagram—on the internal resources of the firm, on its external resources, and on its controllable marketing activities.

Internal Resources

The major internal resources of a firm are its organization; human, financial, research and development, production, and marketing resources; reputation; and experience. The quantity and quality of these internal resources directly influence the firm's performance as a marketing entity. For all practical purposes, the firm controls these resources and the ways they are used.

Organization. A firm must have good people organized in an effective and efficient manner, and set to tasks that they have been trained to handle.

Human Resources. All firms are made up of people, although the competencies of these people may vary widely from firm to firm, and even within the firm itself. The selection, training, supervision, and compensation of a firm's human resources is one of the most critical areas of its operation.

Financial Resources. Most new businesses fail because they have insufficient financial resources to survive their first few months of operation. Many established businesses fail because they dissipate their financial resources on a multiplicity of products, or on poor investments. Obviously, companies differ widely in their financial resources. There is no comparison between the financial capabilities of Procter & Gamble and those of the local doughnut shop. Yet, for both, financial resources are a company resource that can be squandered or used wisely.

Research and Development (R&D) Resources. Firms vary widely in their R&D capacity. Yet, in a competitive industry, the success or failure of R&D activities is eventually mirrored in the success or failure of the firm. Not all firms have a R&D facility. Not all firms can afford one. Often, firms with limited or nonexistent R&D facilities turn to outside suppliers for this function.

Production Resources. Production resources often confer benefits and impose restrictions on a firm's capabilities. A company with modern, efficient production resources can turn out competitive products at competitive prices. Conversely, the firm that permits its manufacturing facility to become outmoded, inflexible, or inefficient is at a competitive disadvantage. At any given point, production facilities may be an asset or a liability depending upon the firm's marketing needs.

Marketing Resources. Some firms have excellent marketing capabilities; some virtually none. Some companies are extremely capable of marketing certain products or to particular customer groups, while lacking the skills to market other products or to other audiences.

Reputation. The reputation of a firm may be an asset or a liability. For example, the Sara Lee name is an asset in marketing frozen foods, particularly frozen desserts. However, the name Sara Lee would be a liability in marketing industrial equipment because it is not known in this field. Although reputation refers to ways in which others perceive a firm, the company's reputation is an internal asset because the activities of a company shape it.

Experience. The experience of a company, as reflected in the knowledge and competencies of its people, is a real but somewhat intangible asset. An experienced company avoids mistakes that a less experienced rival may blunder into. And, production experience has been demonstrated to be a major factor in reducing production costs.

Marketing cannot be divorced from the internal resources of a firm. These resources determine the character of a firm's marketing programs. In the short term, lack of internal resources often act as a restraint on a firm's marketing activities. In the long term, internal resources are under the direct control of the firm, are shaped by management policies and decisions, and affect the degree of marketing success that will be achieved.

External Resources

In addition to its internal resources, a firm also has access to a number of external resources. (See Figure 1–2.) The existence of these resources, as well as the extent to which they are used by a particular firm, has a direct influence on the nature and scope of the firm's marketing activities. For example, a system of channel intermediaries—wholesalers, jobbers, brokers, retailers, and so forth—exists in most product fields. If a firm chooses to use these channel intermediaries—and often it has no viable alternative—it must gear its internal organization to work with them. In some instances, a firm may choose to bypass existing channel structures and devise its own system for getting products to the ultimate consumers. This approach is used by firms that sell by direct mail; firms that sell door-to-door, such as Fuller Brush, Avon, and Amway; firms that establish their own company-owned stores; and firms that establish franchises. Direct selling to consumers is not feasible for most consumer products, however, and various channel intermediaries must be used.

Similarly, all firms are dependent to a greater or lesser extent upon existing transportation facilities to transport raw material to their place of manufacture and to ship products to distributors. Most firms are dependent upon financial institutions for generating capital funds and some, but not all firms, use external sources for advertising counsel and for technology.

Although firms cannot control the activities of external resources, they may be able to exert a great deal of influence over the services offered by them. For example, Safeway, as a valued customer, can obtain greater service and more concessions from outside suppliers than can the proprieter of a small, independent grocery outlet; General Motors, because of its economic power, can influence the policies of many of its suppliers; and any firm that has an excellent record of profitability can obtain capital funds more easily, and often at less cost, than firms with a poor history of earnings.

Controllable Marketing Activities

Controllable marketing activities (Figure 1–2) are those marketing variables over which a firm has direct control. Jerome McCarthy has referred to these variables as the *four P's,* a designation that is widely used in marketing circles.[10] The four P's—*Product, Place, Promotion,* and *Price*—represent basic areas of marketing decisions. To the four P's, I have chosen to add a fifth P—*Planning*—to emphasize that an effective marketing

10. E. Jerome McCarthy, *Basic Marketing: A Managerial Approach,* 6th ed. (Homewood, IL: Richard D. Irwin, Inc., 1978), p. 7–8.

program doesn't happen by chance; it is a thoughtfully designed undertaking. Although separate chapters will be devoted to each of these variables, let us examine each of them briefly in order to better understand their dimensions.

Product. The term *product,* as it is used in the four P's, is an inclusive term which contains three separate, but interrelated variables, namely:

- The physical product itself and some combination of product services.
- The product name.
- The product package.

In order to be successful, a firm must develop a product, product name, and product package that are appealing to a large enough group of consumers to justify developmental and marketing costs. Not all consumers are interested in the same products. A dry dog food, for example, has little value to consumers who do not own dogs. Even among dog owners, the product attributes sought by consumers vary widely. The owner of a "working dog" requires a dog food with a higher food value (calories) than the owner of a household pet. For adequate nutrition, puppies require more protein and other nutritional ingredients than do mature dogs. And, some dog owners prefer canned foods for their pets rather than dry foods because of greater palatability. Similar differences exist in other product fields, so that individual firms have considerable discretion in formulating the specific products that will be sold. Even wider discretion exists in package design and product name. The point is that the producer controls this aspect of the marketing effort, and wise decisions are essential to marketing success.

Decisions, decisions, decisions. (Photo by Rick Smolan)

PLACE. A second, controllable marketing variable is the place of sale. Some firms sell directly to the ultimate consumer through direct mail, company representatives, or company-owned outlets. Others use a chain of channel intermediaries, such as wholesalers, jobbers, and retail stores. The particular sequence of intermediaries used in getting a product from the producer to the ultimate consumer is called the *channel of distribution.*

Conceptually, at least, producers have control over the particular channels of distribution they employ. Practically, they often do not. The producer of grocery products who wishes to reach the mass grocery market has little choice but to sell through food stores. Further, distribution does not occur automatically by executive fiat. Channel intermediaries often refuse to stock a producer's product because they already carry similar products and do not believe it would be profitable to add another.

In other instances, however, choosing the correct channel of distribution is critical to reach particular consumer groups. The firm that markets fashion merchandise to sophisticated consumers would be wise to select I. Magnum, Sak's Fifth Avenue, and Bonwit-Teller rather than K-Mart, Fed-Mart, or Yellow Front. And, deciding whether to seek *intensive* distribution through mass outlets rather than *selective* distribution through a small number of specialty stores is often a critical marketing decision.

PROMOTION. The term *promotion,* like the term *product,* is an inclusive one that involves a number of activities. Traditionally, personal selling, advertising, sales promotion, and product publicity are included in the definition of promotion. The value of these different promotional activities vary by product and industry, however. Firms that market highly technical products to a limited number of industrial customers may find that advertising is of little value, and choose to concentrate their promotional efforts in personal selling by technically trained salespeople. By contrast, producers of household detergents may find that extensive advertising is essential to influence the ultimate consumer.

PRICE. Price is the fourth marketing variable over which a firm has control. Within limits, a firm may price its products at whatever level it chooses. The limits, of course, are *costs* and *consumer acceptance.* No firm can price its products below cost for any extended period of time and expect to remain in business. At the same time, there are limits to what consumers are able and willing to pay for various products. Since pricing and pricing strategies will be discussed in a later chapter, we need only note at this point that pricing is a competitive tool that carries implications of quality as well as economy. In addition, pricing is an important variable in formulating an effective marketing strategy.

PLANNING. The purpose of planning is to enable a firm to make judicious decisions, and to carry them out well. Planning has a number of functions and dimensions that will be discussed in later chapters. However, one important dimension of marketing planning involves the ways in which marketing practitioners manipulate the controllable marketing variables—Product, Place, Promotion, and Price—in an effort to develop an effective marketing program. The term *marketing mix* has been coined to describe this manipulation.[11]

Products may have many different physical and performance characteristics; packages may be designed in a variety of ways; the possibilities for brand names are infinite; different channels of distribution can be used; different prices can be charged; advertising can take many forms, both in the appeals used and the media in which it appears; and sales promotion activities are almost endless in form and variety. The task of the marketing firm is to find the proper mix for these ingredients to appeal to particular consumer groups.

The number of possible marketing mixes is exceedingly large, and the task of the marketing planner is to devise the right mix for the right market at the right time.

The use and coordination of a firm's resources in order to develop an effective marketing plan is not a simple undertaking. Further, marketing is done best in firms specifically designed to perform marketing's tasks. This brings us to the idea of a marketing organization.

ORGANIZATION FOR MARKETING

Whenever two or more people are engaged in a common enterprise, they are bound to have problems of coordination. Agreements have to be reached about who will do what, when, and where. All business firms must deal with the problems of coordinating the activities of their members and, as firms grow in size, the problems of coordination increase geometrically. The arrangement of a firm's internal relationships is referred to as *organizational structure.*

A firm may be organized in many ways and the particular form used depends upon the firm's primary functions. For firms that adopt the marketing concept, traditional organizational forms are often inadequate and must be modified to coordinate marketing activities to the degree required for effective marketing. Figure 1–3 shows a traditional organization, organized on the basis of function. From a marketing standpoint, a number of problems occur with this form of organization:

- Many key marketing functions, such as marketing research, sales promotion, and physical distribution, are not explicitly recognized.
- Major marketing functions such as advertising and sales, are separated into different departments and no one, except the president, is responsible for their coordination.

11. Neil H. Borden, "The Concept of the Marketing Mix," *Journal of Advertising Research* (June, 1964): 2–7.

- Responsibility for individual products is split among several functional departments. A basic tenet of organizational theory states that, when everybody is responsible, no one is responsible.

Figure 1–4 shows one way in which the firm might be reorganized as a more effective marketing organization. Note that:

- Major marketing activities are grouped under a marketing department in order to facilitate coordination.
- Several key marketing functions have been added to the organization.
- Individual product managers have been assigned responsibility for individual products.

The size of the company, the number of products, the types of products, and the markets served will influence the form that a particular firm's organization takes.

CONFLICT IN THE FIRM

Marketing activities often make demands upon a firm that conflict with the values and beliefs of the people managing the firm's resources. People tend to view problems in terms of their own self-interests and areas of expertise. Thus, financial people view a firm's operation from the standpoint of purely financial considerations; production people, from the standpoint of production operations; and marketing people from the standpoint of marketing needs.

Further, each internal department seeking efficiency in performing a limited function, may create severe problems in other areas of the firm. The sacrifice of overall company effectiveness to maximize efficiency in a particular department is referred to as *suboptimization.* For example, let us suppose that the credit department of a firm seeks to minimize credit losses. In performing its job, the credit department may establish credit policies so restrictive that they eliminate a significant volume of profitable business. Many of the customers eliminated may be credit-worthy, but fail to meet the credit department's rigorous standards. This places the credit department in conflict with the marketing department which needs more liberal credit policies in order to achieve sales goals.

Table 1–4 identifies some of the more common conflicts that arise between marketing and other departments. Note that marketing is not the only area that may conflict with other departments. Engineering, for example, may design a part that is difficult or uneconomical to produce, conflicting with the production department by forcing production costs out of line. Or, in order to reduce inventory costs, inventory management

FIGURE 1–3: *Traditional Organization*

may want to order in quantities that are insufficient for purchasing economies. Such conflicts are characteristic of business firms. It is often said that business management is the management of conflict, and that successful business managers are those who have well developed interpersonal relationship and conflict resolution skills.

SUMMARY

All aspects of our daily lives are influenced by marketing. Marketing provides us with products, jobs, transportation, news, and entertainment. Marketing, as a concept and as a business practice, is much more complex than many of us imagine. Rooted in our economic system, marketing is carried out by individual business firms.

The United States is a leading exponent of the marketing system. Freedom of choice for consumers, freedom to produce by manufacturers, and freedom to compete are all basic ingredients of the U.S. economy. Individual business firms are the building blocks of a marketing economy; the operation of these firms makes the marketing system function.

The approximately 14 million business firms in the United States differ in size, form of ownership, and the industries in which they operate. All of these firms have certain things in common, however: all require profit, have internal resources upon which to draw, and depend on marketing and innovation for the attainment of their objectives.

In carrying out marketing functions, firms have direct control over certain marketing variables: the product, its place of sale, its promotion, its price, and planning. The ways in which a firm manipulates these controllable variables is a key responsibility of marketing managers.

To coordinate marketing activities and develop and execute effective marketing plans, firms often must modify their traditional organizational structures. They also must develop skills in conflict resolution since marketing requirements often conflict with traditional values of those who manage the firm's resources.

FIGURE 1–4: Organization of a Marketing Firm

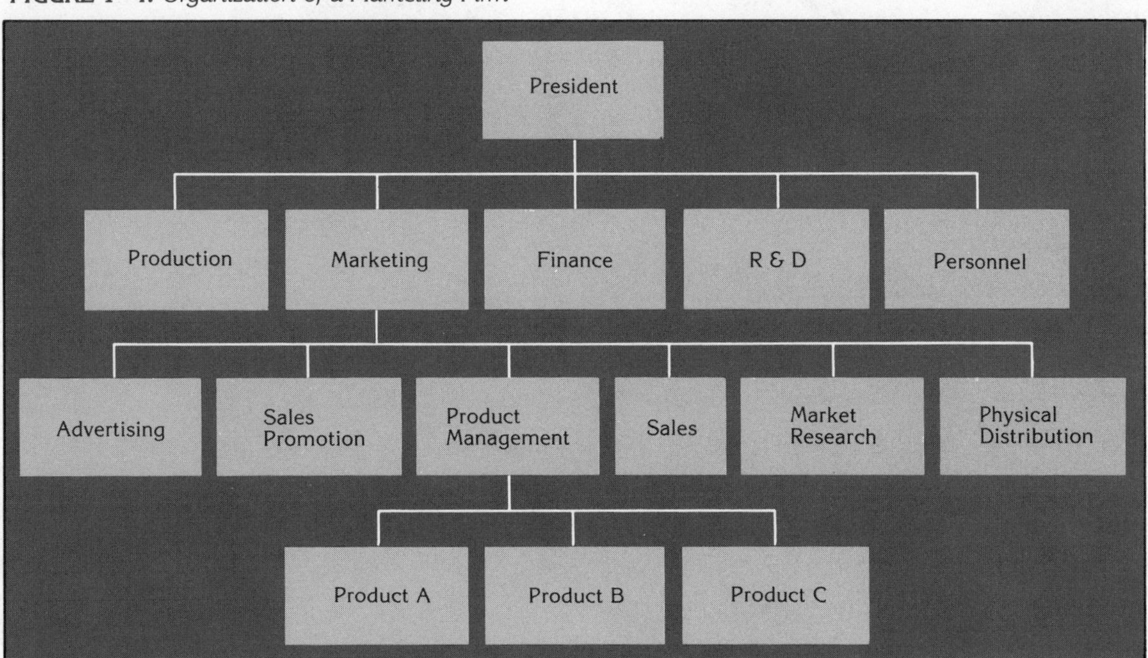

TABLE 1–4: Organizational Conflicts Between Marketing and Other Departments
SOURCE: Philip Kotler, *Marketing Management*, 4th edition, © 1980, p. 593. Reprinted by permission of Prentice-Hall, Inc., Englewood Cliffs, New Jersey.

DEPARTMENT	THEIR EMPHASIS	MARKETING'S EMPHASIS
R&D	Basic research	Applied research
	Intrinsic quality	Perceived quality
	Functional features	Sales features
Engineering	Long design lead time	Short design lead time
	Few models	Many models
	Standard components	Custom components
Purchasing	Narrow product line	Broad product line
	Standard parts	Nonstandard parts
	Price of material	Quality of material
	Economical lot sizes	Large lot sizes to avoid stockouts
	Purchasing at infrequent intervals	Immediate purchasing for customer needs
Manufacturing	Long production lead time	Short production lead time
	Long runs with few models	Short runs with many models
	No model changes	Frequent model changes
	Standard orders	Custom orders
	Ease of fabrication	Aesthetic appearance
	Average quality control	Tight quality control
Finance	Strict rationales for spending	Intuitive arguments for spending
	Hard and fast budgets	Flexible budgets to meet changing needs
	Pricing to cover costs	Pricing to further market development
Accounting	Standard transactions	Special terms and discounts
	Few reports	Many reports
Credit	Full financial disclosures by customers	Minimum credit examination of customers
	Low credit risks	Medium credit risks
	Tough credit terms	Easy credit terms
	Tough collection procedures	Easy collection procedures

1. What is meant by distributive justice? Why is it a perplexing national problem and what are its practical implications?
2. What are the basic dimensions that distinguish planned economies from marketing economies?
3. How does "self-interest" automatically determine resource allocation in a marketing economy?
4. Identify the basic concepts of freedom upon which a marketing economy is based.
5. Why did the marketing economy of Adam Smith fail to perform as smoothly as its promise implied? How have these faults been dealt with?
6. Explain the role of profits in a business enterprise. How does this role relate to the concept of profit maximization?
7. Why are activities such as manufacturing, finance, accounting, personnel, and data processing considered expenses and not basic functions of a business?
8. Explain the marketing concept.
9. What are the controllable marketing variables and how are they related to the concept of the "marketing mix?"
10. Explain, using two or three examples, how marketing may conflict with other areas of a firm.

1. Assume that you are a member of the economic planning committee in a planned economy. What problems would you encounter in allocating resources and determining equitable compensation systems for workers? How might you approach these problems?
2. Does the marketing concept apply to organizations such as state universities? Private universities? Churches? Why or why not?
3. A contention of free market economists is that, as individuals serve their self-interests, the needs of society will also be served. Is this a valid contention?
4. How would you define the product for a business such as McDonald's Restaurants?
5. How might you organize the marketing function in a company that had the following characteristics: (1) a number of profitable consumer products, some of which are sold through department stores and some through hardware stores; (2) a number of highly technical, industrial products sold to the automotive, appliance, and the steel industries; (3) a small, but rapidly growing European market for some of its industrial products. Draw up an organizational structure for such a company.

THE BUSINESS OF MARKETING

Ordway is a small, coeducational, private, liberal arts college located adjacent to popular skiing and outdoor recreational areas (hiking, canoeing, rock climbing) in one of the Mountain States. Founded in 1915, its curriculum emphasized the humanities, basic sciences, and religious and ethical training. Because the college has maintained high academic standards, Ordway enjoys a good academic reputation, has an outstanding roster of successful graduates, and is recognized in academic circles for the accomplishments of its faculty. The school has remained relatively small and, in the late 1970s, had an enrollment of approximately two thousand students, drawn from all parts of the United States.

Ordway's curriculum has changed somewhat in response to changing emphases in education. A social sciences department was added in 1933, and a business department in 1955. Both of these departments have been well accepted, and currently account for almost 25 percent of the school's majors. Nonetheless, Ordway has maintained its original emphasis as a liberal arts college.

About 75 percent of Ordway's graduates continue postgraduate education at other universities. Because of its academic reputation, Ordway has had no trouble in gaining acceptance for its graduates in law schools, schools of medicine, and other postgraduate areas of study. As a point of record, Ordway's director of placement has noted with pride that no Ordway graduate had failed to gain admission to schools of medicine or law.

The late 1970s brought a series of problems to Ordway. Although the school had been relatively successful in increasing its endowment, income from this source was insufficient to keep pace with rising operating costs caused by inflation. As a consequence, tuitions had been sharply increased. Although the problem was serious, it was not considered critical since a modest increase of 10 to 15 percent in enrollment would be sufficient to offset the deficit and put the college on a sound financial basis.

During 1978 and 1979, however, enrollments decreased by about 5 percent each year. Further, between 1975 and 1985, it was estimated that the number of high school graduates would shrink from 4.2 million to 3.6 million. In addition, an increasing number of applicants failed to meet Ordway's admission standards, or were considered marginal by Ordway's director of admissions.

A nationwide survey of high school seniors by Ordway officials indicated these potential problems: High school seniors from warmer climates were concerned about cold weather and snow during the winter months. Prospects in the east were concerned over whether Ordway was prestigeous enough. West coast prospects were concerned that Ordway might be too formal, and offer too little opportunity for outdoor recreation.

College officials also noted that recruiting practices of other private colleges were becoming increasingly competitive, and that some were hiring marketing experts to help them. Many of these schools were buying mailing lists of high school seniors, broken down by zip code, ethnic group, family income, class rank, college entrance examination scores, anticipated majors, and planned careers. In addition, the more successful schools were sharpening their identities in order to differentiate themselves from other schools. In marketing, this process is known as "product positioning." For example, one school that was known for teacher education was positioning itself with a new program designed to help graduates teach economics at the grade school level. Another was positioning itself with its courses in clinical psychology. Still a third was emphasizing its financial programs, and its ability to prepare students for the "realities of the business world."

Ordway's officials disagreed about the course that the school should follow. Some felt that "marketing" education was inappropriate for Ordway, insisting that the school was an educational institution rather than a business. This group believed that Ordway should continue to operate as it had in the past, but that the college should redouble its efforts to solicit endowment and operating funds from private sources. They acknowledged, however, that such funds were becoming more difficult to raise. Others felt that Ordway should lower its entrance requirements and performance standards in order to appeal to a broader range of students. Still others felt that Ordway should embark upon an extensive marketing program.

Assignment

What course of action should Ordway officials follow? In preparing your answer, consider the following questions:

1. *Should Ordway be considered as a business? Why or why not? If it were a state-supported university instead of a private school, would the same answer apply?*
2. *If it is a business, what is its product?*
3. *If Ordway were to embark on an extensive marketing program, how should it proceed?*
   - *Should it lower its admission and performance standards to broaden its appeal to students?*
   - *How might Ordway officials position the school?*
   - *What appeals should they use to attract students?*
   - *Should the same appeals be used in all areas of the country? If not, how should they differ?*

2

Uncontrollable Environmental Variables

- *The uncontrollable variables influencing a firm's marketing activities.*
- *The legislative philosophies that have influenced business legislation.*
- *Major legislation governing marketing activities.*

MARKETING EXAMPLES

THE COST OF REGULATION

By the late 1970s, the cost of government regulation of business in the United States was estimated at $100 billion—about 25 percent of the entire national budget and nearly three-quarters of the annual private investment in plants and equipment. The private sector was forced to fill out more than 4,000 different federal forms each year, an activity that required almost 143 million hours. On the federal level alone, an army of 100,000 workers staffed 41 regulatory agencies.[1] Speaking to the National Association of Manufacturers, a GM executive stated that compliance with federal, state, and local regulations cost the General Motors Corporation $1.9 billion—not including the cost of extra equipment required on its products—and required the full-time work of the equivalent of 25,000 GM employees.[2]

Few areas of economic activity are immune to government regulation. Pricing, advertising, product safety, pollution control, hiring practices, and working conditions are only a few of the areas in which the United States government has intervened in the economy. Although no single piece of regulation may be crippling, the private sector often feels that it is being nibbled to death by minnows.

ROBOTS? YES, ROBOTS

Robots have invaded industry.

> Robots, in fact, are the latest form of automation . . . a typical model can be fitted with a variety of "hands"—e.g., a mechanical "gripper" that enables it to pick up parts and pass them along, a sprayhead that converts into a painter, or an arc that turns into a welder. Such robots load and unload parts from furnaces, stamping presses, and conveyers—and a few of them even perform the job while riding on conveyers. . . . Most wonderous of all, robots are starting to assem-

1. Williard C. Butcher, "The Stifling Cost of Regulation," *Business Week* (Nov. 6, 1968):22–23.
2. "Red Tape Costs $1.9 Billion in 1979 G. M. Executive Says," *The Arizona Republic* (Oct. 11, 1980):C1.

> ble components in factories. Over the next twelve months, General Motors will install ten Pumas, which, among other things, will partly assemble armatures for electric motors, screw small electric bulbs into instrument panels, and help put windshield wipers together. . . . Robots are getting smarter all the time. . . .[3]

In 1979 the United States market for robots was approximately $60 million. By 1989 sales are expected to be somewhere between $700 million and $2 billion. Robots are simply one of the latest developments in technology, a development in a dynamic economy which seems to have a life of its own. Technology often seems to exist as an "outside force" that revolutionizes production, obsoletes products overnight, and plays havoc with marketing planning.

TENNIS, ANYONE?

In the mid-1970s, tennis was booming. From 1972 to 1976, regular adult players increased from 14 million to some 26 million, and sales of racquets, shoes, tennis balls, and clothes grew apace.

> Now, the game has gone soft, at least as a business. . . . Team tennis is dead, and the networks have sharply cut their coverage of matches. Philip Morris no longer has its Virginia Slims circuit, once the keystone of the women's tour. Fully one-third of last year's corporate sponsors for the U.S. Open, which is held every September in New York City, have failed to renew their pledges. Most telling of all, the sales of racquets, which peaked at $184 million in 1976, skidded to $137 million last year, and is expected to fall another 30 percent this year [1979]. Wilson Sporting Goods, the PepsiCo subsidiary that introduced the first steel racquet in 1967, has been losing money and is widely rumored to be up for sale. . . . Many of those who tried tennis during the boom time but found it tough to

3. Gene Bylinsky, "Those Smart Young Robots on the Production Line," FORTUNE Magazine

master have moved on to jogging or simpler racquet sports. In fact, some of the nation's 1,000 indoor tennis facilities, which cost about $165,000 a court to build, have converted their underused courts to racquetball.[4]

In their pursuit of social pleasure and physical fitness, millions of consumers tried tennis and many found it wanting. In response to consumer demand, sales of tennis-related products bloomed—and then faded. Nor could wishful thinking nor corporate investment restore the bloom to the rosy years of the tennis heyday.

Government regulations, technology, and consumer interests are but three of the uncontrollable environmental variables that sometimes make mock of business planning and turn market forecasting into a guessing game.

4. "Net Loss," reprinted by permission from TIME, The Weekly Newsmagazine (Sept. 3, 1979); Copyright Time Inc. 1979.

In Chapter 1, we identified the major marketing variables a business firm controls in preparing its marketing programs—planning, product, place, promotion, and price. Now, let us turn our attention to the major uncontrollable variables that introduce a distressing amount of uncertainty into the marketing enterprise.

UNCONTROLLABLE VARIABLES IN MARKETING

Were it not for the uncontrollable variables, market planning and execution would be a piece of cake. Because of these variables, however, the best laid plans often go awry and many marketing programs end up as an exercise in frustration and disappointment. *The major, uncontrollable variables in marketing are the consumers themselves, the level of economic activity, technology, resource availability, competition, and government and consumerism.* These uncontrollable variables are shown in relation to the controllable marketing activities of the firm in Figure 2–1. Let us examine each of these uncontrollable variables more carefully to understand the impact they may have on a marketing firm.

Consumers

All markets are made up of people—individuals and population groups. As a consequence, the salient characteristics of a society's population are of central interest to the marketer of goods and services. Two aspects of U.S. society will be examined briefly in this section—the United States culture and population demographics.

THE UNITED STATES CULTURE. Societies differ in the beliefs, values, and expectations held by their members. The term *culture* refers to the particular patterns of beliefs, values, and expectations that characterize a society, differentiating it from other societies. The ways in which we dress, the foods we eat, our attitudes toward competition, and our social activities are a part of our cultural heritage.

Culture defines and prescribes accepted behaviors; many of these prescriptions, however, are general rather than specific. That is, instead of demanding a specific behavior, culture prescribes a range of acceptable behaviors. And, although a cultural norm may exist, considerable variation around that norm is allowed. Behaviors that fall outside the acceptable range tend to be eliminated simply because they do not achieve their intended results.

FIGURE 2–1: Uncontrollable Variables Influencing Marketing

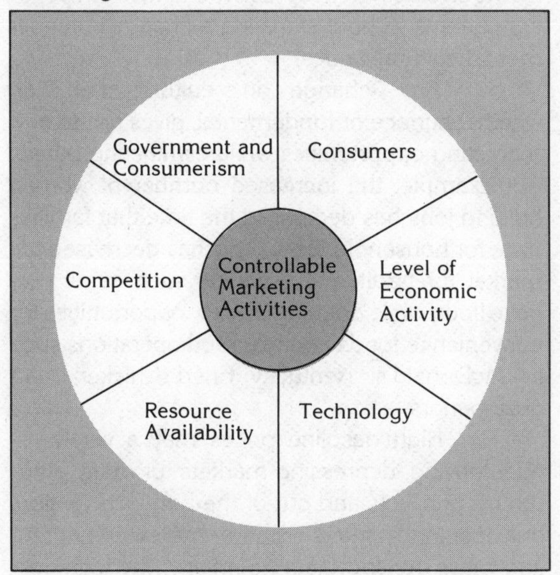

Culture is an uncontrollable marketing variable because it is a given, which simply exists. Marketers are well advised to familiarize themselves with the dominant strains of the United States culture if they expect to devise products and programs that will be successful. There are three characteristics of the United States culture that pose special problems for marketers: cultural pluralism, basic cultural change, and surface changes.

Cultural Pluralism. A nation as large and complex as the United States, includes subcultures with beliefs, values, and institutions that differ in some significant way from the dominant cultural themes characterizing the mainstream of society. The existence of these subcultures creates *cultural pluralism.* The United States is a pluralistic culture; tolerance of a relatively large degree of pluralism is rooted in its historic traditions.

Many of these subcultures—Hispanic, black, Jewish, and American Indian—represent significant markets for many products, and are particularly important in certain sections of the country. The large influx of Cubans into the Miami, Florida, area, for example, has led many marketers to refer to Miami as "Little Havana." The Mexican-American and American Indian populations in the Southwest, and the black populations in the South and in major urban areas, particularly in the East and Midwest, also constitute significant markets for many products.

Although major marketers often ignore minor subcultures, they are conscious of those which, because of their size and purchasing power, represent major marketing opportunities. Since subcultures often hold different beliefs and values than the dominant culture, marketing programs may have to be adapted or changed in significant ways to be effective with these groups. The increased use of black models in television commercials and print ads in the 1960s represents one such adaptation. The use of special media programmed for blacks, Hispanics, and the Navajo represents another. Marketers of food products who expect to capitalize on the large and relatively affluent Jewish market in major cities know that ethnic tastes and dietary laws prescribe many of their purchases. In order to gain acceptance in this market, many food products, particularly meats, must be kosher. That is, prepared in accordance with Jewish dietary laws, and carry rabbinical approval.

In addition, at any given time, relatively small groups of people in revolt against traditional values will adopt life-styles that run counter to dominant cultural beliefs. The hippies of the 1960s represent such a group. Other groups include those who promote gay rights, communal living, cohabitation, and radical environmentalism. The early 1980s saw the emergence of the "moral majority," deeply religious groups that protested the decline of morality in the U.S. and boycotted products advertised on television shows of which they disapproved. Although such groups often receive disproportionate press coverage, they generally constitute a relatively small part of society. As a consequence, major marketers often ignore them and devote their attention to the major themes of the U.S. culture, leaving these special or peripheral markets to smaller producers. Nonetheless, such groups are a factor in market planning.

Cultural Change. Cultures change. Sometimes they change slowly, almost glacially, as a process of evolution. Sometimes they change rapidly as a result of internal strife or the impact of external factors. The culture of the United States is no exception.

The impact of the youthful revolt of the 1960s and early 1970s, described by Charles Reich in *The Greening of America,*[5] has led to a somewhat greater tolerance of alternative life styles that has been accommodated in the programs of alert marketers. The women's liberation movement, combined with the economic necessity of women working outside of their homes to keep pace with inflation, has modified attitudes toward the traditional roles of women, requiring adaptations on the part of marketing practitioners. The advent of the birth control pill has led to more casual living arrangements. And, although these informal relationships are not condoned by the mainstream of society, greater toleration of them has been recognized in marketing communications.

Perhaps the biggest threat to the stability of the United States culture is the impact that the shortage of petroleum-based fuels has had on the economy. Failure to recognize the importance of this phenomenon and sluggishness in responding have seriously hurt the U.S. automotive industry, threatened the survival of Chrysler and Ford, and strained the resources of General Motors. The effect of the energy shortage on the economy of the United States is, at this point, unclear because it depends upon the country's ability to discover additional petroleum reserves or to develop alternative sources of energy.

In any event, basic cultural change is an uncontrollable variable that tests the adaptability of individual marketers.

Surface Changes. In addition to basic cultural changes, minor changes shift the focus of consumer interests and direct spending patterns from one type of consumer activity to another. Nothing, for example, in the growing interest in physical fitness threatens dominant cultural values, although this interest has given rise to lucrative markets for bicycles, jogging paraphenalia, racquet sports, backpacks, and various other physical fitness supplies. Such changes in the focus of consumer interests may be referred to as *surface changes* since they represent changes in spending patterns without signaling a change in fundamental cultural values.

Any change in cultural behavior, whether surface or fundamental, gives rise to new marketing opportunities while eliminating others. For example, the increased number of women holding jobs has decreased the time that families have for household tasks. This has decreased the market for traditional products such as all purpose flour, while opening up new opportunities for convenience foods and fast-food operations such as McDonald's, Kentucky Fried Chicken, and pizza parlors.

High gasoline prices may severely reduce driving, depressing markets for many automotive products and out-of-the-home recreation, but opening markets for in-home entertainment and mass transportation. Similarly, the high cost of home repairs has created substantial markets for do-it-yourself products, and has made product guarantees and warranties a more important component for a wide range of durable products.

Forecasting Cultural Change. The economic effects of even minor cultural changes are such that a market has developed for *cultural forecasting* among business firms. Major corporations often devote a significant portion of their marketing research resources to ascertaining future buying trends, and independent marketing research companies are showing an increasing interest in this area. The forecasting of cultural change, unfortunately, is highly tentative and often characterized by speculation rather than defensible predictions.

CONSUMER DEMOGRAPHICS. Demographics refer to structural dimensions of a population such as age distribution, income distribution, family composition, occupational characteristics, births, deaths, and so forth. Although individual marketers have no control over these factors, they are subject to their effects.

The children born within a given year, for example, limits the market for baby products. The adults between the ages of 18 and 35 largely determines the size of the beer market, and the number of new family formations has clear impli-

5. Charles Reich, *The Greening of America* (New York: Random House, Inc., 1970).

cations for housing and home furnishing markets.

The demographic structure of a society is seldom static for long, and changes in demographic composition often test the resiliency of a marketing firm. Unless management has the foresight to diversify into other products in order to protect sales and earnings, a decline in birthrate may be a disaster for some firms, such as Gerber's which claimed for years that "Babies are our business—our only business." This same decline may be a boon to other firms that cater to adult recreation, travel, and other activities indulged in by those who are not hampered by the presence of small children.

A later chapter will be devoted to identifying and analyzing some of the more significant demographic trends in the U.S. population. At this point, note that consumer demographics is an uncontrollable environmental variable to which successful marketers must adapt.

The Level of Economic Activity

One characteristic of free economies is their tendency to oscillate between boom and bust. Planned economies exhibit this same characteristic; although in a rigidly controlled economy, the effects of economic swings can be softened or disguised, at least in the short run. In a relatively free economy, such as the United States, government attempts at economic stabilization through monetary controls (control of money supply) and fiscal controls (taxation and government expenditures) often seem to exacerbate the problem rather than solve it. This is the reason why free market economists, such as Milton Friedman, are critical of government intervention in economic affairs. Major economic swings, according to this point of view, are more often caused by government mismanagement than by any inherent instability in the economic system itself.[6]

In any event, economic swings affect marketing activity because they affect purchasing power. During an economic recession, purchasing power is limited and patterns of expenditures change. Consumers, for example, may shift their food store purchases away from higher priced brands to lower priced store brands. During the recession of 1973–74, a survey by *Better Homes and Gardens* indicated that 72 percent of the respondents were buying more store brands in order to save money.[7] In 1979, under the impact of falling purchasing power, many consumers turned to *generic brands* (unadvertised, "plain label" grocery items) that often sold for 30 to 40 percent below advertised products. Also, during periods of economic recession, consumers often curtail or postpone their expenditures for luxury and high-ticket items—washing machines, automatic dryers, automobiles, and housing, for example. Conversely, during times of relative affluence, consumers are much less conscious of small price differentials, and the sales of luxury and expensive items boom.

Not all industries are affected the same way by economic swings. Nonetheless, the expected state of the economy should play a major role in market planning. During the 1950s and 1960s, real incomes grew at a record rate, creating a psychology of affluence and optimism. During this period, Sears, Roebuck and Company—the nation's largest merchandiser—upgraded product lines and raised prices. When the 1970s ushered in a period of declining real income, Sears was no longer competitive. Despite massive promotional efforts to dispose of excess inventories and regain its market position, this giant retailer is still suffering from a miscalculation of the future of the U.S. economy.[8] W. T. Grant, a major variety chain which overextended itself financially during the late 1960s and early 1970s, was unable to survive the recession of the mid-1970s. In 1976 Grant declared bankruptcy, the largest retail bankruptcy in U.S. history.[9]

No company is immune to the vagaries of the economy, although some are less vulnerable than others. For all, however, the level of economic activity is an uncontrollable variable that

6. Milton Friedman, *Capitalism and Freedom* (Chicago: The University of Chicago Press, 1962), Chapters 3, 4, and 5.

7. "Private Brands Seek Growth in Falling Economy," *Grey Matter* (June, 1974):1.

8. Wyndhem Robertson, "How Sears' Retailing Strategy Backfired," *Fortune* (May 8, 1978):103.

9. Rush Loving, Jr., "W. T. Grant's Last Days—As Seen from Store 1192," *Fortune* (April, 1976):108-114.

demands anticipation of future economic conditions and flexibility in devising marketing strategies that will enable adaptation to unanticipated economic swings.

Technology

Business Week introduced an article on technology with this quotation:

> Industrial America in 2029 will bear only a surface resemblance to industrial America of 1979. Some corporations will still be the same. Some products will be recognizable . . . but by 2029, some of today's major producers of consumer goods such as apparel and home appliances will have virtually disappeared in their present form. . . .[10]

Eberhard Scheuing, in a book titled *New Product Management,* estimated that ". . . 80 percent of today's products will have disappeared from the market ten years from now, while an estimated 80 percent of the products that will be sold in the next decade are as yet unknown."[11] Joseph Schumpeter, a renowned economist, saw technology as a force for "creative destruction," and Joel Dean, also an economist, identified technology as the primary factor leading to the demise of existing products.

There is little question about the impact of technology on the survival of existing products and the development of future ones. There is also little question that the growth rate of an economy is intimately related to the growth of its technology. Many of the products we take for granted today were either nonexistent or exceedingly primitive at the beginning of the century. Automobiles, airplanes, talking moving pictures, radio, television, transistors, color film, jet engines, electronic computers, synthetic fibers, antibiotics, and many, many others are of relatively recent origin.

Not all technological developments are equally beneficial, nor equivalent in terms of the impact they have on the economy. Computers, for example, represent a major advance in humanity's capacity to organize, process, and present information, and to solve complex problems. Spray cans for dispensing deodorants—as well as the deodorants themselves—are, on the other hand, somewhat trivial. Nonetheless, from the standpoint of marketing, even the most trivial technological development may have the potential for launching a multimillion dollar industry and for obsoleting current products. Consider the following examples: instant baking mixes, a multibillion dollar market, have virtually replaced all purpose flour in most consumers' homes. Frozen foods have made deep inroads in dry grocery items. Synthetic fibers have virtually replaced cotton and wool for many textile needs. Television demoted radio from a leading form of entertainment to a support medium. Plastics have revolutionized the houseware and toy industries. Word processing systems are replacing typewriters in many major corporations and in the nation's newsrooms. Antibiotics have changed the complexion of health care. Computers are assuming an increasingly important role in medical diagnosis. Versatile robots are appearing on assembly lines and in steel mills. The list is endless.

Technological progress represents both an opportunity and threat for individual companies. As an opportunity, technology is a source of new and better products. As a threat, technological developments by competitors may result in lost markets.

Technological progress does not come cheap, however. Total U.S. expenditures for Research and Development in 1980 were estimated to exceed $57 billion, with about half of that amount being funded by individual companies. The remainder was funded by the U.S. government, which contracted out some research to private firms.[12]

Further, from the standpoint of individual firms, technology is a highly speculative undertaking. For example, there is no way of knowing how long it will take to develop a new product,

10. "New Growth Industries—and Some of the Dropouts," Reprinted from *Business Week* (Sept. 3, 1979), by special permission, © 1979 by McGraw-Hill, Inc. New York, NY 10020. All rights reserved.

11. Eberhard E. Scheuing, *New Product Development* (Hinsdale, IL: The Dryden Press, 1974), p. 1.

12. Becky Barna, "Innovate or Wither," *Datamation* (August, 1979):54.

Production by technology. (Photo courtesy of Mercedes-Benz of North America, Inc.)

or whether the product will be profitable. If a new product or process requires a basically new technology, development time and costs may be exceedingly high. Television, for example, required fifty-five years from the time development started until its commercialization. Table 2–1 shows the time that elapsed between the start of development and introduction to the market for a selected list of consumer and industrial products.

In view of technology's high cost in money and time, and its uncertainty, many small companies are ill prepared to invest in future product development. Further, the United States is losing the technological advantage that it has traditionally held, as this advantage is being seized by foreign competitors. For example:

- The number of patents granted to U.S. citizens declined 21 percent between 1971 and 1976, while patents to foreign residents grew by 16 percent. In the 1950s, the United States brought forth approximately 82 percent of the world's major inventions. By the late 1960s, this figure had dwindled to 55 percent.[13]

13. Ibid, pp. 54–55.

TABLE 2–1: *Elapsed Time From Start of Product Development to Marketing*
SOURCE: Lee Adler, "Time Lag in New Product Development," *Journal of Marketing,* Vol. 30 (June 1966), pp. 17–22.

Product	*Company*	*Years*
	Consumer Products	
Birdseye frozen foods	General Foods	15
Ban (roll-on deodorant)	Bristol Meyers	6
Calm (powder deodorant)	Alberto Culver	5
Clorodent (toothpaste)	Lever Bros.	21
Citroid (cold compound)	Grove Laboratories	2
Coldene (cold remedy)	Pharma Craft	1
Crest (toothpaste)	Procter & Gamble	10
Decaf (instant coffee)	Nestle	10
Flav-R-Straws	Frontier Foods Corp. and others	3
Gerber (strained baby foods)	Gerber	1
Hills Bros. (instant coffee)	Hills Bros.	22
Johnson shoe polishes	S. C. Johnson	3
Lustre Creme (liquid shampoo)	Colgate Palmolive	8
Marlboro (filter cigarettes)	Philip Morris	2
Maxim (concentrated instant coffee)	General Foods	10
Minute Maid (frozen orange juice)	Minute Maid	2
Minute Rice	General Foods	18
Purina Dog Chow	Ralston Purina	4
Red Kettle (dry soup mixes)	Campbell Soup	19
Stripe (toothpaste)	Lever Bros.	6
Wisk (liquid detergent)	Lever Bros.	1
Bendix (washer/dryer)	Bendix	12
Eversharp (ball-point pen)	Eversharp	2/3
Floron (plastic floor tile)	Pabco Products	6
Polaroid Land Camera	Polaroid Corp.	2
Polaroid Color Pack Camera	Polaroid Corp.	15
Scripto Tilt-Tip (ball-point pen)	Scripto	2
Smith Corona (portable typewriter)	Smith Corona	5
Sunbeam Electric Tooth Brush	Sunbeam Corp.	5
Talon zippers	Corporate predecessor of Talon, Inc.	30
Television	Many companies	55
	Industrial Products	
Dictet (portable recording machine)	Dictaphone Corp.	1 2/3
Isothalic (chemical compound to improve paints)	Oronite Corp.	7
Krilium (soil conditioner)	Monsanto	12 1/2
Page Master (pocket-sized paging system)	Stromberg Carlson	2
Penicillin	Many companies	15
Transisters	Bell Laboratories	16
Xerox copier	Xerox Corp.	15

FIGURE 2–2: World Population Growth
Copyright by Donald J. Bogue, Ph. D., The University of Chicago, 1969.

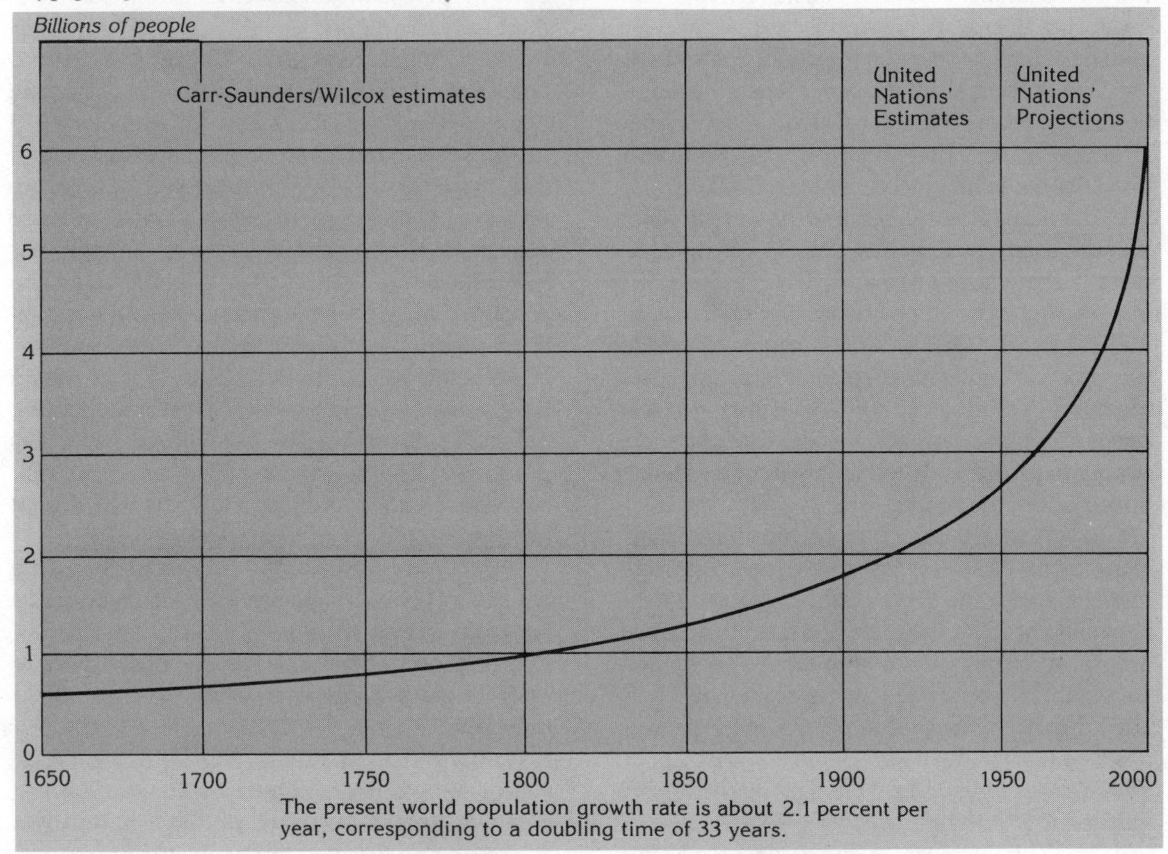

- The focus of R&D in the United States appears to be shifting away from basic research and toward inventive research (application of existing technology) to generate quicker profits; and defensive technology into toxicology, pollution, work safety, and quality control.[14]

In any case, technology is a major force in business and industry. A new development can give birth to a new industry, or make an existing, profitable product obsolete. From the standpoint of the individual firm, technology is an uncontrollable factor in the environment. Although individual firms can and should invest in R&D, they have no control over what is being done by domestic competitors, by the U.S. government, or by foreign countries.

14. Eugene P. Schonfeld, "Some Trends in R&D," *Industrial Research* (Sept., 1979):50–51

Resource Availability

A complex economy requires a dependable supply of natural resources to support its productive capacity. Yet, natural resources are often in short supply and, in some instances, this shortage is critical. Figure 2–2 shows the growth in world population, a population that is growing at an exponential rate. The natural resources required to meet the needs of this population are being used at a similar rate. Resources laid down by geological forces over billions of years are being gobbled up at a rate that makes gluttony resemble restraint.

Technology has, and is being used to extend and replace natural resources. But, existing technology has its limits. Further, advanced technology often requires large amounts of energy, and energy is a resource that is experiencing a critical shortage. Robert Heilbroner, an economic historian and philosopher, has also pointed out that, with the exception of solar energy, a by-product of energy production is heat. An accelerated discharge of heat into the atmosphere resulting from substantially increased energy production could threaten the ecosystem—that delicate envelope surrounding the earth that protects it from the devastating force of the sun.[15]

Natural resources, and the ways in which they are used, create both problems and opportunities for marketing firms. Two such areas are increasing costs and environmental pollution.

INCREASING COSTS. As the supply of natural resources is depleted, costs rise. This increases the costs of production and is reflected in higher prices to consumers. Eventually, a product dependent upon scarce resources may be literally priced out of the market.

A case in point is petroleum-based fuels. Many of us can remember when gasoline cost between thirty and forty cents a gallon. By the beginning of 1980, the price had risen to well over a dollar a gallon and some authorities were predicting that it would rise to two dollars a gallon by 1981. For example, in Portugal where the price of gasoline has not been kept artificially low by price controls—as it has in the United States—the price reached four dollars a gallon in 1980.

This increase in the price of gasoline and other petroleum-based fuels has not only increased the cost of all manufacturing and contributed to an outrageous inflation, but also played havoc with the market for automobiles and recreational vehicles that are notorious gas hogs. As noted earlier, United States' automobile producers, who have been slow in developing fuel-efficient cars, are facing disasterous times. In the meantime, fuel-efficient foreign cars—particularly Toyota, Datsun, Honda, and Volkswagen—have been enjoying a bonanza.

Rising costs because of scarcity are not confined to gasoline and heating oil. Plastics, as well as the entire petrochemical industry, are experiencing similar pressures. Further, platinum, gold, zinc, and lead—essential industrial metals—are in short supply, and silver, tin, uranium, and other irreplaceable resources face a similar fate in the forseeable future.

At the same time, however, these shortages also represent opportunities for marketing oriented firms—opportunities for more efficient use of existing resources and the development of new materials. Fuel-efficient cars, of course, are an example of the more efficient use of existing resources. Wood and coal burning stoves for home heating, solar energy, gasohol, methane produced from coal and organic wastes, and batteries powered by plentiful hydrogen are examples of substitute resources that can be and are being developed. The development of new materials is a continuing challenge for a technology that has produced plastics, synthetic fibers, synthetic rubber, and a variety of other materials that do not occur in nature.

In the meantime, individual firms are caught in a profit squeeze as production costs increase and as consumers resist higher prices. Thus, resource availability is an uncontrollable environmental variable to which business firms must adapt.

ENVIRONMENTAL POLLUTION. Pollution is an inevitable by-product of industrialization. Exhaust pollution, smoke pollution, and particle pollution fill the air and threaten to strangle us in our own filth. Sewage disposal, agricultural chemicals, solid and liquid waste discharged by factories, thousands of tons of manure accumulated by commercial feedlots, as well as nonbiodegradable bottles, cans, plastics, packages, and detergents turn our oceans and waterways into sewers and transform our landscapes into garbage dumps.

A growing concern for environmental pollution throughout the world has caused governments to take active roles in environmental protection. This concern has also led to the formation of international commissions under the auspices of the United Nations to identify common concerns and coordinate international solutions. Although substantial progress has been made in many areas, the solutions sometimes create their own problems. For example, automobile emission controls, which are effective in reducing the hydrocarbons in the atmosphere, in-

15. Robert Heilbroner, *An Inquiry into the Human Prospect,* (New York: W. W. Norton and Co., Inc., 1974).

crease the sulphuric acid in the air, an occurrence that has unfortunate effects on some agriculture.

In addition, government requirements for pollution control—while necessary and desirable—divert funds from capital investment into expensive pollution control devices and programs, and raise the cost of production.

Certainly, the foregoing examples of pollution are depressing. However, pollution also creates three kinds of marketing opportunities. *First,* markets for scrubbers, improved methods of waste treatment, and methods for recycling materials. *Second,* a marketing challenge to devise alternative ways of packaging goods and to develop inexpensive, biodegradable packaging materials. *Third,* an opportunity to find productive and socially beneficial uses for industrial, animal, and human wastes.

The point is, of course, that resource shortages and pollution are uncontrollable environmental variables for the individual business firm. But, these very problems also create opportunities for those firms that have the foresight to address these difficulties, and the imagination and technical skill to solve them.

Competition

A fifth, uncontrollable variable is competition itself. Competition is a national policy of the United States government and, for most companies in the United States, competition is intense.

Competition exists not only between similar products, such as different brands of soup, or different makes of automobiles, but also between dissimilar products. The desires of most consumers exceed their budgets. They have to make choices between a new refrigerator and a washing machine, between a new car and a vacation, between a color television set or a hi-fi system, between a pair of shoes or a suit. In a marketing economy, each producer competes with others for a share of consumer purchases.

During times of economic affluence, or in a newly developing market, sometimes all competitors increase their sales and profits because there is enough business to go around. Even under the most favorable conditions, however, some competitors succeed and others fail. During times of economic stress, when purchasing power is depressed, competition becomes more intense. The price of success goes up and the penalty for failure becomes more punishing. A similar situation exists in mature markets. That is, markets that have leveled off or are beginning to shrink. Competition in such markets is a zero-sum game; an increase in sales for one firm means a decrease in sales for others.

Firms compete on many bases: price, quality, product features, advertising appeals, sales promotion, product availability, and service. An individual firm designs its marketing program around these variables to appeal to a particular group or groups of consumers. Competing firms do the same thing. And, no firm has any control over what other firms do.

A carefully-designed marketing strategy and a carefully-executed program can be negated by a competitor who introduces a superior product, lowers prices, devises a more effective distribution system, or develops an especially appealing advertising or sales promotion program. A firm can only try to anticipate what competitors will do; it has no control over them. As a consequence, competition exists as a major uncontrollable variable in the marketing environment.

The Legal Environment

Prior to 1890, no business legislation had been enacted as such. Firms were constrained by *common law,* an ambiguous body of doctrine that governed commercial activities. Violence, fraud, and criminal activity in business practice were frowned upon, but the mechanics for obtaining redress even in these spheres were left to private initiative. Monopolies, cartels, price-fixing, stock-rigging, and other activities deemed unsavory by today's standards were not uncommon. Robber barons flourished, and the Rockefellers, Mellons, Goulds, Fricks, and Harrimans built family fortunes that enabled their descendents to pursue vocations of public service.

Private excess by powerful capitalists led to even greater business excess. Philip Danforth

Armour, founder of the company by the same name, made his fortune by providing rotting beef to the Union Army. Railway tycoons enriched themselves by price discrimination and coercive contracts with farmers and cattlemen dependent upon the railroads to get their produce to eastern markets. People increasingly resented what they perceived as the great disparity in wealth between the capitalists and the masses; government intervention in the economic process became a political necessity.

By 1888 public revolt against monopolies had increased to the point that the political platform of the Democratic party contained a condemnation of trusts and conspiracies to restrain trade, and the Democratic party campaign promised to restore the benefits of price competition. The Democrats lost the election, but Republican victor Benjamin Harrison asked Congress to pass the first antitrust law governing competition.

The *Sherman-Antitrust Act,* enacted in 1890, had two major provisions:

- *It made monoplies illegal.* Specifically, "Every contract or combination in the form of a trust or otherwise, or conspiracy, in the restraint of trade or commerce among the several states or the foreign nations, is hereby declared to be illegal."
- *It made efforts to monopolize illegal.* ". . . every person who shall monopolize, or combine or conspire with any other person or persons, to monopolize any part of the trade or commerce among the several states or foreign nations, shall be deemed guilty of a misdemeanor, and on conviction thereof shall be punished by fine not exceeding five thousand dollars, or by imprisonment not exceeding one year, or by both said punishments, in the discretion of the court."

As a piece of legislation, the original Sherman-Antitrust Act was a poor and puny thing, thought by many to have been enacted as a political sop to public demand rather than as a piece of enforceable legislation. Indeed, the ambiguity of the Sherman Antitrust Act in defining "monopoly" or "conspiracy to monopolize," combined with its failure to establish a legal mechanism for dealing with problems of monopoly, seriously limited its effectiveness. Nonetheless, the Sherman Antitrust Act is a landmark piece of legislation for three reasons:

- This act was the first major government intervention into the workings of the economic system. As such, it opened the way for what, in the 1960s and 1970s, became a veritable flood of legislation designed to eliminate or control business abuses.
- Through a series of amendments and supplementary legislative acts, the Sherman Antitrust Act has been strengthened until today it stands as the foundation for antitrust enforcement.
- Attempts to clarify the meaning of the legislation led to the formulation of "the rule of reason" in the Standard Oil Case in 1911. The "rule of reason" suggested that the Sherman Antitrust Act applied only to "unreasonable" restraints of trade, and has been interpreted to mean that each case must be judged upon its own merits, a practice that prevails today.

THREE LEGISLATIVE PHILOSOPHIES. The history of business legislation during the past ninety years has been characterized by three distinct legislative philosophies:

To prevent monopoly and protect competition.

To protect individual consumers.

To protect society.

Let's look at each of these legislative philosophies more carefully.

Legislation to Protect Competition. Beginning with the Sherman Antitrust Act, a number of legislative acts have emerged to protect competition. Four of the most important are: the Federal Trade Commission Act, the Clayton Act, the Robinson-Patman Act, and the Celler–Kefauver Antimerger Act.

The Federal Trade Commission Act (1914)
Because of the ambiguity of the Sherman Antitrust Act and its lack of an administrative mechanism, the U.S. Justice Department was reluctant to initiate antitrust suits, and was relatively unsuccessful in those that it did initiate. So in 1914, Congress passed the Federal Trade Commission Act. The primary purposes of the act were to:

- Establish the Federal Trade Commission (FTC) to:
  (1) investigate matters involving antitrust proceedings, and to issue cease and desist orders when, in the commission's judgment, they were warranted.
  (2) serve as a "friend of the court" on technical and economic issues relating to antitrust.
- Declare that "unfair methods of competition in commerce, and unfair or deceptive acts in commerce" were unlawful.

The Clayton Act (1914)
The Clayton Act also strengthened the Sherman Antitrust Act by defining practices as unlawful "where the effect . . . may be to substantially lessen competition or to create a monopoly." In addition, it singled out four specific practices as unlawful *provided* they tended to lessen competition or create monopoly. The Clayton Act

- Prohibited price discrimination.
- Prohibited tying agreements, making it illegal to require customers (distributors and wholesalers) not to handle competitors' products.
- Prohibited the acquisition of the capital stock of competitors where such acquisition would restrain competition.
- Prohibited interlocking directorates of companies in competition with one another.

Again, these acts are *not* illegal per se; they are only illegal when they tend to substantially lessen competition or create monopoly. Also, the Federal Trade Commission was left with the task of determining guidelines for the term *substantially lessen competition.*

The Robinson-Patman Act (1936)
Although the Federal Trade Commission and the Clayton Act strengthened the Sherman Antitrust Act, they did not solve all of its problems. This became particularly apparent with the rise of large corporate chains in the late 1920s, and the threat they posed for small retailers. Large retail chains, with A&P being a specific example, were able to gain price concessions from suppliers by threatening to withdraw their business. In addition, A&P collected brokerage fees from totally owned subsidiaries, giving it a further price advantage. A&P and other large retail corporations also asked for and obtained special promotional allowances which resulted in a further competitive advantage over small retailers. In 1936 Congress dealt with these problems by passing the Robinson-Patman Act, which has become one of the most influential pieces of federal legislation affecting business. Specifically, the Robinson-Patman Act:

- Prohibited price discrimination—that is charging different prices to different customers for goods of like grade and quality—subject to certain defenses.
- Prohibited paying brokerage fees to totally owned subsidiaries.
- Required that promotional allowances be offered on a "proportionate" basis to all customers, not just to large accounts.
- Stated that a buyer is culpable if a discriminatory price has been knowingly induced or received.

The real impact of the Robinson-Patman Act, however, lay in its modification of the phrase "to substantially lessen competition or tend to create a monopoly." To this phrase, the Robinson-Patman Act added "or to injure, destroy, or prevent competition." Thus, a business practice no longer had to "substantially reduce competition" to be illegal. It only had to "injure" competition. The addition of these words opened a real bag of worms because the FTC, and many court decisions, have interpreted "injury to competition" to

The United States Congress—where marketing rules are made by people who do not know much about marketing. (Photo by Paul Conklin)

mean "injury to an individual competitor." Obviously, demonstrating that an individual competitor has been injured is easier than demonstrating that competition in general has been injured. The problem arising from this interpretation is that almost any marketing activity undertaken by a firm is designed to improve that firm's market position at the expense of competition. Companies that successfully innovate injure individual competitors all of the time. And, inefficient firms are constantly being injured. Thus, one criticism of the Robinson-Patman Act is that, instead of promoting competition, it protects inefficient marketers from legitimate competition. The Robinson-Patman Act has made business firms extremely cautious, and discouraged the use of price competition, thereby penalizing consumers—a far cry from the original intent of antitrust legislation.

The Celler–Kefauver Antimerger Act (1950). The Clayton Act prohibited the acquisition of capital stock in a competitive company if this acquisition would reduce competition. The Celler–Kefauver Act extends this prohibition by preventing the acquisition of the assets of competitive firms, if the result is to lessen competition.

A summary of major legislation designed to protect competition, along with the primary purposes of this legislation, is shown in Table 2–2.

Legislation to Protect Consumers. Prior to 1906, the prevailing philosophy of business was *caveat emptor*—"let the buyer beware." And, buyers had a lot to beware of. Some food and drug companies were selling dangerous drugs and contaminated or adulterated foods. Meat packers were endangering public health by selling diseased meat, and ground meat replete with animal offal,

TABLE 2–2: *U.S. Legislation to Protect Competition*

Sherman Antitrust Act (1890) Prohibits contracts, combinations, and conspiracies restraining trade. Also declares monopolies or attempts to create monopolies illegal.

Federal Trade Commission Act (1914) Established the Federal Trade Commission (FTC) as an administrative agency to study and investigate antitrust matters. Also declares unfair methods of competition to be unlawful.

Clayton Act (1914) Prohibited certain specific practices (price discrimination, tying clauses and exclusive dealing, intercorporate stockholding, interlocking directorates) where the effect "may be to substantially lessen competition or tend to create monopoly." Provided that individual corporate officials could be held liable, and eliminated labor and agricultural organizations from its provisions.

Robinson-Patman Act (1936) Amended the Clayton Act. Prohibits price discrimination (subject to certain defenses), provided the FTC with the authority to limit quantity discounts, forbids brokerage allowances except to independent brokers, and prohibited discriminatory promotional allowances.

Miller-Tydings Act (1937) Amended the Sherman Antitrust Act to exempt interstate fair-trade (price fixing) from antitrust prosecution. The purpose of the act was to protect small retailers from predatory pricing practices of chain stores.

Celler–Kefauver Antimerger Act (1950) Amended the Clayton Act to prohibit the acquisition of assets (as opposed to capital stock) if the effect were to lessen competition.

McGuire Act (1952) The basis of fair-trade (Miller-Tydings Act) rested in a nonsigners clause which held that if one retailer in a state signed a fair-trade agreement with a manufacturer, all other retailers were equally obligated to observe the agreement. The nonsigner clause was struck out in a court decision. The McGuire Act reinstated the nonsigner clause.

Consumer Goods Pricing Act (1975) Repealed the fair-trade laws (Miller-Tydings Act and McGuire Act). These acts were repealed because Congress felt that they added to inflation and penalized any large business that operated efficiently.

Other Legislation A number of laws have been enacted affecting specific industries.

rotten meat, mouse droppings (and even the mice themselves), sawdust, floor sweepings, and every other imaginable form of filth and contamination.

In his book *The Jungle,* Upton Sinclair, wrote a searing exposé of the managerial tyranny and brutality rampant in the meat packing industry and, almost incidentally, described the contamination of meat products. Sinclair intended his book as a social protest against brutal and inhuman treatment of workers. *The Jungle* led to widespread public indignation—not over the brutal inhumanity it portrayed—but over the contamination of the meat products which it described. As Sinclair himself later said, "I aimed at the public's heart—and hit its stomach."

About the same time, Harvey W. Wiley, the chief chemist of the U.S. Agriculture Department, became appalled by the dangerous drugs that were being sold, and by the contamination, adulteration, and mislabeling that he found in food and drug products. His protests, combined with the public indignation aroused by Upton Sinclair, led to the passage of the first consumer protection legislation—the *Pure Food and Drug Act* and the *Meat Inspection Act.*

Subsequently, legislation to protect consumers has appeared in an increasing torrent. Table 2–3 identifies some of the major consumer protection legislation enacted by the federal government.

In addition, states and many municipalities have enacted consumer protection legislation, and major cities have established departments of consumer affairs and given them teeth through consumer protection acts that cover a wide range of deceptive marketing practices.[16]

Legislation to Protect Society. Earlier, we noted that manufacturing firms, in an effort to keep production costs low, often pollute the environment with smoke particulate and industrial wastes. By the 1960s, the public concern over industrial pollution was becoming increasingly strident. Rachel Carson, in her book *The Silent Spring,* inveighed against industrial practices that destroyed wildlife, raped the earth, and contaminated the environ-

16. "The New Centurians," *Time* (Sept. 18, 1972).

TABLE 2–3: Major Legislation Designed to Protect Consumers

Pure Food and Drug Act (1906) Forbade the manufacture, sale, or transport of adulterated or fraudulently labeled food and drug products in interstate commerce.

Meat Inspection Act (1906) Provides for enforcement of sanitary conditions and federal inspection of slaughtering, packing, and canning plants that ship meat products in interstate commerce.

Wheeler Lea Act (1937) An amendment to the Federal Trade Commission Act which gives the FTC jurisdiction over advertising of food, drugs, cosmetics, and therapeutic devices.

Cosmetic Act (1938) Extends FTC authority over packaging, branding, and labeling to include cosmetics and therapeutic devices.

Wool Products Labeling Act (1939) Requires that wool products be labeled to show the percent of virgin wool, reprocessed wool, and reused wool.

Fur Products Labeling Act (1951) Prohibits false advertising and mislabeling of fur products.

Flammable Fabrics Act (1953) Prohibits the manufacture and sale of wearing apparel that is dangerously flammable.

Automobile Information Disclosure Act (1958) Designed to prevent deceptive pricing, the act requires automobile dealers to affix a statement on new cars showing the suggested retail price for the automobile and factory installed accessories.

Textile Fiber Products Identification Act (1958) Requires that labels of textiles identify fibers used by percent of content, the name of the manufacturer or distributor (if imported), and requires that synthetic fibers be identified by generic names assigned by the FTC.

National Traffic and Safety Act (1966) Directs the Secretary of Transportation to issue compulsory safety standards for automobiles and tires.

Fair Packaging and Labeling Act (1966) Establishes regulation for the packaging and labeling of consumer goods. Manufacturers must show what the package contains, its quantity, and who made it. Permits industries to establish and adopt uniform packaging standards.

Child Protection Act (1966) Prohibited the sale of hazardous toys and other products to children.

Federal Cigarette Labeling and Advertising Act (1967) Requires cigarette packages to carry the following statement: "Warning: The Surgeon General Has Determined That Cigarette Smoking Is Dangerous To Your Health."

Consumer Credit Protection Act (1968) Requires disclosure of credit terms and annual interest rates on loans and installment purchases.

Fair Credit Reporting Act (1970) Requires that consumer credit reports contain only accurate, relevant, and recent information, and requires that such information be handled confidentially.

Consumer Product Safety Act (1972) Established the Consumer Product Safety Commission and authorized it to set safety standards for unsafe products, and to establish penalties for failure to meet standards.

Magnuson-Moss Warranty/FTC Improvement Act (1975) Establishes minimum standards for written consumer product warranties, and provides for methods of redress such as "class action" suits. Also authorizes FTC to prescribe regulations governing the use of warranties.

Other Legislation Other federal laws, as well as state and local statutes have also been enacted in the interests of consumers.

ment. Organizations, such as the Sierra Club and The Friends of the Earth, took up the cry and in 1969, The *National Environmental Policy Act* was passed by Congress. This legislation established a national policy toward the environment and authorized the formation of the *Council on Environmental Quality*. In 1970, this council was superceded by the *Environmental Protection Agency*.

EVALUATION OF MARKETING LEGISLATION. Undoubtedly much of the marketing legislation that has been enacted is desirable. To protect competition, to protect consumers, and to protect society are laudable endeavors.

In many instances, however, government legislation has had undesirable and unintentional consequences. Governments, throughout history, have been known for their excesses.[17] Earlier, for example, we noted that FTC interpretation of the Robinson-Patman Act has served to protect inefficient competitors, and to raise

17. For a discussion of this issue, see Walter Guzzardi, Jr., "A Search for Sanity in Antitrust," *Fortune* (Jan. 30, 1978):72–73.

prices—a violation of the intent of the legislation. Similarly, consumer protection legislation in the food and drug field has resulted in excessive caution by government agencies that has increased the cost of developing and bringing a new drug to the marketplace from $500,000 in the early 1960s to $54 million in 1978.[18] One result has been a sharp reduction in the development of new drugs in the United States. The problem is further complicated by the fact that the Food and Drug Administration (FDA) typically does not accept evidence from abroad as proof of effectiveness. Thus, many effective drugs sold in Europe may not be sold in the United States, and thousands of U.S. patients die unnecessarily as a result.

Many believe that government agencies exceed their authority by enforcing administrative decisions that go beyond the intent of Congress. This concern caused the U.S. Congress to enact the *legislative veto* in 1979. Through this device, Congress retains the right to overturn any administrative decisions that a sufficient number of its members do not favor.

The enactment of the legislative veto has been greeted with cheers and criticism by politicians and consumers alike. Proponents laud the legislative veto because it returns legislative authority back to Congress where it belongs. Opponents contend the legislative veto emasculates the authority of administrative agencies, and turns the control of business back to the political arena where it is subject to the politics of special interest groups, business lobbies, and political chicanery.

On balance, I suspect that the legislative veto is desirable. Those who staff the government's administrative agencies are not less subject to malice, bias, error, and political ambition than elected representatives. Further, the tyranny of administrative agencies is about as close as one can come to an authoritarian government in a representative democracy.

In any event, government legislation is, for the most part, beyond the control of individual firms. An uncontrollable element in the environment, government legislation adds uncertainty to the practice of marketing.

18. Milton and Rose Friedman, *Free to Choose* (New York: Avon Books, 1979), p. 196.

Consumerism

Along with the growth of government legislation to protect consumers, a multitude of activist, consumer interest groups has emerged at the national, state, and local levels. These groups, in fact, have inspired much of the consumer-protection legislation that has been enacted.

Taking their cue from President John F. Kennedy's "rights of consumers"—the right to safety, the right to be informed, the right to choose, and the right to be heard—consumer groups have become a powerful force in demanding and obtaining more responsible behavior from the business community. Although consumer groups are usually responsible and constructive, they may also be irresponsible and destructive. A case in point is Ralph Nader and the Corvair. In 1965 Nader published *Unsafe at Any Speed,* a scathing indictment of General Motor's Corvair. Public outcry gave rise to congressional hearings that resulted in the *National Traffic and Safety Act* of 1966. Some six years later, one of the agencies set up under the National Traffic and Safety Act got around to testing the Corvair against comparable cars. Their conclusion? "The 1960–63 Corvair compared favorably with the other contemporary vehicles used in the test."[19]

Many marketers tend to view consumer-interest groups as wholly unreasonable and a threat to marketing freedom. In some instances, consumer groups are unreasonable and irresponsible, and they *do* impose restraints on marketing freedom, particularly for those marketers who are insensitive to, or contemptuous of consumer concerns.

Realistically, however, like government, consumerism should be viewed as an uncontrollable environmental variable. While consumerism may indeed create problems, it also provides opportunities for the marketing firm willing to note

19. *Evaluation of the 1960–63 Corvair Handling, Stability* (Washington DC: U.S. Department of Transportation, National Highway Traffic Safety Administration, July, 1972), p. 2.

Consumerism—threat or benefit? (Photo by Paul Rosenfeld)

consumers' concerns and, where possible, incorporate them into product offerings and marketing practices.

SUMMARY

Were it not for the uncontrollable variables in the marketing environment, marketing planning and execution would not be difficult. Because of these uncontrollable variables, however, the best laid plans often go awry and many marketing programs end up as an exercise in frustration and disappointment. The major uncontrollable variables affecting marketing are consumers, the level of economic activity, technology, resource availability, competition, government, and consumerism.

To function effectively, marketing managers must be aware of the beliefs, values, and expectations held by consumers, and sensitive to trends in consumer behavior and buying interests. Similarly, marketing managers need to use demographic data as a basis for forecasting changes in the composition of the U.S. population because of the influence that demographic changes have on buying patterns.

The level of economic activity will also influence buying patterns, and marketers should be aware of the possible effects of prosperity, recession, and inflation on consumer spending.

Technological developments, resource availability, and competition are also uncontrollable elements that can affect production costs, product quality, and competitive strategies.

Marketing managers must be aware of legal restrictions affecting virtually all marketing activities, and responsive to the concerns of consumers as expressed by consumer interest groups.

Although uncontrollable variables do impose restrictions on marketing freedom, they also give rise to marketing opportunities for alert and imaginative firms which seek them out.

REVIEW QUESTIONS

1. Explain *cultural pluralism* and why it is important to marketing.
2. Distinguish between *basic* and *surface* changes in the U.S. culture and explain why they are important to marketers. Demonstrate your answer with specific examples.
3. Explain demographics and give specific examples of how demographic composition might affect a company's sales.
4. Explain with examples how the level of economic activity may affect marketing.
5. How does technology in the United States appear to be changing? What effect should these changes have on the competitiveness of American products?
6. Under the section on *resource availability,* the text identifies two areas of problems and opportunities: *rising costs* and *pollution.* Show how each of these areas presents both problems *and* opportunities for marketers.
7. Explain why the Sherman Antitrust Act, although a relatively weak legislative act, is a landmark in business legislation.
8. Identify and explain the three distinct legislative philosophies that characterize business legislation.
9. Identify and characterize the basic purpose of each of the major legislative acts designed to prevent monopoly and protect competition.
10. Explain why the Robinson-Patman Act has been charged with protecting inefficient marketers rather than promoting competition.

DISCUSSION QUESTIONS

1. As a producer of microwave ovens, discuss how the uncontrollable marketing factors might influence your operation.
2. Because of the high costs and risks involved in technological research, it may be argued that small firms should adopt a strategy of copying what larger firms do. Do you agree with this strategy? Why or why not?
3. In 1980 Chrysler was facing bankruptcy. In order keep it in business and to save ten thousand jobs, the U.S. government guaranteed loans to the company. Do you agree with this action? Why or why not? How does this government action relate to the U.S. policy of encouraging competition?
4. Free economists argue that government interference in business does more harm than good. Do you agree with this point of view? Why or why not?
5. In 1978 the FTC proposed major restrictions on children's television. Specifically, FTC recommended:
   - Ban all advertising from TV shows seen by substantial audiences of children under 8 because they are too young to understand the selling intent of the message.

- Ban advertising of sugary foods that pose dental health risks from TV shows seen by significant numbers of children between 8 and 11.
- Allow continued TV advertising of less hazardous sugared foods to the 8 to 11 year-old-group, but only if individual food advertisers used "balancing" nutritional and/or health disclosures.

Do you agree with this proposal? Why or why not?

UNCONTROLLABLE ENVIRONMENTAL VARIABLES

Advertising has long been a target of the Federal Trade Commission (FTC). Charges against advertising have ranged from the contention that advertising is a "barrier to competition" to accusations of fraudulent and deceptive advertising.

Basing its actions on the Wheeler-Lea Act (1938), the FTC has brought charges of false advertising against many well-known brands. Section 12 of the Wheeler-Lea Act states, in part, "It shall be unlawful for any person, partnership, or corporation to disseminate, or cause to be disseminated any false advertisement. . . ." In section 15, false advertising is defined in these words:

> *The term* false advertisement *means an advertisement, other than labeling, which is misleading in a material respect; and in determining whether any advertisement is misleading, there shall be taken into account (among other things) not only representations made or suggested by statement, word, design, device, sound, or any combination thereof, but also the extent to which the advertisement fails to reveal facts material in the light of such representations or material with respect to consequences which may result from the use of the commodity to which the advertisement relates under the conditions prescribed in said advertisement, or conditions as are customary or usual.*

Below, in summary form, are some of the cases which have arisen under the FTC's interpretation of the Wheeler–Lea Act.

- *A commercial for Cranapple, a breakfast drink, claimed that the product provided extra energy because it was high in "food value." The FTC claimed that the commercial was deceptive because most consumers did not know that, in nutritional terms, "food value" means "calories."*
- *In a demonstration for Campbell's vegetable soup, marbles were placed in the bottom of the bowl to make the vegetables rise to the top. The FTC charged that the commercial was deceptive because it exaggerated the amount of vegetables in the soup. Campbell's defense was that, if marbles were not used, the vegetables sank to the bottom, giving the impression that the bowl contained less vegetables than it actually did.*
- *An advertisement for Wonder Bread claimed that its enriched bread "Helps build strong bodies 12 ways." The FTC charged that the advertisement was deceptive because, even though the claim was true, it was not unique since other brands of enriched bread had the same benefits. And, by using this claim, the Wonder Bread advertisement implied that it was nutritionally superior to other enriched breads.*
- *Profile Bread advertising claimed that it had fewer calories per slice than other brands of bread. The FTC charged that the advertisement was deceptive because it failed to point out that each slice of Profile Bread was thinner than the slices of other breads.*
- *Sears attracted customers to its stores by advertising an attractive sewing machine for $58. FTC charged Sears with deceptive practices because, when customers inquired about the advertised model, Sears salespeople tried to trade them up to a higher priced model by disparaging the advertised model with such statements as: "the advertised sewing machines are noisy and are not guaranteed for as long a time as the firm's more expensive models; certain of them will not sew a straight stitch, zigzag stitch, or in reverse; none of the advertised sewing machines is available for sale and, if ordered, there will be long delays in delivery."*
- *Manufacturers of Rapid Shave produced a television commercial that purported to show the moisterizing effects of the brand by applying it to sandpaper and then removing the sand with one stroke of a razor.*

Actually, sandpaper was not used in the demonstration. Instead, loose sand was spread on Plexiglas to simulate sandpaper. The FTC charged the company with deceptive advertising.

- *When Dry Ban, one of the first "dry" deodorants was introduced, advertisements claimed that it was superior to existing spray deodorants because it was a dry spray and left no wet residue when applied to the body. The FTC charged deceptive advertising because the spray, while drier than existing products, was not entirely dry.*
- *Advertising for Chevron gasoline claimed that an ingredient, F-310, helped reduce pollution. The FTC charged the company with deceptive advertising because, although F-310 did indeed reduce pollution, the total amount of pollution reduction was not significant and, therefore, could not be claimed in advertising.*
- *Advertising for STP, an oil additive, claimed that use of the product would reduce oil consumption by 20 percent. The FTC charged the company with deceptive advertising, claiming that the tests upon which the advertising claims were based were faulty. The company's defense was: "Nowhere (in the FTC complaint) is there any challenge to the efficacy of the product. It's merely a question of some defective tests done years ago."*

Assignment

Do you think that the FTC's charges of deceptive advertising in each of these cases are reasonable? Why or why not?

3

Markets and Marketing Strategy

- *The nature of markets.*
- *The concept of market segments.*
- *The strategies of product differentiation and market segmentation.*
- *Bases for segmenting markets.*

MARKETING EXAMPLES

Thus far, we have used the term *market* in a general sense; the way you and I use the term in our everyday conversation. But, in order to turn our attention to the day-to-day tasks of marketing, we need to look at the concept of a market more closely in order to understand what a market really is. Actually, it is a somewhat ambiguous term. Consider the following examples:

AUTOMOBILES

1979 was a mixed year for the automotive industry. Spiraling gas prices finally convinced most Americans that the days of low cost fuel were over. Sales of fuel-efficient imports were booming. Long waiting lists resulted from consumers flocking to their retail outlets. Prices for imports were relatively high because of demand and a devalued dollar. Few bargains could be found and profits were high because foreign car agencies were in a *seller's market.*

At the same time, sales of large, fuel-inefficient U.S. cars were in the doldrums. Sales were down, discounts on new cars were rampant, and dealers were offering every imaginable kind of premium to get car buyers to visit their showrooms. Consumers interested in doing so could make some good buys because large, American cars were in a *buyer's market.*

BABIES

Babies are a big market. Baby foods, disposable diapers, baby shampoos, pants, powders, pacifiers, and nursing bottles alone account for more than $2.5 billion in retail sales. And, this figure does not include dozens of other products purchased solely for babies—clothes, toys, furniture, and so forth. So, babies are a market.

TUCSON, PITTSBURGH, AND NEW YORK CITY

According to *Advertising Age,* Tucson, Pittsburgh, and New York City are among the one hundred largest markets in the United States.[1] Tucson passed the 500,000 population mark in 1979, ranked 83rd among U.S. markets, and had an aggregate personal income in excess of $2.9 billion. Tucson's housing industry was hard pressed to keep up with the influx of snowbirds who deserted the frozen northeast and upper Midwest in search of a more benign climate.

Pittsburgh, Pennsylvania, ranks thirteenth among U.S. cities with a population exceeding 2.3 million and an aggregate personal income over $17.1 billion. And then there is the "Big Apple"—New York City—the granddaddy of all U.S. markets. New York's population is over 9.2 million, its aggregate personal income over $76 billion, and it is still growing.

SOUP

Soup is also a market. Dried soups, frozen soups, canned soups, and soup starters. Canned soups alone account for over a billion dollars in retail sales and Campbell's, with its sixty or so different varieties in easily recognizable red and white cans has a lock on more than 80 percent of this large and growing market.

1. *Advertising Age* (Dec. 19, 1979). Information on the top 100 U.S. markets is listed alphabetically throughout the issue.

Conditions of sale, people, places, and products are all referred to as markets. What *is* a market?

DEFINITION OF A MARKET

Generically, a market is a group of people with purchasing power who are willing to spend money to satisfy their needs. Three aspects of this definition should be noted: people, purchasing power, and willingness to spend. These are the essential dimensions of a market. Let's look at each more closely.

People

All products and services are acquired by people, and these people are the object of all marketing activity. This is true whether we are speaking of a pet owner buying food for the family dog, an industrial buyer making a purchase for a company, a householder buying for other members of the family, or an individual making a personal purchase.

Purchasing Power

The second element in the concept of a market is purchasing power. Without purchasing power, there is no market in the business sense. Many of us are not part of the market for many products because we lack purchasing power. For example, most people are not part of the market for a Rolls-Royce simply because they do not have the $80,000 or so that is required to buy the economy model.[2]

Willingness to Spend

The third element in the concept of a market is willingness to spend. People must be willing to spend their purchasing power for a product before they may be considered a part of its market. Thus, most of us are excluded from many markets through choice. We have neither need for nor interest in hundreds of products that we can well afford.

These three elements—people, purchasing power, and willingness to spend—are all necessary conditions for a market. Without any one of them, no market exists in the business sense.

A *seller's market,* has an excess of demand. That is, an excess of people with money to spend who are not only willing, but eager, to spend their money for a product in short supply. Under these conditions, the seller is in control and sets the conditions of sale, as in the case of fuel-efficient automobiles. A *buyer's market,* has an excess of supply in relationship to demand. The supply of the product in question is greater than the people who are willing to spend their money for it. Under these circumstances, buyers control the conditions of sale, and sellers resort to price cuts, premiums, and other devices to dispose of inventories.

When we speak of the *baby market,* we are speaking of a group of people who buy products that are used for babies. We may also speak of the geriatric market (elderly people), or the youth market, or the pet market (made up of pet owners), or the Catholic market, or any other identifiable group of people who are willing to spend money in the satisfaction of their needs. A *product market*—the soup market, the dog food market, or the cake mix market—refers to those people who buy these products. And, Tucson, Pittsburgh, and New York are markets because they represent places where buying and selling occurs—implying the existence of people, purchasing power, and willingness to spend.

Throughout the text, the term *market* is used in all of the senses described above, with the particular meaning of the term being given by the context in which it is used. Regardless of how the term *market* is used, it always involves people with purchasing power and a willingness to spend.

PRODUCT MARKETS

The generic definition of a market must be refined and made more specific to be truly useful as a marketing concept. Thus, we need to focus on

2. This is an interesting example of the effects of inflation. When I first started using this example in class in 1975, one could buy a Rolls-Royce for $42,500.

TABLE 3–1: Households Using Selected Products.
SOURCE: "1979 Guide to Product Use," *Progressive Grocer* (July 1979), pp. 39ff.

	Households Using
Flour	*95.2%*
Cake Mixes	*77.8*
Pancake Mixes	*71.1*
Candy Bars	*47.1*
Powdered Breakfast Drinks	*19.6*
Cold Cereals	*90.8*
Hot Cereals	*76.3*
Regular Tea	*80.5*
Iced Tea Mixes	*31.4*
Dry Gravy and Sauces	*33.3*
Margarine	*91.9*
Peanut Butter	*90.5*
Instant Pudding	*66.9*
Frozen Vegetables	*78.4*
Salad Dressing	*87.9*
Vegetable Juices	*55.1*
Canned Cat Food	*11.5*
Canned Soup	*91.1*

particular groups of people who are willing to spend their money for particular products.

A product may be defined *as a bundle of attributes capable of satisfying human needs. A product market, then, consists of all those people whose needs may be satisfied by the particular bundle of attributes possessed by the product in question.* Note that, in marketing, the term *product* is used in an inclusive sense. Considered as a bundle of attributes, a product may be a physical thing, like a radio, a camera, or a tube of toothpaste. Or, a service, such as that offered by a mechanic, a television repairperson, or a dentist. Or, an idea, such as a scheme to get rich.

Most people in the United States are part of many markets. Nevertheless, not everyone is part of each market for all products. All of us eat food, but not everyone eats tapioca pudding. Some people don't eat brussel sprouts, and vegetarians don't eat meat. In truth, the market for most products is limited. *Supermarketing,* in an annual study of consumer expenditures, lists over two hundred different categories of food.[3] Table 3–1 shows the percent of U.S. families buying some of the various products listed in this study.

Note that none of these product categories enjoy universal use. Some—flour, cold cereals, margarine, peanut butter, and soup—are bought by over 90 percent of the families, but the usage of these products is not universal. Others, such as powdered breakfast drinks (19.6 percent usage), iced tea mix (31.4 percent) and canned cat food (11.5 percent), are used by relatively few families. Even among those categories that enjoy widespread usage (soup, for example) not everyone likes the same flavors. Thus, Campbell's manufactures more than sixty varieties of soup, each designed to appeal to different tastes, and each constituting a market in its own right. Thus, we may speak of the market for vegetable soup, the market for cream of tomato soup, or the market for cream of mushroom soup.

So it is with most products. People's interests vary, funds are limited, and choices have to be made. A business firm has to identify groups of people interested in and able to buy the products it produces, or is able to produce, and to direct marketing activities toward these groups. That is, firms need to consider markets from the standpoint of the products required to meet the diverse needs of various groups of people. The existence of these various groups of people with diverse needs introduces the concept of market segments.

MARKET SEGMENTS

Few product markets are entirely homogeneous. Rather, they tend to be composed of groups of people who seek somewhat different attributes in the products they buy. Let's examine a couple of product markets in order to clarify this thought.

The Cigarette Market

The cigarette market is a product market made up of people who smoke cigarettes. But, not all

3. "Annual Consumer Expenditures Study," *Supermarketing* (September, 1978).

FIGURE 3–1: *Cigarette Markets.*
SOURCE: Computed from *Advertising Age* (December 17, 1979): 56–57

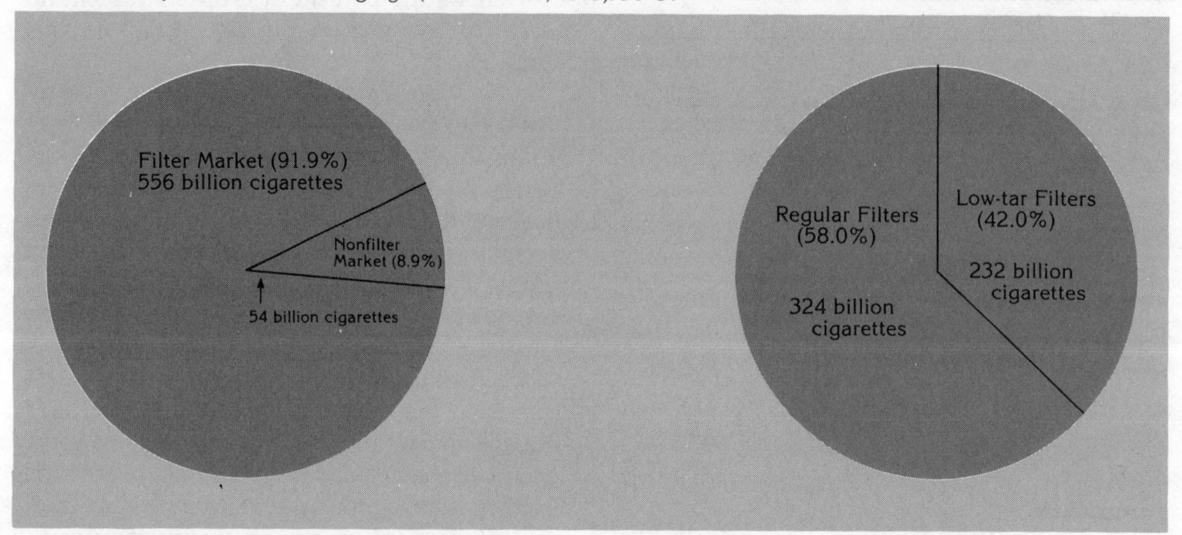

cigarette smokers are interested in the same product attributes. To begin with, the cigarette market consists of two distinctly different segments—people who smoke nonfilter cigarettes, possibly because of their stronger flavor—and people who smoke filter cigarettes, presumably because of concerns over health or preference for a milder taste. Both market segments are substantial, although the filter market is by far the larger. (See Figure 3–1.)

The filter market, itself, is not a homogeneous market, but can be broken into at least two segments based on the effectiveness of the filter—regular filter smokers and low-tar filter smokers. The difference between these two groups probably lies in the extent of their concern over the dangers of smoking. (See Figure 3–1.)

The cigarette market can also be dissected into segments based on other variables, such as menthol or nonmenthol, regular or king size, hard pack or soft pack, and on the basis of masculinity or femininity. Marlboro, for example, is the epitome of masculinity among cigarettes, whereas Virginia Slims and Eve are clearly designed to appeal to the feminine segment of the market. The feminine segment of the market can be subdivided even further. Virginia Slims is marketed to the liberated woman; Eve, to the more traditional one. The point is that the cigarette market is not homogeneous, but segmented by different groups of people who want different attributes in the cigarettes they smoke.

FIGURE 3–2: *Dog Food Market*
SOURCE: "31st Annual Consumer Expenditure Study," *Supermarketing* (September 1978).

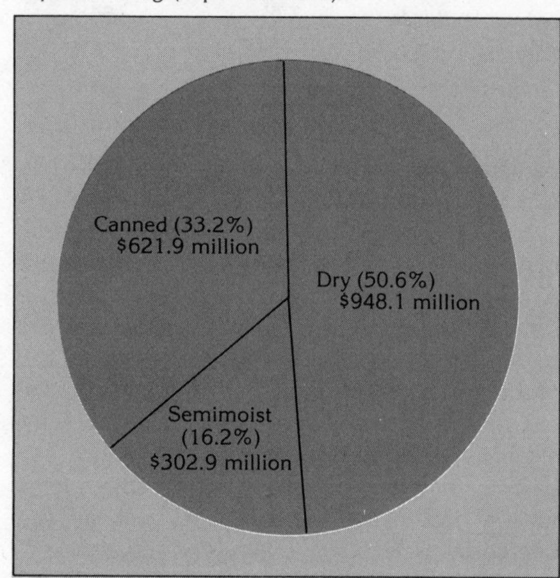

The Dog Food Market

Using product form as a segmentation variable, the prepared dog food market can be subdivided into three separate segments—canned, dry, and semimoist. (See Figure 3–2.) Still a fourth segment of this market is referred to as mixed feeders. That is, people who buy two or more forms of prepared dog food. In fact, a fairly recent development in the dog food market is the emergence of a dry-moist category, presumably developed for the mixed feeders who want the convenience of buying two kinds of dog food in the same package. The dry-moist category which, as the name implies, is a combination of dry and moist food, contained three brands in 1979—Tender Chunks (Quaker Oats), Moist & Chunky (Ralston Purina), and Tender Moist Chunx (Jim Dandy)—with a combined volume of $154 million.

The dog food market can also be divided into other segments using different variables than product form as the basis for segmentation. For example, segmentation on the basis of price, the age of the pet (puppies or mature dogs), the occasion of feeding (treats or full nutrition dinners), and energy value (working dogs or household pets).

Again, as in the case of cigarettes, the dog food market consists of submarkets or segments, each composed of groups of people who want a slightly different bundle of attributes.

MARKETS AND MARKETING STRATEGY

Essentially, marketers use two strategies in approaching product markets: product differentiation and market segmentation.

Product Differentiation

Product differentiation, also referred to as *undifferentiated marketing,*[4] *market aggregation,*[5] and *market combination,*[6] is an appropriate strategy:

- When markets are indeed homogeneous.
- When subdividing a market into smaller segments is not economically feasible.
- In new markets with little competition where market growth often exceeds production capacity.

Under this strategy, a firm chooses *not* to recognize the possible existence of market segments. Instead, the seller designs a product that will appeal to most buyers, and directs its promotional activities to the whole market.

Often, in the face of stiff competition, the firm may attempt to create consumer preference for its brand by making unique advertising claims, or by modifying the brand in some insignificant way so that it *appears* different, and can be distinguished from competitive brands. Styling differences in the automotive industry provide an example of this approach.

ADVANTAGES OF PRODUCT DIFFERENTIATION. The primary advantage of this strategy is that it minimizes production, promotion, inventory, administrative, and other costs that may be increased by producing several brands designed for different market segments. Producing one brand rather than many is simply cheaper.

In addition, by concentrating marketing expenditures behind a single product, the brand may achieve market domination in consumer awareness and sales. This latter defense of a product differentiation strategy is summed up beautifully in this anecdote:

> The animals of the jungle were gathered around the watering hole during the twilight hours and conversation soon turned to their children. "I have two children," bragged the monkey, "and they are beautiful." "I have eight children," bragged the field mouse. "That's nothing," said the rabbit. "I have twelve children. How many do you have, Mr. Lion?" The lion surveyed the other animals contemptuously, and answered: "I have only one, but *he is a lion*."

DISADVANTAGES OF PRODUCT DIFFERENTIATION. Product differentiation has been widely criticized because of its failure to recognize that

4. Philip Kotler, *Marketing Management,* 4th edition (Englewood Cliffs, NJ: Prentice Hall, Inc., 1980), p. 207.
5. William J. Stanton, *Fundamentals of Marketing* (New York: McGraw-Hill Book Company, 1978), p. 73.
6. E. Jerome McCarthy, *Basic Marketing,* 6th edition (Homewood, IL: Richard D. Irwin, Inc., 1978), p. 70.

different consumers seek different attributes in the products they purchase. Few brands are capable of serving the needs of all consumers equally well, and those that attempt to be "everything to everybody" run the danger of becoming "nothing to anyone." By far, the most telling criticism of product differentiation is that the brand becomes vulnerable to other marketers more sensitive to consumer needs.

The U.S. automobile industry is a case in point. For years, the industry produced only large cars, with each succeeding model becoming larger, more powerful, and less efficient. Between 1955 and 1970, the typical U.S. car increased in size and weight by about 30 to 35 percent. By catering to the "majority" of car buyers, the industry virtually ignored a small, but growing segment of buyers who wanted a smaller, more maneuverable, more efficient, and less expensive mode of transportation. Certainly, there were reasons for this decision. Larger cars are more profitable, and the market for them was bigger. Nonetheless, U.S. producers' strategy enabled foreign manufacturers to gain a foothold in the lucrative U.S. automobile market by exploiting the unsatisfied segment of the market. Even when domestic producers awoke to this challenge, they attempted to meet it for the most part by "cutting down" large cars—a wholly unsatisfactory approach—rather than designing a small car from the ground up.

Another classic example is the Coca-Cola Company. For years the company sold the same product in a familiar one size hourglass–shaped bottle, which consumers could buy by the case or separately.[7] Pepsi Cola exploited the vulnerability of Coca-Cola by offering a cola product with a somewhat different flavor at a lower per ounce price. Pepsi Cola also catered to heavy users by introducing family-size bottles and six–packs. When Coca-Cola found its market share slipping significantly, the company's first response was to fire the advertising agency that had helped build a small, unknown maker of syrup into a national institution. But, someone had to be the scapegoat, and admitting their own marketing shortsightedness was difficult for Coca-Cola executives.

7. Coca-Cola did not totally ignore market segments. The company also distributed its syrup to soda fountains, thereby meeting the needs of out-of-home users. Local soda fountains catered to individual consumer preferences by adding citrus and other flavored syrups to the basic Coca-Cola syrup, so that consumers were offered cherry cokes, lemon cokes, lime cokes, chocolate cokes, and so forth.

Marketing Segmentation

Market segmentation (sometimes referred to as target marketing) differs from product differentiation in that the marketer recognizes market segments and deliberately takes them into consideration in devising marketing strategies. Market segmentation comes in two forms: differentiated marketing (or multisegment marketing) and concentrated marketing.[8]

DIFFERENTIATED MARKETING. Under differentiated marketing, the firm divides markets into two or more segments, and offers each a different product, a different marketing program, or both. This strategy is appropriate when:

- Markets are heterogeneous.
- Subdividing the market into smaller segments offers an opportunity for increased sales and profits.
- The firm has sufficient resources to market two or more products simultaneously.

Cigarettes, for example, are offered by the same company in both filter and nonfilter forms, as mentholated and nonmentholated, in different lengths, for men and women, and for different personality types.

Prepared dog food is offered by a single company in canned, dry, and semimoist forms; as full-nutrition and as treat products; for puppies and for mature dogs; and so forth. Automobiles are offered in different price ranges and for different purposes with four doors or two doors, four-wheel or front wheel drive; as station wagons,

8. Philip Kotler and others use the terms "differentiated" and "concentrated" marketing. Pride and Ferrel substitute the term "multisegment" marketing for "differentiated" marketing. Marketing practitioners often use the term "multiple-product" marketing to refer to "differentiated" marketing.

sports cars, recreation vehicles, dune buggies, and trucks. This latter segmentation is referred to as *end use* segmentation. Note that, in all of these examples a *different form* of the product is specifically designed for different market segments.

One may also engage in differentiated marketing with the *same product.* In these instances, the same product form is promoted to several market segments through separate marketing programs. For example, the evaporated milk industry has historically recognized three different market segments for its products—infant feeding, cooking, and coffee creaming. Historically, different promotional programs have appealed to each of these three groups. Arm & Hammer baking soda is also marketed to two markets through different advertising programs. One market uses the product for baking; the other for eliminating odors. While these market segments may overlap because some people will use the product in several ways, from a marketing standpoint, they represent different markets, requiring different advertising programs.

At this point, note that markets and market segments are seldom as discrete as many marketers would like to think. Women smoke cigarettes marketed for men and men smoke cigarettes marketed for women. Women wear pants, and men use perfume. I have both a family car (a Cordoba) and a fuel-efficient pickup (a Datsun). Confirmed cigarette smokers will smoke anything, including grapevine and cornsilk, when they are having nicotine fits.

Perhaps it is just as well that markets and market segments are not as discrete as we would like to think because many, if not most, of the media vehicles available for reaching markets are not that selective either. Hunters and nonhunters read *Field & Stream,* some women read *Playboy* and some men read *Mademoiselle.* Finally, the average soap opera, recognized and touted as a women's medium, will reach an audience of 58 percent women over the age of 18, and 42 percent men, children, and teenagers.

If we keep these limitations in mind and don't expect miracles, differentiated marketing is a useful concept which may improve the effectiveness and efficiency of marketing efforts on a scale ranging from a "great deal" to "a little." And, often small differences distinguish a winner from a loser: The winner of the National Professional Basketball title may beat the runner-up by 101 to 100, a difference of only 1 percent.

CONCENTRATED MARKETING. In a strategy of concentrated marketing, firms select one market segment, become experts on this segment, and direct their marketing activities toward it to the exclusion of other segments. Concentrated marketing is particularly appropriate when:

- A firm has limited resources and cannot afford to attack the entire market.
- A particular segment is being neglected by major competition.

Small local and regional marketers, lacking the resources to compete on a national level for the total market, follow a strategy of concentrated marketing by confining their activities to a limited geographic area.

Datsun and Toyota have selected the *small car segment* of the U.S. automobile market; Hush Puppies once concentrated only on the *casual shoe* segment of the shoe market; and Armour has concentrated on the *deodorant soap segment* of the *bath soap segment* of the *soap segment* of the giant *soap and detergent market* with a highly successful product, Dial. "You use Dial. Don't you wish everyone did?"

REQUIREMENTS FOR MARKET SEGMENTATION. Not all products can be segmented in the same way. Whether a particular form of segmentation is appropriate for a given market depends upon the needs and interests of the consuming groups involved. Furthermore, successful market segmentation generally requires that the segments be measurable, sizable, and reachable.

Measurable. A market segment should be subject to both definition and measurement. If the segment cannot be defined, it cannot be measured; if it cannot be measured, its potential for sales cannot be estimated. Some segments are relatively easy to measure. For example, markets based on age, sex, size of family, and so forth can be measured accurately through census data. On the other hand, market segments based on psychological or behavioral differences between consumer groups may be extremely difficult to measure.

Sizable. The market segment must be large enough to support an independent marketing effort. Many market segments are too small to justify the cost of developing a product to serve their specific needs. Frequently, a segment may be too small to produce sufficient revenue to permit the product to be advertised or promoted. The marketing system does not guarantee that all consumer needs will be served—only those needs that can be served at a profit.[9]

Reachable. A market segment must not only be measurable and sizable, it must be reachable with advertising and promotion costs commensurate with the market's size. Often, specialized media make it possible to reach particular markets. The baby market, a segment of the family market, may be reached through magazines and gift packs distributed in maternity wards of hospitals. Sports car buffs, a segment of the automotive market, may be reached through magazines edited with their specialized interests in mind. In many instances, a market segment may be large enough to justify the use of general media. Blond hair rinses, a segment of the hair care market, provides an example. Despite these requirements, a strategy of market segmentation offers many benefits for marketers.

BENEFITS OF MARKET SEGMENTATION. From the standpoint of the business firm, the primary purposes of market segmentation are to strengthen market position and increase profits. If segmentation does not accomplish these objectives, it is not a viable strategy.

A strategy of market segmentation may help accomplish these objectives in three ways: through the identification of new product opportunities; through more efficient promotion of existing products; and through a greater sensitivity to marketing variables.

New Products. Consider Breck shampoo. The shampoo market consisted of groups of women who perceived their hair differently. Some thought of their hair as dry, some as oily, and some as normal. As a consequence, women were not satisfied with the all-purpose shampoos that dominated the marketplace. Breck gained a competitive advantage by marketing different shampoo formulas for dry, oily, and normal hair. In short, they strengthened their market position and increased their profits by marketing products tailored to the needs of three different market segments.

Or, consider the market for watches. Analysis of this market revealed three clearly distinguishable segments:

- *People who want to pay the lowest possible price for any watch that works reasonably well.* If the watch fails after six months or a year, they will throw it out and replace it.
- *People who value watches for their long life, good workmanship, good material, and good styling.* They are willing to pay for these product qualities.
- *People who look not only for useful product features but also for meaningful emotional qualities.* The most important consideration in this segment is that the watch should suitably symbolize an important occasion. Consequently, fine styling, a well-known brand name, the recommendation of the jeweler, and a gold or diamond case are highly valued.[10]

Obviously, no one product can serve these markets equally well. Again, marketing segmentation offers a reasonable strategy for strengthening market position and increasing profits.

Marketing Efficiency. Market segmentation does not always require new products to pay off. Fre-

9. One notable exception to this statement, and there are undoubtedly others, is found in the pharmaceutical market. Major pharmaceutical firms often develop, produce, and sell rare drugs at a huge loss because these drugs are needed for treatment of obscure illnesses. These companies consider this practice as a part of their social responsibility.

10. Reprinted by permission of the *Harvard Business Review.* Excerpt from "New Criteria for Market Segmentation" by Daniel Yankelovich (March-April 1964). Copyright © 1964 by the President and Fellows of Harvard College; all rights reserved.

quently, its value may lie in identifying highly profitable segments of a market or in discovering new channels of distribution for existing products.

Marketing analysis will sometimes reveal a particular segment of a market has an extremely high per capita consumption rate compared to other market segments. Targeting marketing activities toward this segment, rather than spreading marketing resources across all segments, may lead to increased profits.

Or, consider the gift candy market. Traditionally, gift candies were distributed through drug stores. A market analysis by Russell Stover revealed that a substantial number of gift candy buyers had deep doubts about the freshness of drugstore candies. Russell Stover built a multimillion dollar business by focusing its distribution efforts on alternative channels of distribution—retail candy stores and department stores—channels that were more acceptable to this market segment.

Sensitivity to Marketing Variables. The producer who considers a strategy of market segmentation is forced to analyze markets in depth. This process alone can lead to a better understanding of marketing variables, and facilitate marketing decisions even though no profitable marketing segments are discovered.

DISADVANTAGES OF MARKET SEGMENTATION. Marketing segmentation is not an unmixed blessing. Accompanying potential increased sales and profits, are risks and increased marketing costs. The following costs, for example, will generally be higher under market segmentation than under product differentiation.

Marketing research costs. The research and analysis required for effective segmentation is often expensive. Keeping in touch with several markets through continuing research is more expensive than keeping in touch with only one.

Research and development costs. The development of new products for special market segments is often costly. In addition, new products involve high risks, and many such products fail.

Production costs. In those instances in which a segmentation strategy requires a unique product, production costs usually increase. Normally, a single, standardized product is less expensive to produce than several different products. This is true because of requirements for new machinery, retooling costs, and downtime whenever the product line being manufactured is changed. In addition, when manufacturing several products in the same manufacturing facility, it is more difficult to reduce production costs through "experience curve" effects, and quality control is often a greater problem. In the automobile field, for example, Japanese manufacturers tend to produce fewer models than U.S. car companies. Consequently, workers become more expert at their jobs, and find it easier to maintain high quality.

Administration costs. Separate marketing plans need to be developed for different market segments under a segmentation strategy. Administering these plans generally requires additional marketing research, forecasting, plan development, and program implementation.

Inventory costs. Again, when separate products are required, these products must be inventoried. The additional record keeping involved, as well as the requirement for "safety" stocks (additional stock to cover unanticipated variations in demand), generally exceed the inventory costs for a single, standardized product.

Distribution costs. Sometimes market segmentation requires separate distribution channels for different market segments. The development and servicing of these channels create additional expenses.

Advertising and sales promotion. Finally, separate advertising and promotion plans must be developed and implemented. Frequently, different media must be employed. Fractionalizing media expenditures across a variety of media often leads to the loss of quantity discounts that may be earned by concentrating advertising expenditures in a single, or at least limited media.

THE LIMITS OF SEGMENTATION. The process of market segmentation has limits. The ultimate in segmentation, of course, is a customized product for the individual buyer. However, for volume production, the point must be reached where further

FIGURE 3–3: Product Marketing Strategies and Stages of Market Development

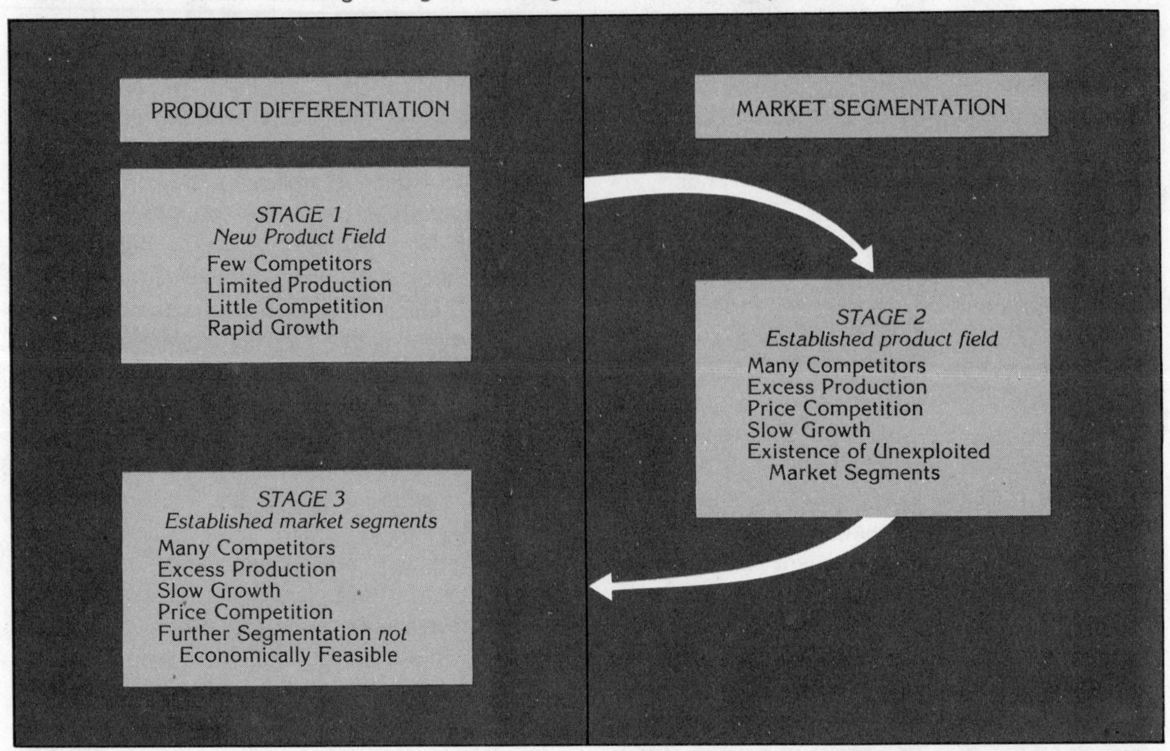

segmentation becomes unprofitable, and a compromise must be made between the company's requirement for volume sales and the individual consumer's desire for a customized product. Whenever the limits of market segmentation are reached, product differentiation, rather than market segmentation, may offer the most appropriate marketing strategy.

SUMMARY NOTE ON PRODUCT DIFFERENTIATION AND MARKET SEGMENTATION. Product differentiation and market segmentation are both viable marketing strategies, depending upon prevailing marketing conditions. Many multiple product companies use both. Which strategy is most appropriate depends upon the stage of market development; the alternating pattern for the use of these two strategies is diagrammed in Figure 3–3.

At the first stage of market development (a new product field), *product differentiation* is an appropriate strategy. At the *second stage* (established product fields), *market segmentation* is the most appropriate strategy. Finally, however, at the *third stage* (established market segments), all of the existing market segments have been fully developed. At this stage, the marketer has little choice: Either returning to a strategy of *product differentiation within market segments,* or getting out of the field.

BASES FOR SEGMENTING MARKETS

A large number of variables may be used in segmenting markets. Table 3–2 lists variables that have been used. Not all of these variables are appropriate for every market. Some markets may be segmented on the basis of geography; others on the basis of sex, income, or education; still others on another basis. Many markets may be segmented by many variables, with each combination identifying a particular group of people sufficiently alike to be considered a market segment.

Although no attempt will be made to discuss all of the variables shown in Table 3–2, we will discuss each of the major categories to demonstrate their application.

TABLE 3–2: Major Market Segmentation Variables

Variables	Typical Breakdown
Geographic	
Region	New England; Middle Atlantic; South Atlantic; East South Central; East North Central; West South Central; West North Central; Mountain; Pacific.
County size	A; B; C; D.
Climate	Northern; Southern
Demographic	
Age	Under 6; 6–11; 12–17; 18–34; 35–49; 50–65; 65 and over.
Sex	Male; female.
Family size	1–2; 3–4; 5 and over.
Family life cycle	Young, single; young, married—no children, youngest child under 6, youngest child 6 or over; older, married—with children, no children under 18, other.
Income	Under $5,000; $5,000–$9,999; $10,000–$14,999; $15,000–$19,999; $20,000 +
Occupation	Professional and technical; managers, officials and proprietors; clerical, sales; craft workers; supervisors; operatives; farmers; retired; students; housewives; unemployed.
Education	Grade school or less; some high school; high school graduate; some college; college graduate.
Religion	Protestant; Catholic; Jewish; other.
Race	White; Black; Oriental; American Indian.
Nationality	American; British; French; German; and so forth.
Social class	Lower-lower; upper-lower; lower-middle; upper-middle; lower-upper; upper-upper.
Psychographic	
Personality Life-style Needs/values	(There are any number of social-psychological factors that can be used. Any particular dimension or cluster of dimensions are usually broken down into thirds, or into upper-half and lower-half.)
Behavioral	
Decision-making unit	Father; mother; both; children; other.
Usage rate	Heavy; light; medium.
Readiness stage	Unaware; aware; interested; intends to try; trier; user.
Benefit sought	Variable and product specific.
End use	Varies with product.
Brand loyalty	Strong; medium; light; none.
Marketing-factor sensitivity	Quality; price; advertising; sales promotion.

Geographic Segmentation

Different regions of the country often provide unique marketing opportunities because of historic, climatic, or physical conditions. Grits, for example, is a food product made from hulled corn that is widely consumed in the southeastern part of the United States, and used sparingly in other sections of the country. Pinto beans and tortillas are indigenous to the Southwest and not widely used in other sections of the country. Lutefisk (codfish processed in lye) and lefse (a potato bread) are popular with Norwegians in the upper-Midwest, and virtually unheard of in other geographic regions. All of the foregoing examples are rooted in historical practices, often influenced by the dominant ethnic groups that settled in particular geographic regions.

The Northeast, Northwest, and Mountain States of the United States are characterized by a climate and terrain that makes downhill skiing a popular winter sport. These conditions do not prevail to the same extent in other sections of the country. Thus, ski resorts, downhill equipment, and ski clothes flourish in the northeastern, northwestern, and mountain regions. The ski industry does relatively poorly in other areas dependent upon artificial snow-making machines and limited by short seasons. As a consequence, manufacturers of ski equipment segment the market geographically, and concentrate their marketing expenditures in areas of greatest sales opportunity.

Many other products differ in their per capita consumption by geographic area—often dramatically. Straight whiskeys, for example, have a much better market in the Southeast, Southwest, and Pacific regions than in other areas. Rice-based cereals, historically, have not sold well in the South. Marine equipment flourishes in areas dominated by large bodies of water. For products that exhibit dramatic differences in per capita consumption by geographic region, geographic segmentation makes sense, and prudent marketing strategy dictates concentrating marketing efforts in areas of high consumption. Areas of low per capita consumption are often treated sparingly, if not ignored.

Demographic Segmentation

Demographic variables such as age, sex, family size, family life cycles, income, and so forth are among the most widely used variables for market segmentation. Reasons for their widespread use include:

Usage rates are often closely associated with demographic variables.

These variables are relatively easy to measure.

The United States Census reports the U.S. population's demographic variables, thereby making it relatively easy to ascertain the size of market segments split along these lines.

Media (magazines, television, etc.) report their audiences' demographic variables, thereby simplifying the process of selecting appropriate vehicles for advertising.

Examples of demographic segmentation abound: economy packages for large families, clothes and games for different age groups, personal care items for women and for men, geriatric products for the elderly, special foods for babies, magazines and books for various age and educational levels, religious artifacts for different religious groups, kosher foods for Jews, varying price levels for different economic groups, and so forth.

A classic example of market segmentation is the economic segmentation recommended by a policy committee of General Motors in the early 1920s. This committee recommended that General Motors market six different automobiles, in the following price ranges:[11]

$450–$600	$1,200–$1,700
$600–$900	$1,700–$2,500
$900–$1,000	$2,500–$3,500

The automobile industry has changed during the past sixty years, and prices have increased phenomenally. In some cases, price distinctions have become blurred as each General

11. Alfred P. Sloan, *My Years with General Motors* (New York: McFadden Books, 1965), p. 65.

Motors division has opted for economic segmentation to sell its different models, and as optional equipment (priced separately) has been added. Nonetheless, the segmentation strategy behind this initial pricing recommendation profoundly influenced the development of the automobile market and contributed to the emergence of General Motors as the market leader. Further, this sixty-year old strategy can still be seen in the comparative price ranges of the Cadillac, the Oldsmobile, and the Chevrolet.

Although segmentation on the basis of a single demographic variable—such as in the foregoing example—is often useful, many sophisticated marketers combine several demographic variables in order to identify target market segments. Pontiac Division of General Motors, for example, combined three demographic variables—marital status, income, and age—to identify likely market segments for the Sunbird and LeMans. Figure 3–4 shows an "exploded" diagram of how these variables were used. Each variable is divided into levels, resulting in eighteen distinct segments. An examination of each segment enabled the company to identify the most profitable markets for these two models. The Sunbird had its greatest potential among single, middle-income consumers in the 18 to 34 age range. The most likely prospects for the LeMans, on the other hand, were married, low-income consumers in the 35 to 39 age group.[12]

FIGURE 3–4: *Demographic Segmentation Variables for the LeMans and the Sunbird*
SOURCE: Adapted from "How Pontiac Pinpoints," *Media Decisions* (Dec. 1977): 81–82

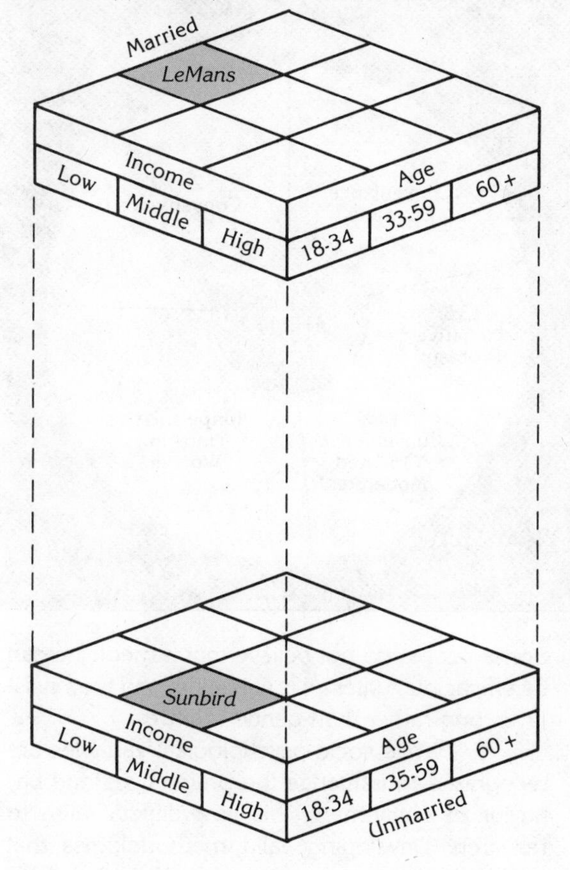

No method of demographic segmentation is infallible, however. Ofttimes, people with quite different demographic characteristics will behave in quite similar ways because of psychological similarities. Thus, the Ford Motor Company designed the Mustang to appeal to young people who wanted an inexpensive, sporty car, and directed Mustang advertising to this group. Subsequent sales analysis indicated that the Mustang was being purchased by all age groups, leading to the conclusion that *psychological age,* not *chronological age,* was the discriminating variable.

Psychographic Segmentation

A relatively recent form of market segmentation, psychographic segmentation, arose because people vary in ways other than those represented by geographic and demographic variables. Some people have a modern, up-to-date orientation and prefer products that reflect this view. Others, more traditional in their outlooks, decorate their homes in early American furniture styles, and respond to products and appeals that emphasize established values. Some, for whom status is a preoccupation, seek prestigious products and designer labels, while others prefer down-to-earth, conventional brands, devoid of frills.

Low-tar cigarette users express more concern for their health than those who smoke

12. "How Pontiac Pinpoints," *Media Decisions* (December, 1977): 81–82.

FIGURE 3–5: Psychographic Segmentation
SOURCE: Ruth Ziff, "Psychographics for Market Segmentation." Reprinted from the *Journal of Advertising Research* © Copyright April, 1971, by the Advertising Research Foundation.

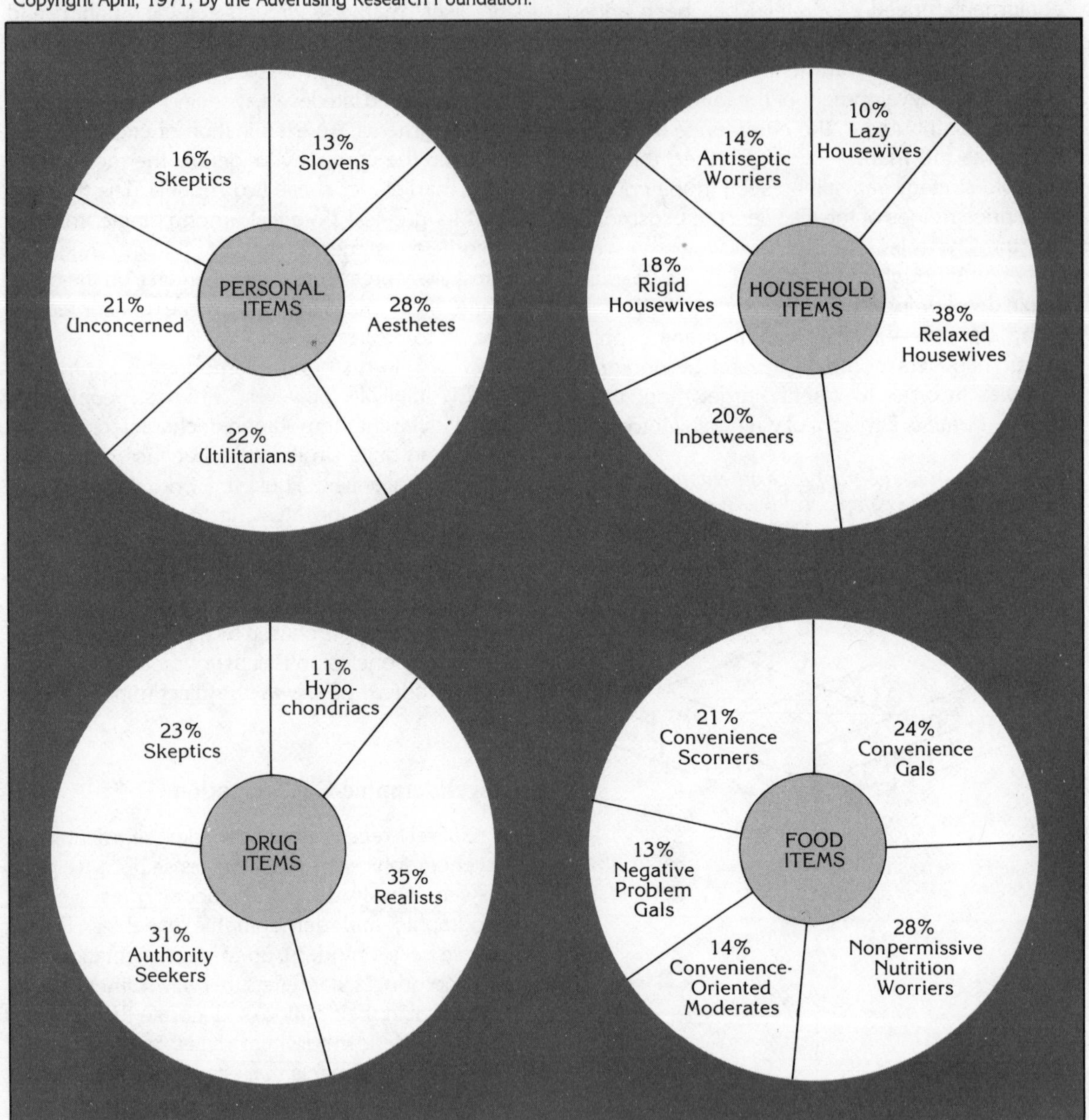

regular filters or nonfilters. Some men insist on brands that project a macho image, with Marlboro providing an example in the cigarette field. An interesting commentary on beer drinkers is that, to date, no beer with a feminine image has managed to capture a significant share of the market. Psychological differences influence our preferences for medicines and therapeutic devices. Some people do not believe that a medicine can be efficacious unless it is ill-tasting, and they insist on strong rather than gentle laxatives.

While socio-psychological variables are recognized to influence the preferences and behavior of consumers, this is a difficult area to research. Developing valid methodologies that enable marketers to exploit these variables effec-

TABLE 3–3: *Who Makes The Buying Decisions? Husbands or Wives?*
SOURCE: *Purchase Influence: Measures of Husband/Wife Influence on Buying Decisions.* Haley, Overholser & Associates, Inc. New Canaan, CT, January, 1975, as abstracted in *Advertising Age* (March 17, 1975).

	Purchased by:		*Direct Influence*				*Indirect Influence*			
			Product		*Brand*		*Product*		*Brand*	
	W	*H*	*W*	*H*	*W*	*H*	*W*	*H*	*W*	*H*
Cereals:										
Cold (Unsweetened)	84	16	74	26	71	29	65	35	67	33
Hot	84	16	67	33	67	33	63	37	59	41
Packaged lunch meat	73	27	60	40	64	36	56	44	57	43
Peanut butter	81	19	70	30	74	26	65	35	68	32
Scotch whisky	35	65	18	82	18	82	22	78	23	77
Bar soap	85	15	65	35	64	36	60	40	61	39
Headache remedies	67	33	67	33	67	33	64	36	65	35
Cat food (dry)	66	34	75	25	81	19	80	20	80	20
Dog food (dry)	76	24	60	40	59	41	60	40	61	39
Fast-food chain hamburgers	68	32	55	45	55	45	53	47	52	48
Catsup	75	25	68	32	68	32	60	40	62	38
Coffee:										
Freeze-dried	68	32	57	43	62	38	56	44	59	41
Regular ground	74	26	65	35	65	35	58	42	60	40
Mouthwash	72	28	56	44	56	44	52	48	53	47

Share of Influence

	Purchase Decision Influence				*Initiation*				*Information Gathering*			
	Product		*Brand*		*Product*		*Brand*		*Product*		*Brand*	
	W	*H*	*W*	*H*	*W*	*H*	*W*	*H*	*W*	*H*	*W*	*H*
Vacuum cleaner	60	40	60	40	80	20	69	31	66	34	65	35
Electric blender	59	41	53	47	67	33	50	50	53	47	52	48
Broadloom carpet	60	40	59	41	82	18	74	26	72	28	69	31
Automobiles	38	62	33	67	22	78	21	79	18	82	18	82

tively is hard to do. Figure 3–5 for example, shows one psychographic breakdown developed for personal care, household, drug, and food items. Unfortunately, there is often a gap between the concept and its application. Thus, exactly how one goes about appealing to a particular segment,

TABLE 3–4: *Children's Attempts to Influence Purchases and Percentage of Mothers Usually Yielding*
SOURCE: Reprinted from Scott Ward and Daniel B. Wackman, "Children's Purchase Influence Attempts and Parental Yielding," *Journal of Marketing Research 9* (August 1972), p. 317, published by the American Marketing Association.

Products	*Frequency of Requests*[a]				*Percentage of Yielding*			
	5–7 Years	*8–10 Years*	*11–12 Years*	*Total*[b]	*5–7 Years*	*8–10 Years*	*11–12 Years*	*Total*[b]
Relevant foods								
Breakfast cereal	1.26	1.59	1.97	1.59	88	91	83	87
Snack foods	1.71	2.00	1.71	1.80	52	62	77	63
Candy	1.60	2.09	2.17	1.93	40	28	57	42
Soft drinks	2.00	2.03	2.00	2.01	38	47	54	46
Jell-o	2.54	2.94	2.97	2.80	40	41	26	36
Overall mean	1.82	2.13	2.16	2.03				
Overall percentage					51.6	53.8	59.4	54.8
Less relevant foods								
Bread	3.12	2.91	3.43	3.16	14	28	17	19
Coffee	3.93	3.91	3.97	3.94	2	0	0	1
Pet food	3.29	3.59	3.24	3.36	7	3	11	7
Overall mean	3.45	3.47	3.49	3.49				
Overall percentage					7.6	10.3	9.3	9.0
Durables, for child's use								
Game, toy	1.24	1.63	2.17	1.65	57	59	46	54
Clothing	2.76	2.47	2.29	2.52	21	34	57	37
Bicycle	2.48	2.59	2.77	2.61	7	9	9	8
Hot wheels	2.43	2.41	3.20	2.67	29	19	17	22
Record album	3.36	2.63	2.23	2.78	12	16	46	24
Camera	3.91	3.75	3.71	3.80	2	3	0	2
Overall mean	2.70	2.58	2.73	2.67				
Overall percentage					25.6	28.0	35.0	29.4
Notions, toiletries								
Toothpaste	2.29	2.31	2.60	2.39	36	44	40	39
Bath soap	3.10	2.97	3.46	3.17	9	9	9	9
Shampoo	3.48	3.31	3.03	3.28	17	6	23	16
Aspirin	3.64	3.78	3.97	3.79	5	6	0	4
Overall mean	3.13	3.09	3.26	3.16				
Overall percentage					16.8	16.3	18.0	17.0
Other products								
Automobile	3.55	3.66	3.51	3.57	2	0	0	12
Gasoline brand	3.64	3.63	3.83	3.70	2	0	3	2
Laundry soap	3.69	3.75	3.71	3.72	2	0	3	2
Household cleaner	3.71	3.84	3.74	3.76	2	3	0	2
Overall mean	3.65	3.72	3.70	3.69				
Overall percentage					2.0	.75	1.50	1.75

a. On a scale from 1 = often to 4 = never.
b. 5–7 years, $n = 43$; 8–10 years, $n = 32$; 11–12 years, $n = 34$; $N = 109$.

TABLE 3–5: Relationship Between Heavy-User Families and Volume Consumed for Selected Products
SOURCE: computed from data given in "1979 Guide to Product Use," *Progressive Grocer*, (July 1979): 39 ff.

		Heavy user families as percent of:			
Product	*Percent of families using*	*All families*	*User families*	*Volume used*	*Ratio of consumption**
Cake mixes	77.8%	29.0%	37.3%	75.4%	5.2
Pancake mixes	71.1	26.6	31.8	74.5	6.2
Candy bars	47.1	14.7	31.1	70.4	5.3
Cold cereals	90.8	37.6	41.4	61.8	2.3
Hot cereals	76.3	19.8	26.0	56.9	3.8
Regular ground coffee	64.7	15.2	23.4	48.6	3.1
Ice tea mixes	31.4	6.6	20.9	49.2	3.7
Catsup	94.5	16.5	17.5	51.2	4.9
Dry gravy and sauces	33.3	7.8	23.6	63.5	5.6
Margarine	91.9	20.8	20.6	41.4	2.7
Peanut butter	90.5	22.6	25.0	67.7	6.3
Soaps and detergents	98.3	21.9	22.3	38.4	2.2
Paper napkins	89.4	21.7	24.2	50.8	3.2
Paper towels	93.0	13.4	14.4	29.0	2.4
Canned dog foods	19.6	7.2	36.7	57.2	2.3

*Using cake mix as an example, the ratio of consumption should be interpreted in the following way: on the average, each heavy user family consumes 5.2 times as much cake mix as each light user family.

while excluding others is not always clear. Further, since these psychological characteristics may be distributed randomly across a variety of demographic characteristics, selecting media to reach a particular segment on a cost-efficient basis is not easy. As a consequence, psychographic segments often must be combined with demographic characteristics to be useful in marketing.

Behavioral Segmentation

The final category of segmentation variables is *behavioral segmentation* which focuses upon the decision making unit, usage rates, benefits sought, end use, and so forth. Many marketers believe that behavioral variables are among the most useful bases for segmentation because they are relatively easy to measure, descriptive of actual consumer behaviors, and easily combined with various demographic dimensions. Three of the most commonly used behavioral variables—the decision making unit, usage rate, and end use—are discussed briefly in the following material.

DECISION MAKING UNIT. Families account for approximately 70 percent of all U.S. households, and control almost 85 percent of consumer income. Many products and brands are purchased by housewives or the heads of households in families without wives. This individual serves as a buying agent, often buying products and brands that result from personal decisions, joint decisions, or decisions by other family members. Little wonder that marketers are concerned with the patterns of family decision making as a segmentation variable!

Table 3–3 shows the family decision patterns for several household items in which the housewife is the primary influence.

Note that, although the wife is the primary influence, the husband exerts both a direct influence (a specific request) and an indirect influence; that is, the wife will buy a product or brand to please the husband without being asked to do so.

One problem with Table 3–3, and most buying-influence studies, is that only husband-wife influences on family purchases are considered, not the influence of other family members. Yet, for many products, children's influence is a significant factor. One study by Ward and Wackman of children's influence distinguishes between the frequency of children's requests and the extent to which mothers yielded to these requests. In this study, self-administered questionnaires were sent to 132 mothers of 5 to 12-year-old children in the Boston Metropolitan Area. The products investigated were all heavily advertised, but varied in price, frequency of purchase, and relevance to the child in terms of direct consumption.[14]

Table 3–4 summarizes some of the findings of this study. This data indicates that: 1) children's influence attempts and parental yielding occurs across a broad range of products; 2) the older the children, the more likely mothers are to yield to influence attempts; and 3) parental yielding is higher on food products and on those products relevant to children as direct consumers.

Although the Ward and Wachman study is based on a small sample and restricted to the Boston area, the findings appear reasonable and are consistent with industry practices of promoting products relevant to children—cereals, snack foods, candy, soft drinks, toys, and records—through children's media and children's premiums.

An analysis of the size of the market segments represented by various family decision patterns may well result in the identification of a particular segment that deserves primary attention to increase the effectiveness and efficiency of the marketing effort.

---

13. "Buying Study Called Good Support Data," *Advertising Age* (March 17, 1975): 72.
14. Scott Ward and Daniel B. Wackman, "Children's Purchase Influence Attempts and Parental Yielding," *Journal of Marketing Research* (August, 1972): 317.

USAGE SEGMENTATION. Most markets can be segmented on the basis of the quantity of product used, a segmentation variable referred to as *volume segmentation.* Commonly, heavy users of a particular product will use twice as much as light users because of a higher frequency of use, larger family sizes, or a combination of both. Table 3–5 reflects the importance of heavy users for household products. Taking cake mix as an example, the table shows that 77.8 percent of all families use cake mix. Yet, 37.3 percent of user families (29.0 percent of all families) consume 75.4 percent of all cake mix sold. Further, the average heavy-user family consumes 5.2 times as much cake mix as the average light-user family.

Identifying heavy users' common demographic characteristics and media patterns helps marketers select media and allocate advertising and promotion funds most effectively. Further, when considering package, product, or price changes, alert marketers check the proposed changes against heavy users to make sure that the proposed changes will not alienate this important group of consumers. A case in point occurred when Pet, Inc. test marketed a proposed package change for its leading product, evaporated milk. When the company found that heavy users were deserting the brand because they were afraid that the package change also meant a product change, Pet quickly abandoned the proposed new package.

END USE. Often markets can be segmented by the end use to which the product is put because the same product may be used by different markets in quite different ways. Arm & Hammer baking soda and evaporated milk are examples mentioned earlier. Historically Kellogg's has marketed Cracklin' Bran, 40% Bran Flakes, Bran Buds, and All-Bran as ready-to-eat cereals. As the advertisement on Plate 3–1 shows, however, these products also have a market as cooking ingredients.

The same is true of Campbell's soups that are marketed to people for whom "soup is just soup" as well as to others who use soup as a cooking ingredient. Angostura Aromatic Bitters, traditionally used in making cocktails and advertised to a dominantly male market, may also be

PLATE 3–1 *Kellogg's Ad.*

used by gourmet cooks as a flavor enhancer (See Plate 3–2). Thus, a knowledge of alternative end use possibilities for a product often generates new markets requiring different marketing strategies.

The basic point is, of course, that few markets are entirely homogeneous. Most can be segmented along some dimension or combination of dimensions. Further, experience has shown that market segmentation often leads to increased sales and profit.

SEGMENTATION RESEARCH

The emphasis given to market segmentation by marketing practitioners during the past two decades has led many marketing research firms to devise new approaches to discovering viable bases for segmenting markets. Under the umbrella of *segmentation research,* a variety of sophisticated and pseudosophisticated analytical techniques have been promoted. Despite the at-

PLATE 3–2 *Angostura Aromatic Bitters ad reprinted with permission.*

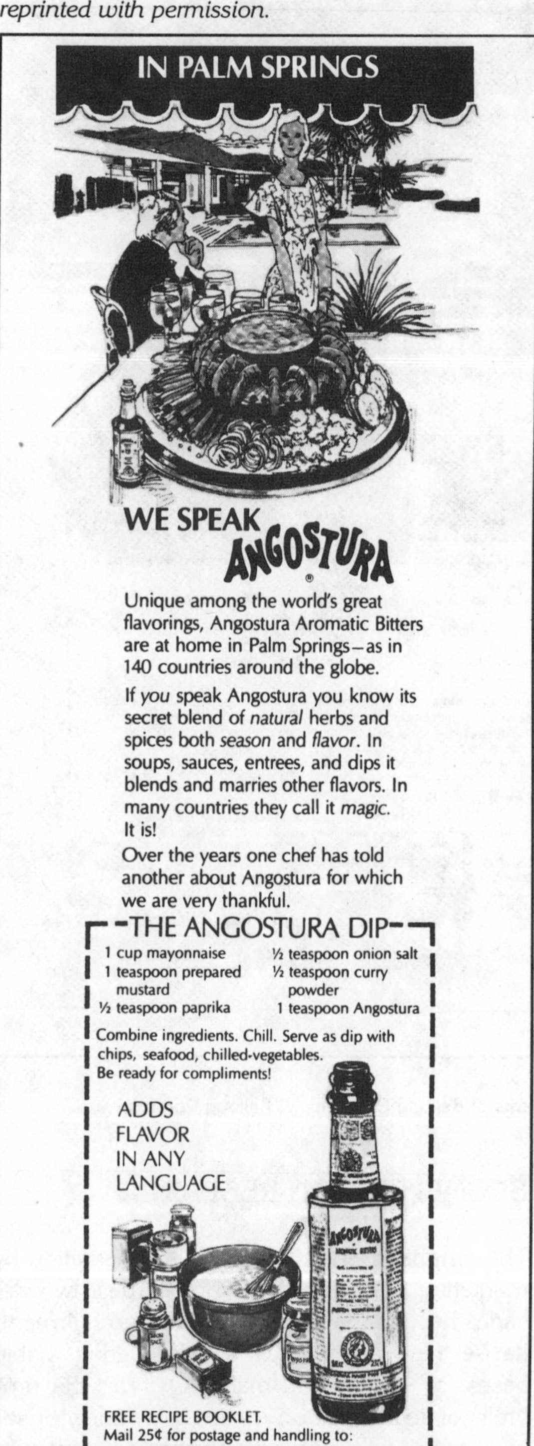

tention these approaches have received, they yield indifferent results more often than not. Perhaps this is one of the reasons that a survey of marketing executives found that "recognizing, defining, understanding, and segmenting markets" is one of their most worrisome problems.[15]

Marketing practitioners and marketing scholars cannot agree about how the problem of market segmentation should be approached. Thus, one author notes:

> Academic segmentation research has been one of the most advanced areas of research in marketing. Many of the new analytical techniques proposed in marketing have been applied to and tested in the segmentation area. Real-world segmentation studies, in contrast, have followed . . . prototypical research patterns with little creativity in design or analysis. . . .[16]

By contrast, a journal article, written by members of a major advertising agency, observes:

> After determining that the segmentation of the market is the right strategy to pursue, the researcher must decide the basis upon which to segment. Too often this decision is made by examining several alternative mathematical or statistical approaches in terms of which one can best reproduce itself. Though there is much scientific argument for such a procedure, it fails to account for the marketing utility of a segmentation approach. Statistical considerations are important only in assessing those alternatives that are relevant from a marketing standpoint.
>
> In the authors' experience, segmentation based on benefits desired is usually the most meaningful type of use from a marketing standpoint, as it directly facilitates product planning, positioning, and advertising communications. Though life-style, psychographic, or general attitudinal approaches

---

15. C. N. Waldo, "What's Bothering Marketing Chiefs Most?" *Advertising Age* (June 4, 1973): 77.

16. Yoram Wind, "Issues and Advances in Segmentation Research," *Journal of Marketing Research* (August, 1978): 317.

work well statistically, they are *not* always helpful in marketing.[17]

Conflicts such as this have led one marketing scholar to suggest that: "The advancement of market segmentation research requires . . . narrowing the gap between the academically oriented research on segmentation and the real world applications of segmentation research."[18]

A discussion of the various approaches used in segmentation research is beyond the scope of this text. For those interested in pursuing this area, however, the *Journal of Marketing Research* has devoted a special issue to this subject.[19]

SUMMARY

The term *market* is a somewhat ambiguous term that refers to the relationship between supply and demand, to places where marketing takes place, to products, and to groups of people. Underlying all of these uses, however, is a generic definition of a market that has three elements—people, purchasing power, and willingness to spend. Marketing planning deals primarily with "product markets," that is, groups of people with purchasing power who are willing to spend this purchasing power for particular products.

Few markets are entirely homogeneous. Rather they can be broken into segments or submarkets each of which consists of people seeking similar attributes in the particular products they buy. Everyone is a part of many markets, but no one is a part of the market for all products.

Two basic strategies are used in dealing with product markets: product differentiation and market segmentation. Under product differentiation, a market is treated as though it were homogeneous and a single marketing program, directed at the entire market, is prepared. Under market segmentation, the market is divided into segments, and separate marketing programs are developed for each segment. Each of these strategies is appropriate under certain marketing conditions, and each has advantages and disadvantages.

Markets may be segmented according to many variables, although all markets are not segmentable along the same lines. The variables along which markets may be segmented can be grouped into four major classifications: geographic, demographic, psychographic, and behavioral.

17. Shirley Young, Leland Ott, and Barbara Feigin, "Some Practical Considerations in Market Segmentation," *Journal of Marketing Research* (August, 1978): 317.

18. Yoram Wind, "Issues and Advances in Segmentation Research," p. 317.

19. See *Journal of Marketing Research* (August, 1978).

1. Explain what is meant by the following uses of the term *market:* (A) market as a relationship between supply and demand; (B) market as a place; (C) market as a group of people; (D) product markets.
2. What is the generic definition of a market?
3. Distinguish the strategies of *product differentiation* and *market segmentation.*
4. Under what conditions is the strategy of product differentiation appropriate?
5. Under what conditions is the strategy of market segmentation appropriate?
6. What are the advantages and disadvantages of a strategy of product differentiation?
7. What are the advantages and disadvantages of a strategy of market segmentation?
8. Distinguish between differentiated marketing and concentrated marketing. Support this distinction with an example of each.
9. Identify and explain the requirements for successful market segmentation.
10. What are the major bases along which markets may be segmented? Give an example of each.

1. Discuss ways in which the following product markets might be segmented: (A) ready-to-eat cereals; (B) time measuring devices; (C) cameras.
2. Discuss some of the ways that the market for a retail sporting goods store might be segmented.
3. Identify some product markets which you believe are essentially homogeneous, and not subject to segmentation.
4. Markets can sometimes be segmented by a number of variables simultaneously. What are some of the problems that might be encountered in segmenting a market under such conditions?
5. Select a product with which you are familiar. Indicate how the market for this product might be segmented in terms of *end use.* What are some of the other variables upon which the market for this product might segmented?

CHAPTER PROBLEM

MARKETS AND MARKETING STRATEGY

Western Wear is a small, retail clothing store that specializes in western clothing located in Windrip. A university town of 35,000 in one of the western states, Windrip is adjacent to an Indian reservation which has a population of approximately 100,000. The university has over 12,000 students who buy much of their casual clothing from local merchants.

Western Wear was founded in 1973 by Cyrill Brown, a former department store executive from Chicago who decided to move to a small town in the Southwest in search of a less hectic life-style. Brown was attracted by the scenery around Windrip, and also by its casual life-style. He noted the strong preference for western-styled clothing in the area and, because of his experience in retail merchandising, felt that a western wear clothing store could be successful. Although several such stores were established in the area, Brown believed that a western wear store that featured leading brand names, tailoring service, and moderate to high prices could attain a significant share of the market.

Western Wear met with limited success, falling well below Brown's expectations; in 1978 he sold it to John Hopewell, a local insurance man who was interested in opening a retail clothing store.

Hopewell believed that the primary problem with Western Wear was inadequate advertising. For several months, he used various advertising media—the local newspaper, radio, television—with indifferent results. Finally, in an effort to get some help, he called a friend who taught marketing in the university and who had worked for several years in a major advertising agency.

Over lunch with the marketing professor, Hopewell explained the store's background and said, "You know, I thought that a little advertising would solve the problem, but it doesn't seem to help that much. Besides, even in a town this size, advertising can get expensive. Whenever I feature a sale, I get a lot of people in the store and sell a lot of merchandise at cut-rate prices, but I can't make a profit selling at cut-rate prices."

The professor asked, "Who are your customers?" "Everyone," Hopewell answered. "Business people, workers, university professors, university students, Indians. I get them all. And that's another problem. Everyone wants something a little different, and a small retail store like Western Wear can only handle a limited line of merchandise. With your experience, I hoped that you could give me some ideas."

Assignment

1. *How would you define Hopewell's strategy to date?*
2. *What other strategies might Hopewell have used?*
3. *If you were the marketing professor, what would you suggest?*
4. *What will be some of the questions that Hopewell will have to deal with if he follows your suggestions?*

4

The Marketing Plan

- *The importance and role of market planning.*
- *The functions of market planning.*
- *The content of the product marketing plan.*
- *How to prepare a product marketing plan.*

MARKETING EXAMPLES

CREST

Crest toothpaste burst into the dental care field with all of the subtlety of an atomic bomb. Spearheaded by massive door-to-door sampling, publicized by heavy consumer advertising extolling the benefits of fluoride, and supported by the endorsement of the American Dental Association, Crest made American consumers cavity conscious and "Look, Mom! No cavities" became a national byword. But it didn't happen by chance.

Procter & Gamble had carefully identified cavities and expensive dental work as a major consumer concern. The company had developed a product containing fluoride that effectively inhibited cavities. Then, Procter & Gamble postponed the product introduction for several years while they carefully amassed clinical tests necessary to obtain the American Dental Association's approval for their advertising claims. The success of Crest was a triumph for thorough planning. Crest is not an exception in Procter & Gamble's stable of products, which includes successes such as Tide detergent, Crisco shortening, Scope mouthwash, Pampers diapers, Charmin toilet tissue, Duncan Hines baking mixes, and Folger's coffee. The one thing that all of these products have in common is thorough planning.

NOBLE ROMAN'S

Most Americans have never heard of Noble Roman's. There is little reason they should. In the burgeoning fast-food market, Noble Roman's is a pigmy among giants such as McDonald's with over 4,000 outlets, or Pizza Hut with 3,000 stores. Yet, Noble Roman's progress is remarkable. Beginning in 1969, with an almost defunct pizza restaurant and limited capital, Noble Roman's has over 1,000 employees and sales in excess of $22 million. The company expected to have 225 outlets in 1981.

> As one would suspect, planning is an important managerial function at Noble Roman's. Plans are formulated for periods of one, two, three, and five years. The detail of the plan is inversely correlated with its length. As a result, the one-year plan has some "hard numbers" broken down monthly that are periodically reviewed and updated quarterly . . .[1]

Although Noble Roman's is a pigmy in an industry of giants, a systematic approach to growth and emphasis upon careful planning may yet enable it to become the noblest Roman of them all.

1. Joseph M. Waldman, "Making It Big in the Fast Foods Industry," *Business Horizons* (June, 1978): 65–71.

Few topics have received as much attention as planning in the marketing and management literature. In most management texts, planning is treated as one of the primary functions of management. Yet, too frequently, planning is haphazard, and many so-called plans represent little more than the thoughtless perpetuation of past management errors.

THE SCOPE OF PLANNING

During times of economic affluence when market demand is high, the penalties for failing to plan marketing activities may be minimal. The incompetent often succeed despite themselves, and the benefits of planning are not readily apparent. By contrast, during times of economic stress when a premium is placed on using company resources wisely, less able firms are weeded out, and market planning comes into its own. To be realistic about the future, economic stress is forecast for the next two decades. High energy costs, intense competition from domestic and imported products, and a decline in technological innovation in many areas should transform marketing planning into a criterion for survival.

Much of the literature on market planning deals with top management decisions on the broad strategy that a company should follow in determining the fields in which it should compete, how the company should be organized, and how resources should be utilized to insure survival and growth.

Although such decisions are indeed crucial, corporate level decisions do not occupy most of the time and energies of those who engage in the day-to-day practice of marketing. Nor do high level corporate decisions demand the skills and attention of today's marketing students during the first ten to twenty years of their business careers. Instead, planning, development, and execution of marketing activities at the product level will occupy student's minds and challenge their ingenuity.

Most of the activity that we normally refer to as market planning occurs at the product level. Here strategic decisions are made concerning product attributes, packaging, brand names, pricing, distribution, and marketing communications. Once a company's basic direction has been set, most of the real work of marketing is done at the product level. As a consequence, the main thrust of this text will be devoted to market planning at the product level.[2]

MARKET PLANNING AT THE PRODUCT LEVEL

Basically, market planning at the product level enables the marketer to use the resources of the firm wisely in promoting sales of company products. This can best be done by:

- Assessing the marketing environment to identify problems and opportunities.
- Establishing realistic sales objectives and levels of spending.
- Devising competitive strategies for the controllable marketing variables—product, price, place, and promotion.
- Developing detailed plans for carrying out these strategies.

The key to market planning at the product level is the product marketing plan.

The Importance of the Marketing Plan

Marketing is a complex activity requiring the participation of many people, and the use of diverse skills. Truly complex tasks, such as marketing, can only be accomplished by breaking them down into their component parts, and working on each part separately. This is the key to the success of the modern business organization and the secret of mass production. When the parts are reassembled they will not fit together properly unless they have been constructed according to a single overall design. In the manufacture of a physical

2. This does not imply that corporate strategy is unimportant or should be neglected in an introductory marketing text. Chapter 21 deals with corporate strategy, so that students will have some understanding of its role.

product, such as an automobile, this problem is solved through the use of engineering plans that specify how each component is to be constructed and the magnitude of the tolerances that will be allowed.

Since marketing is a complex task, it too must be broken down into its component parts, and each part constructed according to an overall design. The instrument that provides this unity of design for the marketing effort is the marketing plan. Through the marketing plan everyone involved in the marketing effort knows what to do and is given assurance that, once individual tasks are completed, each part of the plan will fit together properly.

THE MARKETING PLAN VERSUS THE SALES PLAN. The sales plan is, of course, part of the marketing plan—the part that organizes and directs the activities of the sales force, and coordinates these activities with other aspects of the marketing effort. In a *single product company,* the sales plan may indeed be a part of the document referred to as the marketing plan.

In a *multiple-product company,* however, the product marketing plan and the sales plan are usually *separate, but interdependent documents.* The reason for this is that many companies market a number of products, each handled by the same sales force. Thus, there may be a product marketing plan for each product, but only one sales plan that allocates sales activity to each product as needed.

By convention the marketing plan deals with variables such as the product, the product name, packaging, pricing, distribution, advertising, and sales promotion. The *sales plan,* on the other hand (often referred to as the *call plan*), details the activities of the sales force, defines the pattern of sales calls on customers, and allocates sales effort to individual products.

TIME FRAME OF THE MARKETING PLAN. In most companies, the product marketing plan is a short-term document, usually covering one year. Some companies prepare three-year product marketing plans, updating them and extending them on a yearly basis. This is not a common practice, however. Product marketing plans tend to be short-term documents because the dynamic marketing environment often changes so rapidly that long-term, detailed planning at the product level is not productive.

At the corporate management level, broad company plans may be made for five years or more. But, detailed plans for individual products are generally short-term in nature.

The Functions of the Product Marketing Plan

Although its basic purpose is to enable the marketer to use the resources of the firm wisely in promoting the sales of company products, a product marketing plan also:

- Brings together in one place all of the important facts, conclusions, and operating decisions which bear on the marketing problem and its solutions.
- Provides a complete operating guide to all personnel working on the product, both within the firm and in other participating organizations, such as the firm's advertising agency.
- Provides a summary of basic facts and conclusions for review by new personnel, and by personnel who are not directly or intimately involved in the preparation or implementation of the plan.
- Establishes benchmarks against which marketing accomplishments can be judged.
- Finally, provides a history of a brand's marketing plan development, of the strategic decisions made, and of their outcomes.

Terminology in the Marketing Plan

No universally agreed upon terminology has been developed to describe the concepts used in a marketing plan. Instead, there are a profusion of terms: goals, objectives, missions, strategies, plans, tactics, copy platform, image, program, promotion, sales promotion, merchandising, public relations, and publicity. Some of these terms are used interchangeably, and some have unique and sometimes highly idiosyncratic meanings. To avoid confusion, key terms are defined below.

Presenting the marketing plan to the sales force. (Photo courtesy of Nationwide Insurance Company)

Objective. The term *objective* is used to describe the end result to be achieved by a specific time. The statement of objectives at any level (that is, marketing objectives, media objectives, sales promotion objectives, etc.) *always* identifies *what* is to be accomplished, *not how* it is to be accomplished. The terms *goal* and *objective* are often used synonymously.

Strategy. The term *strategy* is used to describe *how* objectives are to be accomplished. Thus, strategy statements communicate the principles used in selecting and/or utilizing various marketing techniques or devices; we speak of marketing strategy, media strategy, product strategy, copy strategy, and so forth.

Plan. The term *plan* is used in two ways: When preceded by the word *marketing,* plan refers to the entire document. When preceded by such words as *advertising, media, copy, package, sales promotion,* and so forth, plan refers to the detailed presentation of recommended actions in these areas. This latter use of the word *plan* is synonymous with the term *tactics.*

Sales Promotion. The term *sales promotion* describes special incentives or other activities directed toward consumers, the trade, or the sales force designed to stimulate action by one of these groups—*excluding* advertising, packaging, publicity, and normal pricing. Point-of-purchase material is considered sales promotion. By convention, marketers often use the word *merchandising* when they mean sales promotion, but technically this is an improper use of the term. Technically, merchandising refers to the activities of *merchandise houses,* which is what department stores were originally called. Merchandising originally referred to the selection, pricing, display, and promotion of the goods or merchandise offered by these stores. Merchandising is still used in this way in the retail trade. However, marketers and advertising agencies have appropriated the word and often use it as a synonym for sales promotion.

FIGURE 4–1: *Detailed Flow of the Marketing Plan*

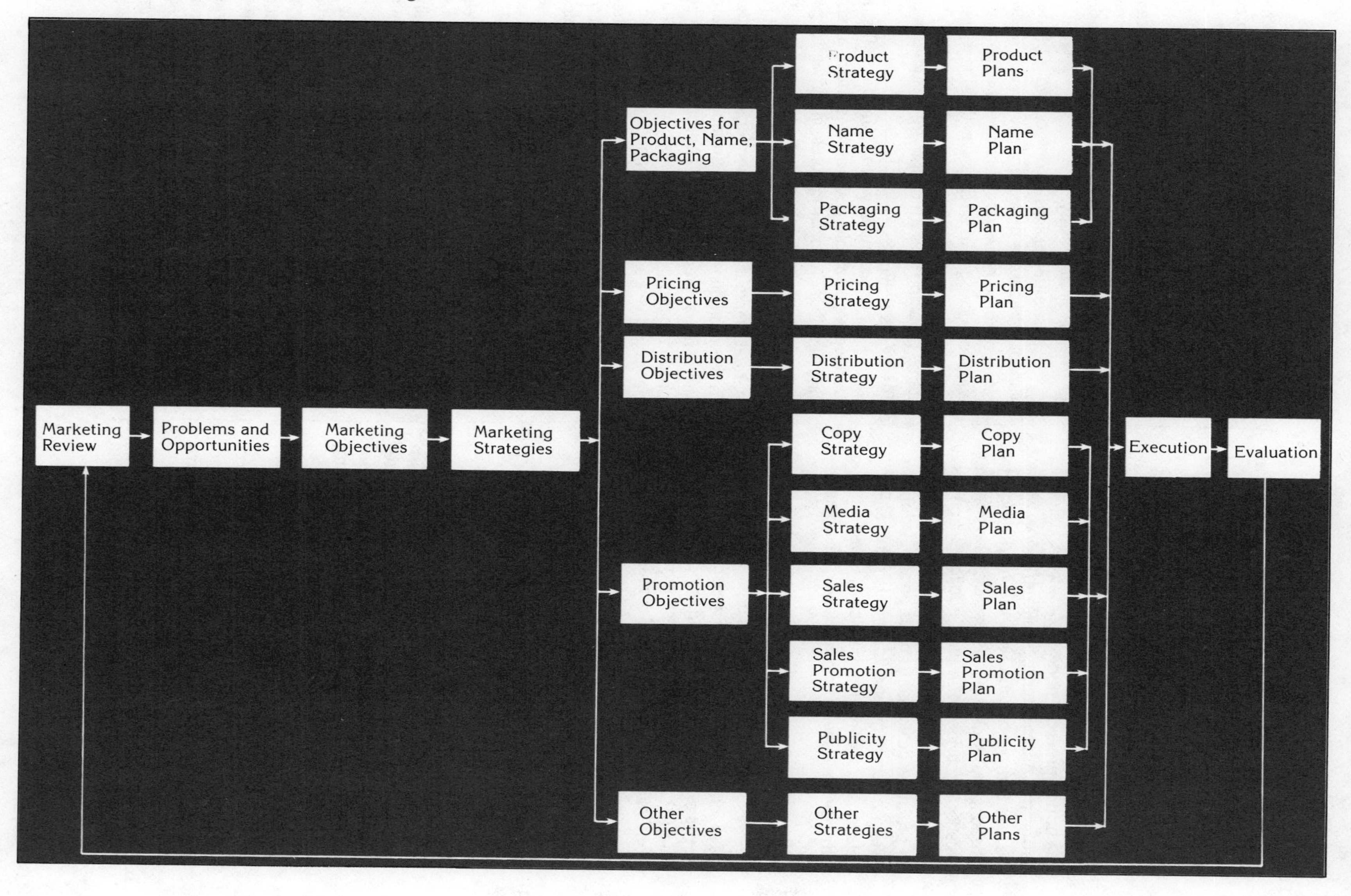

Advertising. Advertising includes only paid media advertising, including direct mail.

Publicity. Publicity is a form of promotion, often referred to as *product publicity.* It differs from advertising in that publicity is not paid for at standard rates, and the sponsor is not identified. Usually publicity (unidentified as such) appears in the editorial or news columns of printed media or in the noncommercial portion of radio and television programs. Another term, *public relations,* will *not* be used in connection with the marketing of a product, although it often describes the communications activities of a firm. Public relations is a broader term than publicity and involves a variety of practices designed to build good relations between a company and its various publics. Public relations may involve publicity, advertising, or other techniques in accomplishing its objectives.

While these definitions are arbitrary, I have chosen them for two reasons: (1) these terms are widely used by marketing practitioners; and (2) agreement upon these terms and definitions will avoid a great deal of confusion in discussing the content of the marketing plan.

THE CONTENT OF THE MARKETING PLAN

The marketing plan is a systematic document that proceeds from the general to the specific—from an assessment of the marketing environment (referred to as the *market review* or *situational analysis*) to a detailed summary of the marketing budget. Each step logically leads to the next, and each specific marketing recommendation is firmly rooted in the material that precedes it.

The marketing plan for a *new product* usually contains the parts, and interrelationship shown in Figure 4–1, as well as a budget summary and a calendar of events.

The outline in Figure 4–1 is for a new product. For an *established product*—one that has been on the market for some time—product objectives, pricing objectives and distribution objectives are usually eliminated from the *annual* marketing plan. These items are usually omitted from the annual marketing plan for an established product because *they exist as basic, long-term decisions that have already been made.* In short, they are givens, and normally, further discussion of them is unnecessary.

If a discussion of one or more of these variables becomes necessary—and such discussions become necessary whenever the marketing situation changes in such a way that these previous decisions should be reconsidered—then the items requiring reexamination are included in the marketing plan.

For example, when Contac was first introduced, a strategic decision was made to confine distribution to drugstores in order to gain support of pharmacists and to enhance Contac's image as an ethical drug product. In the next few annual marketing plans, a section on *distribution* in the marketing plan was unnecessary because the same strategy was still appropriate. After the product had become well established and its initial objectives attained, expanding distribution to food stores in order to take advantage of these marketing opportunities became desirable. At this point, the whole question of distribution strategy was reexamined in the marketing plan and a new distribution strategy developed, along with a rationale explaining the reasons for the change.

Similarly, a company may need to reexamine product formulation, or pricing structure, or package. In such instances, these reexaminations, bolstered by the thinking behind them, should appear in the annual marketing plan.

Few marketing decisions are cast in bronze. Competitive activity, technological developments, economic pressures, and changing consumer preferences may force a reexamination of marketing decisions that are considered relatively permanent. Ivory Soap has been sold under the same name for over a hundred years. During this period, Ivory's package has been modernized (see Figure 13–6), and the product form has been extended to include Ivory Flakes and Ivory

Liquid. If you were to go back through P&G's files, you could find the marketing plans in which these changes had been made, and the reasons behind them.

In the following material, each major section of the product marketing plan will be described and clarified. This material, which is designed to show the student how to write a marketing plan, should be approached in three ways. *First,* read it all the way through in order to get an impression of the various parts and how they fit together. *Second,* study each section of the marketing plan in order to understand its purpose and construction. *Third,* read the sample marketing plan in the Appendix to see how a marketing plan looks in its final form. Finally, while the foregoing procedure will provide a base for understanding the structure and content of the marketing plan, it will not teach you to write a marketing plan. *One learns to write marketing plans by writing them—over and over again.*

Nonetheless, the following material will provide a guide and some direction along the way. Realistically, that's about all one can expect from the classroom study of marketing. The reason for this is that learning to market products is a little like learning to play golf. You can spend the rest of your life reading about golf, and you can pick up a lot of pointers, but you will never learn to play until you get out on the golf course and start swinging some clubs.

The sections of a marketing plan are discussed from the standpoint of an *established product* in the following material. As a consequence, product, pricing, and distribution objectives have been omitted. Later chapters deal with these topics from a strategic viewpoint.

THE MARKET REVIEW

The market review, or first section of the marketing plan, provides the factual basis for the definition of problems and opportunities, for the marketing objectives, and for the marketing strategies that follow. The market review summarizes the relevant information that will shape marketing decisions.

The preparation of a marketing review is not simple and routine. This part of the marketing plan is critical, and its value depends wholly on the analyst's ability to select facts relevant to the current situation, to be objective in selecting and reporting these facts, and to report them in a manner that is concise, yet fully intelligible to a reader who is not intimately involved in marketing the product on a day-to-day basis.

Generalizing about the content of the marketing review section is difficult because the dynamics of individual markets will vary widely for different products and because there are major differences in the kinds and amount of information available to the marketing analyst. For example, the analyst who has access to detailed competitive information on brand shares, pricing, sales promotion activity, and advertising expenditures on a regional basis will be able to make a more comprehensive analysis than one who does not have such information. Similarly, the market planner who has recently completed a test market, a promotion test, or a major consumer survey will have relevant data to include in the market review section that will not be available to the planner who has not undertaken such activities.

In any case, analysts make do with what they have, identify gaps in the information available and, if feasible, make provisions in the marketing plan for obtaining this information before the next planning period.[3]

The purpose of the marketing review section is to describe the *current* marketing situation. To this end, historical data should be summarized and used only to the extent that it explains or highlights the present market condition and its trends. For example, an analysis of historical data may show that the product's total market or the brand share is increasing or decreasing at a regular rate, at an accelerating rate, or at a decelerating rate. This fact, revealed by historical analysis, may be useful in making forecasts of the market and brand performance. Generally, however, the

3. A basic list of data sources (many of them free) that are often useful in preparing the market review section of the marketing plan is given in the marketing research chapter.

market review concentrates on developments in the market *since* the last marketing plan. Thus, its focus is on developments of the past year.

The major areas of interest from which relevant facts are extracted in the preparation of the marketing review section are:

The Market

- Definition of the relevant market. For example, if the marketing plan is being prepared for a dog food product, the part of the dog food market considered relevant should be clear. Is it the *total* market for dog food, or a particular segment of the market, such as canned, moist, or dry foods? If it is dry dog food, is the marketer primarily concerned with baked products, meals, kibbles, snacks, or some combination of these.
- Market size and growth trends.
- Forecast of market growth.
- Makeup of the market by product type, brand, package size, price, and other relevant characteristics.
- Distribution of the total market by region, season, city or county size, sales by outlet type, and so forth.
- Significant trends or changes in any of the above areas.

Competitive Position

Frequently, key points can best be emphasized by contrasting the brand's strengths or weaknesses with those of the competition. Relevant considerations here are:

- Product quality, both technical and as judged by consumer tests.
- Pricing, sizes available, and packaging features.
- Distribution of the product category in retail outlets, as well as the distribution for individual brands and for the various package sizes that are offered.
- Brand shares of market and/or per capita consumption data. If possible, this information should be examined for the total market, by outlet type, by geographic area, and by city size.
- Trends or recent changes in any of the above areas.

The Consumer

- The size of the consumer market in persons, households, or families, whichever is the most relevant.
- Frequency of purchase, usage rates, trial, repurchase rates, etc.
- Definition of the consumer market by socioeconomic groups and by sociopsychological characteristics. Combined with usage rates, this data serves to identify target markets.
- Consumers' knowledge and/or attitudes toward the product category and individual brands.
- Consumer usage habits. This includes the occasion of use, where the product is consumed, and so forth.
- Factors influencing brand selection: Within the family who selects, purchases, and uses the product? What are the decision patterns for the brand?
- Trends or recent changes in any of the above factors.

Dealers/Distributors/Brokers

- Buying patterns, including such characteristics as seasonal loading.
- Attitudes toward the company, its product, pricing, advertising, and other aspects of its marketing program.
- Markups, promotional practices, and so forth.
- Trends or new developments in the above areas.

Advertising History

This information should be obtained for the company's brand as well as for competition.

- Advertising expenditures, in total, per unit or case, and as a percent of sales. If possible, this information should be broken down by markets, regions, seasonal periods, package sizes and other relevant considerations such as flavors, models, etc.
- Copy. An analysis and comparison should be made of basic appeals, claims, themes, and the mood or tone of presentation.
- Media. An analysis should be made of the major media used, media mix, coverage, reach, frequency, scheduling, selectivity among primary target groups, and media efficiency.
- Advertising results. Analysis should be made of any copy tests, media tests, research findings on awareness, registration of specific selling points, and attitudes.

Sales Promotion

Again, the company's brand should be analyzed as well as the competition, insofar as competitive information is available.

- Types and amounts of sales promotion activity.
- Estimated promotional expenditures in total, by item, by region, and by season.
- Traceable results of past promotions: trade and sales force comments, special pricing, displays, retail advertising, and consumer action.
- Trade attitudes toward various forms of promotion for the product type.

The presentation of marketing facts in the review section should proceed from the general to the specific, starting with the market as a whole and ending with a discussion of individual brands. This procedure contributes to objectivity and facilitates the reader's understanding. Remember that the presentation should be clear, concise, logical, and easy to understand.

PROBLEMS AND OPPORTUNITIES

This section of the marketing plan is linked directly to the market review section and consists of the conclusions derived from it. As a separate entity, the problems and opportunities section highlights key findings derived from the background analysis by setting them apart and allows additional latitude for interpreting the meaning and implications of these key findings.

The problems and opportunities section provides the bases for the marketing objectives as well as for key points of marketing strategy. Points appearing in this section generally fall into one of the following groups:

- Identification of specific marketing *problems* that need to be corrected.
- Identification of specific marketing *opportunities* that can be exploited.
- Basic conclusions or judgments that have a major bearing on the action which will be recommended in later sections.

This section of the report should be quite brief. All major points can usually be made concisely on a single page since these points have been mentioned in the marketing review section and represent key conclusions from the foregoing analysis.

MARKETING OBJECTIVES

The marketing objectives section follows immediately after the conclusions section. This section should be brief and spell out the commitment which will be made to management in return for the allocation of resources that are requested. At a minimum, the objectives section should specify sales for the marketing period for which the plan is being prepared and the amount of money that will be spent in obtaining the sales objectives.

Other objectives, if relevant, may also be included; for example, the commitment to develop a new package, to introduce new flavors or a new model, or to initiate product improvements. A major marketing research project may also appear in the objectives section. Keep in mind that the purpose of the objectives section is to state what will be accomplished during the next marketing period.

Marketing objectives should always be *specific, actionable,* and *achievable.* Objectives which do not meet these three criteria provide little guidance for marketing activity, and no basis at all for evaluating the marketing program. If objectives are not specific, they are not subject to measurement. If they are not actionable, no specific activities can be undertaken to achieve them. Whether objectives are achievable may be more difficult to assess because this is essentially a matter of judgment, based on knowledge of the market and past experience. An objective is achievable when, based on the company's resources and present marketing position, it appears *reasonable.*

MARKETING STRATEGY

The marketing strategy section stands at the heart of the marketing plan as the basic statement of *how* the various controllable marketing variables will be used to achieve marketing objectives. Strategy statements define the roles of advertising, sales promotion, pricing, packaging, distribution, personal selling, and other marketing variables.

Earlier, we noted that the problems and opportunities section of the marketing plan was directly related to the marketing strategy section. Now we can make this relationship more clear. *At least one marketing strategy statement should be made for each problem and opportunity listed in that section.* Why? Simply because the purpose of the marketing strategy section is to make summary statements about *how* company resources will be used to solve the problems and to take advantage of opportunities to achieve marketing objectives.

Marketing strategy is the first real test of the competence of the marketing planner who, up to this point, has analyzed the current situation and set objectives. Marketing strategy is the test that brings together understanding, imagination, vision, and decisiveness to give direction to the entire marketing effort. A marketing strategy which is ill-conceived or ambiguous, has little chance to be successful. While a well-conceived strategy can be sabotaged by inept execution, key marketing strategy decisions can spell the difference between a brilliant marketing program and one that is just mediocre.

Marketing strategy provides the framework within which specific strategies and plans are developed for each area of marketing activity. An important part of this framework is the clarification of the interrelationships between the various elements of the marketing mix; between advertising and sales promotion; between distribution and pricing; between product and packaging.

Remember that marketing strategies provide only a *general direction.* Marketing strategies do not attempt to specify what media will be used, what price will be charged, what specific sales promotion devices will be employed, what the package should look like, or precisely how advertising should be written. These decisions are left to the experts in these fields. The strategy statements do place certain constraints on the experts, however. Boundaries are given for how much money may be spent for a particular activity, the kinds of people to be reached, the areas of the country in which media will be used, what will be featured in advertising, and the role that pricing will play. Within these constraints, however, creative groups, sales promotion experts, media buyers, sales management, and others are free to exercise their imagination, judgment, and experience.

PROMOTION OBJECTIVES

Promotion objectives are an extension of the general marketing strategy. The purpose of this section is to define further the role of promotion in the total marketing effort, and to establish specific promotion objectives for the current planning period. The promotion objectives should not repeat anything that has been stated in the marketing strategy section. Instead, the promotion objectives should add new dimensions to the marketing plan. Further, statements in this section should lay the basis for future evaluations of promotional activities.

Normally, the promotional objectives section will include specific objectives only for advertising, sales promotion, and product publicity. Objectives for personal selling are usually omitted because they are covered in a separate *sales or call plan* that is prepared by the sales department and coordinated with the marketing plan. In addition, many companies do not normally include product publicity as a part of the marketing plan, particularly for established products. Experts in the field disagree about the value of product publicity as a part of the marketing program for established products, although they agree that product publicity is a valuable asset for new product introductions.

The promotion objectives section will ordinarily be quite brief. Supported by separate strategies for copy, media, sales promotion and (when present) product publicity, this section should cover only those decisions which affect all of these activities. Normally, promotion objectives do two things.

- Define *who* and *where* the target group or groups are. If these definitions have been made in the marketing strategy section, and they sometimes are, they should not be repeated.
- Provide specific, measurable objectives for the marketing activities that flow from them.

COPY STRATEGY

A single marketing plan may contain more than one copy strategy when the product is advertised to different groups for different reasons. For example, a cereal product might be advertised to both children and mothers, using a flavor or "fun" appeal for the children and a nutritional appeal for the mothers. Or, separate advertising campaigns might be directed to consumers and to the retail trade. Separate strategies may also be required when a product is being advertised for two or more uses. For example, a soap or detergent that is used for both laundry and dishes; or cereal which may be used as a cooking ingredient. In instances of multiple product use, the copy strategy should indicate the relative weight that will be given to each use.

The copy strategy should contain at least four elements:

- A statement of the *principal benefit* offered by the product.
- A statement of the *principal characteristics* of the product—the "reason why" the benefit exists.
- A statement of the *character or personality* of the product which will be reflected in the mood, tone, and overall atmosphere of the advertising.
- A statement of what the product is, and the product's use.

COPY PLAN

The copy plan explains how the copy strategy will be executed in a specific advertising campaign. A short-term document, this plan records the decisions and rationale which have entered into the creation of a recommended copy unit. The copy plan is prepared *after* the copy has been written to give maximum freedom to the creative groups who try to develop a persuasive copy approach. Thus, the chief role of the copy plan is to provide a coherent explanation of *why* the copy was executed as it was. Copy that lacks this kind of logical support is usually highly vulnerable to attack and criticism.

Another value of the copy plan is that it formalizes the creative approach and provides a pattern for the development of further commercials or advertisements by *describing* what the

The end result of thousands of hours of planning. (Photo courtesy of Bausch & Lomb)

advertising will look like. A separate copy plan is required for each creative strategy statement and for each medium employed; the same plan can seldom be used for printed advertising and television because each media requires different presentation techniques.

Thus, the copy plan describes the key elements and the basic format of the advertisement or commercial. If the copy plan is truly well written, a new creative team, with no previous experience with the product, can use the copy plan to develop advertising that will fit smoothly into the campaign.

MEDIA STRATEGY

The media strategy is subordinate to the *marketing strategy* and *promotion objectives* which have already established general media constraints such as the money available, the target groups of consumers, the relative emphasis to be given to the various target groups, and what time of the year advertising support is to be delivered. The basic function of media strategy is to show how media will be selected and used to meet these criteria.

Generally, media strategy statements cover the following areas:

- Decisions concerning the media to be used, such as television or magazines, along with a rationale for these decisions.
- Decisions concerning the types within broad media classifications that will be used, such as home service magazines or women's magazines, and the rationale for these decisions.
- Decisions concerning space and time units, such as half pages or full pages, and the reasons for these decisions.
- Decisions concerning the ways in which other marketing factors—such as a major promotion, or the introduction of a new package—will influence media planning.

MEDIA PLAN

The media plan shows how the media strategy is to be executed by recommending specific purchases. Since the media strategy sets forth the principles upon which the media plan is based, the plan itself shows how these principles are brought to bear in individual buying decisions. However, the media plan as it appears in the marketing plan is a summary—rather than detailed—statement. Necessary rationale or other background discussion comparing various media alternatives should be relegated to separate support documents.

SALES PROMOTION STRATEGY

As noted earlier, sales promotion refers to activities outside the areas of media advertising and product publicity. Sales promotion includes such things as point-of-sale material, sampling, couponing, contests, trade incentives, and sales force incentive programs.

The section on sales promotion should be rooted in one or more points in the marketing strategy section and the promotion objectives section of the marketing plan. Thus, the marketing strategy and promotion objectives establish the sales promotion objectives. Typically, sales promotion strategy will contain:

1. Statements of the promotional techniques (couponing, sampling, contests, etc.) that offer the most effective and efficient means of meeting marketing objectives.
2. Statements of how total promotion weight will be allocated by product, by marketing area, by season, and so forth.

SALES PROMOTION PLAN

The sales promotion plan explains how the promotion strategy will be executed with specific offers or other activities, geographic areas of application, the key audiences to which the sales promotion is addressed, and the specific times during the marketing year in which the promotion will be used. In addition to outlining the details of the recommended activities, the sales promotion plan also summarizes the estimated cost of the recommendations.

Generally, the selection of a particular sales promotion technique to accomplish a particular objective is based on: company experience, traditional practices in a given industry, and/or the results of specific sales promotion tests that have been run. A later chapter discusses various sales

Market planning starts here. (Photo courtesy of Nationwide Insurance Company)

promotion techniques and the unique values of each.

PRODUCT PUBLICITY STRATEGY

Product publicity is an optional part of the marketing plan for the simple reason that many marketers believe that product publicity is neither necessary nor efficient. Others disagree. Because the effects of product publicity are particularly difficult to measure, many marketing practitioners hold it in low repute.

Product publicity strategy does identify the basic form that the publicity program will take. The strategy section for product publicity generally includes:

- A purpose and rationale statement for the publicity program.
- An identification of the specific audiences to be reached.
- An identification of the types of product publicity that will be most effective.
- A statement of how product publicity will be coordinated with other marketing activities.
- Finally, although this point is often neglected, a statement describing how the effectiveness of the product publicity program will be evaluated.

PRODUCT PUBLICITY PLAN

The product publicity plan details the nature of the proposed publicity activities, the specific audiences for these activities, the timing of each activity, and the costs to be incurred.

SPECIAL OBJECTIVES, STRATEGIES, AND PLANS

This section of the marketing plan for *established products* is devoted to recommendations about the product itself, packaging, pricing, marketing research, and test marketing. As pointed out earlier, the marketing plan for established products does not normally deal with these areas *unless* the market review section has identified specific problems or opportunities. If the market review reveals weaknesses in any of these areas, these weaknesses must be dealt with in some way—by recommending consumer tests, by initiating developmental work on product improvements or package design, by recommending test markets, or by proposing some other appropriate activity.

Often weaknesses in one or more of the controllable marketing variables will be detected during the course of the marketing year—that is, between plans. Such developments often arise because of competitive activity, such as a product improvement, a redesigned package, or a change in pricing practices. In such cases, the marketer cannot afford to delay action until the next formal planning period. Instead, existing objectives, strategies, and plans must be examined immediately,

TABLE 4–1: *Budget Summary*

Advertising		
1. *Consumer Magazines* 6 to 9 4-color bleed pages in each of 8 magazines: total circulation of 38.5 million. Net unduplicated coverage of 56% of U.S. households.		$940,000
2. *Spot Television* 60 to 100 Gross Rating Points weekly for 26 weeks in 38 markets.		720,000
3. *Spot Radio* 15 to 20 sixty-second commercials weekly for 39 weeks on estimated 26 Black stations in 21 major markets.		173,000
4. *Production, Preparation*		
Magazines:	$15,000	
Television:	8,000	
Radio:	4,000	27,000
Total Advertising		$1,860,000
Sales Promotion		
1. Major tie-in promotion based on 50¢/case display allowance; national magazine support.		200,000
2. February-March: Repeat fall tie-in promotion:		200,000
3. "Pay Day" Black promotion—SE Region		40,000
4. Promotion materials		30,000
Total Promotion		470,000
Reserves		
1. For test marketing 2 new packages		125,000
2. General reserves (5% of budget)		125,000
Total Reserves		250,000
GRAND TOTAL		$2,580,000

FIGURE 4–2: Calendar of Marketing Activities

	A	M	J	J	A	S	O	N	D	J	F	M
Consumer Magazines:												
(Page 4-C Bleed)												
LHJ	x	x	x			x	x	x	x	-x-		x
GH	x	x	x			x	x	x	x		x	x
Redbook	x	x	x			x	x	x	x		x	x
FC	x	x	x			x	x	x	x		x	x
WD	x	x	x			x	x	x	x		x	x
Ebony	x	x				x		x		x		x
TS	x	x				x		x		x		x
MR	x	x				x		x		x		x
Spot Television												
GRP Weekly	60	60	-	-	-	100	100	60	-	-	100	100
Spot Radio												
15-20 Spots—Wk.	x	x				x	x	x	x	x	x	x
Fall Tie-in Promotion						x	x					
Winter Tie-in Promotion											x	x
Black "Pay Day" Promotion												
(S.E. Region Only)						x	x	x	x	x	x	x

and adjustments made. For this reason, every marketing plan should contain a budget reserve. The budget reserve is a contingency fund that defrays unanticipated expenses so that the planned contribution to profits will not be reduced, or any reduction will be minimized.

Even under the best of conditions, the market planner cannot anticipate all of the contingencies that may arise in a competitive marketing situation. This factor, which surrounds marketing with an aura of uncertainty, makes marketing an exciting, dynamic occupation.

BUDGET SUMMARY AND CALENDAR OF EVENTS

At some point in the marketing plan, all recommended expenditures should be brought together to enable the reader to quickly grasp the full implications of what has been proposed and to show the interrelationships of the various parts of the marketing plan. This summary usually works best at the end of the plan because the preceding material provides justification. The budget summary should be limited to a single page. Major, related expenditures should always be grouped together so that the outline of the spending plan is clear. An example of a budget summary appears in Table 4–1.

Following the budget summary, a calendar of marketing activities gives a visual picture of how the various activities fit together. A calendar of events is shown in Figure 4–2.

SUMMARY

Few topics are more important than market planning. This is particularly true in times of economic stress when effective market planning often becomes a criterion for survival. Much of the literature on market planning deals with top management decisions on the broad strategy that a company should follow in determining the fields in which it should compete, how the company should be organized, and how resources should be utilized to insure survival and growth.

Although such decisions are indeed crucial, decisions at the corporate level do not occupy the time and energies of those who engage in the day-to-day practice of marketing. Most of the activity that we normally think of as market planning occurs at the product level.

Market planning at the product level enables the marketer to use the resources of the firm wisely in promoting the sales of company products. This can best be done by: (1) assessing the marketing environment in order to identify marketing problems and opportunities; (2) establishing realistic sales objectives and levels of spending; (3) devising competitive strategies for the controllable marketing variables—product, price, place, and promotion; and (4) developing detailed plans for carrying out these strategies. The key to market planning at the product level is the product marketing plan.

The product marketing plan is a systematic document that proceeds from the general to the specific—from an assessment of the marketing environment to a detailed summary of the marketing budget. The marketing plan for a *new product* usually contains the following sections: (1) market review; (2) problems and opportunities; (3) marketing objectives; (4) marketing strategies; (5) product objectives, strategies and plans; (6) pricing objectives, strategies, and plans; (7) distribution objectives, strategies, and plans; (8) promotion objectives, strategies, and plans; (9) other objectives, strategies, and plans; (10) a budget summary; and (11) a calendar of events.

For an *established product,* some of these sections may be omitted. For example, if no changes are required in the product, its name, or its package, this section can be omitted from the annual plan. If changes in the market require that these elements be reexamined, then they must be included.

REVIEW QUESTIONS

1. What is the basic purpose of the product marketing plan, and how can this purpose best be accomplished?
2. How does the marketing plan differ from the sales plan, and why are they usually separate documents?
3. What are the functions of the marketing plan?
4. Distinguish between the terms *objectives, strategies,* and *plans.*
5. Identify the basic parts of the marketing plan.
6. How does the marketing plan for a *new product* differ from the marketing plan for an *established product?*
7. What is the relationship between the problems and opportunities section of the marketing plan and the marketing strategy section?
8. Identify the major areas covered in the market review section of the marketing plan.
9. Identify the basic elements that should appear in a copy strategy.
10. Identify the basic elements that should appear in a media strategy.

1. Many companies do not prepare formal marketing plans. Discuss some of the problems inherent in this approach.
2. In view of the current economic climate and the intensity of competition, discuss some of the problems that the market planner faces. How might the market planner minimize the impact of an unstable marketing environment.
3. Select a consumer product with which you are familiar. From an examination of its advertising, packaging, pricing, distribution, and sales promotion activities, identify its key marketing strategies.
4. Most product marketing plans are written for one year. Some are written for three years, and updated and extended annually. What do you feel are the advantages and disadvantages of these two approaches?
5. Select a magazine advertisement for a consumer product. On the basis of the information presented in this advertisement, write a copy strategy for it.

THE MARKETING PLAN

The Boxstitch Candy Company is a leading producer of expensive boxed chocolates. Established in Boston in 1897, Boxstitch has developed into a national marketer of fancy chocolates that are distributed through chain drugstores, independent drugstores, and candy departments in department stores. By the mid-seventies, annual sales approximated $40 million, and the company employed a sales force of eighty salespeople who called on wholesalers, drugstore chains, large independent drugstores, and department stores. The company spent approximately 10 percent of its sales on advertising and sales promotion.

Each year the company president, Bruce Ruble, approves an advertising and promotion budget based on a sales forecast made by the sales department. The budget is administered by an advertising manager who, working with the company's advertising agency, decides on a copy approach and a media schedule. Funds are allocated geographically on the basis of retail drug sales, and the bulk of the funds are spent on magazine advertising, although recently some funds have been diverted to spot television in major markets.

Sales grew steadily until the late 1960s when they began to level. Competition has increased significantly in the past few years, particularly from regional brands and from national brands that have concentrated their distribution in franchised candy stores and in leased departments in department stores.

In 1978 Boxstitch was purchased by a major tobacco company that was seeking to diversify its holdings. You, as the marketing director of the tobacco company, have been directed to study the marketing practices of the new Boxstitch division, and to persuade the president of the division to adopt any modifications in planning procedures that you believe appropriate. In preliminary discussions with Ruble, you find that he is receptive to talking about market planning, and has asked you to put together a short presentation on the values of planning and how a marketing plan can help the division.

Assignment

1. *Evaluate the current marketing practices of the Boxstitch Candy Company.*
2. *Prepare a brief presentation—about 10 or 15 minutes in length—on the nature and values of market planning for Ruble. Use any charts or visual material that will help make the presentation effective.*
3. *Based on information given in the case, what kinds of marketing data will the company need to acquire and analyze in order to develop a systemic marketing plan?*

Three markets visible from one corner.
(Photo by Freda Leinwand)

THE TOOLS OF MARKETING

Earlier, we noted that the preparation of the marketing review section of the marketing plan requires objectivity, understanding, and a high level of analytical skill. In this part of the text, we will examine some of the tools of marketing that make this task easier.

Chapter 5 describes some of the methods that are widely used in analysis—ways of looking at marketing data that facilitate an understanding of the current marketing situation.

Chapter 6 focuses on consumer demographics, and examines some trends emerging in the U.S. population, and in U.S. purchasing power.

Chapter 7 examines industrial markets and the buying patterns that characterize them. In this chapter, we will briefly examine producer markets, reseller markets, and government markets; where these markets are located; and their structures. We will also examine such questions as "When they buy," "Why they buy," and "How they buy."

In Chapter 8, we will turn our attention back to consumers in order to consider their behavioral dimensions. As marketing becomes more competitive—and as competitors become more sophisticated—an understanding of the behavioral characteristics of consumers becomes more important.

Chapter 9 is devoted to marketing research and other sources of marketing data. A marketer without good sources of marketing information is a little like a blind man stranded in the middle of a freeway during the rush hour. He knows he is in danger, but he doesn't know what to do about it.

Finally, Chapter 10 deals with forecasting and the marketing budget, both of which are critical areas for the marketing manager.

These chapters deal with the basic tools and background knowledge essential to the practice of marketing.

5

Some Useful Methods of Analysis

- *Per capita consumption and index numbers.*
- *The concept of market saturation.*
- *Brand share analysis.*
- *All commodity and store-count distribution.*
- *Comparative advertising expenditures.*
- *Comparative sales promotion expenditures.*
- *Advertising effectiveness.*

MARKETING EXAMPLES

PERRIER

When is bubbly water not bubbly water? When it is a soft drink. United States consumers, riding a wave of concern for health and snobbishness, discovered the virtues of mineral water as a soft drink in the late 1970s.

Perrier, a naturally carbonated mineral water imported from France, was a minor specialty product sold through exclusive restaurants and specialty shops. Perrier's distribution was limited, its market select, and its price high. In 1976 Perrier's sales in the United States were only 3.5 million bottles.

Bruce Nevin, president of Great Waters of France (the U.S. subsidiary of the Perrier Group) put two pieces of marketing information together and struck a bonanza. *First,* the market for mineral water in the United States was relatively small whereas the market for soft drinks was huge—over $6 billion. *Second,* in Europe the situation was reversed. Mineral water outsold the leading cola drink by two to one. According to Nevin, "research showed the product itself had potential if only the company could improve its distribution system and lower the price. . . ."[1]

This potential was realized through two strategies: (1) the product was repositioned as a refreshing, healthful soft drink and promoted heavily to consumers, distributors, and retailers; (2) distribution was switched from direct deliveries to selected local outlets to centralized distribution through soft drink bottlers and beer wholesalers. The distribution change, which was made in mid-1977, opened up a mass market and reduced the retail price of a 23-ounce bottle from over a dollar to about sixty-nine cents. By the end of 1978, Perrier sales exceeded 90 million bottles, and a new mass market was born.[2]

---

1. *Sales and Marketing Management* (January, 1979): 16–17.
2. Ibid.

PUREX

Purex markets a line of household cleaners, including Brillo, Old Dutch, Sweetheart, and Fels, in competition with companies such as Procter & Gamble and Lever Brothers. Two problems faced by Purex were inability to match the advertising expenditures of its major competition; and a sales force heavily outnumbered by the two thousand or so sales representatives deployed by Procter & Gamble.

An analysis of the grocery store business revealed that 17 percent of the food stores do 72 percent of the grocery volume, and 6 percent of Purex's customers accounted for two-thirds of the sales of their product categories. These findings were seen by Purex management as an opportunity to offset some of the disadvantages created by its giant competitors.

Purex developed a "national accounts" program, a promotional program aimed at the buyers and top executives of the major food stores. This program, which includes mail promotions, telephone calls, and face-to-face meetings, keeps buyers and other retail executives informed about new products, retail and consumer sales promotions, and special services offered by Purex. By concentrating its sales efforts on its major customers, Purex has a highly successful, minimal cost promotional program.[3]

FROZEN PIES

In preparing a marketing review, a major producer of frozen pies found that the market share for its product was considerably below the national average in many major markets. Management's first inclination was to increase advertising expenditures in these markets in an effort to bolster sales. However, further analysis revealed two separate problems.

---

3. "Purex Borrows from Cosmetics to Market Household Cleaners," *Product Marketing* (February, 1977): 10

In one group of markets, brand distribution was good; the brand was distributed in stores selling 80 to 85 percent of the total grocery volume; however, market share per point of retail distribution was well below the national average. In the second group of markets, share per point of distribution was equal to or above the national average, but the brand was only distributed in stores doing 50 to 60 percent of the grocery volume.

Since the problems in these two groups of markets were distinctly different, they required different solutions. In the first group of markets—where distribution was high—additional consumer advertising was mandated. In the second group of markets, however, the problem was to increase retail distribution; advertising, as such, is generally an inefficient tool for this purpose. The strategy employed in these markets was: (1) to continue the normal advertising support; (2) to increase sales coverage of retail outlets by the sales force; (3) to offer stocking allowances of fifty cents per case to encourage retailers to stock the brand; and (4) to use a consumer couponing effort in order to provide initial sales to reassure retailers that, if the brand were stocked, sales would be forthcoming.

Each of these three examples demonstrates the role of marketing analysis in determining strategy. In the case of Perrier, an examination of research findings led to a repositioning of the product and a basic change in its method of distribution. For Purex, an analysis of customers led to an innovative and low cost sales strategy that enabled the company to compete effectively with competitors utilyzing greater resources. In the case of frozen pies, a company was able to tailor its promotional program to deal with two distinctly different sales problems, thereby using its promotional funds more wisely.

Since careful marketing analysis is essential to developing sound marketing plans, let's turn our attention to this subject. In the following material, we will discuss: the scope of analysis, analyzing the total market, analyzing company sales, distribution analysis, analyzing advertising expenditures, analyzing sales promotion activity, analyzing advertising effectiveness, and special research.

THE SCOPE OF ANALYSIS

The scope of marketing analysis depends upon the amount and variety of factual data. Some companies will draw on relatively little marketing data. Others will have a great deal. Generally, the data available will depend upon the individual company's ability and willingness to invest in marketing information. Extensive marketing data can be expensive, but it is often worth the cost.

Private research firms, such as A. C. Nielsen, provide information on consumer purchases obtained from periodic audits of retail stores. Other firms, such as the Market Research Corporation of America, provide information on consumer purchases obtained from daily consumer diaries that are sent to the company on a weekly basis for tabulation and analysis by 7,500 families across the nation. Such services are expensive, often costing well over one hundred thousand dollars a year; many companies cannot afford them. Most companies, however, have access to a surprisingly wide variety of data which, when used properly, can provide valuable insights into the structure and current conditions in the marketplace. Trade associations routinely assemble facts and figures about their industries; an amazing range of data is available from the United States Department of Commerce; newspapers and broadcast media conduct surveys in major metropolitan areas; *Merchandising* Magazine prints the annual sales for selected department store products; *Supermarketing* Magazine does the same for grocery store products; *Progressive Grocer* devotes an issue each year to consumption patterns for leading food and drug products; warehouse withdrawal figures are available for most major markets at a relatively low cost; and syndicated research services, such as W. R. Simmons, provide current survey information on product usage and media habits of consumers. The point is that a wide variety of information is available for the marketer who will bother to seek it out. In Chapter 9 (Marketing Research), sources of marketing data are given in some detail.

The basic purpose of this chapter is to examine some of the basic analytical approaches that can be used in making sense out of the wealth of available statistics.

While many statistically sophisticated ways of analyzing marketing data exist, about 95 percent of all marketing analysis is based on relatively simple, easy to use methods. We will focus our attention on these easily understood tools of analysis. Later courses in marketing—courses in marketing research and quantitative techniques in marketing—will cover more sophisticated analytical methods.

ANALYZING THE TOTAL MARKET

As pointed out earlier, the market review section of the marketing plan proceeds from the general to the specific. The analyst starts with a broad consideration of the market and progressively narrows the analysis down to specific factors affecting the problems and opportunities of a particular brand.

Analysis of a product market begins with the known demand for a particular product at a given time, and under known marketing conditions.[4] For example, the market demand for passenger cars in the United States in 1979 was approximately 10.6 million cars. Under conditions of economic recession, the market demand may drop to as low as 8 million cars, as it did in 1981. Or, during periods of full employment, consumer optimism, and heavy promotional expenses, the market demand may rise to over 12 million units. Thus, at any given time, the market demand reflects the total size of a particular market in units or dollars.

Some markets are volatile because they are strongly influenced by a variety of economic and personal factors; others are relatively stable. The market forecast (to be discussed in Chapter 10) is highly critical in volatile markets. A forecast that is too low can lead to a severe loss in market position since often raw materials must be ordered, and production plans formulated, months or even years ahead of time. A case in point is the problem faced by the Chrysler Corporation with the Aspen and Horizon in 1979 and 1980. Because of the demand for fuel-efficient cars, Chrysler could not make enough Aspens and Horizons to fill customers' orders. The reason? Chrysler had to order the engines several years ahead of their need from Volkswagon. Underestimating their demand, Chrysler ordered only about 300,000 engines—far short of what could have been sold. By contrast, if the market forecast is too high, unsold inventories erode profits and may result in severe losses.

Although the market forecast is equally important for planning production and spending levels in stable markets, the danger of making forecasting errors is much smaller. Table 5–1 shows industry sales for four product categories. Each category presents different problems and has different implications for the market planner.

---

4. An economic concept, market demand treats demand as a function of the entire set of marketing and environmental variables that influence the total volume of a particular product.

TABLE 5–1: Consumption Statistics
SOURCE: "Alcohol, Tobacco, and Firearms Summary Statistics," Fiscal year 1977, Department of Treasury, Bureau of Alcohol, Tobacco, and Firearms; *Statistical Abstracts of the United States, 1978* and Department of Agriculture *National Food Review.*

	1973	*1974*	*1975*	*1976*	*1977*	*1978*	*1979*
U.S. Passenger Car Sales in Units—Domestic and Imports							
Thousands of Units	—	8,867	8,640	11,111	11,185	11,311	10,064
Change	—	(22.5%)	(2.6%)	17.0%	10.6%	1.1%	(6.0%)
Butter—U.S. Civilian Consumption							
Millions of Pounds	—	964.7	1,013.8	936.1	943.6	933.9	—
Change	—	5.0%	5.0%	(7.3%)	0.8%	(1.0%)	—
Per Capita Consumption in Pounds	—	4.6	4.8	4.4	4.4	4.6	—
Beer							
Millions of Barrels	134.0	142.3	146.8	148.7	—	155.9	—
Change	2.4%	6.2%	3.2%	1.3%	—	4.8%	—
Per Capita Consumption in Gallons	19.8	20.9	21.4	21.5	—	22.4	—
Evaporated and Condensed Milk—U.S. Civilian Consumption							
Millions of Pounds	—	1,174.3	1,056.0	765.9	707.7	626.6	—
Change	—	(6.7%)	(10.1%)	(17.5%)	(7.8%)	(11.5%)	—
Per Capita Consumption in Pounds	—	5.6	5.0	3.6	3.3	2.9	—

The passenger car market is relatively volatile—strongly influenced by economic conditions, the level of employment, and people's expectations of their future economic states. In such a market, demand may shift dramatically from one year to the next. Note that 1974 was off 22.5 percent from the previous year, whereas 1976 was up by 17 percent over the previous year. Butter, on the other hand, is a relatively stable market for the period shown. Per capita consumption was virtually level, and sales changes modest.

Beer represents a relatively strong market. A combination of increases in population and per capita consumption has led to a market increase of 16 percent during the period shown. In contrast to the other markets shown thus far, the market for evaporated and condensed milk is sick. Population growth is being offset by decreases in per capita consumption. Although the market is still large (over 626 million pounds), it decreased by over 46 percent during the five year period shown.

TABLE 5–2: Microwave Oven Sales
SOURCE: *Merchandising* (March, 1979)

Year	Microwave Ovens	Percent Change
1974	635,000	—
1975	840,000	32%
1976	1,661,000	98%
1977	2,175,000	30%
1978	2,422,000	11%

Some markets have a much stronger growth pattern than those shown thus far. Consider the trend for microwave ovens shown in

Table 5–2. From 1974 through 1978, the market increased by 280 percent.

The foregoing discussion, emphasizes that market demand (what is happening to the total market) sets the stage for the marketing plan. Is it a time for optimism or pessimism? A time for investing or retrenching? A time for wooing new customers, or trying to retain current customers? A time for advertising, or a time for price competition?

An analysis of market demand can do more than just set the stage for the marketing plan. Areas of opportunity can be identified that will influence the allocation of the promotional effort, in terms of time and geography. In order to use marketing data for such purposes, however, the raw data must be converted into summary statistics that can be used for comparative purposes.

Use of Per Capita Consumption and Index Numbers

Table 5–3 shows population and beer consumption by region. The method of computing per capita consumption and the index of consumption is shown under the table. Based on the raw data (beer sales), the Pacific region appears to be the best region in which to promote beer because it accounts for 1,339,845 gallons, substantially more than any other region. However, the per capita consumption column indicates that the East North Central region is by far the best region because, on the average, each person in this region consumes 28.6 gallons of beer per year compared to only 19.7 gallons per person in the Pacific region. Or, looking at the index of consumption column, the consumption per person in the East North Central region is 34 percent above the national average, while consumption per person in the Pacific region is 8 percent below the national average (100 − 92 = 8). This means that, all other things being equal, each dollar spent in the East North Central region should produce more sales than each dollar spent in the Pacific region.

Of course, all other things are never equal, and per capita consumption figures and the index of consumption must be used in concert with other marketing data, such as brand share, extent of distribution, and other relevant marketing variables. Nonetheless, the differences in per capita consumption and index of consumption in the two regions discussed are too great to be ignored in marketing analysis.

Table 5–4 shows the seasonal distribution of beer sales. During March through August, monthly consumption is above average. Monthly consumption is average in September, below average during the remaining five months of the year. From the standpoint of marketing, 57 per-

TABLE 5–3: *Comparison of Beer Sales by Region*

SOURCE: "Beer Sales: Alcohol, Tobacco, and Firearms Summary Statistics," Fiscal 1977, Department of Treaury, ATF P 1323.1 4/79. Population statistics: *U.S. Statistical Abstracts,* 1976.

Region	Col. 1 *Population (000s)*	Col. 2 *Consumption (000s of Gallons)*	Col. 3 *Per Capita Gallon Consumption*	Col. 4 *Index of Consumption*
New England	12,198	140,728	11.5	54%
Middle Atlantic	37,263	671,807	18.0	84
East North Central	40,979	1,173,992	28.6	134
South Atlantic	33,717	877,594	26.0	121
West South Central	30,856	348,480	16.7	78
Pacific	68,113	1,339,845	19.7	92
Totals	223,126	4,552,446	21.4	100%

Per capita consumption equals consumption divided by population

The index of consumption is obtained by dividing the per capita consumption for each region by the total per capita consumption.

TABLE 5–4: *Seasonal Patterns in Beer Sales*
SOURCE: "Alcohol, Tobacco, & Firearms Summary Statistics, Fiscal Year 1977," Department of the Treasury, Bureau of Alcohol, Tobacco, & Firearms

1977	*Thousands of Gallons Consumed*	*Percent of Total*	*Index of Consumption*
October	378,770.4	7.9%	95%
November	326,114.8	6.7	81
December	335,838.5	6.9	83
January	310,207.7	6.4	77
February	323,395.1	6.7	81
March	450,978.7	9.4	113
April	442,518.8	9.2	111
May	464,956.6	9.6	116
June	487,010.0	10.0	120
July	458,738.0	9.5	114
August	453,936.1	9.4	113
September	399,521.8	8.3	100
	4,831,986.5	100.0%	100%

Index of consumption was computed by dividing the percent consumed by averaging monthly consumption (100 ÷ 12 = 8.3). A somewhat more precise index of monthly consumption could be derived by computing average consumption per day for each month and for the year, and then dividing the average daily consumption for each month by the average daily consumption for the year. However, the shortcut that was used is adequate to point up existing seasonal patterns.

TABLE 5–5: *Saturation Percentages in Electric Homes for Selected Products*
SOURCE: *Merchandising* (March, 1979), p. 48.

Products	*1968*	*1969*	*1970*	*1971*	*1972*	*1973*	*1974*	*1975*	*1976*	*1977*
Air conditioners (room)	33.5%	36.7%	40.6%	44.5%	46.7%	48.9%	51.6%	52.8%	54.4%	55.3%
Calculators	—	—	—	—	8.9	26.2	46.7	67.6	83.0	92.7
Can openers	39.4	43.2	45.5	48.1	49.5	50.7	52.3	54.6	56.4	57.9
Cornpoppers	21.7	24.9	26.7	29.1	32.1	36.3	37.8	39.3	40.7	42.4
Digital watches	—	—	—	—	—	0.5	1.3	5.1	16.9	32.3
Dishwashers	20.8	23.7	26.5	29.6	32.0	34.3	36.6	38.3	39.6	40.9
Disposals (food waste)	20.5	22.9	25.6	28.4	31.9	35.3	37.2	38.8	40.7	42.8
Fondues, electric	—	—	—	1.1	2.1	2.9	3.7	4.2	4.5	4.6
Hotplates and buffet ranges	23.7	24.1	24.5	24.8	24.0	25.1	25.5	26.2	26.6	26.7
Irons	99.5	99.5	99.7	99.8	99.9	99.9	99.9	99.9	99.9	99.9
Radios	99.7	99.7	99.8	99.8	99.9	99.9	99.9	99.9	99.9	99.9
Refrigerators	99.8	99.8	99.8	99.8	99.9	99.9	99.9	99.9	99.9	99.9
Smooth top ranges	—	—	—	—	—	0.3	0.7	1.1	1.4	1.7
Television, B&W	98.5	98.7	98.7	98.8	98.8	99.9	99.9	99.9	99.9	99.9
Toasters	89.3	91.0	92.6	94.2	95.1	96.5	97.8	98.6	99.4	99.9
Vacuum cleaners	89.1	90.7	92.4	94.4	96.9	97.5	98.4	99.2	99.5	99.9

cent of all beer is consumed during the six spring and summer months, and 43 percent during the remainder of the year. Or, in terms of gallons, the above average consumption months account for 686 million *more* gallons than do the six off-season months. For this reason most beer marketers substantially increase their marketing expenditures during the heavy consumption months.

The Concept of Market Saturation

Although measures of per capita consumption are extremely useful for products that are purchased frequently—products such as those sold through grocery stores, as well as many drugstore items—they are less useful when dealing with products, such as appliances, that are purchased infrequently and used for many years. In their place, the concepts of saturation levels, potential market, and replacement purchase rates are often used.

SATURATION LEVEL. Saturation level refers to the proportion of a defined group of customers who have already purchased one or more units of a product that is known to have a long life. Table 5–5 shows the ten year trend saturation levels of a variety of electrical products in homes that have electrical wiring.

Note that the levels of product saturation vary widely by product type. Irons, radios, refrigerators, black and white television sets, toasters, and vacuum cleaners are present in 99.9 percent of the wired homes. Electric fondues, on the other hand, have a saturation level of only 4.6 percent, and smooth-top (ceramic) ranges are found in only 1.7 percent of the homes.

Not all homes represent equally good markets for all of the appliances shown in Table 5–5. This is demonstrated by the saturation levels for hotplates and buffet ranges. These products have shown little increase in ownership during the past ten years, having increased in saturation from 23.7 percent in 1968 to only 26.7 percent in 1977. By contrast, calculators have grown from zero to 92.7 percent saturation in only six years.

Nonetheless, the prospect for growth would appear to be greater for products with low

TABLE 5–6: *New and Replacement Purchases of Selected Electrical Products in 1978*
SOURCE: *Merchandising* (March 1979): 50.

Product	*Replacement Purchases*	*New Purchases*
Air conditioners (room)	41%	59%
B&W Television	63	37
Color Television	76	24
Dishwashers	57	43
Disposals (food waste)	57	43
Dryers	64	36
Freezers	56	44
Microwave ovens	4	96
Ranges	76	24
Built-in	38	62
Free standing	83	17
Smooth top	40	60
Refrigerators	77	23
Trash compactors	9	91
Washers	68	32

saturation levels than for those that have already attained universal or near-universal usage. This gives rise to the concept of market potential.

MARKET POTENTIAL. Market potential may be defined as the *upper limit of demand approached as the industry effort moves toward infinity in a given marketing environment.* Note the two implications of this definition:

- Under a given marketing environment, demand is a function of marketing effort, up to some undetermined limit. As a consequence, an increase in industry expenditures, price reductions, expansion in distribution, easier credit, or some other change in marketing activity may increase demand.
- If the marketing environment itself changes, demand may increase. Thus, in times of prosperity and consumer optimism, demand may be greater than during economic stress and consumer despair.

The market potential, or upper limit of demand under given marketing conditions, will vary by product. Thus, for some products, a saturation level of 25 percent may represent the upper limit under certain marketing conditions. For other products, the upper limit may be 80 or 90 percent, or higher.

The concept of market potential, or upper limit of demand, is particularly useful when dealing with products that have a long life. And, one way of determining whether a product is reaching its upper limit of demand is the relationship between new buyers and replacement buyers.

NEW BUYERS AND REPLACEMENT PURCHASES. Generally, a high proportion of replacement buyers means that a product is approaching its upper limit, while a low proportion of replacement buyers means that the product has not yet approached its potential. Table 5–6 shows the proportion of total sales of selected electrical products accounted for by replacement and new buyers.

Note the wide variations among products in Table 5–6. The refrigerator market, with 99.9 percent saturation (see Table 5–5), is characterized by a 77 percent replacement rate. The 23 percent of new buyers is relatively low, being composed of new family formations and, to some extent, new housing construction. By contrast, the market for microwave ovens has only a 4 percent replacement rate, with 96 percent of the 1978 sales being accounted for by new buyers.

Any analysis of the total market for these two products should recognize this difference since a high proportion of new buyers compared to replacement purchases forebodes well for future market growth. As a result, increased promotional expenditures may effectively accelerate market growth.

ANALYZING COMPANY SALES

If industry demand sets the stage for the marketing review, company sales reveal how a particular participant is performing on that stage. Company sales records provide a wealth of information which, too often, is neglected. For example, while working with the cigar division of a major tobacco company, I found that the company's failure to perform a simple geographic analysis of its sales led to a serious misallocation of advertising funds to markets in which the company had little or no distribution.

There is no best way to analyze sales data. The type of analysis required depends upon the company and the industry involved. Good sales analysis is an innovative and imaginative task with an ultimate goal of defining problems and opportunities. Sales information can be broken down and compared with past company or industry data by geographic region, by product, by package size or model, by size and type of customer, by method of sales, by size of order, by seasonal patterns, or by financial arrangement.

The analysis of company sales becomes particularly useful when combined with industry data to develop information on brand share.

Brand Share Analysis

Brand share measurement (usually referred to as market share) is one of the most widely used analytical tools for assessing market performance. This widely used measurement is a relatively simple device for evaluating the performance of a particular brand in comparison with the total market *and* in comparison with competition. Used

"Who said that marketing analysis was a nine to five job?" (© 1981 Anne Schullstrom)

TABLE 5–7: *Sales versus Brand Share*

	1974	*1975*	*1976*	*1977*	*1978*
Total market (000s cases)	33,680.0	38,395.2	46,538.4	54,664.5	65,650.5
Brand X sales (000s cases)	8,420.2	9,262.0	10,373.4	11,514.5	13,126.5
Brand X percent increase	—	10.0%	12.0%	11.0%	14.0%
Brand X market share	25.0%	24.1%	22.3%	21.2%	20.0%

TABLE 5–8: *Market Share of the Saunders Company Based on Industry Statistics for 1978*

	Quarterly Sales in 000s of cases				
	1	*2*	*3*	*4*	*Total*
Industry sales	80,326.6	82,516.3	78,915.7	81,416.5	323,175.1
Saunders' sales	18,957.1	22,609.5	24,069.3	25,239.1	90,875.0
Saunders' share	23.6%	27.4%	30.5%	31.0%	28.1%

TABLE 5–9: *Inventory Build-up at Trade Level Resulting from Factory Sales in Excess of Consumer Purchases*

	Quarterly Sales in 000s of cases			
	1	*2*	*3*	*4*
Normal inventory	6,300.0	6,300.0	6,300.0	6,300.0
Saunders' factory sales	18,640.1	22,609.5	24,069.3	25,239.1
Consumer purchases of Saunders' product	18,157.1	18,910.1	18,500.2	18,715.0
Excess inventory	482.9	3,699.4	5,569.1	6,524.1
Accumulated excess inventory	482.9	4,182.3	9,751.5	16,275.6

Note: normal inventory is equal to approximately one month's supply at retail level

properly, market share analysis provides a more critical measure of brand performance than sales alone. This point is demonstrated in Table 5–7.

During the five years represented in Table 5–7, brand X has shown substantial growth in units, increasing sales by over 10 percent each year. Yet, since the industry grew at an even greater rate, brand X failed to keep pace with the market, was outstripped by competitors, and its market share declined from 25 percent to 20 percent. Thus, although sales seemed to indicate that the company was doing quite well, actually Brand X was doing very poorly in comparison to competition.

MISLEADING MARKET SHARE MEASURES. Market share is sometimes misleading. Consider the following example: Most trade associations consider the preparation of industry sales estimates compiled from association members' confidential reports or from government statistics one of their most important functions. When industry estimates are distributed to the association's members, they can compute their market shares and assess individual companies' performances. Table 5–8 reflects the performance of the Saunders Company assessed with industry data. Saunders' sales show a strong growth pattern throughout the year. Market share increases are reflected in every quarter, share position in the final quarter is up over seven points compared to the first quarter, and the company appears to be in a much stronger market position than at the beginning of the year.

In this case, however, market share is a misleading indicator of the company's performance. Saunders' industry sells through distributors to retailers who, in turn, sell to the ultimate consumer. In terms of consumer purchases,

Saunders' sales have remained relatively stable; as a result, the company has excess inventory at the distributor and retail levels of over sixteen thousand cases. Or, almost three months' supply at the current rate of consumer puchases. Until these excess inventories are depleted, distributors and retailers will reduce their purchases, so that Saunders can reasonably expect depressed sales during the next few months. The mechanics of this process is shown in Table 5–9.

This example emphasizes that market share based on sales to channel intermediaries can severely misrepresent the strength of a company's market position. In instances similar to Table 5–9, the discrepancy between factory sales and consumer purchases results in an inventory situation that may signal the need for a consumer promotion to reduce inventory levels and restore stability to factory shipments. The problem described in this example is particularly likely to occur in industries with long channels of distribution; that is, where several intermediaries (distributors, wholesalers, jobbers, and retailers) make up the distribution chain.

The possibility of inventory buildups at distributor and retail levels requires the continual measurement of consumer purchases if feasible. Industries that sell primarily to food and drug stores, can measure consumer purchases through private research companies such as A. C. Nielsen. For most manufacturers of consumer goods, similar information can be purchased from the Market Research Corporation of America. Some companies—such as major floor covering firms and appliance manufacturers—maintain a sample of major retailers who report consumer purchases on a daily basis. Such records of consumer purchases are relatively expensive, and many marketers do not have access to such information. In many product fields, however, special services provide records of warehouse withdrawals by brand at a relatively low cost. Although warehouse withdrawals are not as sensitive for measuring consumer purchases as store audits or consumer diaries, they can be reasonably accurate in those product fields in which retail inventories are kept at a minimum, as in grocery stores.

The point is that factory sales figures, when not reinforced by consumer purchase information, can be misleading and may result in unwise marketing decisions. Two of the most common instances in which market share data may be misleading, are described below.

MISLEADING DOLLAR SHARE. Market share can be computed either in units or dollars. When dollars are used as the basis for computation, a price increase by an individual manufacturer can distort market performance as reflected in the market share. The price increase may give the appearance of an increased market share when the units purchased by consumers, are actually decreasing. This phenomenon is demonstrated in Table 5–10.

Distortions such as this may become calamitous in those industries where retailers nor-

TABLE 5–10: *Distortion of Unit Share Caused by Price Increase*

	Quarterly Sales in 000s of Dollars			
	1	*2*	*3*	*4*
Industry sales ($'s)	$150,465.0	$151,240.3	$152,193.8	$152,983.5
Brand X sales ($'s)	33,533.7	33,877.8	35,765.5	36,869.0
Brand X shares ($'s)	22.3%	22.4%	23.5%	24.1%
Industry sales (units)	143,300.0	144,038.3	138,358.0	139,075.9
Brand X sales (units)	31,955.9	32,120.5	27,809.9	25,311.8
Brand X share (units)	22.3%	22.4%	20.1%	18.2%

Note: During quarters 1 and 2, all brands were priced at $1.05 per unit. Beginning in quarter 3, Brand X increased its price to $1.30 while competitors' prices remained unchanged.

TABLE 5–11: Brand Shares in Two Hypothetical Product Fields

Brands	Product Field 1 Period 1	Product Field 1 Period 2	Product Field 1 Period 3	Product Field 2 Period 1	Product Field 2 Period 2	Product Field 2 Period 3
A	28.8%	28.8%	28.9%	33.2%	33.2%	33.3%
B	26.7	26.7	26.7	28.5	28.5	28.6
C	24.6	24.5	24.4	23.9	23.8	23.8
D	19.9	20.0	20.0	14.4	14.5	14.3
Total	100.0%	100.0%	100.0%	100.0%	100.0%	100.0%

mally evaluate the sales of competitive brands by units or cases, rather than by gross income or profit, as frequently happens in the grocery field. When unit or case sales for a particular product drop below a certain point, that brand becomes a candidate for discontinuation, and distribution may be lost.

MISLEADING UNIT SHARE. Not only may dollar share be misleading, but in some instances the unit share may be misleading. Consider the manufacturer of television sets whose consoles often sell for several hundreds of dollars more than the portable sets, and also carry a higher profit margin. A significant increase in the unit sales of the less expensive model may result in a unit share increase in the total units sold; and a decrease in both dollar sales and profits. This error in interpretation can usually be avoided by computing unit share for each model separately, so that a decrease in share of the more expensive models is not masked by an increase in share by less expensive sets. To avoid this error the marketing analyst must carefully define the particular markets in which the company's products are competing so that appropriate market share calculations can be made.

Market Shares May Conceal Market Instability

Markets often differ dramatically in the amount of brand switching that takes place. Yet, these differences may be concealed by brand share measures. Consider the two hypothetical fields in Table 5–11. Based on brand share measurements taken at different measuring periods, both fields appear to be highly stable, with little change in the brand shares of the competing brands.

Now, let us assume that we interview a representative sample of customers from each field. During the course of the interview, we ask:

What brand did you buy *last* time?

What brand did you buy *time before last*?

We now have a measure of brands bought on the last two buying occasions. Analysis of this data in terms of brand switching might result in the patterns shown in Table 5–12.

Product field 1 is indeed stable. Little brand switching occurred between the last two purchases: 92.6 percent of the consumers who bought Brand A two occasions ago also bought it the last time, and only 7.4 percent of its most recent buyers switched from some other brand. A similar pattern of brand loyalty also prevails for brands B, C, and D.

But now, let us look at product field 2, which represents a completely different picture. Only 30.5 percent of the people who bought Brand A the time before last repurchased it last time. Only 36.7 percent of the people who bought Brand B time before last also bought it the last time. The same general pattern applies to the other two brands as well. In every case, very little repurchase of the same brand took place, with a great deal of brand switching.

Product field 2 is highly unstable; customers consider most of the brands in this field to be pretty much alike. On the basis of brand characteristics, they have no pressing reason to purchase one brand rather than another. As a consequence, they select brands on some other basis—whichever is most convenient, whichever

TABLE 5–12: Comparison of Brand Switching

Buyers the Time Before Last	*Buyers and Source of Buyers Last Time*		
	Source	*Number*	*Percent*
	Product Field 1		
Brand A (650)	From A to A	630	92.6%
	From B to A	50	7.4
	From C to A	—	—
	From D to A	—	—
Brand B (600)	From A to B	—	—
	From B to B	500	86.2%
	From C to B	50	8.6
	From D to B	30	5.2
Brand C (550)	From A to C	20	3.6%
	From B to C	30	5.5
	From C to C	500	90.9
	From D to C	—	—
Brand D (450)	From A to D	—	—
	From B to D	20	4.5%
	From C to D	—	—
	From D to D	420	95.5
	Product Field 2		
Brand A (700)	From A to A	210	30.5%
	From B to A	200	29.0
	From C to A	150	21.7
	From D to A	130	18.8
Brand B (600)	From A to B	150	25.0%
	From B to B	220	36.7
	From C to B	200	33.3
	From D to B	30	5.0
Brand C (500)	From A to C	250	49.0%
	From B to C	80	15.7
	From C to C	100	19.6
	From D to C	80	15.7
Brand D (300)	From A to D	90	30.0%
	From B to D	100	33.3
	From C to D	50	16.7
	From D to D	60	20.0

is on display, whichever they have a coupon for, or whichever has a price-off special.

Such instability sometimes suggests an opportunity for a product improvement. That is, some change in the product to distinguish it from, and give it an advantage over, the competition.

Precisely this situation in the potato chip market caused Procter & Gamble to develop Pringles. The potato chip market was highly unstable. Every product was like every other product, and all had specific disadvantages: *First,* the chips broke into such small pieces that by the time the consumer got to the bottom of the bag, the chips had to be eaten with a spoon or thrown away. *Second,* potato chips were highly hygroscopic, so that in a moist climate they quickly became soggy. *Finally,* most chips were too thin to be used with dips—they broke in pieces when used to scoop up dip. And, fishing around in a communal dip with one's fingers to rescue a potato chip that has disintegrated upon use is not considered good taste!

So, Procter & Gamble reinvented the potato chip by making Pringles stronger, forming chips that nestled in a stack and did not break, and packaging them in a can to protect crispness and prevent them from getting soggy in humid areas.

Not everybody liked Pringles because the manufacturing process produced a potato chip that tasted somewhat different than regular potato chips. But, enough people like Pringles to spend several hundred million dollars a year for the new, improved potato chip.

Two morals are apparent in this example: *First,* market share data *may* conceal instability in the market. *Second,* unstable markets often offer an opportunity for the alert and resourceful marketer.

Misuse of Brand Share Data

Market share data, even when accurately reflecting consumer purchases, can be misused. Many manufacturers use market share as their primary measure of performance and react vigorously to market share decline. In some instances, the cost of maintaining or increasing market share may be excessive and have a deleterious effect on company profits. In some instances, sole reliance on market share performance may inspire marketing decisions that waste company resources and reduce the company's ability to compete effectively, in other, more profitable fields.

Market share is, at best, a descriptive tool which enables the marketer to assess the performance of a brand vis-a-vis competition. Not a diagnostic tool, market share provides no information about *why* market share increases or decreases. This requires further analysis. A declining

TABLE 5–13: *Two Regions Having Similar Shares but Different Shares per Point of Distribution*

	Quarter 1	*Quarter 2*	*Quarter 3*	*Quarter 4*
Region I				
Industry sales	15,463.5	15,376.2	15,560.3	15,701.1
Brand sales	2,814.4	2,783.1	2,847.5	2,857.6
Brand share	18.2%	18.1%	18.3%	18.2%
Distribution (all commodity basis)	90	90	90	90
Share per point of distribution	.202	.201	.203	.202
Region II				
Industry sales	15,000.3	15,216.4	15,110.6	15,198.2
Brand sales	2,640.0	2,723.7	2,629.2	2,659.7
Brand share	17.6%	17.9%	17.4%	17.5%
Distribution (all commodity basis)	68	68	68	68
Share per point of distribution	.258	.263	.256	.257

brand share may be caused by inadequate advertising expenditures; by a weak creative effort; by an improvement in a competitor's product or a new competitor entering the field; or by distribution losses. In some instances, a stable brand share at the national level may hide severe problems in specific regions or in individual markets.

Brand share analysis is only a starting point. But, this important starting point is the best the marketer has available. Remember, however, that a change in brand share only indicates that something has happened in the marketplace. The marketing analyst's task is to discover what that something is and to devise strategies and plans that will either correct an unfavorable situation, or take further advantage of a favorable one.

DISTRIBUTION ANALYSIS

Along with market share analysis, distribution analysis is one of the more valuable techniques in the marketing analyst's kit. Variations in brand share among geographic regions for a mass distributed product are often the result of variations in distribution. Many marketing variables—the product itself, packaging, advertising copy, pricing, and so forth—are similar in all regions. Distribution, along with advertising weight and sales promotion activities, often vary from one region to another.

Market share analysis can obscure variations in distribution that may be critical to a brand's future health. Consider Table 5–13, which illustrates this point graphically by describing two regions which have similar market shares, but distinctly different distribution problems.

Note that the two regions have similar industry sales and brand shares. However, the distribution patterns within the two regions are quite different. In Region 1, distribution is excellent; the brand is sold in stores doing 90 percent of the grocery volume. Share per point of distribution, however, is relatively weak, suggesting increased advertising, in-store promotion, or consumer incentives as possible strategies for increasing market share. In Region II, by contrast, share per point of distribution is excellent—about 25 percent greater than in Region I. On the other hand, all-commodity distribution is relatively poor. An increased sales force effort and stocking allowances, rather than increased advertising, would be appropriate strategies. This situation is similar to the frozen pie example given at the beginning of the chapter.

All Commodity versus Store-Count Distribution

Distribution is often described in two ways: *store-count* distribution and *all-commodity* distribution. Store-count distribution refers to the stores in

FIGURE 5–1: The Average Number of Stores Necessary to Obtain One Point of All Commodity Distribution
SOURCE: James O. Peckham, Sr., *The Wheel of Marketing* (Chicago: A. C. Nielsen Company, 1973), chart 8.

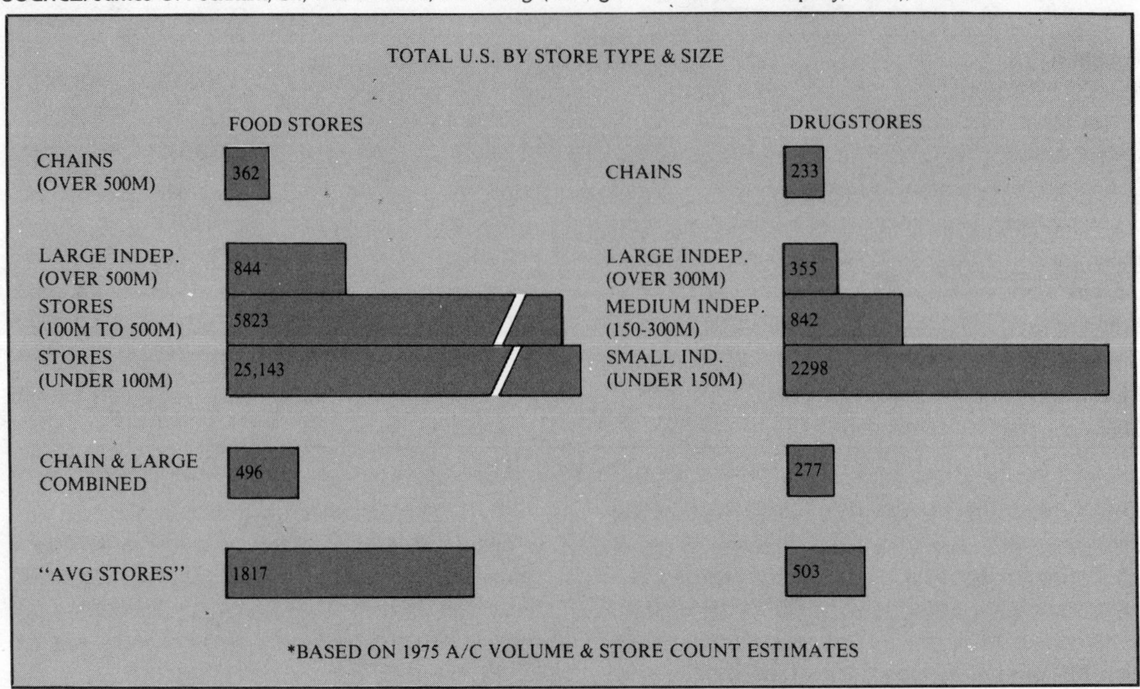

which a brand is distributed; it is computed by dividing the number of stores carrying the brand by the total number of stores available, and expressing the result as a percentage. For example, a brand distributed in 180,000 of the 200,000 grocery stores in the United States would have a store-count distribution of 90 percent (180,000 ÷ 200,000 = .90).

All-commodity distribution, on the other hand, is based on dollar volume. Thus, a brand that had 90 percent all-commodity distribution would be distributed in stores doing 90 percent of the total grocery volume. In this instance, the number of stores required for 90 percent all-commodity distribution would depend upon the size of the stores in which the brand had distribution. For example, the average chain store had an annual volume of $1,445,000 in 1970, while the average, small independent store had a volume of only $40,000. Obviously, many fewer chain stores than small independents would be required to reach a given level of all-commodity distribution.

Figure 5–1, derived from A. C. Nielsen, demonstrates this point graphically. This figure illustrates that 25,143 small, independent food stores (sales under $100,000 annually are required to generate one point of all-commodity distribution, whereas only 844 large independents, and only 362 chain stores could do the same. Similarly, 2,298 small independent drugstores provide one point of all-commodity drug distribution, as would only 233 chain stores.

Manufacturers of mass-distributed consumer products generally concentrate on the large volume outlets because they can obtain a given level of all-commodity exposure at substantially less sales cost than by calling on the smaller outlets. This was the strategy of Purex, discussed at the beginning of the chapter.

Unfortunately, information on either all-commodity or store-count distribution is relatively expensive and often hard to come by for the marketer of consumer goods. The A. C. Nielsen organization provides this information about food and drugstores for its subscribers; similar information

Dogs prefer the taste of new improved Gravy Train® DOG FOOD 3 to 1.

In tests, we gave dogs Gravy Train® and new improved Gravy Train. And you know what happened? 3 out of 4 dogs preferred the new to the old. That's 3 to 1.

You see, we added a natural beef flavor, so it tastes even better, wet or dry. It even looks different. It has a crunchy new shape. And, of course, it's fully nutritious.

So, whether your dog's favorite is Gravy Train or not, he's going to have a new favorite. New improved Gaines® Gravy Train.

Natural beef flavor makes the taste even better.

Gaines

Plate 5-2: *Gravy Train ad reproduced with permission of General Foods Corporation.*

Mealtime.® It's just what your dog's been waiting for.

Dogs love the taste of meat.

That's why Mealtime gets its flavor from meat protein.

35% of the protein in Mealtime actually comes from meat. So it has the flavor a dog loves. And the protein he needs. Plus all the nutrients required for healthy growth and maintenance.

Mealtime is also the only dry dog food with a choice of either large or small crunchy bites.

Either way, why not get some Kal Kan® Mealtime for your dog?

Here's a coupon for 25¢ to make it easy.

Don't you think he's waited long enough?

Tail-waggin' taste from meat protein.™

Save 25¢

on any size package of new Kal Kan® Mealtime®

DEALER: Our representative will redeem this coupon for the face value plus 5¢ for handling charges for each coupon redeemed in accordance with the conditions of this offer. Invoices proving purchase of sufficient stock to cover coupons presented for redemption must be made available upon request to Kal Kan or its agents. The customer must pay any sales tax. This coupon void in states where taxed or restricted by law. Cash value 1/20th of a cent. Restricted to one coupon per family. Kal Kan Foods, Inc. P.O. Box 1836, Clinton, Iowa 52734.

LARGE CRUNCHY BITES

SMALL CRUNCHY BITES

STORE COUPON

STORE COUPON

Plate 5-3: *Mealtime ad reproduced with permission of Kal-Kan Foods.*

can be obtained for other types of retail outlets through specially designed research studies. The cost of such studies tends to be high, however. As a consequence, many smaller companies and those outside of the food and drug fields rely on reports from their sales personnel, or on distribution studies made by local media in major urban areas.

Selective Distribution

Many producers, particularly in the fashion, appliance, automotive, and fast-food categories, rely on a strategy of selective distribution. That is, instead of seeking distribution in all or most stores selling their product type, they seek distribution in a limited number of independent outlets, through company-owned stores, or in franchised stores. This strategy gives the manufacturer greater control over the conditions of retail sale. Such a strategy is appropriate when retail sales personnel have a disproportionate role in influencing consumer decisions (such as in furniture, carpeting, or appliance stores), or when a self-sufficient service (fast-foods, for example) is being offered. Similarly, in the automotive field, where personalized selling, a wide range of models, consumer credit, post-purchase service, and high potential for the product line exists, selective distribution is both desirable and affordable.

Distribution analysis of selective distribution usually involves an examination of the brand's representation in key markets, as well as volume and profit contribution from existing outlets. For example, when General Foods acquired Burger Chef, a profit analysis of each outlet in the chain resulted in the closing of some three hundred unprofitable outlets.[5]

In addition to profit analysis, markets can be compared by the share of market being obtained, if data on industry sales are available on a market-by-market basis. Comparisons can also be made by the sales-per-thousand-households or the dollar share of certain merchandise categories. For example, *Sales Management's Survey of Buying Power,* the bible of the marketing industry, provides estimates of retail sales by metropolitan county areas for total food stores, supermarkets, eating and drinking establishments, department stores, apparel stores, furniture and household appliance retailers, automotive outlets, gas stations, lumber and hardware stores, and drugstores. The survey provides similar information on a county-by-county basis for the entire United States for a more restricted list of outlet types. Similar information can be obtained from the U.S. Census of Business or from industry trade associations which often compile a variety of statistics for the use of association members.

In short, distribution analysis, whether for mass or selectively distributed products, is an essential part of the market review. Since a wealth of marketing data is available from company records, government statistics, *Sales Management's Survey of Buying Power,* trade magazines, and industry associations, the kinds of analyses that can be made are limited only by the imagination and competence of the analyst.

COMPARATIVE ADVERTISING EXPENDITURES

All things being equal, the share of market should equal the share of advertising. Although all things are never equal, this truism still provides a guide for comparing competitive advertising expenditures with market share. Table 5–14 shows a hypothetical comparison of these two variables. On the surface, it would appear that Brand C is underspending both in total and on a per case basis, and that an increase in advertising might reasonably be expected to result in an increase in market share. Such a conclusion is only tentative, however, and could be revised by an examination of competitive pricing, sales promotion, and distribution. If we assume that these variables are relatively equal for leading brands, then Brand C (possibly because of product quality, package, positioning, media patterns, and/or the effectiveness of copy appeals) is a reasonable candidate for increased advertising expenditures, at least in a business-building test. The decision to increase

5. Carol White and Merle Kingman, "Hamburgers? McDonald's Takes It Seriously," *Advertising Age* (May 22, 1972): 3ff.

advertising on the brand, however, must be weighed against company objectives and the profit contribution of the brand.

In the case of Brand A, the relatively unfavorable relationship of advertising and market share *may* result from the brand's high share. Producers in a dominant market position often find that increased advertising expenditures become marginally less effective as their brand approaches the limit of those consumers to whom its marketing approach is appealing. In this instance, a reduction in advertising expenditures could possibly increase the brand's profit contribution while having a negligible effect on its market share position. The relatively unfavorable relationship between advertising and sales for Product D may well signal weakness in some other aspect of its marketing program, and should alert the marketer to search for areas in which corrective action needs to be taken. The point is that a comparison of share of market against share of advertising raises possibilities that need to be explored and may well be an important determinant in developing marketing objectives and strategy.

Obviously, a comparison of these two variables requires a relatively accurate measure of both competitive market share and competitive advertising. As pointed out earlier, reasonably accurate measures of market share are obtainable from a variety of sources. Estimates of competitive advertising expenditures are available from several industry sources. The better known ones are LNA-PIB and Simmons for magazines; Media Records for newspapers; BAR Network TV, Target Group Index, and Simmons Selected Markets for network TV, BAR Barcume and Rorabaugh for spot TV; BAR Radio and Radio Expenditure Report for network and spot radio; and LNA Outdoor for outdoor advertising. Most of these services are subscribed to by major advertising agencies, and smaller agencies often have access to them through affiliation arrangements with larger agencies.

SALES PROMOTION

Like advertising, sales promotion activity is an important ingredient in many marketing programs. Because promotional activities may take a variety of forms, and there is no published record of such activities, the extent and effectiveness of competitive sales promotion is difficult to assess. The field is not a complete desert, however, and reasonable estimates can often be made of the sales promotion activities of competitors.

The advertising trade press, particularly *Advertising Age,* as well as *Promotion* and *Sales Management,* regularly report major promotional activity, frequently in great detail. Of course, a company's sales force is a primary source of information about the existence and extent of sales promotion programs.

Table 5–15, taken from *Advertising Age,* provides a basis for estimating the cost of various coupon offers, a widespread sales promotion involving over 60 billion coupons annually. Current information of this nature is also available from promotional clearinghouses, which specialize in handling coupon redemptions, a task that few advertisers are staffed to cope with.

Note that Table 5–15 indicates wide variations in the effectiveness of the different coupons, with average redemption rates ranging from slightly over 2 percent for a six hundred line newspaper ad to over 16 percent for an individual

TABLE 5–14: *Share of Advertising and Share of Market for a Hypothetical Consumer Product*

	Advertising		*Sales*		
Brands	*Expenditure in 000s*	*Share*	*000s Cases*	*Share*	*Expenditure per Case*
A	$7,388.0	40%	8,971.2	34%	$0.823
B	3,694.0	20	5,804.8	22	0.636
C	2,770.5	15	6,860.3	26	0.404
D	4,617.5	25	4,749.4	18	0.972
Totals	$18,470.0	100%	26,385.7	100%	$0.70

TABLE 5–15: Cost per Coupon Redeemed Based upon Redemption Rates.
SOURCE: *Advertising Age* (October 25, 1976): 112.

Circulation method	*Cost per M printing/-delivery*	*Average redemption*	*Distribution cost (1)*	*Total number of redemptions (2)*	*Redemption costs (3)*	*Total program costs*	*Cost per coupon redeemed*
DIRECT MAIL							
Co-op	$14	11.7%	$ 350,000	2,925,000	$585,000	$ 935,000	31.9¢
Solo	90	16.2 (e)	2,250.000	4,050,000	810,000	3,060,000	75.5¢
MAGAZINE							
Solo	6	3.5	150,000	875,000	175,000	325,000	37¢
Page plus coupon	12	9.1	300,000	2,275,000	455,000	755,000	33.2¢
NEWSPAPER							
600-line r.o.p.	3.75	2.4	93,750	600,000	120,000	213,750	35.6¢
1,000-line r.o.p.	6.25	2.8 (e)	156,250	700,000	140,000	296,250	42.3¢
Co-op r.o.p.							
Coupon only	1	3	25,000	750,000	150,000	175,000	23.3¢
With copy	2	4.5 (e)	50,000	1,125,000	225,000	275,000	24.4¢
Supplements							
Solo	6	3.1	150,000	775,000	155,000	305,000	39.3¢
Free-standing inserts							
Coupon only	2.25	5.4	56,250	1,350,000	270,000	326,250	24.1¢
With copy	3.50	6.4 (e)	87,500	1,600,000	320,000	407,500	25.4¢

(1) Distribution cost based on circulation of 25,000,000; some programs have more, others less distribution.
(2) No allowance made for misredemption, estimated by some industry sources at 20%.
(3) Average cost based on 14¢ face value plus 5c handling charge and 1¢ internal handling charge.
SOURCE: Redemption rates based on A. C. Nielsen Co. figures where available or industry sources; distribution costs based on published rates and industry estimates.
(e) Estimated.

(solo) direct mail coupon. Realistic estimates of the costs for other sales promotions—contests, displays, sweepstakes, and so forth—can be obtained from companies that specialize in these activities.

ADVERTISING EFFECTIVENESS

Advertising effectiveness is a major consideration in the market review, since this factor alone can double or halve the value of the media expenditure. Unfortunately, no one advertising evaluation has the universal support of the marketing fraternity. At the simplest level, an analysis of the content of competitive advertising will indicate whether competitive claims are unique or stereotyped. Such comparisons with major competitors should be made routinely. Table 5–16 shows a possible format for such an analysis, using two dry dog food brands as an example. The advertisements themselves, taken from the same issue of *Good Housekeeping,* are shown in Plates 5–2 and 5–3 opposite page 116.

In addition, more sophisticated measures are desirable and often available. Many companies have their advertisements tested by their own or their advertising agency's research department. The most common measures relate the advertisement's ability to stimulate the consumer's recall of selling points, or to improve attitudes toward the product.

Any number of independent copy testing services are widely used. When independent testing services are used, the services often provide average performance scores for the product type, against which the performance of one's own advertisements can be checked.

SPECIAL RESEARCH

Alert marketers frequently conduct other forms of research which yield valuable information for the

TABLE 5–16: Comparison of Content and Format of Two Dry Dog Food Advertisements

Product:	Gravy Train	Mealtime
Headline:	Dogs prefer the taste of new improved Gravy Train 3 to 1	Mealtime. It's just what your dog's been waiting for.
Illustration:	Side by side: dog ignoring Gravy Train and three dogs eating new improved Gravy Train.	Dog on porch, standing over empty food bowl.
Claims:	Palatability, natural beef flavor	Palatability, meat protein, available in two different sized pellets.
Support:	Close up illustration of texture difference between particles of "old" and "new" Gravy Train; reference to tests in which dogs preferred "new" to "old" Gravy Train 3 to 1	Dogs love meat; "tail-waggin' " taste
Package Illustration:	Lower, right-hand corner	Two packages, lower center—one for large crunchy bite pellets and one for small crunchy bite pellets.

market review. This research includes competitive product tests, package tests, price tests, tests of contemplated promotions, special surveys to gain further information about target markets, business building tests, and concept tests. This test information is analyzed and evaluated, and later summarized in the market review section of the marketing plan.

One major marketer of food and drug products believes that each year the product manager should learn something about the product, its market, or both. As a consequence, a portion of each budget is earmarked for learning, and invested in some form of testing. The outstanding success of this marketer, which has leading products in many product categories, is testimony to the effectiveness of this philosophy.

SUMMARY COMMENT ON MARKET ANALYSIS

Meaningful approaches to analysis have by no means been exhausted in this chapter. Often analysts must devise their own approaches consistent with the data available, that provide insights into the dynamics of the particular marketing situation. This is one of the challenges of marketing analysis, and those who meet this challenge are well rewarded in the marketing industry.

SUMMARY

Careful marketing analysis is essential to developing a sound marketing plan. The scope of analysis used by a particular company depends upon the variety of factual data available. In most instances, though, a surprising amount of data is available from company records, from industry associations, from trade magazines, and from government statistics.

A good analysis goes from the general to the specific. Beginning with an examination of the total market's size and trends, the analysis then examines specific factors affecting the performance of individual products.

At the total market level, a number of analytical tools facilitate the process of analysis. These tools include computation of per capita consumption and index numbers; the concepts of market saturation, saturation levels, and market potential; and analysis of new and replacement buyers.

In analyzing company sales, useful areas include brand share, distribution, comparative advertising expenditures, sales promotion, and advertising effectiveness analyses.

Although the analytical techniques discussed in the chapter are commonly used, the analyst often must develop innovative approaches consistent with the data available, which provide insights into the marketing situation.

REVIEW QUESTIONS

1. Why is the market forecast critical, and how does it help the market planner in preparing marketing plans?
2. Why are per capita consumption computations and indices of consumption useful in marketing analysis? Explain how each might be used in analyzing the market for a consumer product.
3. Explain what is meant by market saturation. Give an example in which this concept might be useful in analyzing a market.
4. Explain why there is no best way to analyze company sales data, and identify some of the typical bases of sales analysis that are used.
5. What is the primary advantage of using brand share analysis, and what can be concluded from such an analysis?
6. What is the value of distribution analysis? Explain how it is possible to have the same brand share in different regions with different levels of distribution.
7. Explain how brand share analysis can be misleading.
8. Distinguish between store-count and all-commodity distribution. Which is more useful and why?
9. What is the assumption underlying a comparison of share of market and share of advertising? Show, by example, how such an analysis might be useful.
10. Under what conditions is selective distribution appropriate? How can the effectiveness of selective distribution be evaluated?

DISCUSSION QUESTIONS

1. Assume that you are the manufacturer of a brand of cold tablets. Brand share in this field is often computed on the basis of dollar sales. A recent report from store audits throughout the country indicates that your market share has dropped by almost 10 points. Outline a method of analysis that will help indicate the nature of this problem.
2. Given the following data on industry and company sales by region, analyze the data and make recommendations for allocating advertising expenditures. What additional information would be helpful?

Sales and population figures in 000s

Region	Population	Industry sales	Company sales
1	49,618.8	6,104	2,050
2	40,597.2	7,630	1,025
3	51,874.2	4,578	1,025
4	11,277.0	3,052	2,050
5	72,172.8	9,156	4,100
Total	225,540.0	30,520	10,250

3. Discuss ways in which a company such as McDonald's or Burger Chef might evaluate the effectiveness of their distribution.
4. The text states that, all things being equal, the share of

advertising should equal the share of market. Yet, more often than not, share of advertising does not equal share of market. How do you account for this?

5. Find magazine advertisements for two competitive products. Make a comparative analysis of these two advertisements following the format suggested in the text. What conclusions can you draw from this comparison?

SOME USEFUL METHODS OF ANALYSIS

The Good-Foods Company is a medium-sized producer of a line of grocery items. One of its major products, Orangefest, is a vitamin fortified powdered drink. When mixed with water, it makes a delicious, nutritious orange drink. Orangefest is sold nationally, and has over 90 percent of all commodity distribution in each geographic region. In 1979 Orangefest sold 8,545,700 cases, or 21.8 percent of the market for a product of its type.

In 1980 an effort was made to increase sales during November through February when sales had been historically weak. In this effort, company management substantially reallocated marketing expenditures for Orangefest by: (1) offering a stocking allowance of seventy-five cents a case to encourage stores to increase their purchases; (2) offering a fifty-cent-per-case display allowance for special store displays; and (3) increasing television advertising during the November-February period. The promotion was judged to be highly successful in increasing company shipments and in obtaining store displays during the four-month period.

Orangefest's sales, shipments, and regional distribution for 1980 are included in the tables.

TABLE 1: *Purchases of Orangefest-type Products*

Period in 1980	Cases
January–February	5,549,400
March–April	6,659,400
May–June	7,399,400
July–August	7,937,500
September–October	7,264,800
November–December	5,549,500

TABLE 2: *Shipments from the Orangefest Factory*

Quarter in 1980	Cases
First	2,190,600
Second	2,182,300
Third	2,290,700
Fourth	3,025,500

TABLE 3: *Market Data by Geographic Region*

Regions	Population	Total Market	Shipments	Purchases
N.E.	12,291,000	2,058,000	520,700	468,600
M.A.	36,377,000	6,619,000	1,800,400	1,620,300
E.N.Cen.	41,287,000	8,718,000	2,013,800	1,812,400
W.N.Cen.	17,118,000	3,552,000	937,700	843,900
S.A.	34,976,000	5,731,000	1,163,400	1,047,100
E.S.Cen.	14,105,000	2,543,000	689,200	620,300
W.S.Cen.	22,470,000	4,924,000	1,083,300	975,000
Mtn.	10,673,000	1,251,000	329,000	296,100
Pac.	30,469,000	4,964,000	1,151,600	1,036,400

Assignment

1. *Evaluate the Orangefest 1980 marketing program.*
2. *Suggest a tentative allocation of marketing funds for 1981, assuming:*
   - *A total marketing expenditure for advertising and sales promotion of $8.8 million.*
   - *Five percent of the marketing budget is to be held as an unallocated reserve against unfavorable forecast variances.*
   - *Eighty percent of the budget is to be allocated in proportion to 1980 consumer sales in order to provide basic marketing support for the product in all regions.*
   - *The remaining 15 percent of the budget is to be used to develop a market share in areas of opportunity.*
3. *Suggest a tentative allocation of 1981 marketing expenditures in terms of seasonal patterns.*

6

Analyzing Consumer Markets— Demographics

- *The nature of demographic analysis and its importance in planning marketing activities.*
- *Population trends in the United States.*
- *Income measures important to market planning.*
- *Major variables influencing consumer expenditures.*

MARKETING EXAMPLES

TWILIGHT OF THE YOUTH CULTURE

The 1950s seem like happy days in retrospect. Inflation was under control, businesses grew, real income increased, and perpetual prosperity seemed a reasonable future. But in the nation's bedrooms a timebomb was ticking away—a timebomb that erupted in a boom—a baby boom—that had explosive results for the 1960s and 1970s. As *Fortune* magazine observed:

> Now that we are putting the Seventies behind us, it is becoming clear how much the bursting fertility after World War II affected us over that decade. In the years from 1946 to 1962, which roughly bracket the baby boom, births frequently came in annual batches exceeding four million; in 1957, one of the peak years, twenty-five Americans were added to every 1,000 then alive. Over the whole span, the population grew by 45 million, a figure never approached in a like period. Since those years, in a process rather unpleasantly compared by demographers to the movement of a pig through the body of a python, those new masses have been traveling through society with devastating effect. After being carried tenderly out of overcrowded maternity wards, the new citizens overloaded educational institutions, subjected society to the excesses of the youth culture, shoved up juvenile delinquency and crime rates, and boosted national unemployment averages—calling forth along the way government programs rippling with distortions of their own. To its possessor, youth may be a joy; to the society that has to accommodate record numbers of them, youths can be an affliction.[1]

Nor does the baby boom stop there. The twilight of the youth culture is the dawning of consuming adults. The teenagers of the

1. Walter Guzzardi, Jr., "Demography's Good News for the Eighties," *Fortune* (Nov. 5, 1979): 92–106.

1960s and 1970s are the consumers and the work force of the 1980s and 1990s. Sometime after the year 2000, they will become retirees, forcing new stresses upon the economic system, and creating a market bonanza for geriatric products and services.

INFLATION, FLOOR SPACE, AND FURNITURE

As the babies of the 1950s became the adults of the 1970s and 1980s, they created an unprecedented demand for new housing. Coupled with double-digit inflation, this demand led to smaller houses. In many instances, the cost of housing has caused many young families to choose apartments and condominiums, often noted for their communal saunas, tennis courts, and swimming pools, but not for interior spaciousness. With smaller houses and smaller rooms, what will happen to the furniture market in the 1980s?

Many furniture manufacturers are betting that smaller pieces will be in demand, and that convertible furniture—sofa beds, chairs that turn into beds, coffee tables that expand into dining tables, or even furniture which collapses for easy storage when not in use—will increase in demand.

JOBS, NOT KIDS

Correlation may not mean causation, but sometimes it's almost as good for forecasting purposes. Certainly, this is true for the correlation between women working outside the home and family size.

As the women in the work force have increased, the fertility rate has decreased. This has occurred, not because working causes sterility (although I am sure that there will be those who will draw this conclusion), but because the extra money that a wife's job brings in, and the challenge of outside contacts, make working a more attractive alternative than staying home, barefoot and pregnant.

Demographics—the shape of society—is the subject of these three examples. The shape of society is an underlying variable that confounds the orderliness of economic planning and influences the size and nature of markets.

THE IMPORTANCE OF DEMOGRAPHICS

This chapter examines the demographic structure of United States society. Demographic data describes the size, distribution, and trends of a society's population in terms of age, sex, location, education, income, households, marital status, employment, and so forth.

Demographic analysis is a basic concern of marketing for four reasons: *First,* as suggested by the examples given earlier, demographics influence the size and nature of markets. *Second,* U.S. censuses provide a wealth of demographic data invaluable to business in planning marketing activities. *Third,* syndicated research services (private companies that develop information on product markets and consumer media patterns) describe this data in consumer demographics. *Finally,* advertising media describe the demographic characteristics of their audiences.

For these reasons, demographic analysis is the starting point for all marketing analysis. A basic understanding of demographic data, and the trends that it foretells, is essential for the aspiring marketer. Therefore, we will examine three broad classes of demographic data that are of particular importance to marketers: population, income, and expenditure patterns.

Understand that these three topics do not exhaust the subject matter of demographics. Nor, will we exhaust the subject matter of these three topics. However, the following material will provide an introduction to an important marketing variable.

POPULATION

The twentieth century has brought an explosive population growth to the world, as well as to the United States. Advances in medicine and nutrition have decreased infant mortality and increased longevity. Technology has multiplied the food supply, increased productivity, and improved transportation. In the developed nations rising incomes have improved living standards and created new markets. Figure 6–1 shows the growth of world population, as well as that of the United States, from 1900 to estimates for the year 2000. Note that, while the world population grew by 297 percent (index of 397), U.S. population grew at a somewhat lesser rate—242 percent (index 342).

FIGURE 6–1: *World and U.S. Populations*
SOURCE: *U.S. Statistical Abstracts*: 1979; *World Almanac*: 1980; *U.N. Population Statistics*: 1979.

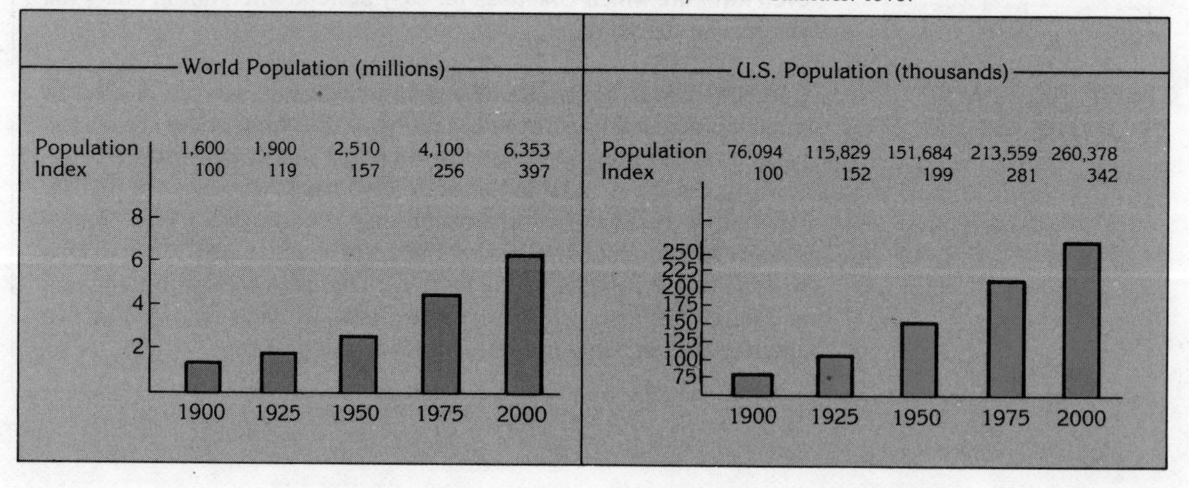

Although growth has created new markets, population has also generated new problems and poses a positive threat for the future. Uncontained population growth is a pressing concern of governments and demographers throughout the world who fear that continued growth will exceed the earth's capacity to sustain its peoples, and lead to breakdowns in the world's productive and economic structures.[2]

Population growth problems are further aggravated because growth is not equal throughout the world. Instead, those nations least able to support larger populations are gaining at a more rapid rate than the developed nations of the world. Data supporting this observation are shown in Table 6–1. Of particular interest in this table is the time required to double the populations of various geographic areas. Time for doubling ranges from 173 years in Europe to 24 years in Africa. Turning now to the United States, let's examine its population characteristics more closely.

Population Size and Trends in the United States

From 1975 to 2000, the U.S. population will grow by almost 47 million people, or 21.9 percent, despite the falling birthrates and the United States' zero-population growth in the mid-1970s. That is, the average number of children born to each woman of child-bearing age decreased to a point just sufficient to replace population. Because of the baby boom the number of women of child-bearing age is so great that the U.S. population will continue to grow until about 2050, provided that no significant reduction in birthrates occurs and that the population is not decimated by some cataclysmic disaster.

Table 6–2 shows the average annual birthrate per 1,000 population from 1930 to 2000.

2. Key references on this point include two Club of Rome reports: Dennis L. Meadows, Jorgan Randers, and William W. Behrans III, *The Limits of Growth* (New York: New American Library, 1972) and Mihajlo D. Mesarović, *Mankind at the Turning Point* (New York: Dutton, 1974). In addition, see: Paul R. Erlich, *The Population Bomb,* 2nd ed. (New York: Ballantine Books, 1971) and Robert L. Heilbroner, *An Inquiry into the Human Prospect* (New York: Norton, 1974).

TABLE 6–1: *Estimated Birthrates and Time Required to Double Populations*
SOURCE: *1979 World Population Data Sheet,* Population Reference Bureau, 1337 Connecticut Ave, N.W., Washington, D.C. 20036.

Country or Geographic Division	*Births per 1,000 Population*	*Years to Double Population*
Developed Areas		
Europe	14	173
United States	15	116
Canada	16	87
Russia	18	87
Developing Areas		
Africa	46	24
Latin America	35	26
Asia	29	38
Oceania	22	53

The number of years required to double population is a function of birth rate, death rate, immigration, and emigration.

TABLE 6–2: *U.S. Birthrate from 1930 to 1999*
SOURCE: *Statistical Abstracts:* 1979

Years	*Average Annual Birth Rate per 1,000 Population*	
1930–34	19.7	
1935–39	18.8	
1940–44	21.2	
1945–49	24.1	Baby boom
1950–54	24.8	Baby boom
1955–59	24.8	Baby boom
1960–64	22.6	Baby boom
1965–69	18.3	
1970–74	16.2	Zero population growth
1975–79	15.0	Zero population growth
1980–84	17.1	Zero population growth
1985–89	16.8	
1990–94	15.6	
1995–99	14.3	

Note the steady decline following the baby boom until 1980–84 when birthrates are estimated to show a significant increase. Following 1985, demographers project a continuing decline in birth rate per 1,000 population through the end of the century. Although population growth would seem to augur well for future market strength, other variables will influence the specific markets that will benefit from this growth.

Age Distribution

Although the population will continue to grow, different age groups will not increase at the same rate. This is particularly important to marketers because age is often used as a segmentation variable. Table 6–3 shows the U.S. population by age group from 1970 to 2000.[3] Four highlights should be noted in this table:

- The U.S. population is growing older as shown by the projected increase in median age. Between 1970 and 2000, the median age of the population is expected to increase by 7.2 years, from 29.4 years to 36.6 years. Thus, we can expect the nation's battle cry to change from "Don't trust anyone *over* 30" to "Don't trust anyone *under* 30."
- The number of people under 25 years of age will remain relatively stable through 2000. Changes in these age groups, whether positive or negative, do not exceed 4.2 percent.
- Significant growth is forecast for the 25 and older population. For example, the 35 to 44 age group is expected to increase by 78.6 percent by the year 2000; the 45 to 54 age group by 53.9 percent; and the 65 and over age group by 58.4 percent.
- The patterns of growth vary significantly between age groups as well as within age groups for the thirty-year period. For example: Between 1980 and 1985, three age groups (25–34, 35–44, and 65+) will have a combined increase of 11.2 million people while all other age groups remain relatively stable. The 25–34 age group is expected to reach its peak of 41.1 million in 1990. In the following ten years, this age group is expected to decrease by 6.6 million.

The foregoing observations about Table 6–3 have been made to emphasize the importance of both long-term and short-term population changes. Thus, the 25 to 34 year age group appears to be a rapidly growing market until 1990, at which point it is expected to go into decline.

Analysis of population trends is an essential part of market planning for firms with age dependent products. For example, the decline in births has forced Gerber, a leading producer of baby foods, to expand into other product lines to maintain sales and profits. The motion picture industry, heavily dependent upon the 18 to 25 age group, can expect little increase in sales during the next ten years unless they can develop entertainment vehicles appealing to other age groups. During the next five years, manufacturers of products for the 25 to 34 age groups—sporting goods, home furnishings, appliances, clothing, and so forth—should enjoy increased demand. Thereafter, these markets will decline sharply. Products for those over 65—adult recreation, apartments, proprietary medicines, crafts, travel, and adult education—should enjoy steady growth for the next twenty years or so.

From the standpoint of marketing, the aging of the U.S. population will not only change the size of various age group markets, but may impact upon the purchasing power of tomorrow's markets. As populations grow older, an increasing burden is thrown on the producing members of society for pension and Social Security payments. This relationship is measured by what demographers refer to as the *dependency ratio,* or the number of workers in relationship to the number of people who are retired. For example, General Motors had ten workers on its payroll for every retiree in 1967. By 1977 the ratio had shrunk to four to one, and by the early 1990s, it may reach one to one. Similarly, the Social Security System, which is already showing signs of strain, will suffer even more in the future. In 1945, the dependency ratio for Social Security was 35 to 1. By 1977 it

3. Population projections are far from being a precise science. The size of the projections made will depend upon births, deaths, immigration, emigration, economic conditions, the permanence of historic trends, and so forth. Because of this, the U.S. Bureau of the Census usually makes at least three projections which are referred to as Series I (high estimates), Series II (intermediate estimates), and Series III (low estimates). Unless otherwise noted, I have used Series II data.

Age demographics. (Photo by Rohn Engh)

TABLE 6–3: *Population by Age Groups in U.S.: 1970–2000 (population in 000s)*
SOURCE: *Statistical Abstracts:* 1980

	Under 5	5–13	14–17	18–21	22–24	25–34	35–44	45–54	55–64	65+	Total	Median Age
1970	17,148	36,636	15,910	14,707	9,980	25,294	23,141	23,310	18,664	20,087	204,878	29.4
1975	15,879	33,440	16,934	16,484	11,120	30,919	22,816	23,769	19,777	22,420	213,559	30.2
1980	17,334	31,268	15,663	15,963	11,765	35,389	27,096	23,113	20,757	24,862	223,220	31.5
1985	18,803	29,098	14,392	15,442	12,441	39,859	31,376	22,457	21,737	27,305	232,880	32.8
1990	19,437	32,568	12,771	14,507	10,642	41,086	36,592	25,311	20,776	29,824	243,513	34.2
1995	18,664	33,824	14,408	14,704	10,152	37,768	38,968	30,593	22,016	30,823	251,910	35.5
2000	17,872	35,080	16,045	14,900	9,663	34,450	41,344	35,875	23,257	31,822	260,308	36.6
Difference: 1970–2000	724	(1,556)	135	193	(317)	9,156	18,202	12,565	4,593	11,735	55,430	7.2
Percent change	4.2%	(4.2%)	0.7%	1.3%	(3.2%)	36.2%	78.6%	53.9%	24.6%	58.4%	27.0%	24.5%

was 3.2 to 1, and by 2035, it is expected to be less than two to one.[4] The increasing burden on society's working members for the support of the aged will create a consequent decrease in their purchasing power. Precisely what effect this will have on the size and vitality of future markets is not clear at this point. But, it is reasonable to expect that the dependency ratio will have some effect.

4. "The Greying of America," *Newsweek* (February 28, 1977): 50–55.

Education

The United States population is also becoming better educated—at least it is staying in school longer. The median years of school attained by adults 25 years and older increased from 8.6 years in 1940 to 12.4 years in 1978. The university

FIGURE 6–2: *Bachelor, Post-Bachelor, and First Professional Degrees Awarded from 1965 and Projected through 1986*
SOURCE: *Projections of Educational Statistics,* National Center for Education Statistics, U.S. Department of Health, Education, and Welfare.

Degree		1965-66	1970-71	1975-76	1980-81	1985-86
Bachelor and Post Bachelor		520,923	839,730	925,746	1,021,000	999,000
	Male	57.6%	56.6%	54.6%	53.6%	53.9%
	Female	42.4%	43.4%	45.4%	46.4%	46.1%
First Professional*		30,124	37,946	62,649	69,700	74,500
	Male	95.2%	93.7%	84.4%	75.3%	71.6%
	Female	4.8%	6.3%	15.6%	24.7%	28.4%

*Includes dentistry (D.D.S. or D.M.D.), law (LL.B or J.D.), medicine (M.D.), theology, veterinary medicine (D.V.M.), chiropody or podiatry (D.S.C. or D.P.P., optometry (O.D.), osteopathy (D.O.).

degrees awarded (Bachelor and post-Bachelor) increased from 709,800 in 1965 and 1966 to 1,334,200 in 1980, an increase of 88 percent, and is expected to increase to 1,545,900 by 1985. Approximately 44 million Americans, or 19 percent of the population, will have attended some college by 1985.

Perhaps of equal interest is the increasing participation of women in higher education. Figure 6–2 shows the increase in university degrees awarded from the 1965–66 school year to those projected for the 1985–86 school year by sex of recipient.

A better educated population not only opens up markets for education related items—books, sophisticated magazines, classical music, art, and travel—but also implies more sophisticated buying practices and a demand for quality consumer products.

A better educated population also means a decline in television viewing since there is an inverse correlation between television viewing and education. Criticism of commercials and advertisements written to appeal to marginally educated consumers will probably rise.

Racial Composition

The nonwhite population (predominantly black) is expected to grow from 18.9 million in 1960 to 41.5 million by 2000, substantially increasing the attractiveness of this market. At the same time, the

FIGURE 6–3: *Projections of U.S. Population by Race*
SOURCE: *Statistical Abstracts:* 1980

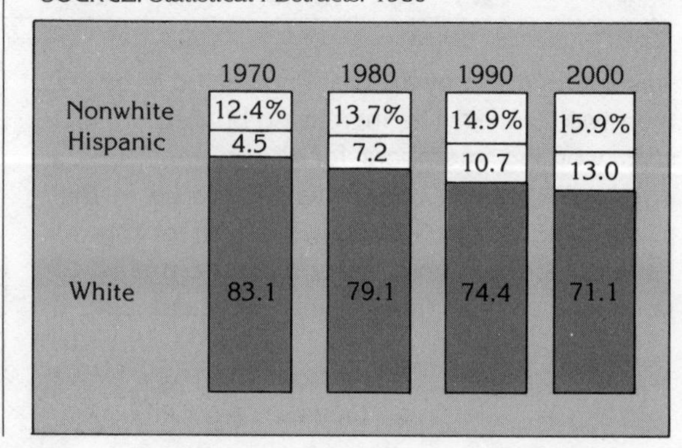

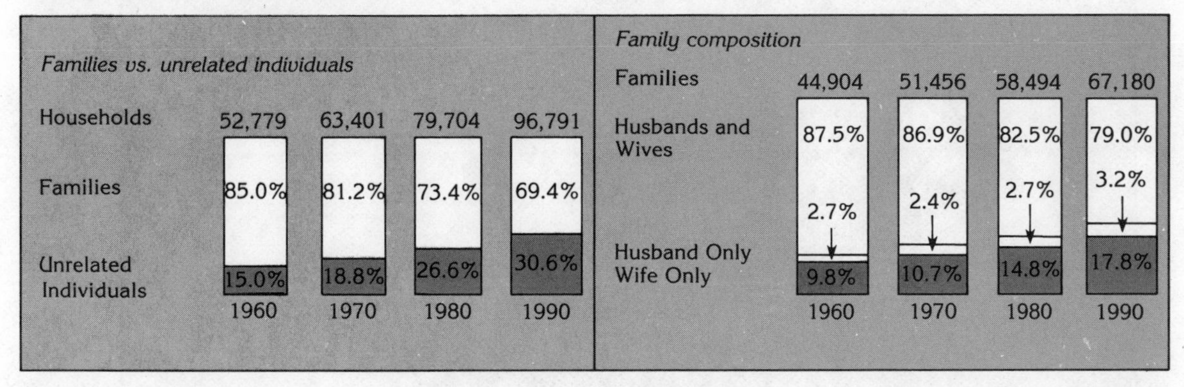

FIGURE 6–4: *Household Composition from 1960 to 1990 (Numbers in 000s)*
SOURCE: *Statistical Abstracts:* 1980

Hispanic market may grow by almost 25 million during the same period.[5] Figure 6–3 shows the projected distribution of the U.S. population by major racial groups from 1970 through 2000.

The nonwhite and Hispanic markets tend to be concentrated geographically. For example, 60 percent of the Hispanics are estimated to live in the Southwest. As a consequence, marketers interested in these market segments need to make detailed analyses of their sizes and distributions.

Household and Family Structure

The 1960s and 1970s witnessed some significant changes in the household and family structures in the United States, changes that are expected to continue into the future. For example, between 1960 and 1990, it is expected that:

- Although the total number of *households* will increase by over 44 million, the number of *families* will decrease by 15.6 million, with a corresponding increase in the number of households composed of unrelated individuals.
- Within families, husband-wife families will decrease and families headed by a single parent only will increase.

This information is summarized in Figure 6–4.

These changes in family and household structures reflect various trends in the United States, such as later marriages, a higher divorce rate, fewer children, more wives working outside the home, and relaxed attitudes toward cohabitation by unmarried couples. As family and household structures change, the demand for various products will also change.

Working wives and families headed by a single parent should continue pressure for convenience foods, fast-food operations, laborsaving devices, child care, and cleaning services. Wives receiving paychecks, now 40 percent of all married women, should increase the markets for women's clothing, travel, and luxury items. In addition, paycheck-toting wives tend to exert a greater influence in the purchase of products traditionally selected by males such as cars, insurance, tires, and vacations. As a result, women need to be taken into consideration in devising marketing and advertising programs for these

5. Data on the Hispanic market in the United States is both scanty and ambiguous. In 1970 the U.S. Bureau of the Census estimated the Hispanic population at 9,073,000, an estimate that is probably low. A special, limited census conducted in 1979 set the 1978 Hispanic population at 12,046,000. Many experts believe that this is a serious understatement. Thus, *CBS Nightly News,* in a special report on March 26, 1980, estimated the Hispanic population at 18 million. *The National Journal* (April 7, 1979) in an article by Neal R. Peirce and Jerry Haystrom titled "The Hispanic Community—a Growing Force to Be Reckoned With" estimated the Hispanic population at 16 million, a figure more in line with the CBS estimate. I have used the Bureau of Census estimate for 1970, recognizing that it is probably an understatement. For 1980, 1990, and 2000, I have made my own estimates based on a number of fragmentary sources. *The National Journal* and CBS believe that by 2000 the Hispanic population will be the largest, single minority group in the United States.

FIGURE 6–5: *1979 Population by U.S. Census Regions*

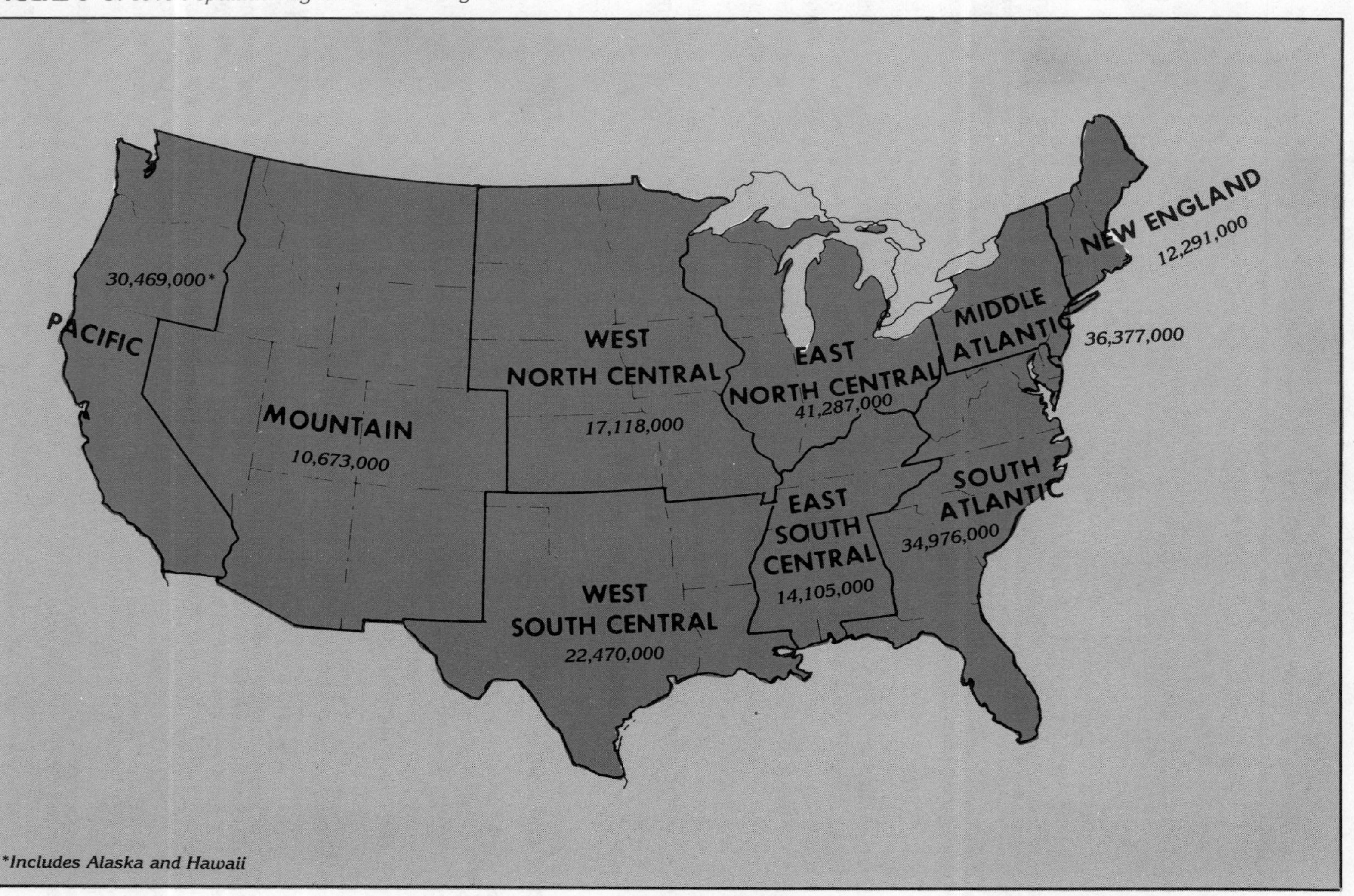

products to a greater extent than they have been in the past.

The temporary nature of many households composed of unrelated individuals should increase the demand for inexpensive furniture and temporary household furnishings, like rental furniture and appliances, and decrease the demand for insurance. In short, changing family and household structures may cause business firms to examine their markets more carefully, and to change their product offerings and marketing programs where such changes appear to be warranted.

GEOGRAPHIC CHANGES

Population growth has been accompanied by changes in geographic distribution which require adaptation by the successful marketer. In this section, we will examine population changes in regions, states, and urban and rural areas.

Geographic Regions

Traditionally, the U.S. Bureau of Census has divided the United States into nine census regions. These regions, and regional populations in 1979 are shown in Figure 6–5.

The regional distribution of population is undergoing some dramatic shifts as Americans flock to the sunbelt and western states in search of milder climates and more relaxed life-styles. Table 6–4 shows regional population changes during the 1970s. Note that the New England, East North Central, and West North Central regions show only modest gains from 1970 to 1979, and that the Middle Atlantic region actually lost population. By contrast, the remaining five census regions show population gains of 10 percent or more.

***TABLE 6–4:** Regional Population Changes from 1970 to 1979*
SOURCE: U.S. Department of Commerce, Bureau of the Census.

Regions	*Population Change*	*Percent Change*
New England	444,000	3.7%
Middle Atlantic	(492,000)	(1.4%)
East North Central	1,034,000	2.6%
West North Central	794,000	14.0%
South Atlantic	4,305,000	10.2%
East South Central	3,148,000	16.3%
West South Central	2,390,000	28.8%
Mountain	3,944,000	14.9%
Pacific	3,000,000	11.0%

Population Changes by States

The dramatic nature of some of the seventies' population shifts is revealed by comparing individual state figures. Table 6–5 shows the ten states experiencing the most dramatic gains as well as the ten slow- or no-growth states. With the exception of Florida, all of the fast-growing states are in the west, seven in the Mountain region. The slow-growth states, including three states that had population losses, are in what is sometimes referred to as the industrial heartland.

Although the rate of growth is important, shrewd marketers don't judge a market by its growth rate alone recognizing that the smaller the starting base, the easier it is to show dramatic percentage gains. Thus, a 1 percent growth in Ohio with a beginning population base of over 10.6 million, represents more additional people than a 31.6 percent increase in Wyoming with a beginning population base of only 332,400.

Differences in the Importance of States

States vary widely in importance due to population. In Table 6–6 states have been divided into five groups based on population. Note that the District of Columbia is treated as a state for statistical purposes simply because one has to do something with it. As a consequence, the nation's capital is included in the last group of states, making eleven in this group.

The ten states with the largest populations account for 54.2 percent of the population, while the ten states with the smallest populations, plus the District of Columbia, account for only 3.3 percent of the population. Keenly aware of these differences, marketing practitioners tend to address their attention to the most populous states.

TABLE 6–5: States with the Fastest and Slowest Growth in the Seventies.
SOURCE: U.S. Department of Commerce, Bureau of the Census.

States	*Population Change*	*Percent Change*	*1978 Population*
Fastest growing states			
Alaska	125,200	41.4%	427,800
Nevada	179,200	36.7	668,000
Arizona	642,800	36.2	2,418,200
Wyoming	105,200	31.6	437,600
Florida	1,975,000	29.1	8,766,400
Idaho	179,000	25.1	892,000
Utah	262,000	24.7	1,321,300
Colorado	500,700	22.7	2,710,300
New Mexico	212,600	20.9	1,229,700
Hawaii	141,600	18.4	911,500
Slow-growth or no-growth states			
New York	(302,700)	(1.7%)	17,938,700
Rhode Island	(14,000)	(1.5)	935,700
Dist. of Columbia	(79,200)	(1.5)	677,500
Pennsylvania	16,500	0.1	11,817,300
Ohio	111,600	1.0	10,769,000
Illinois	176,600	1.6	11,289,400
Massachusetts	112,900	2.0	5,802,100
New Jersey	172,100	2.4	17,938,700
Indiana	165,800	3.2	935,700
Iowa	91,800	0.6	677,500

Generally speaking, these states represent the greatest marketing opportunity—provided, of course, that differences in population between states are not offset by differences in the per capita consumption of the product being marketed.

Urban and Rural Population

Migration from rural to urban areas is characteristic of the process of industrialization; the United States has become an industrialized society. In 1880 approximately 70 percent of the nation's population lived in rural areas. Today, approximately 70 percent live in urban areas. Typically, urban areas have higher incomes and more of the amenities of civilization—the theater, opera, ballet, museums, fine restaurants, more services, a greater selection of goods, a wider variety of prices, and greater employment opportunities—than do small towns and rural areas. These advantages are often offset by a faster pace, higher crime rates, greater competition, and higher costs for housing and transportation. Nonetheless, in the past, the attractions of urban living outweighed any inconveniences for most Americans. Recently, people who find the rigors of urban living too demanding have created a slight shift back to rural America. This shift, though highly publicized, is not yet demographically significant.

Cities themselves underwent a transformation after World War II when middle and upper income residents, encouraged by low transportation costs and a growing network of freeways, fled to the suburbs in search of cheaper housing, green lawns, and open spaces. Retail, manufac-

TABLE 6–6: *States Ranked According to Population in 1979*
SOURCE: U.S. Department of Commerce, Bureau of the Census.

	Population (000s)	Percent of total
California	22,694	10.3%
New York	17,648	8.1
Texas	13,380	6.0
Pennsylvania	11,731	5.4
Illinois	11,229	5.2
Ohio	10,731	4.9
Michigan	9,207	4.2
Florida	8,860	4.1
New Jersey	7,332	3.4
Massachusetts	5,769	2.6
Subtotal	118,581	54.2%
North Carolina	5,606	2.6%
Indiana	5,400	2.6
Virginia	5,197	2.4
Georgia	5,117	2.3
Missouri	4,867	2.2
Wisconsin	4,720	2.1
Tennessee	4,380	2.0
Maryland	4,180	1.0
Minnesota	4,060	1.9
Louisiana	4,018	1.8
Subtotal	47,545	21.8%
Washington	3,926	1.8%
Alabama	3,769	1.8
Kentucky	3,572	1.7
Connecticut	3,115	1.5
South Carolina	2,932	1.3
Iowa	2,902	1.3
Oklahoma	2,892	1.3
Colorado	2,772	1.3
Oregon	2,527	1.1
Mississippi	2,492	1.1
Subtotal	30,899	14.2%
Arizona	2,452	1.0%
Kansas	2,369	1.0
Arkansas	2,180	0.9
West Virginia	1,878	0.8
Nebraska	1,574	0.6
Utah	1,367	0.5
New Mexico	1,241	0.5
Maine	1,097	0.4
Rhode Island	929	0.4
Hawaii	915	0.4
Subtotal	16,002	6.5%
Idaho	907	0.4%
New Hampshire	887	0.4
Montana	786	0.4
Nevada	702	0.3
South Dakota	659	0.3
North Dakota	657	0.3
District of Columbia	656	0.3
Delaware	582	0.3
Vermont	493	0.2
Wyoming	450	0.2
Alaska	406	0.2
Subtotal	7,185	3.3%
Total	218,352	100.0%

turing, and service businesses have followed this outbound population flow, creating suburban shopping centers that have drained trade away from downtown areas.

As middle and upper income families moved to the suburbs, they were replaced in the central cities by lower income people of different ethnic backgrounds—primarily, black and Hispanic. This shift has not only changed the central city as a market, but so lowered the tax base that many central cities are hard pressed to maintain essential services. The social consequences of this phenomenon have been urban blight and high crime rates in downtown areas.

Currently, middle and upper income people are shifting back to central cities. The high cost of gasoline has made commuting from the suburbs more expensive, and crowded freeways have made commuting a chore. The exploding demand for housing in convenient suburbs has

FIGURE 6–6: *Standard Metropolitan Statistical Areas of the United States.*
SOURCE: *County and City Data Book,* U.S. Department of Commerce, Bureau of Census, 1977, pp. xiv and xv.

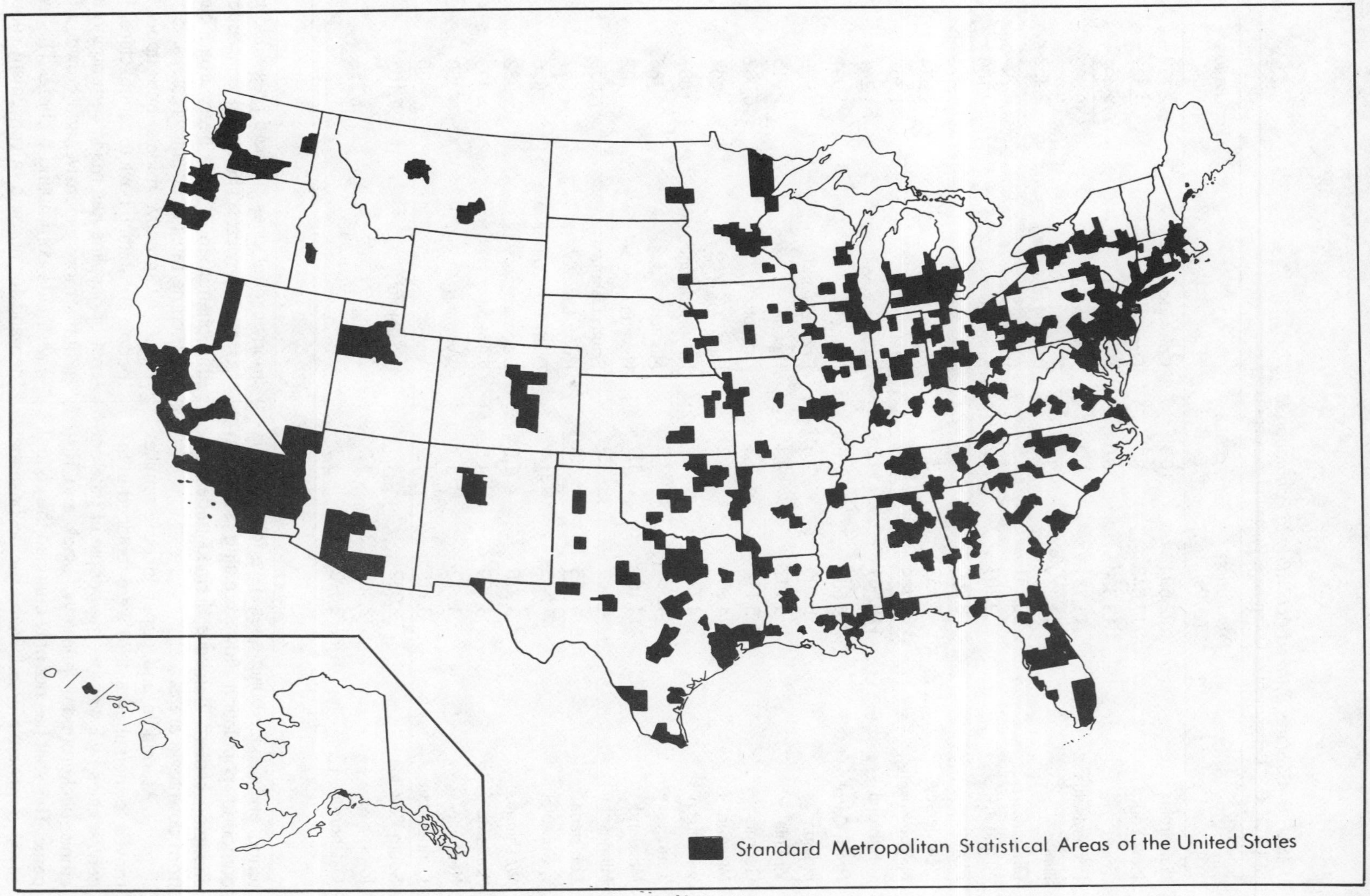

Standard Metropolitan Statistical Areas of the United States

driven suburban land prices beyond the reach of many middle income families and, as children have moved away from home, the attraction of suburban living has lost some of its allure for older people. The move back to the central city is being made predominantly by older people whose children have left home, by young families who find suburban living too expensive, by young marrieds and young singles who want to live where the action is. This movement is being facilitated by the availability of condominiums and highrise apartments in the central city, or nearby areas convenient to downtown offices, shopping, and suburban recreational areas.

The growth of suburbia has led to a reexamination of the traditional concept of a city by the U.S. Bureau of Census and by marketing practitioners, and given rise to the Standard Metropolitan Statistical Area (SMSA), commonly referred to as Metropolitan County Areas.

Standard Metropolitan Statistical Areas (SMSA)

Traditionally, the city has been a political division that became valuable to marketing as an identifiable and isolatable aggregation of people with purchasing power. With the growth of the suburbs, the population of the central city began to lose meaning as a market description. For example, St. Louis had a population slightly over a half million in 1979. But, St. Louis *plus* its suburban population—St. Charles, St. Louis, Jefferson, and Franklin counties in Missouri, and Madison, Monroe, and St. Clair counties in Illinois—had a population of 2,339,700.

In addition, the rise of television as a major medium dealt a blow to the concept of the central city. Television signals are no respecter of arbitrary political boundaries, extending from horizon to horizon, covering the central city, suburbs, and everything else in the vicinity. Further, television stations charge advertising rates in proportion to the population they reach, not in proportion to the central city in which their broadcasting facilities happen to be located. Thus, St. Louis television stations which cover the central city, and its suburbs, charge accordingly.[6]

For these reasons, Standard Metropolitan Statistical Areas have largely replaced central cities in describing major urban areas. *A metropolitan county area consists of a single city of 50,000 or more population plus the county of such a central city or cities and all adjacent counties that are found to be metropolitan in character and economically and socially integrated with the central city.*

Figure 6–6 shows the location of the nation's 212 recognized metropolitan county areas. Over 63 percent of the nation's population and approximately 95 percent of its urban population live in these SMSAs.

The relatively small proportion of a SMSA's population accounted for by the central city is dramatized in Figure 6–7 which shows the central city and suburban populations of all SMSAs of one million or more persons in 1975.

Consolidated Metropolitan Areas, or Beyond Suburbia

The continuing growth of suburban areas has led to a phenomenon variously referred to as *exurbia*, *interurbia*, or the *continuous city*. Exurbia is a urban-suburban strip linking major metropolitan areas. Thus, some demographers visualize a future with a 600-mile long, continuous city running from Boston to Washington, a 300-mile city running from Chicago to St. Louis, and a 500-mile city running from San Diego to San Francisco. The U.S. Bureau of Census has already identified

6. The term *ADI* (Area of Dominant Influence) is used to describe the coverage pattern of television stations. The ADI is developed by the American Research Bureau (ARB) through surveys of the populations of counties surrounding the city where the television signal originates. The following procedure is used for assigning counties to the market. "The hours of viewing of each tv station whose signal reaches the country are totaled; then each station's percentage of share of total viewing hours is calculated. The market of origin of the tv station with the largest share of viewing hours becomes the ADI name of that market, and all counties whose largest viewing share is given to stations of that same market of origin are grouped within the ADI. (*Sales and Marketing Management,* "Survey of Buying Power," July 23, 1979, p. a-46.)

FIGURE 6–7: *Standard Metropolitan Statistical Areas of One Million Persons or More, Ranked by Size: 1975*
SOURCE: *County and City Data Book,* U.S. Department of Commerce, Bureau of Census, 1977, p. xxx.

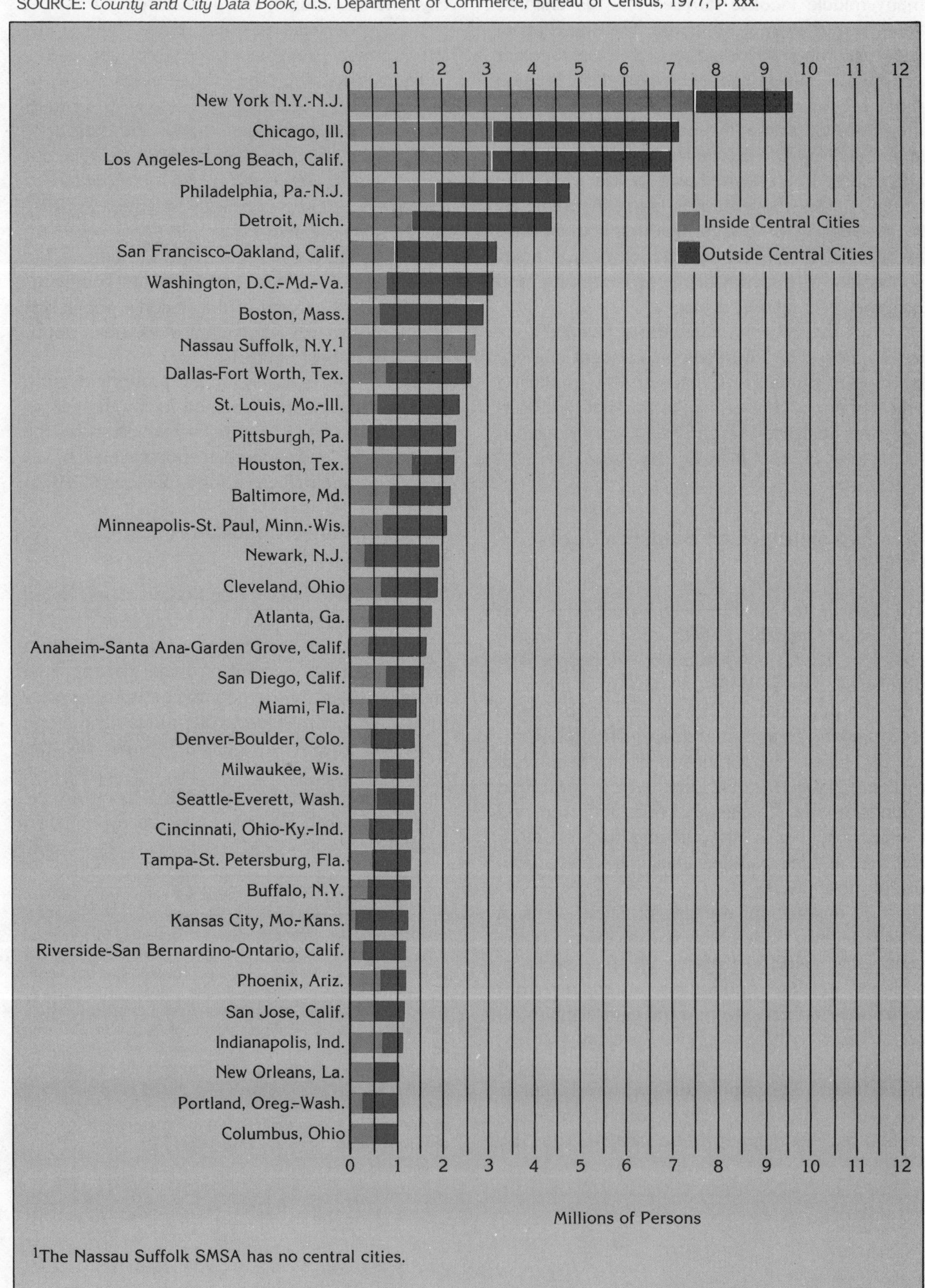

[1]The Nassau Suffolk SMSA has no central cities.

twelve *Consolidated Metropolitan Areas* which are combinations of adjacent SMSAs growing into each other. These twelve areas, which are listed in Table 6–7, account for almost a third of the nation's population.

INCOME

In Chapter 3 we noted that in addition to population, markets also require purchasing power and willingness to spend. In this section, we will deal with consumer income, one of the ingredients necessary to convert a population into a market.

Consumer income soared during the third quarter of this century, rising by approximately 425 percent. Much of this increase was eroded by inflation, however, so that *real income* rose by only about 90 percent during the period. But, 90 percent is not shabby performance. Figure 6–8 shows the relationship between real income (income in constant dollars) and total income (income in current dollars) during this period. Despite inflation, the steady growth of income from 1947 until the early 1970s served as a spur to demand during most of the period.

All income segments benefited fairly equally from the national income growth, although the lower-middle income segments and the top income segment were squeezed slightly. This point is verified in Figure 6–9 which shows the percent of the national income received by

TABLE 6–7: *Consolidated Metropolitan Areas*
SOURCE: *Sales & Marketing Management, Survey of Buying Power* (July 23, 1979): A-13.

Consolidated Metro Market	*Population 000s*	*Percent Change 1970–78*	*Average EBI Per Household*	*EBI Index U.S.=100*	*Buying Power Index*
New York-Newark-Jersey City-Bridgeport	16,967.6	− 3.0%	$21,216	113	8.1683
Los Angeles-Long Beach-Anaheim	10,861.4	+ 8.8	19,792	106	5.4951
Chicago-Gary	7,662.1	+ 0.7	22,352	119	3.9542
Philadelphia-Wilmington-Trenton	5,634.7	+ 0.1	21,132	113	2.6670
San Francisco-Oakland-San Jose	4,769.0	+ 7.8	22,299	119	2.5816
Detroit-Ann Arbor	4,639.7	− 0.6	23,674	126	2.3952
Cleveland-Akron-Lorain	2,875.9	− 4.1	20,884	112	1.3918
Houston-Galveston	2,859.7	+31.8	22,144	118	1.5581
Miami-Fort Lauderdale	2,380.3	+26.1	18,657	100	1.2395
Seattle-Tacoma	1,915.9	+ 4.3	20,543	110	0.9958
Cincinnati-Hamilton	1,632.7	+ 1.2	19,784	106	0.7563
Milwaukee-Racine	1,590.5	+ 1.0	21,109	113	0.7831
Total	63,789.5	+ 3.1%	$21,200	113	31.9860

Note: The EBI Index is calculated by dividing the U.S. average, $18,722, into the market's comparative average EBI per household. The Buying Power Index is a weighted index that converts a market's population, Effective Buying Income, and retail sales into a share of the U.S. potential.

The 12 consolidated metropolitan markets, ranging from 1.6 million (Cincinnati-Hamilton and Milwaukee-Racine) to 16.0 million (New York-Newark-Jersey City-Bridgeport), pose a mixed bag of prospects. Representing collections of contiguous metropolitan areas, they account for almost one-third of the U.S. market potential. But, because they are made up largely of older metropolises in the industrial belt, they're growing less than half as fast as the U.S. as a whole. Despite this, the typical household in these urban areas has an Effective Buying Income that's 13% above the average.

FIGURE 6–8: Money Income in 1977 of Families and Persons in the United States
SOURCE: U.S. Dept. of Commerce, Series P-60, No. 118

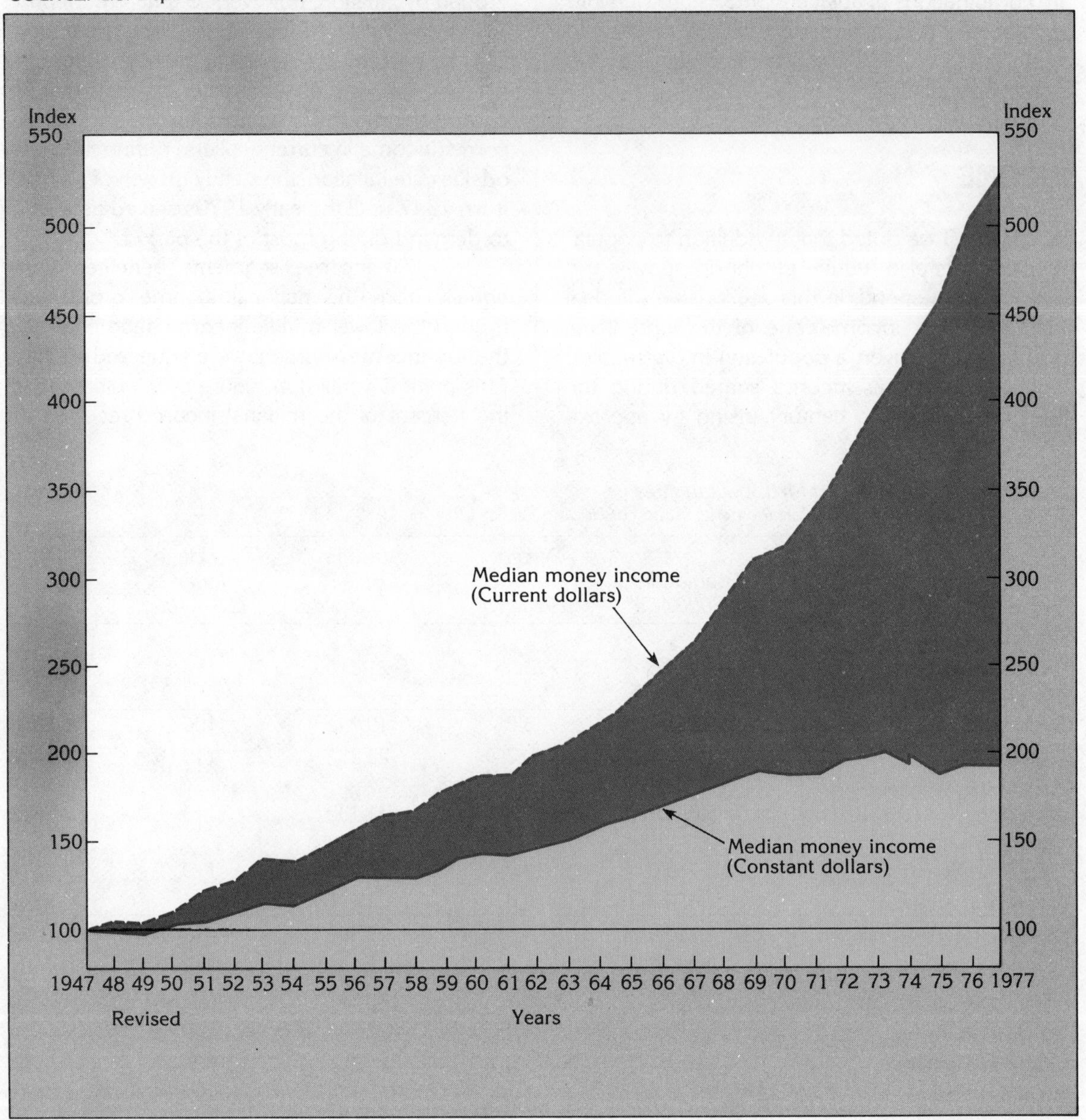

each quintile of the population. Thus, in 1950, the 20 percent of the families having the lowest incomes received 4.5 percent of the nation's total consumer income. In 1977 this same group received 5.2 percent of the nation's income. By way of contrast, the 20 percent of the population receiving the highest incomes received 42.5 percent of the national consumer income in 1950, and 41.5 percent in 1977.

Increases in the cost of energy, credit, public transportation, medical care, food and beverages, and clothing, suggest that real growth in consumer income is coming to a grinding halt. Inflation accelerated in the 1970s, and income

FIGURE 6–9: *Distribution of National Income by Income Group.*
SOURCE: U.S. Department of Commerce, Bureau of Census, National Income Statistics.

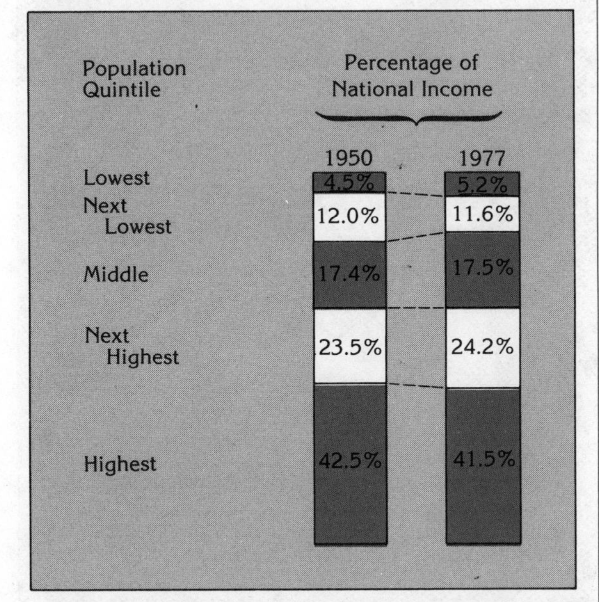

growth was hard pressed to keep pace with the increased costs of living. In order to evaluate this development more carefully, three different ways of measuring income must be differentiated.

Three Measures of Income

In evaluating marketing opportunities, distinguishing between total income, disposable income, and discretionary income is helpful.

- *Total income* refers to all of the income received by a family or individual in the form of wages, interest, dividends, profits, pensions, Social Security payments, and so forth. Not all of this income is available for consumer purchases because a certain portion must be paid out in federal, state, and local taxes; fines, fees, and penalties; and personal contributions to social insurance (Social Security). These payments are required by law.
- *Disposable income* is what remains after the legally required deductions from total income have been made. Thus, disposable income is a measure of what an individual or a family has available to spend. Disposable income must provide necessities such as food, clothing, housing, transportation, medical care, and so forth. Also, any personal savings must come out of disposable income.
- *Discretionary income* is what one has left after necessities are provided for. Consumers have wide discretion over how this residual income can be spent—vacations, luxury items, hobbies, entertainment, gifts, and so forth.

From the standpoint of marketing, disposable income and discretionary income are the most relevant income measures. But, these two measures are not equally relevant for all marketers. Marketers of food staples, of basic clothing, and other necessities are primarily concerned with disposable income. Marketers of luxury goods and other discretionary items—camping equipment, outboard motors, vacations, designer labels, and so forth—will direct their attention to the level of discretionary income.

Looking into the future, the markets for discretionary items will probably suffer during the next few years. For example, in 1980 European vacations were down by almost 50 percent. This will continue to be true because there appears to be no end in sight for inflation. In addition, unemployment is increasing, interest rates are high, and wages and salaries have not kept pace with inflation which has been called, quite properly, the cruelest tax of all. In summary, necessities will require a larger proportion of disposable income, and less will be left for discretionary spending. One of the other factors which forbodes ill for the 1980s is the decrease in consumer savings.

Consumer Savings

A major factor in the stability and growth of a marketing economy is the aggregate level of consumer savings. Consumer savings affect the marketplace in three primary ways:

- Savings constitute a vast reservoir of purchasing power that may supplement income and serve as a major source for financing durable

FIGURE 6–10: *How States Compare in Median EBI per Household*
SOURCE: *Sales & Marketing Management's 1979 Survey of Buying Power.*

Rank	State	Median Effective Buying Income Per Household	% Change 1977-78
1.	Alaska	$23,384	+ 6.1%
2.	New Jersey	20,087	+ 8.5
3.	Hawaii	19,912	+ 9.8
4.	Connecticut	19,098	+ 8.1
5.	Illinois	18,721	+ 3.5
6.	Michigan	18,570	+ 4.9
7.	Nevada	18,017	+ 9.0
8.	Washington	17,656	+ 12.2
9.	Delaware	17,571	+ 7.4
10.	Ohio	17,480	+ 7.3
11.	Maryland	17,446	+ 6.4
12.	Massachusetts	17,425	+ 10.5
13.	Indiana	17,325	+ 9.3
14.	Wisconsin	17,318	+ 10.6
15.	California	17,186	+ 10.0
16.	Wyoming	16,798	+ 11.9
17.	Pennsylvania	16,680	+ 7.0
18.	New Hampshire	16,501	+ 9.3
19.	Minnesota	16,491	+ 11.6
20.	Rhode Island	16,439	+ 6.0
21.	Utah	16,261	+ 10.0
	U.S.	16,231	+ 8.1
22.	Dist. of Columbia	16,201	+ 7.3
23.	Iowa	16,160	+ 8.8
24.	New York	16,068	+ 5.0
25.	Texas	15,914	+ 9.9
26.	Colorado	15,856	+ 9.8
27.	Virginia	15,827	+ 9.0
28.	Oregon	15,504	+ 11.4
29.	Arizona	15,429	+ 12.2
30.	Kansas	15,388	+ 6.6
31.	Nebraska	15,168	+ 7.5
32.	Missouri	14,800	+ 9.0
33.	Georgia	14,513	+ 6.9
34.	Louisiana	14,489	+ 10.1
35.	Idaho	14,347	+ 3.7
36.	North Dakota	14,224	+ 10.8
37.	North Carolina	14,204	+ 7.2
38.	West Virginia	14,104	+ 10.1
39.	Maine	14,056	+ 4.9
40.	South Carolina	14,047	+ 7.9
41.	New Mexico	13,926	+ 11.8
42.	Kentucky	13,791	+ 8.8
43.	Vermont	13,653	− 4.8
44.	Montana	13,483	+ 6.9
45.	Tennessee	13,380	+ 5.3
46.	Alabama	13,279	+ 8.7
47.	Oklahoma	13,208	+ 10.5
48.	Florida	13,178	+ 8.8
49.	South Dakota	12,960	+ 16.5
50.	Arkansas	12,324	+ 10.3
51.	Mississippi	11,991	+ 8.8

Note: Median EBI per household means there are as many households above the stated income figure as below it. It is a more reliable indicator of buying power than average EBI per household because the latter includes income from nonhousehold sources such as institutions and military barracks, hence will always be a higher figure than the median one.

goods such as housing, appliances, and automobiles.

- Savings provide a source of consumer credit through borrowing from banks and other financial institutions.
- Aggregate consumer savings have, in the past, provided up to 30 percent of the capital funds required by businesses to create jobs and increase the output of consumer goods.

Yet, in the past few years, America has become a nation of spendthrifts. In 1970 American consumers were saving slightly less than 8 percent of their annual disposable income. By 1979 this rate had fallen to 3.2 percent. With a continuation of inflation and a rise in unemployment, the savings rate may fall even more. This decrease in the savings rate, combined with an increase in aggregate consumer debt since 1970 of almost a trillion dollars, may well constitute a stultifying mortgage on future expenditures that will depress a wide range of consumer markets.

Using Economic Information in Marketing

Economic information can be useful in forecasting future trends in consumer spending. As pointed out earlier, discretionary purchases will probably suffer a recession in the immediate future, and price competition among products perceived as necessities will play a greater role in market planning than in the past. In addition, economic data can be used in evaluating the relative attractiveness of different geographic areas, in selecting test markets, and in allocating marketing expenditures.

The foregoing statement is true because disposable income and income growth rates vary regionally under the influences of local employment, the level of local economic activity, wage scales, and migrations of people. Figure 6–10, for example, shows the differences in *effective buying income* for the fifty states and the District of Columbia. Effective buying income (EBI) is a measure developed by *Sales and Marketing Management* for its *Survey of Buying Power*, probably the most useful annual marketing data book ever invented. EBI is *disposable income*, minus payments to military and diplomatic personnel stationed overseas. Figure 6–10 shows the wide variations in effective buying power between states. For example, the median household EBI in Mississippi is $11,991, while in Alaska it is $23,384.

As disposable and discretionary income levels change, marketers can expect to see significant shifts in the relative demand for different products and services. This leads to an examination of patterns of consumer expenditures.

PATTERNS OF CONSUMER EXPENDITURES

Historically, consumer expenditure patterns have shifted as income rose. In 1887 Ernst Engel studied the expenditures of working class families and formulated a series of propositions known as *Engel's laws*. Essentially, Engel's laws state that, as family income rises:

1. the percent of income spent on food will tend to decrease;
2. the percent of income spent on housing and household operations will tend to remain constant; and
3. the percent of income spent on other categories (clothing, transportation, recreation, health, and education) will tend to increase.

Note that Engel's laws deal with the *percent of income* spent on different categories, not with the absolute level of expenditures. Thus, as incomes increase, the dollar expenditures in all categories may increase as families buy more delicacies and higher quality food staples. Nonetheless, the percent of family income spent on the various categories tends to change with increasing affluence.

As general propositions, Engel's laws appear to be valid in the aggregate and, as we reflect upon them, they appear logical. For this reason manufacturers of relatively high-priced food products are most often concerned with the

TABLE 6–8: Personal Consumption Expenditures for Selected Product Categories
SOURCE: *Survey of Current Business.*

Product categories	*1973 expenditures (billions)*	*% of total*	*1980 expenditures (billions)*	*% of total*
Total expenditures	$805.2	100.0%	$1,634.1	100.0%
Automobiles and parts	57.5	7.1	94.3	5.7
Furniture and household equipment	55.0	6.8	89.0	5.4
Food and beverages	165.1	20.6	324.3	19.9
Clothing and shoes	70.2	8.7	103.0	6.3
Gasoline and oil	28.3	3.5	83.7	5.1
Housing	116.4	14.4	263.4	16.1
Household operations	47.3	5.9	106.5	6.5
Transportation	23.4	2.9	60.3	3.7
Other	242.0	30.1	509.6	31.3

level of disposable income, while producers of luxury items (vacations, recreational products, gifts, and so forth) are concerned with discretionary income.

Although Engel's laws may serve as a general guide to expenditures, marketers often seek more specific information when preparing marketing plans for specific products. This is necessary because other variables, such as general economic conditions, place of residence, stage in the family life cycle, and consumer expectations, may also influence expenditure patterns.

Economic Conditions

Generally, whenever economic conditions improve and incomes rise dramatically, as they did in the United States between the 1950s and the 1970s, consumers change their definition of what constitutes a necessity. Thus, prior to World War II, a house with a single bath in an urban area was considered adequate. Today, families without two baths, or at least a bath and a half, may perceive themselves as deprived. Automobiles that, before World War II, were clearly luxuries are now considered necessities. Today even homes well below the poverty level are often graced by color television sets.

Further, supply and demand may distort traditional patterns of spending for specific product categories. For example, rapid inflation in the cost of housing in the 1970s has led many families to spend a disproportionate portion of their incomes in this category. Table 6–8 shows the shift in the percent of personal consumption expenditures for selected product categories between 1973 and 1980. Note that gasoline and oil, housing, household operations, and transportation rose from a combined share of 26.7 percent to 31.4 percent, an increase of 4.7 percentage points. While a 4.7 percentage point increase may not seem large, in *constant dollars* it amounted to over $98.7 billion. Obviously, as the proportion of expenditures allocated to these four areas increases, cutbacks have to be made elsewhere. Further, based on economic forecasts, the patterns reflected in Table 6–8 are expected to continue well into the 1980s.

Geographic Area

Geographic areas often have major influences on the types of products bought. Having lived for some twenty years in St. Louis, where few white-collar workers owned pickup trucks, I was amazed when I moved to Flagstaff, Arizona, to find that virtually everyone seemed to have one—even I have one now. Pickups are much more useful than cars for camping, hauling wood for fireplaces and woodburning stores, and traversing the thousands of miles of unmaintained roads that wind through the deserts and mountains of Arizona.

Similarly, mode of dress varies by geographic area. In St. Louis, I wouldn't dream of appearing at a social function without a tie and jacket. By contrast, in Flagstaff I haven't worn a tie in ten years. The wife of a colleague once observed that, if one wants to be well dressed in Flagstaff, one buys a new pair of blue jeans once a year. Thus, forms of recreation, life-style, and the cultural milieu often dictate behavioral norms that vary by geographic area and city size.

Stage in the Family Life Cycle

Most families pass through a sequence of life cycle stages. Each stage has unique needs, creates different patterns of object accumulation, and makes different demands upon the family resources. A young married couple with no children just beginning their married life, has not acquired a house, household furnishings, and the hundreds of items normally accumulated during a lifetime. By contrast, after twenty years that family may include several children, enjoy peak earning power, often own a home, and face the problem of financing a college education for one or more children.

This progression is the basis of the family life cycle which Wells and Gubar have divided into nine stages.[7] A summary of these nine stages is shown in Table 6–9. Note that, at each stage of the family life cycle, patterns of purchase vary as family needs change. The life cycle concept is particularly useful because:

- Income, social perceptions of the family, and demands upon family resources are combined in a single concept.
- Since statistics on families—size, age of head of household, income, number of ages of children, and so forth—are regularly collected and projected in U.S. Department of Commerce population reports, the concept is easy to use as a forecasting device.

Consumer Expectations

A final variable that we will examine in our discussion of consumer expenditure patterns is the role of consumer expectations, also referred to as *consumer buying intentions*.

The existence of consumer credit and installment buying—major forces in the development of the relatively high standard of living in the United States—make it possible for consumers to enjoy luxuries well beyond the immediate capabilities of their immediate incomes. Thus, housing would be unaffordable were it not for long-term mortgages. Fewer cars, major appliances, boats, vacations, and other expensive items would be purchased if it were not possible to finance them on the expectation of future income.

The extent to which consumers are willing to go into debt to purchase desired products is often a function of their optimism or pessimism about future economic conditions, and their personal expectations concerning their future resources. Thus, the buying splurge of the late 1970s that drove aggregate consumer debt to almost a trillion dollars is believed by many to be based on consumers' convictions that inflation would continue, that their future incomes would rise, and that prudence dictated making purchases immediately rather than delaying and being forced to pay higher prices for comparable products at a later date.

Because of the importance of consumer expectations, several organizations undertake periodic surveys of buyer intentions.[8] Survey results

---

7. William D. Wells and George Gubar, "Life Cycle Concept in Marketing Research," *Journal of Marketing Research* (Nov., 1966): 355–63. Other useful references to the life cycle concept are: Talcott Parsons, *Social Structure and Personality* (New York: MacMillan Publishing Co., Inc., 1964), pp. 129–254; M. H. David, *Family Composition and Consumption* (Amsterdam: North-Holland Publishing Co., 1962); S. G. Barten, "The Life Cycle and Buying Patterns," in Lincoln H. Clark (ed.), *Consumer Behavior,* Vol. 2 (New York: New York University Press, 1955), pp. 53–57; John B. Lansing and Leslie Kish, "Family Life Cycle as an Independent Variable," *American Sociological Review* (Oct. 1957): 512–19; and John B. Lansing and James N. Morgan, "Consumer Finances Over the Life Cycle," in Lincoln H. Clark, (ed.), *Consumer Behavior,* pp. 36–51.

8. Among the better known services are the Survey Research Center at the University of Michigan, Sindlinger and Company, The Conference Board, Inc., and the Commercial Credit Corporation. For a discussion of buyer intention surveys, see: "How Good are Consumer Pollsters?" *Business Week* (Nov. 9, 1969): 108–110.

TABLE 6–9: *An Overview of the Life Cycle*

SOURCE: William D. Wells and George Gubar, "Life Cycle Concept in Marketing Research," *Journal of Marketing Research* (Nov., 1966), p. 362.

Bachelor stage; young single people not living at home	*Newly married couples; young, no children*	*Full nest I, youngest child under six*	*Full nest II; youngest child six or over six*	*Full nest III; older married couples with dependent children*	*Empty nest I; older married couples, no children living with them, head in labor force*	*Empty nest II; older married couples, no children living at home, head retired*	*Solitary survivor, in labor force*	*Solitary survivor, retired*
Few financial burdens. Fashion opinion leaders Recreation oriented. Buy: Basic kitchen equipment, basic furniture, cars, equipment for the mating game, vacations.	Better off financially than they will be in near future. Highest purchase rate and highest average purchase of Buy: Cars, refrigerators, stoves, sensible and durable furniture, vacations.	Home purchasing at peak. Liquid assets low. Dissatisfied with financial position and amount of money saved. Interested in new products. Like advertised products. Buy: Washers, dryers, TV, baby food, chest rubs and cough medicine, vitamins, dolls, wagons, sleds, skates.	Financial position better. Some wives work. Less influenced by advertising. Buy larger sized packages, multiple-unit deals Buy: Many foods, cleaning materials, bicycles, music lessons, pianos.	Financial position still better. More wives work. Some children get jobs. Hard to influence with advertising. High average purchase of durables. Buy: New, more tasteful furniture, auto travel, nonnecessary appliances, boats, dental services, magazines.	Home ownership at peak. Most satisfied with financial position and money saved. Interested in travel, recreation, self-education. Make gifts and contributions. Not interested in new products. Buy: Vacations, luxuries, home improvements.	Drastic cut in income. Keep home. Buy: Medical appliances, medical care, products which aid health, sleep, and digestion.	Income still good but likely to sell home.	Same medical and product needs as other retired group; drastic cut in income. Special need for attention, affection, and security.

The Hispanic market. (Photo by Freda Leinwand)

are often used by marketers in forecasting future buying activity, and as an aid in assessing the future demand for their products.

A SUMMARY NOTE ON DEMOGRAPHICS

At the beginning of the chapter we noted that demographics is the starting point for all marketing analysis. The wealth of material produced by the U.S. Bureau of Census, as well as other government agencies, makes demographic analysis both convenient and profitable.

The purpose of this chapter has been to acquaint students with some of the major demographic trends that are emerging, and to emphasize their role in market planning. But, one cannot stop here. The trends we have noted are all rooted in the past. The future will introduce new events and new variables which will modify or even reverse some of the trends that we have observed. As a consequence, demographic analysis is a continuing obligation of marketers who wish to use the resources of their firms wisely.

SUMMARY

Demographic data describes the size, distribution, and trends of a society's population variables: age, sex, location, education, income, size and structure of households, marital status, and employment. Demographic analysis is a basic concern of marketing because it influences the size and nature of markets, because the U.S. government provides a wealth of demographic data invaluable in forecasting and market planning, and because private research companies and media describe markets and media audiences in demographic terms.

Three broad classes of demographic data of particular interest to marketers are: population, income, and expenditure patterns.

The twentieth century has seen an explosive growth in population in the United States and throughout the world. Population growth has been accompanied by changes in the nature and distribution of various populations. In the United States, for example, the population is growing older, and the distribution of population by age groups is changing. Therefore, marketers of age-dependent products often must enter new product fields in order to maintain their sales and profits. In addition, the educational level of the U.S. population is increasing, the distribution of population is shifting from the Upper Midwest and Northeast to the South and Southwest, urban areas are becoming increasingly important, blacks and Hispanics are growing in importance as markets, and household composition is changing. The effects of these changes will vary by product type, but they cannot be ignored with impunity.

Although real income increased during the third quarter of the twentieth century, for the next few years, real income will stabilize or decrease. This will lead to an increase in competition, a greater emphasis on price, and a decrease in discretionary spending. With decreases in disposable and discretionary spending, the patterns of consumer expenditures will change over the next few years. For example, a greater proportion of the national income will be spent on necessities, and spending for luxury items will decrease.

Because of the impact that demographic changes have on markets, marketing practitioners must monitor these changes carefully, and adjust their products and marketing programs to changing marketing conditions.

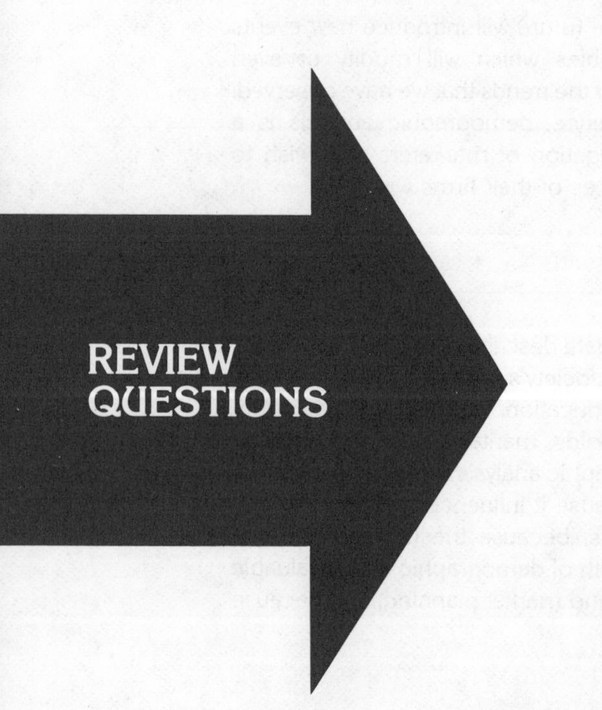

1. Explain why an understanding of demographics is important to marketers of consumer goods.
2. Explain the implications of the baby boom of the 1950s for marketing and for the economy.
3. Identify the major demographic trends in the United States in terms of age, education, and the racial composition of the population.
4. Identify the major ways in which changes in the household structure of the United States will affect product markets.
5. Explain what is meant by a Standard Metropolitan Statistical Area and why it is a more useful marketing concept than the concept of a city.
6. Distinguish between total income, disposable income, and discretionary income. If you were a manufacturer of blue jeans, which of these income measures would you be most interested in, and why?
7. Explain why consumer savings are important for the growth and stability of a marketing economy.
8. Explain and evaluate Engel's laws as guides to consumer expenditures.
9. Explain what is meant by the family life cycle and why it is useful in marketing.
10. Explain the relationship between consumer expectations and marketing activity.

1. Some demographic changes will have a greater impact on the marketing of consumer products than others. Which of the demographic areas discussed in the chapter do you think will have the greatest impact, and why?
2. What effects will the demographic trends discussed in the chapter, have on: suburban shopping centers? major hotels in central cities? expensive restaurants? travel?
3. Identify some of the effects that wives working outside the home will have on spending patterns, decision patterns, and family stability.
4. Based on the changes between 1980 and 1990 in the size of the various age groups, identify three product markets that should increase in size, and three that should decrease in size during this period.
5. During the past two or three years, the cost of fuel for transportation and home heating has risen dramatically. These costs are expected to rise even more in the future. What effects do you believe this will have on transportation, home construction, and the geographic distribution of the population during the next ten years?

CHAPTER PROBLEM

ANALYZING CONSUMER MARKETS—DEMOGRAPHICS

Norwood–Crawford is a major real estate developer in the Southwest with annual sales in the neighborhood of $300 million. Typically, the company buys large areas of undeveloped land in outlying areas of major cities and develops a master plan for a subdivision. Norwood–Crawford homes typically have 2,000 to 2,500 square feet of living space, with three or four bedrooms. The homes are larger than average, well designed, and contain luxury features. Historically, their primary market has been middle-management families with children.

Sales of the company grew steadily during the late 1960s and 1970s. By the late 1970s, however, home sales declined because of increasing land, materials, and labor costs, and because of the high interest rates required for home financing. For example, between 1976 and 1979, the cost per square foot of a Norwood–Crawford home increased from $35 to over $50 per square foot, adding $30,000 to $40,000 to the price of their typical home.

Although the company continues to be optimistic about the future of residential building in the Southwest because of expected population growth in this region, the company is uncertain about the type of home it should build in the future. Company management recognizes, however, that they must formulate marketing plans to guide their activities during the next five years. After considering a variety of alternatives ranging from single family homes to apartments and condominiums, management has identified four alternatives that seem to be most consistent with their experience and capabilities.

- *Continue their present strategy under the assumption that inflation will decrease, land and construction costs will level off, and mortgage rates will drop.*
- *Build smaller—1,600 to 1,800 square feet—no frill, three and four bedroom homes on smaller lots. Under this plan, they could build four homes to an acre, rather than the two they are currently building. Prices would range between $64,000 and $75,000. Under this strategy, extra rooms would be left unfinished, carports would replace garages, and patios would be eliminated or reduced in size. The idea behind this approach is that buyers could finish these areas when they could afford to do so.*
- *Develop retirement communities with quality homes in the 1,200 to 1,400 square feet range. The homes would be placed on quarter acre lots and priced in the $65,000 to $75,000 range.*
- *Develop cluster housing, with individual homes in the 1,800 to 2,000 square foot range. Under this concept, as many as eight homes could be built on an acre of land at a price of $85,000 to $90,000. Management recognized that this approach, in particular, would require changes in zoning restrictions in many areas.*

Assignment

1. *Based on information given in the chapter, what are some of the demographic trends that should influence the decision?*
2. *Which strategy do you believe would be most effective?*
3. *What other information would be desirable in making a decision for the company's future course of action?*

7

Analyzing Industrial Markets—Buying Patterns

- *Differences between consumer and industrial markets.*
- *Basic questions to ask in analyzing markets.*
- *Major characteristics of producer markets.*
- *Major characteristics of reseller markets.*
- *Major characteristics of government markets.*

MARKETING EXAMPLES

THE PEDDLER

A friend and former neighbor was a salesman. He referred to himself as a peddler, but he was not what we usually think of when we use the word *peddler.* He had two advanced degrees: one in electronic engineering and one in business administration. He had only one customer—McDonald Aircraft. And, he had only one product—a multi-million dollar, custom designed computer hardware system for the nose cone of a space missile.

The peddler spent two years making the sale. Periodically, he brought teams of engineers and computer technicians from the home office in New Jersey to consult with engineers, designers, computer experts, and technicians within the McDonald organization. And, after the sale was made, he spent several months obtaining authorizing signatures from company officials, engineers, department heads, and involved government agencies on the purchase contract.

INPUT-OUTPUT ANALYSIS

Late one Wednesday afternoon in the office of the marketing director of a major advertising agency a discussion was held. The marketing director, media director, a media supervisor, and the research director had just come from a meeting with members of the Receiving Tube Division of General Electric. Their problem? To identify the markets for receiving tubes and to develop a media advertising program for reaching these markets.

Marketing Director: "Friends, you could put everything I know about the market for receiving tubes in your ear and not even have an earache. Does anyone have any bright ideas?"

Media Supervisor (after an awkward pause): "Maybe we could use input-output analysis."

Media Director: "What's input-output analysis?"

Media Supervisor: "The U.S. government has a four-digit Industrial

Classification Code which breaks down industries into some 496 groups. Based on this information an input-output table is put together showing how much each industry category buys from every other industry category. Maybe we could use these tables to identify potential receiving tube customers."

Research Director: "Isn't the input-output data pretty much out of date? I think the government is running six to eight years behind in their figures."

Marketing Director: "What about proportions? If we can find out what percent is purchased by various industries, we can get a rough idea of the current market by applying these percentages to current market estimates—unless, of course, there have been major changes in industry purchasing patterns in the past few years."

Media Supervisor: "If there have been, we can probably find that out from other industry sources. At least it's a starting point."

Marketing Director: "Does anyone here know how to interpret input–output tables?"

Research Director: "No, but I can learn fast."

Marketing Director: "All right, let's get at it. I have to go to New York next week, but I should be back by Tuesday evening. Let's get together at 9:00 o'clock Wednesday morning, and see where we are."

The approach worked. Through input-output analysis, the agency identified some twenty separate industrial classifications that represented potential customers, four of which accounted for approximately 80 percent of industry sales. Using the *Census of Business Data,* the agency was able to pinpoint the number of establishments, their sizes, and geographical locations in four key industrial classifications. This information, along with other industry data, was used in developing a marketing approach that became a major part of the agency's presentation to its client.

CAN-CUTTING

The setting: A small conference room in the Graybar Building on Lexington Avenue in New York, headquarters of the Great Atlantic and Pacific Tea Company (A&P).
The participants: Two buyers of dry grocery items for A&P and the general sales manager and the New York division sales manager for a national food marketer.
The occasion: The food marketer was trying to persuade A&P buyers that a new line of applesauce the company had developed should be stocked in A&P stores.

During the meeting, the food company sales representatives made a presentation, developed by their advertising agency, about why A&P should stock the applesauce. Included in the presentation were data on the size of the market, product quality, consumer taste-test results, margins, and estimated profitability per foot of shelf-space, based on test markets in three areas of the U.S. The presentation also included a can-cutting in which cans of the new products and those of leading competitors were cut (opened) so that the buyers could sample the products, noting their appearance, taste, and texture. At the conclusion of the meeting, a fact sheet summarizing key points of the presentation was left with the buyers, and the divisional sales manager agreed to send a case of the new product to A&P's food laboratories for analysis.

If the presentation were successful, the new products would be approved for consideration by individual A&P divisions, and the next stage of the selling process would begin. Representatives of the food company would make the same presentation to buyers in each A&P division. Only after approval at the divisional level could the product be sold to individual store managers, and eventually reach the retail shelves to be purchased by consumers provided, of course, that the manufacturer has persuaded consumers to try it.

Until this chapter, we have talked primarily about *consumer* marketing. The three foregoing examples, however, are not directly concerned with consumers. Instead, they deal with industrial markets—selling a customized computer system to an aircraft manufacturer for a space missile, selling the services of an advertising agency to an industrial advertiser, and selling a new line of applesauce to buyers of a major retail food chain. These examples are also a part of marketing.

DIFFERENCES BETWEEN INDUSTRIAL AND CONSUMER MARKETS

In 1979 the consumption of goods and services by industrial and government markets approximated $1.7 trillion, a somewhat larger total than that spent by consumers. In addition to this size difference, industrial markets (sometimes referred to as *intermediate, business,* or *organizational* markets) differ from consumer markets in a variety of ways that directly offset marketing activities. Some of the more significant differences are:

Market concentration. Industrial markets are more concentrated than consumer markets in terms of customers and geographical locations. A manufacturer of consumer products may number potential customers in the millions. By contrast, the potential customers of an industrial producer may be numbered in the thousands, or hundreds, or (in some cases) less than a dozen. This difference implies:

- Personal selling, rather than advertising, is often the primary form of marketing communication.
- Each customer may become disproportionately important to the producing firm, so that personal relationships between the producer and buyer become much more critical. For example, a producer of consumer products may offend or lose a single customer with no apparent effect on sales. However the loss of a single customer for an industrial producer may result in layoffs, production cutbacks, and financial loss.

Industrial firms do not buy for personal consumption. Instead, they purchase goods and services for the production of other goods and services. One marketing implication of this characteristic is that price is usually more critical in the industrial purchase than in the consumer purchase.

Purchasing decisions are more complex. Often many more people are involved in an industrial purchase than in a consumer purchase. Thus, the purchase of raw materials or equipment used in production may require the participation of personnel in corporate management, design, engineering, production, purchasing and, possibly, other departments. Each of these participants may have different criteria for the product or service being purchased. Therefore, the seller of industrial goods and services must determine which of the customer's personnel are involved in the purchase decision. Often, as many as four to six people are involved. In extreme cases, such as the space missile computer referred to at the beginning of the chapter, as many as forty people may be involved.

Reciprocity is often a factor. Many industrial firms sell to one another. For example, about 30 percent of the sales in the chemical industry are intraindustry sales. Under reciprocity, firms buy from firms that buy from them.

Greater dependence upon objective buying criteria. Many consumer purchases are highly subjective. Although some subjectivity exists in industrial purchases, objective criteria—defined by written purchase specifications—are a major factor.

Dependability of supply and delivery schedules. Since industrial firms often purchase in large quantities, to be delivered at specific times, dependability of supply and scheduled delivery are often major considerations in making a purchase. For example, a manufacturer of light aircraft often must order engines from an independent supplier three years ahead of its production year. Based on a sales forecast, a company might order 24,000 engines to be delivered at the rate of 2,000 per month, three years hence. Failure of the supplier to meet this delivery schedule will result in production disruption and, possibly, financial disaster for the buyer.

The producer market. (Photo by Paul Conklin)

Other differences between consumer and industrial markets exist, but those listed above are critical. In the remainder of this chapter, we will look more carefully at three industrial markets: producer markets, reseller markets, and government markets.

PRODUCER MARKETS

Often the words producer markets or manufacturing conjure up images of huge factories, billowing smokestacks, thousands of workers engaged in repetitive tasks, noisy machinery, assembly lines, and automation. Indeed, the term *manufacturing* is often used for producer markets. In order to understand the size and diversity of producer markets, however, we need to expand our traditional stereotypes of industrial production. Producer markets include not only manufacturing firms, but also advertising agencies that produce advertising, banks that produce credit, insurance companies that produce protection against risks, and restaurants that produce meals. In short, producer markets are so diverse that it is difficult to draw generalizations about them, other than the one given in the following definition. *The producer market is made up of all individuals and business firms that buy products and services used in the production of other products and services that, in turn, are sold, rented, or leased to individual consumers or to other business firms.*

In analyzing producer markets, the marketer should always ask certain basic questions. The same questions should always be asked of consumer markets. While the questions are the same, the answers will be different. These basic questions are:

What is the market? What is its size? What are its trends? What is its competitive structure?

Where is the market? Where is it concentrated geographically?

Who is the market? Does the market spread across all producer classifications, or is it concentrated in relatively few classifications? Is the market dominated by a few firms in the relevant classifications, or are there many?

When is the market? When are the products and services bought? Are there seasonal factors? What is the lead time for purchases?

How does the market buy? How are buying decisions made? Who participates in the buying decisions? What factors influence purchase participation?

Why does the market buy? What are the relevant buying motives in the market? Which ones are most important?

Let's take each of these questions in turn.

What Is the Market?

In the aggregate, producer markets consisting of some 14 million U.S. business firms, employ almost 90 million workers, and generate sales of over $1.6 trillion.

The diversity of products and services used by producer markets is immense. Many classifications of products and services have been established, none of which is exhaustive. Table 7–1 shows one such classification. Note that pro-

TABLE 7–1: Goods and Services Classification for the Producer Market.

Products that become a part of the finished product
- Raw materials
  - Agricultural, forestry, and fishing products (examples: cotton, wool, grains, vegetables, fruits, livestock, wood, raw rubber, fish, seaweed)
  - Extractive products (examples: mineral ores, crude oil, salt, silicates)
- Manufactured material
  - Processed materials (examples: leather, yarn, finished lumber)
  - Manufactured products (examples: synthetic fibers, steel, wire, cement, plastic resins)
  - Fabricated parts (examples: motors, tires, fabricated metals, screws, fasteners, castings)

Production facilities, equipment, and processes
- Land and buildings
- Production equipment (examples: sanders, grinders, punch presses, drill presses)
- Accessory equipment (examples: forklift trucks, hand trucks, pallets)
- Processes (examples: patents and processes upon which royalties are paid such as Sanfordizing and freeze-dry processes)

Maintenance equipment and supplies
- Equipment (examples: hand tools, machinery, paint brushes)
- Supplies (examples: screws, nails, paint, cleaning compounds, lubricants)

Office equipment and supplies
- Office equipment (examples: typewriters, adding machines, copiers, file cabinets)
- Office supplies (examples: paper, staples, paper clips, ledgers, envelopes, typewriter ribbons)

Facilitating products/services
- Financial (examples: banks, insurance companies, brokerage houses)
- Communication (examples: advertising agencies, printing companies, media)
- Transportation and warehousing (examples: trucking companies, airlines, trains, barge companies, public warehouses)
- Advisory services (examples: business consultants, tax consultants, production designers)

ducers use raw and manufactured materials that become a part of their products, as well as other items and services to facilitate the production process; these goods or services do not become a part of the finished product.

For the individual marketer, however, the aggregate is not important. Rather, individual marketers are interested in those segments of the producer market that use the products they supply, or could supply. As a consequence, market analysis is important as a marketing tool searching out producer markets as well as consumer markets.

The size of each market segment for individual industrial products varies widely. For example, the market for diamond saw blades or transistor-bonding nozzles may be extremely limited, amounting to only a few hundred thousand dollars annually. By contrast, the market for processed steel products exceeds $18 billion.

Similarly, different industrial goods or services have varying numbers of suppliers; highly technical fields may have less than a half dozen suppliers while hundreds compete for the existing business in other fields.

Where Is the Market?

Producer markets tend to be much more highly concentrated than consumer markets. Producers cluster in areas close to natural resources, where labor is readily available and transportation inexpensive. Seven states—New York, California, Pennsylvania, Illinois, Ohio, New Jersey, and Michigan—contain over 50 percent of the nation's manufacturing firms. Some industries, such as the petroleum, electronics, and movie industries, are even more heavily concentrated along geographic lines. The geographic concentration problem is aggravated further by the fact that many major companies with geographically dispersed production divisions centralize their buying at the company headquarters.

Many sources can be used in identifying, locating, and obtaining basic statistics on producer markets. Among the more useful are the *Census of Manufacturing,* the *Encyclopedia of Business Information Sources, Standard and Poor's Industrial Index,* trade associations, trade publications, and a variety of industrial directories.[1] In addition to these, two tools for analyzing industrial markets that have already been mentioned, will be discussed more fully—SIC codes and input-output analysis.

STANDARD INDUSTRIAL CLASSIFICATION (SIC) CODES SIC codes break down industries into 496 separate categories. Published by the U.S. Department of Commerce, these codes enable industrial marketers to identify industry groups by their primary activities.

The first two digits of SIC codes identify twenty broad industrial categories. For example, 20 is Food and Kindred Products; 21 is Tobacco Products; 22 is Textile Products; 23 is Apparel; 35 is Machinery, except Electrical; and 36 is Electrical and Electronic Machinery. Each major category is further classified with three- and four-digit codes that become increasingly specific. Figure 7–1 partially traces the sequence of classifications for Food and Kindred Products (SIC code 20) and Electrical and Electronic Machinery, Equipment, and Supplies (SIC code 36).

In order to use SIC codes, the industrial analyst must first identify the four digit SIC categories that represent industries likely to use the company's products. This determination may be made on the basis of knowledge and experience, or through input-output analysis.

INPUT-OUTPUT ANALYSIS Input-output analysis was developed by economist Wassily Leontief to analyze national economic activity. The advent of high speed electronic computers, coupled with the wealth of industrial statistics developed by government agencies, has made the technique feasible for a wide range of econometric and marketing uses. Essentially, input-output analysis shows transactions between different segments of the U.S. economy. Let us assume that a chemical firm has developed a chemical that can be used in the production of paper. Reference to input-output tables will reveal that 75 percent of the paper output is concentrated in paper mills (SIC 2621),

1. Chapter 9, Marketing Research and Test Marketing, provides an annotated list of commonly used sources of industrial and consumer marketing information.

FIGURE 7–1: SIC codes

(20) Food and Kindred Products
(201) Meat Products
(202) Dairy Products
(203) Canned and Preserved Fruits and Vegetables
(204) Grain Mill Products
(205) Bakery Products
(206) Sugar and Confection Products
(207) Fats and Oils
(208) Beverages
(209) Miscellaneous Food Preparations and Kindred Products
(2061) Cane Sugar except Refineries
(2062) Cane Sugar Refineries
(2063) Beet Sugar
(2065) Candy and Other Confectionary Products
(2066) Chocolate and Cocoa Products
(2067) Chewing Gum

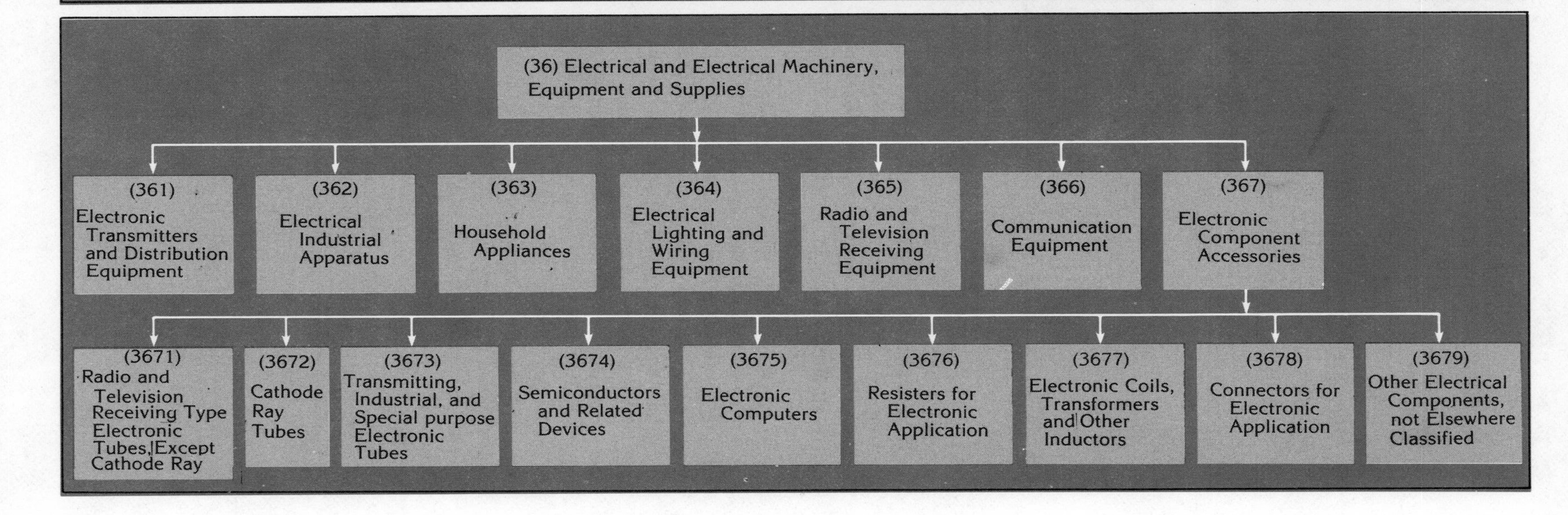

TABLE 7–2: New England Paper Mills
Adapted from *Sales and Marketing Management's* Survey of Industrial Purchasing Power, 1979.

State	Paper Mills	Dollar Volume of Shipments	Percent of U.S. Shipments
Maine	10	$ 965,000	7.55%
New Hampshire	2	87,000	0.68
Massachusetts	20	458,400	3.65
Total	32	$1,510,400	11.88%

Massachusetts Paper Mills

County	Paper Mills	Dollar Volume of Shipments	Percent of U.S. Shipments
Berkshire	7	$133,000	1.08%
Franklin	5	122,900	.97
Hamden	8	202,500	1.60
	20	$458,400	3.65%

15 percent in paperboard mills (SIC 2631), and 10 percent in pulp mills (SIC 2611).

Armed with this information, the chemical producer can use the *Census of Manufacturing* to find the number of paper producers by geographic area. For example, 339 U.S. paper mills with 20 or more employees have aggregate shipments exceeding $12.5 billion. Further, 32 of these mills, with aggregate shipments of $1.5 billion, are located in New England. Table 7–2 shows further breakdowns of the paper mills in New England; specifically, the paper mills in each state, along with the dollar value of their shipments, and percentage of all U.S. shipments. It also shows this same data broken down by counties for Massachusetts.[2] The dollar value figure for shipments can be used to estimate the relative importance of these paper mills. Pulp and paper industry directories provide specific names and addresses of the various mills that have been identified.

The full value of input-output analysis has not, for the most part, been exploited by marketing practitioners. As pointed out earlier, one reason is that input-output tables are often several years behind current developments. Nonetheless, used properly, input-output tables can be a valuable tool for industrial marketers; this value will increase when data becomes available more promptly. Practically speaking, however, major industry patterns usually don't change all that quickly, and some data—even if it is a few years old—is usually better than no data at all.[3]

Who Is the Market?

Often, as demonstrated in the foregoing example, it is easy to determine *who* the market is once one had identified *where* it is. In any case, the total customers in the industry should be determined as well as the size ranges and patterns of concentration. Once specific customers have been identified, many alternatives may be used to gather additional, more precise marketing information.

When Does the Market Buy?

The time pattern of purchases by producers varies by industry and product, based on a variety of fac-

2. *Sales and Marketing Management's Survey of Industrial Buying Power* provides a county-by-county breakdown of industrial establishments by four-digit SIC codes.

3. For a brief introduction to input-output analysis, see M. F. Elliott-Jones, *Input-Output Analysis: A Nontechnical Description* (New York: The Conference Board, Inc., 1971). This reference also contains a good basic bibliography.

TABLE 7–3: Employees Who May Be Involved in the Purchase of "Maintenance Materials, Equipment, and Supplies" in Manufacturing Companies.
SOURCE: Adapted from John H. Frederick, *Industrial Marketing*. Reprinted by Arno Press in New York, 1979, p. 48.

Production and Maintenance Executives
General Managers
Works Managers
Plant Superintendents
Master Mechanics
Maintenance Engineers
Electrical Engineers
Purchasing Agents
Financial and Policy Executives
Presidents
Vice-Presidents in charge of production
Vice-Presidents in charge of sales
Secretaries and Treasurers

tors: the nature of the product, the structure of volume discounts, inventory policies of customers, perishability of the product, cash-flow considerations, and future economic expectations.

Some products, such as office supplies, may be purchased monthly. Others, such as basic raw materials, may be purchased on the basis of a production year. Still others, such as capital improvement equipment, may only be purchased every few years. In any event, every industry—as well as major customers—should be analyzed according to their particular requirements. Sometimes sellers can gain a competitive advantage by adapting their discount policies, billing practices, and shipping procedures to conform to customers' needs.

Information on the timing of purchases can often be obtained through industry associations, or through a survey of the customers themselves. Suppliers' sales representatives are a particularly useful source of information about purchasing patterns as well as other practices within customer companies.

How Does the Market Buy?

This question refers to the patterns of decision making in producer firms. A variety of decision patterns may exist in different companies, and identifying the crucial decision makers is often a frustrating task. A study of buying influences for "Maintenance Materials, Equipment, and Supplies" in manufacturing establishments revealed that almost any combination of the executives listed in Table 7–3 play a role in the purchasing decision.

To some extent, decision patterns depend upon the size of the company. In small companies, one or two people may be responsible for all purchases, but in large corporations, a vice–president of purchasing may head a major department. The authority of the person or persons who actually do the purchasing often varies by the company. In some instances, the buyer determines the product specifications, selects the supplier, and issues the purchasing order. In others, the buyer may only have authority to issue the purchasing order after specifications have been defined and the supplier selected.

Normally, the nature of the product will determine the extent of involvement of different company personnel in the purchasing decision. For example, engineering may have a decisive role in highly technical equipment; production will be deeply involved in purchases that affect its operation; and policy executives will have the determinant voice in major capital investments. In any event, usually the decision process should be broken down into steps, and the participants at each level identified.

One such breakdown identified eight phases of buying.[4]

1. Anticipation or recognition of the problem or need, and identification of a general solution.
2. Determination of the characteristics and quantity of the item needed.
3. Preparation of written specifications for the item, and for the quantity needed.
4. Search for and qualification of potential sources of supply.

4. Patrick J. Robinson, Charles W. Faris, and Yoram Wind, *Industrial Buying and Creative Marketing* (Boston: Allyn & Bacon, Inc., 1967), p. 14.

5. Procurement and analysis of proposals from potential suppliers.
6. Evaluation of the proposals and the selection of one or more suppliers.
7. Development of a routine for ordering the item.
8. Establishment of a procedure for performance evaluation and feedback.

One or more people may participate directly or indirectly in each phase; the number and composition of participants often varies by phase. Marketers must recognize that each participant may bring somewhat different criteria to the decision process with the consequence that buying decisions are often a source of conflict within an organization.[5]

Why Does the Market Buy?

Earlier, we pointed out that the criteria used in making producer purchases tend to be more objective than those used by consumers. Attributes which can be objectively assessed—such as price, quality, dependability of supply, service, and so forth—tend to predominate. Not all industrial sellers, however, possess these attributes to an equal degree. As a consequence, most industrial buying decisions represent a trade-off among a multiplicity of supplier and product attributes. One supplier, whose quality is marginally better than competitors, may have a significantly higher price. Another, with the lower price, may produce goods of questionable quality. A third, offering no price or product quality advantage, may provide outstanding service.

IBM, for example, dominates the computer industry, not because of price or hardware superiority—it has seldom been in the forefront of technological development—but because of outstanding service. From the beginning, IBM management recognized that the key consideration in selling computer hardware was adaptability to the needs of individual customers. Acting on this conviction, IBM has consistently emphasized software, or the application of its computers, and has developed an outstanding service organization to work with its customers in designing software and procedures to best meet their needs.

Although objective criteria tend to dominate industrial buying decisions, subjective criteria are not entirely absent. For example, supplier reputation—a somewhat subjective element in the buyer-seller relationship—often plays an important role. This point is emphasized by a classic advertisement developed by *Business Week*, encouraging industrial advertising in business publications. (See Plate 7–1).

In addition, a variety of influences—environmental, organizational, and interpersonal—introduce a certain amount of subjectivity into all group buying situations. As a conse-

PLATE 7–1: *McGraw Hill Magazines ad*

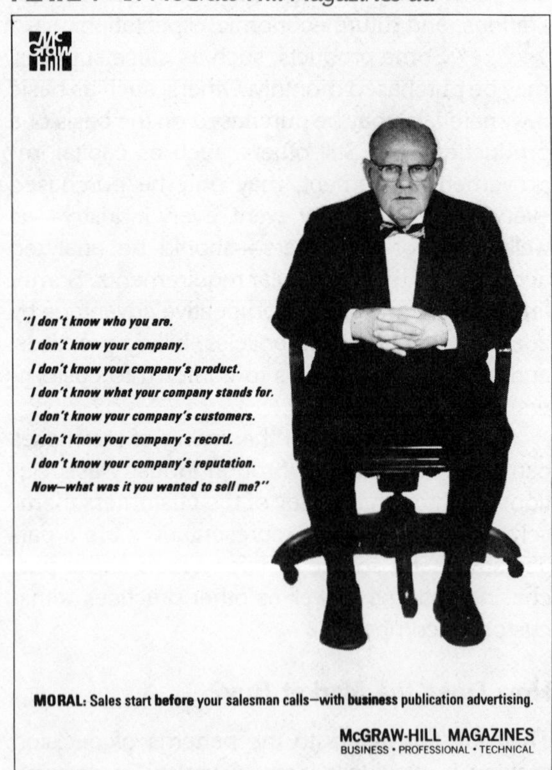

5. Webster and Wind have referred to the decision-making unit of a buying organization as a "buying center," which they define as "all individuals and groups who participate in the purchasing decision process, and who share some common goals and risks arising from the decision." For a further discussion of this concept, see: Frederick E. Webster, Jr. and Yoram Wind, *Organizational Buying Behavior* (Englewood Cliffs, NJ: Prentice-Hall, 1972), p. 6.

quence, the seller of industrial goods and services needs to be sensitive to these variables, and prepared to deal with them.[6]

A Summary Note on the Producer Market

The producer market is a large, complex, and challenging one. Buying practices vary by industry, and by different companies within the same industry. There are no simple solutions or gimmicks for tapping this market. Success in industrial selling, as in all other areas of marketing, requires a systematic approach, thorough analysis, thoughtful use of marketing research, hard work, a willingness to adapt one's approach to market requirements—and a little bit of luck.

RESELLER MARKETS

Normally, resellers, are synonymous with retailers and wholesalers—sometimes referred to as *middlemen* in the economic structure. Some resellers (retailers) sell directly to consumers; some (wholesalers) sell to other resellers; some (industrial distributors) sell to producers. Unlike producer firms, resellers do not modify or change the products which they purchase for resale. Rather, they simply operate as a conduit for transferring products from one group of participants in the economic system to another.

The reseller market may be defined as *all of those firms that purchase products or services for the purpose of reselling, renting, or leasing them to individuals or other business firms.* Thus, resellers serve five functions in a marketing economy:

Bringing together a particular assortment of goods that are of value to a particular group of customers.

Locating these assortments at places more convenient for customers than those provided by producers.

Providing goods and services when they are wanted.

Providing customers with desired products in the desired quantities.

Generally offering a variety of other marketing services such as credit, delivery, sales help, alterations, and service.

What Is the Reseller Market?

In terms of dollars, the reseller market exceeds $1.7 trillion. In terms of numbers, it includes over 275,000 wholesale firms and some 1.5 million retail firms. And, this market is exceedingly diverse. Resellers range from small, family-owned and operated establishments to multibillion dollar firms such as Safeway and Sears. The market is less concentrated geographically than producer markets, but more concentrated than consumer markets.

As in the case of producer markets, individual firms that sell to reseller organizations are not basically concerned with the aggregate market. Rather, they are only interested in those reseller operations that deal in the products they sell. An important part of marketing analysis for those who sell to resellers is to identify the particular reseller organizations that represent appropriate customers.

Note that resellers also represent markets for products other than those they resell. For example, grocery stores are a market for land, buildings, shelving, refrigeration equipment, office equipment and supplies, and many other items needed to run the business. In this sense, resellers are also part of the producer market—they produce a service. In this section, we are only interested in those products they buy to resell.

Who Is the Market?

The market has become so diverse that it defies easy classification because many reseller organizations have evolved to meet the assorted needs of many groups of customers. The U.S. Department of Commerce classifies reseller fields into two major divisions (durable and nondurable goods), and a number of subclassifications for

6. For a discussion of some of the variables that shape the buying process, see: Frederick E. Webster, Jr. and Yoram Wind, "A General Model for Understanding Organizational Buying Behavior," *Journal of Marketing* (April, 1972): 12–19.

The reseller market. (Photo D. Michael Hostetler)

statistical purposes. This classification system is shown in Table 7–4.

The inadequacy of these classifications is obvious since many retail outlets cut across classification lines. Department stores, under nondurable goods, also handle durable goods. Gasoline stations, under nondurable goods, handle automotive parts (a durable good) as well as candy, chewing gum, cigarettes and, in some cases, grocery items. Also, many wholesalers cut across the categories shown, selling to a wide variety of retail outlets.

Earlier, we noted that the marketers of consumer goods should identify those reseller outlets that represent appropriate distribution outlets for their products. Often, the identification of new retail outlets represents an opportunity for increased sales. For example, Nodoz (a mild stimulate to postpone drowsiness) was sold only through drugstores for many years. Analysis of consumer needs and consumer buying trends led to expanded distribution to gasoline stations, grocery stores, and department stores. The result? A significant increase in sales.

When Is the Market?

Two variables—current stock levels and anticipated demand—determine when resellers buy. The stock levels maintained and the frequency of purchase by retailers is always a trade-off. Stock levels are a trade-off between a desire to avoid being out-of-stock with a consequent loss of sales, and to avoid the cost of carrying inventory. During periods of inflation, such as that experienced in 1979 and 1980, the cost of money for investment in stock was 18 to 20 percent. As a consequence, many retailers tended to lower their inventories, and risk the danger of lost sales. During periods when low interest rates make the cost of money cheap, stock levels tend to increase.

TABLE 7–4: *U.S. Department of Commerce Classification of Reseller Markets*

Durable Goods
Automotive
Furniture, home furnishings
Building materials, hardware, garden supplies
Mobile home dealers
Nondurable Goods
Apparel and accessory stores
Drug stores
Eating and drinking places
Food stores
Gasoline service stations
General merchandise, department, and variety stores
Liquor stores
Mail order houses

When interest rates are high, those who sell to the reseller markets can sometimes gain a competitive advantage through *delayed billing* or *consignment selling.* In delayed billing, the supplier bills resellers for products two or three months *after* delivery. In consignment selling, the resellers do not pay the supplier until *after* the product is sold. The effect of these strategies is to transfer much of the cost of carrying inventories from the reseller to the supplier. While this procedure depresses suppliers' profits, consignment selling and delayed billing do maintain distribution and may increase market share, thus contributing to future profits.

Order frequency is a trade-off between inventory costs and reorder costs for the reseller. By placing infrequent, large orders, resellers often gain quantity discounts and reduce order processing costs. At the same time, however, they increase their inventory costs and sometimes incur losses from product spoilage, product obsolescence, or future price reductions by suppliers. By ordering in small quantities, the reseller avoids the foregoing pitfalls, but reorder costs are increased, discounts lost, and the danger of being out-of-stock is increased. In some markets—carpeting being a prime example—suppliers are able to increase order sizes by protecting resellers against unfavorable price changes. Thus, if the supplier's price is reduced after a large purchase by a reseller, the buyer is issued a cash rebate or a credit memorandum equal to the magnitude of the price reduction.

Some markets have distinct seasonal factors. For example, in the home garden market, selling is done in the late fall or early winter in anticipation of a spring-summer consumer market. The apparel field is also particularly susceptible to seasonal buying. Department store buyers order spring fashions in the fall and early winter, and winter fashions in the spring and early summer. The best selling season for hams is just before Easter, and for fancy boxed chocolates shortly before Christmas, Valentine's Day, and Mother's Day. These three occasions account for about 80 percent of the sales of fancy boxed chocolates. Again those who market to reseller organizations must be familiar with the particular buying practices of their customers to develop effective marketing plans.

How Do Resellers Buy?

Buying patterns in reseller firms are usually much less complex than those in producer firms. In a small reseller company, the owner may do all of the buying. In larger firms, buying is a specialized function and, usually a full-time job. Major grocery chains, for example, have produce buyers, meat buyers, dry grocery buyers, frozen food buyers, baked goods buyers, and general merchandise buyers, as well as others. Buyers in reseller organizations have much more authority and freedom than buyers in producer organizations, even though *buying committees* are common in some retail organizations, particularly in retail grocery and drug enterprises.

Buying committees in grocery stores, for example, usually serve two functions: First, they control the new products stocked in company stores. Offered as many as 150 to 200 new items a week, grocery buyers don't have the shelf space to stock all of these new items; often when a new product is accepted, an existing product must be discontinued. In 1978, for example, major grocery chains added 620 new items and discontinued 450 items, for a net gain of 170 items.[7] As a consequence, buying committees accept only the most promising new items referred to them by buyers. Buyers have a powerful influence on the buying committee, and can sabotage a new product offering by failing to present it, by recommending against it, or by presenting it poorly.

The second function of a buying committee is to serve as a buffer between suppliers' representatives and buyers. Thus, the grocery representative doesn't exist who hasn't had a buyer tell him, "I'm sorry, I did my best to get your product accepted by the buying committee, but they turned it down." In many such situations, the product representative strongly suspects that the buyer recommended against the product, but

7. "Distribution and Delivery," *Progressive Grocer* (April, 1979): 149.

there is nothing to say except, "Thanks, Joe. I sure appreciate your efforts on my behalf."

Since suppliers do not meet with buying committees themselves, one of their primary tasks is to arm buyers with persuasive evidence of the new product's probable success. Evidence of probable success includes the results of consumer tests against competitive products, the results of successful test markets, profit potential estimates, and advertising and promotion plans. Producers often enlist advertising agencies to help in preparing presentations to buyers, particularly if the new product represents a major marketing opportunity.

A product does not always find its way to retail stores even after approval by a buying committee. Often, the product is only placed on an "approved" list, and the final order must be placed by individual store managers. In some instances, however, forced distribution will be directed by the buying committee. For example, in order to appease environmentalists, a grocery chain may make a policy decision to offer low-phosphate detergents to its customers. Or, if a new product seems to represent a major marketing opportunity, buying committees will direct store managers to stock it.

Buyers for department stores generally have even more discretion than do buyers in grocery operations. The only real criterion imposed on them by management is "Will it sell?" Buyers are responsible for the purchase and responsible for the sale. If they buy wisely, buyers will prosper. If they buy foolishly, buyers will probably find another job.

Other types of retail and wholesale organizations may have somewhat different buying practices than those outlined above. In most cases, however, buying is a highly specialized function carried out by individual buyers, buying committees, or some combination of the two.

Why Do Resellers Buy?

The basic motivation of buyers in the reseller market is to make a profit. That's what they are in business for. The inventory stocks and administrative procedures required to add a new item to a store's assortment are costly. If the product doesn't sell, or sells less than anticipated, costs accelerate. For these reasons, buyers are particularly responsive to information assuring them that new products will sell in sufficient volume to justify adding them to their inventories. Typically, buyers are interested in this information:

- *Evidence of consumer acceptance.* Preferred evidence is based on actual performance in other markets or other stores. In short, test market results or sales data about the product from competitive stores constitute the most impressive evidence. Other evidence of consumer acceptance includes blind product tests and testimonials.
- *Profit performance.* Profit performance is a combination of the gross margin per item and the number of items sold. In food stores, performance is often measured by profit per linear foot of shelf space. Generally, buyers like products that have high margins and high velocity (a high projected sales rate). Thus, information on profit margins, users, frequency of purchase, and anticipated share of market are of interest.
- *Stocking, display, and advertising allowances.* In many retail fields customarily a stocking allowance—so many cents a case or per item—compensates retail organizations for the cost of adding an item to their warehouses and order lists. Actually, it is a form of blackmail that has become hallowed and institutionalized. In addition, there are often advertising allowances, or allowances for special store displays. Since these allowances can be a significant source of income in a large retail operation, buyers are interested in what is being offered.
- *Advertising and Promotion Plans.* The success or failure of a new product often depends upon the weight of introductory advertising and promotional support. Therefore, details on such programs, dollar expenditures, and types of activity, are wanted.
- *Reputation of the Seller.* Some major producer firms have earned reputations for suc-

cessfully introducing their new products. They are known to be systematic, thorough, and alert marketing practitioners. As a consequence, buyers are often interested in the supplier's track record in introducing new products, and in their reputation for quality.

- *Merchandising suggestions.* Here, buyers are asking for suggestions—preferably tested ones—about where in the store the product should be stocked, how it should be priced, and ways in which it can be most effectively promoted. This is particularly important in grocery stores where many products lend themselves to alternative methods of handling. For example, should Hamburger Helper be stocked near the meat counter, with pastas, with easy to prepare meals, or someplace else?
- *Forecasts of demand.* Profit margins on many retail items are relatively low. A significant decrease in demand can mean the difference between profit or loss. Further, some consumer items are fad items, with relatively short product lives. As a consequence, buyers may want to review demand forecasts, and the logic behind them.

In general, these are things that buyers are looking for. As in the case of producer firms, however, buying decisions are also influenced by economic conditions, organizational constraints, competitive activity, and personal variables.[8]

GOVERNMENT MARKETS

The third type of industrial market to be considered in this chapter is the government. Although the demand for goods and services by government markets is considerably smaller than that of either producer or reseller markets—some $400 billion compared to over a trillion dollars for each of the other two segments—the rate of growth of government markets during the past thirty years has outstripped other segments of the economy.

Government markets include both producer markets, in the sense that governments produce services, and reseller markets since the government operates commissaries and other retail stores for government employees. The diversity and uniqueness of government markets, however, justify their treatment as a separate segment of the economy.

What Are Government Markets?

Government markets consist of federal, state, and local governmental units that acquire goods and services in order to carry out their functions. Approximately 60 percent of government purchases of goods and services are made by the federal government, with the remainder being made by subordinate governmental units at the state and local levels. In the aggregate, the federal government is the largest, single purchaser of goods and services in the economy. This statement is somewhat misleading, however, because government purchases are not made by a single office, but are divided between hundreds of separate agencies and divisions, operating at both national and local levels.

What do governments buy? Virtually everything: military equipment, space missiles, and milk for school lunch programs. They operate police forces, fire fighting services, schools, public utilities, research laboratories, commissaries, offices, hospitals and liquor stores. They are involved in defense, education, social work, health delivery services, insurance, pension funds, construction, communications, transportation, environmental protection and development, recreation, housing, and urban renewal. Virtually all areas of economic activity include government as a producer, a consumer, or a reseller.

Where Do Governments Buy

Government markets are ubiquitous. They exist in Washington, D.C., in state capitals, in major cities, in small towns, and rural areas. Governments buy in all sections of the United States, as well as in

8. Buyers also develop individual strategies or styles for carrying out their tasks. For a discussion of such strategies, see: Roger A. Dickinson, *Buyer Decision Making* (Berkeley, California: Institute of Business and Economic Research, 1967), pp. 15–17.

foreign countries, and often use their purchasing power to stimulate faltering local economies, or even major industries. According to the *Statistical Abstracts of the United States,* approximately 80,000 government units are empowered to make purchases. Even where government purchasing authority is centralized, as is the General Services Administration (GSA), local purchases can be made under open-end GSA contracts. For example, the post office in St. Louis can purchase automobile tires from local dealers of national companies having a GSA contract. The GSA has many open-end contracts for thousands of items that may be purchased locally by government agencies throughout the United States.

Who Participates in Government Purchases?

Although government purchasing authority tends to be concentrated in independent purchasing departments, the number of participants depends upon the government agency involved, and the nature of the purchase. Perhaps one of the greatest differences can be found between federal, state, and local units.

Approximately 75 percent of the dollar value of federal government purchases are for sophisticated weapon and space systems, with the remaining 25 percent being allocated to nonmilitary commodities. At state and local levels, purchases are almost exclusively for nonmilitary commodities, with the largest single expenditure for construction contracts.[9] At the state level, the chief purchasing agent often reports to the governor, or the governor's administrative officer. In most county and city governments, the chief purchasing agent reports to the chief administrator, or to city council.

Purchasing efficiency at local governmental levels is often compromised by excessive decentralization in which individual city departments—school districts, utilities, and other service agencies—are authorized to make purchases subject to inadequate controls. In the case of major purchases, the participation of the mayor, the city manager, and city council often introduces a note of unprofessionalism and political favoritism. Many of these problems are being overcome by revising city charters to centralize purchasing procedures and by establishing a central procurement office under the protection of civil service, staffed by well-paid, experienced professionals.

The government market. (Photo by Julie Estadt)

Of the federal government's many buying agencies, the four most important are the General Services Administration (GSA), the Department of Defense (DOD), the National Aeronautics and Space Administration (NASA), and the Energy Research and Development Agency (ERDA).

The General Services Administration is responsible for all government purchases other than those specifically authorized by the other three buying agencies. However, even these agencies often obtain many commonly used products from GSA which, in these cases, fulfills the role of a reseller.

Needless to say, the magnitude and diversity of the federal government's procurement program requires the participation of thousands of individuals in different parts of the country. This creates severe problems in coordination and communications. One consequence is that many government purchases seem to involve an avalanche of paperwork. In addition to the paperwork, those who do business with the government must also be prepared to deal with the General Accounting Office (GAO). Often referred to as the watchdog of the government, the GAO has the

9. Lemar Lee, Jr. and Donald W. Dobler, *Purchasing and Materials Management,* 3rd ed. (New York: McGraw-Hill Book Company, 1977), p. 541.

responsibility for auditing the expenditures of government agencies for compliance with myriad federal statutes and appropriation acts. The GAO may disallow any improper payments. GAO is authorized to audit supplier books for some fixed-price and all cost-plus contracts. If these contracts violate federal statutes, the GAO can void the contract.

When Are Government Purchases Made?

The same variables that govern purchase frequency in producer and reseller markets also apply to the government because many government procurement agencies are producers, resellers, and consumers. One difference between government purchasing practices and those of private industry involves the frequency of purchases and inventory levels. Since many government purchases depend upon time-consuming "lowest-bid" procedures, purchases may be made less frequently and, as a consequence, higher inventories must be maintained.

How Are Government Purchases Made?

To the uninitiated, government purchasing activity appears to be an impenetrable labyrinth of procedures, forms, regulations, and red tape. For major purchases, and for highly technical ones, this is partly true. In actuality, most government purchases are for less than $10,000, and carried out in a routine fashion. The procedures for major purchases, while more complex, can be mastered with a little effort.

The government is extremely helpful in aiding prospective suppliers. For example, most purchases exceeding $10,000 must be given advance publicity in the *Consumer Business Daily,* a publication issued by the Government Printing Office. The Small Business Administration issues a report which lists thousands of items frequently purchased by the government, cross-referenced by the agencies that use these items most frequently. The GSA operates Business Service Centers in major cities in which government personnel provide information on the procedures employed by the GSA and other procurement agencies. Finally, the offices of congressional representatives and senators are often cooperative in giving directions to constituents who are interested in doing business with the government.

Why Does the Government Buy?

Unlike the private sector, profit is not a primary motivation behind government purchasing. One does not measure the performance of a government by profit, but rather by its ability to provide desired public services, often regardless of the costs involved. Attempts of government procurement officers to be cost efficient—and this is often the primary goal—are sometimes foiled by the thicket of regulations and controls that surround government spending. Governments operate on the public funds voted them by legislative bodies. As watchdogs of the public treasury, legislatures establish constraints, procedures, and specifications that sometimes make efficient operation impossible for government procurement offices. For example, funds are seldom available for an opportunistic purchase in government. By contrast, the private sector will release additional funds if a large quantity of a needed commodity can be bought at a favorable price.

In making appropriations, legislative bodies may specify cumbersome purchasing procedures, uneconomical materials, or unrealistic inventory policies. And, while government buyers seldom get into trouble as long as they follow established procedures, they can be fired if they fail to do so, regardless of how much money they may save, or how cost effective their operation. As a consequence, the primary motivation in government procurement is *conformity.* Within the constraints that have been established, government procurement offices will try to buy efficiently. But, if that is not possible—and often it is not—the office will conform, regardless of the cost.

SUMMARY

Industrial markets (sometimes referred to as intermediate, business, or organizational markets) differ from consumer markets in a variety of ways directly affecting marketing activities. For example, industrial markets are more concentrated in terms of customers and geographical locations, and they do not buy for personal consumption. Purchasing decisions are more complex and reciprocity is often a factor in making industrial purchases. More dependent upon objective buying criteria, dependable supply and delivery are often more critical for the industrial purchaser than for consumer markets.

Industrial markets can be broken down into three major segments—producer markets, reseller markets, and government markets. Each of these segments is sufficiently different from the others to be examined separately.

The producer market is made up of all individuals and business firms that buy products and services used in the production of other products and services that, in turn, are sold, rented, or leased to individual customers or to other business firms.

The reseller market, on the other hand, includes all those firms that purchase products or services to be resold, rented, or leased to individuals or to other firms. Thus, unlike producer markets, the reseller market does not modify the products it buys and sells. Instead, it simply serves as a conduit transferring products from one group of participants in the economic system to another.

Government markets consist of federal, state, and local governmental units that acquire goods and services in order to carry out their functions.

In order to succeed in industrial marketing, regardless of the segment being served, the marketer must analyze customer markets carefully, addressing such questions as: (1) what is the market's size; (2) where is it concentrated geographically; (3) who are the individual customers in the market; (4) when does the market buy; (5) how does the market make purchasing decisions; and (6) what are the market's relevant buying motives.

A great deal of marketing information is available on industrial markets through governmental statistics, industry associations, and business publications. Industrial marketers need to familiarize themselves with this information, and learn to use it wisely.

1. Identify the key differences between industrial and consumer markets.
2. Identify and define the three major segments of the industrial market.
3. Explain what is meant by SIC codes and how they are structured.
4. Explain what is meant by input-output analysis. How can SIC codes and input-output analysis be used in identifying producer customers?
5. Identify the eight phases of buying in producer markets.
6. Identify the five functions served by reseller markets.
7. In what way are resellers also a part of the producer market?
8. What functions does the buying committee serve in the reseller market?
9. Identify the kinds of information that are particularly helpful in persuading reseller buyers to stock a product.
10. Explain why government markets include both producer and reseller markets, and identify the primary buying motivation that pervades government buying. Why is this motivation predominant?

DISCUSSION QUESTIONS

1. The text noted that the authority given to a purchasing agent or buyer in the producer market often varies widely. Discuss how much latitude an industrial buyer should have in purchasing: (A) typewriters for the company; (B) paint for the offices; (C) manufacturered components which will become a part of the product the company produces; and (D) a major piece of production equipment. Who, in addition to the purchasing agent, should participate in each of these purchases?
2. The text identifies eight phases of industrial buying. Discuss why identifying participants in each stage is important. Select a particular product, such as a lathe or some other product, to demonstrate your answer.
3. Many companies often obtain bids for the products that they purchase. Often, however, they do not buy from the supplier with the lowest bid. Discuss some of the reasons why this is so.
4. Discuss some of the differences in the motivations of consumers and industrial buyers in making purchases.
5. Based on your understanding of decision buying motives for producers and resellers, outline the basic ingredients of a sales presentation to each type of customer.

CHAPTER PROBLEM

ANALYZING INDUSTRIAL MARKETS—BUYING PATTERNS

Robert C. Runyon, an inventor and entrepreneur, had evolved a profitable procedure for making money. Specializing in precision tools, he would search for an industrial process in which he saw an opportunity to improve an existing tool. He would then invent a new tool for the process, patent it, and form a company to produce it. After developing a market he would sell the company at a substantial profit, usually negotiating royalty payments for his basic patent.

One product he developed was a diamond saw blade for sawing silicon chips used in the computer industry. A traditional diamond saw blade has diamond particles formed into a paper-thin blade which is bonded to a slightly smaller stainless steel disk that has been drilled so that it can be mounted on the spindle of a high-speed diamond saw. A single blade sold for about $25, with the steel disk accounting for about $4 to $5 of the cost of manufacture. The problem with this blade is that it is paper-thin and brittle. Under normal use, a worker would *break the cutting edges of four to five blades a day, resulting in a cost for blades of $100 to $125 for each diamond saw in use.*

Runyon saw an opportunity to reduce this cost by mounting the blade between two slightly smaller disks; he planned to sell the blade and the disks separately. In addition, he planned to sell sets of disks in three different sizes. When the blade broke with the largest disks, the worker could shear off the diamond blade against a hard surface, reducing it to the size of the largest disk. The same blade could then be mounted on the medium size disks. When that broke, the same blade could be sheared off and mounted on the smallest disks.

A producer of computer chips would buy one set of disks for each saw in operation. Each set of disks could be used over and over for years. Saw blades could then be sold separately at a price competitive with existing saw blades, but each saw blade would have a use-life three times longer than existing saw blades. The net result was a significant savings in the cost of diamond saw blades.

After developing the saw blade and checking out its operation in his own workshop, he called on the purchasing agents of a couple of major computer chip producers. The purchasing agents were cautiously enthusiastic about Runyon's product. They recognized its cost-saving potential, but they didn't know how it would be accepted by production. Since it required a different procedure than was currently being used, they didn't know how workers, foremen, and production managers would react to it.

Runyon didn't see this as an unsolvable problem, however, and started thinking about how he would market the product. He didn't know much about the size of the market, nor where it was located. He was under the impression that there were hundreds of computer chip producers, located around San Francisco in an area that has become known as silicon valley, and in the Southwest.

Assignment

How should Runyon proceed?

8

Behavioral Dimensions of Consumers

- *The role of consumer behavior in planning marketing activities.*
- *The nature of motivation.*
- *Social variables that influence consumer behavior.*
- *Intrapersonal variables that influence consumer behavior.*

MARKETING EXAMPLES

WATCHES

Why do people buy watches? To keep time? Yes, but according to research conducted by Daniel Yankelovich:

> . . . Approximately 23 percent of the buyers bought for the lowest possible price.
> . . . Another 46 percent bought for durability and general product quality.
> . . . And 31 percent bought watches as symbols of important occasions.[1]

Yankelovich goes on to say:

> Defining and quantifying such segments is helpful in marketing planning . . . especially if a watch company's product happens to appeal mostly to one segment or if the line straddles the three segments, failing to appeal effectively to any. Without such an understanding, the demographic characteristics of the market are most confusing. It turns out, for example, that the most expensive watches are being bought by people with the highest and lowest incomes. On the other hand, some upper-income consumers are no longer buying costly watches, but are buying cheap, well-styled watches to throw away when they require servicing. Other upper-income consumers, however, continue to buy fine, expensive watches for suitable occasions.[2]

These two examples have been chosen to dramatize a crucial point in marketing: *different people buy products for different reasons.* And, finding the appeal or appeals that will be most effective in

---

1. Reprinted by permission of the *Harvard Business Review.* Excerpt from "New Criteria for Market Segmentation" by Daniel Yankelovich (March-April 1964). Copyright © 1964 by the President and Fellows of Harvard College; all rights reserved.
2. Ibid, p. 85.

attracting consumers is a never-ending search in the marketing community.

David Ogilvy, the founder of Ogilvy, Benson, and Mather and a highly acclaimed advertising practitioner, begins his discussion of how to build a great advertising campaign with the following statement:

> Once upon a time I was riding on the top of a Fifth Avenue bus, when I heard a mythical housewife say to another, "Molly, my dear, I would have bought that new brand of toilet soap if only they hadn't set the body copy in ten-point Garamond."
>
> Don't you believe it. What really decides consumers to buy or not to buy is the *content* of your advertising, not its form. Your most important job is to decide what you are going to say about your product, what benefit you are going to promise. Two hundred years ago Dr. Johnson said, "Promise, large promise is the soul of an advertisement." When he auctioned off the contents of the Anchor Brewery he made the following promise: "We are not here to sell boilers and vats, but the potentiality of growing rich beyond the dreams of avarice."
>
> The selection of the right promise is so vitally important that you should never rely on *guesswork* to decide it. At Ogilvy, Benson, and Mather, we use five research techniques to find out which is the most powerful.[3]

TOOTHPASTE

Why do people buy toothpaste? To brush their teeth, of course, but it isn't that simple. According to research done on behavioral segmentation of the toothpaste market, different people buy different kinds of toothpaste for quite different reasons. Russell Haley has identified four

3. David Ogilvy, *Confessions of an Advertising Man* (New York: Atheneum, 1964), p. 93.

TABLE 8–1: Toothpaste Market Segment Description
SOURCE: Russell J. Haley, "Benefit Segmentation: A Decision Oriented Research Tool," *Journal of Marketing* (July, 1968): p. 33.

Segment Name	The Sensory Segment	The Sociables	The Worriers	The Independent Segment
Principal benefit sought:	Flavor, product appearance	Brightness of teeth	Decay prevention	Price
Demographic strengths:	Children	Teens, young people	Large families	Men
Special behavioral characteristics:	Users of spearmint flavored toothpaste	Smokers	Heavy users	Heavy users
Brands disproportionately favored:	Colgate, Stripe	Macleans, Plus White, Ultra Brite	Crest	Brands on sale
Personality characteristics:	High self-involvement	High sociability	High hypochondriasis	High autonomy
Life-style characteristics	Hedonistic	Active	Conservative	Value-oriented

separate segments of the toothpaste market as the *Worriers*, the *Sociables*, the *Sensory* segment, and the *Independents*.[4]

The Worriers: This segment is primarily concerned with cavities and the prevention of tooth decay. They show a definite preference for fluoride toothpaste.

The Sociables: Brightness of teeth is important to this group. They want a toothpaste that will make their teeth white.

The Sensory Segment: Flavor and appearance are the key benefits sought by this group, and their use of spearmint flavored toothpastes is well above average.

The Independents: Members of this segment think most toothpastes are pretty much alike. They switch brands more than do the other segments, and economy plays a major role in their purchases. They are most likely to buy the brand that is on sale.

Table 8–1 summarizes some of the information that is known about these market segments. Note the differences between segments on the dimensions shown.

4. Russell J. Haley, "Benefit Segmentation: A Decision-Oriented Research Tool," *Journal of Marketing* (July, 1968): 30–35.

Marketing is rooted in consumer behavior. And, as competition has become more intense during the past thirty years, marketers have turned to the social sciences to gain a better understanding of why people behave as they do, and what product appeals will be most effective in moving consumers to buy their brands.

AN OVERVIEW OF CONSUMER BEHAVIOR

Think of consumers as problem solvers with a problem defined as a *perceived difference between an existing state of affairs and a desired state of affairs.* Thus, consumers' needs, wants, and desires often present problems which they attempt to solve through the purchase of goods and services. A young man feels awkward and ill at ease in social situations, so he enrolls in a Dale Carnegie course to improve his self-confidence and social skills. A young woman who believes that her hair color is unattractive, solves this problem by purchasing a hair dye or tint. Appalled by the increase in gasoline prices, a young couple attempts to solve this problem through the purchase of a fuel-efficient car. A young woman just entering the job market wishes to impress her new employer with her professionalism, so she purchases a tailored, dark suit and, perhaps, an impressive attaché case. The problems that consumers encounter in the act of living are endless. Their solutions are equally diverse.

Obviously, where the purchase of goods or services is concerned, problems may be solved in a variety of ways. Consumers are faced with many choices, presented by manufacturers insisting that their particular product is the best solution. Clairol, Revlon, Max Factor, Elizabeth Arden, Charles of the Ritz, and Helena Rubenstein are but a few of the alternatives available in the cosmetics and personal care fields. Ford, Chevrolet, Plymouth, Pontiac, Oldsmobile, Chrysler, Volkswagen, Datsun, Toyota, and Subaru are not even half of the alternatives available among automobiles. Other product fields have similar arrays.

Through product design, packaging, pricing, advertising, and other communication variables, each manufacturer attempts to motivate consumers to choose its particular products. Those who are successful in this endeavor prosper; those who are unsuccessful do not. Little wonder that motivation is a buzz-word in marketing, and that consumer behavior is a subject of intense interest. In this chapter, we will isolate consumer behavior as a subject of study, and briefly examine human motivation and the variables that influence it.

MOTIVATION

Motivation is one of the more complex areas of human behavior. Like the weather, everyone talks about motivation but there is a great deal of confusion about what one should do. Employers worry about motivating their workers; teachers fret about the lack of student motivation; and marketers spend inordinate time trying to find effective ways to motivate consumers to buy their products.

One of the problems is the ambiguity of the words used to discuss motivation. We use the terms *motivation, motives, needs, drives, wants,* and *goals,* often intermixing technical and popular language and sometimes confusing both ourselves and others. To complicate matters further, we sometimes make distinctions between *conscious* and *unconscious* motives, between *rational* and *irrational* motives, and between *needs* and *wants.*

A second problem in studying motivation is that, like most psychological concepts, motives cannot be directly observed. Only behavior can be observed. For example, we observe someone eating and we *infer* that the person is hungry. Yet, hunger may not be the reason for eating at all. Most of us have had the experience of joining someone for a sandwich and a cup of coffee, not because we were hungry, but for social reasons. We want companionship. Sometimes we eat, not because we are hungry, but because it is time to eat. By virtue of our daily routine, we usually eat at a particular hour, whether we are hungry or not. And then there is the compulsive eater—the person who, because of some psychological conflict, eats continually, thereby endangering health and gaining unwanted weight.

In the following material, we will do four things: *First,* we will define motivation. *Second,* we will suggest some terminology that can be used to eliminate ambiguity when discussing the subject. *Third,* we will discuss some of the key issues relating to motivation. *Fourth,* we will identify some conclusions that can be drawn about motivation.

Definition of Motivation

Generically, motivation can be defined as: *a theoretical construct involving an internal need state (sometimes referred to as an energizing force or tension system) that gives impetus to behavior, and a directional component that gives general direction to a variety of responses serving the same general function for the organism.*

Although there are many theories of motivation, most agree with the stipulations in this definition. Let's look at these stipulations more closely.

- *Theoretical construct.* Motivation is a theoretical construct that cannot be directly observed. We cannot see inside peoples' heads. We can only observe behavior from which we *infer* motives. Thus, a motive is an abstraction intended to explain behavior.
- *Internal need state.* Generally, the concept of motivation requires an internal energizing force which causes us to act. Further, this need state may vary in intensity.
- *Directional component for a variety of behaviors.* Generally, a motive provides direction for a variety of behaviors. The emphasis on a directional component for a variety of responses suggests that motivated behavior is adaptive and influenced by environmental and personal variables. The child who is unable to gain attention by tugging at a parent's hand may do so by having a temper tantrum. The student who cannot achieve recognition through scholarship or athletic prowness may do so through antisocial behavior. Or, in terms of marketing, members of a deprived subculture whose strivings for prestige are blocked by barriers of prejudice and discrimination may gain some measure of self-esteem through the purchase of expensive cars or prestige brands of products.

  Similarly, a safety motive could be used to explain the purchase of flight insurance, the acquisition of steel-belted radial tires, the installation of a smoke detector, the purchase of a burglar alarm, fleeing in the face of danger, or even aggressive behavior used to subdue the observed threat. This latter example is in keeping with the cliché that, sometimes, the best defense is a good offense.

With this definition of motivation, let us turn to the language of motivation. In the process, we will relate the psychological concept of motivation to the economic concept of demand because, ultimately, marketing practitioners are interested in demand. Consumer motivation is of concern to marketers only insofar as it creates demand for their products.

The Language of Motivation

Inherent in the concept of motivation is the concept of a goal. The need states in our definition of motivation are internal. Yet many, if not most, of our need states must be satisfied through things in the external world. These external things that have the capacity to satisfy internal need states are called goals, and much of our behavior is directed toward their attainment. A goal may be an *object,* such as food, water, or a product. Or, a *state of affairs,* such as an occupation, marriage, or being held in admiration and esteem by others.

The intent of marketing is to persuade consumers to perceive products and services as goals that will satisfy their needs. And, as marketing succeeds in this task, it transforms psychological needs into the economic concept of demand.[5] The process by which this transformation

5. Johan Arndt has suggested that, for clarity of thinking in marketing, a conceptual distinction should be made between the concepts of needs, wants, and demand. See, Johan Arndt, "How Broad Should the Marketing Concept Be?" *Journal of Marketing* (Jan., 1978): 101–103.

Plate 8-1: *Johnnie Walker Black Label ad reproduced with permission of Somerset Importers, Ltd.*

All toothpastes are not alike. No. 3 in a series.

Over a million bacteria bombard his teeth with cavity-causing acid every day. Can you rely on just any toothpaste?

Colgate says "no"!
Teeth are constantly under attack. That's because the mouth is a natural breeding ground for bacteria which produce decay acids. Even tough teeth can have imperfections where decay can get a foothold. But it's a proven scientific fact that tooth enamel can be strengthened to resist cavities.

Colgate's fluoride strengthens.
Just as decay acids can penetrate enamel and cause damage, Colgate® with MFP® fluoride penetrates to strengthen tooth enamel and resist these acids. Regular brushing with Colgate can mean fewer cavities. This has been proven in test after clinical test.

Not all toothpastes are alike.
If your toothpaste doesn't have fluoride like Colgate does, you're taking chances with your children's teeth. A proven effective fluoride formula like Colgate should be part of your family's oral health program, along with regular dental checkups, watching sweet snacks, and thorough brushing with Colgate after every meal.

The clean in your mouth is Colgate.
Get Colgate for your family. The fresh, clean taste is rated number one among fluoride toothpastes by parents all over America. And it fights decay acids. Reduces cavities.

The Penetration Principle: Painting a piece of chalk with colored liquid illustrates how, with regular brushing, Colgate's fluoride penetrates the surface of tooth enamel to strengthen it against decay.

Colgate helps stop cavities before they start.

Colgate
WITH MFP
FLUORIDE TOOTHPASTE

"Colgate® with MFP® fluoride has been shown to be an effective decay-preventive dentifrice that can be of significant value when used in a conscientiously applied program of oral hygiene and regular professional care." Council on Dental Therapeutics, American Dental Association.

Plate 8-3: *Colgate ad reprinted with permission of Colgate-Palmolive Company.*

takes place can be conceptualized through the following four-stage progression:

1. *Internal Need States.* This is what we normally mean when we use the term *need*—the hypothetical need state referred to in our definition of motivation. At this stage, the need state (or need) is nonconscious in the commonsense use of the term, and broad enough to accept a variety of related goals or solutions. An example of such a need state might be the general safety of the individual.

There is no universal agreement, and no way of experimentally validating the precise nature or number of internal need states. However, the late Abraham Maslow, an eminent psychologist, suggested that man has five basic needs—physiological, safety, affiliation, esteem, and self–actualization. For the purposes of an example, let us assume that these five basic needs are substantially correct. If we do, then the general safety of the individual may be considered a need state.

2. *Need Recognition.* This is what we normally mean when we use the word *motive.* At this stage, the need appears as a conscious identifiable idea. The particular form of manifestation will be influenced by both the individual's psychophysical characteristics and by factors in the external environment. Thus, for someone living in a high crime area, the need for safety might surface in consciousness with the realization that one's home could be burgled. In this instance, the *motive* would be to take action to prevent this eventuality from occurring. With a different individual, or under different environmental factors, the internal need for safety might appear in consciousness as a concern for health, fear of injury from an automobile accident, fear of flying, or as some other concern.

3. *Product Identification.* This is what we usually mean when we use the term *want* in connection with marketing.[6] At this stage, a product or service is identified that appears to offer a solution to the fear of being burgled. Actually, a number of alternatives may suggest themselves—additional locks on doors and windows, a security service, a burglar alarm, a watchdog, a gun, and so forth.

Product identification or wants may occur at different levels of specificity. The first level is generalized: a *protection* device of some kind is desired. At a second level, after thinking about it or after preliminary investigation, a security service may be selected. Finally, after investigating alternative security services, a particular security service may be chosen because of their procedures and personnel.

4. *Product Demand.* At this point, a *want* is converted into demand by the act of purchase. A particular security service is decided upon, and a financial commitment is made.

The progression reflected in the foregoing discussion is shown graphically in Figure 8–1. In this diagram, we can see how a need for safety might be converted into demand for a particular security service. With a different individual, or under different environmental circumstances, the need for safety could have taken a different form and resulted in different market behavior. Further, each of the other basic needs may also give rise to a variety of motives, wants, products considered, and demand outcomes.

Although successful marketers should have a basic concept of what constitutes internal need states (Stage 1 in the progression), the effects of marketing activity are most apparent at Stages 2, 3, and 4 of the motivational progression. For example, an individual's need for affiliation (a need state) may appear in consciousness as a desire "not to offend" (a motive). The advertising for a particular brand of deodorant may create a preference (a want) by promising "long lasting" protection as evidence of its superiority over alternative deodorant soaps, colognes, and other brands of deodorant. When this brand is purchased, demand has been created.

Key Issues Relating to Motivation

Two issues relating to the subject of motivation are of particular interest to marketers: the number

6. Psychologists tend to use the words "peripheral needs" or "instrumental needs" when referring to this motivational level.

FIGURE 8–1: Progression of a "Need for Safety" to the Purchase of a "Security Service"

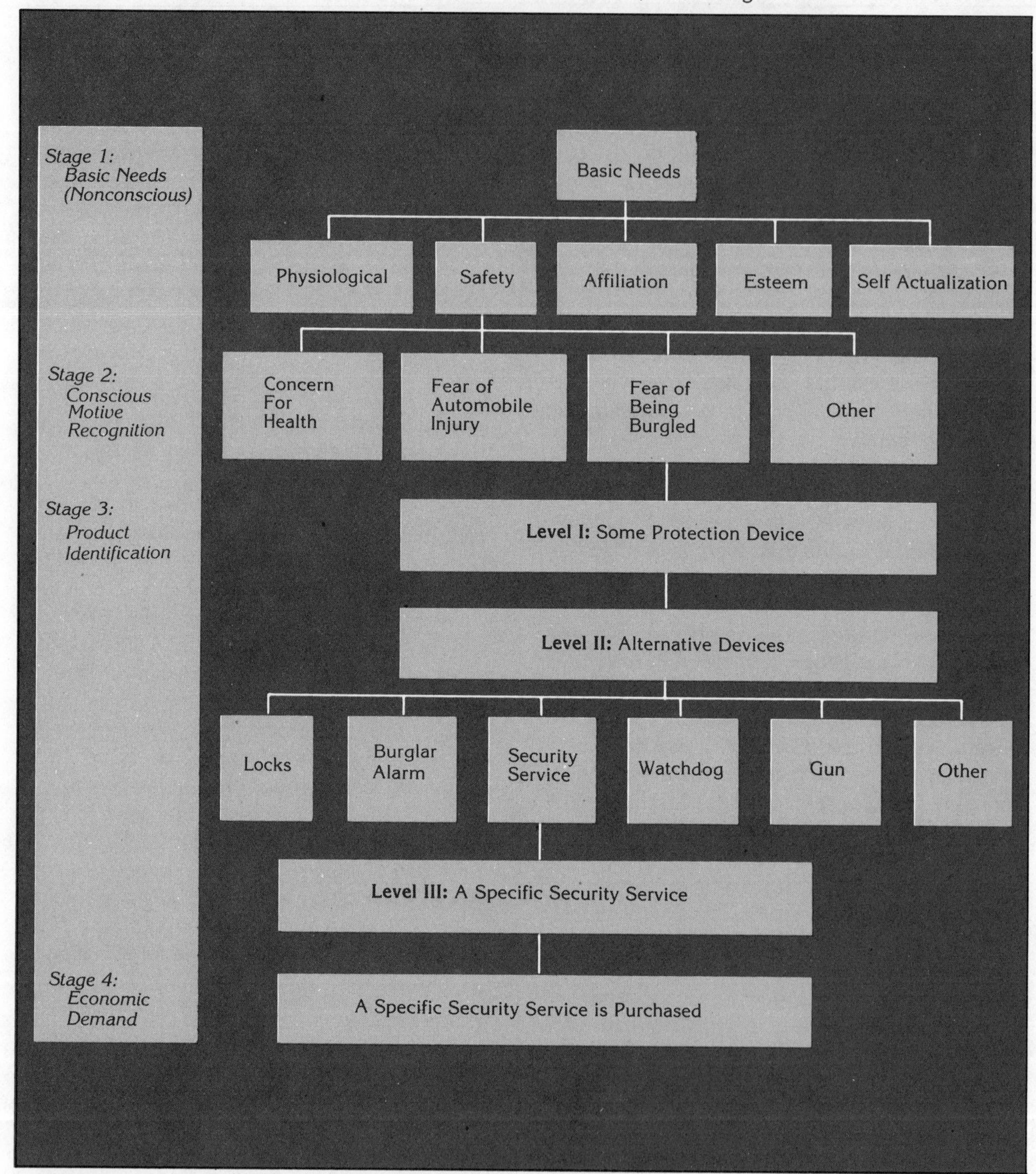

and nature of the basic needs, and the intensity of motivated behavior.

BASIC NEEDS. Earlier, we pointed out that there is no universal agreement upon, and no way of experimentally validating the precise number and nature of basic needs or need states. Different psychologists suggest different answers. One formulation, however, that has attracted a great deal of attention is that of Abraham Maslow. Maslow has described human beings as "wanting" animals, and has suggested that human needs are insatiable because, as quickly as one set of needs is satisfied, another set of needs arises.

Maslow postulates that human beings have a hierarchy of needs, and that lower level needs must be largely satisfied before needs higher in the hierarchy become salient. This hierarchy, arranged from lower to higher needs, is summarized below:

Physiological Needs. If the organism is to survive, physiological needs must be met. Essentially, these biological needs are hunger, thirst, waste elimination, and so forth.

Safety Needs. Included among the safety needs are security, protection, avoidance of pain, and order and structure in the environment.

Affiliation Needs. These are social needs. Human beings need warm and satisfying relationships with other people—needs for association and affection.

Esteem Needs. These are needs for recognition, self–respect, and esteem. There are two kinds of esteem needs: (1) needs for achievement, for personal adequacy in dealing with the environment and other people, for confidence, and for independence; and (2) needs for reputation, respect, attention, and appreciation.[7]

Self-Actualization Needs. These are needs for self–fulfillment. The need to become relatively independent from environmental demands, and to develop fully all abilities.

At a primitive level, where no needs are being met, physiological needs dominate human behavior. The other needs remain unrecognized until physiological needs are largely met. Once physiological needs have been largely satisfied, and no longer exert an influence on behavior, the next higher order needs, those of safety, emerge. At this level of need satisfaction, the safety needs become predominant and remain so until they are largely fulfilled. In order for needs at a higher level to emerge as motivating factors, those at lower levels must be largely satisfied.

When needs at a particular level are frustrated, or only partially satisfied, they persist as an influence on the individual's motivational patterns. Unfortunately, the circumstances of human existence often prevent the satisfaction of all lower–order needs, so that relatively few people ever become self–actualizers, although most of us engage in some self-actualizing behavior.

A key point in Maslow's theory is that *our needs are never satisfied*—at least as long as we are alive. As needs at a particular level in the hierarchy are satisfied, other higher order needs emerge to take their place. This answers the question of whether marketing creates needs. According to this theory, it does not. Diverse and emerging needs are a unique human experience. Marketing may, indeed, contribute to the creation of "wants" by portraying products as instrumentalities that can be used to satisfy basic needs. Since material products and services only partially satisfy most human need states, however, human motivational patterns are remarkably persistent.

A second implication of Maslow's theory is that, *in an affluent society such as the United States, lower order needs are largely met.* Accordingly, the higher order needs—those for affiliation, esteem, and self–actualization—should be prepotent. An examination of commercials and advertisements quickly shows the importance of higher-need levels in product design and in the motivational appeals. We seldom buy food *just* because we are hungry. Few of us are starving. We have many choices in what we eat, and even the most mundane food products are sold on the basis of a variety of social and personal appeals.

THE INTENSITY OF MOTIVATED BEHAVIOR. A second issue in motivation lies in the recognition that some motives require more energy to be expended in their service than others. We may spend a great deal of time and energy to satisfy some of our motives, while we devote relatively little time and effort to satisfy others. In addition, people will differ dramatically in the effort they will put forth to achieve what appears to be the same motive. For example, let us assume that two people of similar ability and means express desires to

7. Abraham Maslow, *Motivation and Personality,* 2nd. ed., (New York: Harper & Row, Publishers, 1970), pp. 35–36.

become medical doctors. One, through self-discipline, hard work, and long hours of study eventually is graduated as an M.D. The other, unwilling to make the personal sacrifices or put forth the effort required, drops out of the program. In comparing their behaviors, most people would agree that the student who completed the program was more highly motivated toward becoming a doctor than the one who did not.

In order to explain the differences in intensity that characterize motivated behavior, cognitive psychologists often invoke the concept of central and peripheral needs.

- *Central needs* are those needs closely related to our sense of identity and survival. In our definition of motivation they were termed basic need states, and include physiological needs, safety needs, affiliation needs, esteem needs, and self–actualization needs.
- *Peripheral needs,* sometimes referred to as *instrumental needs or wants,* consist of the preferences one has for alternative means of satisfying central needs.

For example, a minimum amount of liquid is required for survival (a central need). A variety of liquids will satisfy this minimal requirement—water, beer, tea, coffee, and fruit juices. The individual's preference order for each of these alternatives represents a personal order of instrumental needs or wants. If one liquid is not available, even though it is preferred, another will suffice.

Similarly, from a psychological standpoint, status may represent a central need. Status may be satisfied in a variety of ways—through money, housing, excellence in any variety of activities, becoming a member of a profession, holding office in an organization, and so forth. An individual's particular order of preference for these alternatives represents a hierarchy of peripheral needs and, if the preferred alternative is blocked, the next preferred is acceptable, although perhaps not as satisfying.

Normally, since peripheral needs represent alternative ways of satisfying central needs, specific peripheral needs tend to be less critical to the identity and survival of the individual than do central needs that have no alternatives. Occasionally, however, in a psychologically disturbed individual, the central-peripheral nature of the need structure breaks down, and normally perceived peripheral or instrumental needs assume the intensity of central needs. Such instances are always distressing, and sometimes lead to tragedy.

The distinction between central and peripheral needs is important in marketing. Central needs or need states tend to be absolute and not subject to substitute satisfactions. Thus, prestige is no substitute for food, and food is a poor substitute for prestige. Peripheral needs or wants, on the other hand, *are* subject to substitute satisfactions. Pork will serve the same function as beef in alleviating hunger and promoting the survival of the individual. And, athletic prowness and success in scholarship are alternative ways of gaining prestige.

For the normal person—and most of us are normal, or nearly so—commercial products and services are merely alternative ways of satisfying peripheral needs or wants. Many products and services are interchangeable in their ability to satisfy consumers' wants and desires. As a consequence, marketing activities—advertising, packaging, pricing, and sales promotion—can be effective devices in persuading consumers to purchase one product or brand rather than another.

The point is that a theory of motivation requires an energizing force that varies in intensity to validate the empirical observation that motives do, indeed, vary in strength. The exact nature of this energizing force is, however, uncertain. For some psychologists, affect (emotion) is the energizing factor.[8] Thus, needs of high centrality will be accompanied by strong emotional commitment, while peripheral needs are invested with less emotional content.

A Summary Note on Motivation

A survey of motivational theories and research permits us to draw certain generalizations about motivation that are relevant to marketing.

8. Bernard Weiner, *Theories of Motivation* (Chicago: Markham Publishing Company, 1972), pp. 173–74.

- Consumer behavior is purposeful, goal-directed activity.
- Basic consumer needs are diverse including physiological, safety, affiliation, esteem, and self-actualization needs—and perhaps others.
- Consumer needs are insatiable. As needs at one level are largely satisfied, higher order needs come into play. In addition, products and services may only partially satisfy basic human needs. As a consequence, these needs are never wholly satisfied, and continue to exert an influence on behavior.
- Needs vary in intensity, with the basic or central needs generally having a greater influence on behavior than instrumental or peripheral needs sometimes referred to as *wants* in the popular language.
- Since most products and services represent wants, many products and services are substitutable in their ability to satisfy human requirements. Thus, marketing activities can be used to persuade consumers to accept one product rather than another.
- In a relatively affluent society, such as the United States, the higher level needs—needs for affiliation, esteem, and self-actualization—tend to be prepotent. As a consequence, marketing appeals to these needs tend to be successful.
- Emotions (affect) are intimately involved in the concept of motivation, and emotional appeals often serve as cues for motivational arousal.

Throughout our discussion of motivation, we have emphasized the diversity of behavior which different individuals may express in the service of the same basic need. We have also noted that the same individual, under different environmental constraints, may exhibit different behaviors in the service of the same motive. One way of expressing these relationships is shown in Figure 8–2. Note that the central or basic needs are filtered through social-psychological variables, and that the emerging motivational patterns are surrounded by environmental constraints which also influence the specific behavior that occurs.

In the remainder of this chapter, we will briefly examine some of the major social-psychological variables that influence our motivational patterns. Along with motivation, these areas are the subject matter of texts on consumer behavior. Students interested in exploring some of these areas should refer to the library for any number of excellent texts on consumer behavior.

SOCIAL VARIABLES

Man is a social animal; the very notion of human behavior implies interaction with other people. Studies of feral children (children abandoned in infancy and adopted by infrahuman species) find that such children are virtually devoid of characteristics normally thought of as human.[9]

Thorstein Veblen, an economist of the early twentieth century, is generally credited as the originator of *social determination* in human behavior. Veblen questioned the Victorian economists' assumptions that behavior was primarily the result of economic forces. In *The Theory of the Leisure Class,* he theorized that much behavior is the consequence of social competition and emulation, and coined the term *conspicuous consumption* to describe the behavior of consumers. Veblen argued that we purchase products in order to enhance our social prestige, and turned attention to such things as culture, reference groups, and the family as prime determinants of consumption patterns. Taking their cue from Veblen's insights, during the past thirty years, marketing practitioners and theorists have turned their attention to such social variables as culture, social class, social groups, and the family as possible bases for segmenting markets and developing effective motivational appeals.

---

9. For discussions of feral children see: Joseph Amrito Singh, *Wolf Children and Feral Man* (Handen, CT: Archon Books, 1966), and Jean Claude Armen, *Gazelle-Boy,* translated by Stephen Hardmen (New York: University Books, 1974).

FIGURE 8–2: Graphic Representation of Central Needs Filtered Through Sociopsychological Variables and Environmental Constraints Before Emerging as Behavior

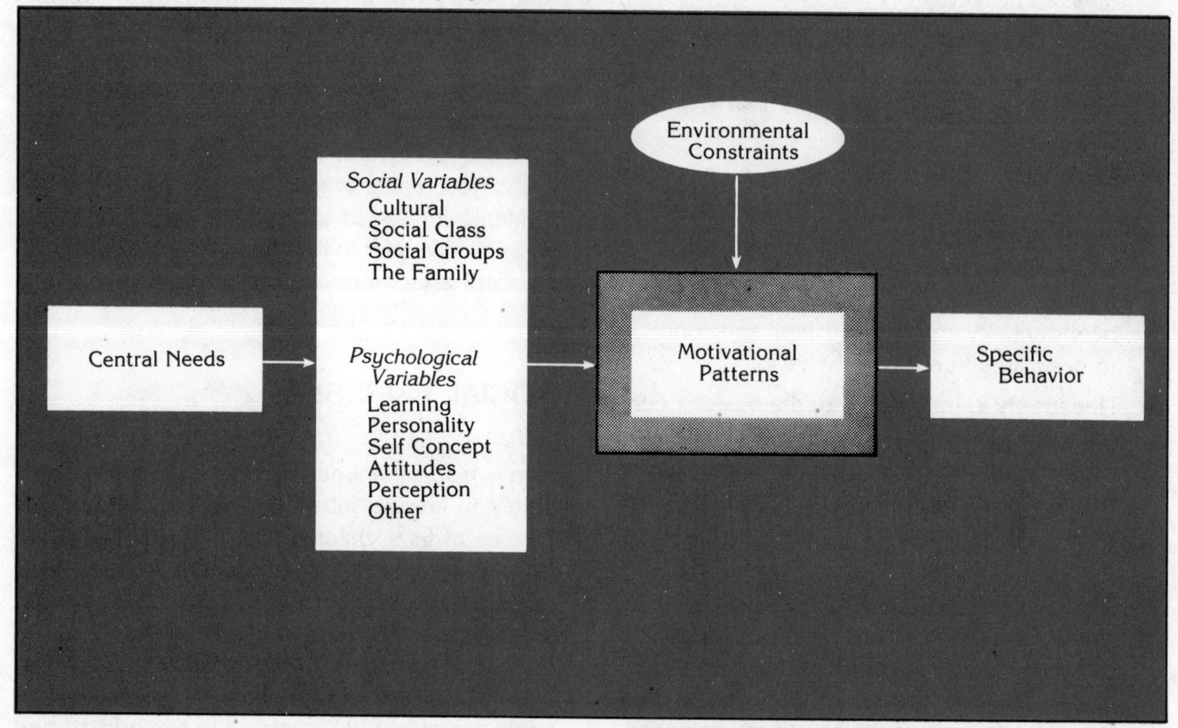

Culture

All of us are prisoners of our own culture. By this I mean that every individual lives in a society that prescribes certain broad patterns of behavior. These patterns extend to such diverse areas as sexual roles, dress, food habits, recreational activities, patterns of authority, status symbols, artifacts, attitudes, acceptable motivational patterns, the use of space, and the structure of language. Some of the differences between cultures are trivial. For example, in the United States, we play football and baseball. In England, one plays cricket and soccer. Some differences are profound. In the United States, for example, we worship individualism. In Russia, social cooperation is the dominant mode.

Normally, when marketing to the dominant U.S. culture, U.S. marketers have no problems; they simply do what comes naturally. But, the United States is becoming more pluralistic. Major ethnic groups are emerging whose values, language, and motivational patterns differ from those of the dominant U.S. culture. Some of these groups—such as blacks, Hispanics, Jews, and Indians—represent significant markets in certain regions of the country. These groups often require special marketing communications because of the danger that, unless care is taken to appeal to their value systems, they will be offended or even alienated. And, while marketing may need many things in order to achieve perfection, alienation of potential customers is not one of them.

This problem becomes even more acute when a United States based company markets products in a foreign country with more cultural differences than similarities. In these situations, beliefs and values appropriate in the United States may run aground on the reefs of cultural differences. Some of the problems of international marketing will be detailed in Chapter 20 on "International Marketing."

In the meantime, the solution to the problem is to utilize marketing research to gain an understanding of the values, decision–making processes, buying practices, marketing institutions, and motivations of the unfamiliar cultural groups. When marketing in a foreign country, "nationals" may be employed to provide guidance in marketing communications, and to help us understand local customs.

Social Class

All societies are structured or stratified into social groups. Such stratification arises because, many different societal functions must be performed in order for a society to survive; some functions are valued more highly than others and, as a consequence, accorded higher status. In a simple hunting society, where survival is dependent upon skill in slaying game, the hunters most proficient in this skill will be accorded higher status. In a society under constant threat from outside invasion, or dependent upon conquest for its survival and well–being, warriors and military leaders occupy status positions. And, in a theocracy, the priesthood emerges as a dominant and influential social group.

In a complex society, several status systems may exist. In the United States, for example, males have traditionally been accorded higher status than females—an attitude that has led to the equal rights movement. Adults are accorded higher status than children, a distinction often resented by the young. Successful people in all endeavors—business, the professions, art, politics, the theater, sports, and so on—are accorded higher status than those who are less successful. Another way of stratifying a complex society is social class.

Social class may be defined as *two or more orders of people who are perceived by members of society to occupy socially superior and socially inferior positions. Social classes differ in their values, interests, and motivational patterns, and members of a social class tend to marry within their own order. Unlike social castes, the values of society permit movement up and down the social ladder.*

In the United States, social class distinctions are usually based on occupation, source of income, house type, and dwelling area. A typical breakdown of social classes in the United States, along with a brief characterization of each, is shown:

- *Upper-upper class* (1.4 percent of the population). This is the cream of society. People within this group represent inherited wealth, and the key word is "inherited." They are confident of their position in society, and live comfortably with a sense of security and permanence.
- *Lower-upper class* (1.6 percent of the population). This group is sometimes referred to as the nouveau riche. They differ from the class above them in that, instead of inheriting their wealth, they have earned their fortunes themselves. They are "high achievers"—high income professional people, presidents of major corporations, and highly successful entrepreneurs. While they are not members of the socially elite, their children probably will be if they go to the right schools and marry wisely.
- *Upper-middle* (10 percent of the population). These are successful business people and professionals. They are active, striving people whose social status is dependent upon the husband's or wife's career. Should this career falter, they have few resources to fall back on. For this reason, they are security conscious, and are heavy buyers of health and life insurance.
- *Lower-middle* (29 percent of the population). Traditionally, this group has been known as "white–collar" workers—small tradespeople, office workers, civil service employees, technicians, teachers, and many salespeople. They tend to be home or church centered people, and their desire to see their children get college educations and good jobs are important values in their lives.
- *Upper-lower* (34 percent of the population). This is the largest of the social groups. Often referred to as the "working class" it consists largely of moderately skilled and semi-skilled workers. Members of this class are subject to the vaguaries of the job market, such as being laid off during times of recession. They tend to

be home and family centered, and to have short time horizons.

- *Lower-lower* (24 percent of the population). This class is at the bottom of the social heap. They are the unskilled workers, the chronically unemployed, and the disinherited of society. Their education is poor, their housing crowded, and their living relationships often communal, with more than one family living in the same quarters.[10]

Before examining the marketing implications of social class, two key points should be emphasized:

- *Social class is not based on income.* Although income tends to increase as one moves up the social ladder, the anomalies between classes are too widespread for income to be the differentiating variable. For example, a cross–country truck driver (upper–lower) will earn as much or more than a college professor (upper–middle). The junior executive with an MBA may earn no more than a skilled or semiskilled worker. No, the difference isn't income. It is life–style—the interests and values—and the ways in which income is spent.
- *The concept of social class is a descriptive concept, not an evaluative one.* There is no implication in the notion of social class that a member of an upper class is any better as a person than a member of a lower class. After all, St. Peter was lower class while Caligula, one of the most vicious and depraved of the Roman caesars, was upper class.

The primary focus for the marketing of mass consumer products in the United States is the lower-middle and upper-lower classes. Together, these two classes comprise approximately 60 to 70 percent of the U.S. population, and are referred to as the *middle majority.*

Social class has been found to be a discriminating variable for segmenting markets in the retail shopping field, leisure activities, savings and credit, and in media. Since social class is not a useful segmentation variable for all products, its value for a particular marketer must be decided on a product by product basis through the use of marketing research.

10. W. Lloyd Warner and P. S. Lunt, *The Social Life of the Modern Community,* Yankee City Series, Vol. 1 (New York: Harcourt Brace, Jovanovich, 1964), p. 460.

Social Groups

Social groups are the fundamental units of the social system. They are formed to promote survival, carry out work, achieve goals, provide solace and comfort, entertain, and relax their members. Much of our consumption occurs in groups; even products that are considered intensely personal are not immune to group influence. Thus, we buy toilet tissue color coordinated with the decor of our bathrooms in order to impress friends and neighbors with our exquisite taste. And, facial tissue is bought in decorated boxes that can be displayed in public areas in the home. No wonder groups play an important role in marketing!

Although groups may be defined and analyzed in many ways, the group that holds the greatest interest for marketers is the *reference group.* A reference group may be defined as *a group with which an individual wants to be associated and whose beliefs, attitudes, values and behaviors the individual will seek to emulate.* Sociologists generally speak of reference groups; we may also speak of a *reference person.* A reference person is an individual who serves as an ideal or model, and generally embodies admired salient group characteristics.

Many advertisers portray their products being used in group settings with which consumers can easily identify. Most soft drink advertising makes it difficult to tell whether the advertiser is selling soft drinks or "lovable people having fun." The same thing can be said of chewing gum advertising, beer advertising, and even bank advertising. Most bank advertisements, in fact, say little about the services of the bank, but emphasize the lovely social experience we will have if we do business with them.

Products such as breath fresheners, toothpaste which promises to whiten teeth, and deodorants are sold solely on social value. Women's cosmetics and men's shaving products and cologne carry a promise of romance which, by definition, is a social activity. And, let's face it, designer-label clothes—most of which are outrageously expensive—are purchased for their prestige value, not for their durability or skillful construction. Finally, the Johnnie Walker Black Label ad (Plate 8–1) says very little about the product, but a great deal about social prestige.

Along with the use of groups in advertising communications, is a widespread use of reference persons. Sports figures, television stars, and other celebrities grace both the airways and the newsstands; one of the benefits of winning a gold medal in the Olympics is the accompanying opportunity for profitable product endorsements. In a recent year, no less than sixty-four network television performers starred in commercials, either as spokespersons for, or endorsers of, a wide variety of products. Financial rewards to members of the Screen Actors Guild for appearing in television commercials exceed what they earn from television programs and movies combined. Reference figures are not restricted to television stars and celebrities. IBM, Cryovac, and others feature business leaders with whom potential customers can identify, and whose success they would love to emulate.

Some companies, such as General Mills, create their own reference persons. Created in 1921, Betty Crocker has reigned as "a sort of 'First Lady of Food,' the most highly esteemed home service authority in the nation and a real friend to millions of women."[11] Ann Pillsbury for Pillsbury Mills and Ann Page for A&P are other examples of corporate personalities created to communicate with consumers. And then, of course, there is Brother Dominick, one of the most wistful and appealing of them all (Plate 8–2). In summary, the power of social groups in influencing our motivational patterns and in selling products and services is too great for any marketer to ignore.

11. Julian L. Watkins, *The 100 Greatest Advertisements* (New York: Dover Publications, 1959), p. 205.

The Family

The family is a unique reference group that, perhaps more than any other, shapes the individual and influences decision patterns and purchase behaviors. Among young adults, for example, initial brand preferences are often simply continuations of family preferences. The family is unique because the relationships between family members are usually more intimate, the emotional attachments more intense, and the forces holding the group together stronger than in other groups. Shared consumption and joint decision making are characteristic of family living; the latter characteristic is particularly important in marketing.

In Chapter 6, the family life cycle was described as a demographic variable determining the products purchased at each stage of family development. Chapter 3 referred to the fact that often markets can be segmented by family decision processes. The point is that the family is an important consuming unit, and that knowledge of family consumption characteristics and decision patterns is a necessary precondition for successful marketing.

INTRAPERSONAL VARIABLES

Although human beings are inherently social, social variables do not account for all consumer behavior. Consumers are also individuals who express their individuality within the social context of society in a variety of ways. For an understanding of the intrapersonal variables that influence behavior, we must turn to the field of psychology.

Major areas of psychology include learning, personality, the self–concept, attitudes, and perception. Each area contains clues to guide the marketing practitioner in tapping motivational veins.

PLATE 8–2: *Xerox Ad*
SOURCE: *Fortune,* Sept 24, 1979

When you push a few buttons on a Xerox high-speed duplicator, a miracle occurs.

A multitude of complicated jobs are converted instantly into simple ones.

For example, you can get a Xerox duplicator that copies on both sides of a piece of paper, automatically.

That reduces, automatically. Collates, automatically.

Feeds and cycles up to 200 originals, automatically.

And even makes two-sided 8-1/2″ x 11″ copies from unburst computer printouts, automatically.

But of all the virtues of simplicity, the greatest is this:

It increaseth productivity.

Since Xerox duplicators are so easy to use, people can spend more time using them, and less time figuring out how. Anyone who can master the technology of pushing buttons can operate one of our duplicators.

So if you appreciate the virtues of simplicity, look into the virtues of a Xerox 9200 or 9400 duplicator.

We'll even arrange a simple demonstration at your convenience.

Just in case you don't accept miracles on faith alone.

XEROX

XEROX®, 9200® and 9400 are trademarks of XEROX CORPORATION.

Learning

Learning is central to understanding behavior, and to devising effective marketing communications. None of us is born with brand names and product attributes engraved on our central nervous system. Our knowledge of brands and their attributes is learned, and a major function of marketing communications is to facilitate learning. An examination of learning theories identifies certain principles useful in helping consumers learn. Four central principles are repetition, continuity, reinforcement, and meaning.

REPETITION. The principle of repetition—the repeated exposure of a product message or brand name—is widely used in almost all media scheduling and within the copy of advertisements. Conventional wisdom in the advertising industry holds that thirteen insertions a year—or every four weeks—in a magazine represents an optimal media schedule. Experiments have also demonstrated that thirteen exposures, four weeks apart, generate awareness among 48 percent of study participants by the end of the year. A higher awareness can be obtained by using the same number of exposures over a briefer period of time, although the duration of the learning effect is sharply reduced. Thus, one advertisement a week for thirteen weeks resulted in 63 percent awareness; however, the advertisement had been forgotten by the end of the year. Figure 8–3 is a graphic expression of these findings.

The use of repetition to register a product name within a single advertisement is demonstrated by the Colgate advertisement shown on Plate 8–3 (opposite page 180). The name Colgate appears fourteen times within the advertisement.

CONTIGUITY. Contiguity is most often achieved in marketing communications by associating a product with a pleasant or attractive situation through spatial or temporal proximity. Jewelry is displayed in attractive settings; trim manikins are used to display clothing to the best advantage; and selective distribution is often employed to associate quality products with prestige stores. Beer is shown being enjoyed in a happy social setting, such as a picnic, barbecue, or "night out with the boys"; food products are shown being enjoyed by happy and congenial families; dozens of products are associated with sex by placing attractive and often scantily clad models in the advertisement, even though their presence may have little or nothing to do with product use; and the Johnnie Walker Black Label ad shown in Plate 8–1 (opposite page 180) has no other purpose than to associate the product with the sweet smell of success.

REINFORCEMENT. Reinforcement or *reward* is the primary learning principle underlying operant conditioning, a leading learning theory. The underlying idea in operant conditioning is that people will engage in activities that are rewarding and avoid situations that are punishing. A wide range of rewards are promised or implied to those who use the product being marketed—instant romance, economic security, freedom from pain, good health, hedonistic pleasure, popularity, personal confidence, trouble-free service, monetary savings, and a host of others.

MEANING. The concept of meaning is a central pillar in cognitive learning theory. Cognitive theory views the individual as a *problem solver* who seeks the attainment of personal goals. Applied to marketing, cognitive theory emphasizes subjec-

FIGURE 8–3: *Weekly Percentage of Housewives who Could Remember Advertisements*
H. A. Zielske, "The Remembering and Forgetting of Advertising," Reprinted from *Journal of Marketing* 23 (January 1969): 239–43. Published by the American Marketing Association.

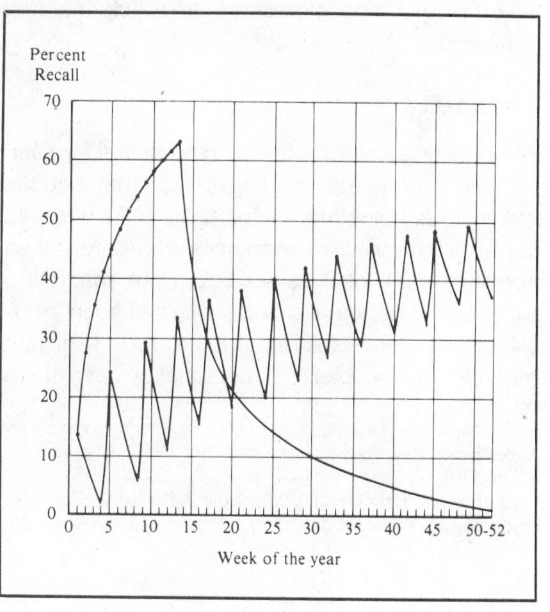

tive feelings and perceptions, and provides product information that will enable consumers to relate the marketer's product to themselves and to their goals: Fuel-efficient car makers emphasize how consumers can avoid high gasoline expenses. Insurance companies explain how their policies can provide a comfortable retirement. Steel-belted radial tire advertisements demonstrate how these tires can provide driving safety. Food recipes show housewives how they can please their families and guarantee domestic tranquility. And, the Joe Karbo advertisement (Plate 8–4) explains how easy it is to become a millionaire overnight—certainly a meaningful goal for millions of frustrated jobholders who enjoy spending money more than they enjoy working.

In all of these examples, the emphasis is on consumer goals—not on products. The product is only a means to an end much more precious in the eyes of consumers. Fundamentally, the ultimate key to unlocking the power of personal motivation is to find out what a person's goals are and to show how these goals can be achieved.

There are many other direct applications of learning theory to marketing communications. Mel Hatwick devotes three chapters of his book *How to Use Psychology for Better Advertising* to this topic,[12] and Steuart Henderson Britt describes twenty applications of learning theory to advertising communications in an article that first appeared in *Printer's Ink*.[13]

Personality

Personality is a word with which we are all familiar. We use it frequently in describing other people; many of us have taken personality tests. Despite our familiarity with the term *personality*, few of us normally think of it as an important marketing variable. Yet personality is a subject of keen interest among marketers. Not all attempts to segment markets on the basis of personality have been successful, but personality differences have been successfully exploited in the development of products and in the devising of appeals.

A classic case of market segmentation that seems to have its roots in personality differences exists in the market for mouthwashes and gargles. Listerine is a straw–colored, astringent, unpleasant tasting mouthwash advertised as the "taste you hate two times a day." Scope, by contrast, is deep green and pleasant tasting. Both products have the same function, with the only apparent differences being in taste and color. The Listerine user does not believe that a pleasant tasting mouthwash can be effective. The Scope user cannot understand why people would subject themselves to the taste of Listerine when better tasting alternatives are available. The differences in preferences seem to lie in the personalities of the users. Similar differences appear to apply to the proprietary medicine field where some consumers believe medicines must be ill-tasting and harsh to be effective, while others prefer a gentler approach to medication.

Ads for detergents, cosmetics, cigarettes, beer, alcoholic beverages, automobiles, clothing, and many other products often play on basic differences in the personalities of consumers in achieving acceptance. A number of advertising agencies use psychologists and psychoanalysts as consultants to help them develop advertising appeals. Earnest Dicter and his Institute for Research on Motivation gained both fame and fortune by identifying unconscious motives which are, by definition, hidden facets of the personality.

However, personality theory is not easy to use in marketing. Difficult to research, sometimes hard to translate into product features and promotional appeals, personality theory's history probably includes more failures than successes. Which is to say that personality, like many behavioral variables, should be used cautiously, and carefully tested through marketing research.

The Self–Concept

The self–concept or subjective self refers to the way in which individuals regard themselves. As a

12. Melvin S. Hatwick, *How to Use Psychology for Better Advertising* (New York: Prentice-Hall, Inc., 1950), Chapters 14, 15, and 16.

13. Steuart Henderson Britt, "How Advertising Can Use Psychology's Rules of Learning," *Printer's Ink* (Sept. 23, 1955): 77 ff.

PLATE 8–4: *Joe Karobo Ad*
SOURCE: *Time,* March 10, 1980.

Too Busy Earning a Living To Make Any Money?

You think you've got problems?

Well, I remember when a bank turned me down for a $200 loan. Now I lend money to the bank — Certificates of Deposit at $100,000 a crack.

I remember the day a car dealer got a little nervous because I was a couple of months behind in my payments — and repossessed my car. Now I own a Rolls Royce. I paid $43,000 for it — cash.

I remember the day my wife phoned me, crying, because the landlord had shown up at the house, demanding his rent — and we didn't have the money to pay it.

Now we own five homes. Two are on the oceanfront in California (I use one as my office). One is a lakefront "cabin" in Washington, (that's where we spend the whole summer — loafing, fishing, swimming, and sailing.) One is a condominium on a sunny beach in Mexico. And one is snuggled right on the best beach of the best island in Hawaii — Maui.

Right now I could sell all this property, pay off the mortgages, — and — without touching any of my other investments — walk away with over $750,000 in cash. But I don't want to sell, because I don't think of my homes as "investments." I've got other real estate — and stocks, bonds, and cash in the bank — for that.

I remember when I lost my job. Because I was head over heels in debt, my lawyer told me the only thing I could do was declare bankruptcy. He was wrong. I paid off every dime.

Now, I have a million dollar line of credit; but I still don't have a job. Instead, I get up every weekday morning and decide whether I want to go to work or not. Sometimes I do — for 5 or 6 hours. But about half the time, I decide to read, go for a walk, sail my boat, swim, or ride my bike.

I know what it's like to be broke. And I know what it's like to have everything you want. And I know that you — like me — can *decide* which one it's going to be. It's really as easy as that. That's why I call it "The Lazy Man's Way to Riches."

So I'm going to ask you to send me something I don't need: money. Ten dollars to be exact. Why? Because I want you to pay attention. And I figure that if you've got $10 invested, you'll look over what I send you and decide whether to send it back...or keep it. And I don't *want* you to keep it unless you agree that it's worth at least a hundred times what you invested.

Is the material "worth" $10? No — if you think of it as paper and ink. But that's not what I'm selling. What I am selling is information. *More* information than I give when I'm paid $1000 as a guest speaker. *More* information than I give in a one-hour consultation for $300.

But you're really not risking *anything*. Because I won't cash your check or money order for 31 days *after* I've sent you my material. That's the deal. Return it in 31 days — and I'll send back your check or money order — uncashed.

How do you know I'll do it? Well, if you really want to be on the safe side, post-date your check for a month from today — *plus 2 additional weeks.* That'll give you plenty of time to receive it, look it over, try it out.

I know what you're thinking: "He got rich telling people how to get rich." The truth is — and this is very important — the year before I shared "The Lazy Man's Way to Riches," my net income was $216,646. And what I'll send you tells just how I made that kind of money...working a few hours a day...about 8 months out of the year.

It doesn't require "education." I'm a high school graduate.

It doesn't require "capital." Remember I was up to my neck in debt when I started.

It doesn't require "luck." I've had more than my share. But I'm not promising you that you'll make as much money as I have. And you may do better. I personally know one man who used these principles, worked hard, and made 11 million dollars in 8 years. But money isn't everything.

It doesn't require "talent." Just enough brains to know what to look for. And I'll tell you that.

It doesn't require "youth." One woman I worked with is over 70. She's travelled the world over, making all the money she needs, doing only what I taught her.

It doesn't require "experience." A widow in Chicago has been averaging $25,000 a year for the past 5 years, using my methods.

What does it require? Belief. Enough to take a chance. Enough to absorb what I'll send you. Enough to put the principles into *action.* If you do just that — nothing more, nothing less — the results will be hard to believe. Remember — I guarantee it.

You don't have to give up your job. But you may soon be making so much money that you'll be able to. Once again — I guarantee it.

I know you're skeptical. Well, here are some comments from other people. (Initials have been used to protect the writer's privacy. The originals are in my files.) I'm sure that, like you, these people didn't believe me either when they clipped the coupon. Guess they figured that, since I wasn't going to deposit their check for at least 31 days, they had nothing to lose.

They were right.

And here's what they gained:

'Wow, it does work!'
"Oddly enough, I purchased Lazy Man's Way to Riches some six months ago, or so, read it..and really did nothing about it. Then, about three weeks ago, when I was really getting desperate about my financial situation, I remembered it, re-read it, studied it, and this time, put it to work and WOW, it does work! Doesn't take much time, either...I guess some of us just have to be at a severe point of desperation before we overcome the ultimate laziness, procrastination."
Mr. J.K., Anaheim, CA

'Made $50,000 just fooling around'
"In February 1974 you sent me (for ten bucks) your Lazy Man's Way to Riches. Since then I have made approximately 50 grand ($50,000) just fooling around on the basis of your advice. You see, I really am lazy — otherwise I could have made 50 million! Thank you!"
Mr. R. McK., Atlanta, GA

'$24,000 in 45 days'
"...received $24,000.00 in the mail the last 45 days. "Thanks again."
Mr. E.G.N., Matewan, W.VA

Made $70,000
"A $70,000 thanks to you for writing The Lazy Man's Way to Riches. That's how much I've made...
"I use this extra income for all of the good things in life, exotic vacations, classic automobiles, etc. Soon I hope to make enough to quit my regular job and devote full time to making money the easy way..."
Mr. D.R., Newport Beach, CA

$260,000 in eleven months
"Two years ago, I mailed you ten dollars in sheer desperation for a better life...One year ago, just out of the blue sky, a man called and offered me a partnership...I grossed over $260,000 cash business in eleven months. You are a God sent miracle to me."
B.F., Pascagoula, Miss.

'There's no stopping me'
"Since I've got your (Lazy Man's Way to Riches) in July, I've started 4 companies...there's no stopping me and I'm so high I need chains to keep me on the ground."
M.T. Portland, OR

What I'm saying is probably contrary to what you've heard from your friends, your family, your teachers, and maybe everyone else you know.

I can only ask you one question.

How many of them are millionaires?

So it's up to you.

A month from today, you can be nothing more than 30 days older — or you can be on your way to getting rich. You decide.

The wisest man I ever knew told me something I never forgot: "Most people are too busy earning a living to make any money."

Don't take as long as I did to find out he was right.

I'll prove it to you, if you'll send in the coupon now. I'm not asking you to "believe" me. Just try it. If I'm wrong, all you've lost is a couple of minutes and a postage stamp. But what if I'm right?

©Joe Karbo - 1979, 17105 South Pacific, Sunset Beach, Calif. 90742

PROOF!
Don't take my word for it. These are excerpts from articles in newspapers and magazines:

Time:
He only works half the year in his stunning office on California's Sunset Beach, and even when he's there he puts in short hours...In other words, Joe Karbo, 48, is the prototype for..."The Lazy Man's Way to Riches."

Seattle Times:
Is it all honest? A man who has done business with him says Karbo's reputation is excellent, and that he has managed to conduct mutually beneficial deals with him with nothing but a handshake and an oral agreement.
Want to be rich? Take my advice and follow his.

Boston Herald-American:
The book has drawn hundreds of letters from persons who have profited by it...

Los Angeles Herald-Examiner:
An unpretentious millionaire, Joe Karbo of Huntington Harbor is a vibrant, living testimonial to his intellectual, pragmatic conviction.

Forbes:
After bouncing around show biz, advertising, and real estate, he made his fortune...Last year (1972) he made $250,000.

Money Making Opportunities:
Maybe Joe Karbo has the secret. Don't you think you owe it to yourself to find out what it is all about?...I just finished it — and I'm off on a vacation myself. Get the idea?

The Boston Globe:
Jay Haws of Chico, Cal. said the pep talk...in "The Lazy Man's Way to Riches" has "changed my life," and upped his freelance graphic designer income from $2000 to $30,000 annually.
"I'm not rich yet," said Haws, "but I see the light at the end of the tunnel...It gave me the swift kick in the pants that I needed."

Long Beach Independent:
He's programmed the path to riches for the lazy man.

Sworn Statement:
"On the basis of my professional relationship as his accountant, I certify that Mr. Karbo's net worth is more than one million dollars."
Stuart A. Cogan

Bank Reference:
Home Bank
17010 Magnolia Avenue
Fountain Valley,
CA 92708

Joe Karbo
17105 South Pacific, Dept. 437-B
Sunset Beach, California 90742

Joe, you may be full of beans, but what have I got to lose? Send me the Lazy Man's Way to Riches. *But don't deposit my check or money order for at least 31 days after it's in the mail.*

If I return your material — for *any* reason — within that time, return my *uncashed* check or money order to me. On that basis, here's my ten dollars.

Name ____________________
(Please Print Clearly)
Address ____________________
City ____________________
State __________ Zip __________

SORRY — NO COD'S

behavioral concept, it is narrower than the concept of personality dealing only with conscious perceptions of what we believe about ourselves, and not with the unconscious facets of behavior that play a significant role in psychoanalytic psychologies. As a consequence, many psychologists deride the self–concept as being too limited in scope to explain behavior. Nonetheless, leading self–concept theorists believe that one cannot understand and predict behavior without a recognition of how individuals perceive themselves in their environments.

All of us have self–concepts. We may think of ourselves as attractive or unattractive, as socially skilled or socially inept, as extravagant or penurious, as being capable in some areas and incapable in others. Some individuals have an exceedingly high opinion of themselves, and others an extremely low opinion. In extreme cases, these high or low opinions are psychopathic and described as manic-depressive psychosis.

The self–concept includes individuals' attitudes, feelings, perceptions, and evaluations of themselves. This learned response arises over a period of time from our experiences in social situations and from other peoples' reactions to us and to our behavior. Once formed, however, the self–concept influences the ways in which we behave, and the products which we buy. This is why the self–concept should be of interest to marketers. We tend to buy products that reflect our self–images, and avoid products which contradict them. One marketing writer has noted: "A consumer may buy a product because, among other factors, he feels the product enhances his own self image. Similarly, a consumer may decide not to buy a product or shop at a particular store if he feels that these actions are not consistent with his own perceptions of himself."[14]

All of us are aware that we use possessions as a way of making statements about ourselves. The teenager who smokes cigarettes or drinks alcoholic beverages is using these products to say, "I'm an adult." The adult who drives a Cadillac or Lincoln Continental is telling others that he is important. And the host and hostess who serve imported wine are exhibiting their discriminating tastes to their guests. The teenager who insists on the particular brand of blue jeans or tennis shoes worn by the peer group, or who dresses as other members of the group do, or who buys records and other products that conform to group tastes is saying, in effect, "See, I'm just like you. You can tell by the clothes I wear and the products I use."

This is not to say that all consumption is determined by the self–images that consumers hold. Self–concepts do exist, and may influence many consumer purchases, particularly for those products that have high visibility and are primarily consumed in social settings.

Attitudes

Thus far, we have dealt with a variety of variables that exert an influence on consumer behavior. We have identified social factors such as culture, social class, groups, and the family. We have recognized intrapersonal variables such as learning, personality, and the self–concept. Although all of these variables may exert an influence on behavior, the psychological mechanism through which they operate has not been specified. One useful approach is to consider the concept of attitude as this mechanism. From this point of view, the net effect of social and intrapersonal variables is to create a structure of attitudes that ultimately govern behavior.

Attitudes may be defined as predispositions to respond in a consistently favorable or unfavorable manner in respect to a given object.[15] In the context of marketing, the goal of marketing communications is to affect attitudes, thereby creating a predisposition to purchase a particular product or service. For this reason, the measurement of attitudes toward products is a multimillion dollar business, and changing attitudes is a major preoccupation of the marketing industry.

14. Steuart H. Britt, *Consumer Behavior and the Behavior Sciences: Theories and Applications* (New York: John Wiley & Sons, Inc., 1966), p. 186.

15. Martin Fishbein and Icek Ajzen, *Belief, Attitude, Intention and Behavior* (Reading, MA: Addison–Wesley Publishing Company, 1975), p. 6.

Traditionally, attitudes have been perceived as having three components: *cognitions,* or what we know about an attitude object; *affect,* or what we feel about the object; and *behavior,* or a predisposition to behave in a particular way toward the attitude object. Further, these three components tend to be consistent with one another. For example, if we have a favorable feeling toward a brand, we generally believe favorable things about it, and are inclined to purchase it.

Since these three components tend to be consistent, if we can change one of them, the others will tend to shift in the same direction. Thus, if we can change an individual's emotional response toward a brand from negative or neutral to positive, she may start perceiving the brand differently and be persuaded to purchase it. Or, if we can provide favorable information about a brand, thereby changing beliefs about it, there will be a tendency for feelings to change, and the probability of purchase is increased. Finally, if we can change behavior, that is, induce a consumer to use a product she has not previously used, then both the feelings toward the brand and her knowledge about it will also change.

These three strategies—changing feelings through emotional appeals, changing knowledge or beliefs by providing information, and changing behavior by inducing trial—are the primary strategies used by marketers to change attitudes. Generally, the more of these variables we can affect, the greater will be the probability of attitude change. For this reason, most marketers use a combination of strategies.

Automobile marketers, for example, use informational advertising and brochures to change beliefs, emotional advertising to change feelings, and demonstration rides to change behavior. Further, the major automobile companies compete vigorously to sell their cars to Hertz, Avis, National, and other car rental firms because these firms give potential customers a chance to drive their brands. Marketers of other products use similar strategies.

In summary, attitudes are a primary variable in consumer behavior, and marketers who want to stay in business are well counseled to give proper attention to this variable.

Perception

The ways in which people behave depend upon how they perceive the world around them. For this reason, many psychologists believe that an understanding of behavior requires an understanding of perception. Perception begins with the stimulation of the sense receptors—eyes, ears, nose, skin, tongue, and kinesthetic receptors—by a pattern of energy. Each receptor transforms this energy into neural impulses that are received by the central nervous system. There, the impulse is modified and elaborated to create a meaningful experience.

Note that incoming stimuli are not passively received by the organism. Rather, these stimuli are organized, interpreted, and given meaning. Thus, perception may be defined as *a process through which incoming stimuli are given meaning,* or *the process through which we make sense of the world.*

The role of marketing communications is to help consumers perceive particular products in desired ways. We do this by surrounding a product or brand with *cues* that identify it and give the product a desired character. Words, colors, shapes, sounds, odors, weight, and other symbols are some of the cues we use: Pictures facilitate product recognition, as do distinctive packaging, and easy to recognize, distinctive names. Pastel colors are used to appeal to women; dark colors attract the attention of men. Table settings draw attention to food, and children in the background symbolize a family situation.

The cues we use in advertising communications are designed to work together; to point in the same direction, as it were. When, through oversight or ignorance, we use incompatible cues, consumer confusion and uncertainty may result. Note the ways in which the headline, the illustration, the body copy, the package, the room furnishings, the family setting, the clothing worn by the models, the wood-burning fireplace, the old–fashioned coffee-grinder, and the solid homey coffee cups work together in the advertisement for Mellow Roast coffee and grain beverage (Plate 8–5, opposite page 468).

This advertisement creates a warm, informal, nostalgic vision of traditional American values wholly compatible with the name Mellow Roast, and with the fact that it is a blend of coffee and grain. The use of warm browns, the wood tones, and the richness of the coffee complimented by the yellow sweater worn by the woman, the gold in her hair, and reds and yellows in the blazing fire say "Mellow Roast."

CONSUMER BEHAVIOR AND MARKETING

No one of the variables discussed in this chapter holds the magic key to motivating consumers. There is no such key. One product may be primarily subject to group influences. Another may be more closely tied to personality, or to the self-concept. Learning, attitudes, and perception are also important variables in influencing consumers. Most generally, consumers are acted upon by a number of variables simultaneously, and the marketer must tease out those that are the most significant.

Human behavior is complex, and consumer behavior is no simpler. There are no easy answers or short cuts. Knowledge, analysis, sensitivity, intuition, and plain hard work are all ingredients in successful marketing. But, marketing does involve consumer behavior, and an appreciation of the complexity of consumer behavior implies recognition that not all consumers see the world as we do, nor are they necessarily motivated by the same things that inspire us.

SUMMARY

Marketing is rooted in consumer behavior; in the past thirty years, marketers have turned to the social sciences in order to gain a better understanding of why people behave as they do, and what product appeals will be most effective in moving consumers to buy their brands. Each manufacturer, through product design, packaging, pricing, advertising, and other communication variables attempts to motivate consumers. As a consequence, motivation is a buzz-word in marketing, and consumer behavior is a subject of intense interest.

Motivation may be defined as a theoretical construct involving an internal need state that gives impetus to behavior, and a directional component that gives general direction to a variety of responses serving the same function for the organism. The conversion of motivation from internal need states to economic demand occurs in four stages: (1) internal need states, which are unconscious; (2) need recognition, wherein need states appear in consciousness as an identifiable idea; (3) product or object identification as a possible solution to the need that has been recognized; and (4) economic demand, which exists when a product or service is purchased in order to satisfy a conscious need.

The particular form that need recognition takes depends upon the psychophysiological history of the individual and environmental forces. Further, a number of social-psychological variables influence motivational patterns. Of particular interest to marketers are: social variables, such as culture, social class, social groups, and the family; and intrapersonal variables such as learning, personality, the self-concept, attitudes, and perception.

No one of these variables holds the magic key to motivating consumers. One product may be primarily subject to group influence; another may be more closely tied to personality or the self-concept. Most generally, consumers are acted upon by a number of variables simultaneously, and the marketer must tease out those that are most significant.

1. Explain what is meant by the statement that motivation is a theoretical construct.
2. Identify and explain the stages through which internal need states are transformed into the concept of economic demand. Demonstrate this process by an example.
3. Identify and explain Maslow's hierarchy of needs.
4. What are the two major implications of Maslow's theory of motivation for marketing?
5. Distinguish between central and peripheral needs. What is the relevance of this distinction insofar as products and services are concerned?
6. Why is an understanding of culture important for marketing practitioners?
7. Explain what is meant by "reference groups" and "reference persons." How are these concepts used in marketing?
8. Identify the major learning principles used in marketing, giving examples of how each is used.
9. Explain what is meant by the self–concept. Why is this concept important to marketing?
10. Explain the strategies marketers use in attempting to change attitudes. What is the thinking upon which these strategies is based?

1. Assume that the need for esteem is an internal need state. Using the stages of motivational development described in the text, explain how this need might manifest itself in the acquisition of a medical degree by one person, the purchase of a Cadillac by another, a subscription to the *New Yorker* magazine by a third, and the purchase of a guitar by a fourth.
2. According to the text, marketing does not create needs. Do you agree with this point of view? Why or why not?
3. In the United States culture, a great deal of emphasis is placed on economic success. Discuss whether or not economic success is a basic need. If you conclude that it is not, why do people commit crimes and risk imprisonment in order to obtain money?
4. Thorstein Veblen argued that we purchase products in order to enhance our social prestige. Do you agree with this point of view? Why or why not? Identify five product fields in which brands might be purchased for this purpose. Now, identify five product fields in which social influence plays no part in brand preference.
5. Do you agree that social classes exist in the United States? Develop an argument in defense of your point of view.

BEHAVIORAL DIMENSIONS OF CONSUMERS

Motivating consumers is a basic objective of marketing. Marketers use a variety of appeals to sell products that serve essentially the same function. Motorcycles, for example, might be sold on the basis of economy, excitement, adventure, freedom, power, safety, independence, and so forth.

In this chapter, references are made to Maslow's hierarchy of needs. According to Maslow, human beings have five basic needs—physiological needs, safety needs, affiliation needs, esteem needs, and self-actualization needs.

Assignment

Select an advertisement from a current magazine. Good magazines for finding ads for a variety of products are Good Housekeeping, Woman's Day, Family Circle, Sunset, Better Homes and Gardens, Redbook, Cosmopolitan, *and* Glamour. *Analyze the advertisement in terms of (1) the basic function that the product type fulfills; (2) the primary motivational appeal used in the advertisement; (3) secondary motivational appeals that are employed. Then, classify the motivational appeals being used in terms of Maslow's hierarchy of needs.*

9

Marketing Research and Test Marketing

- *Marketing information system.*
- *Analysis of internal records.*
- *Scope of marketing research.*
- *Barriers to marketing research.*
- *Distinction between primary and secondary research.*
- *Basic sources of secondary research.*
- *Major techniques in primary research.*
- *How to plan primary research projects.*
- *Basic considerations in planning test markets.*

MARKETING EXAMPLES

THE PRODUCT THAT ALMOST WASN'T

Today, semimoist dog foods represent an established segment of the dog food market with sales of over $300 million. Yet, without marketing research, the entire product category might have died aborning.

The first semimoist product introduced to consumer markets was Gaines·burgers, a new form of dog food that looked like a raw hamburger patty. The product concept was based on research findings that many consumers believed dogs needed meat—or at least something that looked like meat. The product name was an inspiration, echoing consumers' perceptions of the product's appearance. Feeding tests had indicated the new product was highly palatable, the packaging was well designed to show the product in its best light, and the introductory advertising played heavily on the theme of hamburgers—a product as hallowed as mother, apple pie, and the U.S. flag in our culture. Yet, Gaines·burgers performed poorly in test markets. Volume projections were not met, and Gaines·burgers appeared to be a prime candidate for the almost endless list of new product failures.

General Foods, however, had a long tradition of marketing research, and the profit potential of the dog food market was too great to be discarded lightly. Extensive marketing research had accompanied the test market effort. Analysis of this research found the root of the problem.

Consumer surveys revealed three telling points: 1) although large numbers of consumers purchased Gaines·burgers, they purchased it infrequently; 2) Gaines·burgers was not being used by dog owners as a full-course dinner for their pets, but as a dog treat; and 3) the hamburger analogy used in the advertising conjured up visions in consumers' minds of a snack item, not of a food staple.

Using this information, a second round of test markets was planned. The advertising was modified to emphasize the full nutrition character of the product, and to clearly portray Gaines·burgers as a complete meal, not a snack. The new test markets were successful;

Gaines-burgers became the prototype for a new category of pet foods; and dozens of competitors, less innovative than General Foods, rushed similar products to the marketplace.

DIMINISHING RETURNS

While I was a research director of an advertising agency, the agency was approached by a regional soft drink manufacturer in the second year of an expansion program. Both the president of the company and its sales manager were devoting the bulk of their time to recruiting new bottlers in major cities throughout the United States. Their results were impressive: sales had tripled and the company's future appeared rosy. Although pleased with their progress, company management believed that even more progress could be made with a more dramatic and persuasive advertising program.

The agency was invited to make a presentation showing how it would handle the account, with particular emphasis on a strong advertising theme. In preparing for the presentation, the agency asked for a month—by—month record of sales by bottler. This information was turned over to the agency's research department for analysis. The results of the analysis were unpleasant, but revealing.

Sales analysis indicated that the entire growth in sales was being sustained by the rapid rate at which new markets were being added. Sales in established markets were declining and, the older the markets, the greater the sales decline. As a result of these findings, the agency recommended that further expansion be delayed, and proposed a program of marketing research to identify the nature of the problem. This wasn't what the company management wanted to hear, and the agency did not get the account.

A year or so later, the company was in deep trouble. Losing bottlers faster than it could appoint new ones, sales began to decline. Company refusal to face reality, and to use marketing research as an integral part of its marketing program, prevented diagnosis of its problems and corrective action.

FIGURE 9–1: Overview of the Marketing Information System
SOURCE: Larry J. Rosenberg, *Marketing,* © 1977, p. 549. Reprinted by permission of Prentice-Hall, Inc. Englewood Cliffs, New Jersey.

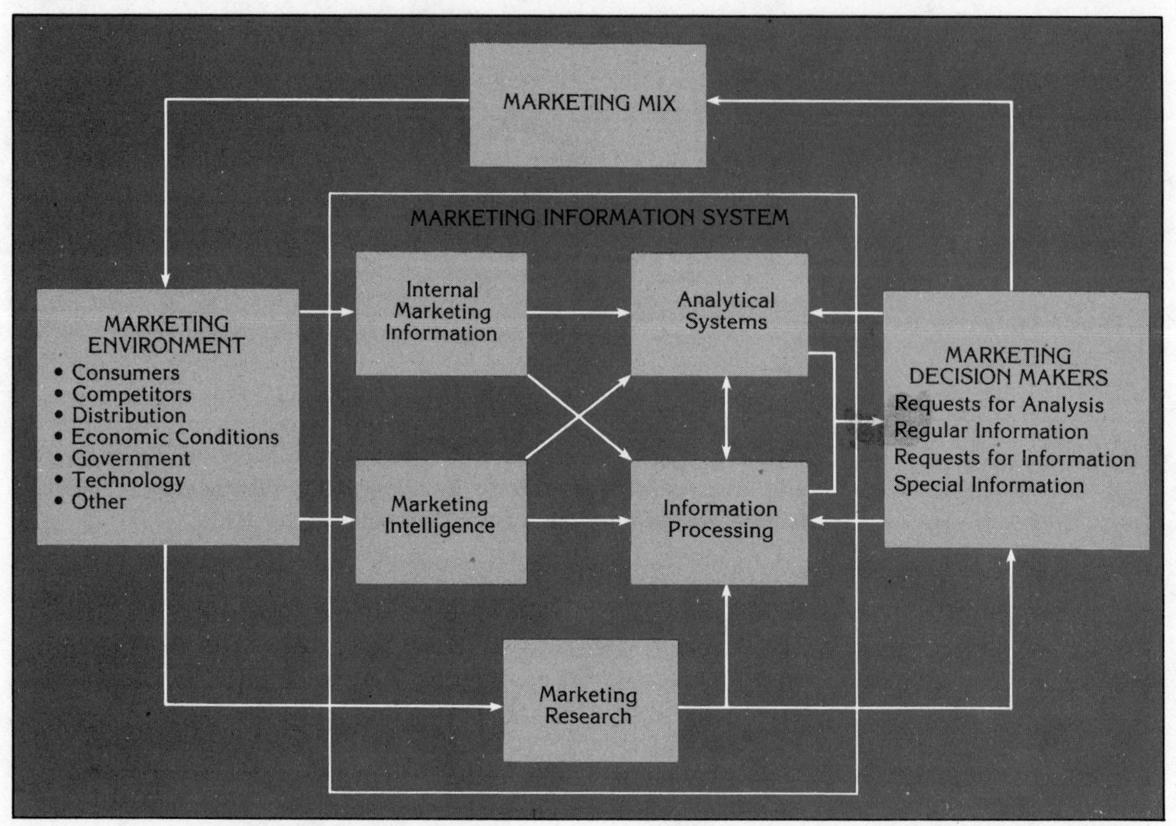

The point of these two examples from the real world is that marketing research is the lifeblood of modern marketing. With marketing research, marketing managers can make decisions. Without it, they can only make unconfirmed guesses. A marketing program based on unconfirmed guesses is a disaster looking for a place to happen.

This chapter will be devoted primarily to marketing research and to test marketing, a specialized form of marketing research widely used by marketing practitioners. Of course, marketing research is not the only form of marketing information used by businesses. To place marketing research in its proper perspective, we should look briefly at the concept of a marketing information system.

THE MARKETING INFORMATION SYSTEM

The purpose of the marketing information system is to gather, process, analyze, and disseminate information that will be of *value* to marketing executives in developing products, in preparing marketing plans, in assessing the various elements of the marketing mix, and in evaluating product performance.

The key word in the foregoing description is *value.* Information which is of no value—and the world is full of valueless information—must be weeded out and discarded for the marketing information system to serve its purpose. Distinguishing between useful and useless information requires a systematic approach, analytical skill, judgment, practice, and a sense of relevance. That is, a clear understanding of marketing objectives and the ways in which marketing information can be helpful.

Generally, marketing information emanates from three subsystems or sources: internal records, marketing intelligence, and marketing research. Data from these sources must be processed or organized in some way, analyzed, and made available to appropriate company executives. Figure 9–1 shows the interrelationships that should exist between the marketing environment, sources of marketing data, processing, analysis, and marketing decision makers.

Companies differ widely in the sophistication of the marketing information systems they use. In some companies, the structure of the system and its procedures for coordinating and transmitting data are so primitive that they are of little value. In still other companies—generally the larger ones—the marketing information system is a well–designed, well–integrated process that makes use of computer technology for information storage and retrieval. For example, some of the major companies in the floor-covering industry have on-line computer tie-ins with major dealers to provide daily reports on how various patterns are selling. General Electric bases its daily production schedule of major appliance models on end-of-day reports from its distributors. And a number of major companies use computers to summarize and compare periodic data received from commercial research services such as A. C. Nielsen.[1] These systems employ performance criteria which "red flag" or call attention to unusual or systematic variances between reporting periods. For example, if the market share in a particular geographic area or store type changes more than five percentage points in a single period, it is red-flagged for attention. Or, a consistent series of smaller share losses (or gains) over three consecutive reporting periods will be red-flagged, as well as significant changes in channel inventories or average retail price.

"I don't know why I need a college education to check prices.". (Photo courtesy of The Kroger Company)

No marketing information system, however, is perfect. Even in the best designed systems, critical information may be overlooked, lost, interpreted incorrectly, or transmitted too late or to the wrong people. No system—no matter how well designed—is any better than the people who oversee it and, as pointed out in Chapter 1, good people are in short supply. Let's turn now to the sources of marketing information.

Internal Records.

Internal records can provide marketing executives with an almost endless array of information on sales, costs, inventories, customers, and cash flow. Marketing executives are particularly interested in sales and profits, broken down by individual products, geographic regions, customers, and sales representatives. Most of this information is available from current accounting records, which must be reorganized and interpreted to be of value to marketing executives. Typical information obtainable from internal records includes:

- *Sales.* Sales may be summarized by customer type and size, individual product and product

1. The A. C. Nielsen Company conducts bimonthly audits in samples of drug and food stores. For each reporting period, the company summarizes information on sales, share, price, inventories, and sales promotion activity for subscribers' products and for their competition.

line, geographic area, salesperson, size of order, and method of payment.

- *Customer.* Information may be obtained on individual customers in terms of order size and frequency as well as promptness in paying bills. This last bit of information is often useful in determining cash flow requirements and in evaluating credit risks.
- *Inventories.* Information on the size of product inventories and in total is available from company records. This information is particularly useful in planning promotions and/or determining whether sufficient inventories are on hand to meet planned promotional activity or known seasonal variations in sales.
- *Costs.* Functional costs by product, by customer, and by sales activity can be analyzed in a variety of ways to assess profitability.
- *Profit and variation from plan.* Finally, internal data provide a running record of profitability by product and by customer, as well as comparisons between actual and planned performance.

The monthly operating statement (profit and loss statement), a routine production of the accounting department, is often the central control document employed in assessing the performance of company products. A simplified operating statement is shown in Table 9–1. Note that, at a glance, one can tell whether a product is profitable for the period covered, where favorable and unfavorable variances from plan are occurring, and possible problem areas that may exist.

In Table 9–1, for example, note that an unfavorable variance in the cost of raw materials has reduced the planned profit. This observation should trigger an inquiry into the cause of the unfavorable variance to determine whether it is a short-term aberration, or one that may be expected to persist. In the latter case, profit requirements and pricing decisions should be reviewed.

Minor variances in the monthly operating statement are not uncommon because of the different number of production and sales days in a month, minor operating problems, delayed shipments, and so forth. Normally, minor variations are not a cause for alarm; they only become a cause for alarm when they appear excessive—in terms of past experience—or when they persist month after month. These two criteria—excessive and persistent variances—usually signal a problem. Because of this, many marketing managers give only cursory attention to the monthly operating statement—checking them only for excessive variances—and reserve thorough analysis for quarterly statements, or for some other time period that is long enough to produce a reasonably stable picture of operating results. The point is, however, that internally generated data is a valuable tool in assessing company performance.

Marketing Intelligence

Marketing intelligence includes all those procedures that a company routinely uses to keep abreast of developments in the external environment. Common sources of marketing intelligence are company sales representatives, syndicated research services such as A. C. Nielsen, trade and technical journals, industry associations, industry newsletters, and so forth.

Generally, company sales representatives are the prime sources of marketing intelligence on competitive pricing, promotions, and new products. Major companies train their field sales staff to be alert to competitive activities, and to be prompt in reporting such information to the sales manager. In addition, companies and their executives exhibit a great deal of variety in the ways they acquire information; in some instances, they use techniques reminiscent of the CIA, FBI, and James Bond. I recall one time, when we were working on a major packaging revision for a consumer product, one of our production people picked up a rumor from a package supplier that a major competitor was working on a similar package revision. To find out the direction that the competitive efforts were taking, we hired an investigator in the competitor's home-office city to rummage through the company's trash cans at the end of each day in search of discarded design roughs. We didn't find any. They shredded it all.

TABLE 9–1: Simplified Monthly Operating Statement Comparing Actual and Projected Performance

	Planned		Actual		Variance
Net sales		$2,560,800		$2,594,094	1.3%
Cost of goods		1,232,600		1,384,210	12.3
Gross margin		$1,328,200		$1,209,884	(9.0)
Expenses					
	$220,520		$218,756		
Sales	0		6		(0.8)
Advertising	340,890		344,639		1.1
Freight/warehousing	23,436		23,717		1.2
Administrative	322,050		327,401		(1.4)
Total expenses		$ 906,896		$ 914,513	(0.3)
Profit before taxes		$ 421,304		$ 295,371	(28.3)

Some companies, particularly in highly technical and fashion dependent industries, have been known to place spies in competitive companies to report on developments. Most ethical businesses, however, refrain from illegal spying as well as other dubious practices, and will cooperate with competition in order to eliminate them. For example, a few years ago, a young product manager for a large packaged goods company contacted a major competitor, offering to sell the marketing plan for a product being marketed by his company. The competitor immediately contacted the product manager's superiors and cooperated with them and the police in apprehending the product manager in the act of selling the plans.

Marketing Research

The third source of marketing information is the marketing research department whose specific task is to custom design research projects to obtain information needed by company marketing executives. The marketing research department may be intimately involved in analyzing internal records and other forms of marketing intelligence, but this department is uniquely involved in conducting surveys, product, and packaging tests; determining consumer preferences and consumer profiles; and evaluating advertising. Because of the importance of marketing research, our discussion will be expanded in the following material.

MARKETING RESEARCH AND THE MARKETING CONCEPT

Rapid acceleration in the growth of marketing information in general, and marketing research in particular, occurred following World War II. This growth was stimulated by the emergence of the marketing concept as a fundamental philosophy of product competition. The marketing concept—which recognized that consumer satisfaction was the ultimate key to survival, profits, and growth—placed a premium on marketing information that could guide management in segmenting markets; developing products; preparing marketing plans; and devising advertising, promotion strategies, and themes.

Some indication of the importance attached to the marketing research function can be obtained from a survey conducted by the American Marketing Association in 1978.[2] Figure 9–2 shows, by company size, the percentage of companies in various categories having formal marketing research departments. For example, 20 percent of the advertising agencies with billings under $5 million have formal marketing research departments, whereas all advertising agencies billing $25 million or more have such departments. Similarly, 25 percent of consumer product

2. Dick Warren Twedt, *1978 Survey of Marketing Research*, (Chicago: American Marketing Association, 1978). The 1978 survey is the sixth in a series of similar surveys (1947, 1959, 1963, 1968, and 1973).

FIGURE 9–2: *Frequency of Marketing Research Departments—By Company Type and Size*
SOURCE: Dick Warren Twedt (ed.), *1978 Survey of Marketing Research* (Chicago: American Marketing Association, 1978), p. 15.

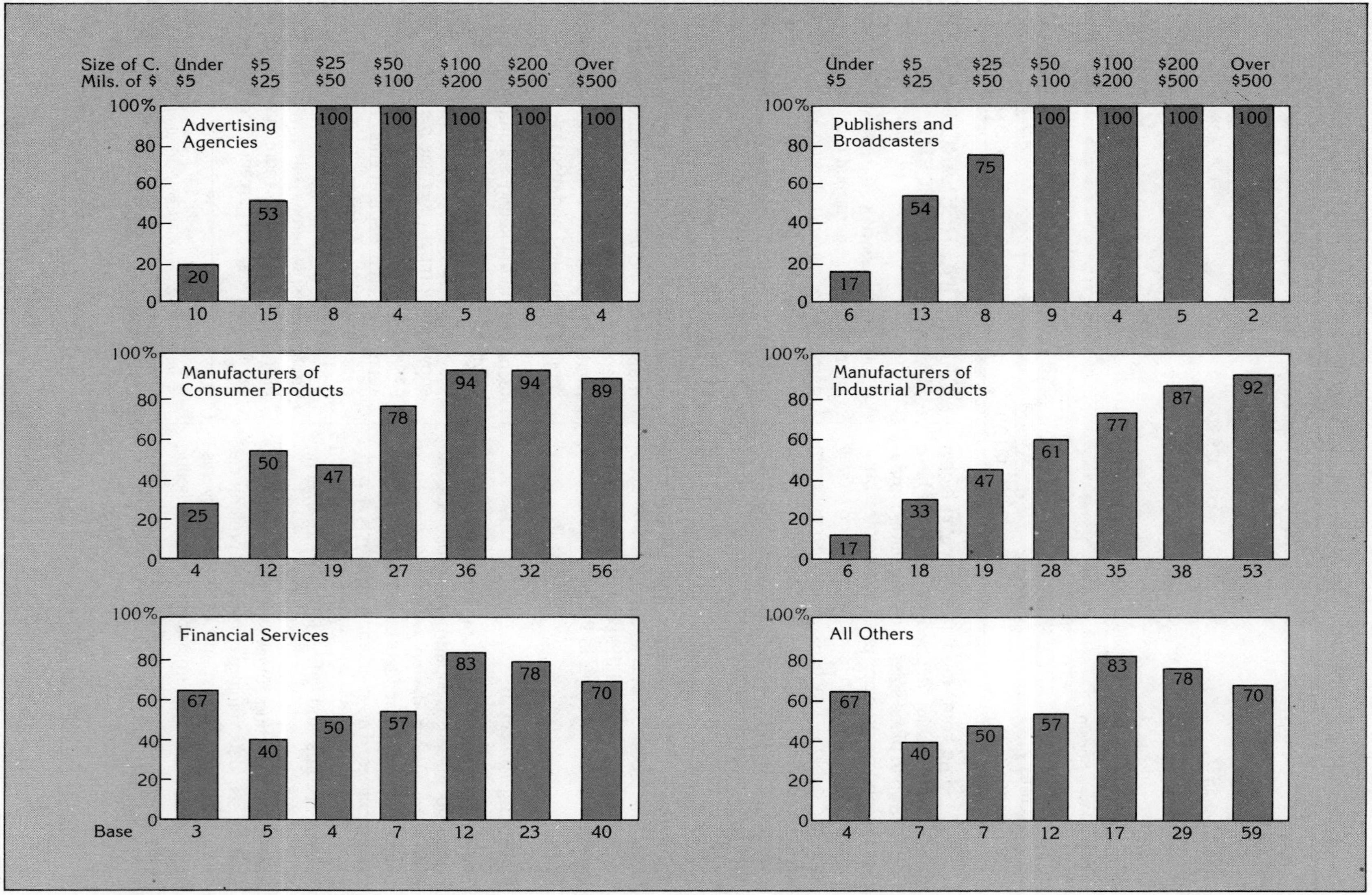

Size of C. Mils. of $
Under $5 | $5 $25 | $25 $50 | $50 $100 | $100 $200 | $200 $500 | Over $500

100%
80
60
40
20
0

Advertising Agencies
20 | 53 | 100 | 100 | 100 | 100 | 100
10 | 15 | 8 | 4 | 5 | 8 | 4

Publishers and Broadcasters
17 | 54 | 75 | 100 | 100 | 100 | 100
6 | 13 | 8 | 9 | 4 | 5 | 2

Manufacturers of Consumer Products
25 | 50 | 47 | 78 | 94 | 94 | 89
4 | 12 | 19 | 27 | 36 | 32 | 56

Manufacturers of Industrial Products
17 | 33 | 47 | 61 | 77 | 87 | 92
6 | 18 | 19 | 28 | 35 | 38 | 53

Financial Services
67 | 40 | 50 | 57 | 83 | 78 | 70
Base 3 | 5 | 4 | 7 | 12 | 23 | 40

All Others
67 | 40 | 50 | 57 | 83 | 78 | 70
4 | 7 | 7 | 12 | 17 | 29 | 59

companies with sales under $5 million have formal departments, while 94 percent of those with sales between $100 and $200 million have formal departments. Generally, the percentage of companies having formal marketing research departments increases with company size, with the exception of the "financial services" and "all others" categories. The erratic patterns found in these two categories may arise because marketing research is a relatively recent innovation in many of these organizations.

The Scope of Marketing Research

Since marketing research is the primary tool used to gather relevant marketing information, we need to examine the scope of the discipline in order to recognize the major areas in which it can be used.

Marketing research has been defined as the *gathering, recording, and analyzing of facts about problems relating to the transfer and sales of goods and services.*[3] Within this definition, the activities of a marketing research department are limited only by the information needed, the imagination and ethics of the research personnel who devise ways of obtaining needed information, and budget considerations. And this is essentially true. Because of its versatility, marketing research offers many values for market planning and the determination of marketing strategies. As a result, marketing research personnel are often a functional part of the marketing group. Table 9–2 provides some insight into the variety of tasks undertaken by marketing research departments by listing some thirty-two different research tasks, divided among five major research areas.

BARRIERS TO THE USE OF MARKETING RESEARCH

The rapid growth of marketing research in recent years implies that marketing research has universal acceptance among marketing practitioners, and that it is a panacea for marketing woes. Unfortunately, neither of these statements is true. Many marketing executives rely heavily on marketing research in making marketing decisions; others do not. Two major reasons for these diverse reactions are the limitations to what marketing research can do; and the fact that the world is full of bad research.

Limitations to What Marketing Research Can Do

Four limitations to marketing research are discussed in the following material.

MARKETING RESEARCH CAN ONLY MEASURE THE PAST—NOT THE FUTURE. Marketing research can only measure what exists—not what may exist in the future. All of its predictions are extrapolations of past data. Not surprisingly, these extrapolations are sometimes inaccurate because situations change, new variables are introduced into the equation, and people do not always behave tomorrow the way they did yesterday. True, marketing research may attempt to get a handle on the future by asking respondents "What they *plan* to do in a given situation" or "What they *would* do in the future under certain conditions." And one can get answers. The trouble is that the answers one gets are not always reliable. People don't necessarily know what they will do in the future—it all depends upon a variety of factors. As a consequence, the best guide to future intentions is often past behavior, with all of its limitations.

RESEARCH CAN ONLY REPORT FINDINGS—IT CANNOT MAKE DECISIONS. Too often, executives have unrealistic expectations of marketing research. They expect research to make decisions for them, to provide guarantees, and to eliminate complexity. Yet, marketing research may do none of these things.

Marketing research can provide information upon which to base decisions, but it can't make the decisions. Decision making is an executive prerogative and responsibility—what executives are paid for.

3. *Marketing Definitions: A Glossary of Marketing Terms,* compiled by the Committee on Definitions of the American Marketing Association, Ralph S. Alexander, Chairman (Chicago: American Marketing Association, 1960), p. 210.

TABLE 9–2: Research Activities of 798 Companies
SOURCE: Dick Warren Twedt (ed.), *1978 Survey of Marketing Research* (Chicago American Marketing Association, 1978), p. 41.

Activity	*Doing*
Advertising Research	
Motivation Research	48%
Copy Research	49
Media Research	61
Studies of Ad Effectiveness	67
Business Economics and Corporate Research	
Short Range Forecasting (Up to 1 year)	85
Longe Range Forecasting (Over 1 year)	82
Studies of Business Trends	86
Pricing Studies	81
Plant and Warehouse Location Studies	71
Acquisition Studies	69
Export and International Studies	51
MIS (Management Information Studies)	72
Operations Research	60
Internal Company Employees	65
Corporate Responsibility Research	
Consumers "Right to Know" Studies	26
Ecological Impact Studies	33
Studies of Legal Constraints on Advertising and Promotion	51
Social Values and Policies Studies	40
Product Research	
New Product Acceptance and Potential	84
Competitive Product Studies	85
Testing of Existing Products	75
Packaging Research: Design or Physical Characteristics	60
Sales and Market Research	
Measurement of Market Potentials	93
Market Share Analysis	92
Determination of Market Characteristics	93
Sales Analysis	89
Establishment of Sales Quotas, Territories	75
Distribution Channel Studies	69
Test Markets and Store Audits	54
Consumer Panel Operations	50
Sales Compensation Studies	60
Promotional Studies of Premiums, Coupons, Sampling, Deals, Etc.	52

Neither can marketing research provide guarantees or certainties; only probabilities based on past experience. There are no certainties in this world—except birth, death, and taxes.

Finally, research may indeed simplify decision making by eliminating alternatives on some occasions. Yet, on other occasions, research may make decisions more difficult by uncovering alternatives that heretofore had been unrecognized.

In short, some executives fail to recognize that research is only a tool to help them make decisions—not a decision-making machine.

RESEARCH CAN ONLY DEAL WITH THE PROBLEM IT IS GIVEN—NOT WITH THE PROBLEM IT SHOULD HAVE BEEN GIVEN. Marketing problems are often so complex that a marketing executive may define a problem improperly or incompletely. In these instances, research findings are likely to be trivial, useless, or (even worse) misleading. For example, let us assume that the market share for a given product is trending downward, despite strong sales coverage, heavy advertising expenditures, and aggressive promotion. The vice-president in charge of sales, concerned by the situation and not enthusiastic about the advertising campaign, charges the research department with finding out what is wrong with the advertising. The vice-president may be right, of course. The problem may be the advertising appeals used. On the other hand, he may have misidentified the problem. The problem could be the result of product inadequacy caused by competitive improvement, lack of retail cooperation, unfavorable pricing, packaging failure due to a change in packaging materials made in the name of economy, losses in distribution, or any number of other marketing variables. A leading brewer, for example, once suffered a severe share loss in one of the southern states. Company executives were confident that the problem was caused by a recent promotion run by a major competitor. Investigation, however, revealed that the primary cause was retailer and customer offense over the company's highly publicized contribution to the National Association for the Advancement of Colored People.

Although the possibility of assigning the wrong problem can never be completely eliminated, it can be minimized by having research personnel participate in problem definition, making them aware of the decision alternatives that management faces. Usually, the most critical stage in the development of marketing research is the definition of the problem to be researched.

RESEARCH TECHNIQUES ARE SOMETIMES INADEQUATE FOR THEIR TASKS. Many research techniques, particularly in the areas of consumer motivation and advertising research, are primitive and provide only gross and tentative measures of consumer motivations or of communications effectiveness. This is unfortunate, but true. A great deal of progress has been made in developing more adequate research techniques to gather data from consumers, but further development is still needed. In the meantime, motivation and communications research must be supplemented by the intuitive feelings or creative hunches of competent people. One major packaged goods advertiser, for example, will not run a commercial or print advertisement that has not been subjected to consumer tests. On the other hand, if a particular advertisement or commercial scores poorly in tests but the advertising agency insists this is the right approach and is willing to fight for it, the advertiser follows the agency's recommendation. Recognizing the value and legitimacy of creative judgment, the advertiser is aware that its research techniques are fallible.

Taken together, these four factors have limited the acceptance of marketing research among executives disappointed in their expectations of what marketing research could contribute. A case in point is a feature article by Lois Ernst, an outstandingly effective copywriter and advertising practitioner. The article, titled "703 reasons why creative people don't trust research," details eight grievances against research.[4] Of course, 8 isn't 703, but then Ernst is highly creative. Most of the grievances in this article are triv-

---

4. Lois G. Ernst, "703 Reasons Why Creative People Don't Trust Research," *Advertising Age* (Feb. 10, 1973): 35–36.

ial and relate to the four factors we have identified as limiting the acceptance of marketing research. Nonetheless, Ernst and other marketing and advertising executives, are sometimes disappointed by the contributions that research has been able to make. Granted that their expectations are often unrealistic or that their use of marketing research is inappropriate, the fact remains that their disappointment weakens their acceptance of marketing research as an essential element of the marketing process.

The World Is Full of Bad Research

A second barrier to the use of marketing research resides in the field itself and is caused by the fact that the field of marketing research, like every other field of human endeavor, has its share of charlatans, ripoff artists, and incompetents. Much of the marketing research that is done is excellent. A great deal is adequate. Far too much is badly conceived, poorly executed, or misrepresented.

Professionals in the field are conscious of these problems and strive mightily to eliminate them. The American Marketing Association has worked steadily and effectively to establish standards of research and to upgrade the quality of the work. Nonetheless, problems continue. The litany of research abuses range from unnecessary use of research through faulty research design, poor questionnaire development, inadequate sample selection, careless interviewing procedures, superficial data analysis, and blatant misrepresentation of findings. Sometimes abuses arise out of ignorance and incompetence. Sometimes they occur because inadequate funds are budgeted for the research project and unwise compromises are made. Occasionally, research integrity is deliberately subverted for selfish and irresponsible interests. But that's life, and nobody promised you a rose garden. Nonetheless, the fact that abuses exist have offended many and created distrust of research among executives who could benefit from its use.

MARKETING RESEARCH AND THE CONSUMER

One form of marketing research that is particularly important, is *consumer* research. Dealing solely with consumers, consumer research does not include sales analysis, forecasting, store audits, and other, more impersonal forms. In the area of consumer research, the three broad research traditions that differ in their focus or emphasis are the *distributive, morphological,* and *analytical* approaches.[5]

Distributive Research

Distributive research focuses attention on the outcomes of consumer behavior and is essentially concerned with *who* buys and *what* is bought. The emphasis of distributive research is on demographics—who customers are in terms of geographic and sociological characteristics. Profiles of buyers and nonbuyers are built from age, income, marital status, family size, and geographic location information. Distributive research computes per capita and per family consumption rates for relevant products and brands and defines markets in terms of geographic and sociological descriptions. Both quantitative and descriptive, the distributive approach is the beginning of wisdom.

THE VALUE OF DISTRIBUTIVE RESEARCH. Distributive research is the starting point for all understanding of the consumer; more sophisticated approaches are simply refinements or supplements to the distributive approach. Relatively simple and straightforward in research techniques, distributive research is often less expensive than other forms of consumer research. A further advantage is that its results can be compared with U.S. census data for purposes of estimating market potentials and projecting future trends. Essential for the geographic allocation of advertising dollars, and media selection, distributive research often provides a rough guide for creative development. This is particularly true when income, family life cycle, or social class are key dimensions influencing product use and/or consumption rates.

LIMITATIONS OF DISTRIBUTIVE RESEARCH. Despite its values, distributive research has three major limitations.

5. R. H. Dahl, M. Haire, and P. F. Lazerfeld, *Social Science Research on Business: Product and Potential* (New York: Columbia University Press, 1969), pp. 103–104.

First, the distributive approach is purely descriptive and fails to deal with the nature of the decision process that underlies the purchase. Often, unless this process is understood, sound marketing strategies cannot be developed. Buying a carpet, for example, involves a completely different decision process than buying a pound of coffee. Since different sources of information, different shopping behaviors, and different influence patterns characterize these two purchases, the marketer of carpeting and the marketer of coffee should allocate their marketing resources differently—each developing a marketing mix that is appropriate for its particular product. While the differences in the decision process for carpets versus coffee may appear obvious, important differences that are not immediately apparent exist for other products as well.

Second, the distributive approach fails to deal with the dynamics of behavior. In order to understand consumers, and communicate effectively with them, the marketer must know something about their motivational patterns, something about the relative importance of various psychological and sociological influences, and something about their media and promotional susceptibilities. In short, she needs to know why consumers behave as they do. Distributive research does not provide this kind of information.

Third, as markets become more competitive, segmentation along demographic lines becomes less adequate for purposes of product positioning. Instead, in order to remain competitive, the marketer must look to psychosocial dimensions as possible bases for segmentation.

Morphological Research

The morphological approach starts where distributive research stops. After consumers are identified and described, the morphological approach focuses on the various ways in which different products are bought or the differences in the way the same products are bought by groups of people. Morphological research might be described as *how* research since it concentrates on how decisions are made.

In the carpeting versus coffee example given earlier, the purchaser of carpeting will generally visit a number of outlets to see competitive carpeting samples and to gather information. She may consult consumer reports to learn more about fibers, she will undoubtedly talk with friends who have purchased carpeting recently, she will be strongly influenced by retail sales personnel, and share the final decision with her husband. The decision process will tend to be drawn out over a considerable period of time, possibly several weeks. By contrast, the buyer of coffee will probably rely on her own judgment and experience, augmented, perhaps, by advertising and recommendations from friends. Obviously, the marketer of carpets has different points of influence than does the marketer of coffee. Each, however, must know what the points of influence are before company resources can be used well.

Analytical Research

Analytical research, like the morphological approach, starts where distributive research stops. Differing from morphological research, it involves causal assessment. That is, "why" consumers purchase the products and brands they do. This causal assessment may reveal that the purchase was based on apparent product differences, or primarily influenced by psychosocial aspects of the product's image.

Generally, analytical research is the most difficult and is more fraught with ambiguity and error than the other forms of marketing research. Because of this, indirect techniques have been developed to determine consumer motivations.

Turning to the coffee and carpeting example may help to distinguish between morphological and analytical research. In the case of carpeting, our hypothetical consumer visited carpeting dealers, read consumer reports, talked with friends, and discussed the decision with her husband. This is a morphological description of *how* she went about making the decision, but it doesn't indicate which information source was most influential or why the consumer chose the brand of carpeting she finally bought. Analytical research, on the other hand, might reveal that (1) she pur-

TABLE 9–3: Selected Sources of Secondary Research Information

Source Bibliographies

American Statistical Index. This is a comprehensive descriptive index to the statistics published by U.S. Government agencies. A basic guide to government produced statistical, social, and economic information.

Encyclopedia of Business Information Sources. This source contains a detailed listing of primary subjects of interest to managerial personnel. Over 20,000 entries in 1,300 subject categories; includes references to sourcebooks, periodicals, organizations, directories, handbooks, bibliographies, and other sources of information on each topic covered.

Statistical Sources. A subject guide to data on industrial, business, social, educational, financial, and other topics for the world. Arranged in dictionary style, with frequent cross-references, it cites annuals, yearbooks, directories, and other publications.

Subject Index to Sources of Comparative International Statistics. Referred to as SISCIS, this source covers the whole field of economic and social activity with over 53,000 entries indexed under some 4,000 subject headings.

Periodicals/Studies

Business Periodicals Index. Issued monthly, this source indexes articles appearing in a wide range of business and technical publications. This index covers marketing and its various topics better than any other. An excellent source of contemporary and historic articles.

The Conference Board (Cumulative Index). The Cumulative Index lists studies completed, alphabetically by subject matter or major industries, products, issues, and so forth.

F & S Index of Corporations and Industries. This source is a guide to articles on products, industries, and companies appearing in over 750 financial publications. Divided into two sections, Section I (green pages) is arranged numerically by SIC codes. An alphabetical list of SIC numbers is provided at the beginning of the section. Section II is arranged alphabetically by company name. Generally, it provides good information on the marketing of products.

Industry Surveys. Published quarterly by Standard and Poors, this is a useful source for data on sixty-nine major domestic industries. Includes an analysis of trends and problems in historical perspective. Statistical tables and charts are used for assessing the subjects presented. Also contains a comparative analysis of the leading companies in each industry.

Predicasts. Predicast, Inc., scans over one thousand magazines and trade publications for statistics. In two volumes, *Predicasts* provides a base period statistic, and a short–term and long–term statistical forecast. *Basebook* gives a statistical measure of market size for the current year and figures for the past ten to fifteen years.

Sources of Demographic, Economic, and Product Information

Consumer Attitudes and Buying Plans. Monthly publication of the Conference Board presents a *Consumer Confidence Index* and a *Buying Plans Index* which contains survey results.

Demographic Yearbook. Annual publication contains international statistics on population, birth rate, mortality, life expectancies, marriage and divorce for some 200 geographic and political divisions.

Editor & Publisher Market Guide. Contains data about transportation, population, households, banks, automobiles, gas and electric meters, principal industries, climate, tap water, retailing, and retail outlets in every market in the United States and Canada in which a daily newspaper is published. Also contains information on the aggregate circulations of daily and weekly newspapers.

Guide to Consumer Markets. Statistics presented in this source are gathered from government and trade publications. Provides detailed information about population growth and characteristics, consumer income and expenditures, distribution and prices of consumer goods and services.

Progressive Grocer. This trade magazine publishes annual editions addressed to relevant subjects. One issue, for example, shows the percent of people using various consumer products, the percent of heavy users, and the percent of volume accounted for by heavy users. Another edition surveys the grocery trade in terms of the number of stores, and the dollar volume of chains, independents, and supermarkets.

Merchandising. This trade publication issues an annual edition with current and historical data for a wide number of household appliances. Also provides data on percent household saturation for these same items.

Rand McNally Commercial Atlas & Marketing Guide. This annual publication gives population estimates for Metropolitan County Areas and principal cities on a state by state basis. A Trading Area Map divides the United

TABLE 9–3: Continued

States into fifty major trading areas which are subdivided into smaller areas. Maps are detailed and up to date.

Sales and Marketing Management. The *Survey of Buying Power,* published in July and October is a "must" for the marketer, and is often referred to as the "bible" of the marketing industry. Provides current statistics on population and selected retail categories by states, counties, cities, and Metropolitan County Areas. Also provides a *Buying Power Index* for each of the areas covered. Two other annual editions are devoted to the *Survey of Industrial Purchasing Power* in which the establishments and dollar volume are presented by geographic area, by SIC codes, and *Survey of Selling Costs,* which presents current statistics on this marketing function.

Social Indicators. This publication of the U.S. Government Printing Office covers statistics and trends on health, public safety, education, employment, income, housing, leisure and recreation, and population.

Standard Rate and Data Service. Published monthly, SRDS is a basic working tool of advertising agencies and advertisers. Summarizes the rate cards for newspapers, magazines, business publications, radio, and spot television. A special volume is issued for each major media category, including direct-mail lists. In addition to providing rate and discount information, also gives the mechanical requirements for advertising materials sent to the media it lists.

Statistical Abstracts. An annual compilation of a wide range of summary statistics gathered by the U.S. government. Includes information on business firms, commodities, population, and innumerable other topics.

Supermarketing. This trade publication has an annual issue that lists the dollar sales for a wide range of consumer products sold through grocery stores. An excellent source for the market size of products.

World Almanac. Annual publication giving economic, demographic, and political data for the world's nations.

U.S. Government Source Statistics

County and City Data Book. Compilation of statistical information for counties, Standard Metropolitan Areas, and cities.

Basic Census Documents. Publications by the U.S. government contain detailed census information derived from these censuses conducted by the government:

Census of Agriculture
Census of Construction Industries
Census of Housing
Census of Manufacturers
Census of Mineral Industries
Census of Population
Census of Retail Trade
Census of Selected Service Industries
Census of Transportation
Census of Wholesale Trade

Other Sources

Individual States. Most states publish statistical abstracts on population, industry, economics, agriculture, transportation, and so forth within the state.

Industry Associations. Most major industries have trade associations such as the Evaporated Milk Association, the Frozen Foods Association, the Distilled Spirits Institute, the Brewers' Institute, and so forth. These associations are often sources of basic statistical data for their products and business firms.

Major Media. The research departments of trade publications and major consumer media are often sources for a variety of data on products and consumers. Newspapers in many major markets develop market data on consumer products.

chased a particular type of carpeting because the fiber was resistant to stain and quickly recovered from crushing; (2) she bought the brand she did because of the fashion appeal used in the advertising; (3) she bought from the store she did because it was a high prestige store; and (4) she bought from the salesperson she did because she reassured her in her choice of colors and patterns. By contrast, in the case of coffee, the consumer may have purchased a particular brand because of an endorsement by a celebrity, because of a particular advertising claim such as Folger's "mountain grown" slogan, because of a uniquely appealing package design, because of a price-off coupon offer, or because of a variety of other reasons.

The point is that distributive, morphological, and analytical research all answer different questions.

Distributive research asks "who?"
Morphological research asks "how?"
Analytical research asks "why?"

All of these questions are important, and the marketing manager should consider all of them when developing a marketing plan for a product.

One danger that exists is that the novice marketer, intrigued by the "how" and "why" questions and fascinated by esoteric research techniques, will be tempted to bypass the more mundane province of distributive research and go dashing off into the wild blue yonder of motivation research. Forget it! Successful marketing is systematic and founded on proper regard for the fundamentals. Distributive research is fundamental; morphological and analytical research, while important, should be added when and where they are applicable. As markets become more competitive, market segmentation and product differentiation depend more on psychosocial distinctions. Under these conditions, the descriptive data of distributive research, while still fundamental, is inadequate to provide marketing direction and must be supplemented by the morphological and analytical approaches.

PRIMARY VERSUS SECONDARY RESEARCH

One distinction often made in marketing is that between *primary* and *secondary* research. This distinction is not always clear. Primary data is generally considered as data originated in view of a specific need; secondary data is already in existence in some organized form, having been searched, organized, and stored by someone else. For example, if *Time* Magazine were to undertake a survey to define their subscribers' demographic characteristics, the study would be primary research. This same information provided to advertisers and advertising agencies in published form would be secondary research insofar as the advertisers and advertising agencies were concerned, because they did not originate the data.

Secondary Research

An immense amount of useful secondary data pertaining to industries, markets, products, and consumers is available in the United States; those interested in marketing should know of its existence. Table 9–3 gives an annotated list of major data sources. Although this list is far from comprehensive, it is an excellent start.

Among the more useful references for day-to-day marketing statistics are three annual issues of *Sales and Marketing Management.* The July and October issues are called *Survey of Buying Power;* these volumes provide a plethora of population, household, and income statistics, as well as retail sales for several merchandise groups. This data is broken down by states, counties, selected cities, and Standard Metropolitan County Areas.

The April issue is titled *Survey of Industrial Purchasing Power.* This annual issue reports the number of companies in the United States and their aggregate dollar volume by Standard Industrial Classification (SIC) codes. These data are also reported for states, counties, selected cities, and Standard Metropolitan County Areas. A sample listing from the April issue of *Sales and Marketing Management* is shown in Table 9–4.

Finally, the January issue of *Sales and Marketing Management* is devoted to a *Survey of Selling Costs,* and provides current information on the average cost of sales by major industrial groups as well as other relevant data on the sales function.

Obtaining secondary information is primarily a matter of digging it out. With perseverance, a great deal of information relevant to almost any marketing problem can be found. One problem, however, is that often secondary data is not specific enough to the problem at hand, and must be supplemented by primary research.

Primary Research

Primary research, unlike secondary research, does not rely on published data. Instead, original data is developed through some form of experimental or survey design. Essentially, primary data,

TABLE 9–4: Sample Listing for New Hampshire from *Sales and Market Management's* Survey of Buying Power *(July 27, 1981)*

N.H. S&MM ESTIMATES — POPULATION—12/31/80 — RETAIL SALES BY STORE GROUP 1980

METRO AREA / County / City	Total Population (Thousands)	% Of U.S.	Median Age of Pop.	% of Population by Age Group: 18–24 Years	25–34 Years	35–49 Years	50 & Over	Households (Thousands)	Total Retail Sales ($000)	Food ($000)	Eating & Drinking Places ($000)	General Mdse. ($000)	Furniture/ Furnish./ Appliance ($000)	Automotive ($000)	Drug ($000)
MANCHESTER - NASHUA	**280.8**	**.1228**	**30.0**	**12.3**	**18.1**	**16.9**	**24.2**	**98.3**	**1,217,090**	**272,708**	**100,447**	**148,267**	**62,666**	**200,132**	**32,475**
Hillsborough	280.8	.1228	30.0	12.3	18.1	16.9	24.2	98.3	1,217,090	272,708	100,447	148,267	62,666	200,132	32,475
• Manchester	91.0	.0398	32.5	12.4	14.8	17.1	29.1	34.7	449,208	82,890	45,382	52,571	20,815	91,716	14,372
• Nashua	68.7	.0301	29.2	12.3	19.4	17.2	21.6	24.3	406,104	88,088	28,461	46,533	23,786	80,176	10,871
SUBURBAN TOTAL	121.1	.0529	29.1	12.3	19.6	16.5	22.0	39.3	361,778	101,730	26,604	49,163	18,065	28,240	7,232
PORTSMOUTH - DOVER - ROCHESTER	**423.3**	**.1852**	**29.8**	**12.9**	**17.9**	**16.6**	**24.0**	**149.2**	**1,837,917**	**455,761**	**174,345**	**155,308**	**72,518**	**290,766**	**57,797**
Rockingham	*194.5*	*.0851*	*29.5*	*11.5*	*19.6*	*17.3*	*21.9*	*68.2*	*993,134*	*260,310*	*89,155*	*94,885*	*43,877*	*150,329*	*23,826*
• Portsmouth	26.3	.0115	26.1	13.8	13.5	16.7	21.3	9.4	214,379	35,620	23,778	11,468	11,662	42,230	3,197
Strafford	86.6	.0379	28.5	17.3	16.3	16.4	23.1	29.9	342,384	79,391	29,793	29,150	13,559	57,497	14,542
• Dover	22.5	.0098	29.0	9.7	12.2	18.4	24.3	8.2	115,606	18,788	11,518	8,786	8,499	20,034	3,175
• Rochester	27.0	.0118	30.0	8.7	12.1	18.2	25.8	10.1	138,279	35,564	9,270	11,936	2,100	25,103	9,471
York, Me.	142.2	.0622	31.1	12.0	16.2	16.0	27.7	51.1	502,399	116,060	55,397	31,273	15,082	82,940	19,429
SUBURBAN TOTAL	347.5	.1521	30.0	13.3	18.9	16.4	24.2	121.5	1,369,653	365,789	129,779	123,118	50,257	203,399	41,954
OTHER COUNTIES															
Belknap	43.8	.0191	31.9	10.4	15.8	16.7	28.4	16.1	230,288	57,520	17,446	16,530	11,071	37,044	4,617
Carroll	28.7	.0126	34.6	9.9	14.2	16.2	33.3	11.5	146,762	36,125	17,273	6,432	5,537	13,577	2,567
Cheshire	62.8	.0275	30.3	14.2	16.6	16.4	25.8	22.3	214,945	59,678	18,063	18,912	9,675	30,947	3,710
Coos	35.2	.0154	33.0	9.6	14.1	17.8	29.5	13.1	144,159	37,052	10,961	13,329	4,144	21,228	3,206
Grafton	66.7	.0292	29.6	17.6	15.6	15.3	26.3	23.8	329,923	88,622	25,893	34,942	13,353	35,917	6,674
Merrimack	99.9	.0438	32.0	12.3	16.4	16.2	28.9	35.6	471,176	107,700	34,108	55,735	13,547	86,642	12,650
Sullivan	36.5	.0160	32.1	10.3	16.4	16.6	28.7	13.6	135,568	36,821	7,789	6,780	6,057	23,955	4,804
TOTAL METRO COUNTIES	**561.9**	**.2458**	**29.6**	**12.8**	**18.3**	**17.0**	**23.1**	**196.4**	**2,552,608**	**612,409**	**219,395**	**272,302**	**120,102**	**407,958**	**70,843**
TOTAL STATE	**935.5**	**.4094**	**30.3**	**12.8**	**17.3**	**16.7**	**25.2**	**332.4**	**4,225,429**	**1,035,927**	**350,928**	**424,962**	**183,486**	**657,268**	**109,071**

N.H. S&MM ESTIMATES — EFFECTIVE BUYING INCOME 1980

% of Hslds. by EBI Group: (A) $8,000–$9,999 (B) $10,000–$14,999 (C) $15,000–$24,999 (D) $25,000 & Over

METRO AREA / County / City	Total EBI ($000)	Median Hsld. EBI	A	B	C	D	Buying Power Index
MANCHESTER - NASHUA	**2,220,467**	**20,858**	**4.2**	**12.1**	**30.7**	**36.6**	**.1235**
Hillsborough	2,220,467	20,858	4.2	12.1	30.7	36.6	.1235
• Manchester	714,973	18,604	4.9	13.6	29.9	30.7	.0416
• Nashua	583,107	22,291	3.9	10.7	31.3	40.6	.0347
SUBURBAN TOTAL	922,387	21,876	3.9	11.5	31.1	39.3	.0472
PORTSMOUTH - DOVER - ROCHESTER	**3,096,395**	**18,640**	**5.0**	**14.9**	**33.1**	**29.3**	**.1796**
Rockingham	*1,586,803*	*21,377*	*4.1*	*12.5*	*31.4*	*38.4*	*.0917*
• Portsmouth	190,943	17,705	5.4	16.4	32.8	27.2	.0142
Strafford	590,597	17,597	5.6	15.9	35.0	24.6	.0345
• Dover	161,377	18,091	5.7	16.2	35.1	26.5	.0100
• Rochester	180,343	16,638	5.7	17.0	35.4	20.8	.0116
York, Me.	918,995	16,181	5.7	17.4	34.5	20.1	.0534
SUBURBAN TOTAL	2,563,732	18,916	4.8	14.5	32.8	30.4	.1438
OTHER COUNTIES							
Belknap	344,367	18,386	4.7	14.7	31.3	29.5	.0205
Carroll	193,734	14,551	6.4	20.8	31.3	17.0	.0125
Cheshire	482,641	19,319	4.5	14.5	34.2	30.9	.0254
Coos	237,711	16,485	6.0	15.9	34.5	20.8	.0141
Grafton	537,143	18,255	5.3	15.5	30.7	29.8	.0310
Merrimack	756,800	18,505	5.1	15.0	33.5	28.5	.0442
Sullivan	279,835	17,823	5.2	15.8	33.3	26.7	.0151
TOTAL METRO COUNTIES	**4,397,867**	**20,473**	**4.4**	**12.8**	**31.7**	**35.4**	**.2497**
TOTAL STATE	**7,230,098**	**19,408**	**4.7**	**14.0**	**32.1**	**32.1**	**.4125**

is collected in three ways although each may appear in a variety of forms and, in fact, may be combined in order to solve a particular research problem. The three ways are observation, experiments, and surveys.

OBSERVATIONAL TECHNIQUES. Many marketing questions can be answered by simply observing some aspect of the marketing process at work. For example:

- The Pet Milk Company at one point radically changed its evaporated milk label and introduced the new label in the Detroit market. Researchers posted themselves near the evaporated milk section of supermarkets and observed how customers responded to the new label. Since they observed that the label was causing a great deal of consumer confusion, and since retail orders were severely depressed, the label was withdrawn from distribution.
- A major magazine regularly concealed a television camera in its waiting room to observe which magazine articles were read by people who were waiting to see someone in the company. The object was to find out which articles commanded the greatest consumer attention.
- Investigators set up a hidden television camera in the ceiling of a supermarket to follow the movements of shoppers through stores. The object was to develop generalizations on the customer flow pattern that would lead to a more effective arrangement of merchandise and increased customer purchases.
- Twenty-four sheet poster (billboards) companies regularly observe traffic flow in various parts of major cities in order to develop statistics about the number of automobiles passing billboard sites.

The opportunities for observation are endless: pantry checks, garbage can checks, concealed microphones which reveal how sales reps respond to questions, and a variety of other observational techniques can be employed when they are appropriate, and when they provide insight into consumer behavior.

One of the major shortcomings of the approach is that observation is restricted to overt behavior and provides only inferential material about the consumer's thoughts. This approach also tends to be expensive and requires careful observation by the investigators.

One criticism of the observational technique is an ethical one. Normally, consumers are not aware that they are under observation; as a consequence, such observation may be considered an invasion of privacy. Not all of the observational techniques constitute an invasion of privacy, but some do. Since, at this point, legal guidelines are ambiguous, the researcher must formulate personal standards of conduct.

EXPERIMENTAL DESIGNS. Another problem of the observational method is that behavior usually takes place under natural, uncontrolled conditions. As a consequence, drawing meaningful conclusions or testing a marketing hypothesis is difficult. In order to test hypotheses about some marketing stimuli or some form of marketing behavior, the experimental method is often employed, and experimental controls introduced. The experimental method involves a systematic introduction of selected stimuli into a marketing situation and careful measurement of the effects these different stimuli exert on the dependent variable. Extraneous factors that might influence experimental results are controlled by experimental design, by statistical analysis, or both.

A simple example of a marketing experiment would be an in-store test of the effectiveness of a product display in generating additional sales. One approach to such an experiment would be to use two groups of stores, *control* stores and *experimental* stores. The control and experimental stores might be given the treatment shown in Figure 9–3. Unit sales of the product would be measured during the pretest, the test, and the posttest periods in both control and experimental stores. In the control stores, the conditions would be the same in all three periods. By contrast, in experimental stores, the display would be erected

FIGURE 9–3: A Simple Marketing Experiment

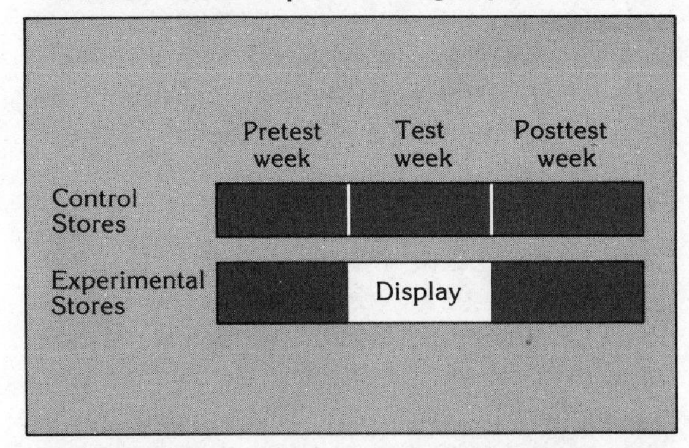

during the test period. The effectiveness of the display in generating additional sales would be determined by comparing the sales patterns in the control stores to sales in the experimental stores and testing the significance of the statistical differences found.

The example just given is a simple experimental design for a controlled experiment in marketing. Other experimental designs could have been used for the same experiment, some of which would be more sophisticated and others less sophisticated. A variety of experimental designs can be employed in testing marketing hypotheses, although a discussion of them is beyond the scope of this text. Some designs are more defensible than others, which means that they use more effective controls. Some designs are highly sophisticated, and some are relatively crude. The highly sophisticated experimental design is not always the best, nor is the relatively crude design necessarily the worst. The nature of the problem, the nature of the data, and the nature of the decisions to be made are always the deciding factors. This is why marketing managers should have at least some experience in experimental design and scientific methodology. With such experience, they will be better able to evaluate the adequacy of a particular experimental design and assess the validity of the results.

SURVEYS. The third, and most common, method for developing consumer information is the survey. Compared to direct observation and experimental designs, surveys are more versatile, produce a wealth of information, and are applicable to a greater variety of research problems. Surveys may be used to develop distributive, morphological, and analytical data and are the workhorses of consumer research.

Since surveys are so widespread and their use is so commonplace, people often assume that surveys require no great skill to design and execute. This is not true. The design of the survey, the development of the questionnaire (sometimes referred to as a schedule), the identification of the appropriate population, the selection of a sample, the interviewing procedure, and the coding and analysis of data constitute one of the most demanding and technically advanced areas of marketing research. The design and execution of a survey requires a great deal of skill and judgment.

Because of the complexity of planning, executing, and analyzing surveys, an extensive literature has developed which details procedures and cautions against common errors. Innumerable books and articles have been written about questionnaire development, sample design, interviewing procedures, coding, analysis, and presentation of results. One of the better basic references is McGraw-Hill's *Handbook of Marketing Research* edited by Robert Ferber, which devotes some thirteen hundred pages to marketing research, a good portion of which relates to surveys.

Planning Primary Research

The success of primary research generally depends upon the planning that goes into it. Poorly planned reesearch has the unfortunate habit of generating misleading or useless data. Fortunately, as a guide to planning, a research project can be structured into five major steps: definition of the problem, design of the research, field work, analysis and interpretation, and presentation of the findings.

Definition of the Problem

As pointed out earlier, definition is probably the most critical step in the process because, if the problem is defined improperly or fuzzily, little useful data will result. In defining the problem, one must strike a balance between defining too broadly or too narrowly. For example, to say that one wishes to survey attitudes toward blue jeans is distressingly vague. Whose attitudes? The general population? Men? Women? Teen-agers? Subteens? Distributors? Retailers? What kinds of attitudes? Attitudes toward construction and quality? Brand preferences? Styling? Price? Versatility? Attitudes toward blue jean advertising?

Precisely how the problem should be defined depends upon the marketing decisions that will be made on the basis of the data. Depending on the purpose for which the survey data will be used, any of the population groups or types of attitudes indicated above could be addressed.

Because of the critical role of problem definition in obtaining useful data, marketing research personnel—as well as marketing executives who will use the data—should participate in the problem definition stage. One of the most important topics of discussion should be *how* the data will be used, and the kinds of decisions that will be based upon it.

Design of the Research

After the problem has been defined satisfactorily, critical questions arise. For example, how much money can be allocated to the research job? If too little is available to obtain reasonably valid results, the task should not be undertaken. If the cost of obtaining valid results exceeds the benefit to be derived from the research, forget it. Spending $50,000 for a research project when the decision to be made is only worth $10,000 has little value. Beyond this, many research projects lend themselves to a variety of research techniques. Some are more accurate and more expensive than others. The research design finally selected will be influenced by the level of accuracy required and the available budget. Virtually all marketing research is a tradeoff between cost, accuracy, and the amount of data to be gathered. Compromises have to be made. However, they should always be reasonable compromises, not compromises that will seriously threaten the integrity of the findings.

Research design involves sample size and selection, choice of research technique, questionnaire development, method of supervision, compensation for not-at-homes or people who fail to respond, and the plan of analysis.

Field Work

After an acceptable research design has been devised, it must be executed. While this may be done by research department personnel, this stage of the project is usually subcontracted to independent research firms. Close supervision of fieldwork is a must because sins of omission and commission in this stage of the project are rampant. Thus, while associate research director of D'Arcy-MacManus & Masius (a Chicago–based advertising agency), William T. Field observed:

> I've acquired a strong distrust of interviewers, field supervisors, coders, recruiters, and all those shadowy, middle-classed, middle-aged suburban housewives in whose hands research analysts all over the country, and in every rank, put their questionnaires and other field documents for implementation.
>
> And this distrust is really justified. The field cuts corners, pads expenses, and doesn't follow instructions. In a word, it cheats, but only if you let it.[6]

Analysis and Interpretation

The fourth step in the research process is doing something sensible with the data; what is often done, isn't always sensible. The kinds of analyses that can be made depend upon the nature of the data. As pointed out earlier, the research design stage should include the plan of analysis. Unless some thought is given to the ways in which the data will be analyzed in designing the research, chances are very good that unanalyzable garbage will result.

Analysis may be as simple as tabulating the answers to individual questions. Or, as complex as using some form of multivariate analysis. Some research findings—*analytical research,* for example—is more difficult to analyze and

6. "Research Users Must Check Work of Field Interviewers," *Marketing News* (Jan. 11, 1980): 15.

"Please don't close the door, I have only one more question." (Photo by Paul Conklin)

interpret than other forms, such as *distributive research*. The key point to keep in mind is that analysis should be done in such a way that relevant conclusions may be reached. This often requires an analyst with imagination, judgment, and skill. And, *all* of these characteristics are necessary. I once had an analyst working for me who had a great deal of imagination and skill, but absolutely no judgment. Unable to distinguish what was important and unimportant, he would spend hours teasing out the details of some trivial finding. Needless to say, all of his work had to be turned over to someone else for interpretation.

Presentation of the Findings

Finally, the report is presented in a form useful to the marketing executives who make the decisions. A written research report is usually organized into five sections: (1) the definition of the problem; (2) major findings and conclusions; (3) limitations of the data; (4) detailed tables and discussion; and (5) an appendix containing a detailed description of the study design and a tabulation of the raw data.

Various companies may use different formats for research reports than that given above, although they will seldom depart very far from this format. In any instance, each of the sections indicated in this format should appear somewhere in the final report.

TEST MARKETS

Test markets, often referred to as market testing, have been broken out as a separate area of research because of their widespread use in modern marketing. Test markets are used for many reasons—to introduce new products, to test different price levels, to test sales promotion programs, to test advertising themes, to test new packages, and so forth. The particular variables being tested will determine the design of the test market effort, and the kinds of research to be conducted. *The primary purpose of a test market is to find out how a new product, or some change in the marketing mix, will perform under normal, competitive marketing conditions.*

Attempting to discuss all the various forms that test marketing might take would be extremely unwieldy. So, let us confine ourselves to a brief discussion of the most exciting kind of test marketing—the test marketing of new products. I have designed and/or participated in many test market operations. Some, like Purina Dog Chow, Purina Cat Chow, Jack Daniel's, Busch Bavarian Beer, Duncan Hines Cake Mixes, and Sego Liquid Diet Food were highly successful. Some, I would like to forget. They were so bad that, at the time, suicide seemed like a reasonable alternative. And, no two were alike. Nonetheless, certain generalizations can be drawn about test market selection and measurement.

Selecting Test Markets

In the selection of test markets, consider two factors: the number of test markets to be used, and the identification of specific markets. Let's look at each of these variables.

NUMBER OF MARKETS. How many markets should be used depends upon what is being tested, how much money is available, and how critical the decision is that will be made from the results. At this point, note that the number of markets one selects is *not* a scientific, statistically defensible operation. For example, for truly projectable results from test markets, one would need to randomly select at least twenty markets from the universe of all markets available. From the standpoint of affordability, such an approach would be excessively expensive, so compromises have to be made.

When testing only one variable—say a marketing plan for a new product—marketing practitioners sometimes use a single market. Normally, this is undesirable because uncontrollable variables may distort test market results. For example, a strike by a major industry in the market selected may generate consumer anxiety and reduce willingness to spend on new products; or a competitor may schedule an unusual activity in the market selected; or reaction to the marketing program may differ in various parts of the country. Generally, marketing practitioners prefer to schedule at least three markets in different geographic areas. In some instances, depending upon circumstances, an entire region may be selected for a test market operation. Thus, I was involved in one test market that included Texas, Oklahoma, Arkansas, and New Mexico. Tests of this magnitude are rare because they are expensive and the risk is high. After all, one of the primary functions of a test market should be to gain information while limiting financial risk.

If three markets are required to test a single variable, six would be required to test two variables. For example, let us assume that we are introducing a new product, and planning to use three markets. Then, because uncertainty arises about the price to be charged, a decision is made to test two price levels. Now, six markets are

TABLE 9–5: Typical Criteria Used in Selecting Test Markets for a Popular Food Store Product

- *Market size.* Population between 250,000 and 500,000 in the primary media coverage area. Larger markets tend to become too expensive; smaller markets may be atypical in competitive activity.
- *Media availability.* Two criteria are generally applied: all major media should be available in the market; the market should be self-contained; that is, not be dominated by media originating in nontest areas.
- *Distribution channels.* Three criteria are often used: First, the distribution of sales between chain stores and independents should approximate the national distribution of sales between store types. Second, no single chain should dominate the market. The reason for this criteria is that failure to obtain distribution in the dominant chain could jeopardize the test program. Third, markets selected should be regional headquarters of the chain stores in the market because restricting product distribution to the test area in markets where chains have their headquarters is easier than in out-lying markets. An alternative is to drop ship to individual stores. That is, the marketer assumes the responsibility to deliver the test product to individual stores, rather than distributing through the chain warehouses. This procedure increases the cost of the test market, however.
- *Product potential.* Per capita sales for the product type should be average or above. Below average per capita sales may mean that competitive advertising will be below normal levels, and may mean that total sales will be disappointing.
- *Geographic dispersion.* Markets should be dispersed geographically, if more than one market is used.
- *Demographic characteristics.* The markets should be reasonably balanced in terms of demographic factors—age, income, and diversity of industry.
- *Economic conditions.* The market should not be economically depressed because of widespread strikes or layoffs.
- *Competitive use.* Because they meet the foregoing criteria, some markets become popular as test markets and are widely used. As a consequence, two problems may be encountered: tests by other companies may detract from the test market program; consumers in the market may become blasé about new products because of excessive testing.
- *Other.* Depending upon the particular situation, other criteria may also be set.

required. Now, let us introduce still another variable—two different advertising themes. If each appeal were tested at each price level, twelve markets would be required. As you can see, as the number of variables to be tested increases, the number of markets required can quickly get out of hand.

Statistical methods permit testing a number of variables with limited markets. From a practical point of view, however, statistical methods are seldom satisfactory because of the uncertainty of the interaction of different variables. Although one can gain scope and breadth by using these procedures, the risk of atypical results is increased, and the interpretation of the findings is not nearly as simple as textbook models imply. For these reasons, most marketing practitioners restrict the variables being tested when running test markets on new products. Most often, they content themselves with testing the effectiveness of a single marketing program, with no variations between markets.

CHOOSING SPECIFIC MARKETS. No single market, nor limited group of markets, is a microcosm of the United States. As a consequence, specific markets are selected by taking into consideration market size, patterns of product demand, the nature of the test, the structure of competition, availability of distribution channels, and the demographic and economic characteristics of the markets being considered. Table 9–5 identifies typical criteria used in selecting test markets for a widely used, new food store product. The selection of good test markets is neither routine nor foolproof. For this reason, more than one market is usually recommended.

Length of the Test

Again, how long a test market should run has no universal answer. Some tests may run only a few months. Some may run for over a year. Generally, test markets for a new product should be long enough to give consumers an opportunity to repurchase the product at least once. In the case of products that are relatively expensive in comparison to competition, which require new methods of use or have a novelty appeal, the test market should be continued long enough to permit a second, third, or even fourth repurchase. Three test products with which I was involved—a cold cereal, one of the first frosting mixes, and a chocolate syrup dispensed from an aerosol can—did exceedingly well through the first and second repurchase. Thereafter, as the test market continued, repurchases dwindled and sales virtually disappeared.

Generally, with a frequently purchased product, where one or two repurchases are sufficient to evaluate test market results, test markets should last at least six months. If, at this point, the new product is judged a success, a rollout or expansion program will commence. Often two or three years are necessary to rollout a new product from test markets to national distribution. The actual time depends upon production facilities, sales coverage, and financial resources. Even after the rollout has begun, original test markets are often monitored closely for another six months or year to detect any possible signs of weakening.

Spending Strategies

An examination of spending patterns for new products reveals three different test marketing spending strategies: a heavy spending strategy, a limited spending strategy, and a compromise strategy.

HEAVY SPENDING STRATEGY. In a heavy spending strategy, the intent is to spend at whatever level necessary to give the new product the best possible chance of succeeding. The assumption underlying this strategy is that a product which fails under the most favorable spending conditions, should be abandoned. If the product gains a significant share of market, and consumers are pleased with its performance, additional markets will be scheduled at lower spending levels until an optimal level is found.

The heavy spending strategy was most apparent in the early 1950s when test marketing was becoming popular. Of course, this strategy may result in overspending and the consequent waste of company resources if, despite early indications of success, an affordable spending level cannot be found.

LIMITED SPENDING STRATEGY. In a limited spending strategy, careful forecasts are made of the total market and the anticipated market share. Money is allocated on the basis of an affordable amount per case or per unit, based on estimated sales. For example, assume that over a given period of time—usually one to three years—an estimated 200,000 cases can be sold in selected test markets. Also assume that the marketer can afford to spend three dollars a case within the planned pricing structure. Then, $600,000 (200,000 cases × $3.00 per case) is budgeted for test marketing. A product which fails to meet its sales goals, is rejected as unprofitable. If it succeeds, the marketer has reasonable expectations that the product can be expanded nationally as a profitable addition to the line.

This approach is probably the most widely used today. But, even this strategy is not without fault. Forecasting the sales of a new product is far from an exact science. If the forecast is too low, too little may be spent, and the product will either fail completely, or fail to achieve its potential.

COMPROMISE SPENDING STRATEGIES. By employing a compromise spending strategy, sophisticated marketers recognize the limitations of the foregoing approaches. To guard against the weaknesses of each, they compromise. First, they plan test markets on a *limited spending strategy*. Then, to protect against the danger of underspending, marketers may schedule one or two markets under a heavy spending plan deliberately spending at a higher level. Quite frequently, this strategy pays off, and the higher spending level generates more than enough additional sales to pay for itself.

MEASURING TEST MARKET RESULTS

The research measurements used in test markets depend upon the purpose of the test. For example, let us assume that the test is a simple business-building test for a product with established distribution and market share. The purpose of the test is to determine whether an increase in marketing expenditures will bring about a profitable increase in sales and market share. In this instance, the only measures that may be used are company shipment records, warehouse withdrawals, or store audits.

If, on the other hand, the purpose is to test market a new consumer product, more comprehensive measures are used. Basically, four questions should be answered when test marketing a new product:

- Can adequate distribution be obtained?
- Can sales and share goals be achieved?
- Will the repurchase rate be sufficient to insure the continued success of the product?
- Are there any weaknesses in the marketing plan that need to be corrected?

A variety of research measures will be used to answer these four questions. Distribution surveys may be made to measure the extent of distribution. Company shipment records, warehouse withdrawals, and/or store audits may be used to measure unit sales and market share. Consumer surveys and consumer panels may be used to measure purchases, repurchases, reactions to the product, awareness of the advertising, reasons for purchasing or not purchasing, and so forth.

Distribution surveys are generally made fairly early in the test to detect problems in this area. Subsequent repeat surveys make sure that any problems uncovered in the first survey have been corrected. Warehouse withdrawals and/or store audits are generally made weekly or biweekly throughout the test period. Consumer panels may be established at the beginning of the test, and interviewed weekly throughout the test period. Consumer surveys are generally made between the fourth and sixth month of the test, although they may be made earlier or later as well.

The point is that a wide variety of information is gathered to analyze the details of the test market's performance. This information is carefully analyzed to learn as much as possible about what happened in the test market. Some test market results are clear-cut failures; some, clear-cut successes. For others, interpretation of the results is more ambiguous. In cases of ambiguity, where possible weaknesses in the program have been detected, the program may be modified and additional test markets scheduled.

WHEN TO TEST

As devices for gaining direct experience in the marketplace under normal conditions, test markets are invaluable and irreplaceable. They are also relatively expensive, however, and involve risks. A product that does well in test markets is not guaranteed to do well when marketed nationally. Between test market results and national sales, too many variables can intervene: economic conditions may change; new competitive products may enter the market; achieving the same national advertising exposure achieved in test markets may not be possible no matter how carefully one attempts to match the effort; the test market may tip-off competitors concerning company activity, and, thereby, enable them to develop counter strategies.

Of course, on some occasions test marketing is deemed too risky, or unnecessary. The question to test or not to test is one of marketing judgment, and sometimes prudence will dictate against a test. Probably the most frequent reason for not test marketing is that this method enables competitors to develop competitive products and counter strategies. Sometimes this may be true, but more often than not, it is not and the benefits of test marketing far outweigh the risks.

TEST MARKETING AND INDUSTRIAL PRODUCTS

Note that test marketing, as such, is primarily a consumer product phenomenon, which is not widely used for most industrial products. This is true for several reasons: (1) the expense of producing an inventory of industrial goods—heavy equipment, computers, production machinery, and so forth—for testing purposes is prohibitive; (2) many industrial products are made to specifications which do not lend themselves to standardization; (3) industrial customers are often divided among several markets—for example, two in Pittsburgh, one in Philadelphia, and four in Chicago—and do not lend themselves to the market testing concept.

This is not to say that test marketing is *never* used by industrial marketers. When the nature of the product and the distribution of users are appropriate for test market treatment, even on a regional basis, then such testing may be used. Most often, however, industrial marketers tend to test their products in other ways. First, they use extensive laboratory and in-use tests to develop performance standards, desirable design characteristics, and cost efficiency. Second, they will often seek agreement from a list of selected customers who use the product on a trial basis for a limited time, often at no cost, in order to get some idea of the product's performance under normal production conditions. After passing this test successfully, the product is usually turned over to the sales force and introduced to the market through normal selling channels, or through a trade show.

SUMMARY

Marketing research is the lifeblood of marketing—a major source of marketing information that enables marketers to make sound decisions. Marketing research is not the only source of marketing data used by businesses, however. Rather, it is simply one part of the marketing information system that includes three subsystems: internal records, marketing intelligence, and marketing research.

Internal records provide a great deal of useful data that can be analyzed to determine sales, customers, inventories, costs, and profits. The monthly operating statement is often the central control document in assessing performance of company products.

Marketing intelligence includes all of the procedures a company routinely uses to keep abreast of developments in the external environment. Common sources of marketing intelligence are company sales representatives, syndicated research services, trade and technical journals, and industry associations.

Although the value of marketing research has been amply demonstrated, some executives have been disappointed in their use of research, either because they had unrealistic expectations or because they have had unfortunate experiences with research badly done.

Three primary research traditions are distributive research, morphological research, and analytical research. Distributive research asks "What?" Morphological research asks "How?" Analytical research asks "Why?" Each, however, has a role in the research program.

A distinction may be made between *secondary* and *primary* research. Secondary research refers to research data obtained from published sources. Primary research refers to research undertaken to originate data. Within primary research, the three major approaches for gathering data are through observation, experiment, and survey. The particular method used depends upon the nature of the research problem.

A specialized form of marketing research, test marketing forecasts how a new product, or some change in the marketing mix, will perform under normal, competitive marketing conditions. Key problems in conducting test markets are: (1) determining what is to be tested; (2) selecting markets; (3) specifying the marketing research to be undertaken; (4) determining spending patterns; and (5) deciding upon the length of the test. Although test markets always incur risks, their benefits generally outweigh the risks.

1. Explain what is meant by the marketing information system. Identify its components, and characterize the information that each of these components produces.
2. Devise a simple operating statement to show how it might be used as a control document.
3. Identify the major limitations of marketing research discussed in the text.
4. The text identifies three traditions in marketing research—distributive research, morphological research, and analytical research. Explain each type of research. Also indicate which type is most basic, and why.
5. Distinguish between primary and secondary research.
6. Distinguish between "observation" and "experiment" as methods for obtaining primary data.
7. Identify the various stages in planning a primary research project. Which stage is the most critical, and why?
8. Explain the primary purpose of test marketing, giving a specific example of an occasion in which test marketing might be used.
9. Identify the key variables which must be considered in selecting test markets.
10. Identify and explain the various test market spending strategies discussed in the text.

DISCUSSION QUESTIONS

1. You are the marketing director of a company that sells a dry dog food product in grocery stores through a network of food brokers. Your boss has asked you how many stores carry your product. You do not have this information. How would you go about answering this question?
2. As a product manager, you have received the following monthly operating statement on your product. How would you interpret it? What steps would you take in preparing a report on it?

	Planned	*Actual*
Net sales	$1,362,200	$1,225,980
Cost of goods	863,400	880,668
Gross margin	$ 498,800	$ 345,312
Expenses		
Sales	40,975	41,384
Advertising	125,144	131,401
Freight/warehousing	8,465	7,618
Administration	127,754	126,476
Total	$ 302,338	$ 306,879
Profit before taxes	$ 196,462	$ 38,433

3. You have recently been employed as the research director for a company that sells expensive home furniture. Historically, the company has not used marketing research, and has virtually no data available on its products or markets. Outline a research program to start assembling comprehensive data on the company's products and markets.
4. You have been asked to develop a spending strategy for test markets for a new frosting mix developed by your company. How would you proceed with this assignment?
5. Your company is planning to introduce a new shampoo in three test markets. You have been asked to identify the kinds of marketing research that should be undertaken in the test markets. How would you approach this problem? What would you recommend?

MARKETING RESEARCH AND TEST MARKETING

Southwest Dairies, a large regional dairy company in Texas, markets a variety of dairy products—milk, skim milk, buttermilk, cream, butter, cottage cheese, ice cream, and so forth—through grocery stores and supermarkets. Milk products are marketed in traditional, square cardboard cartons. Although the cardboard carton proved to be satisfactory for most of its milk products, the company had a problem, as did competitors, with its gallon milk carton. The weight of the milk in the gallon carton often caused the package to leak, causing consumer complaints and a high incidence of product returns from grocery stores. In the most recent year, product returns were approximately 8 percent of gross sales. A summary operations statement for the dairy company's gallon-sized container for this year is shown below.

	Dollars	Units
Gross sales	$226,598	202,320
Returns because of leakage	18,127	16,185
Net sales	$208,471	186,135
Cost of goods sold (80.0%)	183,091	
Gross margin	$ 25,380	
Expenses	22,180	
Net profit before taxes	$ 3,200	

After several unsuccessful attempts to correct the leakage problem with conventional packaging, management was considering a plastic package for the gallon container. Since the plastic package cost $0.188, substantially more than the current package which cost $0.104, management realized that the plastic package would have to increase their market share to justify its cost.

In order to test the plastic package, the sales manager made arrangements with an independent grocery store to stock the plastic package for a week. As a control, sales in the test store were measured for one week—Monday through Saturday. The following week—Monday through Saturday—the plastic package was substituted for the current package. The results of the test showed that the plastic package outsold the conventional package 312 to 280 units.

On the basis of this finding, the sales manager recommended that the company replace the conventional package with the plastic package in all of its grocery outlets.

Assignment

1. *Do you believe that the testing method used by the sales manager was adequate? If not, why not?*
2. *If you do not agree that the test was adequate, design a test that would overcome its deficiencies.*
3. *How much of a sales increase would be required in order to justify a change to the plastic package? (Suggestion to students: In order to answer this question, set up the following equation: Present net sales − cost of goods = X − [(% cost of goods × X) + .084 (X/1.12)]. Solve for X which represents the sales of the plastic package required to maintain the same gross margin currently earned.)*

10

Forecasting and the Marketing Budget

- *The importance of forecasting in market planning.*
- *Major types of market forecasts.*
- *Major methods of forecasting.*
- *Methods of determining the marketing budget.*
- *The nature and use of payout plans.*

MARKETING EXAMPLES

OH, THE PRECISION OF INVENTORY CONTROL!

The U.S. automobile industry is a volatile industry. In the 1974 recession, lightning struck—sales dropped some 2.6 million units, factory rebates to clear out excessive inventories became a painful necessity, and Detroit wept. Sales continued to drop slightly in 1975, and then began to recover. In 1979 lightning struck again, and again Detroit was stuck with excessive inventories. Let's look at *Fortune's* comment on the double whammy:

> Ever since the 1974 recession, when they woke up to find their warehouses bulging with unsold merchandise, a lot of businessmen have paid special attention to their inventory controls. Nowhere was this trend more evident than in the automobile industry, which has always pioneered in sophisticated inventory–management systems, and which got badly hurt all the same in the 1974 collapse.
>
> So what happened this time around? As late as the end of April, when the first gasoline lines were already snaking their way across California, General Motors' Chairman Thomas Murphy was still predicting that Detroit would sell a record 15.5 million cars and trucks in 1979. Instead, by July the industry had accumulated a stockpile of 2.15 million unsold vehicles—a record all right, but not the kind Chairman Murphy had in mind. Which raises a couple of interesting questions. First, what went wrong with those vaunted control systems? Second, now that things are leveling off in Detroit, what are the odds that the same sort of runaway inventory buildup could afflict other industries?
>
> The quick answer to the first question is that an inventory –management system, however sophisticated, is no better than the sales forecast on which it is based. . . . A sales forecast, in turn, is nothing more than an educated guess about the future.[1]

1. Edward Meadows, "How Detroit Got Stuck with All Those Cars," *Fortune* (Oct. 22, 1979): 54.

By year's end, Chairman Murphy had missed his forecast by some 5 million units—a multibillion dollar forecasting error.

IF IT AIN'T BROKE, DON'T FIX IT

A small, but highly successful, midwest manufacturer produced a line of household items. Forecasts for each product in its line were made by a statistical analyst in its sales department who, for the sake of anonymity, we will call Joe Greene.

After several years in his job, Joe's knowledge of the company's products, markets, and distributors had made him an excellent forecaster, although, like most forecasters, he made an occasional blooper. Generally, management was well satisfied with Joe's forecasts which were quite adequate—with occasional exceptions—for annual budgeting and production scheduling. With the rise in the popularity of computers, and the development of econometric forecasting models, company management decided to take advantage of this new technology. So, a Chicago management consulting firm was retained for $50,000 to develop a computer model, and to provide quarterly and annual forecasts. Joe was relegated to providing sales data to the consulting firm, and serving as the company's liaison with the consultant.

A couple of years after the automated forecasting system had been installed, I asked the comptroller of the company how it was working. "Fine," he said. "I think it was a good investment."

Later, I dropped by Joe's office and asked him how the forecasting system was working. "I suppose it's all right," Joe said. "The consultants send me the forecasts and I look them over. If they look okay, I send them on to management. If they seem to be out of line, I adjust them and send them back to the consulting firm. The consulting firm modifies the forecasts in terms of my suggestions, and we send them on to the management. It's really a pretty good system,"

Joe said. "I still make the forecasts, but I don't get blamed when they are wrong."

FORECASTING BEER

A major brewing company traditionally used a two-step sales forecast. The first step involved a forecast of sales by distributor territory which was made by the company's research department. This forecast took into consideration both industry and company trends. Using population data from the U.S. Department of Commerce to estimate the eighteen-year-olds coming into the beer market, the forecast also involved other economic indicators that, historically, had influenced the sale of beer.

The second step involved research department members visiting each distributor so that the distributors could review the forecasts for their areas in the light of their knowledge of competitive activity and local market trends. During these visits, the forecasts were sometimes revised to provide a more realistic reflection of the research department's estimates and the distributors' local knowledge. The result was a realistic forecast that served well as a basis for market planning.

Each of these examples deals with one of the more arcane facets of marketing—forecasting. The automobile industry example demonstrates that even the most sophisticated of inventory control systems ultimately depends upon the accuracy of the forecast upon which it is based. The second example suggests that even sophisticated forecasting systems need be ameliorated by an intimate knowledge of products and markets. Finally, the beer example shows how a thoughtful and systematic approach to forecasting provided a brewery with realistic estimates upon which to base its marketing programs.

This chapter examines two critical variables in the marketing plan—forecasts and the establishment of the variable marketing budget. Intimately bound together, these variables govern the magnitude of the marketing effort.

FORECASTING

Overestimating the importance of accurate sales forecasts in planning company activities is difficult. The company sales forecast serves as the basis for planning levels of production, the raw materials that will be required, the extent to which capital investments in production capacity must be made, the salary budgets the company can afford, and the marketing expenditures that can be budgeted. If the forecast is too high, unnecessary expenses will be incurred and company resources dissipated. If the forecast is too low, sales and profit opportunities will be irretrievably lost. And, forecasting is not an exact science; misjudgments are made. Even under the best of circumstances, an accurate forecast is often a delicate balance of errors.

Forecasting is a *top management* responsibility. Although the mechanics of forecasting can be delegated to the marketing research department, the sales department, or some other area in the company, the ultimate responsibility falls on the shoulders of management. The final sales forecast used for planning company activities carries the sanction of management to whom has been entrusted the welfare of the company.

A detailed discussion of forecasting and forecasting techniques is beyond the scope of this book. Yet a general review of forecasts that are often made and the major methods used is desirable because the marketing forecast is an indispensable part of the marketing review section of the marketing plan.

Types of Forecasts

Generally speaking, four forecasts may be made for individual products, depending upon the nature of the product and the competitive environment within which it is marketed. These are: forecasts of general economic activity, industry forecasts, product or brand forecasts, and company forecasts.

GENERAL FORECASTS OF ECONOMIC ACTIVITY. The general level of economic activity in the United States is reflected in the *Gross National Product* (GNP). The GNP is the value of all goods and services sold in the United States within a given year. Each year, estimates of the GNP are made by the President's Council of Economic Advisors, by leading economists, and by major companies.

Predictions of an increase in GNP indicate an increase in general economic activity which, in turn, signals increased sales and optimistic forecasts for individual industries and companies. Some industries, such as the automotive industry, major appliances, and construction are closely related to fluctuations in GNP. For these industries, forecasts of GNP should play a prominent role in making estimates of industry sales. For other industries less closely tied to general economic activity, fluctuations in GNP may not be a major consideration.

INDUSTRY FORECASTS. Regardless of whether GNP is the basis of a forecast for a particular industry, the industry forecast is of critical importance in determining sales of the individual companies making up that industry. Generally, when an industry is depressed the forecasts of the companies composing that industry are also depressed. Conversely, when increased industry sales are anticipated, optimistic forecasts and increased promotional activities characterize the behavior of individual producers. A case in point is the market for coffee in 1977–78. High and rising coffee prices resulted in decreased per capita consumption as consumers decreased their coffee purchases and switched to other beverages. By mid-1977, the market for regular coffee was estimated to decrease by 20 to 25 percent. These estimates led to a sharp reduction in the volume forecasts and promotional activities for traditional brands of coffee and an increase in product development and test marketing of lower-priced coffee substitutes such as General Foods' Mellow Roast (half coffee and half natural grains) and Nestle's Sunrise (54 percent coffee and 46 percent chicory).

Occasionally, an individual brand will buck industry trends and plan increased volume despite declining industry sales. In such instances, however, the review section of the marketing plan should contain persuasive reasons to justify optimism, such as: (1) clear-cut product or program superiorities that are expected to lead to substantial brand switching; (2) recent test market evidence that the brand is gaining share at a rate that offsets industry declines; or (3) firm evidence that a number of minor brands will drop out of the market as a result of economic pressures arising from the declining industry, and that the brand in question will be a major beneficiary of their demise.

PRODUCT FORECASTS. Examining GNP and industry forecasts should result in a realistic forecast for individual products. Industry changes, of course, are not the only factors entering into the brand forecast, although they are major considerations. The performance of a brand in a particular market always relates to the anticipated effectiveness of its marketing effort vis-a-vis competition. Knowledge of unusual development by competitors as well as the private knowledge that a company has of the effectiveness of its own marketing activities will influence the share of market the company expects to obtain. For example, assuming no significant changes in the magnitude or effectiveness of the marketing programs of a particular brand and its competitors, it is reasonable to assume the brand will hold approximately the same share of market for future periods as it held in the period just completed. On the other hand, any significant changes in marketing programs may lead to shifts in market share. Normally, one of the primary responsibilities of a marketing group is to strengthen its market and/or profit

"I don't know why we needed a $100,000 computer to make that forecast." (Photo by Billy E. Barnes)

position through the development and implementation of effective strategies. That's what they are paid for.

COMPANY FORECASTS. If a company is a single product company, the company forecast is the same as the brand or product forecast. In multiple product companies, however, the company forecast is the aggregate of its brand forecasts. Frequently, company strategy will require a reduced effort behind a particular brand (a holding action) so that the company resources may be placed behind brands that hold greater promise. Each product manager generally competes with other product managers for a share of the company resources. This competition recommends the product manager system to many companies. Ultimately, the overall welfare of the company, not the individual brand, is the overriding concern of top management. As a consequence, company strategy may sometimes invoke policy decisions that constrain the activities of individual brands.

Methods of Forecasting

None of the various methods for forecasting industry sales is infallible. For this reason, forecasters will often use a number of approaches, hoping for convergence within a narrow range of values. In the last analysis, however, a certain subjectivity occurs in the sales forecast, regardless of the sophistication of the forecasting techniques employed. Common forecasting techniques are briefly described in the following material.

TREND EXTENSION. One group of forecasting techniques, frequently used because of simplicity, can be classified as *trend extensions.* The trend extension approach may be highly successful for markets that have exhibited a historic pattern of stability, but it is full of pitfalls for volatile markets. Trend extension requires a history of relevant data. For example, if sales data for several years are available, future sales may be forecast by extrapolating the historic sales trend. The assumption underlying trend extensions is that the future will be similar to the past, with no major changes in the variables that influence sales. This assumption, of course, is the weakness of trend extensions. If any of the variables upon which the forecast is based changes in the future, inaccuracy will be introduced into the forecast.

Trend extension includes several approaches, some more sophisticated than others, but all subject to assumptions that the future will be similar to the past.

Proportion of GNP. For industries which tend to fluctuate with GNP, the forecaster can identify the nature of the relationship. For example, steel production tends to vary with GNP because the demand for steel in a variety of durable goods rises as national income rises, and decreases as national income declines. However, the relationship is seldom a one-to-one relationship. GNP can provide a rough gauge of steel sales, but steel industry forecasts must be refined through the use of other factors related to demand.

Simple Regression Analysis. Regression analysis is a statistical technique used to extrapolate historical trends. Step-by-step procedures for its calculation can be found in most introductory statistical texts. Through simple regression analysis, one can identify the slope of a line that best describes historical data. Figure 10–1 shows a scatter diagram that reflects time on the horizontal axis and unit sales for a hypothetical product on the vertical axis. Sales for each year are plotted in this diagram. The line in the diagram represents that line that best describes or "fits" the sales points. One

FIGURE 10–1: Scatter Diagram and Regression Line

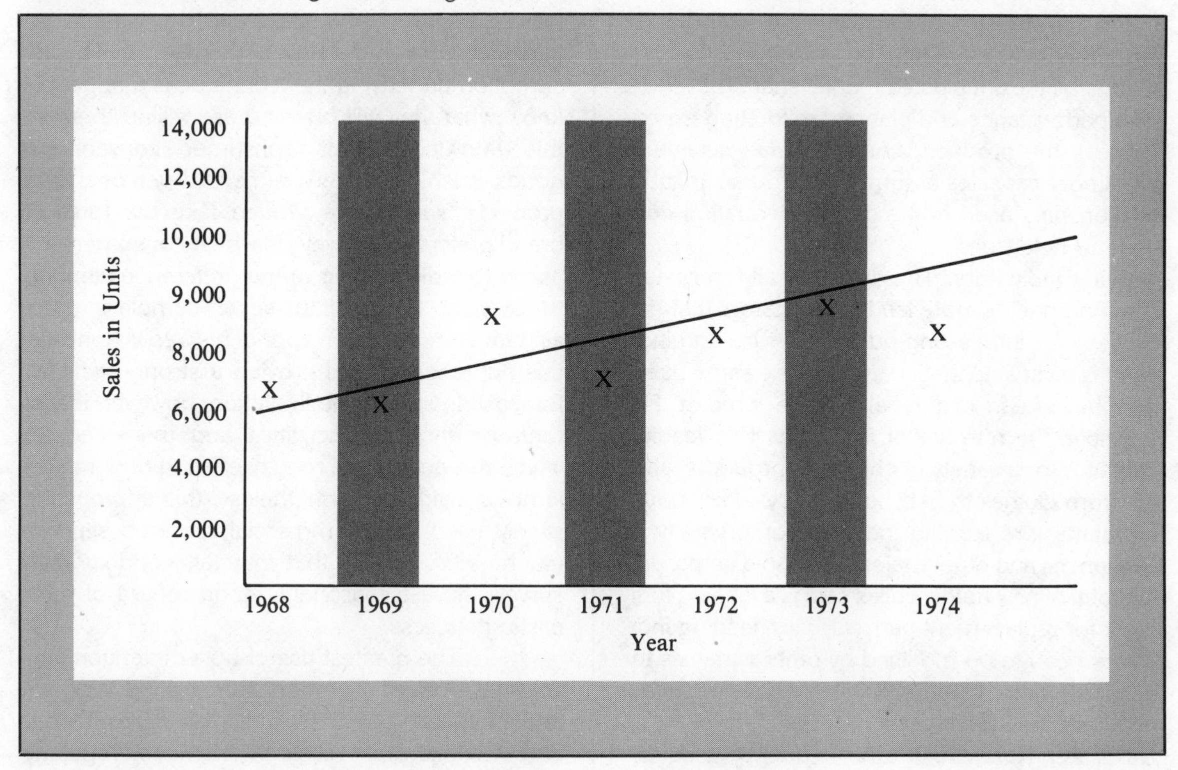

can, of course, prepare a scatter diagram and sketch in a line on the basis of visual inspection. Such a projection may be fairly accurate, but not as precise as the line derived from regression analysis.

Multiple Regression Analysis. A somewhat more sophisticated procedure for forecasting sales uses multiple regression. Whereas the simple regression example shown in Figure 10–1 uses only two variables—time and unit sales—multiple regression seeks to build a forecasting equation using several variables. For example, a demand equation for evaporated milk might be built by considering the price of whole milk, the price of evaporated milk, historical sales of evaporated milk, disposable income, sales of other milk substitutes, the number of children under the age of one year (because of the use of evaporated milk for infant feeding), and the sales of prepared infant formulas. The particular variables used are generally selected on the basis of judgment, and various combinations are manipulated mathematically until an acceptable fit is found.

One example of the use of multiple regression is that developed by the U.S. Department of Commerce for forecasting the sales of passenger cars.[2] The demand equation is:

$$Y = 0.0003X_1^{2.5} X_2^{2.3} X_3^{-1.4} (0.032)X_4$$

where:

Y = new private passenger car registrations per 1,000 households.

X_1 = real disposable income per household in base year dollars.

X_2 = current annual real disposable income per household as a percentage of the preceding year in base dollars.

X_3 = the percentage of average retail price of cars to all consumers' prices as measured by the consumer price index.

X_4 = the average scrappage age.

---

2. "Consumer Markets for Durable Goods," Survey of Current Business (April, 1958): 19.

Given this demand equation, an automobile producer could forecast the total market for passenger cars. Then, by multiplying the total market by the anticipated market share (based on past performance and planned marketing expenditures), the producer could estimate its future passenger car sales assuming, of course, that the relationships used in the demand equation continue to hold true.

Leading Indicators. The dream of all forecasters is to find one or more leading indicators that can be used for forecasting purposes. A leading indicator is a variable that changes in the same direction, but *ahead* of the sales to be forecast. For example, the number of live births is a leading indicator for a variety of children's products ranging from clothes to baby food to toys. New housing starts is a leading indicator for a variety of appliances and other major household items, and the total of new automobiles sold is a leading indicator for replacement parts. Usually, leading indicators need to be modified by other variables for accurate forecasting purposes, yet they provide a general framework for the forecast.

Sales Per Household. One frequently-used device is sales per household. Based on historic data, the sales per household for many commonly used consumer products can be projected. This projection, multiplied by the number of households projected for future years by the U.S. Department of Census, creates the estimated total sales for future years.

SUBJECTIVE METHODS. The trend extension methods referred to above are all based on the extension of past data. People may or may not behave the same way in the future. As a consequence, forecasting techniques have been devised that attempt to find out, either directly from customers or from other knowledgeable individuals, what the future promises. Often referred to as *subjective methods,* these methods are based on opinions rather than on hard, objective data. Three frequently used subjective methods are: surveys of buyer intentions, sales force opinion, and expert opinion.

Surveys of Buyer Intentions. Since all forecasting is an attempt to estimate what buyers are likely to do in the future, one approach is to survey all potential buyers for a given product or a representative sample of potential buyers to obtain this information from the buyers themselves. The assumption underlying the technique is that people know what they will buy and are willing to share this knowledge. For consumer convenience goods, such as grocery items and personal care products, such surveys often take the form of brand preference surveys in which consumers are asked to indicate their brand preferences among the available brands. If the survey sample is representative and if the respondents reply honestly, this approach should provide a strong basis for forecasting sales. One limitation, however, is that future competitive activities and the extent to which this activity will modify existing preferences is not considered. Nonetheless, this approach is widely used, and commercial research services (such as *Product Q*) that routinely conduct such surveys have a reasonably good record of forecasting success.

The greatest use of buyer intention surveys has been made for consumer durable goods and industrial products. In terms of consumer durables, several research services regularly produce reports of buying intentions.[3] These reports have proven themselves useful, but not wholly accurate, for short-range consumer durable forecasts. In the field of *industrial buying,* intention surveys for plant, equipment, and materials have been carried out by a number of agencies. The best known capital expenditure surveys are conducted by the U.S. Department of Commerce in collaboration with the Securities and Exchange Commission, and by McGraw-Hill's publication, *Business Week.*

Surveys of buying intentions have been used for a variety of products, but they are generally most satisfactory where the number of customers is small, the relationship between buyers and the seller is relatively close, and the cost of

---

3. Among the better known services are the Survey Research Center at the University of Michigan, Sindlinger and Company, the Conference Board, Inc., and the Commercial Credit Corporation. For a discussion of buyer intention surveys, see: "How Good Are Consumer Pollsters?" *Business Week* (November 9, 1969): 108–10.

obtaining the data is relatively low. For example, a chemical company with less than a hundred customers for a particular chemical purchased in large quantities would generally find intention surveys more useful and economical than a consumer product manufacturer such as Coca-Cola which has millions of potential customers, most of whom buy in relatively small quantities.

Sales Force Opinion. Many companies obtain estimates from their sales forces as part of their forecasting procedure. The assumption underlying this practice is that sales representatives are more likely to be familiar with customers' reactions and more aware of competitive activity than personnel in the home office. This assumption has a great deal of merit since sales reps, in their day-to-day activities, are intimately involved with customers, or with retailers where extended lines of distribution are employed. Sales reps are also more aware of the extent to which point-of-sale material or other forms of local promotion are being used and often have a more current (although unsystematic) picture of sales than do analysts in the home office. On the negative side, sales reps are often "overinfluenced" by purely local activities and usually unaware of larger economic developments and of company plans. Further, their perceptions are often distorted by their own proclivities for optimism or pessimism and by their recent experiences in the field.

Few companies use sales personnel's estimates without some modification, and most frequently they are used as checks against home office forecasts. Involving salespeople in the forecasting procedure provides them with a sense of participation; they are often more willing to accept the final forecast and the sales quotas derived from it.

Expert Opinion. Closely related to sales force opinion is the use of opinions from experts in the product field. These experts may be company executives who, by virtue of their experience, are able to make valuable contributions to the forecast; they may be company distributors; or they may be members of independent consulting firms. In the brewery example used at the beginning of this chapter, opinions of company distributors were sought.

Automobile manufacturers routinely solicit estimates of sales directly from their dealers, and many companies regularly subscribe to forecasts from public and private agencies that sell periodic forecasts of both short-term and long-term business conditions. The advantages of obtaining expert opinions are that estimates can often be obtained quickly; diverse points of view can be obtained and reconciled to gain a "balanced" forecast; and often, particularly in the case of new products, there is no alternative source of data upon which to base forecasts.

One problem with expert opinions is how to reconcile differences among experts. If all of the experts' forecasts converge within a relatively small range, this is no problem. If, however, they are widely divergent (and they sometimes are), some method of resolving these differences must be found. Methods of resolution may be broken down into two groups: *single estimates* and *reiterations.*

Dealing With Single Estimates. In single estimates, experts are asked to forecast sales for a particular period. Discrepancies may be resolved by discussion, averaging, or weighting.

- *Discussion.* This approach works best when only company personnel are involved. During a meeting, the various estimates and the thinking behind them are explained; the group attempts to resolve any discrepancies through discussion. Although the goal is to obtain consensus, resolution may have to be made by majority agreement.
- *Averaging.* In this approach, estimates are given to an individual who assumes that all estimates are of equal validity, and simply averages them to obtain a single value.
- *Weighting.* As in averaging, the estimates are given to an individual; however, they are not assumed to have equal validity. Instead, each estimator is weighted in terms of experience, knowledge, and history of accuracy. For example, one estimator may be given a weight of .3; still another, a weight of .1; and a third, who merits a great deal of confidence, may be given a weight of .6. The weighted values are then averaged to arrive at a final estimate.

Reiteration Methods. A second approach to reconciling expert opinions is to use a sequential series of estimates from the same panel of experts. Each expert is asked to submit an estimate with a rationale. The various estimates are summarized; often an average or medium estimate along with the range of estimates, is computed. This data is sent back to each expert who reviews the data, and submits a second estimate. The same procedure is repeated over and over again until either reasonable consensus is reached, or further iterations are determined to be unproductive.[4]

For the most part, subjective methods are used to supplement other sources of data, to serve as a check on trend analysis estimates or to supply information where no historic data is available. Since forecasting is always an uncertain undertaking, forecasters try to bring as many sources of information as possible to bear on their task.

Special Problems of Forecasting

Market forecasting becomes particularly difficult in highly volatile markets or in the case of new products where no historic data is available. Because there is no good answer in these instances, the marketing group must devise an acceptable method of its own. For example, when diethylstilbestrol—a hormone for fattening cattle—was introduced, there was no past history for forecasting its rate of acceptance and the future growth of the market. The marketing group working on the project, however, came up with an extremely imaginative approach.

- First, they assumed that acceptance by cattle feeders would be dependent upon the return on investment produced by product use. For example, a product that produced five dollars in incremental revenues for each dollar invested would be accepted more quickly than a product producing only two dollars in incremental revenues for each dollar invested.
- Next they computed the return on investment for a wide range of farm innovations—fertilizers, herbicides, antibiotics, and so forth—and the rate of growth for each of these products. An illustrative result of this is shown in Figure 10–2.
- Then, they computed the estimated return on investment for diethylstilbestrol, based on experimental data, and compared it to the data illustrated in Figure 10–2. From this, they estimated the percent of acceptance that would be accorded diethylstilbestrol.
- Finally, they applied this percentage to the known universe of cattle feeders and came up with an estimate of the market that proved remarkably accurate.

4. The best known of the iteration techniques is the Delphi Method developed by the Rand Corporation for forecasting technological developments. See: R. J. Tersine and W. E. Riggs, "The Delphi Technique—A Long Range Planning Tool," *Business Horizons* (April, 1967): 51–56; Norman Dalkey and Olaf Helmer, "An Experimental Application of the Delphi Method to the Use of Experts," *Management Science* (April, 1963): 458–67; Roger J. Best, "An Experiment in Delphi Estimation in Marketing Decision Making," *Journal of Marketing Research* (November, 1974): 447–52.

Test markets are also useful in estimating demand for new products where there is no historic data from which to draw. The results of the test market are then extrapolated to the entire U.S. population. For example, let us assume that the test markets used had a population of 930,000 people, or 0.372 percent of the total U.S. population. Let us also assume that, during the first year, 18,600 cases of product were sold in the test markets. Estimated sales for the total U.S.

FIGURE 10–2: *Illustrative Relationship Between Acceptance of Agricultural Innovations and Incremental Revenue*

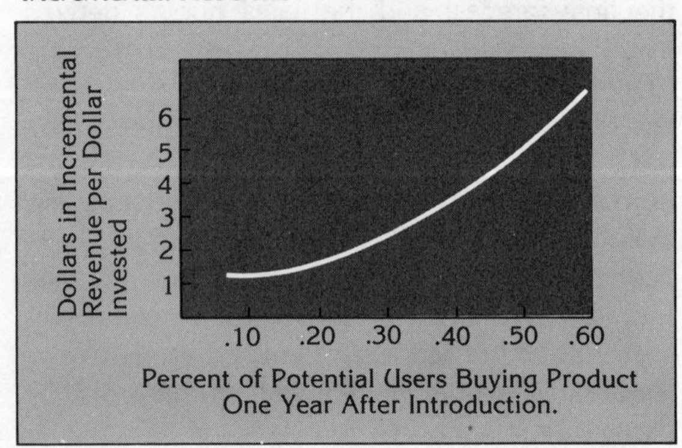

could then be projected as 5 million cases (18,600 ÷ .00372).

One problem with this procedure, as pointed out earlier, is that test market response may not be representative of the total United States. Compensating for this problem by using test markets in different regions, is, at best, a poor compensation. Yet, sometimes, this is all one has, and forecasting decisions have to be made.

REGIONAL AND SEASONAL FORECASTS

Sometimes, in making a national forecast, marketers will make separate forecasts for individual regions, and combine these regional forecasts to reach a national total. Such a forecasting procedure has been referred to as the *buildup* method of forecasting. Quite frequently, however, a national forecast is made first, and then broken down into various regions. This step is necessary to provide guidance in allocating marketing expenditures in various geographic regions.

Many products vary in sales by regions. Straight whiskeys, for example, have their highest per capita consumption in a band of states extending across the southern part of the country and up the west coast. Blended whiskeys tend to sell best in the upper midwest, and Scotch whiskeys have the bulk of their sales in the major metropolitan areas of New York, Washington, D.C., Miami, Cleveland, St. Louis, Chicago, Los Angeles, and San Francisco. The per capita consumption of dry dog food is 20 to 50 percent over the U.S. average in the East Central, North Central, and South Central states. Rice cereals do not sell well in the south.

The regional variations for many products are ideosyncratic and based on obscure, historical developments. Nonetheless, these variations are of the utmost importance to the advertiser whose success depends upon the wise allocation of available funds. Where geographic patterns are unique to an industry, knowledge of regional variations must be derived from industry sources such as trade associations, from a variety of government or private sources, from consumer surveys, or from national retail audits.

In the absence of industry sales figures for specific geographic areas, companies often develop *indexes of buying power.* Thus, a marketer might assume that the pattern of sales for a product will follow the distribution of population, retail sales, automotive sales, general merchandise sales, or some other measurable factor. The distribution of the variables listed above can be obtained from *Sales Management's Survey of Buying Power.* For example, a producer of headache remedies might assume that users of this product type are distributed uniformly throughout the population. If the state of Virginia accounted for 2.31 percent of the U.S. population, it would account for 2.31 percent of the headache remedy market. Generally, a single factor such as population is an inadequate indicator of sales opportunity. Other variables such as disposable income, population density, retail drug sales, or doctors per thousand families might be important variables in this particular case. This possibility leads to the development of multiple-factor indexes, with each factor being assigned a specific weight in the index.

One of the better known, general-purpose, multiple-factor indexes of area demand is that published in the *Survey of Buying Power.* This index is given by the formula:

$$B_i = .5y_i + .3r_i + .2p_i$$

where:

B_i = percentage of total national buying power found in area *i*.

y_i = percentage of national disposable personal income originating in area *i*.

r_i = percentage of national retail sales in area *i*.

p_i = percentage of national population located in area *i*.

Sales Management does not contend that this general purpose index will apply to all products; it does contend, however, that this index does reflect the market for many goods that are neither luxury items nor low-priced staples.

Regional market potential estimates reflect the opportunity for an entire industry, not for the individual company. The individual company must estimate its market share based on distribution, the level of competitive activity, and past performance in the area. In other words, given the market potential in a particular area, companies still must estimate the share of that potential they can acquire. This share represents the company's sales estimate.

In addition to variations by regions, the sales of many products vary by season. Swimming suits, for example, are sold primarily during the spring and summer months, although they may enjoy a year long market in extreme southern areas blessed with mild winters. Diet foods also have a seasonal pattern that picks up in the spring and summer. Hot drinks, such as coffee and hot chocolate, enjoy sales peaks in the winter months. Gift chocolate and greeting card sales concentrate 80 percent of their annual figures around Christmas, Valentine's Day, and Mothers' Day. This is the reason why greeting card companies, such as Hallmark, do not employ year around advertising schedules. Instead they concentrate their advertising appropriations in television "specials" immediately preceding peak demand periods. Few products are completely immune to seasonal variations, although many seasonal variations are less extreme than the examples cited above.

As a consequence, annual forecasts often have to be decomposed on a seasonal basis to determine the seasonal allocation of marketing expenditures.

DETERMINATION OF THE MARKETING BUDGET

The purpose of forecasting is to arrive at a sales projection that will enable a company to compute income, expenses, and profit. A major part of the expense side of the budget, particularly for consumer product companies, is expenditures for marketing. Marketing expenditures can be divided into two categories:

- *Fixed and semifixed expenses.* These expenditures include such things as salaries, office space, utilities, supplies, and so forth. Remaining relatively fixed from year to year, they are difficult to reduce on a short-term basis.
- *Variable marketing expenses.* These expenses vary from period to period or year to year in support of the company's products. Included are advertising, sales promotion, special marketing research projects, product publicity, package design, test markets, trade shows, and so forth.

Our primary concern in this chapter will be with the second of these two expense categories—*variable marketing expenses.* These expenses are the focus of the yearly marketing plan.

Table 10–1 shows a simplified pro forma budget for a hypothetical company. In Table 10–1, after all expenses *except* advertising and promotion have been subtracted from income, the residual of $9,033,000 is sometimes referred to as "contribution to profit." The contribution figure is what the company has to promote the brand *and* to make a profit. Obviously, the more that is spent for marketing, the less the profit will be. In this particular instance, 60 percent of the contribution has been allocated for marketing, leaving a profit before taxes of $3,613,200. The critical role of forecasting can now be seen. Let us assume that actual sales were 10 percent less than forecast, or $48,220,200 instead of $53,578,000. Cost of goods would also be decreased by 10 percent, of course, but gross margin would be decreased by $1,668,600, to $15,017,400. Assuming that no reductions were made in advertising and sales promotion expenditures, profits before taxes would drop from $3,613,200 to $1,944,600—a decrease of approximately 46 percent.

Is $5,419,800 the proper amount to spend for marketing in this case? That all depends. It depends upon the nature of the market and the level of competitive activity. It depends upon how much profit the company needs. It depends on the objectives of the company. It depends upon the effectiveness of the company's programming and the persuasiveness of its creative effort. In short, there is no easy answer. Eldridge has pointed out:

TABLE 10–1: *Pro Forma Operating Budget*

Sales (000's cases)	6,230,000	
Income ($8.60/case)	$53,578,000	
Minus: cost of goods (including packaging)	36,892,000	
Gross Margin		$16,686,000
Expenses		
Sales expense (including sales force, freight, and warehousing)	$ 3,682,500	
Administrative overhead	2,162,000	
Other fixed and semifixed expenses	1,808,500	
Total expenses		7,653,000
Contribution to profit		$9,033,000
Less: Marketing expense (60%)		5,419,800
Profit before taxes		$3,613,200

Management is called upon to make no decisions that are more important, or that can more significantly affect the health, growth, and profitability of the business than those involving the marketing budget. In many companies whose success depends upon effective marketing programs, the cost of marketing is the largest controllable expense; in some companies the cost of marketing a product is even greater than the cost of producing it—including raw materials, labor, and packaging costs.[5]

A number of methods are used to establish the communications appropriation, some are better than others, but none wholly satisfactory. Each of them, however, speaks to some aspect of the allocation process. Five such methods, along with their advantages and disadvantages are discussed below.

The Affordable Method

One of the least effective methods of determining the advertising and sales promotion budget is to spend what the company can afford. Generally, the determining factor is the level of profit required by the company. In such cases, management earmarks a given amount for profit, and any excess funds in the contribution portion of the budget may be spent for marketing communications. Joel Dean, an economist, has puckishly suggested that everything above a respectable return on capital could be spent for advertising "... since excess earnings have low utility to management as such, compared with the *possible* contribution of continuous advertising to the eternal life of the firm."[6] Generally, this approach is most frequently used in companies where advertising objectives are poorly defined and advertising serves a public relations function, as is sometimes the case with public utilities.

The problem is that the affordable method fails to take into consideration the marketing job that has to be done. Consequently, the amount appropriated for advertising and sales promotion may be excessive for the task or sadly inadequate.

At the same time, though, this approach tacitly recognizes the role of budget constraints. Profit *is* a necessary function of a firm. Without an adequate level of profit over the long term, businesses simply do not survive. True, the profit required may vary year by year, and on some

5. Clarence E. Eldridge, *The Marketing Budget and Its Allocation in the Advertising Budget* (New York: Association of National Advertisers, Inc., 1967): 25.

6. Joel Dean, *Managerial Economics* (Englewood Cliffs, NJ: Prentice-Hall, Inc., 1951): 368.

occasions a firm may forego profit entirely because of investment requirements or marketing demands. Nonetheless, the requirement for profit normally places an upper limit on the marketing appropriation.

Percentage of Sales Method

Many companies prefer to set their communications budget as a percent of sales, or a fixed amount per case or unit. Automobile manufacturers typically budget a certain amount per car, and oil companies tend to set their communications budget as a fraction of a cent for each gallon of gasoline sold. Similarly, packaged goods manufacturers often appropriate a certain amount per case.

When such appropriations are based on projected or forecast sales, the approach appears to have a certain merit in that the greater the forecast, the greater the expenditure. Conversely, during times of depressed forecasts, communications expenditures are cut accordingly. In addition, when by tacit agreement all factors in the industry utilize a similar percentage, advertising wars are averted and a certain stability is enjoyed by the industry.

Although many companies use this approach, it does have major limitations. First, appropriations are set by anticipated sales or availability of funds rather than by marketing opportunities. Second, the percentage spent, or the amount allocated per unit, is often arbitrary and may bear little relationship to the amount that must be spent to develop the total market effectively. Finally, competitive positions tend to become fixed since all competitors are utilizing similar advertising to sales ratios, and real competition is at a minimum.

On the positive side, this approach recognizes the need for a minimum expenditure level demanded by competition. As demand increases, competitive appropriations generally increase; the firm that fails to keep pace may anticipate a decline in share. Thus, it is reasonable for a firm to establish a standard expenditure rate based on a percentage of sales or a fixed allocation per unit with the provision that marketing opportunities and problems may require a deviation from this standard. One advantage of having a standard is that the firm can evaluate deviations from the standard costs involved in pursuing a particular marketing opportunity.

Share of Advertising Method

A truism in marketing states "all other things being equal, share of market will equal share of advertising." And, while "all other things" are seldom equal, this concept serves as the basis for the share of advertising method of allocating advertising expenditures. This approach, based on empirical studies in the food and drug fields, was offered by J. O. Peckham, executive vice-president of the A. C. Nielsen Company in the mid-1960s. If a marketer keeps product and advertising appeals competitive with the rest of the field, the best insurance for maintaining or increasing market share is to keep share of advertising at a point somewhat ahead of share of sales. For *new* brands being introduced into the market, Peckham found that the initial rate of expenditure should be approximately double the share of sales desired. For example, assume that a new brand is being marketed in a product field in which annual sales are $60 million and annual advertising expenditures are $8 million. Also assume that the market share objective for the new brand is 25 percent. Then

Annual sales goal (25 percent of $60,000,000) = $15,000,000
Annual advertising allocation (50 percent of $8,000,000) = $ 4,000,000

The *disadvantages* of this approach are that: all other variables are seldom equal; it tends to focus on advertising to the exclusion of other marketing variables; and it does not take profit needs into consideration.

The *advantages* of this method are that it emphasizes the need to be aware of competitive activity as one aspect of market performance; it deals with measurable quantities and provides a rough basis for setting the advertising appropriation; and it provides a rough diagnostic tool. For example, if market share consistently lags significantly behind share of advertising, some other aspect of the marketing mix (copy appeals, media selection, product, price, distribution, package, and so forth) is out of kilter and should be reexamined. Or, market share significantly above advertising share may signal an opportunity for improving market position through an increase in advertising expenditures.

Objective and Task Method

In the objective and task method, the firm establishes a sales goal, asks what tasks need to be done to achieve this goal, estimates the cost of each task separately, and then totals these costs to arrive at the marketing allocation required. The objective and task method has a certain logic and appeal that accounts for its growing popularity. Charles A. Mortimer, who rose through advertising and marketing to the presidency of General Foods, has stated:

> The task method is built brick by brick; not pulled out of a hat, or devined with a willow wand. . . . It is based on a concrete estimate of the job to be done. It uses extensively past advertising experience—all that is available—but never accepts any rule of thumb or past statistical relation as a sufficient guide for expenditures without reexamination of the nature of the task and the most promising method of accomplishing it *this* year—not *last* year. It involves constant awareness of what the competitors are doing with respect to advertising themes and expenditures, but it does not blindly follow the competitors' program.
>
> The only safe assumption to make in determining advertising expenditures is that each year—or campaign—involves a task that is *new* in some important respect. Old measurements and old answers, accepted uncritically, are not good enough.[7]

On the surface, the task and objective method appears to be the answer to prayer. But it's not. Its major strengths are emphasis on situational analysis, recognition of the dynamic nature of marketing, and the need to identify the job to be done. The task and objective method introduces a note of realism into marketing allocations by relating the variety and magnitude of the marketing tasks with the size of the allocation. And this is all to the good.

On the negative side, this method has two shortcomings: it fails to consider the need for profit and whether a particular objective is worth pursuing in terms of its costs; and it oversimplifies, by implication, the difficulty of determining how much effort will be required to accomplish a given task. Marketing is filled with risks. That is one of its charms. And the best laid schemes do not always accomplish intended goals. That is one of its frustrations.

A Practical Point of View

From a practical point of view, most sophisticated companies use all of these methods in arriving at their marketing allocation.

- As in the affordable method, availability of funds and the need for profit are considerations.
- As in the percent-of-sales method, management identifies a standard or normal rate of expenditure based on a percent of sales or fixed allocation per unit or case.
- As in the share of advertising method, they recognize the relationship between share of market and share of advertising, and they often use this rough relationship in defining the level of the marketing appropriation.
- Finally, all of these approaches are consolidated in the task and objective approach which specifically takes into consideration the variety of tasks that must be done in order to accomplish marketing objectives.

Let's take a look at how this pragmatic approach might be applied by a sophisticated company. To do this, we will introduce three new terms: *return on investment, economic profit,* and *payout plan.*

7. Charles G. Mortimer, Jr., "How Much Should You Spend on Advertising," in Roger Barton, (ed), *Advertising Handbook* (Englewood Cliffs, NJ: Prentice-Hall, Inc., 1967): 113–15

RETURN ON INVESTMENT (ROI). Return on investment is a profit criterion frequently used by firms to determine whether they should or should not compete in a particular product field. ROI is a ratio between the capital investment required to enter a business and the annual profit the business will produce. Take the simplified operations statement used in Table 10–1 to demonstrate this concept. The sales income in Table 10–1 is $53,578,000. Let us assume that it costs the company $10,000,000 in capital investment to build the plant and buy the equipment needed to produce this product. Let us also assume that the firm requires an annual ROI of 20 percent before taxes. In order to meet its profit requirements, the $53,578,000 in sales must produce a profit of $2,000,000 ($10,000,000 × .20 = $2,000,000). This $2,000,000 may be considered as a cost of doing business since this level of profit is a policy requirement for making the necessary capital investment.

ECONOMIC PROFIT. Economic profit refers to that profit a firm makes over and above its minimal profit requirements. The firm in Table 10–1 made a contribution to profit of $9,033,000. Since the firm only needs $2,000,000 in profits to meet its ROI objectives, it is earning an *economic profit* of $7,033,000 ($9,033,000 − $2,000,000 = $7,033,000) *before* marketing expenses. This $7,033,000, referred to as *available funds,* is the amount available for economic profit and marketing expenditures.

Now, let us assume that, normally, the firm expects to realize 30 percent of the available funds for economic profit, and to allocate 70 percent of the funds for marketing. Then, normal expenditures for a sales level of $53,578,000 would be $4,923,100. These relationships are:

Sales (1000s cases)	6,230,000
Income from sales	$53,578,000
Contribution to profit	9,033,000
Less: required ROI	2,000,000
Available funds ($1.13/case)	$ 7,033,000
Less: economic profit (30%)	2,109,900
Normal marketing allocation (70%)	$ 4,923,100
Normal marketing allocation as a percent of sales	9.2%
Normal marketing allocation per case	$0.79

Now, as long as the marketing request for funds falls within the area of $0.79 per case or 9.2 percent of sales, the marketing department and top management will not have any problems; provided, of course, that the marketing forecast appears realistic, the brand is doing reasonably well, the strategies and plans seem to be well conceived, and the creative approach doesn't offend anyone. From management's point of new, the marketing appropriation is in the *normal* range of the cost of doing business, they are getting their profit goodies, and all's well with the world.

But now, let's blow up utopia. Let us suppose that the market is in a real turmoil. A major competitor has just come up with a smashing creative approach; another competitor has launched what appears to be an extremely effective sales promotion program; the company has developed a product improvement that marks a real opportunity for increased sales. In short, the price of doing business has just gone up. And, in the judgment of marketing management, a significant increase in the marketing expenditure is required. This leads us to the concept of payout plans.

Payout Plan

Payout, as it is used here, refers to the time required to recover an *investment* in marketing. A *payout plan* is a projection that shows funds available, funds spent, and the resulting economic profit. Payout plans seldom exceed three years because of the difficulty of projecting sales and income with reasonable accuracy beyond this period. Generally, the length of payout plans has been decreasing during the past decade or so because technology and competitive response has tended to shorten time that a product or marketing advantage can be maintained. In the 1950s and early 1960s, for example, three year payout plans were common. More recently, one and two year payout plans have become the norm. Table 10–2 illustrates the mechanics of a three year payout plan using the figures we have developed

Table 10–2: Three-year Payout Plan

	Units and Dollars in Thousands		
	Year 1	Year 2	Year 3
Total market (cases)	31,150.0	32,705.5	34,669.9
Share of market	20.0%	23.1%	25.0%
Company forecast (cases)	6,230.0	7,552.7	8,667.5
Funds available ($1.13/case)	7,039.9	8,534.6	9,794.3
Expenditures	9,950.0	8,571.5	6,847.3
Economic profit/loss	(2,910.1)	(36.9)	2,947.0
Cumulative economic profit/loss	(2,910.1)	(2,947.0)	–0–
Cost per case	$1.60	$1.13	$0.79

thus far. Note that, in this table, total *available funds* for the entire three-year period are allocated for marketing expenditures; substantial investments in the first two periods cause losses to be incurred. In the third year, marketing expenditures have returned to normal ($0.79 per case), and the investment has been recovered. For the entire period, no economic profit is earned. However, at the end of the three-year period, the firm holds an increased share of an expanded market, and future economic profits will be substantially greater than they have been in the past.

The payout plan clarifies three things for management: the money that will have to be invested to achieve desired results; time required for the investment; and the benefits that will accrue from the investment. With this information, management can decide whether the risks and potential gain are worth the required investment. The payout approach is commonly used by sophisticated marketers for all new products as well as for other major marketing investments such as business building tests.

Hedging the Marketing Budget

Both forecasting and budget determination are central considerations in the development of marketing plans. Although sophisticated quantitative models are sometimes used in making these determinations, the dynamics of the marketing situation precludes total reliance on such mechanical approaches. Consequently, the role of experience, judgment, and a sense of marketing opportunity make budget determination as much an art as a science.

Since marketing forecasts contain some uncertainty, many firms choose to hedge their marketing allocation. A common way of doing this is to hold some amount, say 10 percent, of the budget in reserve, with the stipulation that this reserve will be released for spending if sales follow the forecast after the first six months of the fiscal year. This procedure minimizes cutting back the marketing program to meet profit objectives if sales lag somewhat behind forecast.

Allocation of the Marketing Budget

Thus far we have talked about determining the total marketing budget. The allocation of the total budget to particular marketing activities will be dictated by strategic considerations and based on the tasks to be done. For most consumer goods, the bulk of the budget is normally allocated to advertising and sales promotion. Where special objectives and strategies are an important part of the marketing plan, substantial expenditures may be made in research, market tests, or other special activities.

SUMMARY

This chapter examines two critical variables in the marketing plan—forecasts and the communications budget. These variables are intimately bound together and govern the magnitude of the marketing effort.

Overestimating the importance of accurate sales forecasts in planning company activities is hard, because such forecasts serve as the basis for all financial planning in the company.

Generally, four forecasts may be necessary for individual companies: forecasts of general economic activity, industry forecasts, product or brand forecasts, and company forecasts.

No method of forecasting is infallible. As a consequence, forecasters often use a number of approaches, hoping for convergence. Two basic methods of forecasting are *trend extensions* and *subjective.*

Sometimes, forecasts are first made for regions, which are combined to obtain a national forecast. This approach is referred to as the *build-up* system of forecasting. On other occasions, a national forecast is made first, and then decomposed into regions to provide guidance for regional marketing expenditures.

The forecast determines a sales budget that will enable the company to compute its income, expenses, and profits. A major part of the expense budget is expenditures for marketing. Marketing expenditures can be divided into two groups: fixed and variable. This chapter is primarily concerned with variable marketing expenses because these expenses are the focus of the yearly marketing plan.

A number of methods are used to establish the variable marketing appropriation. The *affordable method,* which emphasizes the importance of profits; the *percentage of sales* method, which recognizes the need for a minimum expenditure to keep abreast of competition; the *share of advertising* method, which recognizes the relationship between share of market and share of advertising; and the *objective and task* method, which focuses on the task to be accomplished. Because no one approach is completely satisfactory, the sophisticated marketer usually uses them all.

Since marketing forecasts are, at best, uncertain, many marketers hedge their marketing budget by setting aside a portion as a reserve against failure to achieve projected sales.

1. Explain why the forecast is crucial in planning company activities. What are the penalties for a forecast that is too high? For one that is too low?
2. Explain what is meant by GNP. In which industries does a GNP forecast play a major role in making industry and company forecasts? Why?
3. Identify some of the conditions that would cause a company to forecast sales increases for a brand in an industry that is stagnant or declining.
4. Explain what is meant by trend extension forecasting. What is the primary assumption that underlies its use, and what are its primary limitations?
5. Explain what is meant by *leading indicators.* Give an example of such an indicator, showing how it might be used.
6. Under what conditions might a survey of buyers' intentions be most helpful and least helpful in preparing a forecast for a company's products?
7. Identify the primary advantages and disadvantages of sales-force opinion in preparing forecasts. How are sales force opinions generally used?
8. What are the advantages and disadvantages of each of the following methods for setting the variable marketing budget: affordable method; the percent-of-sales method; the share of advertising method; and the objective and task method?
9. Explain ROI and economic profit. Relate these concepts to the terms: profit contribution and available funds.
10. Explain a *payout plan.* Identify how a payout plan helps management evaluate a decision to invest additional funds in a marketing program.

1. Two forecasters working for the same home appliance company arrived at substantially different forecasts for the company's line of refrigerators. Does this imply that sales forecasting is largely guesswork?
2. Suggest some plausible explanations for year-to-year fluctuations in the sales of: automobiles, play pens for children, automobile tires, racquet ball equipment.
3. The following table shows the sales of skis in units for the past seven years for a manufacturer of sports equipment. Based on this data, what would you forecast for the eighth year? How did you arrive at your forecast? What other information would improve your forecast?

Year	Unit sales	Year	Unit sales
1	10,250	5	13,100
2	14,000	6	13,300
3	9,130	7	14,000
4	12,860		

4. A brewer wants to develop a multiple regression equation to explain state-by-state variations in sales. What variables should be tested? If the resulting equation explains most of the state-by-state variations, would the equation be a good method for forecasting future sales of the company's brand?
5. Your company has developed a significant improvement in a nationally-marketed grocery product. Based on test markets, you have found that the improved product increased your market share significantly. The current total market for your product field is 42 million cases, and your company sales are 9,240,000 cases (a 22 percent share of the market). Your funds available are $1.30 per case, and your normal marketing expenditure is $0.80 per case, leaving $0.50 per case for economic profit. Based on the test market results, you have put together the following payout plan for a national expansion of the test market program.

	Year 1	Year 2	Year 3
Total market (000's cases)	44,100.0	46,305.0	48,620.2
Company market share	25%	25.5%	26.0%
Company sales (000's cases)	11,025.0	11,807.8	12,641.2
Funds available ($1.30/case)	$14,332.50	$15,350.10	$16,433.60
Marketing expenditure	$21,500.00	$14,503.20	$10,113.00
Profit/loss	($7,167.50)	$846.90	$6,320.60
Cumulative profit/loss	($7,167.50)	($6,320.60)	(0)
Expenditure per case	$1.95	$1.23	$0.80

Decide whether you should recommend this payout plan to management. What is your decision? How did you arrive at it? What are the assumptions upon which the payout plan is based?

CHAPTER PROBLEM

FORECASTING AND THE MARKETING BUDGET

Mark Linden, product manager for Cook's Choice Instant Pudding Mix was preparing a marketing plan for the next fiscal year. The pudding market was a relatively stable market, and Cook's Choice held a dominant share. Sales and brand share for the past five years are shown in Table 1.

TABLE 1: *Cook's Choice Instant Pudding Sales and Brand Share*

	Total Market	Cook's Choice	Market Share
1976	30,550,000	7,484,700	24.5%
1977	31,466,500	7,740,800	24.6%
1978	32,095,800	7,863,500	24.5%
1979	33,219,200	8,205,100	24.7%
1980	34,547,900	8,533,300	24.7%

Instant pudding mixes, popular both for puddings and pie fillings because of their ease of preparation, were considered by many consumers to be in inferior in texture and flavor to regular puddings which took longer to prepare. These shortcomings of instant pudding mixes had put a ceiling on the market. Cook's Choice research and development department had been working on an improved formula of the product for several years. In 1979 they developed an instant pudding product that was comparable to regular puddings in richness, texture, and flavor.

The new mix had been introduced as "new and improved" product in three test markets in 1980. While performance varied on a market-by-market basis, the overall results were highly encouraging. The funds available for instant pudding mix were $1.20 per case, of which 65 percent was normally allocated to advertising and sales promotion and 35 percent was retained as profit. In the test markets, however, the company had spent at double the normal rate. A comparison of test market sales compared to the rest of the country is shown in Table 2.

Mark Linden wondered whether, on the basis of test market results, he should recommend a program of investment spending to introduce the new product nationally in 1981. And, if so, he wondered how long a payout he should recommend.

TABLE 2: *Cook's Choice Test Markets*

	Total Market	Cook's Choice	Market Share
Combined Test Markets			
1979	664,400	162,800	24.5%
1980	730,800	208,300	28.5%
Rest of Country			
1979	32,554,800	8,042,300	24.6%
1980	33,817,100	8,325,000	24.6%

Linden knew that competition had been alerted to the product change by the test markets in 1980, but discussions with research and development personnel had partially assured him that the competition would take at least eighteen to thirty months to duplicate the new product. The reason for this long developmental time was that the product improvement involved a formula change that would be time consuming to duplicate, a change in the way in which the dry milk ingredient was processed, and a change in cooking temperatures. Even after the competition had duplicated the process, it would take at least six months to acquire the special equipment required to manufacture in volume.

Based on the relative consistency of the three test markets, on some consumer tests, and his own evaluation of the new product, Linden felt pretty confident about the test market results.

Assignment

Develop a forecast and spending plan for the national introduction of the new product, recognizing that some kind of payout plan will be required. Suggestion to students: In preparing a payout plan, use the following procedure:

1. *Estimate the total market for each year of the payout plan.*
2. *Estimate market share for each year.*
3. *Compute company sales in cases for each year.*
4. *Determine funds available for each year of the payout plan by multiplying expected company sales in cases by funds available per case.*

5. *Combine the funds available in each year of the payout plan to obtain total funds available.*
6. *Determine planned expenditure for the last year of the payout plan by multiplying the estimated company sales in cases during this year by the normal expenditure per case.*
7. *Subtract the planned expenditure in the last year of the payout plan from the total funds available to determine how much is available for the preceding years. Allocate this amount over the preceding years on the basis of judgment.*
8. *Compute economic profit and loss and cumulative profit and loss.*
9. *Compute cost per case for expenditures for each year of the payout plan.*

Marketing communications.
(Photo by Freda Leinwand)

MARKETING COMMUNICATIONS AND THE ELEMENTS OF MARKETING

In a mass production economy, marketing is communications. But, it is communications with a special purpose, and that purpose is persuasion.

If marketing does not persuade consumers to try a product or service, or to accept a new idea, then marketing has not fulfilled its function. A product marketing program that leaves consumers indifferent to its product has not only failed, but has also wasted company resources.

Persuasive marketing does not start and end with advertising, which is widely recognized—and often criticized—as an instrument of persuasion. Instead, effective persuasion involves every element of the marketing program.

When a product performs poorly, or a package design fails to attract consumers' interests, or a pricing structure discourages trade support and consumer purchase, then the process of persuasion has broken down as surely as when an advertising program leaves the consumer unmoved.

Indeed, every element of the marketing program has a task in the persuasion process. In this section of the text, we will examine each major element of the marketing plan as an instrument of persuasion.

Chapter 11 sets the stage for the succeeding chapters by focusing on the communications process and the importance of both verbal and nonverbal communications in forming the brand image.

Chapter 12 is concerned with the product itself, with the role of consumer expectations in product satisfaction, with product development, and with product strategies.

Chapter 13 devotes its attention to branding and packaging as communication variables, clarifying their functions in the marketing mix, and identifying basic strategies for their use.

Chapter 14 deals with pricing, one of the most complex areas of marketing decision making. In this chapter, both traditional and modern pricing concepts are examined, and basic pricing strategies are discussed.

Chapter 15 explores the field of distribution channels, describes different types of channel arrangements, introduces the concept of channel design and management, and identifies key distribution strategies.

Chapter 16 introduces one of the most neglected areas of marketing—physical distribution. After defining the nature and scope of physical distribution, the chapter identifies the major components of the physical distribution system, explains what is meant by the "total cost of distribution," and provides guidelines for planning and managing the physical distribution system.

Chapter 17 turns to personal selling as an avenue of marketing communications. The importance of personal selling is emphasized, the complexity of the modern sales job is described, and problems in organizing and managing the sales force are discussed.

Chapter 18 singles out advertising as its subject. In addition to providing an understanding of the dimensions and structure of the advertising industry, the chapter clarifies the role of advertising agencies, explains the uses of advertising, and shows how advertising objectives and strategies give direction to the advertising effort.

Finally, Chapter 19 examines sales promotion and product publicity as a part of the marketing mix. The uses of these marketing variables are discussed, and their roles in the marketing program explained.

Taken together, the subjects of these chapters are the visible activities of marketing, each of which has a unique role in marketing communications. Properly coordinated, they are powerful tools of communication. If they are not coordinated properly, resources will be wasted and disappointment will result.

An Overview of Marketing Communications

- *The nature and importance of marketing communications.*
- *The communications process.*
- *Verbal and nonverbal communications in marketing.*
- *Major marketing variables controlling the brand image.*
- *The stages of marketing communications.*

MARKETING EXAMPLES

THREE WHITE POWDERS

Rudy Czufin, formerly executive art director of the Gardner Advertising Company, had a presentation which he called "The Story of Three White Powders." The three white powders were similar in form and undistinguished in appearance. One powder was a cake mix; the second was nonfat dried milk; and the third was a soil conditioner. Czufin's presentation was about packaging. The problem, however, was one of communications. The story he unfolded was how to design packages for each of these products so that the packages would quickly communicate what the package contained, and how it was used. Communications!

HOW DOES ONE MAKE A FEMININE BEER LOOK LIKE A MASCULINE BEER?

Beer drinkers like their beers to have a masculine character. No feminine beer has ever been successful in achieving a significant share of the huge—4.5 billion gallons—annual beer market. Yet, one of the most successful entries into the beer market in recent years has been light beer, a product low in calories and light in body—clearly appealing to weight-conscious women. The problem facing beer companies was one of *communications*. How could they communicate masculinity with a feminine product?

Partly, they did it with packaging, using bold, masculine typography and masculine colors. Partly, they did it with advertising by using male sports figures in their advertising—football players, baseball players, bowlers. One commercial shows a bowler ripping the top half of the can off and commenting that one thing he liked about the product was the "easy opening can." The popularity of light beers is a testimony to the persuasive effectiveness of their communications.

WHY MANY PREMIUMS FAIL

Premiums are widely used in marketing. In some fields, they represent an important part of the annual marketing expenditure. Marketers who are dependent upon successful premium offers use a variety of research techniques to make sure that the premiums they select will be appealing to the consumers in the target market. Yet, premiums that do well in consumer tests often fail miserably in the marketplace, and the marketer ends up with a warehouse full of unwanted merchandise. Why? Carol Boudreau, Vice-President and Premium Director for Dancer, Fitzgerald and Sample (a major advertising agency), made the following comments about premiums in *Advertising Age.*

> How often have you spent time and money testing premiums only to have the chosen item not live up to the test results? When this happens, many blame the premium or fault the testing procedure. But the fault isn't always the premiums.
>
> If it has happened to you—as it has to most promotion people—go back and analyze the premium advertisement or the in-store presentation. You might discover the premium offer was not communicated effectively.
>
> The keys to communicating premium offers effectively are clarity, conciseness, directness, and honesty.[1]

---

1. Carol E. Boudreau, "Success Hinges on Communication," reprinted with permission from May 7, 1979 issue of *Advertising Age.* Copyright 1979 by Crain Communications, Inc.

Communications! Warren Kratky, former president of the Gardner Advertising Company, has noted that in a mass production society, *modern marketing has become primarily a matter of mass communications.* And, unless marketing communications are effective, there is little chance that the marketing program will be successful.

Marketing communications are particularly critical because, for the most part, they are one-way communications. That is, we seldom have a two-way flow of information between the seller and the buyer except, of course, in personal selling where the potential customer has an opportunity to ask questions, to exchange information, and to clarify what is being communicated.

Generally, however, consumers do not have this opportunity. All they can do is to listen to what is said, look at what is shown, and respond to the marketer's message in terms of what they understand. Unfortunately, consumers do not always understand what marketers are trying to say. The American Association of Advertising Agencies recently presented the first part of a three-year study in which they measured the extent to which consumers understand television advertising. Their findings? More than 80 percent of the consumers surveyed misunderstood at least part of the television advertising they viewed.[2] Now, maybe they weren't listening. Maybe they were doing something else—reading, talking, raiding the refrigerator, or puttering around the house. But, if they were, that doesn't solve the problem. It only makes it more critical because communicating with consumers is a necessary condition for successful marketing. Without persuasive communications, no marketing takes place. For this reason, we need to examine the role of mass communications in marketing strategy.

THE NATURE OF MARKETING COMMUNICATIONS

In a self-service, mass-production economy, marketing *is* communications. The producer of consumer goods no longer enjoys the benefits of knowing customers personally and being able to respond directly to their questions and complaints. Communications with consumers are mediated by nonpersonal media, unresponsive point-of-sale material, and—too frequently—uncaring retail salespeople. The marketer's initial message must be direct and clear because opportunities to clarify ambiguities or to correct misunderstandings are limited. Consumers only know producers through their products and what is said about them.

Faced with this situation, producers of consumer goods must identify their points of contact with consumers so that they can use these points effectively in communicating product con-

Personal contact is the most effective channel of communication. (Copyright © 1976 The Courier Journal and Louisville Times Company)

2. "Narrow Focus," *Advertising Age* (May 26, 1980): 16.

cepts. Basically, there are two points of view regarding what constitutes communications with consumers: a *limited* point of view that identifies communications with advertising, sales promotion, personal selling, and product publicity; and an *extended* point of view that recognizes that all aspects of a firm's marketing activities represent an opportunity for communication. Assuming that consumers are only influenced by what marketers say in their advertising, sales promotion, and product publicity releases is unrealistic. Edmund Burke, the eighteenth-century Irish statesman, once observed: "I can't hear what you say. Your actions drown out your words." So it is with marketers. What they say in advertising may be drowned out by what they do with the product, the package, the price, or some other aspect of visible marketing activities.

Visible marketing activities are those activities that are open to the consumers' view. Through these visible marketing activities, the producer has an opportunity to communicate a product concept to consumers. On the basis of these visible marketing activities the consumer forms the brand images that ultimately determine buying behavior in the marketplace. These visible activities make up the communications side of marketing.

In this chapter, we will examine five aspects of marketing communications. *First,* we will examine the communications process itself. *Second,* we will examine both the verbal and nonverbal dimensions of communications. *Third,* we will identify and discuss the visible marketing variables that are most influential in determining the brand image. *Fourth,* we will examine the various stages of marketing communications. Finally, we will discuss the communications mix.

The Communications Process

We can describe communications in a variety of ways, depending upon the persons involved, the method of communication employed, and the purpose for which the communication is intended. The particular form of communication with which we are concerned in this section is *mass communications.* We are primarily concerned with the messages that the producer of consumer products directs to large numbers of consumers, and we are also concerned with the messages that these consumers send back to the producer.

Effective communication takes place when the receiver of the communication perceives the message that was intended by the sender. If the message is perceived differently from the way it was intended, communication has failed. Mass communications are particularly subject to failure because the lack of face-to-face contact between the sender and receiver eliminates or delays feedback from the receiver indicating the message is being received, misread, or ignored.

A MODEL FOR MASS COMMUNICATIONS. A model for mass communications is shown in Figure 11–1. The model has eight elements: (a) the sender, (b) the intended message, (c) the transmitted message, (d) the channel, (e) the received message, (f) the receiver, (g) the response, and (h) feedback.

The Sender. The sender in mass communications is the originator of the message—in this case, the producer of a consumer product. The purpose of the communication is to reach a particular group of consumers with a message about the product that will predispose them to buy it. Assuming the marketing concept has been followed, this should not be difficult because the product has been designed with the interests of this particular group of consumers in mind.

The Intended Message. The intended message is the product concept, including all of the physical and psychological attributes believed appropriate for the target market. The goal of the communication is to create a brand image that will appeal to the market segment for which the product is intended.

The Transmitted Message. Before the intended message can be sent, it must be put in a transmittable form appropriate to the channel of communication being used. If the channel is radio, the transmittable form will be sounds—words, music, and/or other sound effects. If the channel is a magazine, the transmittable form will be visible—printed words, colors, pictures. The form in which

FIGURE 11–1: *Mass Communication Model*

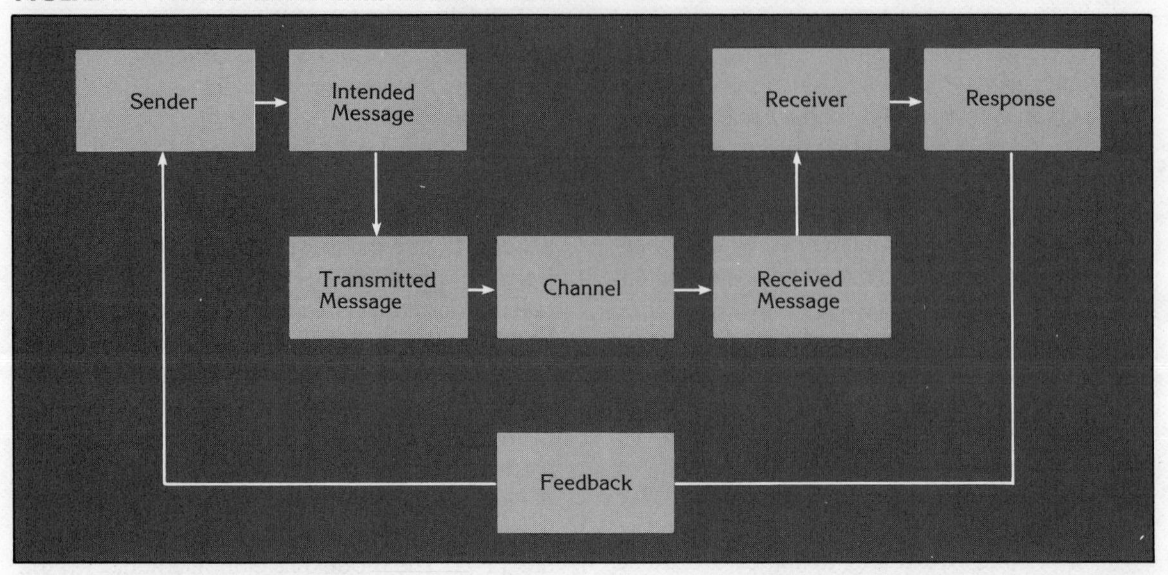

a message is transmitted always involves symbols that stand for thoughts that the sender wishes to transmit. If sufficient care is taken in translating the intended message into the transmitted message, there will be a reasonable correspondence between the two although a certain amount of slippage will probably occur. Most of us have had the experience of being unable to express an idea or describe a thing as precisely as we experience it. The more abstract the idea or the more personal the experience, the more difficult it is to communicate precisely. By definition, brand concepts are both abstract and personal, thereby challenging precise communication. To guard against this problem in marketing communications, communications specialists—copywriters, artists, package designers, and so forth—compose the transmitted message.

The Channel. The channel is the medium or the carrier of the message. Marketing communications employ a number of channels simultaneously. Commercial media, such as radio, television, magazines, newspapers, and outdoor posters, are the most widely recognized channels of communication. However, point-of-sale material is also a channel, as is the package, and the product name, and even the product itself. Care must be taken that the same message is sent over each channel used; otherwise, confusion by the receiver is inevitable.

The Message Received. The message received may not be the same as the message sent because the channel itself influences the message content. Sometimes, the channel influence is simply the result of poor message reproduction. For example, a four-color newspaper advertisement developed for Duncan Hines Chocolate Cake featured a chocolate-coconut icing. Great care was taken to obtain a photograph that conveyed appetite appeal. Unfortunately, not all of the newspapers carrying the advertisement were capable of high-quality color reproduction. In some newspapers (generally the smaller ones), the cake illustration was decidedly unappetizing, and in one newspaper in particular it appeared as a nauseating purple lump, covered with bilious green worms.

Aside from poor message reproduction, the character of the channel itself may profoundly affect the persuasiveness of the message. Early experiments in message effectiveness exposed matched groups of subjects to an identical argument about a controversial subject. One group would get the argument in the form of a personal lecture; another would hear it on the radio; a third would read it in print. Each group was tested to see what attitude changes had taken place. In experiment after experiment, the results were consistent: the face-to-face lecture was more persuasive than radio, and radio was more persuasive than print.[3] Subsequent experiments have shown that television and film are both superior to radio, but still less effective than personal contact.[4]

The editorial setting of a medium may also make it more appropriate for some messages than for others. For example, the *New Yorker,* with its urbane, sophisticated, eastern-seaboard orientation, provides quite a different environment for product advertising than does *Sunset* magazine with its provincial, west-coast, home-service view of the world. Media analysts are acutely conscious of these editorial differences and select media compatible with the product being advertised and the specific message being sent.

The Receiver. The receiver also influences the message that is perceived because of expectations, situational factors, or simply because of inattentiveness. A case in point is a newspaper advertisement prepared by a division of the Bell Telephone system to encourage use of the yellow pages. The advertisement showed a worn shoe with a hole in the sole. The headline and body copy urged the consumer to save time and shoe leather by using the yellow pages to locate needed goods and services, rather than engaging in wasteful, trial and error shopping. Advertising research revealed, however, that a large number of consumers, who only glanced at the advertisement without really reading it, interpreted the worn shoe as an appeal by the telephone company for a rate increase. Thus, the advertisement not only failed to communicate the intended message, but also raised the spectre of telephone rates, a delicate subject that most public monopolies prefer to keep submerged.

The Response. Receivers may respond in a variety of ways to a message; they may accept it, reject it, question it, show interest, resent it, or ignore it entirely. Yet, for the one sending the message, the response is often critical, and an integral part of the whole communications process. In marketing, a message is only effective when it gives rise to some positive response, either overt or covert.

Feedback. Feedback is the response that flows back to the sender from the recipient and serves as a control mechanism for the accuracy of the communication. Ideally, feedback occurs quickly and takes the form of questions requesting clarification, or evidence that the message is or is not being received. In marketing communications, feedback typically occurs in the form of letters of satisfaction or complaint, product purchase, returned merchandise, lack of sales, and so forth. Feedback, if received and properly interpreted, provides a basis for evaluating the effectiveness of the communication, and for making changes in the message, if changes are needed.

Unfortunately, marketing feedback is often delayed, misleading, or ambiguous. Few consumers express their satisfactions or complaints directly to the producer, and those who do are frequently not typical of the target market. Consumers are more inclined to express satisfaction and dissatisfaction quietly by simply purchasing or not purchasing the product. This is, after all, the ultimate weapon of the individual against an impersonal corporation in a marketing society. Sales changes, as a measure of communications effectiveness, are often inadequate because sales may be influenced by factors other than communications, and inventories at different levels in the distribution chain may delay recognition of shifts in consumer buying practices. For these reasons, the marketer of consumer goods must usually initiate and maintain independent and continuing research to monitor consumer responses to the various parts of the marketing program.

NOISE IN THE COMMUNICATIONS SYSTEM.

Noise refers to any type of interference with the communications process. It can occur anyplace in the system. For example, the product concept may be fuzzy or ambiguous. Noise may occur because the intended message is improperly encoded, because of channel distortions, incompatibility between the channel and the message, receiver distractions, or receiver disinterest. In short,

3. James T. Clapper, "The Effects of Mass Communications," (New York: Free Press, 1960), p. 106.
4. P. M. Sandman, D. M. Rubin, and D. B. Sachsman, *Media* (Englewood Cliffs, NJ: Prentice-Hall, Inc., 1972), p. 231.

anything that interferes with communication is considered noise.

The difficulty of mass communications and the everpresent threat of noise within the system has led Schramm to identify certain conditions that are essential to the success of communications:

1. The message must be so designed and delivered as to gain the attention of the intended destination.
2. The message must employ signs which refer to experience common to source and destination, in order to "get the meaning across."
3. The message must arouse personality needs in the destination and suggest some ways to meet these needs.
4. The message must suggest a way to meet these needs which is appropriate to the group situation in which the destination finds himself at the time he is moved to make the desired response.[5]

With this background on the communications process, let's turn now to the signs and symbols which we use to communicate.

VERBAL AND NONVERBAL COMMUNICATIONS

Marketing is based on ideas, and communicates these ideas through signs—words, phrases, pictures, and actions—that give rise to meaning. A *sign,* as it is used in communications, is merely a stimulus that represents an object or an idea. The sign *apple* for example, means a certain kind of fruit. The sign *run* means a certain kind of action. Thus, a sign is a label that is associated with the object or idea it represents. Signs gain their meanings through learning; as people have the same learning experience they use the same signs to represent the same things. Without common signs there can be no communication; anyone who has traveled in a foreign country without knowing the local language knows how awkward communications can become.

5. Wilber Schramm, *The Process and Effects of Mass Communication* (Urbana, IL: University of Illinois Press, 1954), p. 13.

FIGURE 11–2: *Fields of Experience of the Sender and Receiver of a Message. (Only signs that fall within the region of shared experience will be understood.)*

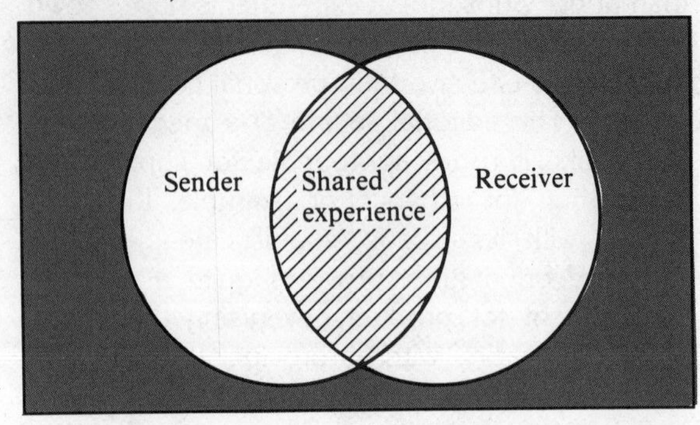

People reared within the same culture have certain common experiences (in the home, in school, and in society at large) that facilitate their communication. But because no two people ever have an *identical* history of experience, even common signs may become distorted. For example, the sign, father, has a core meaning in our culture that is shared by most people. Yet, even this sign will have a somewhat different meaning to two people if the father of one was loving and concerned and the father of the other was harsh and critical. To the first person, the sign, father, will give rise to feelings of affection; to the other, it will trigger feelings of hostility and resentment. Since even common signs can have somewhat different meanings, communications are seldom perfect. The problems that arise in communications are represented in Figure 11–2.

The sender of a message can communicate with the receiver of the message to the extent that their fields of experience overlap. Signs that fall outside the area of shared experiences will either not be understood, or will be misinterpreted. Since signs may have different meanings to different people, we need to more closely examine the concept of *meaning.* Generally, signs have four kinds of meanings: denotative, connotative, structural, and contextual.

Denotative Meaning

Through learning we associate signs with objects, actions, and ideas. The sign, *chair,* denotes a particular class of objects with certain characteristics

Nonverbal communications. (Photo by Rick Smolan)

which, by common agreement, is called *chair*. Denotative meaning involves a relatively simple sign-object relationship. Words high in denotative meaning most often refer to concrete objects. The dictionary definition of a word refers, essentially, to its denotative meaning.

Connotative Meaning

Many objects and ideas are much more complex than that represented by a simple sign-object relationship. The idea or object becomes surrounded by a complex constellation of meanings so that the meaning of the sign varies somewhat among different people. *Communism, socialism,* and *capitalism* all have a denotative meaning as a form of economic organization. At the same time, these words have rich connotative meanings among different people and are often associated with strong feelings. Many people, for example, respond to *communism* as *bad, threatening, oppressive,* and *undesirable.* Others, by contrast, respond to it as *good* and *desirable,* and perceive it as a reasonable attempt to introduce rationality, equity, and justice into economic relationships. Sometimes, words that have the same denotative meaning may have somewhat different connotative meanings. For example *naked* and *nude* denotatively mean "to be without clothing." Yet, connotatively, *naked* is a masculine word and *nude* is a feminine word. When great precision in communication is desired, one should try to use words that are high in denotative meaning and low in connotative meaning. Conversely, when *persuasion* is the object of communications, words high in connotative meaning become more important.

Since the object of marketing communications is persuasion, words high in connotative meaning are its basic tools. Herein lies a danger in the communications process. Words should be chosen carefully so that they complement each other. When words with noncomplementary connotative meanings are used together, confusion and ambiguity mar attempts at communication. There is generally a "right" word to express every thought, and the careless use of a single word can destroy a carefully constructed argument. Marketers need to be adept with words, sensitive to their nuances, and conscious of their power.

Structural Meaning

Single words are insufficient for most communications. Normally, we need to use combinations of words to express our meanings. Syntax and grammar provide the rules for stringing words together in a meaningful relationship. These rules permit us to express complex ideas through sentences and paragraphs. The receivers of messages respond to sentences in the same way they respond to individual words. A sentence has a coherent unity if it is properly constructed. Again, advertising writers need an understanding of syntax and grammar.

Writers of advertising sometimes deliberately violate the rules of syntax and grammar in order to gain impact and euphony. "Winston tastes good like a cigarette should" is grammatically incorrect. It should read "Winston tastes good as a cigarette should." Yet, this grammatical violation adds force to the slogan, even though it may offend some grammarians. Violations of syntax and grammar need to be used judiciously if at all. When syntax and grammar are used either carelessly or ignorantly, the intended meaning may be lost or the reader may be confused.

Contextual Meaning

Signs often derive their meanings from the context in which they occur—that is, from the signs that surround them. Consider the following sentences:

We crossed the river on the *bridge* north of town.

I have never played worse *bridge* in my life.

It was a difficult billiard shot. Even with the *bridge,* I could hardly reach the cue ball.

Did the dentist have to install a *bridge?*

I'm having trouble building a *bridge* between the key ideas of the presentation.

In each case, the word *bridge* has a different meaning, depending upon the context within which it appears.

Context is extremely important in marketing. The meaning that a sign carries is often clarified and sometimes enhanced by the context within which it occurs. Context is often obvious in the illustration selected for the advertisement. For example, a proprietary medicine shown in a hospital setting takes on an air of legitimacy that it might not otherwise possess. A high fashion line of clothing advertised in *Vogue,* or a piece of jewelry advertised in the *New Yorker* has its value enhanced by the medium in which it appears. Similarly, a necklace sold in Tiffany's will appear to have greater value than the same necklace sold in K-Mart simply because of context.

Thus far, I have dealt primarily with words as signs, although some of the examples that I have used indicate that signs can also be nonverbal. And they can, of course. Pictures, actions, colors, and shapes are signs also. The Eagle Printing Company printed the following suggestions for enhancing the appetite appeal of food illustrations.

> Orange is one of the dominant hues of high appetite appeal. The color is rich and luminous. Avoid yellow–orange. Clear yellow, however, slightly warm in tone, is savory. But again avoid the goldenrod cast (which appears rancid) and the greenish cast (which appears raw).
>
> Among the reds, use bright vermilion, suggestive of porterhouse steaks and ripe apples. Purplish reds seem "tough" and unfit for human consumption.
>
> As to greens, select clean ones, crisp and clean in quality. Avoid yellowish greens which are bilious, and bluish greens which seem poisonous.
>
> Your other colors will then consist of warm browns and tans, remindful of well-cooked meats and breads. For a definitely "sweet" color choose pink. For wines and liquors choose transparent purples. This is the appetite palette. Blues may be used to set them off, for while blue is not a good food color it does seem to suggest cleanliness and freshness.

> However, purples, grays, magentas, chartreuse greens, and the like are to be avoided. We would not care to "eat" them—so why should they feature any products meant for our tables.[6]

Shapes are also used for communications. Classic examples, of course, lie in the styling of automobiles, furniture, and appliances. Some shapes are heavy, bulky, and masculine. Others, graceful, delicate, and feminine. Even something as simple as a line can be used for communication purposes. For example, McNeal notes:

> Some lines are strong and decisive, some weak and timid, and still others, thin and precise. Thus, without forming any representational object, a line may still be descriptive of an idea or mood. For example dark angular lines are generally recognized as being symbolic of strength. Smoother flowing lines symbolize femininity. Straight lines convey a feeling of formalism, while kinky lines represent an informal situation.[7]

McNeal further points out that vertical lines symbolize growth and life, horizontal lines express stability and repose, and diagonal lines are symbolic of action.[8]

In addition to colors, shapes, and lines, we may also use objects, animals, and people to convey ideas and meaning. The Rock of Gibralter, used by the Prudential Insurance Company as a trademark, is intended to convey strength and dependability. The cougar used by Mercury symbolizes power and speed. People are used in many ways by marketers—babies to suggest innocence and softness; children and teen-agers to convey vitality; couples to communicate intimacy; and older people to communicate calmness, wisdom, and serenity.

Words, colors, lines, shapes, objects, animals, and people are all instruments for conveying meaning, and all are used lavishly in marketing communications. With this background on communications, let's now see how the major marketing variables can be used to translate a product concept into a desired brand image.

6. Eagle Printing Company, "What Colors Look Good Enough to Eat," No. 5, *Facts from the Research Department of the Eagle Printing Company,* 100 Sixth Ave., New York, NY

7. James U. McNeal, *An Introduction to Consumer Behavior* (New York: John Wiley & Sons, Inc., 1973), p. 102.

8. Ibid, p. 103–4.

MAJOR MARKETING VARIABLES CONTROLLING THE BRAND IMAGE

The producer controls six major variables that can be used to shape the brand image: the product itself, the package, the brand name, the brand price, advertising and promotion, and distribution. These are the primary variables that the consumer sees and upon which judgments about the brand are based. Each is a *channel* for communicating meaning about the brand and, as such, all must communicate the same message to create a clear brand image.

In the following material, we will examine each of these variables as a channel of communication with the consumer, always emphasizing the importance of using each channel prudently and in careful concert with the other channels. Remember, however, that the intended message of communication is the product concept. If the product concept is ill-chosen or unattractive to consumers, no amount of communication will make it attractive. Marketing success is predicted on a product concept that is designed around consumers' perceptions of their needs. The purpose of marketing communications is to translate the product concept into an appealing brand image that will cause consumers to select that product over competition.

The Product

The product is the embodiment of the product concept. In the last analysis, it is the final point of communication with consumers. If the product does not live up to the promises that have been made, consumer disappointment and dissatisfaction are inevitable.

For many product fields, however, physical attributes may not be the unique variable in the product concept that distinguishes one brand from another. Beer is such a product. Most con-

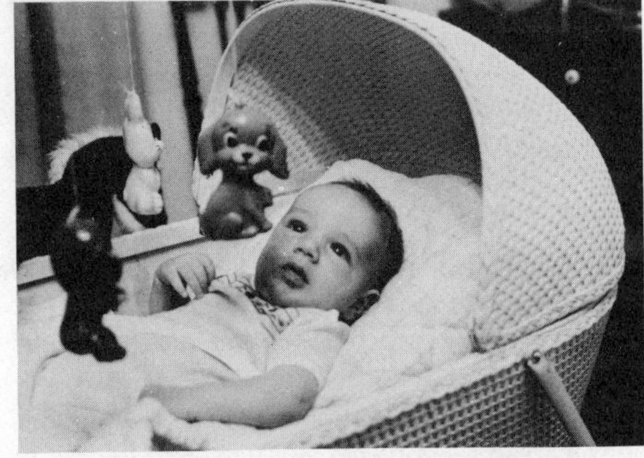

People can convey innocence, wisdom, intimacy, and vitality. (Photos by Steven Smith, ACTION/Foster Grandparent Program, Hank Young, Stix Pix)

sumers cannot distinguish one brand of beer from another on the basis of appearance and taste. This is the case because the prevailing taste preference for beer in the United States is for Pilsener and Dortmunder beers, which are characterized by a pale color, a medium hop flavor, a relatively strong carbonation, and an alcoholic content of 3.0 to 3.8 percent by weight. As a consequence, the bulk of all beers marketed in the United States are brewed to these standards. Little wonder, then, that they are similar in taste.

Since different brands of beer are not clearly differentiated by their physical characteristics, their distinguishing features are imputed psychological and sociological attributes. In such instances, the physical product must not contradict the psychological product. The product concept for most U.S. beers specifies a light, refreshing beer—a product concept wholly compatible with the Pilsener and Dortmunder beers. If, however, the product concept specified a dark, heavy, full-bodied, and somewhat sweet beer, the Pilsener and Dortmunder beers would be completely inappropriate, and some variety of a Munich beer would have to be used instead. In this case, however, the marketer would be bypassing the mass market for beer in the United States, because most consumers prefer a light, refreshing beer. Instead, the marketer would be aiming at what, to date, has been a small, generally neglected, and probably ethnic segment of the overall market for beer.

The brewing industry is not alone in the physical similarity of the various competing brands. Cigarettes, detergents, personal-care products, food staples, and many other product categories suffer from the same affliction. In such cases, the burden of marketing is heavy indeed, since the claimed brand differences must be wholly supported by intangible, symbolic representation, unreinforced by concrete, observable product characteristics. This state of affairs led *Advertising Age* to criticize the marketing of the 1970s by noting:

> . . . it seems to us that (lack of real product differences) puts an unfair burden on advertising—pumping up minuscule benefits of me-too products to the point where advertising itself is used as a substitute for products with meaningful advantages of their own. . . . The '70s were a bummer as far as innovative product marketing was concerned. We have higher hopes for the '80s.[9]

More fortunate is the marketer whose product concept calls for a product that is clearly differentiated from competition on the basis of observable physical characteristics and/or product performance attributes. The experience of Purina Cat Chow and Ivory Snow demonstrate this situation.

PURINA CAT CHOW. At the time Purina Cat Chow was conceived, the market for cat food was dominated by canned products, by cats who were reputedly fussy eaters, and by cat owners who looked aghast at the thought that their pets would eat a dry ration. But canned foods had serious shortcomings: they were ill-smelling (to humans, not cats), they were bothersome to prepare, and after cans were opened, they had to be refrigerated, which did not enhance the odors inside cat owners' refrigerators very much. The product concept for Purina Cat Chow called for a product that was highly palatable, odorless, and convenient to prepare. In contrast to canned foods, Purina Cat Chow met these specifications. The advertising claim "Flavor's gone wild; odor's gone mild" was a succinct expression of the product concept. Today, Purina holds 60 percent of the dry cat food market.

IVORY SNOW. The story of Ivory Snow, a granulated soap powder, is the story of an old, established product that was successfully repositioned in the face of devastating competition from detergents. Shortly after World War II, the detergent revolution threatened to demolish the laundry soap industry, and with good reason. For both hand and machine washing, synthetic detergents simply cleaned better than traditional soaps. As a result, the laundry market virtually became the private domain of the Tides, Cheers, and Fabs. Concurrently, the soap portion of the market declined precipitously as the detergents took over.

9. "The marketing process: Painful lesson of the '70s," reprinted with permission from Aug. 18, 1980 issue of *Advertising Age*. Copyright 1980 by Crain Communications, Inc.

Ivory Snow was the dramatic exception to this trend; its sales not only resisted this decline, but actually grew, while sales of similar soap products deteriorated sharply. This remarkable marketing feat took place because somewhere between Procter & Gamble and its advertising agency, Ivory Snow was repositioned in light of a thorough review of the product, its name, its advertising and promotion, and its competition.

Essentially, this successful product repositioning transpired in the following manner. From a product standpoint, soap products left a residue on fabrics known as *limesoap,* which gave them a feel of softness, in contrast to the effect of synthetic detergents, which cleaned the fabric so thoroughly that the material was stiff and rough. This product characteristic of soaps was turned to a brand advantage by Ivory Snow as tangible evidence of the greater softness that could only be achieved with a product of its type. Historically, the name "Ivory Snow" had always connoted mildness. The question became, "Where were Ivory mildness and fabric softness particularly important?" Once the question was asked, the answer was obvious: baby diapers and fine fabrics.

Ivory Snow was positioned as a mild soap that left fabrics soft and pliable, particularly suited for diapers and fine fabrics. The product itself performed in demonstrable contrast to detergents that left fabrics harsh to the touch. Through its performance attributes the product clearly reinforced its product concept.

Thus, the product itself is an important channel of communications with the consumer, a fact well recognized by marketing practitioners.

The Package

The product package is an obvious, but sometimes neglected, channel of communications. Through proper design of packaging, the marketer can show the product in living color, portray it in various use situations, provide instructions for its proper use, and feature promotions, such as premiums or price-off deals when appropriate. Through its shape, color, illustrations, and typography, the package can give character to a product and help distinguish it from competition.

At the beginning of the chapter, reference was made to the story of "three white powders," wherein packaging communicated the ideas of a cake mix, a nonfat dry milk, and a soil conditioner. The burden of communications in each instance was carried by the package design—truly a powerful communications tool, and one that is highly visible to consumers.

The Brand Name

The role of the brand name in communicating brand attributes is well recognized. The name "Slender," used by Carnation, is a natural for its diet food, as are "Instant Breakfast" for the company's instant breakfast, and "Coffeemate" for its nondairy coffee creamer. Brand names are used to give brands dimension and character. Consider these names gathered during a walk through a supermarket: dishwashing compounds—Cascade, Finish, Crystal Clear; laundry detergents—Whisk, Dynamo, White Magic, Cold Power; aluminum foil—Handi-wrap, Reynolds Wrap, Eskimo Freezer Paper; cat food—Crave, Country Blend, Tender Vittles, Meow Mix (the only cat food cats ask for by name), Fish Ahoy, Chef's Blend, Mealtime; dog food—Butcher's Blend, High Protein, Gravy Train, Tender Chunks, Gains·burger, Puppy Chow; diapers—Pampers, Luvs, Huggies. The list is endless. Each manufacturer tries to find a name that unerringly projects the appropriate product concept.

Price

The fourth channel for communicating information about the brand is price. Traditionally, price has been a primary basis for market segmentation, with a "price range" figuring prominently in the brand concepts of many product fields. Thus, Rolls-Royce, at over $80,000, is clearly positioned for a different market segment than are Volkswagen, Datsun, Honda, and other relatively low-priced cars.

Apart from its role in market segmentation, price may be used to position a product within a given economic segment. A brand may be priced slightly above competition, along with competition, or below competition, depending upon whether it is being positioned as a quality or economy item.

Contrary to general expectations, price has no necessary relation to costs in many product fields. In personal-care products, distilled spirits, cosmetics, proprietary medicines, hard goods, home furnishings, art objects, and even in food and clothing, price is more often a reflection of product positioning than of product costs.

Price is seen as a guarantor of confidence for many consumers who do not have the technical knowledge and experience to assess product quality. Because of this function and because of the flexibility that exists in many price-cost relationships, the marketer should view price as a psychological device for communicating the value of the brand.

Advertising and Sales Promotion

Perhaps the most apparent channel of communication with the consumer lies in advertising and sales promotion, which disseminate information about the brand and surround it with psychological overtones that appeal to consumers. Advertising, to be effective, must be coordinated with the other channels of communication and clearly project the product concept upon which it is based.

Advertising is most effective when it has something tangible to work with—a clearly demonstrable product superiority or an observable product difference. In highly competitive markets, where products are often similar, such differences may be negligible or nonexistent. Under these conditions, advertising must rely wholly on psychological positioning, creative technique, or sheer weight of expenditures to attract the attention of consumers and persuade them to try the product.

One product field in which competition has vitiated the uniqueness of product differences is the home detergent field. Three major competitors—Procter & Gamble, Lever Brothers, and Colgate–Palmolive Company—dominate the field, competing with themselves and with each other through a dazzling galaxy of brands. Product claims for different brand entries focus on such minor and unobservable differences: "gets clothes whiter," "gets clothes brighter," "makes colors brighter," "gets clothes cleaner," "leaves clothes fresher," "safe sudsing," "it's concentrated," and so on and so forth, ad nauseum.

Indeed only a brilliant housewife could sort out all of these claims, fit them to particular brands, and decide which one best meets her needs. Enter psychological positioning and creative technique: "ring around the collar," the white knight, the white tornado, giant arms thrusting through washing machines, washing machines that grow eight feet tall, and the little kid that does all of the laundry properly while mother is away at college. All of these are examples in which product differences are relatively insignificant, so that advertising must communicate intangible virtues and benefits that are about all the product concept has to offer.

When considering advertising as a channel of communication, note that advertising claims should not be contradicted by other channels, particularly the product channel. Overstatement in advertising becomes more dangerous than understatement, whenever consumers' inflated expectations cannot be satisfied. David Berstein, a successful British advertising practitioner, has widely pointed out that advertising can sell a product once, but that an unkept advertising promise loses repeat sales.

Distribution

A final channel of communication used by marketers is distribution, although it is often not recognized as such. Nonetheless, a little reflection on the differences between Neiman-Marcus and Sears, or Saks' Fifth Avenue and K-Mart, or Tiffany's and Woolworths should make this point apparent.

For many product fields, place of distribution does not offer an opportunity to make a unique statement about a product. For example, most grocery items are sold through grocery stores, and no attempt is made by the producer to exclude grocery outlets because they do not complement the brand concept. In many other product fields, however, place of distribution is an important consideration in surrounding the brand with psychological overtones. For example, when first introduced, Contact was restricted to drugstores in order to project a "pharmaceutical" rather than a "proprietary" image. Sego, a diet food, was first introduced into grocery stores, rather than drugstores, to project an image of a food rather than a medicine. And, of course, in the high fashion field, place of distribution is often a critical consideration.

The point that I have been trying to emphasize in the foregoing discussion is that marketing is a complex process that involves different channels of communication. The product, its package, the brand name, price, advertising and promotion, and place of sale are all highly visible ways in which marketers, intentionally or unintentionally, make statements about the products they offer for sale. Further, these statements must be coordinated if consumer confusion is to be avoided.

STAGES IN MARKETING COMMUNICATIONS

The goal of marketing communications is to affect consumer attitudes—to convert nonbuying consumers into customers. At any given point in time, however, different consumers may be in different stages of attitude formation. For example, a consumer who is unaware of a particular product is less likely to buy it than one who is aware of it, favorably impressed with its attributes, and considering its purchase. One can, in fact, conceptualize a progression of stages from "unawareness of the product" to purchasing it for the first time.

Several marketing writers have suggested models for this progression. Five such models, referred to as "hierarchy of effects" models, are shown in Figure 11–3. The similarity of these models is apparent. They differ only in the number of steps involved and the particular words used to describe the steps. In order to examine the hierarchy of effects concept more closely, let's consider one of the models in detail. Although any of the models could be used equally well, let's use the Industrial Conference Board model since: (1) its terms are relatively unambiguous; (2) it has an intermediate number of steps that, in my experience, seem to parallel the stages that consumers often go through; and (3) its authors explicitly recognize that the role of advertising tends to decrease as one approaches the actual purchase.

This model, like the others, assumes that the progress from awareness to purchase is a laborious one that takes place over a period of time, that the consumer moves only one step at a time, and that each step increases the probability of purchase. Although these assumptions may hold true in many cases, the rule is not inviolate. Many of us can recall personal experiences that required repeated exposures to a brand before we finally made a decision to purchase it. If the consumer benefit is strong and relevant to needs that are prepotent, one may traverse the ladder from awareness to purchase in a single leap. Kristian Palda has also questioned the assumption that each step up the ladder increases the probability of purchase.[10] Certainly, one can imagine situations in which Palda's criticism is valid. For example, I have clearly progressed from "awareness of" to a "preference for" a Rolls-Royce with no increase in the probability that I will ever buy one. Not only do I not have the money, but the thought of spending over $80,000 for an automobile (even though I recognize its excellence) violates my sense of propriety. This simply means that marketing communication often has effects on individuals who lie outside the target market for whom the communication is intended.

Aside from these exceptions, the hierarchy of effects models seem reasonably descriptive and offer a way to monitor the extent to which marketing is creating customers. So, let's appraise each of the steps in the Industrial Conference Board model to see how it works in practice, and to see how a knowledge of these stages can aid in assessing the effectiveness of the marketing effort.

Awareness

As a first step in the purchase process, broad awareness among relevant consumer groups is

10. Kristian S. Palda, "The Hypothesis of Hierarchy of Effects: A Partial Evaluation," *Journal of Marketing Research* (February, 1966): 13–24.

FIGURE 11–3: Hierarchy of Effects Models

Dagmar	Lavidge-Steiner	AIDA	Adoption Process	Industrial Conference Board
Action	Purchase	Action	Adoption	Provoking sale
Conviction	Conviction	Desire	Trial	Intention
Comprehension	Preference	Interest	Evaluation	Preference
Awareness	Liking	Attention	Interest	Acceptance
	Knowledge		Awareness	Awareness
	Awareness			

critical. Few brands are positioned to appeal to an entire market; each, on some basis, identifies a target segment to which it is directed. The extent to which brand awareness is achieved among these target segments can be measured fairly simply through market surveys.

Although any or all of the visible marketing activities discussed earlier may contribute to achieving awareness, the burden of this task often falls on advertising. The challenge that advertising faces in achieving awareness is often herculean because it means breaking through the fog of lethargy, apathy, and distraction that surrounds consumers. In order to create awareness, the advertisement or commercial must first attract attention, usually with a dramatic device of some sort. In magazine advertising, the advertiser has only a fraction of a second to arrest the attention of readers before they flip the page. Dramatic headlines, provocative illustrations, and the ostentatious use of color all attract attention. This is undoubtedly one of the reasons for the excessive use of scantily clad and provocative women in advertising illustrations, even though their relationship to the products is not always clear. After all, it may be argued that there is nothing like sex to attract the attention of members of a society in which sexual hang-ups are the national neurosis.

In broadcast advertising, the first five seconds of the commercial must capture the active attention of viewers. Otherwise, their attention will wander, they will flip to another channel, or they will engage in some other activity. All of this places a premium on developing dramatic devices that test the ingenuity of advertising writers and illustrators.

Sometimes, preoccupation with gaining attention becomes so single-minded that not enough thought is given to other tasks that an advertisement or commercial should perform. Thus, there are advertisements which have achieved wide awareness of specific brands, but done little to move consumers to the next step in the hierarchy, namely, that of acceptance.

Although advertising generally carries the main burden for creating awareness, product sampling, in-store displays, and packaging may also contribute to this role. Major introductions of new products are often accompanied by widespread sampling, a relatively expensive promotional device that has the advantage of placing the product, along with an advertising message, in the hands of consumers. In-store displays are also an effective attention-getting device, particularly in food stores that enjoy high consumer traffic. When such displays are accompanied by advertising as well as coupons or price features, their awareness-creating capability is considerably enhanced. Finally, dramatic packaging, which causes a product to stand out on retailers' shelves, may be an effective awareness creating device.

Despite the contributions made by these other marketing variables, the role of advertising in creating awareness is so elementary that failure to achieve an adequate level of awareness is generally considered a sign of advertising weakness in appeal, media adequacy or both.

Acceptance

When a product has achieved acceptance, it is seen as an alternative brand. That is, as a brand that might be bought if the preferred brand is not available. In some product fields, where leading brands are seen as similar, gaining acceptance may be about as much as advertising alone can accomplish. In the gasoline industry, for example, the brands with which consumers are familiar fall into two groups. The *golden circle* group includes brands that are considered acceptable and interchangeable. Individuals will use any brand in their golden circles without concern and with equal confidence. The *off-brand* group includes those brands about which the consumer is a little suspicious and will avoid using if possible.

The level of acceptance generally requires a greater familiarity with, and more information about the brand, than the level of awareness. Familiarity and information are often achieved through *reason why* advertising copy, or by showing the brand in appropriate use situations. Sometimes, sheer repetition of the brand name will move it to the level of acceptance. This is an expensive way to gain acceptance, but it is sometimes effective because the consumer's logic seems to be: "I've seen that brand name so often, it must be all right. If it weren't, the manufacturer couldn't sell enough to justify its continued advertising."

"Reason why" copy may take many forms: The form of a secret ingredient—"The mysterious beauty fluid" in Oil of Olay that "works with your skin's own natural moisture to quickly ease away dryness, leaving your skin feeling soft and smooth." The form of a product endorsement by a celebrity. Thus, Chris Evert Lloyd, the tennis star, describes Everynight Astringent Shampoo by Helene Curtis saying: "It super cleans oily hair without drying it out." And lastly the form of demonstrations or simple reassurances. Whatever form reason why copy takes, it enables consumers to make the subjective decision that "This brand is all right. I won't go far wrong if I use it."

The stage of acceptance can be facilitated by other marketing variables as well. Package information, brochures, personal selling, price, sampling, and place of sale may all contribute to the acceptance of the product. In any event, however, these variables function by providing additional information about the product or brand, and by offering reassurance of its adequacy. Failure to gain acceptance after widespread awareness has been achieved suggests that the basic product concept is either weak or being communicated poorly.

Preference

The goal of most marketing communications is to gain preference—to bring consumers to the point where they prefer a particular brand above all others. For a new product—one that has not been purchased before—preference is always tentative because product performance may result in disappointment, with the consequence that the product will fall back to the bottom rung of the ladder and not be repurchased. For this reason product quality and product performance, *as perceived by the consumer,* should *always* be a primary concern of marketers. I once knew an outstanding marketing practitioner who insisted that, given control over advertising, package, product name, price, and sales promotion, he could sell anything *once.* But, he could never sell it *again* unless the product lived up to the promises that he made in its behalf. This same marketing practitioner also insisted that the most powerful piece of marketing communication that is ever made about a product is the *actual performance of the product in its normal use situation.*

The marketing communication variables used to create preference for a product that has not been previously purchased are those used to promote acceptance—advertising, package information, brochures, personal selling, price, sampling, and place of sale. The extent of preference can be measured by marketing research—the proportion of the target market preferring the brand and preference strength (how strongly the brand is preferred over competitive brands). If consumer research finds that relatively few consumers prefer a particular brand compared to competition, the problem may lie in many areas: the product concept, the product itself, the brand name, packaging, pricing, advertising, service, and so forth. Each area, then, should be examined carefully for evidence of weakness.

Sometimes, a brand's "share of preference" may exceed its "share of sales." Such a finding may mean that the brand is progressing nicely and that the difference is simply a time lag between effective marketing communications and consumer purchases. On the other hand, it may indicate a weakness in some portion of the marketing program. A case in point is that of a major household appliance. Consumer surveys consistently revealed that 40 to 45 percent of the potential customers preferred the brand *before* they began shopping for their actual purchase. Yet, the brand obtained less than 30 percent of sales in the field. Investigation in this instance revealed that lack of sales support at the retail level was the culprit. The company had neglected retail salespeople in its marketing program—the same salespeople who were switching potential customers to other brands.

Intention to Buy

This stage refers to the psychological commitment to purchase a particular brand. For many low-priced packaged goods, preference and intention are virtually synonymous. In such cases, advertising may play a major role in inducing intention to buy. For more expensive items where price is a limiting factor, the role of advertising may be diminished, and other marketing variables increase in importance.

For some relatively expensive products, advertising may still have a contributing role. For example, the advertising of warranties for an extended period, such as "Five years or 50,000 miles" for an automobile, may move a consumer from the preference stage to a psychological commitment to buy. Or, advertising the lifetime guarantee of the J. C. Penney sealed battery may be sufficient assurance. However, in these instances, the motivating element is the warranty or guarantee, and advertising is simply publicizing their existence. More often than not, however, the decision to buy a relatively expensive product requires more information and more reassurance than is normally possible through advertising alone. At this point personal selling often plays a major role. Also at this point variables over which the marketer has little control—such as the experience and advice of friends and acquaintances—often complicate the decision process and require special marketing activities to provide further information and to answer specific questions.

Provoking the Sale

The role of different marketing activities in provoking the sale vary widely, depending upon the product class and the methods of distribution employed. For relatively inexpensive, frequently purchased items, advertising may be a sufficient incentive, although even in these cases point-of-purchase material, price incentives, and packaging emerge as major considerations. For expensive items, or for products that require demonstrations and/or personal selling (automobiles, appliances, insurance, clothing, furniture, carpeting, and a host of other products), the contribution of advertising in closing the sale is minimal. Advertising can make consumers receptive to a particular brand, but other marketing variables usually occupy the dominant role in closing the sale. Price inducements, service, warranties, and financing assume major importance at this stage of the purchasing decision.

Summary Observations on the Hierarchy of Effects Models

Hierarchy of effects models cannot provide pure, unadulterated descriptions of the stages leading up to the purchase of products. There are too many confounding variables and too many differences between product fields to permit neat, simplistic descriptions. Nonetheless, these models are useful for three reasons:

The hierarchy of effects models explicitly recognize that effective marketing communications may involve discrete stages.

The models allow for the possibility that each stage may require a somewhat different mix of visible marketing activities.

The models provide an analytical framework for diagnosing the extent to which marketing communications are accomplishing their various tasks.

Any model that possesses these virtues commends itself to the attention of serious marketing practitioners.

In Chapter 1, we noted that marketing practitioners are "mixers of ingredients." The ways in which they mix these ingredients constitute a major dimension of marketing strategy. In this chapter, we have considered the major marketing variables as elements in, or channels of communication. The product, the brand name, the package, pricing, advertising and promotion, and the place of sale (distribution) are all highly visible ingredients that must be mixed in the proper proportions to communicate with consumers effectively. In industrial marketing—producer markets, reseller markets, and government markets—personal selling also becomes a highly visible marketing activity and an important avenue of communications.

In the following chapters of this section of the text, we will examine each of the foregoing marketing variables separately, pointing out their unique characteristics, and identifying strategic ways in which they may be used.

SUMMARY

Modern marketing has become primarily a matter of mass communications. Unless marketing communications are effective, there is little chance that the marketing program will be successful. Marketing communications are particularly important because for the most part, they are one-way communications with little opportunity to clarify the message if it is improperly understood.

The communications process involves eight steps: the sender, the intended message, the transmitted message, the channel, the received message, the receiver, the response, and feedback. Each of these stages influences the communications message, and the message may be distorted by noise at any of these points. "Noise" refers to anything that interferes with the communications process.

Marketing is based on ideas, but it communicates these ideas through signs—words, phrases, pictures, and actions—that give rise to meaning. Four kinds of meaning should be noted: (1) denotative meaning, which is a sign-object relationship; (2) connotative meaning, which arises from personal experiences; (3) structural meaning, which involves grammar and syntax; and (4) contextual meaning, wherein a sign takes its meaning from the context within which it appears.

All of the major marketing variables under the control of the marketer—the product, the package, the brand name, the brand price, advertising and promotion, and the place of sale (distribution)—are channels of communications because they are highly visible to consumers, and because what the marketer does with each of these variables influences how the product being marketed is perceived.

The process of marketing communications has several recognizable stages. These stages have been formalized, and are referred to as "hierarchy of effects" models. Although the various models differ slightly, characteristic stages in the "hierarchy of effects" models are: awareness, acceptance, preference, intention to buy, and provoking the sale.

Different marketing variables are most effective at each of these stages. Advertising is generally more effective in the "awareness" and "acceptance" stages, and decreases in effectiveness in the later stages. In the later stages, personal selling, price inducements, warranties, demonstrations, and so forth are generally most effective.

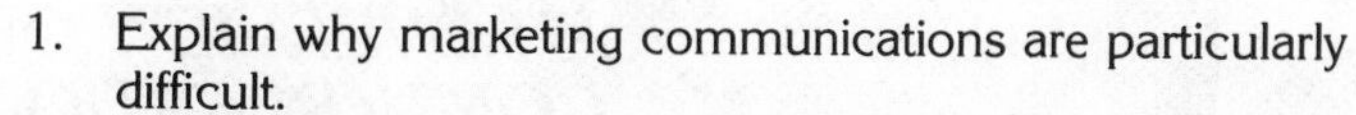

1. Explain why marketing communications are particularly difficult.
2. Distinguish between a limited view of marketing communications and an extended view. Why is this distinction important?
3. Explain what is meant by "noise" in the communications system. Give an example of noise at each stage of the communications process.
4. Explain the differences between denotative, connotative, structural, and contextual meaning.
5. Identify the six primary channels of communication involved in marketing. Why is it important that the messages being sent through these channels be coordinated?
6. Why are distinguishable product differences important in marketing communications?
7. Explain how distribution can be a channel of communications. Support your answer with an example.
8. Explain what is meant by the hierarchy of effects. Give an example of a hierarchy of effects model, identifying each of its stages.
9. Explain why acceptance is about as much as advertising alone can accomplish in some product groups, and support your explanation with an example.
10. Identify the three reasons that hierarchy of effects models are useful.

1. Select a package for a grocery product. On the basis of the "signs" used on the package—colors, typography, design, illustrations, and words—relate the package to the product and the primary benefit(s) it offers, and to the type of consumer (male, female, all family, children) to which the product is designed to appeal.
2. Select a magazine advertisement for a consumer product. Analyze the ways in which "signs" have been used to describe the product, its primary appeal(s), and the audience to which the advertisement is addressed.
3. Select two or three product fields in a grocery store. Write down the brand names for all of the brands stocked in this classification. Analyze the denotative and connotative meanings of these brand names.
4. Select a magazine advertisement for a consumer product. Identify words in the ad that are rich in connotative meanings, and discuss what these words connote.
5. Identify three or four different retail stores of the same general type—i.e., department stores, or sporting goods stores, or shoe stores. Discuss how these stores are alike or different in the way they are positioned. Consider such variables as price, quality, breadth of merchandise, and the types of consumers to which the stores would most likely appeal. What is the basis of your conclusions about these stores?

AN OVERVIEW OF MARKETING COMMUNICATIONS

Advertising utilizes a variety of signs, both verbal and nonverbal to convey meaning. Most of us are not aware of the ways in which signs are used because we seldom look at advertisements or commercials analytically to discover how their elements contribute to the overall impression.

Assignment
Select a magazine advertisement. Analyze the overall impression it creates and the particular signs and symbols employed in the ad. Elements to analyze are settings, action, people, groups, objects, colors, typography, and so forth. Indicate how each element contributes to the overall impression of the advertisement.

12

The Product

- *The meaning of the term product in marketing.*
- *Ways in which products may be classified.*
- *The role of consumer expectations in product satisfaction.*
- *How companies organize to develop new products.*
- *Stages in the development of new products.*
- *Why new products fail.*
- *Product strategies for new products.*
- *The product life cycle.*
- *Strategies for extending the product life cycle.*

MARKETING EXAMPLES

SURE

Sure is an antiperspirant marketed by Procter and Gamble in an aerosol can. According to its label, the product is aluminum chlorohydrate in an antiperspirant base of propellant 11S, propellant 12, isopropyl myistrate, quaternium-18 hectorite, S.D. alcohol 40, fragrance, citric acid, and water. According to its advertising, the product is confidence. And, according to its use, the product is an antiperspirant, although many consumers think of it as a deodorant. What *is* the product?

PURINA DOG CHOW

When introduced in the 1950s, Purina Dog Chow was a new form of dry dog food that was more palatable than competitive brands, and contained the sixteen basic nutrients that a dog was known to need. Based on an advertising theme, "New Purina Dog Chow makes dogs eager eaters," it quickly became the nation's number one dry dog food.

During the past twenty-five years, Ralston Purina has made many changes in Purina Dog Chow. Nutritional research at Purina's research farm has led to the discovery of other nutrients, with the result that nutrients have been increased from sixteen to over forty. Manufacturing and ingredient changes have made Purina Dog Chow even more palatable than the initial formulation; ingredients have been added to facilitate the transition from other commercial dog foods to Purina Dog Chow without untoward effects on the dog's digestive system. This was done because, frequently, dogs experience a period of diarrhea when their diet is changed. As a result of these formula modifications, Purina Dog Chow is now dramatically different from its initial formulation. The package design has undergone a number of minor changes and different advertising themes have been used during the history of the brand. Even the name has been changed—it used to be *New* Purina Dog Chow. Through it all Purina is still the nation's number one dry dog food. Is Purina Dog Chow the same product it was twenty-five years ago? Many consumers who have been buying it for years, think that it is.

AUTOMOBILES

Consider the following hypothetical—but not impossible—situation. Jose Ramirez and Sue Jackson bought the same model new car on the same day, from different dealers. The cars were identical in color, trim, upholstery, and accessories. Within a month, both cars developed carboration problems. Both owners took their cars back to the respective dealers. Ramirez's dealer was friendly, cooperative, and helpful. She fixed the car without charge and gave Ramirez another car to drive while his car was in the shop. Jackson's dealer was uncooperative and suspicious. He fixed the car reluctantly, without charge, but did not give Jackson a car to drive while her car was in the shop. Neither car had recurrent problems with the carboration. During the next five years, both cars had the same mechanical failures—all minor—at about the same time. Ramirez always took his car to the dealer from whom he had bought it and was always satisfied with the work. Jackson did not go back to the dealer from whom she had purchased her car. She took it to another garage, and she was always satisfied with the work. After five years, Ramirez said that the car was the best one he had ever owned and that he was going to buy the same brand again. Jackson said that it was the worst car she had ever owned, and she would never buy that brand again. Were they talking about the same product?

The concept of product is not a simple one, as shown by the preceding examples. Without a product, however, there is no marketing. Without a good product, there is little chance of marketing success. The primacy of the product in the marketing enterprise is both an act of faith and a fact of life among successful marketers. Howard M. Morgens, former chairman of the board of Procter & Gamble, the nation's largest advertiser, has observed:

> The only way you can succeed in business is with a good product. You can't do it with advertising. It all gets down to the fact that if you've got a good product, you can be successful with a reasonable marketing expenditure, but if you haven't got the product, the surest way to go broke is to pour your money behind it.[1]

DEFINITION OF A PRODUCT

The foregoing examples are designed to point up the complexity of the term *product.* Broadly speaking, a product might be defined as a *bundle of satisfaction.* Actually, however, it is somewhat more complicated than that. Every product is really three products—a generic product, a physical product, and a psychological product.[2]

The Generic Product

As I am using the term, the *generic product* refers to the basic product type, and the primary function it serves. Thus, in the examples given, *Sure* is an antiperspirant in an aerosol can which is expected to keep one dry. *Purina Dog Chow* is a dry dog food that is expected to provide nutrition for the family pet. And an automobile is a particular type of vehicle that is expected to be comfortable and to stop and start when one wants it to. Consumers have certain general expectations concerning generic products—expectations relating to their primary function, their general appearance, and their prices. A product that does not conform to consumers' general expectations in these regards may meet with resistance or rejection. For example, back in the early 1930s, Chrysler introduced a new model called the Airflow. Its streamlined appearance was at least thirty years ahead of every other car on the market. Even though it was an excellent automobile, consumers rejected the Airflow because it did not conform to their expectations of what a generic automobile should look like.

The Physical Product

The physical product is the actual physical entity or service that is offered to consumers—the *object* that is sold. In the case of *Sure,* the object is an antiperspirant that is composed of aluminum chlorohydrate in an antiperspirant base of propellant 11S, propellant 12, isopropyl myistrate, quaternium-18 hectorite, S.D. alcohol 40, fragrance, citric acid, and water. In the case of *Purina Dog Chow,* the physical product is a dry dog food that has a particular appearance and is composed of a variety of nutrients, cereal grains, meat by-products, preservatives, and so forth. In an automobile, the physical product is a vehicle designed in a certain way and composed of wheels, formed metal, circuits, valves, cylinders, a distributor, filters, brakes, upholstery, colors, accessories, and particular performance characteristics. In short, it is the physical thing that is manufactured.

The Psychological Product

The psychological product is the physical product along with the entire galaxy of services, warranties, and psychological overtones that accompany it. Theodore Levitt has suggested that competition

> is not between what companies produce in their factories, but between *what they add to their factory output in the form of packag-*

1. John S. Wright, Daniel S. Warner, Willis L. Winter, Jr., and Sherilyn K. Ziegler, *Advertising,* 4th ed. (New York: McGraw-Hill Book Company, 1977), p. 81

2. Other marketing writers have dealt with the complexity of the product in various ways. McCarthy refers to the *physical* product and the *total* product. See, E. Jerome McCarthy, *Basic Marketing,* sixth ed. (Homewood, IL: Richard D. Irwin, Inc., 1978, p. 238). Kotler has variously referred to the *tangible* product, the *extended* product, and the *generic* product; the *core* product, the *augmented* product, and the *symbolic* product; and the *core* product, the *formal* product, and the *augmented* product. See Philip Kotler, *Marketing Management* (Homewood, IL: Richard D. Irwin, Inc.), 2nd. ed., 1972, p. 424; 3rd. ed., 1976, p. 184; and 4th. ed., 1980, p. 352.

ing, services, advertising, customer advice, financing, delivery arrangements, warehousing, and other things that people value.[3]

According to this definition of a product, Ramirez and Jackson were *not* talking about the same product in the automobile example given earlier. The difference was dealer attitude and service. They were indeed talking about the same *physical product,* but the *psychological product* created the satisfactions and dissatisfactions that resulted in different perceptions of the physical product. Jackson's generic expectations were disappointed; as a consequence, she said it was the worst car she had ever owned. By contrast, Ramirez's generic expectations were satisfied; he said it was the best car he had ever owned.

In the case of *Sure,* the psychological product is social confidence. In the case of Purina Dog Chow, the psychological product is the health and well-being of the family pet.

CLASSIFICATIONS OF PRODUCTS

Obviously, not all products are alike. Instead they differ in significant ways. Some marketing writers have examined these differences in an effort to devise broad product classifications that could serve as guides to preparing marketing strategies. One such classification is the distinction between industrial and consumer goods. The basis of this classification is the purpose for which products are used. *Industrial products and services are used in the production of other goods and services. Consumer goods and services, by contrast, are used for personal consumption.*

To some extent, this classification is useful when considering marketing strategy. Price, for example, is often more critical in marketing industrial goods than in the consumer field. Advertising tends to be less important. Personal selling is often more important in the industrial field. Customers, buying motivations, and decision patterns also differ. Regardless of these strategic generalizations, however, effective marketing strategies require a much more thorough study of individual products, their users, and their marketing environments than these generalizations suggest.

Similarly, classifications systems have also been established for the consumer goods segment of the market in the expectation that they might guide the development of marketing strategies.

Convenience, Shopping, and Specialty Goods

One of the earliest classifications of consumer goods distinguishes three types—convenience, shopping, and specialty. Definitions of these three types of goods are:

- *Convenience Goods.* Those consumer goods which the customer usually purchases frequently, immediately, and with the minimum of effort in comparison and buying. Examples of merchandise customarily bought as convenience goods are tobacco products, soap, newspapers, magazines, chewing gum, small packaged confections and many food products.
- *Shopping Goods.* Those consumer goods which the customer in the process of selection and purchase characteristically compares on such bases as suitability, quality, price, and style. Examples of goods that most consumers probably buy as shopping goods are millinary, furniture, dress goods, ready-to-wear and shoes, used automobiles, and major appliances.
- *Specialty Goods.* Those consumer goods with unique characteristics and/or brand identification for which a significant group of buyers are habitually willing to make a special purchasing effort. Examples of articles usually bought as specialty goods are specific brands and types of fancy goods, hi-fi components, certain types of sporting equipment, and men's suits.[4]

3. Theodore Levitt, *The Marketing Mode* (New York: McGraw-Hill Book Company, 1969), p. 2.

4. Ralph S. Alexander and the Committee on Definitions of the American Marketing Association, *Marketing Definitions: A Glossary of Marketing Terms* (Chicago: American Marketing Association, 1960).

STRATEGIC IMPLICATIONS. Each class of goods has somewhat different implications for marketing strategy planning. For example, *convenience goods* are widely distributed, generally inexpensively priced, carry relatively low retailer margins, and employ mass consumer advertising and appealing packaging as their primary promotional efforts. *Shopping goods* are less widely distributed than convenience goods, are moderate to high priced, have moderate retail margins, focus on trade advertising and personal selling. *Specialty goods* generally employ selective distribution, are high priced, carry high retail margins, and employ consumer advertising in specialty media and personal selling as the major emphasis in their marketing strategies. Table 12–1 summarizes these promotional characteristics.

LIMITATIONS OF THE CONCEPT. From the standpoint of strategy, this classification system has several limitations.

- The criteria for placing a product within a particular classification are too general to provide much guidance for marketing practitioners. For example, in the definitions given, ready-to-wear and shoes are placed in the *shopping goods* classification and men's suits are placed in the *specialty goods* classification. Why? An examination of the ways in which these products are distributed, the markups they carry, and the ways in which they are bought suggest that the classification system is somewhat ambiguous.
- From the consumers' point of view, the same products may be perceived as belonging to different classifications. For example, a pair of tennis shoes for a low-income family may be a *shopping* good; for a middle to high income family, a *convenience* good; for a teen-ager or a jock, a *specialty good.*[5]
- Broad classification systems such as this are too rigid to accommodate the variety of strategies that may be successful in the marketplace. Ready-to-wear is classified as a shopping good, yet, many designer clothes that are obviously ready-to-wear are sold as specialty goods. Carpet sweepers would logically be considered as a shopping good, and should employ a strategy of intermediate distribution. Yet, some of the most successful marketers in the field have achieved success through door-to-door selling. Kirby is an example.

A basic goal of marketers of branded products, regardless of their products' characteristics, is to portray their products as specialty goods. Their marketing activities are designed to achieve this goal, although few are as successful in this endeavor as they would like to be.

As a consequence, the primary value of the convenience–shopping–specialty goods classification is broadly descriptive, rather than strategic.

Other Classification Systems

Attempts have been made to overcome the foregoing criticisms of product classification systems, generally by defining the criteria for classification more precisely. For example, Leo Aspinwall used five criteria—replacement rate, gross margins, adjustment, time of consumption, and searching time—as a basis for classifying goods.[6] Gordon Miracle used nine product characteristics as a basis for defining marketing strategy: unit value, significance of each purchase to the consumer, time and effort spent in purchase, rate of technological and fashion change, technical complexity, consumer need for service, frequency of purchase, rapidity of consumption, and extent of use.[7]

5. Indeed, it might be more appropriate to classify the behavior of consumers in terms of their proclivities for convenience, for shopping, and for forming strong attachments to brands. Some such classification of consumers might then be used as a basis for market segmentation. See: Barnette Greenberg and Danny Bellinger, "The Classification of Consumer Goods: An Empirical Study," Georgia State University School of Business Administration, Research Monograph No. 56 (1975), pp. 36–41.

6. Leo V. Aspinwall, "The Characteristics of Goods Theory," in William Lazer and Eugene J. Kelley, eds., *Managerial Marketing: Perspectives and Viewpoints,* revised ed. (Homewood, IL: Richard D. Irwin, Inc., 1962), pp. 633–43.

7. Gordon E. Miracle, "Product Characteristics and Marketing Strategy," *Journal of Marketing* (Jan., 1965): 18–24.

TABLE 12–1: Marketing Characteristics for Convenience, Shopping, and Specialty Goods.

Type of Good	*Breadth of Distribution*	*Pricing*	*Retail Margins*	*Primary forms of Promotion*
Convenience	Intensive	Inexpensive	Low	Mass advertising
Shopping	Intermediate	Moderate to high	Moderate	Trade advertising/personal selling
Specialty	Selective	High	High	Selective advertising/personal selling

Both of these approaches represent significant refinements over the traditional classification of convenience–shopping–specialty goods. Nonetheless, the value of these classifications may be limited for specific strategy formulations because different marketing opportunities often dictate that similar products be sold in quite different ways.

RETAIL STORES AND SERVICES AS PRODUCTS

Thus far, we have discussed products as though they were only tangible objects, such as cars, refrigerators, baking mixes, or loaves of bread. From the standpoint of marketing, however, retail stores are also products, as are services provided by doctors, dentists, television repairpersons, bankers, or automobile mechanics.

A retail store is a product that sells other products. As such, it has generic, physical, and psychological dimensions. A department store, for example, represents a store about which consumers have generic expectations. The failure of a department store to meet these expectations—a diversity of hard and soft good lines, liberal exchange policies, credit, delivery, and so forth—may relegate it to the limbo of uncertainty as to store type, or give rise to an entirely new type of store classification. This is precisely what happened in the early days of discount houses. Early discount houses resembled department stores because they stocked many merchandise lines. However, their lack of liberal exchange policies, requirement for membership applications from potential customers, pricing policies, failure to extend credit, and lack of delivery and other services normally considered characteristic of traditional department stores caused many people to avoid them, even though their prices were substantially lower than department stores' for the same items. And, a new store classification—discount houses—was devised to designate this particular type of store.

The *physical* dimension of retail stores consists of their appearance, layout, assortment of merchandise, pricing practices, parking facilities, and so forth. Their *psychological* dimension involves their symbolic character as projected by their services, decor, pricing policies, and the style of their advertising and promotion.

Similarly, the services provided by a doctor, mechanic, or banker are also products, and marketed as such by those in these professions. The individuals or organizations that offer these services succeed or fail in relation to their abilities to provide consumer satisfaction.

From the standpoint of marketing and market planning, operators of retail stores or services face precisely the same problems as the manufacturers of tangible products. They should define their target market, determine the essential store or service characteristics that will appeal to this market, and develop an economically efficient way of communicating with this market. Most large and successful retail stores do this. Few small retailers or service people do, which may be one of the reasons for the high rate of failure for small retail stores and service businesses.

CONSUMER EXPECTATIONS AND PRODUCT SATISFACTION

If the concept of a product is complex, consumer satisfaction is no less so. Two consumers may buy the same brand of a product. Each of the products purchased performs equally well. Yet one consumer is satisfied and the other is not. Or, consumers often make purchases with which they are initially well pleased. Yet, a few weeks later their initial pleasure turns to dissatisfaction and they lament that they ever made the purchase.

The key to the problem of consumer satisfaction seems to lie in the concept of *expectations.* Satisfaction with a purchase often lies less in the actual performance of the product itself than in the "expectations of performance" held by the purchaser. A number of theories of consumer satisfaction and dissatisfaction—all based on the concept of expectations—have been devised.[8] Perhaps one of the most useful theories of consumer satisfaction, and one that lends itself to marketing analysis and action, is the two-factor theory suggested by Swan and Combs.

Swan and Combs suggest that consumers judge products on a limited set of attributes, some of which are relatively important in determining satisfaction. Still other attributes, which are not critical to satisfaction, create dissatisfaction when their performance is disappointing. In making this distinction, the authors speak of two aspects of performance.

- *Instrumental performance* refers to a means to a set of ends. This is essentially the performance of the physical product, per se.
- *Expressive performance* is the performance that consumers consider an end in itself. It involves psychological attributes such as style and expression of the self concept.

The determinant attributes of a given purchase may be the *expressive* attributes, while the *instrumental* attributes may not be an explicit part of the purchase decision. However, inadequate performance of the physical product (instrumental attributes) may lead to dissatisfaction with the purchase. For example, a woman may buy a dress because of its style, and be well pleased with her purchase. Style, an expressive attribute, is the determinant attribute of her purchase. After she has worn the dress a few times, she finds that the material begins to stretch, and lose its form; or seams are constantly tearing loose. In making the purchase, she did not consciously consider these factors. She tacitly assumed that the dress was of good quality and would perform well. However, she becomes bitterly dissatisfied with her purchase—not because of the style (the expressive attribute for which she bought it), but because of its physical failure (instrumental attributes) that were not consciously considered at the time of purchase.

The instrumental performance of Swan and Combs (the performance of the physical product, per se) is the performance equivalent of the *physical* product. Thus, Swan and Combs isolate the *physical* product from the complexities of the *psychological* and emphasize the role of the *physical* product in consumer dissatisfaction, although it may not have been a determinant factor in making the purchase.

Howard Morgans, who was quoted at the beginning of the chapter, was undoubtedly talking about the *physical* product with his observation that: "You can only succeed with a good product. You can't do it with advertising." A direct implication for marketers is that, regardless of the psychological attributes with which a product is imbued, the performance characteristics of the physical product always remain as key determinants in product satisfaction or dissatisfaction. Thus, the quality of the physical product should *always* be a major concern of marketers although, I'm deeply afraid that often it is not. One constantly sees evidence of this in products whose expressive attributes are delightful to behold, but whose physical performance is, at best, shoddy.

8. Ralph E. Anderson, "Consumer Dissatisfaction: The Effect of Disconfirmed Expectancy on Perceived Product Performance," *Journal of Marketing Research* (February, 1973): 38–44.

9. John E. Swan and Linda Jones Combs, "Product Performance and Consumer Satisfaction: A New Concept," *Journal of Marketing* (April, 1976): 25–33. This theory was anticipated by Irving S. White who made a distinction between "expressive products" and "utility products" in 1969. See, Irving S. White, "New Product Differentiation: Physical and Symbolic Dimensions," in *Marketing in a Changing World,* Bernard A. Morin, ed. (Chicago: American Marketing Association, 1969), pp. 99–103.

NEW PRODUCT DEVELOPMENT

New products are the future of a business. Without a continuous flow of new products, the marketing system as we know it would probably atrophy and die. In *New Product Management,* Eberhard Scheuing estimates that "80 percent of today's products will have disappeared from the market ten years from now, while an estimated 80 percent of the products that will be sold in the next decade are as yet unknown."[10]

Yet, the development of new products is expensive, and the risks are relatively high. Ford is estimated to have lost $350 million on the Edsel, Du Pont lost $100 million on Corfam (a synthetic leather), Scott Paper Company lost $12 million on Baby Scott (disposable diapers), and Standard Brands spent $6 million in marketing support alone during the brief year that its Smooth & Easy Sauce and Gravy Mixes unsuccessfully struggled for survival. Today, under the impact of inflation and depressed real profits, the cost is even higher. During the early 1970s, the cost for designing and producing a new automobile was estimated to be $750 million; by 1980, Ford spent $3 billion developing the Ford Escort and Mercury Lynx, Ford's answer to fuel-efficient imports, and this does not include the high cost of introducing a new entry into the automobile market.[11]

Few products are as expensive to develop as automobiles, but all are relatively expensive and a succession of new product failures is sufficient to depress the profits and weaken the financial structure of even the most vigorous of companies.

While few reliable figures are available on the failure rate of new products, a number of attempts have been made to assess failure rates, with estimates ranging from 90 percent to 30 percent. Unfortunately, the definition of what constitutes a new product in these studies, and the criteria of success used, raise more questions than they answer. Some studies, for example, have concentrated on "major" new products, while others have included every single item marketed, including new sizes and colors. Some studies have used successful commercialization as the criterion of success, while others have used "performance in test markets" as the criterion. Still others have considered a product a failure even if the product idea is dropped as unfeasible at an early stage in its development.

Some new products are old products. (Photo by Paul M. Shrock)

C. Merle Crawford analyzed some thirty-two reports of new product failure and found that twenty-five of the reports should be rejected because they were based on unsupported opinion or seriously flawed methodology. Only seven of the thirty-two reports appeared to have value, and even these studies may be questioned because of their methodology.[12]

Among the seven studies in which Crawford considered the methodology reasonably acceptable, the failure rates ranged from 27 to 42 percent, with an average failure rate of 36.2 per-

10. Eberhard E. Scheuing, *New Product Development* (Hinsdale, IL: The Dryden Press, 1974), p. 1.

11. "Detroit's Uphill Battle," *Time* (Sept. 8, 1980): 46.

12. C. Merle Crawford, "New Product Failure Rates—Facts and Fallacies," *Research Management* (Sept., 1979): 9–13.

cent. The universe of products included in these studies was restricted to those that reached the commercialization stage. That is, of all new products that reached the commercialization stage, an average of 36.2 percent failed. Only a tiny proportion of all new products that enter the developmental pipeline ever reach the commercialization stage, however, since most are rejected at various stages of their development up to and including test marketing.

Anyone who has worked on new products in industry knows that discovering, developing, and commercializing new products is an arduous and risk-filled task. Dozens of new product ideas are often rejected in the preliminary screening process before one is found worthy of further investigation. Many of those rating further investigation are found to be either technically or economically unfeasible. And only a few of those considered feasible survive concept testing or actual consumer tests of prototypes. Among those that achieve test marketing, still more are eliminated. The *Wall Street Journal* has referred to new product development as one of the "highest risk and highest reward activities in the business world," and has pointed out that "substantial companies may launch only a few new products in a narrow field during their entire history."[13] It is little wonder that the development of new products is a subject of concern for marketing practitioners.

Companies vary widely in the level of sophistication with which they approach the development of new products. Some seem to operate on a catch-as-catch-can basis and, among these companies, failures tend to be high. Others develop systematic and sometimes elaborate procedures for new product development, instituting controls at a variety of levels in the developmental process to avoid failures and to conserve company resources.

Organizational Arrangements for New Product Development

Companies have devised a variety of organizational arrangements to facilitate the development of new products. At the simplest level, new product responsibility is delegated to product managers of existing company products, or perhaps, to a *new products manager* whose only responsibility is new product development. The problem with the first of these two approaches (using managers of existing products) is that new product activity is often shunted aside by the day-to-day demands of managing existing products. The problem with the second approach (a special new products manager) is that the hierarchical level of this person in the organization often doesn't command enough clout to assure that high priorities will be given to developmental work. Nonetheless, this approach may work reasonably well in smaller companies where organizational structures are flexible and intracompany relationships relatively informal.

Large companies, however, usually require a more elaborate organizational arrangement. Among those that have received the most attention are new product committees, new product departments, and new product venture teams.

NEW PRODUCT COMMITTEES. New product committees are usually composed of top level executives from key company departments such as marketing, engineering, production, and finance. The primary function of such a committee is to establish a system that will provide a flow of new product ideas, to review the ideas generated, to identify ideas for further development, and to assign this work to the appropriate departments of the organization. Because of the importance of the people serving on the committee, their decisions have sufficient authority to assure that priorities will be given to new product areas. Unfortunately, however, since the members of the committee have other demanding responsibilities within the company, their meetings are often infrequent and follow-up erratic. As a consequence, new product committees often have to be replaced or supplemented by more dependable organizational arrangements if an effective new product program is to be developed.

NEW PRODUCT DEPARTMENTS. Some organizations, with General Mills and S. C. Johnson serving as examples, establish a formal new products

13. "Seeking a Winner: Success Comes Hard in the Tricky Business of Creating Products," *Wall Street Journal* (Aug. 23, 1978): 1.

department, headed by a high ranking executive who usually reports to the chief executive officer or to the marketing vice-president. This department is charged with generating and screening new product ideas, conducting feasibility studies, developing products, and completing all of those tasks required to prepare a product for commercialization. At that point, the product is turned over to a brand manager or to a company division for commercialization.

Although new product departments often work quite well, they have one drawback: responsibility ends when the product is ready for commercialization. At this point, responsibility passes to some other group or division within the company, and this group or division may or may not devote sufficient resources to the commercialization phase. For example, a major chemical company specializing in industrial marketing turned new products developed by its new product department over to appropriate company divisions for commercialization. The trouble was that commercialization is often an expensive and lengthy process, with the full economic benefits often several years in the future. At the same time, divisional vice-presidents knew that they were being evaluated by corporate management according to the annual profits they produced, and that favorable evaluations led to promotions to head larger divisions or to corporate headquarters. Since commercialization of new products depressed short-term profits, divisional vice-presidents were reluctant to devote major divisional resources to new products. As a consequence, the new products turned over to the company's divisions tended to be neglected, and to do poorly. In an effort to avoid this kind of a situation, some companies have turned to new product venture teams.

NEW PRODUCT VENTURE TEAMS. New product venture teams are groups of experts brought together and charged with the development of a specific product. Unlike new product departments, however, they carry the product through the commercialization stage, turning the product over to the product managers or other divisions only *after* it has been successfully commercialized. This relieves company divisions of the initial cost of commercialization, with its consequent depression of division profits. The team spirit in the venture team often leads to increased dedication, greater creativity, and speeds up the work. Even dedication has its limitations. Team members sometimes become so involved in the product upon which they are working that they lose their objectivity, take unnecessary risks, and often carry product work past the state where it should have been abandoned.

No structural arrangement is without fault. Companies need to develop different organizational arrangements depending upon each company's needs and resources, the particular products and industries involved, and the environmental situation that prevails.

Regardless of the particular organizational structure employed, there are certain logical steps or stages in the development of new products. This is not to say that these steps are always followed, or must be followed. However, they do represent a systematic process designed to minimize risk and protect company resources.

Stages in New Product Development

Writers conceptualize the stages of new product development in different ways. Some identify as few as four major stages, while others identify as many as eight.[14] Regardless of the stages identified, most of the conceptualizations involve the following essential activities:

- *Ideal development.* The first step is to develop a pool of ideas for new products. Such ideas come from many sources—from a company's basic research, company employ-

14. Benton & Bowles (a major advertising agency) and *Printer's Ink* identify four stages: idea stage, development stage, concept stage, and test market stage. See *Printer's Ink* (April 13, 1962): 22–23. Booz, Allen & Hamilton (a management consultant organization) identifies six stages: exploration, screening, business analysis, development, testing, and commercialization. See Booz, Allen & Hamilton, *Management of New Products,* 1968. Philip Kotler identifies eight stages: idea generation, screening, concept development and testing, marketing strategy, business analysis, product development, market testing, and commercialization. See Philip Kotler, *Marketing Management* 4th ed. (Englewood Cliffs, NJ: Prentice-Hall, Inc., 1980), p. 315.

ees, distributors, consumers, competitors, inventors, scientists, universities, industry publications, and so forth. The generation of ideas is often one of the most difficult steps in the entire process, and a variety of techniques for idea generation have been developed by individuals, companies, and consulting firms.[15]

- *Idea Screening.* Not all new product ideas are good ones. Most, in fact, are pretty bad. The purpose of idea screening is to eliminate weak ideas that have little promise for development. Booz, Allen and Hamilton, a major management consulting firm, say that they commonly consider one hundred ideas in order to find six or eight worth pursuing. And, for every ten or twelve ideas considered worth pursuing, only one will reach the marketplace.[16]

  Ideas are discarded for many reasons. Some because they are technologically unfeasible; some because their cost would be exhorbitant; some because they have been tried and failed; some because they are incompatible with company goals and resources; and some because they are not new.

  Some companies employ evaluation matrices such as those shown in Tables 12–2 and 12–3. While these matrices differ somewhat in form and detail, they both have the same purpose. Namely, to find some way of assigning a numerical rating to new product ideas so that they can be compared, and those having the highest ratings selected for further exploration. Of course, assigning numbers to the various dimensions of these matrices is a subjective, judgmental process; but quite practically, judgment is an essential ingredient in idea screening.

  Whatever the process employed in screening ideas, the primary goal is to avoid eliminating good ideas and to avoid pursuing poor ones.

- *Product Concept.* A product idea is simply a potential product described in functional terms—a cold preparation that will give long-lasting relief; a hunger suppressant that will help one to lose weight; a concentrated powder that, when mixed with water or milk, will make a delicious drink; a protein paste that can be used in food preparation; a detergent that will remove ground in stains. These are all product ideas. Consumers, however, don't buy product ideas. They buy benefits.

  In the product concept stage, the product idea must be transformed into a physical product that will appeal to a definable group of consumers. Decisions must be made concerning the product form and the particular attributes that it should possess. In the case of the cold preparation mentioned above, one could develop a capsule with "hundreds of tiny time pills," as was done in the case of Contac. Or, one could develop a soothing, nighttime drink, as was done with Nyquil. These two product concepts are different in form, in occasion of use, and in appeal. The hunger suppressant could take the form of a full-nutrition meal, a pill to be taken before meals, or as a between meal snack. The concentrated powder to be mixed with water or milk to provide a delicious drink could be turned into a breakfast drink, a food supplement, a diet drink, or (as Carnation demonstrated) into an Instant Breakfast. A protein paste could be turned into a spread for children's snacks, an adult sandwich spread for picnics or lunch box use, or a food ingredient to be used in a variety of dishes. And, the heavy-duty detergent could appear as a powder, a liquid, a tablet, or, possibly, in other forms. The detergent could also be positioned for general use, or for a use as specific as "ring around the collar."

---

15. See John E. Arnold, "Useful Creative Techniques," in *Source Book for Creative Thinking* by Sidney J. Parnes and Harold F. Harding, eds. (New York: Charles Scribner's Sons, 1962). Alex F. Osborn, *Applied Imagination,* 3rd. ed. (New York: Charles Scribner's Sons, 1963); Edward M. Tauber, "HIT: Heuristic Ideation Technique—A Systematic Procedure for New Product Search," *Journal of Marketing* (January, 1972): 58–70; Charles L. Alford and Joseph Barry Mason, "Generating New Product Ideas," *Journal of Advertising Research* (December, 1975), 27–32. In fact, there is a fairly voluminous literature on how to be creative, much of which isn't particularly creative.

16. "Seeking a Winner: Success Comes Hard in the Tricky Business of Creating Products," *Wall Street Journal* (August 23, 1978): 1 and 29.

Many product ideas lend themselves to a variety of product concepts which will involve decisions concerning form, flavors, convenience, price, and method of use. The way in which these questions are resolved will depend upon the way the product concept is defined and the market to which the product is to be addressed. Extensive market analysis and consumer research are often required to determine the alternative that offers the greatest promise of sales and profits.

- *Feasibility Analysis.* The development of the product concept enables marketers to develop their first clear fix on the market to which the product will be directed, and the product characteristics that will be required. As a consequence, feasibility analysis usually takes two forms: one, a business analysis of the probable size of the market, possible price ranges, competitive barriers, and profit. The other, a technological analysis designed to determine whether the proposed product is technologically feasible within a reasonable time span, and an estimate of developmental costs.
- *Developmental Stage.* During this phase, actual product development takes place, a prototype is produced, and pilot plant production undertaken to work out bugs in the production process and to gain a firmer estimate of product costs. Extensive consumer testing is often used and, sometime during this period, work is begun on the package, product name, pricing structure, distribution strategy, advertising and promotion. By the end of this phase, if the product has not been washed out because of cost or technological problems, both a product and a marketing plan exist.
- *Test Marketing.* In most instances, test markets are now undertaken to determine how well the product will perform in the marketplace, to detect possible weaknesses in the marketing plan, and to gain more precise information on expected volume upon which to base production and economic planning.
- *Commercialization.* This is the final stage in the new product development process. Test markets are expanded into a "roll-out" program and major marketing investments are called for. Note that success is not yet assured. About a third of all products that survive test marketing fail in the commercialization stage and are eventually abandoned.

TABLE 12–2 *Evaluation Matrix—Product Fit.*
SOURCE: Barry M. Richman, "A Rating Scale for Product Innovation," *Business Horizons* (Summer, 1962), p. 43. Copyright, 1962, by the Foundation for the School of Business at Indiana University. Reprinted by permission.

		(B) Product Compatibility Values											
Sphere of Performance	(A) Relative Weight	0	.1	.2	.3	.4	.5	.6	.7	.8	.9	1.0	(C) A × B
Company personality and goodwill	.20							x					.120
Marketing	.20										x		.180
Research and development	.20								x				.140
Personnel	.15							x					.090
Finance	.10										x		.090
Production	.05									x			.040
Location and facilities	.05				x								.015
Purchasing and supply	.05										x		.045
Total	1.00												.720*

*Rating Scale: 0–.40, poor; .41–75, fair; .76–1.0, good. Present minimum acceptance rate: .70

TABLE 12–3: New Product Marketing Index.
SOURCE: Reprinted by permission of the *Harvard Business Review.* Table from "Selecting Profitable Products," (January-February, 1961).

	Very good	*Good*	*Average*	*Poor*	*Very poor*
MARKETABILITY					
Relation to present distribution channels	Can reach major markets by distributing through present channels.	Can reach major markets by distributing mostly through present channels, partly through new channels.	Will have to distribute equally between new and present channels, in order to reach major markets.	Will have to distribute mostly through new channels in order to reach major markets.	Will have to distribute entirely through new channels in order to reach major markets.
Relation to present product lines	Complements a present line which needs more products to fill it.	Complements a present line that does not need, but can handle, another product.	Can be fitted into a present line.	Can be fitted into a present line but does not fit entirely.	Does not fit in with any present product line.
Quality/price relationship	Priced below all competing products of similar quality.	Priced below most competing products of similar quality.	Approximately the same price as competing products of similar quality.	Priced above many competing products of similar quality.	Priced above all competing products of similar quality.
Number of sizes and grades	Few staple sizes and grades.	Several sizes and grades, but customers will be satisfied with few staples.	Several sizes and grades, but can satisfy customer wants with small inventory of nonstaples.	Several sizes and grades, each of which will have to be stocked in equal amounts.	Many sizes and grades which will necessitate heavy inventories.
Merchandisability	Has product characteristics over and above those of competing products that lend themselves to the kind of promotion, advertising, and display that the given company does best.	Has promotable characteristics that will compare favorably with the characteristics of competing products.	Has promotable characteristics that are equal to those of other products.	Has a few characteristics that are promotable, but generally does not measure up to characteristics of competing products.	Has no characteristics at all that are equal to competitors' or that lend themselves to imaginative promotion.
Effects on sales of present products	Should aid in sales of present products.	May help sales of present products; definitely will not be harmful to present sales.	Should have no effect on present sales.	May hinder present sales some; definitely will not aid present sales.	Will reduce sales of presently profitable products.

TABLE 12–3: *New Product Marketing Index—continued*

	Very good	*Good*	*Average*	*Poor*	*Very poor*
DURABILITY					
Stability	Basic product which can always expect to have uses.	Product which will have uses long enough to earn back initial investment, plus at least 10 years of additional profits.	Product which will have uses long enough to earn back initial investment, plus several (from 5 to 10) years of additional profits.	Product which will have uses long enough to earn back initial investment, plus 1 to 5 years of additional profits.	Product which will probably be obsolete in near future.
Breadth of market	A national market, a wide variety of consumers, and a potential foreign market.	A national market and a wide variety of consumers.	Either a national market or a wide variety of consumers.	A regional market and a restricted variety of consumers.	A specialized market in a small marketing area.
Resistance to cyclical fluctuations	Will sell readily in inflation or depression.	Effects of cyclical chances will be *moderate,* and will be felt *after* changes in economic outlook.	Sales will rise and fall with the economy.	Effects of cyclical changes will be *heavy,* and will be felt *before* changes in economic outlook.	Cyclical changes will cause extreme fluctuations in demand.
Resistance to seasonal fluctuations	Steady sales throughout the year.	Steady sales—except under unusual circumstances.	Seasonal fluctuations, but inventory and personnel problems can be absorbed.	Heavy seasonal fluctuations that will cause considerable inventory and personnel problems.	Severe seasonal fluctuations that will necessitate layoffs and heavy inventories.
Exclusiveness of design	Can be protected by a patent with no loopholes.	Can be patented, but the patent might be circumvented.	Cannot be patented, but has certain salient characteristics that cannot be copied very well.	Cannot be patented, and can be copied by larger, more knowledgeable companies.	Cannot be patented, and can be copied by anyone.
PRODUCTIVE ABILITY					
Equipment necessary	Can be produced with equipment that is presently idle.	Can be produced with present equipment, but production will have to be scheduled with other products.	Can be produced largely with present equipment, but the company will have to purchase some additional equipment.	Company will have to buy a good deal of new equipment, but some present equipment can be used.	Company will have to buy all new equipment.

TABLE 12–3: *New Product Marketing Index—continued*

	Very good	*Good*	*Average*	*Poor*	*Very poor*
Production knowledge and personnel necessary	Present knowledge and personnel will be able to produce new product.	With very few minor exceptions, present knowledge and personnel will be able to produce new product.	With some exceptions, present knowledge and personnel will be able to produce new product.	A ratio of approximately 50–50 will prevail between the needs for new knowledge and personnel and for present knowledge and personnel.	Mostly new knowledge and personnel are needed to produce the new product.
Raw materials' availability	Company can purchase raw materials from its best supplier(s) exclusively.	Company can purchase major portion of raw materials from its best supplier(s), and remainder from any one of a number of companies.	Company can purchase approximately half of raw materials from its best supplier(s), and other half from any one of a number of companies.	Company must purchase most of raw materials from any one of a number of companies other than its best supplier(s).	Company must purchase most or all of raw materials from a certain few companies other than its best supplier(s).
GROWTH POTENTIAL					
Place in market	New type of product that will fill a need presently not being filled.	Product that will substantially improve on products presently on the market.	Product that will have certain new characteristics that will appeal to a substantial segment of the market.	Product that will have minor improvements over products presently on the market.	Product similar to those presently on the market and which adds nothing new.
Expected competitive situation—value added	Very high value added so as to substantially restrict number of competitors.	High enough value added so that, unless product is extremely well suited to other firms, they will not want to invest in additional facilities.	High enough value added so that, unless other companies are as strong in market as the firm, it will not be profitable for them to compete.	Lower value added so as to allow large, medium, and some smaller companies to compete.	Very low value added so that all companies can profitably enter market.
Expected availability of end users	Number of end users will increase substantially.	Number of end users will increase moderately.	Number of end users will increase slightly, if at all.	Number of end users will decrease moderately.	Number of end users will decrease substantially.

The foregoing material outlines the major steps in the development of new products. Needless to say, the sequence is not as rigid as its presentation implies, and exceptions may often be made for sound business reasons. For example, several years ago General Foods developed and tested a fruit-filled waffle (Toast'em Popups) in several markets. Kellogg, a major competitor of General Foods, monitored the test results and discovered that the General Foods' product had gained wide consumer acceptance. Since the product technology was fairly simple and investment costs low, Kellogg immediately developed its own product, named it Pop Tarts, introduced it nationally, and gained market leadership in a significant market. It is always possible that Kellogg's product development simply paralleled that of General Foods. It is much more probable, however, that Kellogg saw a good idea, grabbed it, and commercialized it without going through the laborious pains of the product development scheme outlined above.

WHY NEW PRODUCTS FAIL

Why do new products fail? Many reasons are given—a weak product concept, inadequate testing, insufficient spending, faulty pricing, unexpected competitive strength, failure to obtain distribution, poor advertising, packaging failure, unexpected production problems, supply problems, and almost any other reason that can be imagined. And, indeed, any of these reasons may bear the brunt of responsibility in a particular case.

However, *the most common reason for new product failure is the lack of a significant difference in the physical product, as viewed by the consumer, from products already in the marketplace.* Thus, Theodore Angelus, who made a study of seventy-five new product failures in the food and drug industries, found that the major cause of failure was lack of a significant product difference, as viewed by the consumer.[17]

17. Theodore L. Angelus, "Why Do Most New Products Fail?" *Advertising Age* (March 24, 1969): 85–86.

TABLE 12–4 *Comparison of Successful and Unsuccessful Products.*
SOURCE: Adapted from J. Hugh Davidson, "Why Most New Consumer Brands Fail," *Harvard Business Review,* 54 (March-April, 1976), p. 119.

Differences from Competition	*Successful Products*	*Unsuccessful Products*
Better than competition	74%	20%
Same as competition	26%	60%
Worse than competition	—	20%
Total	100%	100%

Hugh Davidson supports this conclusion in a study of one hundred new products, fifty of which succeeded.[18] The results of this study, summarized in Table 12–4, clearly show that most of the successful products (74 percent) were *better* than competition, while most of the products which failed (80 percent) were either no *different* or *worse* than the competition's physical product performance.

These findings, which are well supported by the pragmatic experience of marketing and advertising practitioners, emphasize the importance of a *perceivable* product superiority in the success of new products. This is not to say that new products that are no different from existing competition always fail. However, the success of such products is relatively rare and, after all, sound marketing decisions are based on playing the odds.

PRODUCT STRATEGY FOR NEW PRODUCTS

Basically, there are two strategies for new products—market segmentation and product differentiation.

Market Segmentation

Not all forms of market segmentation fall within *product* strategy. Many of the bases for market segmentation do not require an actual modifica-

18. J. Hugh Davidson, "Why Most New Consumer Brands Fail," *Harvard Business Review* (March-April, 1976): 119.

tion of the physical product. Markets may be segmented into distribution channels, geographic areas, income, and so forth without any change in the physical product, although minor product changes are often made to avoid confusion. This is particularly true when segmentation is based on consumer income or distribution channels. For example, a major manufacturer of carpet sweepers sold the same sweeper under two different pricing structures. In order to avoid consumer confusion and retailer complaints, the higher priced sweeper was decorated with a narrow strip of chrome on the sweeper head and sold through department stores; the lower priced sweeper, sans the chrome strip, was sold through discount stores. The basis of segmentation was price. The product difference (the chrome strip) between the two models was a minor, inexpensive concession to provide visual support for the premium price of the more expensive sweeper.

In the discussion of market segmentation in Chapter 3, reference was made to the evaporated milk market which is segmented by use: infant feeding, cooking, and coffee creaming. These three distinct markets may overlap since some families may use evaporated milk for all three purposes. The *physical* product is the same for all three markets, but these three segments require different copy appeals, different directions for use, and different media.

Product strategy, as such, is only involved in marketing new products when an actual difference in the physical product is deemed necessary. The particular form that product strategy takes depends upon the product field involved and consumer preferences. The difference may be in appearance, method of use, performance characteristics, size, shape, and so forth. In any case, the judgment as to whether market segmentation requires a unique physical product must be made on a product-by-product basis in view of company resources, competitive activity, and market characteristics.

Product Differentiation

As pointed out earlier, product differentiation differs from market segmentation in that marketers utilizing this strategy direct their activities toward the entire market, competing with all other entries, rather than directing their activities to one or more subsets of the total market. Product differentiation is a viable strategy when the market is truly homogeneous or when its size precludes profitable segmentation. As in the case of market segmentation, actual differences in the physical product may or may not play a role in the strategy of product differentiation. Much product differentiation is simply based on preemptive claims in the sense that the same claim could be made for every competitor in the field; and this approach is sometimes successful. Wonder Bread's "Helps build strong bodies twelve ways" is such a claim.

Product strategy enters into product differentiation when an actual change is made in the physical product and this difference is used as support for advertising claims. The "secret" ingredient approach is an example, as are minor, visible product differences. For example, a major manufacturer of lawn and garden fertilizers laced its product with green particles to support its claim of "Green Power." Oxydol is sprinkled through with green crystals as tangible evidence of its product difference; and the blue color of Cheer supports its claim of "blue magic." As a generalization, product differentiation is simplified and made more believable when there is a *visible* product difference. Many consumers may be gullible, but even the most gullible of consumers are more comfortable when they have something visible to be gullible about.

PRODUCT STRATEGY FOR ESTABLISHED PRODUCTS

Product strategy plays a major role in established products, as well as in the development of new ones. In order to understand the role of product strategy for established brands, we need to examine the concept of the product life cycle.

Product Life Cycle

Every day, new products are born into the marketplace. And every day, old products, no longer in sufficient demand to justify their continued promotion and distribution, disappear from the marketplace. The period between the birth and death of a product has become known as the *product life cycle.* The concept of the product life cycle is an attempt to recognize that every product has distinct stages in its sales history and that each stage presents unique problems and opportunities for marketing strategy.

STAGES IN THE PRODUCT LIFE CYCLE. The product life cycle is generally portrayed as having four stages: introduction, growth, maturity, and decline. The traditional form of the product life cycle is shown in Figure 12–1. Note that the product profitability curve does not parallel the life cycle curve but tends to peak earlier. This phenomenon is, essentially, a function of pricing practices and increased competitive activity.

Some authorities portray the life cycle as having five stages rather than four. Chester Wasson inserts a *competitive turbulent* stage between growth and maturity.[19] Booz, Allen and Hamilton insert a *saturation* stage between maturity and decline.[20] Regardless of the number of stages, the general form of the life cycle is essentially the same, although William E. Cox, in a study of 754 drug products, identified six different life cycle curves. The differences resulted from technical developments and promotional activities during the products' lives.[21] The most common variation found by Cox has a second, although smaller rise which results from a final, promotional push during the decline stage. This suggests that marketing activities may modify, or even prolong product life cycles.

The most common reasons for the demise of products are technological or psychological obsolescence, and poor product management. In technological obsolescence, a new technology arises that performs the essential function of existing products better or at less cost. The replacement of the horse and buggy by the automobile is an excellent example of technological obsolescence. Fashion is an example of psychological obsolescence since a new fashion—while no better, and certainly no cheaper—may turn last year's wardrobe into a contribution to the Salvation Army overnight. Examples of poor product management are almost too frequent to mention, but once-great names like Pear's Soap, Packard, Uneeda Biscuit, and Twenty Grand have been dead so long that they are no longer mourned.

19. Chester R. Wasson, *Dynamic Competitive Strategy and Product Life Cycles* (St. Louis: Challenge Books, 1974), p. 3.

20. *Management of New Products,* p. 4.

21. William E. Cox, Jr. "Product Life Cycles as Marketing Models," *Journal of Business* (October, 1967): 375–84.

FIGURE 12–1: *Typical Four-Stage Product Life Cycle and Product Curve.*

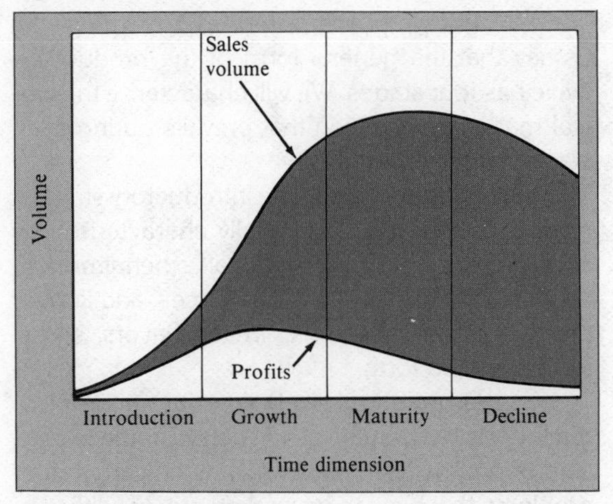

Some products, such as glass, never die because technology has not produced an economical and superior replacement for mirrors, windows, and dozens of other functional uses. Other products, such as coal (a victim of petroleum, natural gas, and other forms of cheaper, cleaner energy) may have their funerals interrupted by a shortage of their replacement products and be "born again."

Thus, the product life cycle concept is not a good predictive indicator of either product longevity or product vigor. Technological, economic, and managerial variables may influence both the cycle's duration and magnitude. Further, the concept of product life cycle does not specify whether the *product* is a product class (vegetables), a product form (canned vegetables), or a product brand (Del Monte). Obviously, different considerations will apply to these three interpretations of *product.* Nonetheless, the product life cycle may have some value in giving us insights into marketing strategy.

For purposes of marketing strategy, let us say that the general form of the product life cycle has four stages. We will characterize the typical marketing situation that prevails during each stage of the life cycle.

The Introductory Stage. The introductory stage of a product life cycle is generally characterized by slow growth, heavy promotional expenditures in relation to sales, relatively high prices, and limited product offerings; that is, limited flavors, styles, forms, and so forth.

Growth is relatively slow during the introductory stage because of: (1) delays in the expansion of productive capacity; (2) technical product problems that have to be worked out; (3) difficulty in gaining widespread distribution; and (4) inertia on the part of consumers in trying the new product.[22] Promotional expenditures are high in relation to sales because of the heavy sales costs involved in obtaining distribution and because of the need for an advertising investment to create consumer awareness and trial. Prices are relatively high because of the need to recover investment costs in plant and equipment and because a relatively low volume of sales characterizes the introductory period leading to high production costs. Limited product offerings exist because initial volume is not sufficient to justify a wide variety of flavors, sizes, forms, styles, and so forth.

The Growth Stage. If the introduction is successful, sales start climbing rapidly as distribution increases and as consumers are persuaded to try the product. Promotional expenditures remain high in absolute volume, although their ratio to sales decreases because sales are increasing rapidly. Prices tend to remain high unless they are reduced to stimulate demand or to discourage competition from entering the field. During the growth period, production capacity becomes both more plentiful and more efficient. Competitors enter the field, and major product improvements appear as a response to competition. Product differentiation and market segmentation emerge as marketing strategies, competition for distribution becomes intense, and dealers adopt multiple-line policies (that is, they stock several competitive brands). Sales promotion activities increase, and new forms of the product appear.

The Maturity Stage. Eventually, the rate of growth slows down when most of the potential customers have tried the product. The reduction in growth rate exerts a downward pressure on prices, dealer margins, and profits. Weak competitors and less than adequate brands drop out of the market. Their places are taken by the surviving brands, and sales settle down to the repurchase rate of consumers who are satisfied with the product's performance. Any continued growth tends to parallel population growth.

The maturity stage lasts much longer than the preceding stages and, indeed, may continue for many years. Most products on the market are in the maturity stage, which is characterized by well-entrenched brands, consumer loyalty, and relatively stable market shares. Prices are relatively stable because the margin between cost and selling price has dropped to normal levels. Any significant increase in sales for a particular brand must come at the expense of competitive brands, not from growth of the total market.

The manufacturing costs of most competitors are comparable, and promotional expenditures reach a stable ratio to sales. There is little opportunity for price increases because of the existence of established competition. Price decreases offer only a temporary advantage because they will be met by competition with the consequence that profit levels for the entire field will be reduced even further. Deals and price promotions are used on a periodic, short-term basis to clear inventories, to attract customers from other brands, and to increase retail visibility.

The maturity stage is marked by increased efforts to find unique, dramatic, and compelling ways of presenting advertising claims. A larger proportion of the budget is devoted to sales promotional activities. Media analysis, designed to increase the efficiency of the advertising budget, becomes more intense. The maturity stage is often characterized by frenzied efforts to increase

22. Robert D. Buzzell, "Competitive Behavior and the Product Life Cycle," in *New Ideas for Successful Marketing*, John S. Wright and Jac L. Goldstucker, eds. (Chicago: American Marketing Association, 1966), pp. 46–68.

usage by current users, to discover new users, new uses for the product, and new channels of distribution.

The Decline Stage. Eventually, most product forms and brands enter a period of declining sales. The decline period may be rapid, particularly in a case where technology devises a new product form functionally superior to existing brands. Or, the decline period may continue for years as consumers gradually lose interest and as a variety of substitute forms of the product emerge. The decline stage for most industries and brands is characterized by both dwindling sales and a decrease in competition as more and more competitive companies seek lucrative uses for their productive capacity and company resources.

MANAGING THE PRODUCT LIFE CYCLE. For the marketing manager, the major question is whether the *brand* life cycle is inevitable, or whether the cycle can be managed in such a way that the vitality of the brand is prolonged. Certainly, many once bright brands have lost their luster. On the other hand, Ivory Soap has been around since 1878, and Kodak cameras have a similar longevity. Kellogg, Ford, RCA, Remington, Chase and Sanborn, Hires, Coca-Cola, Woodbury, Cadillac, Hershey, and many other brands seem to defy the life cycle concept and retain their vigor long past the age of reasonable senescence. Some have done so while keeping their original form and formula—Coca-Cola, for example. Others have done so through a variety of brand modifications and marketing strategies. Our focus in this chapter is on *product* strategies that are used to extend the product life cycle and maintain the health of the brand. These strategies focus on the physical form of the tangible product.

Strategies for Extending the Product Life Cycle

The creation of a successful brand is an expensive undertaking that represents a major commitment of company resources and often takes years of concentrated effort. As a consequence, the demise of a brand represents the loss of an important company asset. A number of product strategies are employed to prolong the life of an established brand. The more common ones—product quality, product differentiation, line extensions, and product obsolescence are briefly discussed in the following material.

PRODUCT QUALITY. Product quality, as perceived by the consumer, is unquestionably the most fundamental product strategy for maintaining the health of a brand. Major companies such as Coca-Cola, Anheuser-Busch, Procter and Gamble, Ralston Purina, Maytag, and many others are sticklers for product quality. These companies maintain extensive systems of quality control, augmented by periodic consumer tests, to make sure that manufacturing standards are being met and that their brands continue to satisfy consumers. Maytag, at one point, closed down the production line of one of its major appliances—at considerable inconvenience and expense—on

"This is a product?" (Photo by Paul Conklin)

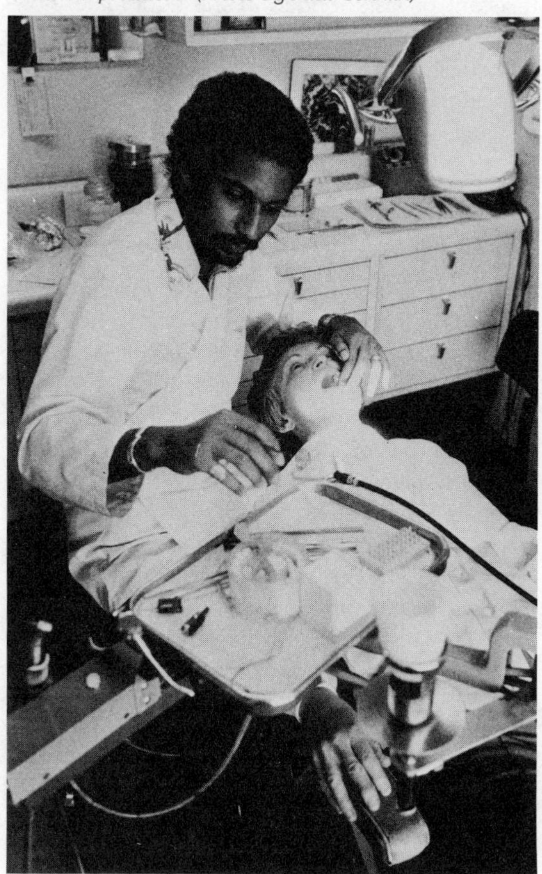

the basis of three letters of complaint from consumers. All production was halted while plant engineers investigated the complaints to make sure that the problem was a nonrecurrent one and not the fault of material specification, design characteristics, manufacturing procedures, or quality control standards. Production was not resumed until plant engineers were satisfied that the problem was not likely to recur. This same company has used the "high quality" of its products as the theme for an extremely effective advertising campaign—"The Maytag repairman is the loneliest man in town."

The maintenance of product quality often involves many small product improvements, any one of which is imperceptible to consumers, and none of which are significant enough to mention in advertising. It may involve a better preservative, a manufacturing procedure that provides better quality control, a coating that is more stain resistant or lasts longer. In the aggregate, however, often these small improvements truly maintain quality and keep the brand competitive in the marketplace. Making continuous, undramatic product improvements that result in only minor changes in the tangible product may, indeed, be one of the most fundamental of product strategies in prolonging the brand life cycle.

PRODUCT DIFFERENTIATION. Companies employing a strategy of product differentiation often insist that the differentiated claim be based on a perceivable difference in the tangible product and not simply on a preemptive or psychological claim. The "Green Power" example given earlier, in which green crystals were added to a lawn and garden fertilizer, is an example of this approach. Gillette's *Promax Compact* hair dryer is another. Here, the product difference is one of size, with the *Promax Compact* being substantially smaller than competitive models.

The product differentiation strategy sometimes involves a systematic program of physical variations, introduced on a periodic basis and designed to create an impression of continuous modification and improvement.

LINE EXTENSION. Line extension is a strategy wherein new products are introduced into the line to provide variety, add shelf facings, and increase sales. Line extensions may or may not employ a strategy of market segmentation.

The most common example of line extensions is adding flavors to a food product such as Campbell's soups, Jello, or cake mixes. A classic example of the addition of new flavors to increase sales and gain market dominance occurred in the cake mix market in the mid to late 1950s. At that time, prepared cake mixes as a product form were in the late growth stage of their product life cycle. The major brands offered four basic mixes—white, yellow, chocolate, and spice. Analysis of marketing activities at that time suggests that General Mills launched the following, three-stage strategy of flavor proliferation.

First, the company undertook a major research and development effort to create new cake mix flavors.

Second, the company cut the price of the basic mixes, virtually eliminating all advertising and promotion funds. Competitive brands quickly followed suit from fear that the price differential would cause them to lose volume and market share.

Finally, General Mills' Betty Crocker brand started introducing its new flavors on a periodic basis—Peanut Delight, Confetti Angel, Lemon Custard Angel, Black Walnut, Marble Chiffon, and so forth. Advertising funds were generated from the promotional investments for the new flavors, and copy was designed to introduce the new flavors and support the entire product line.

Competitors were caught flat footed. By virtue of the price cut, they had no advertising and promotion funds in their pricing structures to fight back. Neither did they have an inventory of new flavors with which to counterattack. If this analysis is correct, it was a highly effective strategy, brilliantly conceived, and beautifully executed.

The most common form of line extension that involves market segmentation is introducing new models or new forms of the product designed to appeal to different consumer groups or different uses. The television manufacturer may extend its product line by adding portable models, thereby appealing to a market segment seeking portable entertainment. Or an automobile maker may augment its product line by adding a station wagon, a dune buggy, a truck, and so forth. Or a soap manufacturer may add a liquid or bar or powder form to a brand which initially consisted of soap flakes.

A specific example of a line extension strategy is shown in the Coppertone ad (Figure 12–2), which offers three Coppertones—for fair skin, for normal skin, and for dark skin. This is an adaptation of a strategy employed by John H. Breck, Inc.; for over twenty-five years the company has marketed different formulas of Breck Shampoo for dry, normal, and oily hair.

PRODUCT OBSOLESCENCE. Product obsolescence is a marketing strategy that involves the use of features, style, or materials that cause a product to become prematurely obsolete to increase its frequency of purchase. It applies, primarily, to durable and fashion goods with relatively long use lives, usually several years. Sometimes referred to as *planned obsolescence,* this strategy is highly controversial, and is often unfairly criticized. Basically, there are three forms of product obsolescence: functional, style, and material obsolescence.

Functional Obsolescence. In functional obsolescence, a new feature or a new function is added that makes the older model less desirable despite its continued use value. Historically, in automobiles the inclusion of electric starters, hydraulic brakes, automatic transmissions, power steering, radios, tape decks, and so forth are examples of functional obsolescence. New refrigerators with freezer compartments, automatic defrosting mechanisms, shelves in the doors, rotatable shelves to provide easy access to refrigerated foods, ice dispensers, and ice water spigots may not destroy the functional value of older models without these features, but they certainly make them appear shoddy and old fashioned.

When such improvements are the intermittent result of technological research and are made available as soon as the "bugs" have been worked out of them and manufacturing costs make them affordable, then the strategy of functional obsolescence is both desirable and socially

FIGURE 12–2: *Coppertone Ad*
©1977 Plough, Inc. Reprinted with permission.

defensible. In following this strategy, manufacturers invest substantial resources in research and development, always with the goal of meeting consumers' needs. In the process, they extend the lives of their brands.

On the other hand, if a manufacturer has had such improvements on hand at an affordable cost and *deliberately* withheld some of them from the market so that they could be introduced separately in successive model years, a strategy of *planned obsolescence* would be in effect, and the marketer is open to criticism for exploiting consumers. Such a strategy, however, entails substantial risk because of the danger that competitors will introduce the improvement first and gain a competitive advantage.

Style Obsolescence. Style obsolescence involves periodic style changes deliberately made to provoke consumer dissatisfaction with last year's purchase. The garment industry was the pioneer in this form of obsolescence, and the automobile industry was quick to follow suit. Yearly model or style changes, with no perceptible product improvements but with design changes that date the product at a glance, have a long history in these industries. Whether or not we consider this strategy to be ethically reprehensible depends largely on whether we view cars and fashions as purely functional items or as psychological expressions of their owners. Marketers as well as economists disagree on this point. If, however, we consider the consumer as sovereign, recognizing that the choice to purchase or not to purchase is a personal decision that is made freely, then style obsolescence is a legitimate marketing strategy. Any business firm that uses this strategy does so with the risk that consumers may reject its most recent offering. Such was the case of the "midi" in 1970. As Chester Wasson has pointed out:

> Generally, of course, the fashion offerings available in any given season are really quite diverse. In one instance . . . that of the midi introductions of 1970, such was not the case. For once the industry spoke with one strong voice. If customers were manipulatable, the midi should have been a smashing success . . . however, it was pure disaster, and one fashion that caught on strong that season was one which both designers and merchants had been rather reluctant to sell—the pants suit.[23]

Material Obsolescence. Material obsolescence means that the manufacturer deliberately chooses inferior materials subject to breakage, corrosion, rot, and wear. Presumably, the purpose in making such a choice is to hasten the return of the purchaser to the market. In a competitive economy, this is *not* a viable marketing strategy. It is a recipe for failure.

The Death and Burial of Sick Products

No brand is ever completely immune to obsolescence or competitive defeat. Even under the best of marketing managements, occasions arise when prudence dictates that a brand should be withdrawn from competition. It is often a painful process because company personnel become personally involved in the products they handle, and killing a product seems analogous to drowning a kitten. A great deal has been written about the death and burial of sick products.[24] Marketing and advertising managers should be alert to the possibility that a brand should be eliminated, devise a strategy for brand elimination, act decisively, and then stop worrying about it.

23. Chester R. Wasson, *Consumer Behavior: A Managerial Viewpoint* (Austin, TX: Press Educational Division of Lone Star Publishers, Inc., 1975), p. 415.

SUMMARY

The concept of a *product* is a complex one. Every product is really three products—a generic product, a physical product, and a psychological product. The generic product refers to the basic product type, and its primary functions. The physical product is the actual physical entity that is offered to consumers. The psychological product is the physical product along with the entire galaxy of services, warranties, and psychological overtones that accompany it.

Marketing writers have devised broad product classifications to serve as guides in devising marketing strategies. One such classification is the distinction between industrial and consumer goods. Another is the distinction among consumer products, of convenience goods, shopping goods, and specialty goods. To some extent these classifications are useful when considering marketing strategies; however, effective marketing strategies generally require a more thorough study of individual products, their users, and their marketing environments than these classification systems provide.

From the standpoint of marketing, retail stores and services are also products, and should be treated as such when developing marketing programs.

24. Ralph S. Alexander, "The Death and Burial of 'Sick' Products," *Journal of Marketing* (April, 1964): 1–7; Walter J. Talley, Jr., "Profiting from a Declining Product," *Business Horizons* (Spring, 1974): 77–84; Philip Kotler, "Phasing Out Weak Products," *Harvard Business Review* (March-April, 1965): 107–18; Conrad Berenson, "Pruning the Product Line," *Business Horizons* (Summer, 1963): 63–70.

Consumers' satisfaction with a product may depend more upon their expectations than on the actual performance of the product itself. One theory of consumer satisfaction notes that the reasons for purchasing a product may not be the reasons that lead to product dissatisfaction. Thus, consumers may buy a product because of style, but be dissatisfied because of the product's physical performance.

New products are the future of a business. Yet the development of new products is expensive and the risk is high. Companies differ widely in the levels of sophistication with which they approach new product development. Generally, larger companies require more complex organizational arrangements for new product development than do smaller ones, although none of the organizational arrangements are without fault.

The development of new products includes certain logical steps or stages: (1) idea development; (2) idea screening; (3) product concept; (4) feasibility analysis; (5) development stage; (6) test marketing; and (7) commercialization.

New products fail for a variety of reasons. The most common reason for new product failure, however, is the lack of a significant difference in the physical product, as viewed by consumers, from products already on the market.

Market segmentation and product differentiation are the two basic strategies used by marketers in developing new products. These approaches involve product strategy only when an actual difference in the physical product is present.

Product strategy is often involved in extending the life cycles of brands. Major strategies for extending the brand's life cycle are: (1) product quality; (2) product differentiation; (3) line extensions; and (4) product obsolescence. No brand is completely immune to obsolescence and competitive defeat. Even under the best of conditions, occasions arise when prudence dictates that a brand should be withdrawn from the market. Although killing a brand is often a painful process, marketing managers should always be alert to this possibility and, when the need arises, devise a strategy for doing so, and get on with it.

1. Explain what is meant by the statement that every product is really three products. Explain each of the products identified in the text.
2. Explain and critique the "convenience-shopping-specialty" classification of consumer goods.
3. Explain the Swan and Combs two factor theory of consumer satisfaction. What is the implication of the two factor theory in terms of the physical product?
4. Explain and identify the limitations of the following organizational arrangements for the development of new products: product managers, new product managers, new product committees, new product departments, and new product venture teams.
5. Identify and explain the seven stages of new product development outlined in the text.
6. Why do new products fail? What is the most common reason?
7. Discuss the role of the product in the strategies of market segmentation and product differentiation. Under what conditions does product strategy become involved?
8. Explain the product life cycle, identifying and characterizing each of its stages.
9. Identify and explain the four basic strategies for extending the life cycle of a brand.
10. Identify and explain the three forms of product obsolescence discussed in the text.

1. Discuss each of the following products as a generic product, a physical product, and a psychological product: McDonald's, a pediatrician, Cadillac, a custom builder of homes, or a university.
2. As noted in the text, the present form of Purina Dog Chow is quite different from its original form. Is it still the same product? Why or why not?
3. Explain how each of the following products might be seen as a convenience product, a shopping product, or as a specialty product by different groups of consumers: a motel, a bottle of wine, an automobile, or a cake mix.
4. Identify three products that you believe are purchased for their expressive performance and three that you believe are purchased for their instrumental performance. How do you think the marketing programs of these products differ?
5. Devise an organizational arrangement for developing new products for a large company, representing it by an organizational chart. How would you avoid the shortcomings of the different organizational arrangements discussed in the text?

CHAPTER PROBLEM

THE PRODUCT

The Stoddard Drug Company is a moderate sized producer of lotions, cleansing agents, and hair preparations sold primarily through drugstores. The company maintains a sales force of eighty sales representatives who call on drug wholesalers and drug chains. Attempts to gain food store distribution for its products through grocery wholesalers have not been particularly successful. Management is concerned because sales have leveled during the past five years, and the company has introduced no new products during this period.

In 1978 a new product committee was established consisting of the sales manager and the directors of manufacturing, marketing, and the company's clinical research department. Although the committee only met sporadically because of time demands on the participants, whenever it met new product ideas submitted by employees and wholesalers were considered. Most of these ideas have been rejected because they were considered technically unfeasible or because they were not sufficiently different from competitive products to have a reasonable chance of success.

Recently, the new product committee has been investigating the possibility of marketing a skin lightener or fade cream. Traditionally, the fade cream market has been associated with: (1) elderly consumers who were embarrassed by dark skin spots which are associated with aging, and (2) members of ethnic groups who wanted a lighter skin color. In 1978 the retail market for fade creams was estimated at $10 million. By 1981 however, the market had grown to $30 or $40 million, and an even more dramatic growth was expected as more consumers were exposed to the product field through advertising.

Several reasons accounted for the growing popularity of fade creams: One had to do with the aging of the American population and the increasing 50–and–over population category. Another had to do with widespread use of birth control pills, a side effect of which may be a darkening of the skin in localized areas. In some cases, the skin around the lower portion of the face darkens slightly, giving the appearance of a mask. A third reason is overexposure to the sun and artificial tanning lights in tanning parlors. Overexposure frequently results in skin damage and the development of localized dark spots.

A number of firms have recently become interested in the fade cream market. Porcelana, a product of Jeffrey Martin, Inc., spent $5.5 million on fade cream advertising in 1979 and, during the first half of 1980, had already spent $7 million. Observers in the industry credit the aggressive marketing expenditures of Porcelana as a major reason for the market's growth. Other major entries in the field are Esoterica, produced by Norcliff-Thayer, and Fade-Fast, marketed by Alleghany Pharmaceutical.

Since fade creams contain hydroquinone, a drug ingredient that penetrates the skin, these creams have been sold primarily through drugstores. However, department stores and food stores are potential outlets as well.

Product margins are high, and there are wide variations in pricing. For example, Porcelana sells a two-ounce size for $6 and a four-ounce size for $8.25.

Frank Calderwell, director of Stoddard's clinical research department, has indicated that a fade cream could easily be produced by the company in its traditional form, or in combination with a sunscreen or suntan lotion.

Assignment

1. *Evaluate Stoddard's new product development procedures. Should they be changed? If so, how?*
2. *What action should Stoddard take about marketing a fade cream? In answering this question, deal with such issues as:*
   - *Their probability of success.*
   - *Their target market.*
   - *The form the product should take—a regular fade cream or a product that combines a fade cream with a sunscreen.*
   - *The type of distribution that should be sought.*
3. *If you believe Stoddard should market a fade cream:*
   - *Define a product position—that is, how it would be presented to consumers.*
   - *Suggest a brand name.*

Branding and Packaging

- *The importance of the brand name.*
- *Guidelines to use in selecting brand names.*
- *Legal considerations in selecting brand names.*
- *Brand name strategies.*
- *Private labels and generic products.*
- *The importance of packaging in modern marketing.*
- *The functions of packaging.*
- *Packaging strategies.*
- *Package design and changing packages.*

MARKETING EXAMPLES

"EAST" IS JUST A REGION

Jack Trout and Al Ries, authors of a controversial series of articles in *Advertising Age* titled "The Positioning Era Cometh," insisted then (1972) and now that the name of a company or product is of primary importance in its success.[1] Writing in 1979, they continued to emphasize the importance of product names with the following observation.

> Our 1969 example was Eastern Airlines. Among the four largest domestic airlines, Eastern consistently ranks at the bottom on passenger surveys.
>
> Why? Eastern has a "regional" name that puts them in a different category than the big nationwide carriers (American, United, Trans World). The name Eastern puts the airline in the same category with Southern, North Central, Piedmont, and Allegheny. The regional airline category.
>
> After ten years of effort, Eastern still ranks at the bottom of the big four.
>
> You see what you expect to see. The passenger who has a bad experience on American or United says, "It was just one of those things." An exception to the good service he or she was expecting.
>
> The passenger who has a bad experience on Eastern says, "It's that darn Eastern Airlines again." A continuation of the bad service he or she was expecting.
>
> One prime objective of all advertising is to heighten expectations. To create the illusion that the product or service will perform the miracles you expect. And presto, it does.

1. Jack Trout and Al Ries, "The Positioning Era Cometh," *Advertising Age* (April 24, 1972): 35–38; "Positioning Cuts Through Chaos in Marketplace," *Advertising Age* (May 1, 1972): 51–54; "How to Position Your Product," *Advertising Age* (May 8, 1972): 114–116.

Recently, Allegheny Airlines has seen the light. The new name: USAir . . ."[2]

Are these comments about the importance of the product name justified? Perhaps. Certainly, most successful marketing practitioners act as though they are. Consider: Depend (a glue); Pampers (disposable diapers); Sure (an antiperspirant); Edge (a shaving cream); Butcher's Blend (a dog food); Crave (a cat food); Taster's Choice (a coffee). The list is endless and the search for appropriate product names, a major industry.

AMERICAN LOWENBRAU? HOW QUAINT.

Even the best of marketers sometimes do silly things. Consider *Advertising Age's* editorial comment on the Miller Brewing Company.

During the period when everyone, including *Advertising Age,* was lauding Miller Brewing Co. for its marketing prowess—in particular the classic Lite beer success—the brewer made what may turn out to be a likewise-classic mistake.

Although the facts aren't all in yet, it appears that Miller blew it when it acquired the Lowenbrau brand from its German owners to mount an assault on Anheuser-Busch's Michelob in the superpremium beer segment. Not that acquiring Lowenbrau was a wrong move; far from it. But the decision to use that valued name and image for taking on an *American* category seems wasteful. Miller can argue that it could not economically import Lowenbrau in the volume it wanted to generate. Thus, the decision to brew it here. We can't argue with its sales goals, or the advertising with which it sought to accomplish it. But consumer and competitor complaints about its

---

2. Jack Trout and Al Ries, "The Positioning Era Cometh," reprinted with permission from April 24, 1972, issue of *Advertising Age.* Copyright 1972 by Crain Communications, Inc.

U.S. origin have finally dictated that commercials declare it to be "a truly great *American* beer." And that's not the image the name conjures up.

Pre-Miller, the name meant top-of-the-line, quality, Germany—as did the less well-known Wurzburger. A limited market at the time, to be sure—not what Miller was after. But since the decision to launch Lowenbrau into the superpremium race, the import category has been growing nicely. Anheuser is going into the category through an agreement with Wurzburger. And where is the brand that should dominate the business? On the air calling itself "a truly great American beer."

So Miller must now combat Wurzburger by creating a new brand, Munich Oktoberfest. That's as close as you can get to a truly German name, if you don't have one. Isn't it a shame the name Lowenbrau no longer represents a truly great German beer?[3]

BURN THE PLANT, BUT SAVE THE NAME

A brand name is often the most important asset that a company possesses. Although this statement may seem exaggerated, it is amply born out by the following comment from the legal counsel of Coca-Cola:

> The production plants and inventories of the Coca-Cola Company could go up in flames one night, yet the following morning there is not a bank in Atlanta, New York, or any other place that would not lend this company the funds necessary for rebuilding, accepting as security only the goodwill of its trademark.[4]

These three examples emphasize the role that the brand name plays in the positioning of a product, in communicating salient product characteristics to consumers, and as a valuable resource of an industrial enterprise. In the case of Eastern Airlines, Trout and Ries suggest that the regional connotation of the company name has limited the company's ability to represent itself as a major airline. In the case of Miller, *Advertising Age* has suggested that the company has wasted a great brand name by applying it to an American-brewed beer, and now has to create a new brand, Munich Oktoberfest, for its own entry into the import beer market. The quotation by the legal counsel of Coca-Cola reveals the value that a multibillion dollar corporation attaches to the brand name of its major product.

---

3. "A Miller Miscue," reprinted with permission from September 10, 1979, issue of *Advertising Age.* Copyright 1979 by Crain Communications, Inc.
4. *Trademarks: Orientation for Advertising People* (New York: American Association of Advertising Agencies, Inc., 1971), p. 1.

Although branding has been around for a long time—it was used in the middle ages by craft guilds to control the quantity and quality of production—the importance of brand names as a marketing tool has emerged with the growing sophistication of marketing. Many of the early brands on the American marketing scene were simply the family names of the producers—Westinghouse, Swift, Kohler, Campbell, Ford, Chrysler, and so forth—and were intended as a guarantee of product quality. Even then, however, alert and sensitive marketers were cognizant of the communication value of a product name. For example, in 1878 a Cincinnati company perfected a formula for a revolutionary new soap. It was white and pure, and it floated. Initially, Procter & Gamble called the product "P&G White Soap," a reasonably descriptive but totally unimaginative name. Harley Procter, son of cofounder William Procter, persuaded the firm to let him launch a proper campaign to introduce P&G White Soap to consumers.

Young Harley did not like the name. He wanted a brand name that would capture the fancy of the public, give the product an identity, and communicate the essence of the product to potential users. He searched for weeks for a name that would communicate the product's attributes and finally found his inspiration in church when the minister read from the eighth verse of Psalm 45: "All thy garments smell of myrrh, and aloes, and cassia, out of the ivory palaces, whereby they have made thee glad." And Ivory Soap was born—99 and 44/100 pure. So pure, it floats.[5]

GUIDELINES FOR SELECTING PRODUCT NAMES

Today, selecting product names for their communication value is common practice. The pursuit of appropriate brand names for new products is an unending and often frustrating task. These guidelines are fundamental to the selection process:

- *If at all possible, select a brand name that communicates the essential attributes of the product concept.* If one can find such a name, the problems of communicating with consumers will be simplified. The Carnation Company has been extremely successful in this regard, devising names such as *Instant Breakfast, Coffeemate, Slender,* and *Little Friskies.* Clairol's *Born Blond,* Bausch & Lomb's *Soflens,* Purina's *Meow Mix,* Procter & Gamble's *Pampers,* General Foods' *Hamburger Helper* and *Shake 'n' Bake* are other outstanding examples of this approach.
- *If it is not possible to select a name that communicates the essential product concept, select a neutral name into which the desired meaning can be built through advertising and promotion. Sego, Ford, Campbell,* and *Exxon* are examples. Ford and Campbell, of course, are family names that, over the years, have been given meaning by the millions of marketing dollars that have been invested in their support. *Sego* was deliberately chosen for a diet food because research indicated that it was meaningless to most people, and an introductory advertising line "See the pounds go with Sego" was developed to give it meaning. *Exxon* was the result of a mammoth name search to find a name that had no negative connotations in any of the countries in which the company currently operated, or in which it was likely to make investments.

  Under this guideline, initial communication may be more difficult, and promotion costs will be higher, but the task is not an unreasonable one.
- *Avoid selecting names that contradict the essential product concept.* Such names erect barriers to communications, and normal competitive activities create enough barriers to product success without compounding the problem through unwise name selection. I suspect, for example, it would be a waste of time and money to introduce a diet food called *Fat,* a brand of tires called *Blowout,* or an automobile named *Lemon.*

5. Hannah Campbell, *Why Did They Name It...* (New York: Fleet Press Corp., 1954), pp. 58–64.

Finding real-life examples of really bad brand names is difficult because no sane marketing practitioner would even consider them. Sometimes, though, it inadvertantly happens. For example, when Chevrolet introduced the *Nova* into South America, it laid an egg. Why? Phonetically, Nova in Spanish is *No Va* which literally means "It doesn't go." Sales improved when Chevrolet changed the name to *Caribe.*

LEGAL CONSIDERATIONS IN SELECTING BRAND NAMES

Before we proceed further in the discussion of brand name strategy, perhaps we should define some of the key terms associated with branding, and mention some of the legal requirements that govern the use of brand identification.

Definition of Terms

Confusion often arises in the use of the terms *trade name, brand name, brand mark,* and *trademark,* although each has a distinctive meaning.

Trade name The name under which a company conducts its business. General Motors, General Mills, Procter and Gamble, Ralston Purina, and Anheuser Busch are all well-recognized trade names.

Brand "A name, term, sign, symbol, or design, or a combination of them which is intended to identify the goods or services of one seller or a group of sellers and to differentiate them from those of competitors."[6]

Brand name That part of the *brand* that can be vocalized, such as Instant Breakfast, Sego, Charlie, Winston, Pampers. A brand name may be, but need not be, a trade name. For example, Coca-Cola is a trade name that is also the brand name of the company's leading product. Pampers is a brand name, but the trade name of the company that manufactures Pampers is Procter and Gamble.

Brand mark That part of the *brand* that can be recognized but can not be vocalized, such as a design or symbol, or distinctive coloring or lettering. The Plymouth ship, the Metro-Goldwyn-Mayer lion, and the Playboy bunny are all brand marks.

Trademark A brand or part of a brand (a brand name or brand mark) that is given legal protection because it is capable of appropriation. A trademark is, essentially, a legal concept which protects the seller's exclusive rights to use a brand name and or a brand mark. A product may have several trademarks; thus *Coca-Cola* and *Coke* are both trademarks referring to the same product.

Legal Requirements for a Trademark

Trademarks are normally registered with the U.S. Patent Office, although they need not be officially registered in order to be given protection under the Lanham (trademark) Act, passed in 1946. However, the registering of the trademark helps in protecting it by establishing priority of use, which is a major consideration in trademark ownership. A trademark may be registered for twenty years and is renewable. A number of legal restrictions apply to the use of trademarks; the major ones are:

A trademark must be used in connection with an actual product. A design or name that is only used in an advertisement or on a factory does not constitute a trademark within the definition of the law unless it is clearly applied to a particular product, appearing on the product itself or, if that is not possible, on the package or on a dispensing unit such as a gasoline pump.

A trademark may not cause confusion or deceive purchasers as to the source of the product. The patent office will not register trademarks that are so similar to existing trademarks that they might cause confusion. The test of confusion is not that the trademarks, when presented side by side, appear similar; but rather that the consumer might be confused when making a purchase. For example, Promise furniture spray was disallowed because it was confused with the

---

6. *Marketing Definitions: A Glossary of Marketing Terms,* Ralph S. Alexander and the Committee on Definitions of the American Marketing Association (Chicago: American Marketing Association, 1960).

***Table 13–1:** Trademarks in Conflict.*
SOURCE: *The United States Trademark Association Year End Report,* 1970, pp. 8–15.

Successfully Defended Trademarks	*Unsuccessful Challenges*
AFRIN topical nasal decongestant	FA-DRIN chlorphenpyridamine maleate tablets
AFTER TAN lotion for skin grooming	APRES SUN skin lotion
AIR COMMAND air conditioners and parts	CLIMATE COMMAND heating, cooling and air conditioning units
AIREX cellular material of artificial and natural elastomers and plastomers	SEREX plastic forms for use in insulation
AIRVAC dental aspirators and apparatus	VACUUM/AIRE dental equipment and accessories
ARMALON coated fabrics	ARMALONVEST armored vests
AWAKE frozen concentrate for imitation orange juice	ARISE liquid breakfast drink
BALL PARK frankfurters	BALL GAME wieners
BEER NUTS shelled and salted peanuts	BEER POTATO CHIPS potato chips
BIG BOY stick-candy	BIG BOY! powder for soft drinks
BY GEORGE men's toiletries	GEORGE V toilet water
THE CATTLEMAN restaurant and food services	CATTLEMAN canned chopped beef, luncheon meat
CHICKEN KING drive-in restaurant services	WHERE CHICKEN IS KING restaurant services
COFFEE BREAK nondairy cream substitutes	COFFEE BREAK nondairy cream substitutes
COMSAT satellite communications system	COMCET communications computer
CONDITION beauty pack treatment for hair	CURL & CONDITION permanent waving lotion
CORVETTE automobiles	VETTE fiberglass repair panels for automobiles
DISNEY, WALT DISNEY PRESENTS and DISNEYLAND motion picture films, educational parks and services	DISNEY AREA ACREAGE, INC. real estate
DOT fasteners, connectors and attaching devices of various types used in construction, etc.	RED DOT DOLLY fastening devices used in construction
DURO-LITE incandescent and fluorescent lamps	DURAGLOBE globes for electric lighting fixtures
DUMPMASTER lifting mechanism for true dumping	TRASHMASTER heavy-duty vehicles
EXECUTIVE razors and blades	EXECUTIVE after-shave, pre-shave lotions
FLECTO protective coatings for paint, etc.	FELCO paint
GALLAHER smoking and chewing tobacco, etc.	GALAHAD cigars
GANT SHIRTMAKERS dress and sport shirts	GHENT ON SCROLL, designer shirts, pajamas, etc.
GP lubricating oil	GP-7 conditioning additives for gasoline, kerosene
HILTON hotels, restaurant and bar services; HILTON HOTELS Scotch whiskey, gin, etc. and CONRAD HILTON Scotch whiskey and bourbon	HILTON'S gin, vodka, bourbon, etc.
HOLLOWAY HOUSE frozen food products and restaurant services	DOC HOLLIDAYHOUSE pecans
ISI magazine	I.A.I. indexes to books
JVC radio receivers and FM multiplex radio receivers	IVC magnetic video tape recorders and reproducers
KENTUCKY FRIED CHICKEN CORPORATION restaurants	OLD KENTUCKY HOME FRIED CHICKEN, INC. restaurants
KUD-L-WRAP, KUD-L-DUDS and KUD-L-NAP nightwear for infants and young children	CUDDLER knitted outerwear for infants

Table 13–1: Trademarks in Conflict—continued.

Successfully Defended Trademarks	Unsuccessful Challenges
LAND YACHT house trailers	SHASTA ROYAL LAND YACHT mobile homes
LAVA soap	LAVANA liquid detergent for fabrics
MAGIC silicone impregnated paper	ITS-MAGIC cleaning pads
MISS MERRY and MY MERRY toy kits	MISS MARY children's tea sets
MISTOMETER metered dose dispensers	METER MIST preparation for asthma
NARCO electronic radio and navigational equipment	NACO radios and tape recorders
NOON HOUR pickled and marinated fish, etc.	12 O'CLOCK dietary food in powder form
OCEAN FREEZE frozen seafood	SEA FREEZE and DESIGN frozen seafood
OLD DOUGLAS whiskey	JAMES DOUGLAS blended Scotch whiskey
OROGLAS synthetic resinous materials in sheets, rods, etc.	PROGLAS plastics, for synthetic injection molding materials
PENNY WISE and GIRL, canned sweet potatoes, hot sauce, etc.	PENNYWISE and OVAL DESIGN cookies
PEXENE liquid floor conditioner	TEXENE germicidal cleaner
PLEDGE furniture polish and cleaner	PROMISE dishwashing detergent
PRESCOTT cotton piece goods	PRESSCOTT sweaters, sport and dress shirts, coats
PRESDFLAKE particle board	CRESFLAKE particle board
Q-TIPS swabs consisting of sanitary absorbent cotton	QUICK TIPS manicure finishing spray
RID-X preparation for liquifying and deodorizing waste materials	RED X insecticides for tobacco crops
SAFGUARD mufflers and exhaust systems for automobile engines	SAFEGUARD automotive engine replacement parts
SANSRUN hosiery	SANS topless footwear
SERENE cold wave permanent kit	CERENA products for care of nails
SI-BONNE fabrics	TRES-BONS hosiery
SPECTRUM decorative paper	SPECTRA gift wrap paper
STOP & SHOP grocery store services	STOP 'N SHOP grocery store services
SUDS WITH MUSCLES detergent	MUSCLE detergent
TARACTAN tranquilizer	TARUXAN preparation for treatment of cardiac insufficiencies
THERMIX magnetic stirrer, hot plate for laboratory use	MIX O THERM magnetic stirrer, hot plate for laboratory use
TIC TAC TOE ice cream and sherbert	TIC TAC candy
TITLIST and FINALIST golf balls	MEDALIST golf balls
TYGON plastic products for surgical use	TYCRON surgical sutures
UNIFLO oils and greases	OMNIFLO motor oil, lubricating greases
UNIVAC tabulating, record handling, computer, etc.	ANAVAC electrically operated entertainment apparatus
VANISH toilet bowl cleaner	BANISH room deodorant
VO 5 and VO 5 CONDITIONER hair conditioner, shampoo, etc.	CONDITIONER # 5 pomade for hair
WHOPPER and HOME OF THE WHOPPER burgers and drive-in restaurant services	WHOPPABURGER sandwiches
ZIRCO catalytic agents	COZIRC driers for paints and varnishes

Johnson Wax Company's Pledge furniture spray. Trademarks that courts have held to be in conflict are shown in Table 13-1.

A trademark may not be deceptive by implying benefits that are invalid. Names that have been legally barred include "Six Months Floor Wax," which did not last that long; "Lemon" soap that contained no lemon; and "Nylodon" for sleeping bags that did not contain nylon.

There are limitations on names that are primarily surnames, geographical names, or merely descriptive names. Many of the surnames applied to products, such as Chrysler, Ford, and Johnson's were in effect before the current trademark laws were enacted. It would be more difficult to get such names approved today. In addition, trademark law does not protect names that are merely descriptive, such as Fresh Bread. Since the word *fresh* is a generic attribute of bread desired by consumers, it may not be used as the name for a particular product of a specific manufacturer. As a consequence, the selection of names that impute the essential quality of the product concept may create problems in trademark registration, and need to be checked thoroughly for their acceptability. For example, Sun Oil Company devised a method of blending gasoline at the pump so that the gasoline buyer could regulate the octane rating of the gasoline purchased. Sun Oil referred to this innovation as Custom Blended gasoline, and spent $30 million over a six-year period advertising Custom Blended gasoline as a Sun Oil Company brand. When the company was challenged in the courts, however, the court ruled that *custom blended* was a descriptive term that could not be appropriated for one company's exclusive use.

BRAND NAME STRATEGIES

The role of the brand name in communicating product attributes is well-recognized in marketing since the brand name not only identifies the product, but also gives the product dimension and character. Pierre Martineau has pointed out:

> The Safeway grocery chain conceived these names for its private label brands: Bel Air frozen foods, Skylark bread, Old Mill vinegar, Oven Glo crackers, Nob Hill coffee, and canned goods with such names as Honeybird, Lalani, Gardenside, Country Home. There is obviously greater sales appeal in these names than in such dry-as-dust labels as "grade A soda crackers." The product in the consumer's mind in some manner becomes different with the mere flick of a name.[7]

The quest for brand names that unerringly project the appropriate product concept is, essentially, a creative act that can and should be confirmed by marketing research, although some marketers have an intuitive knack for sensing the mood of consumers. The late Charles Revson, founder of Revlon, built a $2 billion business on his ability to define appealing brand concepts and develop appropriate names for his brands in the promotion-dependent cosmetics industry. His 1952 "Fire and Ice" promotion for a new cosmetics line was a brilliant success. In 1973 he introduced a fragrance called "Charlie" for "the woman who is sort of liberated but who isn't a bra-burner."[8] While competitors smirked at his folly, sales of Charlie exceeded $10 million during its first year, and by 1975 it had become the largest selling American fragrance in U.S. stores. Subsequently, the name was extended to include makeup.

In choosing a brand name for a new product, marketers have a number of broad strategies that may be employed. They may, for example, use one or more of these approaches.

- *Use the company name plus product identification.* Among companies following this practice are Campbell, General Electric, and Sara Lee. Thus, we have Campbell's Tomato Soup, Campbell's Cream of Chicken Soup, Campbell's Clam Chowder, and so forth. The company name (trade name) acts as a family name or umbrella and is complemented by the brand's generic product name.

---

7. Pierre Marineau, *Motivation in Advertising* (New York: McGraw-Hill Book Company, 1957), p. 109. Reprinted by permission of the publisher.

8. "Merchants of Glamour," *Time* (September 8, 1975): 62.

- *Use the company name plus a brand name.* This practice is characteristic of the personal care and automotive industries, where we find Ford Pinto, Ford Mustang, Mercury Cougar, Buick Regal, Chrysler Cordoba, and so on. The personal care industry brings us Revlon's Charlie, Revlon's Sun Jewels, Clairol's Herbal Essence Shampoo, Clairol's Quiet Touch, Clairol's Balsam Color, Helena Rubenstein's Skin Dew, Helena Rubenstein's Strong and Sheer, and many, many others. The intent under this strategy is to offer a familiar family name, while at the same time, providing each brand an opportunity for differentiated communication through individual brand names.
- *Use a brand name plus product identification.* This approach is often found in large companies with several distinct product lines, some of which have been acquired through purchase or merger. It is also characteristic of large retail organizations that have several lines of private labels. Producers following this practice include Betty Crocker baking mixes (General Mills), Duncan Hines mixes (Procter and Gamble), and Jell-O products (General Foods). Among retailers, examples include the Kenmore and Craftsman lines for Sears, Ann Page and White House for A&P, and Lucerne for Safeway. The logic here is similar to the strategy of using a company name plus product identification. The difference is that companies using a brand name plus a product identification are usually so diverse that the company name may be inappropriate for many of its product lines.
- *Use a brand name only.* Finally, there are those companies that follow a strategy of using only brand names on most of their products. This is common practice in the cigarette field—Camel, Tareyton, Pall Mall, Marlboro, Winston, and so forth; and in the detergent field—Tide, Surf, Fab, Duz, Cheer, All, etc. Such manufacturers insist that each brand stand on its own feet with no help from the parent company name. This strategy provides the greatest opportunity for building a distinct and unique brand image for an individual product, unhampered by historic connotations of a company or family name.

The first three strategies are referred to as *brand-extension* strategies because an existing brand name is extended to cover other products, often with different product concepts. Although the use of a brand extension strategy inevitably blurs the brand image of the products to which it is applied, at least to some degree, brand extension confers three benefits:

- It facilitates the introduction of new products by capitalizing on the halo effect of a well-known and reputable brand. That is, the reputation of the existing brand encourages consumers to try a new product carrying the same brand name.
- It reduces promotion costs since advertising funds spent on any individual product reinforce the entire line through repetition of the family name.
- In-store impact is increased because the same brand name appears on a number of products.

These are mixed blessings however, and the case against a brand extension strategy rests on two arguments. First, the introduction of a less than adequate product under a family name can have a negative effect (negative halo) on the entire line by causing dissatisfied customers to distrust other products in the line. Second, excessive use of a brand extension strategy can dilute the sharpness of brand images and create confusion among customers. Mennen's brand extension of Protein 21 is a case in point. In 1970 the Mennen Company introduced a shampoo conditioner under the brand name *Protein 21.* The concept was strong, and the name was excellent. Within two years, Mennen gained a 13 percent share of the $300 million shampoo market.

> Then Mennen hit the line extension lure. In rapid succession, the company introduced Protein 21 hair spray, Protein 29 hair spray (for men), Protein 21 conditioner (in two for-

mulas), Protein 21 concentrate. To add to the confusion, the original Protein 21 was available in three different formulas (for dry, oily, and regular hair).

> Can you imagine how confused the prospect must be trying to figure out what to put on his or her hair? No wonder Protein 21's share of the shampoo market has fallen from 13 percent to 11 percent. And the decline is bound to continue.[9]

Few hard rules govern whether one should or should not use brand extensions. Their use is always a compromise between dilution of the brand image and possible consumer confusion on the one hand, and advertising efficiency on the other. Generally, brand extensions make a great deal of sense for a line of products that differ primarily in flavor, such as Betty Crocker cake mixes. They make some sense for a line of dessert items, such as those marketed by Sara Lee. They make less sense for a diverse line of baking mixes that ranges from everyday, commonplace items such as cornbread and pancake mix to petits fours. And they make no sense at all for many products.

If a rule for brand extensions exists, it is a three-part rule:

- The more similar two product concepts are, the greater the benefits that will accrue from a brand extension strategy.
- The more different two product concepts are, the greater the risk involved in using such a strategy.
- A brand extension strategy should not be used just to save money. It may turn out to be the most expensive money you have ever saved.

SELECTING A BRAND NAME

The actual selection of a brand name is often a time consuming and frustrating assignment. So much so that Fairfax Cone, in a moment of cynicism prompted by his experience with the ill-fated Edsel, complained: "Naming products is a source of constant and usually fruitless mental exercise in advertising agencies (where the client's wife or a guest at a dinner party usually suggests the name that is finally accepted)."[10]

In the case of the Edsel, his cynicism seems justified. After starting with a list of 16,000 names, judgment and research had reduced the list to four—Corsair, Citation, Pacer, and Ranger. Unfortunately, the Ford board of directors, under a deadline for a name to be used on some vital dies, ignored all recommendations and arbitrarily decided that they would name Ford's new car after the father of the company's president, provided they could obtain the consent of the family. According to Fairfax Cone:

> Consent was forthcoming . . . and so the Edsel was christened in embryo with a name that was at once a surprise and a huge disappointment. As one of our people said, "The name Flab, which had been suggested by a wag in our London office, couldn't have been any less appropriate." Insofar as the public was concerned the name Edsel was devoid of any feeling of action or spirit. It was a proper name, like Elwyn or Ethelbert, and like them, it was faintly effeminate. It had none of the strength of Pontiac or Lincoln, or the spirit of Mercury; nor did it perpetuate a great name in the industry like Chevrolet or Chrysler—or Ford itself.[11]

Fortunately, not all names are selected by boards of directors, client's spouses, or dinner guests. And since the selection of a strong brand name is essentially a creative process bolstered by the judicious use of research, there are few hard and fast rules to go by. Although most of them have been violated at one time or another by some of America's best-known products, some general guidelines are:

- The brand name should *never* contradict the essential attributes of the brand concept. Ideally, the brand name should be supportive of this concept—as are Slender, Coffeemate,

9. Jack Trout and Al Ries, "Positioning Cuts Through Chaos in the Marketplace," pp. 51–53.

10. Fairfax Cone, *With All Its Faults* (Boston: Little, Brown and Company, 1969), p. 249.

11. Ibid, p. 250.

Ivory and other examples that have been given. But, if that is not possible, at least the brand name should be neutral so that the desired meaning can be created with advertising and promotion.

- The name should be simple and clear, easy to spell, write, pronounce, and recognize. Names like Purina Dog Chow, Aztec (a suntan lotion), Crest, Ritz, and Hotpoint.
- The name should be distinctive and not easily confused in sound or appearance with other brand names on the market. This is important not only because of the danger of trademark infringement, but also to avoid possible consumer confusion.
- The name should be usable in package and label design, retaining its identity even when reduced in size, as often is done on the package or in commercials.
- The name should avoid unpleasant connotations that may offend customers. Even in marketing, there is no excuse for poor taste. Perhaps I should say, "Particularly in marketing there is no room for poor taste," because, after all, products do not become successful by offending people.
- Finally, the name should not be too cute, too clever, or too dear. This is difficult. In the search for a distinctive name, there is always the temptation to substitute the clever for the direct, the contrived for the simple, and the phony for the honest.

Despite the difficulty of brand name selection, finding the appropriate brand name is well worth the effort. Everywhere it appears, it communicates some message about the product; the stronger and more appropriate the message, the better the communication.

PRIVATE LABEL

One cannot talk about branding without raising the issue of using *private labels* rather than *national brands.* The terms *private labels* and *national brands* are somewhat awkward because they do not accurately describe the differences between these classes of products. A better terminology is *distributor controlled* brands and *producer controlled* brands.

What are commonly referred to as private labels by marketing practitioners are really distributor controlled brands. That is, the brands are owned and controlled by organizations whose primary business is distribution, such as retailers or wholesalers. Thus, A&P, a major retail grocery chain, owns a number of brands which it distributes only through A&P stores. While A&P produces many of these brands in its own factories, the primary business of the firm is *distribution,* not production.

What are commonly referred to as national brands by marketing practitioners are better described as producer controlled brands. That is, they are owned and controlled by companies whose primary business is production, although they may or may not also own some retail outlets. For example, International Shoe produces Florsheim Shoes which are distributed in company–owned outlets as well as by independent retail outlets. However, the primary business of International Shoe is production, not retailing.

The bulk of all products sold through grocery stores are producer brands. A *Progressive Grocer* study in 1959 indicated that only 10 percent of the items in major grocery chains and 6 percent of the items in regional chains were distributor controlled items.[12] Today, the proportion of sales accounted for by distributor controlled brands is uncertain, but it probably does not exceed 20 percent of all grocery volume. A. C. Nielsen reported in 1972 that only 25.3 percent of all grocery volume was held by a combination of minor advertised brands, sectional brands, and distributor controlled brands, making a 20 percent share for distributor controlled brands an optimistic one.[13] In 1979 *Fortune* noted that the share held by distributor brands was about 20 percent, and that this percentage had not changed

12. "Where We Stand in Private Label Brand Merchandising," *Progressive Grocer* (Aug. 1959): 1–6.
13. J. O. Peckham, Sr., *The Wheel of Retailing* (Chicago: A. C. Nielsen Company, 1973), chart opposite, p. 3.

significantly during the past ten years.[14] However, the success of distributor controlled labels varies sharply by product group, and may range as high as 60 to 70 percent in some product categories, particularly in those in which product differences are minor as is often the case with canned or frozen vegetables or with canned fruit juices. Distributor controlled brands also exist in other merchandise lines, but they appear to be of greater concern in grocery and chain drug outlets than in other fields.

Reasons for Stocking Distributor Controlled Labels

The policy decision to stock distributor controlled labels, and how many such brands to stock, is a difficult one for the retailer. Without presenting an exhaustive list of arguments for distributor controlled labels, the major advantages are:

- Distributor labels generally provide a higher profit margin for the retailer than do producer brands. Thus, the *Progressive Grocer* study referred to earlier found that, while distributor brands accounted for only 8 percent of grocery sales, they accounted for 23 percent of gross margins.
- Individual retail stores have "exclusive" distribution on distributor brands and can use these products to build customer loyalty.
- Distributor brands are generally priced below producer brands, affording the store an image of economy.
- Retail stores have more flexibility in pricing and promoting distributor brands because of larger gross margins and less danger of prosecution for violating state and local minimum profit laws.

All in all, these are formidable arguments in favor of stocking distributor brands. On the negative side, two arguments in support of producer labels are:

- They are presold through advertising and are preferred by the bulk of customers.
- They turn over faster than distributor brands and, as a consequence, may yield a higher profit per linear foot of shelf space for some product groups.

Consumer Attitudes Toward Distributor Brands

Consumer attitudes toward distributor brands are mixed, with no clear patterns of preference. Attempts to differentiate between distributor-brand and producer-brand users on the basis of psychological, social, or economic characteristics have not been particularly successful. Small, but relatively unimportant differences have been found along some socioeconomic dimensions. For example, larger families, better-educated families, and families in which the wife does not work outside the home reflect above-average use of distributor brands.[15]

The reasons for poor socioeconomic correlation with distributor brand usage include:

- Distributor brand availability varies substantially. Some grocery chains such as Safeway and A&P carry relatively broad arrays of distributor labels, whereas many cooperatives and regional chains carry very few.
- Not all distributor label products are of comparable quality when compared to producer brands. Some food products, for example, taste good while others have an inferior taste. Even distributor label consumers would be reluctant to purchase a distributor brand they didn't like.
- Price differentials on distributor labels vary extensively. *Progressive Grocer* found that in large chains distributor labels were priced 14 percent below producer brands on the aver-

14. C. G. Burk, "Plain Labels Challenge the Supermarket Establishment," *Fortune* (March 16, 1979): 70–76.

15. R. E. French and H. W. Boyd, "Are Private–Brand–Prone Grocery Customers Really Different?," *Journal of Advertising Research* (December, 1965): 27–35; J. G. Meyers, "Determinants of Private Brand Attitudes," *Journal of Marketing Research* (February, 1967): 73–81.

age, while in voluntary groups they were only 8 percent below producer brands.[16]

- Experience may be a major factor in distributor brand purchases. That is, as consumers gain experience in shopping, they become less reliant on advertised producer brands, discovering through trial and error that they like some distributor brands as well as producer brands.
- Finally, consumers make many purchases for psychological and social reasons unrelated to the dimension on which producer brands and distributor brands differ, which is essentially price.

Generic Labels

A relatively recent development in the distributor brand field is the appearance of *generic* products. Variously referred to as *generics, plain labels, no frills brands, plain wraps,* and *no-brand brands,* these products are packaged in plain, unadorned packages, with labels that carry only the name of the product type, such as Peanut Butter, Chocolate Cake Mix, Green Beans, and so forth. Their attraction is that they sell for about 30 to 40 percent less than producer brands, and perhaps 20 percent less than distributor labels.

> Generics originated in France in 1976 with the giant Carrefour supermarket chain. Carrefour called them *produit libres*—literally, "free-products," which it explained were as good as the branded products it sold but free from costly promotion and fancy packaging. *Produit libres* scored a phenomenal success, and today, according to Carrefour, they account for 4 percent of total volume, and an average of 40 percent of volume in categories where they compete with branded products.[17]

The relatively low price of generics is achieved through austerity at each level of the production and marketing processes. Low grades of produce are often used in the raw materials. Packaging is simplified as much as possible. For example, a cake mix may be packaged in a plastic bag rather than in a box, thus saving several cents in packaging costs. Selling costs are eliminated since generic products most often originate with supermarket chains which assume the responsibility of lining up suppliers. And, advertising is minimal, often consisting of only a mention in the grocer's weekly advertisement.

Generics first appeared in the United States in Chicago in 1977 when the Jewel supermarket chain introduced forty-four generic products in a limited number of stores. Subsequently, the success of generics was astounding. Early in 1979, it was estimated that generics were being sold by over one hundred supermarket chains in some ten thousand stores, or about 25 percent of the nation's supermarkets. At that time, generics accounted for only about one percent of the total grocery business. Generics' shares of market may vary widely, both in product groups and supermarket chains. Thus, in early 1979, generics appeared to have captured, on the average, about 11 percent of the product categories in which they were represented, although the Stop & Shop supermarket chain—the 26th largest in the United States—reported that, on the average, generics accounted for 30 percent of the product categories in which they were sold.[18]

The future of generic products is uncertain. As inflation persists and food prices continue to rise, many consumers will undoubtedly buy generics to reduce the family food bill. A study published in 1980 predicted that generics may eventually reach a 20 percent share of the grocery business.[19] If this prophecy holds true, generics could eventually represent a small, but important segment of the food industry.

Implications for Marketing

The existence of the distributor controlled brands constitutes a potential threat for most producer labels for four reasons:

16. "Where We Stand...," *Progressive Grocer.*
17. C. G. Burk, "Plain Labels Challenge Supermarket Establishment," p. 70.
18. Ibid, p. 70.
19. "Generics Not a Fad: 20% Market Share Possible," *Marketing News* (August 22, 1980): 6–7.

Generic brands—long-term threat or short-term fad? (Photo by Robert Maust)

- In-store variables such as shelf position, features, and displays exert a major influence on product sales. These variables are clearly under the control of retail management whose distributor labels are in competition with producer brands. It would be naive to expect retail management not to manipulate these variables to favor their own brands.
- Because of their price differential, distributor labels tend to increase in sales during times of economic stress. Most economists forecast a prolonged period of inflation and economic uncertainty that should benefit distributor labels.
- The growth of major chains and the emergence of nationwide distributor brands, such as Topco, for regional chains and independents, may be expected to erode the advertising and distribution advantages traditionally associated with producer labels.
- Consumer legislation, by placing restrictions on advertising claims, package designs, and pricing practices, may further weaken the historic position of producer brands.

The only defense that manufacturers of producer labels have against the encroachment of distributor brands is to establish a strong brand franchise with consumers. Although sales promotion will continue to be a part of their marketing strategy, basically they must rely on innovation, product excellence, product positioning, advertising, and packaging designed to create a strong and unambiguous brand image that will appeal to a significant segment of the consumer market.

PACKAGING

ELMER'S GLUE. Everyone knows about Elmer's glue—it glues everything. But Elmer's sales were coming unstuck. In the face of new competition from a variety of super-glues, Elmer's advertising simply wasn't generating enough retail sales.

In an effort to remedy the situation, the name was changed from *Elmer's Wonder Bond* to *Elmer's Wonder Bond Plus.* But more was needed. Historically, the product had been packaged in a plastic squeeze tube which seemed reasonable enough, but research found that the tube often burst when stored on its side. In addition, the adhesive dried out and the opening, which had to be pricked with a pin, tended to clog after initial use.

The answer? A new package to go along with the new name. Borden, the makers of Elmer's Wonder Glue Plus, developed a new, square dispenser with a clog-resistant tip that made the container easier to open—no pin was needed—and improved storage, reuse, and ease of application.

Although the product itself has not been changed, the company expects the new package to cause consumers who were slipping away to become stuck on Elmer's once again.[20]

GREASY DOG FOOD? Gravy Train has to be one of the more innovative product concepts to hit the dry dog food market in the past twenty years. Billed as a dry dog food that makes its own gravy, the product consisted of basic, dry ration sprayed with a water soluble coating. When water is added to the product, it makes its own gravy. A descriptive name—Gravy Train—and an attractive package supported the product concept. Test markets were highly successful, and the product's future seemed assured. But, during the national roll-out, packaging problems developed.

While gravy looks nice in a dog's feeding bowl, it doesn't look all that appetizing when it soaks through the package. And that's what happened. The coating that produced the gravy bled through the bag, making greasy stains on the packages in grocery stores. Consumers weren't impressed, and the product had to be recalled. A new package with a protective liner was developed, and Gravy Train's debut on the national market postponed for about a year.

A great product concept, a great name, and a great marketing program—all sabotaged by an inadequate package.

IT ONLY HURTS WHEN YOU LAUGH. One of the most interesting new product failures I was ever involved in was *Big Shot.* Big Shot was a chocolate syrup packaged in a pressurized can and dispensed by pressing the side of a nozzle on the top of the can. When the pressure was released, a grommet caused the nozzle to reseat, sealing the can again. A kid's product, the can was designed to look like a soda jerk, with a cap which covered the nozzle looking like a soda jerk's head. To make chocolate milk at home the child filled a glass with milk, inverted the can of Big Shot over the glass, pressed the nozzle and PSSSSST—chocolate milk. Big Shot was test marketed in Phoenix. Then, the packaging trouble started.

The top of the can—the part that looked like a soda jerk's head—was made of two, formed pieces of metal crimped together. The trouble was that the crimp didn't hold very well, the top came apart in the grocery store exposing the nozzle, and children in the grocery store couldn't resist pressing the nozzle and PSSSSST—chocolate syrup all over the display and everything else in the vicinity.

The product manager and I went to Phoenix to check out the test market, and spent two days in grocery stores replacing can tops, washing chocolate syrup off of the cans, and apologizing to store managers.

We corrected that problem by redesigning the can top and placing a plastic sleeve over the nozzle so that it wasn't so easy to discharge. But that wasn't the end of it.

20. "Marketing Facelift Corrects Elmer's Problems," *Marketing News* (February 8, 1980): 8.

Engineering, in an effort to reduce packaging costs, redesigned the nozzle, using a lighter weight grommet under the nozzle. The result? Once the can was used once, the new grommet wasn't strong enough to reseat the nozzle, and all of the propellant leaked out. By the time this packaging mistake was discovered, forty thousand cases had been shipped—and had to be located and recalled.

Eventually, the product was withdrawn from the market. Consumers, somehow, didn't take to it. Partly because the per serving price was too high, but also because children sprayed the syrup every place but in the milk. In retrospect, I don't know how we could have been so dumb. But at the time, it seemed like a great idea. The moral to the story? In marketing, you win some and you lose some.

All three of these examples emphasize the role of packaging in marketing. In the case of Elmer's Wonder Glue Plus, a new packaging design was used to revitalize the sales of an established product. In the cases of Gravy Train and Big Shot, faulty packaging turned new product introductions into minor disasters. Let's examine the concept of packaging more carefully to see how it can be used as an effective tool of marketing communications.

AN OVERVIEW OF PACKAGING

Although billions of dollars are spent on packaging each year, it is one of the most neglected areas of marketing. An examination of marketing texts and journal articles indicates that the subject is either totally ignored or treated in such an offhand manner that it may as well be ignored. A stroll through supermarkets, or simple experience as a consumer, indicates that much packaging is badly designed, cheap, and inconvenient. One sometimes gets the impression that for many manufacturers the marketing concept stopped short of packaging. This is unfortunate because packaging is one of the most obvious channels of communication with consumers. Packages are everywhere—on retail shelves, in displays, in advertising and, after purchase, in the home. The general neglect of packaging has been noted by others. In a speech prepared for the American Management Association's conference on packaging, one speaker said:

> Packaging is the hottest buy in advertising today—and the least understood. First, packaging is the biggest of the advertising media. The message on the package usually reaches far more people than any type of conventional advertising the product can afford. However, businessmen haven't bothered to measure its coverage. Second, it is the least expensive of ad media. Space which costs millions of dollars elsewhere is free on the package; this space is paid for in manufacturing to contain and protect the product. Additional charges to make the package do a better promotional job are usually infinitesimal in relation to audience size. Third, it is the most potentially effective medium. It is seen by those customers who may buy, at the spot where they buy, and at the moment of the buying decision. Packaging has enormous circulation with virtually no waste. Yet, as a marketing tool, it is poorly understood, generally mismanaged, and barely exploited.[21]

The foregoing comment was made in 1965, but things haven't changed much in the past fifteen years. An article in *Advertising Age* titled "Packaging seen as effective marketing tool," notes:

> Old habits die hard, but escalating media costs will spur big advertisers to develop package design as a marketing tool, predicted William J. O'Connor, exec vp, Source/Inc, a Chicago design company.
>
> Packaging traditionally has been the sort of "fickle love object" of marketers who move away from packaging considerations in good times and toward them in bad, or to save a "murky" product. But, as costs have gone up, attitudes have changed, Mr. O'Connor told an ADVERTISING AGE WEEK workshop. . . .
>
> In the future, marketers increasingly will look to packaging for innovative presentations of the product form . . . . Package research and

21. S. M. Barker, "How to Calculate Package Audience," *Profitability and Penetration Through Packaging,* an AMA Bulletin, No. 65, (New York: American Management Association, Inc., 1965), p. 22.

FIGURE 13–1: *L'eggs Display. Used with permission of L'eggs Products, Inc.*

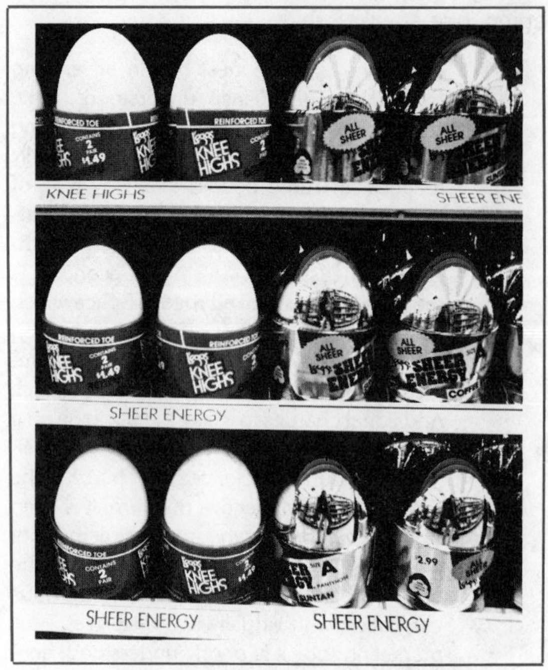

FIGURE 13–2: *Electrasol Package. With permission of Economics Laboratory, Inc.*

testing, a relatively specialized field, will grow in importance in the '80s as more marketers turn to packaging for cost efficiency.[22]

Not all packaging, of course, is poorly done. There are many outstanding packages on the market. L'eggs is a superb example of utilizing packaging to express the essential product concept, to facilitate recall of the product name, and to identify the product with the retail outlets through which it is primarily sold (see Figure 13–1). Electrasol's package is a clean, straightforward package that communicates the product concept at a glance (see Figure 13–2). The Hamburger Helper package, with the ubiquitous Betty Crocker spoon (see Figure 13–3), not only dramatizes the product concept with a picture and a few judiciously chosen words, but also seals it with the stamp of approval of "America's first lady of foods."

Each of the above examples appears to be designed with the product concept in mind, each communicates this concept to consumers, each provides visibility on the retail shelf, each tells its story directly and simply; each is adaptable to print and TV advertising, and each protects the product. In short, each of these packages does what a package is supposed to do and thereby makes a tangible contribution to the marketing effort.

The Functions of Packaging

Traditionally, packaging has played a minor role in the marketing mix. More recently, this role has been expanded, although only a few companies have fully realized its potential. Basically, packages have four functions—protection, economy, convenience, and promotion.

PROTECTION. The least the manufacturer seeks in packaging is the protection of the product during its passage from the manufacturer to the warehouse to the retailer and, eventually, to the consumer. To gain this end, double packaging is used—an outer, shipping carton for transportation and delivery to the retailer, and individual

22. "Packaging Seen as Effective Marketing Tool," Reprinted with permission from September 1, 1980, issue of *Advertising Age*. Copyright 1980 by Crain Communications, Inc.

FIGURE 13–3: *Hamburger Helper Package. Reprinted with the permission of General Mills, Inc.*

packages for shelving and sale to consumers. The minimum requirement for protection is that the package be sufficiently strong to withstand rough handling and sufficiently air tight and leak proof to protect the freshness and integrity of its contents.

ECONOMY. A second function of the package is economy. Unfortunately, many manufacturers regard the package primarily as an expense item, without any redeeming marketing features. This emphasis on cost, more than any other, has retarded the development of the package as a marketing tool and often leads to packaging that is shoddy, unattractive, difficult to shelve, and inconvenient to use. A case in point is the blister packs used for table-ready meats and many other small retail items sold through supermarkets, drugstores, and hardware outlets. The blister pack, indeed, protects the product and keeps it fresh; it is also economical; but it is an abomination to open.

CONVENIENCE. A third function of the package is convenience, both for shipping and shelving and for the consumer. From the standpoint of shipping, warehousing, and shelving, convenience has taken the form of standardization of shipping carton sizes (wherever possible), easy to open shipping cartons, "price spots" for retail pricing and, more recently, the Universal Product Code and Symbols (UPCS) for computerized checkout counters and inventory control. The UPCS promises the elimination of price marking (the price is carried in the computer and scanned at the checkout counter), reduction of checkout costs and errors (a major expense item for supermarkets), and improved inventory control (inventory status is automatically monitored by the computer). Figure 13–4 shows an example of the UPCS, as well as a typical sales receipt automatically printed for the customer.

For consumers, convenience has also taken a variety of forms: easy to open packages; pour spouts, aerosol cans, and other dispensing devices; a wide variety of package sizes for different size families; multiple–packs; heat and serve items; frozen foods packaged in compartmentalized serving trays; shake-and-bake products; boil-in-the-bag foods; dry mixes that the user can mix in the original package; reclosable packages; and so forth. As convenience foods became a big business, the need for convenience packages also grew.

PROMOTION. A fourth function of the package is promotion. Here, the package is recognized for its value in enhancing the brand's appeal through typography, colors, and illustrations; for conveying the desired brand image, describing the product's features, and providing recipes and service suggestions. Often, the package can be designed for use as an attractive dispenser in the home—on the dining table for food products and in the bedroom or bath for toiletries and facial tissue.

A good package, of course, is one that performs all of these functions in an optimal fashion, always being subject to the mutual constraints of each.

FIGURE 13–4: *The Universal Product Code and Symbols, along with an example of a typical sales receipt. (From Grey Matter. Grey Advertising, Inc.)*

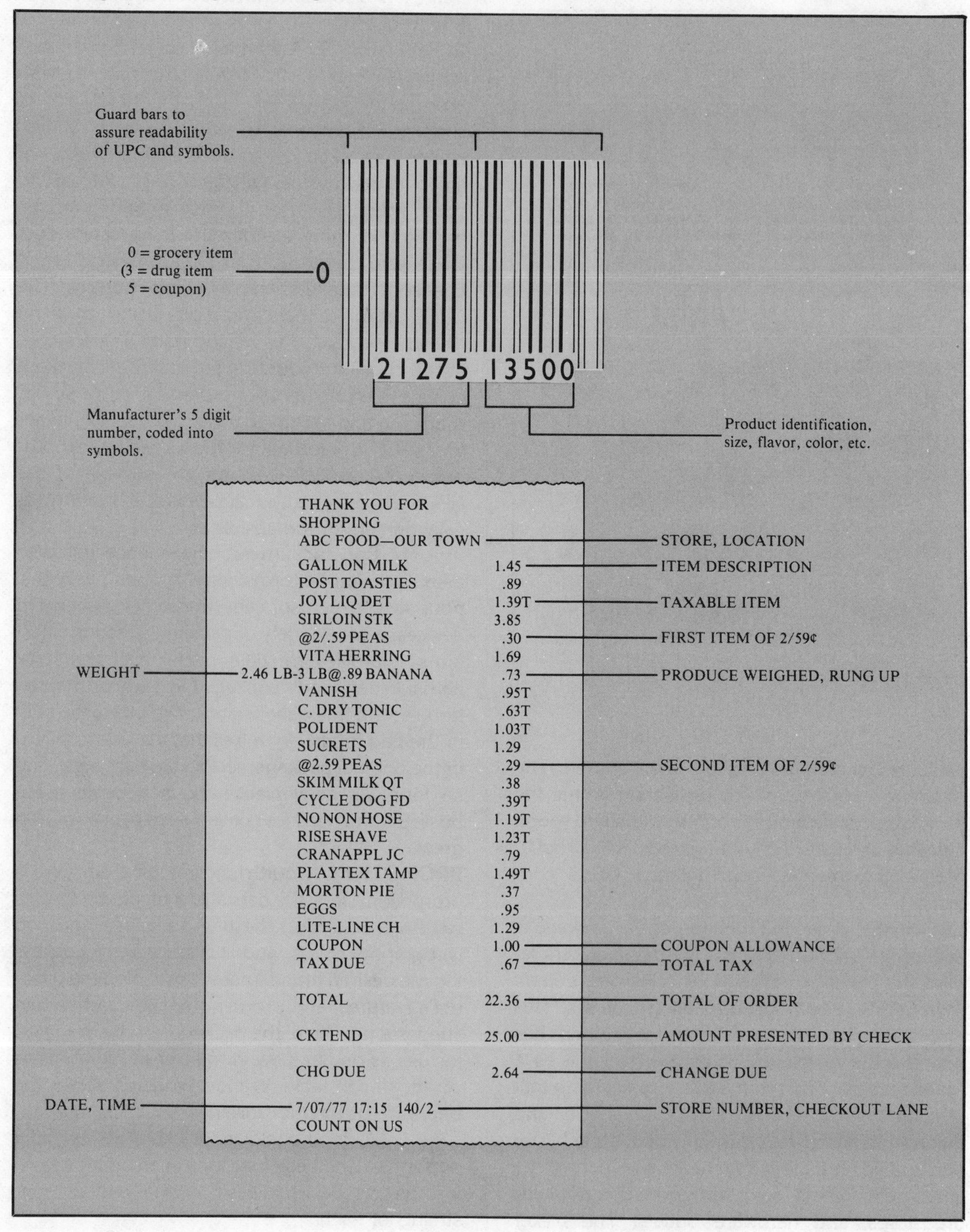

Packaging Strategy

Packaging can be used in several ways as a strategic tool in the marketing effort of a product. The strategies employed should enhance or at least be compatible with the product concept. Among the more important packaging strategies are: size, material, shape, design, convenience, and promotion strategy.

SIZE STRATEGY. Many markets may be segmented by volume users, or by product use. Examples of this may be found in the marketing of both "regular" and "family size" packages, as well as in very small packages produced in some fields (such as toiletries) for the convenience of travelers.

Size strategy also plays a role in new product introductions, both to encourage retail stocking and consumer trial. In the first instance, shipping cartons of six or twelve individual packages may be used to minimize the retailer's investment and to create the impression of high case movement. The use of this strategy also requires relatively intense sales coverage to avoid out-of-stock conditions. After a new product is well established, the shipping carton can be enlarged, perhaps to twenty-four or forty-eight units to decrease packaging costs. For consumers, a small package is usually used for introductory purposes to minimize consumer risk; larger sizes are introduced later to meet the requirements of volume users and to provide additional shelf facings and promotional push.

MATERIAL STRATEGY. The material used in a package may play a major role in marketing strategy. For example, packaging materials may be used to impute *quality*, or to insure *safety*. Examples of the first are tasteful display boxes designed for small luxury goods such as jewelry or electric shavers. The second instance is illustrated by non-breakable shampoo bottles or closures that make it difficult for children to open packages which may be dangerous to them.

SHAPE STRATEGY. Product shape has long been recognized for its perceptual implications. Smooth, rounded shapes, for example, connote femininity; square, solid shapes imply masculinity. Shapes may also be designed to encourage in-home display on the dining table or in another room of the home where it serves as a visual reminder of the brand. Liquid bath soaps have been packaged in the form of animals, fish, and other objects to provide a pleasant distraction for the child undergoing the unpleasant experience of being bathed. A number of years ago, Log Cabin syrup was packaged in a miniature "log cabin." This practice was abandoned, presumably because of costs and difficulties in shelf stacking.

DESIGN STRATEGY. Design strategy may, of course, also involve shapes and materials. But here the emphasis is on colors, typography, pictures, and symbols that enhance the product in the consumer's mind. Design strategy is often used to give identity to a line of packages, such as the Betty Crocker "red spoon," or the picture of a Quaker on Quaker products. And, of course, packaging a product as a gift is a standard practice in the expensive chocolate and distilled spirits industry.

CONVENIENCE STRATEGY. The world is full of convenience packages designed to make life easier for consumers. A number of examples have already been given. When convenience is a relevant consideration in the product concept (and it often is), then it may be possible to use the package to fulfill at least a part of this convenience objective. Sometimes, however, convenience is *not* an attribute that consumers really want. For example, people have complained for years about the difficulty of pouring catsup out of the traditional long-necked, narrow–opening bottle. Yet, when a catsup manufacturer introduced a wide-mouthed bottle that made pouring easier, consumers weren't interested.

PROMOTION STRATEGIES. Packages may be designed or redesigned to tie in with major sales promotions. Back or side panels lend themselves to featuring recipes, service suggestions, and special offers. Cents-off and two-for-one offers are often emblazoned on the package face. All of these strategies are possible through packaging. For these reasons packaging is emerging as a major element in the marketing mix; one that can facilitate or hinder the communication of the product concept.

Designing Packages

A package is not a thing. It is an idea. This thought was aptly expressed by Edward Breck, while president of John H. Breck, Inc., marketer of Breck Shampoo.

> A package is, above all else, an idea. The stronger, the clearer, and the more compelling the idea, the more powerful the package. Many of us in marketing become too absorbed in the details and complexities of package development to realize how important this core idea is to success. Without it the package fails to convey a single impression; its message becomes blurred, and it cannot possibly function with force.[23]

There is no way to tell someone how to design a package. It is a creative, problem-solving process. However, the package designer should ask certain questions. Starting with a clear understanding of the product concept, Walter Margulies, an executive of a leading package design firm, has suggested these:

- How much emphasis should be placed on the brand name? On the product name?
- Toward what segment of the market should the product's basic appeal be aimed?
- In what way will the packaging system best communicate product appeal?
- Should the graphics try to convey the size, shape, color, in-use applications? If so, how?
- In dealing with a food product, is it advisable to include recipes on the package? Which ones? Should they be changed in accordance with the seasons?
- Are all package panels being used to their best advantage? Will they effectively sell the product regardless of the way the package is stacked on the supermarket shelf?
- Can the basic design be extended to logically encompass other items in the manufacturer's line? Is it flexible enough to permit the addition of new products at some future date?
- Is there ample space for the inclusion of extra copy to announce special sales offers?
- What about price marking? Has a specific place been set aside where the product can be priced easily by the retailer so as not to mar the total look of the package?
- Is the design flexible enough to permit the addition of new products?[24]

This list is not intended to be exhaustive. But, it is a good starting point.

Testing the Package Design

The finished package should always be tested. Tests of visibility and ease of recognition under different levels of illumination and from different angles are used to check its adequacy for retail display. Shipping tests may be undertaken to ascertain its ruggedness. Accelerated aging tests measure the package's ability to protect product freshness. Consumer tests are employed to determine ease of use and reactions to the overall package design. Sales tests may be undertaken to see how well the package performs under competitive marketing conditions. Only after a package has been subjected to these scrutinies is it truly ready for use.

CHANGING PACKAGES

Normally, a particular package design is expected to last for years. Yet, packages do require redesigning from time to time. Reasons for change are manifold: repositioning of the product concept; the availability of new packaging materials or new packaging technology; increased costs of existing

23. E. J. Breck, "Function vs. Aesthetics in Packaging," p. 109. Reprinted by permission of the publisher from *Profitability and Penetration through Packaging,* an AMA Bulletin No. 65 ©1965 by the American Management Association, Inc.

24. From pp. 47–48 in *Packaging Power* by Walter P. Margulies (World Publishing Company). Copyright © 1970 by Walter P. Margulies. Reprinted by permission of Harper & Row, Publishers, Inc.

FIGURE 13–5: *Changes in Ivory Soap packages from 1898 to 1965. Courtesy of Procter & Gamble.*

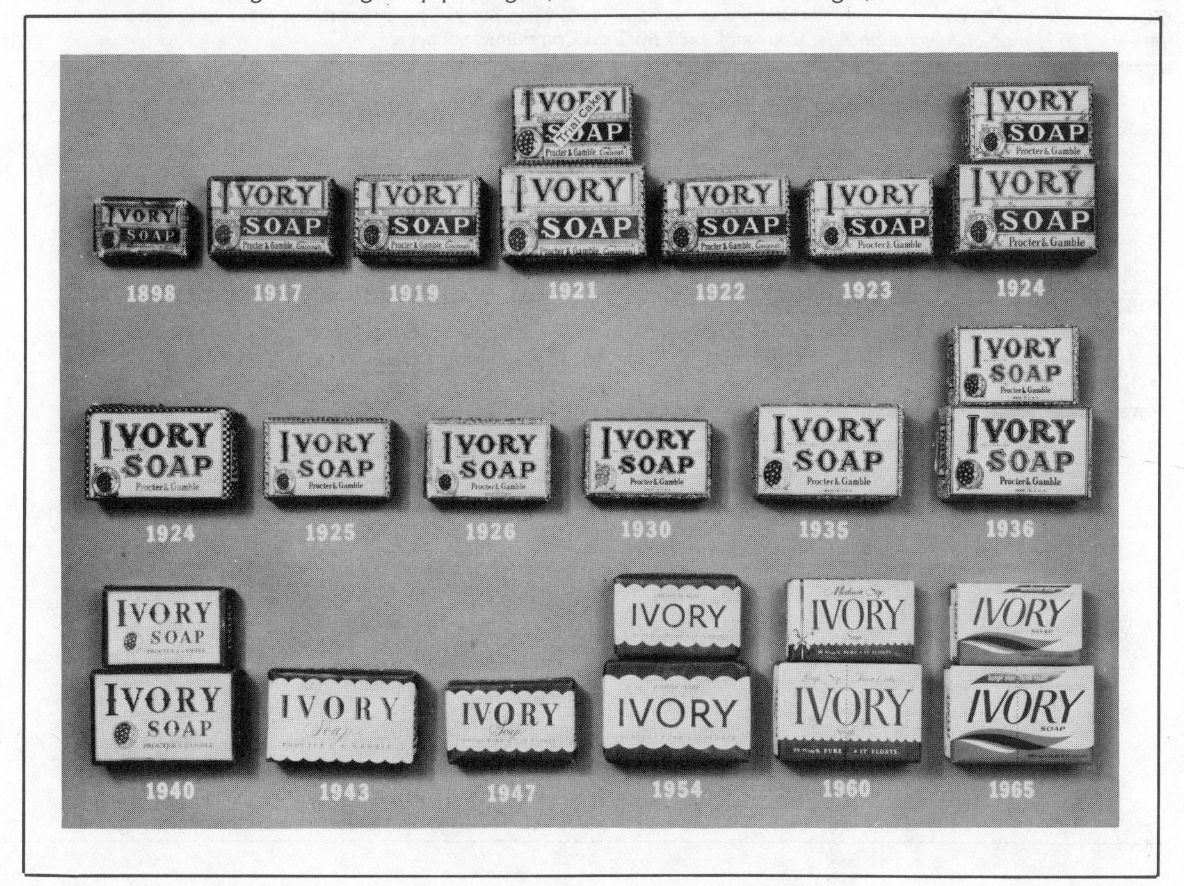

materials; competitive innovations; a change in consumer attitudes and values; modernization of the design. All of these factors may raise the question of package change. But, such changes should not be undertaken lightly. A package *is* an important part of the brand's communication with consumers. The basic question that should always be asked is: "Will this change help or hurt the brand?"

In some fields, package changes are readily accepted by consumers. In others they are not. Several years ago, *Business Week* prepared a presentation for advertising agencies and for distillery managements which demonstrated that, since the turn of the century, no successful distilled whiskey has made a package design change without suffering a decline in sales. At one point, Camel cigarettes attempted to simplify its package by removing some of the pyramids and palm trees from the package face. Consumer complaints were so vocal that the elements were restored. On the other hand, Ivory Soap has changed the package for its bar soap many times in almost a century of marketing. Many of the changes are almost imperceptible, but in the aggregate, the appearance of the package has undergone a transformation (see Figure 13–5).

Stephan Barker, executive of a packaging firm, has offered a checklist of package changes, some of which involve low risk, and some of which involve high risk. This checklist is shown in Table 13–2.

How much a package should be changed, and how frequently changes should be made are questions of marketing judgment that must be made on a product by product basis and

TABLE 13–2: *Packaging Threats to a Consumer Franchise.*
SOURCE: Stephan M. Barker, "When to change your package—and when not to," p. 49. Reprinted with permission from the May 23, 1977, issue of *Advertising Age.* Copyright 1977 by Crain Communications, Inc.

Change	*Low Risk*	*High Risk*
Package Graphics	Directions, cautions*	New name
	Ingredient line, etc.*	New principal color
	Other secondary-panel changes	New illustration, photo
	Legal copy requirements	New logo
	Temporary premium offer	New style
	Temporary deal offer	New design shapes
		Other new design features on main panel
		Directions, cautions*
Package Structure	New convenience feature	New type package
	New cap or fitment**	New shape package
	New material**	Change in only size
	Fewer inks**	Obvious but unexplained change in critical material‡
	Additional packages†	
	Additional sizes†	
	Temporary premium pack	
	Multipack	
	Sample package	
	Display pack	
	New shipping case	
	New distributor pack	
	New unit load	

Notes: *Risk depends on degree of change.
**If appearance is not dramatically different.
†Line extension.
‡As elimination of protective lining.

always in the light of the existing competitive situation.

LEGAL REQUIREMENTS FOR PACKAGING

Within the past few decades, legal restrictions on packaging have increased with the growth of the consumer movement. The Fair Packaging and Labeling Act of 1966 states:

> Informed consumers are essential to the fair and efficient functioning of a free economy. Packages and their labels should enable consumers to obtain accurate information as to the quality of the contents and should facilitate value comparisons. Therefore it is hereby declared to be the policy of the Congress to assist consumers and manufacturers in reaching these goals in the marketing of goods.

The Food and Drug Administration (FDA) is responsible for enforcing the law in regard to foods, drugs, cosmetics, and related goods. The Federal Trade Commission (FTC) has jurisdiction over other consumer products.

Since 1970 FDA regulations require manufacturers to submit data on the safety of food, including the packaging materials with which it may come in contact. These regulations also specify precise labeling requirements, including descriptive words that may be used, how quantities and volume must be stated, the size and placement of type relating to volume and weight, and background colors. Rules govern misrepresentation, slack-fill, health, and a variety of other factors. Obviously, these regulations place restrictions on package design. Some of the restrictions are undoubtedly beneficial; others, merely whimsical. In any case, the package designer subject to today's legislation should have a good lawyer.

SUMMARY

Although branding has been around for a long time—during the middle ages craft guilds used brands to control the quantity and quality of production—the importance of brand names as a marketing tool has emerged with the growing sophistication of marketing. Today, selecting brand names for their communication value is a standard practice.

Certain guidelines are fundamental to the selection process; the brand name should communicate the essential attributes of the product; if this is not possible, select a neutral brand name into which the desired meaning can be built through advertising; and avoid selecting brand names that contradict the essential product concept.

Brands are normally registered with the U.S. Patent Office, although they need not be officially registered to be given legal protection.

The role of brand names in communicating product attributes is well recognized in marketing. In choosing brand names, these approaches are used: (1) use of company name plus product identification; (2) use of company name plus brand name; (3) use of brand name plus product identification; and (4) use of brand name only. The first three approaches are referred to as brand-extension strategies because an existing brand name is extended to cover other products. Brand extensions are often used to save promotional funds and increase promotional impact, but their use often creates problems by blurring the brand image.

One issue that should be noted in the discussion of branding is the distinction between *private labels* and *national brands.* These terms, although in popular use, do not describe the essential differences between the two products. More properly, private labels should be referred to as distributor-controlled brands, and national brands should be referred to as producer-controlled brands. Although distributor-controlled brands are generally less expensive, consumer attitudes toward distributor brands are mixed. Attempts to differentiate between distributor–brand and producer–brand users on the basis of psychological, social, or economic characteristics have not been particularly successful.

Generic labels are a relatively recent development in the distributor-brand field. These products are packaged in plain, unadorned packages, and their labels carry only the name of the product type. The future of generics is uncertain although some analysts believe that eventually, generics may attain as much as 20 percent of the market.

Packaging is one of the most neglected areas of marketing. Packaging has four basic functions in the marketing effort: product protection, economy, convenience, and promotion. Within the framework of these functions, six broad packaging strategies are employed: size strategy, material strategy, shape strategy, design strategy, convenience strategy, and promotion strategy. A new package should always be tested before adoption. Among the tests commonly employed are visibility tests, shipping tests, accelerated aging tests, use tests, and sales tests.

Package designs are usually intended to last for several years, yet changes sometimes have to be made. In some fields, package changes are more readily accepted than in others. How much a package should be changed and how frequently changes should be made are questions of marketing judgment that must be made on a product-by-product basis. Within the past few years, legal restrictions on package design have grown significantly. As a consequence, legal advice is often required when designing packages.

REVIEW QUESTIONS

1. Define each of the following terms: trade name, brand, brand name, brand mark, and trademark.
2. Explain a brand extension strategy. What are its advantages and disadvantages?
3. Identify and explain the reasons for stocking distributor brands.
4. Explain why socioeconomic correlates with distributor brands are weak.
5. How does the existence of distributor-controlled brands constitute a potential threat for most producer labels?
6. How can producer labels best defend themselves against the encroachment of distributor labels?
7. Explain why packaging is an excellent medium for marketing communications.
8. Identify and explain the basic functions of packaging.
9. Identify and explain the various areas of packaging strategy.
10. Identify the various types of package testing utilized before a package is ready for use.

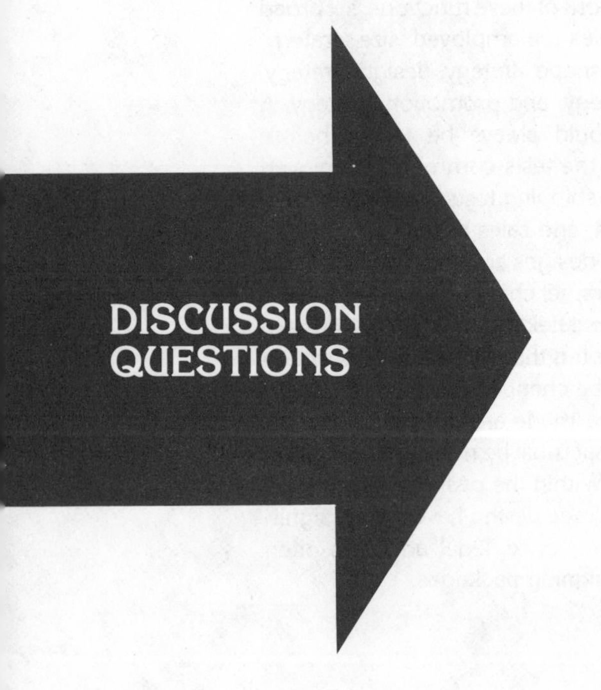

DISCUSSION QUESTIONS

1. Visit a local supermarket or drugstore and select three brand names that you think are particularly good and three brand names that you think are weak. Explain the bases for your selection.
2. Table 13–1 lists brand names that the courts have ruled to be in conflict. Are there any in this group in which you would question the courts' judgments? If you were a judge dealing with a trademark infringement case, how would you go about deciding whether two names were in conflict or not?
3. Select a product field and devise a new product for this field, describing its characteristics and the market for which it is intended. Then coin a brand name which you believe communicates the essential characteristics of this product, and explain your choice of brand names in terms of the criteria for selecting brand names given in the text.
4. Visit a local supermarket or drugstore. Select three packages that you feel are well designed and three that you think are poorly designed. Explain the bases for your selection.
5. Select a product that you think is poorly packaged. How would you change the package in order to improve it? Use the criteria given in the chapter to explain why you made the changes you did.

BRANDING AND PACKAGING

One of the more interesting developments in food marketing in 1981 was the test marketing of New Cookery, a thirty-item line of low fat, low starch, and low sugar food products developed by Nestlé Co.

Based on the belief that sensible eating and weight maintenance was the consumer motif of the 1980's, Nestlé apparently attempted to take the pain out of self-denial with a line of taste treats that included hot cocoa mix, creamy French dressing, strawberry spread, cream of tomato soup, spaghetti sauce, enriched pasta, chili con carne with beans, catsup, mayonnaise, canned fruits, and a number of other products. The new line contained no chemical additives, and the product label carried a side–by–side comparison of the sugar, fat, and starch content of conventional competitive products.

Sales representatives for Conglomerate Foods, Inc., a major competitor, learned of the test markets through trade sources, and picked up samples of the products as soon as they appeared in warehouses in test markets. The management of Conglomerate Foods, Inc., believed that Nestlé could be on target with its new line, and authorized a crash research and development program to develop a competitive line of products.

The basic product concept for the new line was, essentially, the same as that of Nestlé, namely, a line of food products that will be delicious in flavor while having less starch, less fat, and less sugar than conventional products. Specific products in the line have not yet been identified, but the line will include many of the same products as the Nestlé line, as well as others developed by research and development. The target market will be housewives between the ages of 30 and 50 years.

In order to save time, the marketing department has been asked to work with an advertising agency to devise a basic package design that can extend across the line of products as well as a basic brand name. A key admonition was that the product line must be positioned as healthful, sensible eating for the whole family, not as a diet food for people whose primary motivation is weight loss.

Assignment

Develop a brand name and prototype package design for Conglomerate's proposed line of products.

14

Pricing

- *Basic economic concepts influencing pricing.*
- *The traditional role of pricing.*
- *Pricing in contemporary marketing.*
- *Pricing for profit.*
- *Pricing objectives.*
- *The structure of pricing.*
- *Pricing strategies.*

MARKETING EXAMPLES

PRICE ADVERTISING

Usually when we think of price advertising, we think of a company that lowers its product's price and then advertises the price reduction in order to increase sales. But this isn't always the case. *Black Willow Mink* uses a headline that states: "This year only 80 women in America can afford the luxury of a Black Willow Mink." In this advertisement, an exceedingly high price is implied to increase the appeal of the product.

Or consider Curtis Mathes which uses price advertising to guarantee quality for its television sets. Its advertising states: "Curtis Mathes is the highest priced television set in America. And it's worth it."

WILKINSON SWORD, LTD.

For years the market for razor blades was uneventful. Innovations were rare, and razor blade manufacturers were complacent and lethargic. Then, Wilkinson Sword, Ltd., a British firm, changed the name of the game. Wilkinson introduced a stainless steel blade that was clearly superior to American products into the U.S. market. The new blade was heavily supported by advertising and priced at 15.8 cents apiece. The blade was an immediate success. "Overnight, Wilkinson accumulated a staggering backlog of orders, the sort of thing that usually results in delivery delays and expensive crash expansion programs. Had Wilkinson started at 20 cents a blade . . . it would have been much better able to fortify its position."[1]

1. Gilbert Burck, "The Myths and Realities of Corporate Pricing," *Fortune* Magazine © 1972, Time Inc. All rights reserved.

FROM SURPLUS FAT TO SURPLUS PROFIT

The Independent Packing Company of St. Louis, Missouri, had a problem: 11 million pounds of bacon in inventory that the company couldn't sell at prevailing prices. The problem was that, under existing pricing practices, the amount of bacon produced exceeded demand, whereas the other parts of the hog—ham, pork roasts, spareribs, and so forth—were disposed of nicely. The traditional economist's approach to surpluses, of course, would have been to reduce prices, let expanded demand dispose of the surplus, and accept the losses in anticipated revenues with good grace. After all, there is a certain amount of risk in all business. But the Gardner Advertising Company had a better idea. Change the product and raise the price.

How do you change bacon? Cut it into thick slices, give it a heavier-than-usual smoke, put it into a package designed to simulate a hickory log, and name it Hickory Hill Bacon—"a thick sliced, heavy smoked bacon, with a real country flavor." It worked, and a surplus of hog fat was turned into a surplus of profit.

The three foregoing examples are designed to highlight some of the anomolies of pricing that characterize marketing. Black Willow Mink and Curtis Mathes deliberately call attention to their relatively high price to reinforce the concept of quality with which they surround their products. Too low a price for Wilkinson's razor blades produced more consumer demand than the company could handle. In the case of Hickory Hill Bacon, a minor modification of the product, accompanied by a strong and innovative product concept, disposed of an unwanted surplus at a premium price.

Economists and marketers alike have always recognized the complex interrelationship between profits, price, and other marketing variables, but the precise nature of this relationship is often ambiguous. In some instances, relatively high prices lead to increased sales and profits. In other instances, to decreased sales and profits. In still other instances, prices lower than the competitions' lead to high sales and profits. In other cases, they do not.

Heinz catsup, for example, has consistently sold at a wholesale price about 10 percent higher than Hunt's or Del Monte's, and as much as 20 percent more than distributor brands. And, it has consistently held a position of market dominance. A few years ago, Hunt's reduced its price and substantially increased its advertising expenditures in an effort to overtake Heinz's market position. Hunt's did increase its market share, but the effect on profits was so severe that the company had to abandon this strategy.

Pricing strategy is one of the more complex decisions in marketing. To understand the role of price, we need to turn to some of the basic concepts of economics and trace their evolution into today's marketing practices.

BASIC ECONOMIC CONCEPTS

Historically, economics was founded upon the interrelationship of supply and demand as mediated by the price mechanism. The essentials of this interrelationship are shown in Figure 14–1.

Figure 14–1A represents a simplified *demand* curve. It slopes downward and to the right. As price decreases, demand increases because more consumers can afford to buy the product, and because those consumers currently buying the product can afford to buy it in larger quantities. Figure 14–1B represents the *supply* curve. It slopes upward and to the right. As price increases, more suppliers are attracted to the product field because of the increased opportunity for profits. Figure 14–1C represents the *point of equilibrium,* the point where the supply curve and the demand curve intersect and where supply equals demand. A static condition of equilibrium is never achieved because, as prices rise and profit opportunities become more attractive, many suppliers gravitate to the product field and production soon exceeds demand. Production gluts cause suppliers to reduce their prices to dispose of excessive inventories. As prices fall, profits suffer and suppliers desert the field in search of more attractive investment opportunities. This, in turn, leads to a decrease in supply until demand again predominates and consumers begin to bid up the price, creating favorable profit opportunities for suppliers. Then, the cycle begins over again. Thus, the equilibrium point is only a balancing mechanism that keeps supply and demand in an ever-changing relationship.

All of us have experienced the effects of supply and demand. When cattle production is high, producers lower prices to dispose of their production, the price of beef drops, and we all eat steak. However, as prices decrease, the production of beef becomes less profitable. Production is cut back; marginal producers drop out of the field entirely because they can no longer make a profit. Beef becomes scarce. Under the impact of scarcity, demand exceeds supply; prices rise until many consumers can no longer afford to buy beef in the quantities they have in the past and turn to fish, poultry, lamb, pork, cheese, or other substitute products. High beef prices encourage new production, and the cycle begins again.

The Demand Side of Pricing

The foregoing description of the market response to price is based on the assumption that all consumers are aware of price changes and respond to them in the same way. However, from a practical point of view, this assumption is invalid. This gives rise to the concept of price elasticity of demand.

PRICE ELASTICITY OF DEMAND. Price elasticity of demand refers to the effect that a change in price has on total income. It is computed by multiplying price by demand. For example, if the price of a product is $1.00, and the demand is 100,000 units, then total income is $1 times 100,000, or $100,000. The four basic forms of price elasticity of demand are unitary elasticity, price elasticity,

FIGURE 14–1: Interrelationship of Supply and Demand

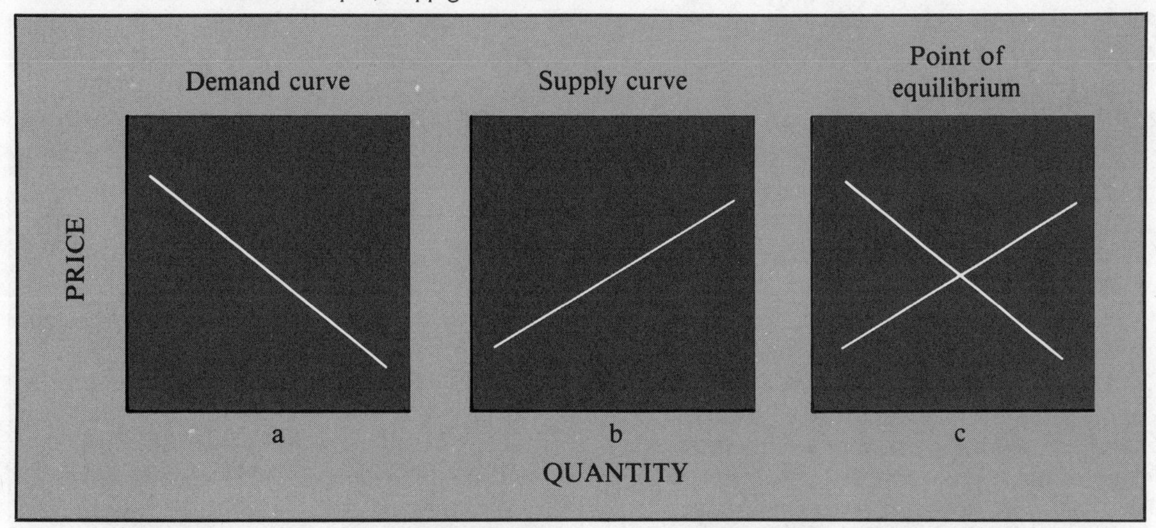

price inelasticity, and negative elasticity. These forms of elasticity are diagrammed in Figure 14–2. They relate to total income in the following ways:

- *Unitary Elasticity (Figure 14–2A).* Under conditions of unitary elasticity, a change in price will be compensated for by a corresponding change in demand so that total income remains the same.
- *Price Elasticity (Figure 14–2B).* Under conditions of price elasticity, a change in price will yield a relatively large change in demand. As a result, a price *decrease* will result in an *increase* in total revenue, and a price *increase* will result in a *decrease* in total revenue.
- *Price Inelasticity (Figure 14–2C).* Under conditions of price inelasticity a change in price will yield a relatively small change in demand. As a consequence, a *decrease* in price will result in a *decrease* in revenue, and an *increase* in price will result in an *increase* in total revenue. A classic example of price inelasticity is insulin, which is used in the treatment of diabetes. If one does not have diabetes, one has no use for insulin. On the other hand, if one has diabetes, one must have insulin regardless of its price. Thus, within a moderate range of prices, the demand for insulin is unaffected by price.
- *Negative Elasticity (Figure 14–2D).* Under conditions of negative elasticity, demand moves in the same direction as price. Thus, an *increase* in price *increases* demand and *total income,* and a *decrease* in price *decreases* demand and total income. Examples of negative elasticity can often be found in the personal care and proprietary medicine fields, where a higher price offers assurance of product efficacy and therefore, makes the product more attractive to consumers. For example, when home permanents were first introduced into the consumer market at a price of twenty–five cents a package, the product was a colossal failure. Women were simply not interested. Then, the same product was repackaged and introduced at $1.25 a package. It was a smashing success. Apparently, women were unwilling to trust their hair to a twenty-five–cent product for fear of hair damage. The higher price increased their confidence in the product's safety.

From the standpoint of the individual firm, prices are too high if demand is elastic because a decrease in price would result in an

FIGURE 14–2: Basic Demand Curves

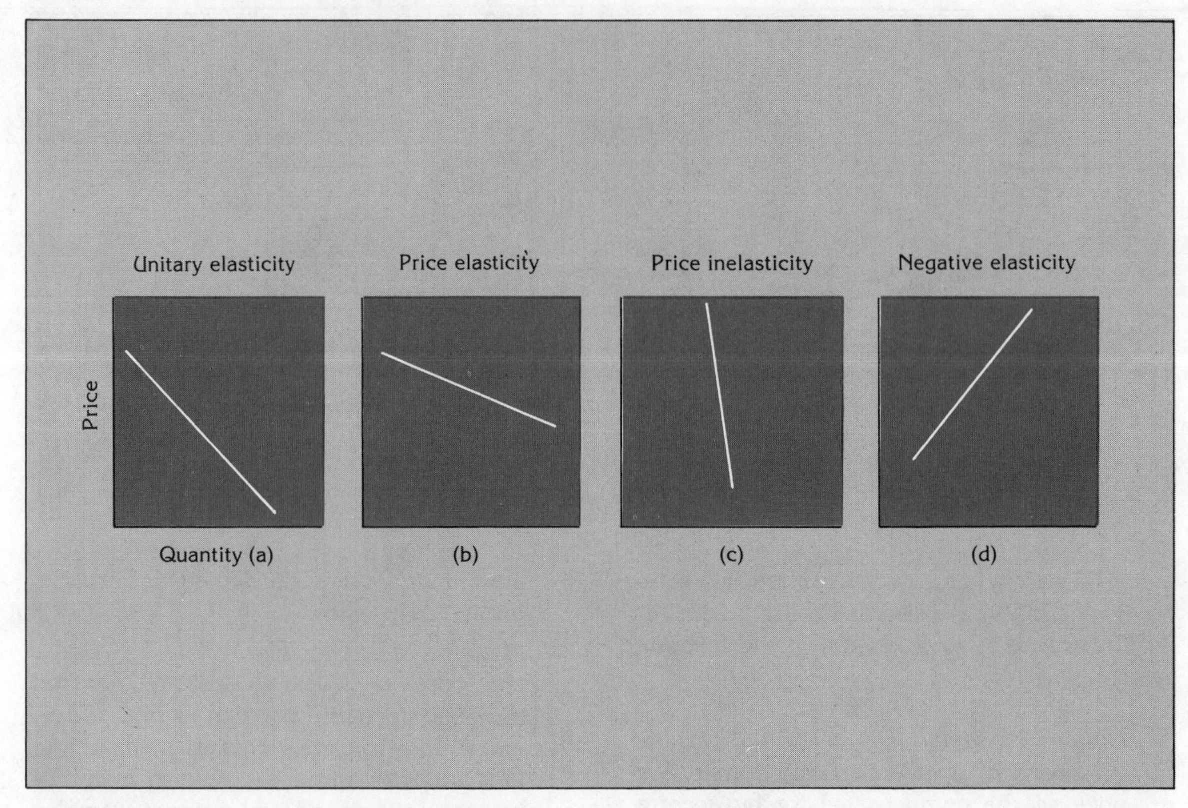

increase in total revenue. Similarly, if prices are inelastic or subject to negative elasticity, so that an increase in prices would increase total income, prices are too low.[2]

COMPUTING PRICE ELASTICITY. In the foregoing discussion, we have illustrated price elasticity with curves of a constant slope (that is, straight lines) for purposes of simplicity. In the real world, demand curves aren't shaped that way. Instead, the slope of the price-demand relationship will vary at different points along the curve. Figure 14–3 shows a demand curve much more typical of those that actually prevail.

Note that the elasticity of demand varies at different points along the curve. At one point, it may be *price inelastic;* at another point, *unitary elasticity* may prevail; while at still another point, it may be *price elastic.* The state of elasticity at any point on the curve may be computed by the following equation.

$$E = \frac{Q_2 - Q_1}{Q_1 + Q_2} \Big/ \frac{P_2 - P_1}{P_1 + P_2}$$

where:

E = the index of elasticity

Q_1 and Q_2 = the quantity sold before (Q_1) and after (Q_2) the price change.

P_1 and P_2 = the price before (P_1) and after (P_2) the price change.

A price elasticity of 1 represents *unitary elasticity,* where demand falls by the same percentage by which the prices rise. An elasticity of less than 1 means that the curve at that point is *price inelastic,* and demand changes by a lesser percent than the percentage change in price. And, an elasticity of greater than 1 represents *price*

2. This statement is contingent upon the behavior of costs at various levels of production since an increase in total revenue does not necessarily result in increased profits. However, for our purposes at this point, we may consider the suggested relationship to be generally valid.

FIGURE 14–3: Price-Demand Curve

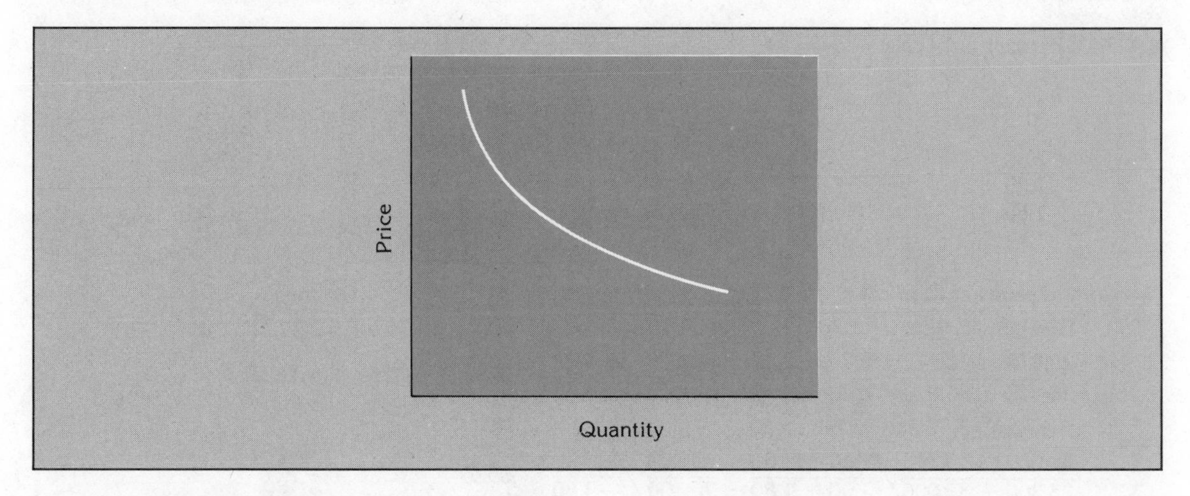

elasticity in which demand changes by a greater percentage than the change in price.

These relationships are shown in Figure 14–4. This figure shows three things. *First,* it gives a hypothetical price-demand schedule which shows demand at six different price levels. *Second,* it shows this same information in the form of a demand curve. *Third,* it shows the computations for the index of elasticity at three different points—between $2.42 and $2.20; between $2.00 and $1.80; and between $1.60 and $1.42. Note that, as the slope of the curve changes, the price elasticity index also changes.

Variables Influencing Price Elasticity

Different products have different elasticities. Why do these differences exist? A number of variables have predictable effects on price elasticity. Chief among them are substitute products, complementary products, quantities purchased, and income.

SUBSTITUTE PRODUCTS. Substitute products are products that can be used in place of another product. Products for which there are easily available substitutes tend to be price elastic. For example, the demand for beef is price elastic. That is, the quantity consumed rises and falls with changes in price. This occurs because of the many substitute products for beef. As the price of beef rises, consumers can easily shift their purchases to substitute products such as poultry, fish, lamb, pork, cheese, and so forth. All are nutritious, all are high in protein, all are edible, and all may be used as a main dish at meals.

Conversely, when there are few substitutes for a particular product type, prices tend to be inelastic. A case in point is salt. There are really no good substitutes for salt. As a consequence, a change in the price of salt will have a minimal effect on the quantity consumed.

The same effect can be observed for different brands of the same product type. When there are many competitive brands, all quite similar in nature, an increase in the price of one will cause consumers to switch brands, resulting in a loss in market share for the brand raising its price. Conversely, a decrease in price for one of the brands will cause consumers to shift their purchases to this brand, resulting in a loss in brand share for competitors—provided, of course, that competitors do not respond by dropping their prices by a comparable amount. If they do, brand shares will tend to remain the same, but the incomes of all competitors will be reduced because of the lower price levels. This is why most producers are wary of making permanent price cuts. Instead, they are more inclined to use temporary measures—such as coupons, special price-off label deals for a short period of time, and so forth—to gain a temporary increase in brand share and to sample new consumers. Producers hope that the new consumers will continue to use

FIGURE 14-4: Demand Schedule, Demand Curve, and Demand Elasticity Computation

1. Price-demand schedule

Price	*Demand in units*
$2.42	28,472
2.20	29,970
2.00	33,300
1.80	37,000
1.60	40,700
1.44	46,805

2. Price-demand curve

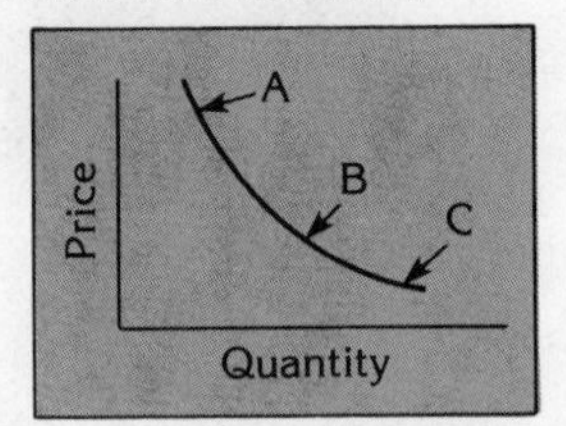

3. Computations of Elasticity

A. Between $2.42 and $2.20

$$\frac{29{,}970 - 28{,}472}{28{,}472 + 29{,}970} \Big/ \frac{2.20 - 2.42}{2.42 + 2.20} = \frac{1{,}498}{58{,}442} \Big/ \frac{-0.22}{4.62} = .0256 \Big/ -.4762 = -.0538$$

B. Between $2.00 and $1.80

$$\frac{37{,}000 - 33{,}300}{33{,}300 + 37{,}000} \Big/ \frac{1.80 - 2.00}{2.00 + 1.80} = \frac{3{,}700}{70{,}300} \Big/ \frac{-0.2}{-3.80} = .0526 \Big/ -.0526 = -1.00$$

C. Between $1.60 and $1.44

$$\frac{46{,}805 - 40{,}700}{40{,}700 + 46{,}805} \Big/ \frac{1.44 - 1.60}{1.60 + 1.44} = \frac{6{,}105}{87{,}505} \Big/ \frac{-0.16}{3.04} = .0698 \Big/ -.0526 = -1.326$$

When determining price elasticity, the minus sign in the answer is ignored.

their brands after the promotions are over and prices have returned to their normal levels.

An example of the dangers of a permanent price cut are illustrated in the following example. The beer market has historically been characterized by "popular-priced" and "premium-priced" brands that are quite similar in nature. The premium-priced beers are generally priced a few cents above popular-priced beers in mass outlets such as supermarkets. As long as the difference in price between popular-priced and premium-priced brands remains within a fairly narrow range, the brand shares of the premium and popular priced beers remain fairly stable.

Falstaff is a popular-priced beer; Budweiser is a premium-priced beer. A few years ago, in the St. Louis market, Falstaff unexpectedly cut its price to retailers by fifty cents a case just before a three-day weekend, and its sales and share of market in food stores rose significantly, hurting both Budweiser and other competitive beers in the market. The following week, Budweiser (apparently in retaliation) cut its price to retailers by a dollar a case and flooded grocery outlets with massive Budweiser displays. The result was disaster. Falstaff's share of market plummeted and, as a side effect, G.B. (a local, marginal, St. Louis beer) was driven out of business.

In the foregoing discussion, we have dealt with similar products in fields with a number of competitors. As I pointed out, in such fields, demand for individual brands tends to be price elastic. Conversely, in product fields with few competitive brands where different brands have unique features, price changes will have a minimal effect on brand shares.

COMPLEMENTARY PRODUCTS. Two products are said to be complementary when a change in the price of one will affect the demand for the other. For example, a significant increase in the price of cameras may cause a decrease in the demand for film, even though the price of film remains unchanged. A sharp increase in the price of film may cause a decrease in the demand for film developing services, even though the price of developing film is unchanged. As a consequence, a firm that markets complementary products must be cautious that a price increase for one product does not have a deleterious effect on the demand for its complement.

PROPORTION OF INCOME. A third factor that affects the elasticity of demand for a product is the proportion of the buyer's income that is required to purchase it. The demand for products that are relatively inexpensive and purchased infrequently tends to be inelastic because the paying of higher prices does not substantially reduce the buyer's ability to buy other things. Matches, light bulbs, and shoe polish are examples of such products. One factor contributing to the inelasticity of demand for products purchased infrequently is that buyers often do not remember how much they paid last time, because of the infrequency of purchase, so that a modest price increase goes unnoticed.

INCOME. Consumers buy more of some products if their incomes increase, and less of when their incomes decrease. For example, a 30 percent increase in the real income of people in the United States may cause a 90 percent increase in the demand for sports cars and pleasure boats. If the demand for a particular product type increases more than the incomes of consumers, it is *income elastic.* Other products are income inelastic. That is, the quantities demanded do not increase as fast as income. Food, for example, is income inelastic. Consumers do not start eating six meals a day when their incomes double.

FIGURE 14–5: *The Shifting Demand Curve*

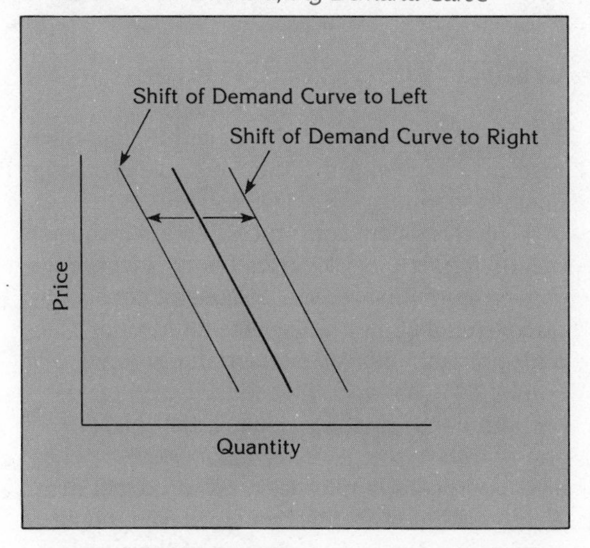

Shifting the Demand Curve

Demand curves can shift. When a product becomes more desirable for some reason, the demand curve will shift to the right. This means that demand at all price levels increases. Conversely, demand curves can also shift to the left when demand at all price levels decreases (see Figure 14–5).

What causes demand curves to shift? For one thing, changes in income. Generally, the demand curve for highly attractive items will shift to the right as income increases. Thus, as real income increases, the demand curve for sirloin steaks tends to shift to the right. Products whose demand curves shift to the right with an increase in income are referred to by economists as *normal* goods. Those whose demand curves shift to the left with increases in income are referred to as *inferior* goods. Thus, sirloin steak is a *normal* good, and hamburger is an *inferior* good.

Marketing can also cause the demand curve to shift. This introduces the concepts of primary demand and selective demand.

Primary Versus Selective Demand

Primary demand is for a product type. Thus, the demand for automobiles, for cake mixes, for peanut butter, or for dog food, is primary demand. Selective demand is demand for a particular brand: for Duncan Hines cake mix, or for Purina Dog Chow, or for Skippy peanut butter. Through product positioning, product quality, advertising, and other marketing activities, producers attempt to increase the selective demand for their particular brands. In fact, this is a primary objective of marketing. Successful marketers shift the selective demand for their products to the right. That's what they're paid for. And, as they succeed, they strengthen the market positions and the profitability of their companies.

Don't underestimate the power of pricing. (Photo by Andy Sacks/Editorial Photocolor Archives)

TRADITIONAL PRICING

Traditionally, economic theory has emphasized the role of price as the primary mediator between supply and demand. In the foregoing material, we have examined some of the basic relationships that generally exist. Practically, however, it doesn't always work that way. Psychological variables also influence demand schedules—note the examples of Heinz catsup, Hickory Hill bacon, and home permanents. Nonetheless, price considerations continue to dominate most traditional economic thinking. Philip Kotler has pointed out that there are persuasive historical, technical, and social reasons for economists to emphasize price.[3]

From a *historical* point of view, economics emerged as a discipline at a time when production was characterized by commodities—wheat, cotton, sugar, and other raw materials; even basic foodstuffs and clothing were largely undifferentiated. Branding, packaging, and advertising were virtually unknown. The major factor differentiating one loaf of bread from another, or one bushel of wheat from another, was price. Further, since most incomes were low, and luxuries were enjoyed only by the wealthy, frugality was a necessary condition for existence.

From a *technical* point of view, price was emphasized because it was easily quantified and unambiguous. Thus, it provided an easy tool for analyzing economic activity. Considerations such as product quality, brand image, promotion, and customer service were difficult to define and even more difficult to measure since they are essentially psychological in nature.

From a *social* point of view, price offered a defensible rationale for the operation of the marketing system. Price fluctuations served as a mechanism to control surpluses and scarcities. When surpluses existed, prices were cut to get rid of excess production. Lower prices increased demand and discouraged further production. When scarcity prevailed, prices were raised to increase profits. This, in turn, attracted new producers to the field. Supply and demand, aided by the price mechanism, automatically controlled the economy and kept it in balance.

CHANGING POINTS OF VIEW

Two factors emerged in the United States which conspired to change the traditional role of pricing: First, economic growth gave rise to a large body of relatively affluent consumers. Mere subsistence was no longer the rule; discretionary income became commonplace, and millions of consumers discovered that they had a taste for luxuries. Second, dramatic increases in productive capacity, combined with an increased rigidity of costs brought about by the mechanization of production and the emergence of labor unions, generated a perpetual surplus for many products. Manufacturers found themselves faced with the need to increase demand to dispose of their produc-

3. Philip Kotler, *Marketing Management,* 2nd. ed. (Englewood Cliffs, NJ: Prentice-Hall, Inc., 1972), p. 515.

tion, and unable to lower prices sufficiently to do so and still make a profit. Market segmentation and product differentiation became a way of life, and these strategies gave rise to two new phenomena: *monopolistic competition* and *symbolic pricing*.

Monopolistic Competition

Pure competition exists when there are many suppliers and all products are homogeneous. Thousands of wheat farmers offering their harvest for sale represent a condition of pure competition. This is one end of the competitive spectrum. At the other extreme is the concept of *monopoly*, where one supplier controls the entire supply of a product that consumers must buy because there are no substitutes. Probably no true monopoly exists because there are generally substitutes of one sort or another. Nonetheless, the *concept* of monopoly is still valid. Between these two extremes, are infinite marketing structures, one of which is *monopolistic competition*.[4]

In monopolistic competition, the product of each competitor differs in *some* way from that of other competitors. In effect, each manufacturer has a monopoly because an exact duplicate of its product cannot be obtained from any other source.[5] True, there are substitute products. For example, one could buy a Ford instead of a Chevrolet and do just as well. But, if the consumer wants a new Chevrolet, the only supplier is the Chevrolet Division of General Motors. Branding, packaging, style, and advertising claims are used by modern marketers to reinforce the concept of a monopoly, and to perpetuate the impression that there is *no real* substitute for the brand being promoted. The major advantage of monopolistic competition for the producer is that it minimizes the need to compete on the basis of price and gives rise to the practice of nonprice competition.

Symbolic Pricing

In monopolistic competition, price is a symbol used by producers to create an *impression* about their products in the minds of consumers. And, as a symbol, price need not function in the traditional manner. For many products, a higher price may lead to an increase in demand rather than a decrease as portrayed by traditional economic theory. In these instances, price serves as a symbol of quality. Similarly, a low price may discourage demand rather than increasing it because the low price connotes inferiority, as in the home permanent example.

PRICING IN CONTEMPORARY MARKETING

Contemporary marketing does not deny the general validity of traditional economic theory. Generally speaking, a lower price *does* result in an increase in demand. More Chevrolets are sold than Rolls-Royces; when the price of steak skyrockets, most of us make do with hamburger, chicken, or fish; and a price reduction on a popular brand can do remarkable things to the sales curve. However, contemporary marketing is no longer a slave to price, having found that product differentiation and consumer psychology can be used to loosen the shackles that traditionally bound supply and demand together in a rigid price relationship. As a consequence, symbolic pricing has *joined* traditional pricing theory as a marketing tool. Together, they make a formidable team.

Symbolic pricing is an effective marketing tool for several reasons. *First,* most consumers believe there is a necessary relationship between the price of a brand and its manufacturing cost. This belief is often expressed through the cliché, "You get what you pay for." Studies by

---

4. Edward H. Chamberlain, *The Theory of Monopolistic Competition* (Cambridge, Massachusetts: Harvard University Press, 1933).

5. Economists generally distinguish between *monopolistic competition* and *differentiated oligopoly*. In monopolistic competition, many competitors have products which differ sufficiently to justify branding, and sales promotion. In a differentiated oligopoly, the same product differences prevail, but there are only a few competitors, rather than many. I have combined monopolistic competition and differentiated oligopoly since my primary focus is on product differences and not the number of competitors.

Leavitt,[6] as well as Tull, Boring, and Gonsior,[7] and by Gabor and Granger[8] support this observation. Unfortunately, this belief isn't necessarily true. A private-label shaving cream that sells for sixty-nine cents often costs no less for product and package than does the advertised brand selling for double the price. The $2.25 proprietary medicine often costs no more than twenty-five cents for product and package; and the bulk of the cost is in the package. In personal care products, distilled spirits, cosmetics, proprietary medicines, hard goods, home furnishings, art objects, and even food and clothing, price is often as much of a reflection of product positioning as it is of product costs. Morris and Bronson correlated price with the quality ratings of *Consumers Union* for forty-eight sets of products (mostly, major household appliances) over a period from 1957 to 1968. They concluded that: "Price and quality do correlate, but at so low a level as to lack practical significance." Further, there was no obvious method by which the consumer could identify the set of products for which price-as-an-indicator-of-quality works.[9]

A second reason why symbolic pricing is effective is that, for many products, consumers do not have the expertise required to evaluate product quality. This is particularly true of major appliances, electronic equipment, fabrics, carpeting, furniture, and many other product fields. It is also true for packaged goods, where the goods are concealed by the package and where the ingredients on the label would require advanced degrees in chemistry and pharmacology to decipher. In these instances, the consumer is forced to rely on surrogate or substitute indicators such as brand reputation, price, or some other, even more extraneous factor.

6. Harold J. Leavitt, "A Note on Some Experimental Findings about the Meaning of Price," *Journal of Business* (July, 1954): 205–10.

7. D. S. Tull, R. A. Boring, and M. H. Gonsior, "A note on the relationship of Price and Imputed Quality," *Journal of Business* (April, 1964): 186–91.

8. Andre Gabor and C. W. J. Granger, "On the Price Consciousness of Consumers," *Applied Statistics* (November, 1961): 170–80.

9. R. T. Morris and C. C. Bronson, "The Chaos of Competition Indicated by Consumer Reports," *Journal of Marketing* (July, 1969): 26–34.

A third reason for symbolic pricing is that quality is often in the eye of the beholder; this psychological phenomenon follows the path of the self-fulfilling prophecy. That is, barring some blatant product failure, consumers *expect* to be satisfied with their purchase and have their expectations fulfilled.

Still a fourth reason for symbolic pricing is the age-old phenomenon of snobbery. Most of us are snobs in one way or another. As a consequence, we buy expensive brands to demonstrate our good taste, to impress our friends and relations, and to distinguish ourselves from the crowd.

All of this does not mean that symbolic pricing is completely free from the traditional strictures of the price mechanism or the pressure of competition. In fact, studies have shown that consumers often have a range of prices which they consider appropriate for a particular product type. For example, the Gabor and Granger study referred to earlier found that buyers have two price limits in mind when they consider a purchase: an upper limit above which the product is judged too expensive, and a lower limit below which the quality of the product would be suspect.[10] Similar findings have been reported by Sherif[11] and by Wassen.[12]

Nor can symbolic pricing offset the obvious inferiority of a pair of tennis shoes that fall apart within a few weeks of purchase, nor a television set that spends it life in the repair shop, nor a garment that tears out at the seams after the first washing, nor a thousand other fragilities of the shoddy product. Product performance and price must be generally compatible, and both should project the product concept.

PRICING FOR PROFIT

The existence of some measure of discretion in setting prices in contemporary marketing places

10. Gabor and Granger, "On the Price Consciousness of Consumers."

11. Carolyn W. Sherif, "Social Categorization as a Function of Latitude of Acceptance and Series Range," *Journal of Abnormal and Social Psychology* (August, 1963): 148–56.

12. Chester Wassen, *Consumer Behavior: A Managerial Viewpoint* (Austin, TX: Austin Press, 1975), p. 391.

the burden of price determination in the hands of management. Further, once this price is determined, the supplier must offer this same price to all potential buyers to avoid charges of price discrimination under the Robinson-Patman Act.[13] Since the price set will influence demand, the goal of management is to *optimize* profit. Too low a price may increase demand but, at the same time, reduce margins so that profits will suffer. On the other hand, too high a price will increase margins, but may depress demand to the point that profits again suffer. This means that producers should try to find the optimal balance between demand and costs in determining the price at which their products will be offered. One approach that is sometimes helpful is marginal analysis.

Marginal analysis

Marginal analysis is concerned with finding the optimal relationship between revenue and cost, so that maximum profits may be obtained. To do this, the behavior of both costs and revenues at various levels of demand must be examined. This requires the introduction of two new terms: *marginal revenue* and *marginal cost.*

MARGINAL REVENUE. *Marginal revenue may be defined as the change in total revenue that results from the sale of one additional unit.* Since the demand curve generally slopes downward and to the right for most products, the price of all units must be decreased to obtain an additional unit of sales. As prices decrease, *total revenue may increase, but marginal revenues may decrease.* Consider, for example, the hypothetical relationship between quantities sold, price, total revenue, and marginal revenue shown in Table 14–1.

At a price of $10, no units are sold, so total revenue is zero. At a price of $9.00, one unit is sold, so

TABLE 14–1: Relationship between Quantities Sold, Price, Total Revenue, and Marginal Revenue

Quantity	Price	Total Revenue	Marginal Revenue
0	$10.00	0	0
1	9.00	$ 9.00	$ 9.00
2	8.00	16.00	7.00
3	7.00	21.00	5.00
4	6.00	24.00	3.00
5	5.00	25.00	1.00
6	4.00	24.00	(1.00)
7	3.00	21.00	(3.00)

that total revenue is $9.00. Marginal revenue (the increase in total revenue resulting from the sale of one additional unit) is also $9.00. When price is decreased to $8.00, two units are sold, producing a total revenue of $16.00. However, marginal revenue decreases by $2.00 because the price of each unit was decreased by $1.00. As we examine Table 14–1 further, we note that as price decreases, total revenue increases and marginal revenue continues to decrease up to and including a price of $5.00. At this point, total revenue reaches its peak of $25, and marginal revenue for the fifth unit is $1.00. Thereafter, marginal revenue becomes negative, and total revenue starts to decrease.

MARGINAL COST. *Marginal cost is defined as the change in total cost that results from producing one extra unit.* Normally, cost per unit decreases somewhat as production increases because as production increases, fixed costs are spread over more units and efficiencies in production and elimination of waste accrue with experience. Also, quantity purchases often reduce the costs of raw materials. Such savings are referred to as *economies of scale.* Eventually, however, the limit of these economies is reached, and costs per unit increase as less efficient methods are used to increase output, or as major investments are required to increase production capacity. Table 14–2 shows a hypothetical relationship between quantity produced, unit costs, total costs, and marginal costs. The relationships shown in Table 14–2 have been deliberately exaggerated by using small quantities to demonstrate the following points:

13. Practically, there are a number of exceptions to this statement. Children, for example, are often charged less than adults for entertainment, transportation, lodging, and so forth. Special rates are also offered to certain groups, such as students or retirees. In some product fields, such as automobiles and housing, bargaining skill may result in different prices for different buyers. This is particularly true where trade-ins are involved. Finally, the Robinson-Patman Act itself permits pricing differences justified by differences in selling costs or by a difference in freight rates.

TABLE 14–2: Hypothetical Relationship between Quantity Produced and Unit, Total, and Marginal Costs

1 Quantity	2 Fixed cost	3 Variable cost/unit	4* Total variable cost	5** Total cost	6 Marginal cost
0	$100	0	0	$100.00	0
1	100	$10.00	$10.00	110.00	$ 10.00
2	100	9.50	19.00	119.00	9.00
3	100	9.00	27.00	127.00	8.00
4	100	8.50	34.00	134.00	7.00
5	100	8.00	40.00	140.00	6.00
6	100	7.50	45.00	145.00	5.00
7	100	7.75	54.25	154.25	9.25
8	200	7.50	60.00	260.00	105.75
9	200	7.50	67.50	267.50	7.50
10	200	7.50	75.00	275.00	7.50

* column 1 × column 3
** column 2 + column 4

- With a fixed investment of $100, variable costs per unit decline through six units because of economies of scale. Throughout this range of production, total costs rise, although marginal costs decrease.
- In order to produce the seventh unit, production inefficiencies are incurred because the optimal production capacity has been exceeded. As a consequence, variable costs per unit increase slightly, but marginal costs increase significantly.
- With unit eight, a substantial investment is made in capital equipment to increase productive capacity. This increases fixed costs from $100 to $200. As a result, variable costs per unit drop back to the level achieved with the sixth unit. However, both total costs and marginal costs increase significantly.
- Finally, with the production of the ninth and tenth unit, variable unit costs remain constant, total costs continue to increase, but marginal costs drop significantly.

Now, let's combine costs and revenues in a single chart to clarify the relationship between these two variables. This has been done in Figure 14–6. Note that for profits to exist, the total cost curve must lie below the total revenue curve. Thus, maximum profits are achieved when the quantity produced is at Q_2, whereas the maximum loss is sustained when the quantity produced is at Q_1. If the firm should produce at a quantity greater than Q_2, the total cost curve is increasing faster than the total revenue curve and profits decrease because marginal costs are increasing faster than marginal revenues. As a consequence, the production level that produces the maximum profit is that point at which marginal costs and marginal revenues are equal. This occurrence is demonstrated in Figure 14–7.

FIGURE 14–6: Relationship between Total Revenues and Total Costs

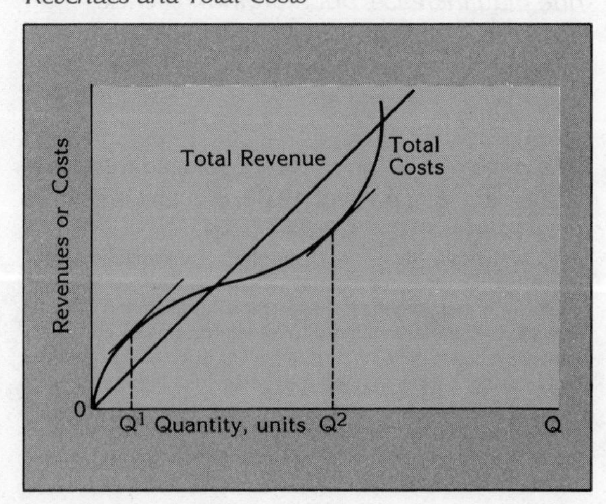

FIGURE 14–7: Relationship between Marginal Cost and Marginal Revenue Curves

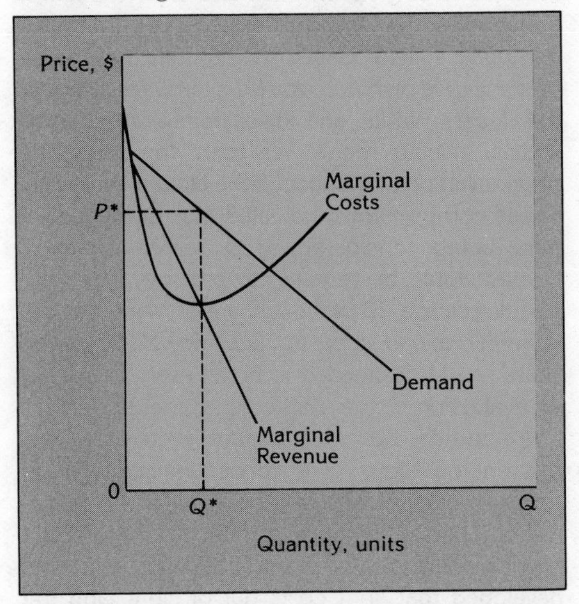

Figure 14–7 shows three things: First, the selective demand for a hypothetical firm's product. Secondly, the marginal cost curve for the firm's production. Thirdly, the marginal revenue curve for the firm at various price levels. The point of intersection of the marginal cost and marginal revenue curves represents the optimal price that will provide the firm with maximum profits.

Marginal analysis is useful because it clarifies the relationship between costs, revenues, and profits across the entire range of relevant demand. However, it has severe limitations when we come to the pragmatic questions of the price that should be charged for a particular product.

Limitations of Marginal Analysis

If prices could be set wholly on the basis of marginal analysis, it would be convenient. The procedure is straightforward, simple, and precise. Unfortunately, determining the optimal price in a competitive world is none of these. The process is seldom straightforward, never simple, and doesn't even know what the word "precise" means. For example:

- Determining a precise demand curve for a particular brand is virtually impossible because competitors may change their prices, thereby changing the demand schedules for all competitors in the field. Further, the reactions of distribution channels and the government may prohibit price optimization as defined through marginal analysis.
- No consideration is given to nonprice variables such as advertising, packaging, promotion, distribution, and so forth. These activities, as well as those of competitors, can have a profound effect on demand schedules from marketing period to marketing period.
- The marginal analysis which has been described is only concerned with the price of a single product. In a multiple product company, the price set for one product may influence the demand schedules for other products. Thus, the price that maximizes profits for one product may detract from the performance of other products and depress the overall profits of the firm. Ideally, while one might take this factor into consideration, it makes marginal analysis extremely complex and terribly uncertain.
- Finally, marginal analysis is based on the assumption that the basic objective of the firm is to maximize profits in the short run. Growth, market share, and other objectives are often given priority over profit maximization, both in the short and long run.

Despite these limitations, marginal analysis has important contributions to make to pricing decisions. The concepts of marginal revenue, marginal costs, and fixed costs are clearly recognized as relevant considerations for pricing decisions. One prominant variation of marginal analysis that is frequently used in price determination is break-even analysis.

Break-Even Analysis

One key consideration in pricing new products is the volume that must be sold to break even. The break-even point in units can be determined by dividing the gross margin per unit into fixed costs. Gross margin is the difference between the selling price and the cost of manufacturing the product. Thus, if the selling price is \$1.00 and manufacturing costs are \$0.40 per unit, the gross margin is \$1.00 minus \$0.40, or \$0.60.

The fixed costs, of course, are the costs for plant and equipment to manufacture the product. They are fixed because they represent costs that must be met whether or not any product is being manufactured. Now, let us take an example to demonstrate the computation of the break–even point. Assume fixed costs to be \$50,000. Assume the gross margin to be \$0.60 per unit. The break-even level of units would be:

$$\frac{\text{Fixed costs}}{\text{Gross margin}} = \frac{\$50{,}000}{\$0.60} = 83{,}333 \text{ units.}$$

Break even in dollars is simply the break-even amount of units multiplied by the price per unit. After break even has been achieved, and fixed costs met, the entire gross margin is a contribution to profit and other expenses, such as selling expenses, advertising, overhead, and so forth.

The relationships between fixed costs, revenue, and contribution to profit are shown in graphic form in Figure 14–8.

By using break-even analysis, one can determine the volume that would be required to make a contribution to profit under known cost and pricing constraints. For example, in working with one client in a new product field, we determined that a 40 percent gross margin would be required to cover promotion and other expenses, and to meet the firm's profit objectives in a highly competitive field. Based on competitive pricing practices, we also determined alternative prices at the upper, middle, and lower points of the competitive pricing range. We then computed the break-even point for each of the alternative prices. These computations indicated that, at the lowest price being considered, a 25 percent share of market would be required to break even. At the middle price, a 20 percent share of market would be required; and, at the highest price, a 16 percent share would be needed to break even. Based on an evaluation of the market, both the 25 percent share and the 20 percent share levels were considered too high. As a consequence, the high price—a 16 percent share of market—was selected. The sequel to the story is that the product never made it to the market. Production problems developed that shot costs out of sight, and the product was abandoned.

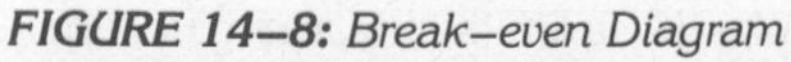

FIGURE 14–8: *Break–even Diagram*

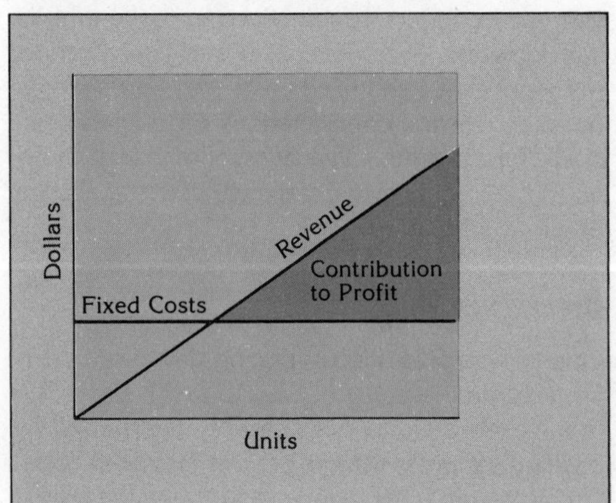

PRICING OBJECTIVES

Based on the foregoing discussion, one might assume that most successful firms have consistent, well-defined pricing objectives. They don't.[14] Despite a considerable literature on the importance of pricing objectives, many, if not most, pricing decisions appear to be made on a catch–as-catch-can basis.[15] Nor is the situation much different in retail outlets. Many retail outlets price

14. Mark I. Alport, *Pricing Decisions* (Glenview, IL: Scott, Foresman & Company, 1971), p. 11.

15. For excellent articles on corporate pricing, each taking a somewhat different approach, see: Robert L. Lanzillotti, "Pricing Objectives in Large Companies," *American Economic Review* (December 1958): 921–40; Joel Dean, "Techniques for Pricing New Products and Services," in *Handbook of Modern Marketing,* Victor Buell, ed. (New York: McGraw-Hill Book Company, Inc., 1970), pp. 5:51–61; Alfred R. Oxenfeldt, "Multi-Stage Approach to Pricing," *Harvard Business Review* (July-August, 1960): 125–33; Gilbert Burck, "The Myths and Realities of Corporate Pricing," *Fortune* (April 1972): 85ff; "The Perplexing Problem of Pricing," *Grey Matter,* published by Grey Advertising, Inc., Vol. 37, no. 12 (December 1966); and Kent B. Monroe and Andris Z. Zoltners, "Pricing the Product Line During Periods of Scarcity," *Journal of Marketing* (Summer 1979): 49–59.

on the basis of traditional margins for their store type and the particular product class involved, although some take a more idiosyncratic approach. For example, when one of my students asked a local retailer how he priced a particular brand of sport shoes, the retailer responded, "I call the local *Athlete's Foot,* find out what they charge for the same shoe, and then charge a dollar less."

What all of this seems to say is that pricing decisions are extremely complex, being influenced by internal and external variables; and market price continues to have a major impact on contemporary pricing practices. These points are reinforced by the following observations:

> Bridging the gap between price theory and the practice of setting prices is difficult. The basic problem is that, to a great extent, conventional price theory does not describe the "real world" in that the assumptions upon which it rests are unrealistic.
>
> One common assumption underlying all traditional theories of price is that the entrepreneur, or businessman, carefully weighs and measures the gains and losses that accrue as a result of the price decisions that he makes. In theory the price maker is assumed to be a rational person who is capable of analyzing the implications of his decisions and deciding accordingly. This is not a realistic assumption, however, because human beings are not as rational in their economic behavior as it supposes and because information concerning costs and demand is often not available to them in the form or to the degree that is assumed in price theory. There is, in fact, a great deal of uncertainty regarding both costs and demand in the real world.[16]

Large companies do appear to have general pricing policies, although these policies are often not explicit, nor are they adhered to in all pricing decisions that these companies make. In a classic study of twenty large companies, Robert F. Lanzillotti compiled a list of the pricing policies of these companies. This list is reproduced in Table 14–3. The following general policies have been abstracted from this table.

Target Return on Investment

One of the most common approaches used by the companies listed in Table 14–3 is to obtain a target return on investment. Under this pricing system, costs and profit goals are based on an average or standard volume of sales rather than on yearly volume which may fluctuate substantially from year to year. Thus, while actual return on investment may vary from year to year, the target expectations will (it is hoped) be achieved over the average life of the plant.

In determining what target returns should be, Lanzillotti found that company managers were influenced by such considerations as: (1) the amount they felt to be a fair and reasonable return; (2) traditional industry performance records; (3) a desire to equal or exceed competition; (4) the amount thought to be practical; and (5) a desire to stabilize industry prices.[17]

Target Market Share

Some companies set a maximum or minimum market share as a key determinant of pricing policy. A maximum share is sometimes set by the management of large corporations because they fear that market dominance will lead to government harassment and charges of monopoly. Such companies, as they approach this maximum, will shift their marketing strategies from price competition to that of emphasizing nonprice variables.

Minimum share goals may be set for a couple of reasons. In many fields, particularly in the food and drug trade, a minimum share is necessary to keep distribution. Once share falls below a given point, distribution is lost and further share losses accelerate. In other instances, a minimum share may be set that is sufficient to make a minimum contribution to profit.

Matching Competition

Companies that use this approach appear to focus on pricing competitively in the marketplace,

16. Donald V. Harper, "The Nature of Prices and Pricing," in *Marketing Management and Administrative Action,* Steuart Henderson Britt and Harper W. Boyd, Jr., eds. (New York: McGraw-Hill Book Company, 1968), p. 444.

17. Lanzillotti, "Pricing Objectives in Large Companies."

TABLE 14–3: Pricing Goals of Twenty Large Industrial Corporations.
SOURCE: Robert F. Lanzillotti, "Pricing Objectives in Large Companies," *American Economic Review* (December 1958): 924–26.

Company	Principal Pricing Goal	Collateral Pricing Goals	Rate of Return on Investment (After taxes) 1947–1955[a] Avg.	Range	Average Market Share[b]
Alcoa	20% on investment (before taxes); higher on new products [about 10% effective rate after taxes]	(a) "Promotive" policy on new products (b) Price stabilization	13.8	7.8–18.7	Pig & ingot, 37%; sheet, 46%; other fabrications, 62%[c]
American Can	Maintenance of market share	(a) "Meeting" competition (using cost of substitute product to determine price)	11.6	9.6–14.7	Approx. 55% of all types of cans[d]
A & P	Increasing market share	(b) Price stabilization "General promotive" (low-margin policy)	13.0	9.7–18.8	n.a.
Du Pont	Target return on investment—no specific figure given	(a) Charging what traffic will bear over long run (b) Maximum return for new products—"life cycle" pricing	25.9	19.6–34.1	n.a.
Esso (Standard Oil of N.J.)	"Fair-return" target—no specific figure given	(a) Maintaining market share (b) Price stabilization	16.0	12.0–18.9	n.a.
General Electric	20% on investment (after taxes); 7% on sales (after taxes)	(a) Promotive policy on new products (b) Price stabilization on nationally advertised products	21.4	18.4–26.6	–[e]
General Foods	33⅓% gross margin: ("⅓ to make, ⅓ to sell, and ⅓ for profit"); expectation of realizing target only on new products	(a) Full line of food products and novelties (b) Maintaining market share	12.2	8.9–15.7	n.a.
General Motors	20% on investment (after taxes)	Maintaining market share	26.0	19.9–37.0	50% of passenger automobiles[f]

TABLE 14–3: *Pricing Goals of Twenty Large Industrial Corporations—continued.*

Company	*Principal Pricing Goal*	*Collateral Pricing Goals*	*Rate of Return on Investment (After taxes) 1947–1955[a]*		*Average Market Share[b]*
			Avg.	*Range*	
Goodyear	"Meeting competitors"	(a) Maintain "position" (b) Price stabilization	13.3	9.2–16.1	n.a.
Gulf	Follow price of most important marketer in each area	(a) Maintain market share (b) Price stabilization	12.6	10.7–16.7	n.a.
International Harvester	10% on investment (after taxes)	Market share: ceiling of "less than a dominant share of any market"	8.9	4.9–11.9	Farm tractors, 28–30%; combines, cornpickers, tractor plows, cultivators, mowers, 20–30%; cotton pickers, 65%; light & light-heavy trucks, 5–18%; medium-heavy to heavy-heavy, 12–30%
Johns–Manville	Return on investment greater than last 15-year average (about 15% after taxes); higher target for new products	(a) Market share not greater than 20% (b) Stabilization of prices	14.9	10.7–19.6	n.a.
Kennecott	Stabilization of prices		16.0	9.3–20.9	n.a.
Kroger	Maintaining market share	Target return of 20% on investment before taxes[g]	12.1	9.7–16.1	n.a.
National Steel	Matching the market-price follower	Increase market share	12.1	7.0–17.4	5%
Sears Roebuck	Increasing market share (8–10% regarded as satisfactory share)	(a) Realization of traditional return on investment of 10–15% (after taxes) (b) General promotive (low margin) policy	5.4	1.6–10.7	5–10% average (twice as large a share in hard goods v. soft goods)

TABLE 14–3: *Pricing Goals of Twenty Large Industrial Corporations—continued.*

Company	*Principal Pricing Goal*	*Collateral Pricing Goals*	*Rate of Return on Investment (After taxes) 1947–1955*[a] *Avg.*	*Range*	*Average Market Share*[b]
Standard Oil (Indiana)	Maintain market share	(a) Stabilize prices (b) Target-return on investment (none specified)	10.4	7.9–14.4	n.a.
Swift	Maintenance of market share in livestock buying and meat packing		6.9	3.9–11.1	Approximately 10% nationally[h]
Union Carbide	Target return on investment[i]	Promotive policy on new products; "life cycle" pricing on chemicals generally	19.2	13.5–24.3	–[j]
U. S. Steel	8% on investment (after taxes)	(a) Target market share of 30% (b) Stable price (c) Stable margin	10.3	7.6–14.8	Ingots and steel, 30%; blast furnaces, 34%; finished hot-rolled products, 35%; other steel mill products, 37%[k]

[a]Federal Trade Commission, *Rates of Return (After Taxes) for Identical Companies in Selected Manufacturing Industries, 1940, 1947–55,* Washington [1957], pp 28–30, except for the following companies whose rates were computed by the author using the methods outlined in the Commission Report: A & P, General Foods, Gulf, International Harvester, Kroger, National Steel, Sears Roebuck, and Swift.

[b]As of 1955, unless otherwise indicated. Source of data is company mentioned unless noted otherwise.

[c]*U.S. v. Alcoa et al.,* "Stipulation Concerning Extension of Tables III–X," dated May 31, 1956, U.S. District Court for the Southern District of New York.

[d]As of 1939. U.S. Department of Justice, *Western Steel Plants and the Tin Plate Industry,* 79th Cong., 1st Sess., Doc. No. 95, p. L 1.

[e]The company states that on the average it aims at not more than 22 to 25 per cent of any given market. Percentages for individual markets or products were not made available, but it is estimated that in some markets, e.g. electrical turbines, General Electric has 60 per cent of the total market. *Cf.* Standard and Poor's, *Industry Surveys,* "Electrical-Electronic-Basic Analysis," Aug. 9, 1956, p. E 21.

[f]Federal Trade Commission, *Industrial Concentration and Product Diversification in the 1000 Largest Manufacturing Companies: 1950,* Washington, Jan. 1957, p. 113.

[g]Target return on investment evidently characterizes company policy as much as target market share. In making investment decisions the company is quoted as follows: "The Kroger Co. normally expected a return on investment of at least 20% before taxes." See McNair, Burnham, and Hersum, *Cases in Retail Management,* New York, 1957, pp. 205 ff.

[h]This represents the average share of total industry shipments of the four largest firms in 1954. *Cf. Concentration in American Industry,* Report of Subcommittee on the Judiciary, U. S. Senate, 85th Cong., 1st Sess., Washington, 1957, p. 315.

[i]In discussions with management officials various profit-return figures were mentioned, with considerable variation among divisions of the company. No official profit target percentage was given, but the author estimates the *average* profit objective for the corporation to be approximately 35% before taxes, or an effective rate after taxes of about 18 per cent.

[j]Chemicals account for 30 per cent of Carbide's sales, most of which are petro-chemicals, a field that the company opened thirty years ago and still dominates; plastics account for 18 per cent—the company sells 40 per cent of the two most important plastics

(vinyl and polyethylene); alloys and metals account for 26 per cent of sales—top U. S. supplier of ferroalloys (e.g. chrome, silicon, manganese), and the biggest U. S. titanium producer; gases account for 14 per cent of sales—estimated to sell 50 per cent of oxygen in the U. S.; carbon, electrodes, and batteries account for 12 per cent of sales—leading U. S. producer of electrodes, refractory carbon, and flashlights and batteries; and miscellaneous—leading operator of atomic energy plants, a leading producer of uranium, the largest U. S. producer of tungsten, and a major supplier of vanadium. *Cf.* "Union Carbide Enriches the Formula," *Fortune,* Feb. 1957, pp. 123 ff.; Standard and Poor's *Industry Surveys,* "Chemicals-Basic Analysis," Dec. 20, 1956, p. C 44; and "Annual Report for 1955 of the Union Carbide and Carbon Corporation."

[k]The range of the corporation's capacity as a percentage of total industry capacity varies from 15 to 54 per cent, as of January 1957. For more detail see *Administered Prices, Hearings Before the Subcommittee on Antitrust and Monopoly of the Senate Committee on the Judiciary,* 85th Cong., 1st Sess., Pt. 2, *Steel,* Washington, 1958, pp. 335–36.

TABLE 14–4: *Margins of Selected Middleman*

SOURCE: Compiled from *1979 Annual Statement Studies* (Fiscal years end 6/30/78 through 3/31/79), Robert Morris Associates, Philadelphia, Pennsylvania. Copyright 1979 by Robert Morris Associates.

Middlemen	*Cost of goods sold*	*Gross margins*	*Expenses*	*Profit before taxes*
Wholesalers				
Automobile and other motor vehicles	82.3%	17.7%	14.8%	2.9%
Tires and tubes	74.1	25.9	22.8	3.1
Radios, refrigerators, and electrical appliances	77.5	22.5	20.2	2.3
Coffee, tea, and spices	79.9	20.1	16.6	3.5
Dairy products and poultry	84.6	15.4	13.7	1.7
Frozen foods	84.1	15.9	13.2	2.7
General groceries	85.6	14.4	13.1	1.3
Floor coverings	74.8	25.2	22.3	2.9
Furniture	72.6	27.4	24.2	3.2
Retailers				
Family clothing	61.2%	38.8%	34.6%	4.2%
Furs	58.7	41.3	34.8	6.5
Shoes	58.5	41.5	37.4	4.1
Department stores	62.8	37.2	34.3	2.9
Drugs	67.5	32.5	29.4	3.1
Dairy products–milk dealers	62.8	37.4	36.9	0.5
Groceries and meats	77.9	22.1	20.1	2.0
Floor coverings	70.3	29.7	26.8	2.9
Furniture	59.8	40.2	37.1	3.1

using prevailing prices as their guide. Actually, this approach offers greater flexibility in pricing than appears at first blush. This is true because, as pointed out earlier, most consumers have a range of prices that they consider appropriate for a given product type. Thus, one may price competitively as long as one is within this range. A product may be priced at the top of the range as a *quality* product, at the bottom of the range as an *economy* product, or anyplace in between.

A Summary Note on Pricing Objectives

Company managers recognize that in an uncertain world and in a dynamic competitive climate, setting pricing objectives is difficult; nonetheless, companies still attempt to do so. Further, these objectives should probably be based on the concept of a target return on investment.

The existence of pricing objectives enables a firm to evaluate the profit contribution of existing products and the potential contribution of new products to the financial needs of the firm. Thus, it provides a general guide for discontinuing products that fall far short of company standards, and for evaluating the attractiveness of new products.

In the absence of profit objectives, there is always the danger that a firm will "drift" into a position where its product portfolio is dominated by low-profit items, so that the overall profitability of the company suffers and its financial stability is threatened.

THE STRUCTURE OF PRICING

Any consideration of pricing must go beyond price as the producer or consumer view it, and recognize the traditional pricing practices of the industry in which a particular product is sold. A key consideration in this respect is the question of channel margins.

In most distributor and retail fields, traditional margins are expected for each product class. If one is selling through department stores, one requires larger dealer margins than if one is selling through discount stores. If one is selling through specialty stores, one needs larger dealer margins than if one is selling through department stores. Further, individual product types have their own traditional margins. Table 14–4 shows typical wholesaler and retailer margins for selected product classes. Note the wide variations in margins between product classes at wholesale and retail levels.

Manufacturers sometimes offer higher than normal margins to the retail trade in the expectation that their products will be given favorable treatment. This can lead to problems. For example, the expected favorable treatment may not be given, but higher margins are still demanded as a form of legal blackmail, with the implications that, if the margins are reduced, the product will not be carried. For this reason manufacturers prefer to increase distributor and retailer margins on a temporary, promotional basis to increase shelf space, obtain displays, encourage sales support for a special promotion, or to achieve cooperative advertising support. In these instances, the duration of the price reduction (which is given in the form of a performance allowance) should be clearly specified.

Although retail margins are sometimes increased to encourage in-store cooperation, they can seldom be decreased with impunity. The maker of a well-established, high demand brand may urge that distributor or retail margins be shaved somewhat, but it is seldom prudent to force the issue if channel goodwill is to be retained. The loss of channel goodwill can lead to a loss of channel cooperation with a consequent decrease in sales.

PRICING STRATEGIES

The purpose of the foregoing discussion of pricing has been to provide a background for examining pricing strategies. A variety of pricing strategies may be used as a part of the marketing program. The overriding consideration in the use of these strategies is that they support or at least be compatible with the product concept. Some of the most frequently used pricing strategies are briefly described in the following material.

Market Skimming

In market skimming, a new product is introduced at a premium price. Its purpose is to recover investment quickly. Market skimming is a viable strategy when: (1) the new brand has a clear superiority over existing brands; (2) the brand is protected by patents, or the lag time for competitors in developing an equivalent product is relatively long because of technological complexities or the need to build new plants and equipment; and (3) the market is price *inelastic,* so that a high price will attract enough consumers to be highly profitable. Normally, market skimming is a temporary strategy in the sense that the price will be lowered to a competitive level when other firms enter the field with a comparable product.

Penetration Pricing

Penetration pricing is an introductory pricing strategy in which the new brand is priced relatively low in order to stimulate market growth and capture a large market share. It is a viable approach when the market is highly elastic, or when lag time for competitors is short and management wants to discourage competition by establishing a relatively low profit margin for the product field.

Market Segmentation

Many markets can be segmented on the basis of price; the automobile market is a prime example. Used in this way, pricing strategy is an effective device for appealing to a particular economic segment of the total market.

Prestige and Economy Pricing

As pointed out earlier, consumers in a particular market segment generally have a *range* of prices which they consider appropriate for the product in question. In *prestige* pricing, the brand is priced in the upper region of this range. In *economy* pricing, it is priced in the lower region of this range.

Break-Even Pricing

Break-even pricing is a viable strategy when a product has two or more components, one of which is purchased infrequently, the other frequently. For example, razors are purchased infrequently; razor blades, on the other hand, are purchased much more frequently. One might, in such an instance, price the razor at break even, or with a slight margin, in order to get the product in use. Blades, then, would be priced with a relatively high margin in order to capitalize on the repurchase pattern of sales. A similar strategy could apply to camera and film, where the manufacturer makes both, or to any other item that requires special refills.

Multiple Pricing

Multiple pricing is, in effect, a quantity discount. A lower price is charged if more than one unit is purchased. This strategy is widely followed by retail stores; grocery and drug outlets in particular offer two-for or three-for combinations. Research has consistently shown that two-for and three-for pricing may double or triple sales over single unit

Multiple pricing = multiple sales. (Photo by Robert Maust)

pricing, even though the price savings may be negligible. In many instances, multiple pricing probably steals sales from future periods and does not lead to an absolute increase in usage. In some cases, however, it does increase consumption, particularly for products such as soft drinks and beer, where availability of the product in the home stimulates use. This is the reason manufacturers of these products use six-packs, or some other multiple unit packages.

Line Pricing

Manufacturers who market a line of similar products (such as different flavors of cake mix or soup) or a line of diverse, but related items (such as pet care products) often find that their manufacturing costs for each item in the line differ. When the differences in costs are substantial, they are usually reflected in the price of the individual items. When the manufacturing costs of the individual items in the line do not vary significantly, a strategy of *averaging pricing* is often used. Thus, the same price is charged for each item in the line, even though the margins will differ somewhat. On the average, however, the manufacturer achieves the desired margin. The purpose of average pricing is to simplify pricing practices for the consumer and create an impression of comparable quality across the entire line.

Another strategy for price lines is sometimes referred to as *lead* pricing. In this strategy, the high volume items in the line carry relatively low manufacturer margins to gain distribution, facilitate consumer purchase, and develop consumer preference. The low volume or specialty items in the line are priced with substantial margins.

Odd Pricing

Odd pricing is most frequently used by retailers, although it may be used by manufacturers who preprice or print the price on the package. Odd pricing is based on the psychological concept that ninety-nine cents is, psychologically, much less than a dollar, or $1.79 is much less than $1.80. One manufacturer of private aircraft consistently suggested odd pricing for its airplanes: $19,990, instead of $20,000; $29,990 instead of $30,000.

Sales Promotion Pricing

In sales promotion pricing, a price discount is used to deplete inventories, sample consumers, and stimulate sales. This strategy is used by both manufacturers and retailers and involves a variety of price reductions: two-for-the-price-of-one sales, penny sales, various forms of multiple pricing, coupons, and so forth. *Loss leaders* are frequently used by retailers to attract customers. A loss leader is usually a high volume, frequently purchased item with an advertised price near, or below cost. The assumption is that loss leaders will attract customers to the store, and while the customers are there, they will buy other items at the regular price.

Bait Pricing

Bait pricing is usually used for hard goods and durable items. In this strategy, a stripped-down model is offered at an attractive, low price. When customers inquire about the bargain, salespeople will attempt to trade them up to a higher priced model with more features and a normal margin. Bait pricing is a defensible technique if customers are permitted to purchase the stripped-down model at the advertised price if they wish to. Often, however, unscrupulous retailers have no intention of selling the bargain and offer an excuse that they had only a limited number of the "sale" item and that those have all been sold.

Any or all of the foregoing pricing strategies may be used. Recognize, however, that pricing strategy is an integral part of the marketing plan and needs to be coordinated with all other elements of the marketing program through the strictures of the marketing plan.

A SUMMARY NOTE ON PRICING

Pricing remains one of the more ambiguous areas of marketing. It is surrounded by uncertainties—uncertainties over actual costs, uncertainties over future costs, uncertainties over competitive pricing plans, and uncertainties over consumer response.

Many studies have purported to show that price is a minor consideration in some product fields. Yet, most of these studies are seriously flawed because, under the conditions in which they were made, consumers had no meaningful price alternatives. As a result, there was no reason why price should be given as a consideration for purchasing.

In approaching the problem of pricing, marketers must deal, of course, with problems of cost, volume, profit, and competition. Nonetheless, they should not forget that price is a channel of communications with consumers, and many consumers do use price as a surrogate indicator, imputing higher quality to those brands carrying a higher price. In addition, consumers often view price as a symbol of status, and willingly pay higher prices for the perceived prestige that such purchases bring. For these reasons pricing decisions need to be made with the product concept clearly in mind, and with an eye on the market for which the product is intended.

SUMMARY

Economists and marketers alike have always recognized the complex relationship between profits, price, and other marketing variables, but the precise nature of this relationship is often ambiguous. As a result, pricing strategy is one of the more complex decisions in marketing.

Historically, economics was founded upon the interrelationship of supply and demand as mediated by the price merchanism. The intersection of the supply and demand curves represent the point of equilibrium, the point where supply equals demand. The point of equilibrium is not static, however, but a point around which supply and demand vary.

A basic concept in pricing is the concept of elasticity of demand. Each of the four basic forms of price elasticity (unitary elasticity, price elasticity and inelasticity, and negative elasticity), describes a different relationship between price, demand, and total income. Different products have different elasticities; the major factors influencing elasticity of demand are substitute products, complementary products, and proportion of income. Demand curves can shift. When a product becomes more desirable, the demand curve shifts to the right. Marketing is one of the factors that can cause demand curves to shift.

Traditionally, economics has emphasized the role of price. However, affluence and dramatic increases of production in the United States have changed the role of price in marketing in recent years, and given rise to the concept of symbolic pricing. In symbolic pricing, price is used as a symbol of the product's worth; its use has introduced more discretion in the setting of prices than has existed in the past.

Both marginal analysis and a derivation of it—break-even analysis—are used by management in determining price. Of the two, break-even analysis is more widely used because it is generally easier to apply in a competitive pricing situation.

Although many companies do not have well-defined pricing policies, most large companies tend to have general pricing policies which they tend to follow. Common pricing policies include target return on investment, target market shares, and matching competition.

The pricing strategies which companies employ include market skimming, penetration pricing, prestige and economy pricing, break–even pricing, multiple pricing, line pricing, odd pricing, sales promotion pricing, and bait pricing.

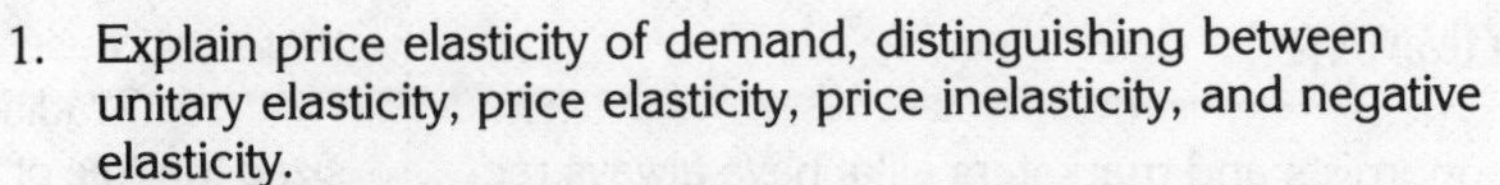

REVIEW QUESTIONS

1. Explain price elasticity of demand, distinguishing between unitary elasticity, price elasticity, price inelasticity, and negative elasticity.
2. Given the following demand schedule, compute the price elasticity index between $3.00 and $2.60. What type of elasticity does this represent?

Price	*Demand in Units*
$3.40	6,000
$3.00	6,500
$2.60	8,000
$2.20	10,000

3. Four variables—substitute products, complementary products, quantities purchased, and income—are said to have predictable effects on price elasticity. Explain each variable and indicate the effect of each on price elasticity.
4. Explain the historical, technical, and social reasons for economics' traditional emphasis on price.
5. Explain why symbolic pricing is an effective marketing tool.
6. Define each of the following terms: marginal analysis, marginal revenue, marginal cost, and point of maximum profit.
7. What are the limitations of marginal analysis?
8. Given the following information, compute the break-even point: selling price = $3.00; variable costs = $2.40; fixed costs = $200,000.
9. Explain why companies should have pricing policies, even though they don't always follow them.
10. Explain each of the following pricing strategies: market skimming, penetration pricing, market segmentation, prestige and economy pricing, break-even pricing, multiple pricing, line pricing, odd pricing, sales promotion pricing, and bait pricing.

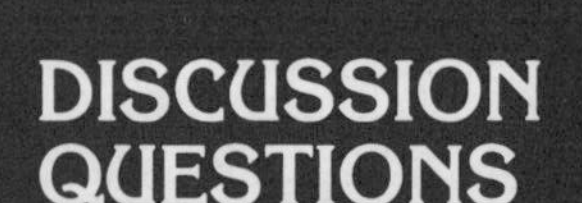

DISCUSSION QUESTIONS

1. In 1980 the market for American-made cars was depressed. Under traditional economic theory, this should have led to a decrease in prices for new American-made cars. Yet, major American auto makers increased the price of their cars over the previous year. Why do you think this was done?
2. Identify three products which you believe are price elastic and three products which you believe are price inelastic. How did you arrive at your selections?
3. Develop a price-demand schedule for a hypothetical brand. From this demand schedule, compute the points at which the index of elasticity is unitary, price elastic, and price inelastic. Would this same demand curve apply to other brands in the same product field? Why or why not?

4. The text states that there is probably no such thing as a true monopoly. Do you agree with this statement? If not, can you think of a true monopoly? What about public utilities, such as electric companies, water companies, natural gas companies, and telephone companies?
5. Visit a local supermarket and select several product fields, such as coffee, canned pears, saltine crackers. Identify the prices charged for three or four brands in each field. How do you account for the differences in prices which you encounter?

PRICING

The American Milling Company is a grocery products company that sells a line of flours and baking mixes through food stores. One of its products, a blueberry muffin mix, holds a 25 percent share of market in a field in which industry sales in 1980 were 2,243,912 cases. The blueberry muffin market is a relatively stable market growing at a rate of about 5 percent a year. The competitive structure of the market is:

	Market share
American Milling	25%
Brand A	26
Brand B	23
All other brands	26
Total	100%

Traditionally, blueberry muffin mixes contained freeze-dried blueberries which reconstituted when water was added to the mix. Although consumers appeared to be satisfied with the mixes on the market, producers of blueberry muffin mixes were aware that freeze-dried blueberries lost some of their flavor and texture in the preservation process.

In 1978 American Milling's research and development department began working on a process by which fresh blueberries could be introduced into the mix. By late 1979 the company had produced a product which, instead of using freeze-dried berries, contained a small plastic pouch of fresh blueberries, preserved in their own juice. In a test of 350 consumers 53 percent preferred the new mix, 35 percent preferred the present mix, and 12 percent had no preference.

The new mix cost about $0.075 more per package than the current formulation. Since normal retail margins for blueberry muffin mixes were 26 percent, this translated into a ten-cent difference in the price of the new product. Jane Knowles, the marketing director for American Milling, was concerned because a ten-cent increase at the retail level would price the new mix at over a dollar in a field where consumers were accustomed to paying $0.89 to $0.91. As a consequence, a price test on the new product was conducted in the fall of 1980.

Six test markets were selected. In three of these markets, the new mix was sold at a manufacturer's price of $8.61 for a case of twelve. In the other three markets, the new mix was sold at a manufacturer's price of $8.96 for a case of twelve. In the rest of the country, the old formulation was sold at an established price of $8.08. The three pricing structures are:

	Present Product ($8.08/case)	New product test markets ($8.61/case)	($8.96/case)
Consumer price	$0.9100	$0.9700	$1.0100
Retail margin (26%)	.2366	.2522	.2626
Manufacturer's selling price	.6734	.7178	.7474
Variable cost of goods	.4377	.5117	.5117
Gross margin	$ .2357	$ .2061	$ .2357

No additional advertising nor sales promotion was employed in the test markets, although advertising copy in the test markets was modified to emphasize "The only blueberry muffin mix with fresh blueberries." Market shares for the two groups of test markets, compared with the rest of the country were:

($8.08/case) Present Product	25.0%
($8.61/case) Markets	28.5%
($8.96/case) Markets	24.3%

After examining the test results, Jane Knowles prepared marketing recommendations for the blueberry muffin mix product for 1981. There were two basic questions she felt she must answer: (1) should the present mix be replaced with the new formulation in 1981? (2) if it should, how should the new mix be priced?

Other relevant data required to answer these questions:

Allocated fixed costs for plant and equipment	$ 460,000
Allocated sales expense and overhead	430,000
Advertising and sales promotion expense	680,000
Estimated total market for blueberry muffin mixes (cases)	2,335,000

Assignment

1. *Assuming market shares of 25 percent for the present product, 28.5 percent for the new product price at $8.61 per case, and 24.3 percent for the new product at $8.96 per case, what should she recommend?*
2. *Do you agree with the way in which test markets for the new product were structured? Why or why not?*

15

Channels of Distribution

- *Distribution channels in marketing.*
- *Channel arrangements used in modern marketing.*
- *Channel design and distribution achievement.*
- *Distribution systems management.*
- *Distribution strategies.*

MARKETING EXAMPLES

MICHELOB

For many years, Michelob, the premium of premium beers, was sold only in draught form. It was neither bottled nor canned because both required pasteurization or constant refrigeration. Pasteurization subtly changed the flavor of the product, and constant refrigeration was expensive, cumbersome, and difficult to control under conditions of mass distribution. So, Anheuser-Busch, the brewer of Michelob, opted for limited distribution in draught outlets. Bars and taverns were carefully chosen for distribution and rigorously controlled. Not only were rigid standards imposed concerning the handling of the product—its temperature had to be controlled within specified limits, the dispenser had to be cleaned on a periodic basis, and a keg had to be consumed within a specified time—but also the brewery imposed standards of cleanliness and appearance on dispensing outlets, as well as standards for the use of promotional material. In short, retailers of Michelob were selected and policed to guarantee the integrity of the product and to enhance the image of the brand.

The strategy of selling Michelob only in draught form was continued until technological developments made it possible to pasteurize the product without injuring the flavor. At that point, distribution strategy was broadened to include a bottled product. Still, control of outlets serving Michelob in draught form remained a strategic concern for Anheuser-Busch.

TUPPERWARE

Tupperware is a line of plastic containers used for the storage of food products. Tupperware has a unique method of closure that seals in odors and protects the contents being stored. The logical places to buy Tupperware products are grocery and variety stores. However, Tupperware had a problem. First, it was relatively expensive compared to competitive products already on the market. Second, its unique method of closure required demonstration to insure proper use, and an explanation in order to justify the price. Yet, demonstration and explanation are not a part of the service offered by normal self-service outlets.

Tupperware's management solved this problem by bypassing traditional outlets and selling directly to consumers through Tupperware parties held in consumers' homes—a method of distribution that has been referred to as "one of the shrewdest, most successful, and most high-powered sales operations in existence."[1]

CHANNEL CONFLICT

The marketing term, *making stores,* means to visit retail outlets to check up on selected products and brands that the stores distribute. When making such store visits, one usually checks distribution, prices, shelf-facings; looks for promotional material; and talks to store managers to get their impressions of how well the various brands are selling and to find out if they have any complaints.

One time I was making stores in New Orleans, checking on the sales of diet foods. In several stores, I noticed that Metracal, one of the leading brands, was not on the shelves of the diet food section where it should have been. So, I asked store managers whether they carried the brand. In every case, I received the same reply. "Yes, I carry it under the counter for customers who ask for it, but I don't display it." When I asked why, this was the response. "Metracal started out in drugstores, and received strong retail support. They owe their success to drugstores. After they became successful, they started selling in supermarkets which undercut drugstore prices and took most of the profit out of the brand. The only reason I didn't drop the brand entirely is because I have a few customers who always ask for Metracal, so I keep a few cans under the counter as a service to these customers. As

1. "Tupperware Parties Create a New Breed of Super Saleswoman," *The Wall Street Journal* (May 21, 1971): 1.

far as I am concerned, Metracal double-crossed drugstores when they started selling through supermarkets, and I'm not going to help that company any more than I have to."

Each of the foregoing examples provides a different insight into the complex problem of product distribution. Michelob represents an instance of selective distribution, used to protect the integrity of the product. Tupperware is an example of a manufacturer that set up its own method of distribution to give the brand a reasonable chance of success. Finally, Metracal is an example of a product whose maker offended an important segment of its channel system, with the subsequent loss of retail support and consumer sales.

Let's look at the concept of distribution channels more closely to gain a better understanding of its role in modern marketing.

AN OVERVIEW OF CHANNELS OF DISTRIBUTION

The variety of channel arrangements makes it difficult to formulate a simple universally applicable generalization about distribution channels. Some firms, particularly in industrial markets, distribute their products directly to their ultimate consumers. Most firms, however, employ one or more intermediaries to achieve this objective. A distribution channel definition is further complicated because it must account for four different activity flows: (1) *product flows,* or the actual, physical movement of the product itself, often referred to as *logistics;* (2) *title flows,* or the path followed by the title to, or ownership of, the product; (3) *negotiation flows,* or the path of negotiations accompanying the sale of the product; and (4) *information flows,* or the path of information regarding market needs.

A simplified diagram showing these four flows for a grocery product is shown in Figure 15–1. This diagram is simplified because it shows only the flows that relate to supermarket chains. This same producer may also employ food wholesalers to reach independent grocery stores, public warehousing in various parts of the country, and institutional distributors to reach institutional markets.

An examination of Figure 15–1 shows that each of the flows involves a somewhat different group of participants. This point becomes even clearer when the participants in each flow are isolated as has been done in Table 15–1.

In order to support the distribution system described in Figure 15–1, *facilitating* agencies are also required. Facilitating agencies are support organizations such as banks and other lending institutions; transportation systems, such as railroads and trucking lines; and communication specialists such as advertising agencies and public relations firms. These agencies provide the special services required to facilitate the distribution process.

Types of Channel Arrangements

Not all producers use the same type of channel arrangements. The particular channel arrangement employed depends both upon the resources and needs of the producer. Broadly speaking, four channel arrangements are commonly used in contemporary marketing: corporate channels,

FIGURE 15–1: *A Simplified Marketing Channel System Illustrating Four Flows*
SOURCE: Adapted from James Heskett, *Marketing* (New York: Macmillan Publishing Company, 1976), p. 268. Copyright © 1976 by James L. Heskett.

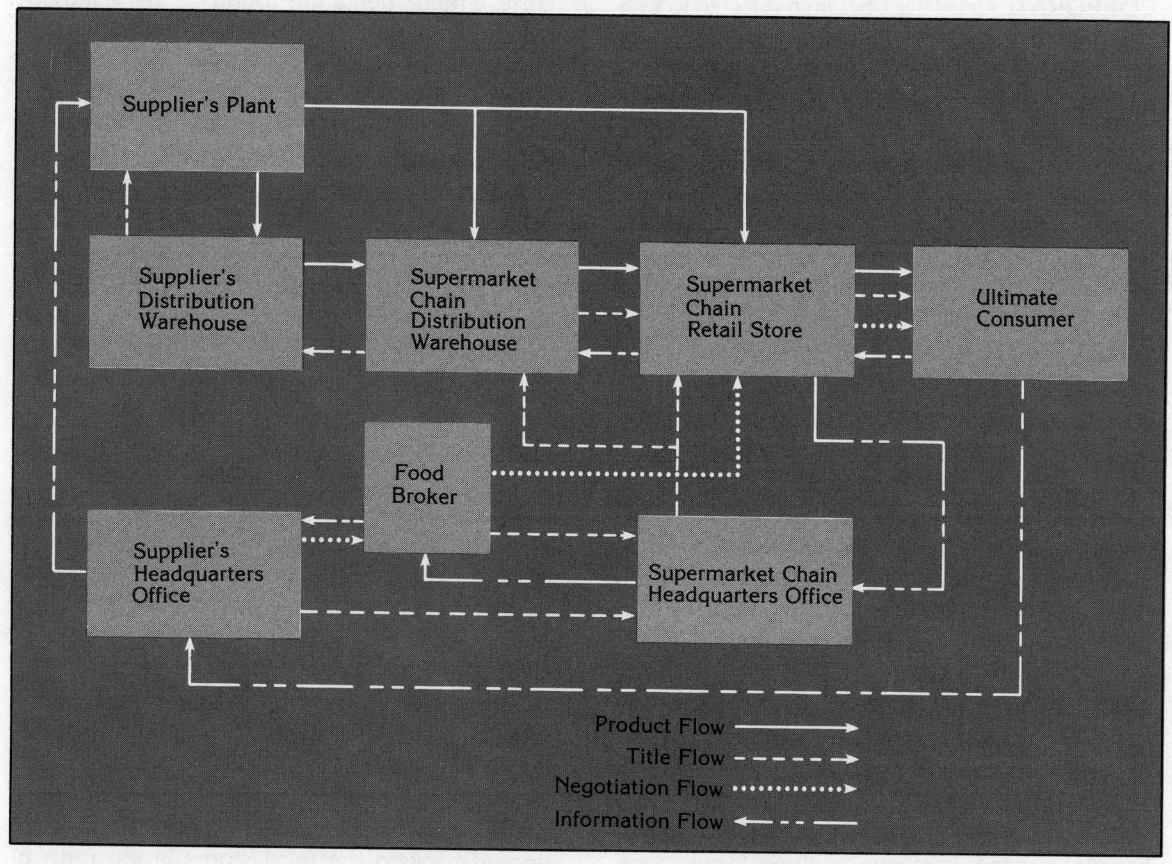

TABLE 15–1: *Channel Participants Related to Each Flow in the Distribution Chain.*

	Flow			
Participant	*Product*	*Title*	*Negotiation*	*Information*
Supplier's Plant	X			X
Supplier's Distribution Warehouse	X			X
Supplier's Headquarters Office		X	X	X
Food Broker			X	X
Supermarket Chain's Headquarters Office		X	X	X
Supermarket Chain's Distribution Warehouse	X	X		X
Supermarket Chain's Retail Store	X	X		X
Ultimate Consumer	X	X	X	X

contractual channels, independent channels, and mixed channels.

CORPORATE CHANNELS. Often referred to as a *corporate vertical marketing system,* this form of channel arrangement provides maximum control by producer organizations because it is characterized by producer ownership of the various stages of distribution. Thus, the producer controls the activity of the channel by virtue of ownership. Examples of corporate channels are Sherwin–Williams, which owns over two thousand paint stores; Hart, Schaffner & Marx, which owns over one hundred clothing outlets; the Delmar Corporation, a retail division of International Shoe which distributes the company's products; U.S. Steel which operates its own stores for distribution of oil field supplies; and major oil companies which own and operate service stations. Although corporate channels are widely used in some industries, corporate channels are not the best way to meet the distribution needs of many consumer products, and most producers do not have the resources to establish company-owned outlets.

CONTRACTUAL CHANNELS. Next in terms of producer control are *contractual vertical marketing* systems. In this type of channel arrangement, outright ownership is replaced by a contractual agreement which creates an integrated and more effective business entity. Contractual organizations commonly take one of three forms: franchises, voluntary organizations, and cooperatives.

Franchises. A franchise has been defined as an arrangement "whereby the franchisor—who has developed a pattern or format for a particular type of business—extends to franchisees the right to conduct such a business provided they follow the established pattern."[2] The franchisor commonly provides the name of the organization, the product or specifications for the product, architectural design of retail premises, record systems, management counsel, and advertising support. The franchisee commonly pays a fee for the franchise, provides capital for constructing the retail outlet, local management, and agrees to operate the franchise in accordance with procedures defined by the franchisor. Outstanding examples of franchise arrangements are found in the fast-foods industry and motel field, although franchise arrangements exist in other industries as well.

Voluntary Organizations. Voluntary organizations are characteristic of the grocery field, although they may exist in other fields as well. In the typical voluntary organization, a wholesaler executes a contractural agreement with independent retailers to supply their grocery needs at a price made possible by large quantity purchases, and to provide warehousing, delivery, and management counsel. In return, the retailers agree to buy a specified proportion of their merchandise from the wholesaler. An example of a voluntary organization is the Independent Grocers Alliance (IGA). Voluntary organizations emerged in the grocery field as an arrangement that enabled independent food stores to be price-competitive with chain grocery stores by providing them with the economies of quantity purchases, made possible by centralized buying.

Cooperative Organizations. Cooperative organizations are similar to, and serve the same function as voluntary organizations. The primary difference is that the wholesale firm is *cooperatively owned* by the independent retailers making up the cooperative, and the profits of the wholesale firm are passed back to the retail stores in the form of patronage refunds or credits on future purchases. Nonmembers of the cooperative are sometimes permitted to buy from the wholesale organization, but they do not participate in patronage refunds.

Independent Channels. A third form of channel arrangement may be referred to as independent channels. Independent channels consist of a loose affiliation of producers, wholesalers, and retail organizations that are independently owned and operate on the basis of short-term, minimal–condition contracts. Thus, a wholesaler or retailer may agree to distribute a producer's product, but may discontinue doing so at any time by simply failing to reorder. Most channel arrangements in the United States are of this type. This is the typical arrangement existing between producers and channel members in the grocery field, the drugstore field, department stores, appliance stores,

2. Edwin H. Lewis and Robert S. Hancock, *The Franchise System of Distribution* (Minneapolis: University Press, 1963), p. 8.

household furnishings, variety stores, lawn and garden supplies, and many other consumer product areas. In this channel arrangement, producers have the least control over the conditions under which their products are sold. Nonetheless, most producers use this form of distribution because it meets the distributional needs of their products, and it's the only form that they can afford.

Mixed Channels. Finally, many producers employ more than one of the foregoing channel arrangements. McDonald's uses franchisees, and also owns some of its outlets outright. Soft drink manufacturers franchise local bottlers to whom they sell syrup and for whom they provide advertising and sales promotion support. Yet, the local bottlers distribute through grocery, drug, and other retail outlets that are independent of both the syrup producer and the bottler. And, wholesaler–retailer groups (voluntary and cooperative arrangements) are a system within a system because they are independent of the producers whose products they handle.

With this background, let us now try to define what we mean by a channel system.

Channel of Distribution Defined

A channel of distribution may be defined as *a sequential arrangement of producer-owned and/or independent organizations established by producers to facilitate the sales of their products or services to the ultimate consumers.* Several key words in this definition should be noted:

- *System.* A channel of distribution is a system in the sense that it involves more than one interrelated firm and/or activities. Even a corporate channel, where the outlets are owned by the producer, has a sequence of interrelated activities.
- *Established by the producer.* Channel systems are established by producers. The firms making up the channel may already exist, but the channel system must be established by the producer through working agreements or formal contractual arrangements. The producer need not produce a physical product; it may produce services. Thus, in a voluntary wholesaler-retailer arrangement, the wholesaler is the producer of a service and is, therefore, a producer in the marketing sense.
- *Facilitate the sales of their products.* This implies that producers have specific objectives in mind when establishing a distribution channel. Namely, to sell their products.

When thinking of channels of distribution, most of us think of *middlemen,* and are often frustrated by their existence. We are frustrated because a product we pay ten dollars for at a retail store can often be purchased directly from the manufacturer for no more than four or five dollars. Thus, we resent middlemen as an unnecessary expense. Actually, they are an economy. Channels of distribution arise because they are *economically efficient* ways of moving goods from producers to consumers. Whenever a particular channel system, or a particular type of middleman becomes economically inefficient, it is replaced by system structures and channel firms that are economically efficient. Let's look more closely at the channel system to see why it is economically efficient.

CHANNEL SYSTEMS AND ECONOMIC EFFICIENCY

Channel systems are economically efficient for a number of reasons. Before we can understand these reasons, we need to introduce the concept of *product assortments.* Product assortments were suggested by Wroe Alderson as the underlying rationale for the development of channels of distribution.[3] *A product assortment is the array of products required by consumers to live a reasonably comfortable existence and to engage in normal human activities.* Product assortments include clothing, a variety of food items, house-

---

3. Wroe Alderson, "Factors Governing the Development of Marketing Channels," in Richard M. Clewett, *Marketing Channels for Manufactured Products* (Homewood, IL: Richard D. Irwin, 1954), pp. 5–22.

hold utensils, home furnishings, tools, vehicles for transportation, and so forth. Unfortunately, basic discrepancies occur because the products manufactured by business firms at their places of production, are required by individual consumers in various other locations. For example, a manufacturer may produce hundreds of thousands of shirts in a plant in Pennsylvania. Individual consumers throughout the United States may require only half a dozen shirts in their product assortments. Further, consumers do not buy their entire stock of shirts at one time. Instead, they usually buy one or two at a time. The problem becomes one of finding a way of balancing out the discrepancy between the hundreds of thousands of shirts manufactured by the producer and the one or two shirts demanded by each individual consumer. This problem centers around the issue of *contact efficiency*. Only a totally impractical and economically inefficient producer would individually contact the hundreds of thousands of consumers to sell shirts. The vision of such an operation is mind boggling. Order processing costs would be phenomenal, the shipping costs horrendous, the credit problems beyond coping with, and the burden on the postal system would destroy it. One solution might be for the manufacturer to establish thousands of geographically dispersed retail outlets (the beginning of a system of distribution), but no manufacturer could afford the financial outlay.

An alternative, then, is to distribute the shirts through independently owned and financed retail outlets. But there is still a problem of assortment discrepancies. Each store needs only a few dozen shirts, while the manufacturer still has hundreds of thousands to dispose of, and the cost to the manufacturer for contacting each individual store would be exhorbitant.

Now, to complicate the problem further. Rather than one manufacturer of shirts, there are dozens of them, each needing to contact the same retail stores. By way of example, let us assume that there are two dozen shirt manufacturers and twenty thousand retail stores. If each manufacturer contacted each retail store only once a year, 480,000 (24 × 20,000) contacts would be required—and each contact costs money. Now, we introduce a wholesaler into the distribution picture. Each manufacturer contacts the wholesaler once a year—a total of twenty-four contacts. The wholesaler contacts each retailer once a year—20,000 contacts. Thus, the total contacts necessary to reach all retail outlets is 20,024 (24 + 20,000), a substantial reduction from the 480,000 contacts required before the introduction of the wholesaler, and a substantial savings in cost. Figure 15–2 demonstrates this point on a much reduced scale. In Figure 15–2, only five shirt manufacturers and six retail stores are shown for demonstration purposes. From this figure, one can see graphically how the introduc-

FIGURE 15–2: *The Wholesaler's Role in the Channel of Distribution*

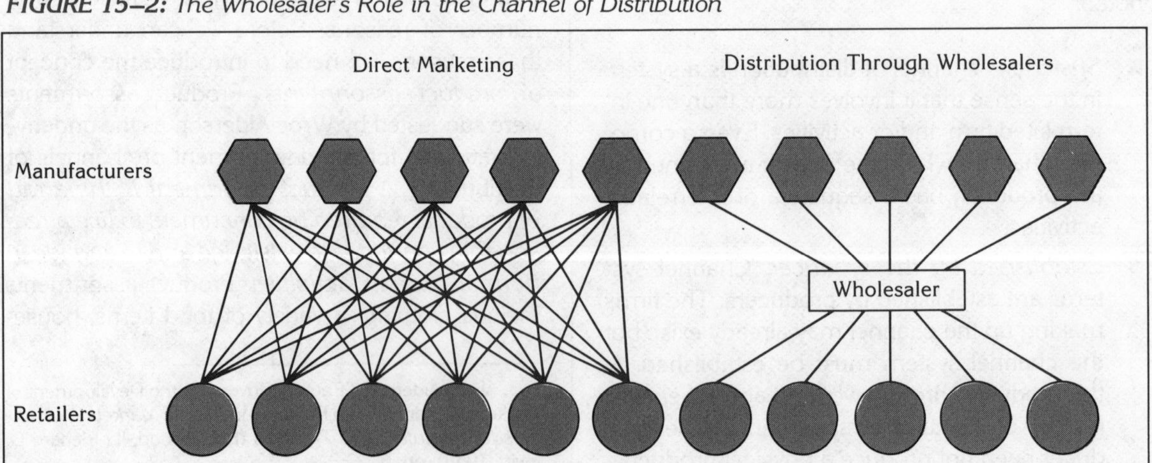

tion of a wholesaler into the channel system reduces the contacts required.

In the foregoing discussion, we have dealt with only one product—shirts. Yet, consumers need many products in their assortments. Thus, further efficiencies are introduced when individual retail stores handle a variety of related products, such as clothing items or food items or, as in the case of department stores, where thousands of products used by consumers are sold through a single retail outlet. Figure 15–3 shows how distribution efficiencies can be gained through channel intermediaries who handle related items. If a different wholesaler and/or different retailers were required for each item in Figure 15–3, the contacts and their related costs would increase enormously.

Contact efficiency is only one of the reasons for the development of distribution channels. In addition to reducing the contacts required, channel systems also provide for specialization, flow of marketing information, and consumer convenience.

Specialization

One of the secrets of mass production is specialization of labor. Specialization occurs when complex production tasks are broken down into relatively simple components, and these component tasks assigned to experts. The result is both an increase in production and a decrease in production costs.

The same principle applies to distribution. Distribution is a complex task that involves such component tasks as buying, selling, transferring of title, transportation, storage, order processing, promotion, and providing information. Further, these tasks are somewhat different at the various levels of distribution. The organizational structure and distribution specialists that may be appropriate for a wholesaling firm may not be most efficient for a retailing firm. Thus, by enabling different organizations in the distributional chain to concentrate on what they do best, a channel system can apply the principle of specialization to the distribution task.

Market Information

Producers are often far removed from the ultimate consumers of their products. This is particularly true when wholesalers, jobbers, and retailers are interposed between the producer and the ultimate consumer in the distribution chain. As a conse-

FIGURE 15–3: Distribution Efficiencies of Handling Related Items

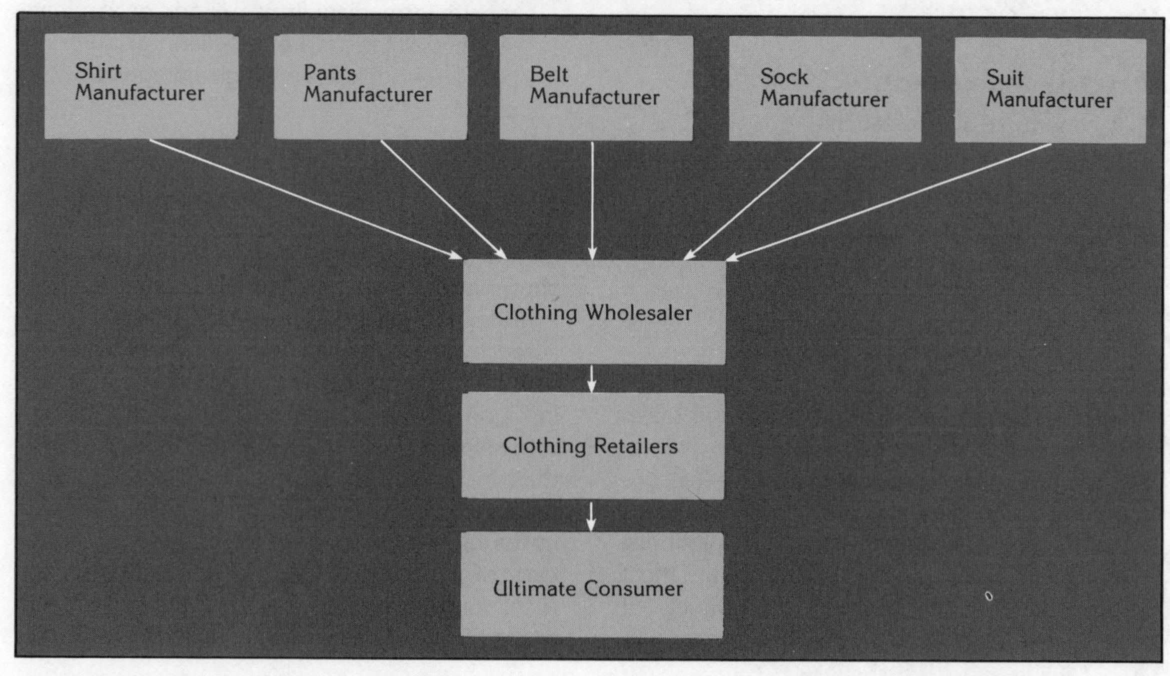

quence, the producer can easily lose touch with what is happening in the marketplace. One may attempt to compensate for this problem through periodic marketing research projects, but obtaining data from this source is often time consuming and expensive. Further, competitors may make changes in prices, discounts, packages, products, and promotion policies that the producer needs to know about immediately in order to take appropriate action. The channel system serves as an economical avenue through which such changes can be relayed to the producer with a minimal loss of time.

Consumer Convenience

Finally, the channel system provides convenience for the consumer. Buying all of your groceries from a single store is much easier and more economical than having to shop at dozens of small specialty outlets to obtain an assortment of foods. Having the products available at a neighborhood store is much more convenient and economical than traveling across town to make a purchase. And, the more convenient it is for consumers to buy a particular product or brand, the more likely they are to do so. In summary, the rationale behind the channel of distribution system rests on the concept of economic efficiency which manifests itself in four basic ways:

- Economy of contacts.
- Economy of specialization.
- Economy and speed in obtaining day-to-day marketing information.
- Economy and convenience for the consumer.

SYSTEMS OF DISTRIBUTION

A number of alternative distribution systems make products available to consumers. These alternatives range from direct mail and catalogue sales to complex distribution systems that involve a hierarchy of intermediary agents, wholesalers, jobbers, and retailers. Table 15–2 lists some of the most common intermediaries which, in a variety of combinations, constitute the distribution channels used by most manufacturers. Note that the functions performed by various intermediaries differ significantly. For example, an agent—who may be a broker, commission merchant, manufacturers' agent, selling agent, or resident buyer (depending upon the field)—negotiates purchases or sales or both, but does not take title to the goods. Remuneration is usually (but not always) in the form of commissions, and the agent may or may not carry out other marketing functions. By contrast, a full-service wholesaler, in addition to selling, also takes title to goods, provides warehousing, and may also engage in delivery, advertising, and sales promotion activities.

In examining Table 15–2 several points should be kept in mind.

- The field sounds much more complicated than it really is because the same type of operation may be called by different names in various industries.
- The range of services offered by a particular intermediary often varies, depending upon the marketing needs of the product or industrial field being served.
- The range of services provided by a particular intermediary is usually negotiable; in order to obtain the business of a desired producer, most intermediary firms will add or eliminate services at the drop of a dollar. For the most part, intermediaries are highly pragmatic people.

Figure 15–4 shows some of the possible distribution systems that are commonly used for industrial and consumer products. This figure shows distribution channels of different *lengths.* The length of a particular channel system is measured by the *stages* or intermediaries that exist between the producer and the ultimate consumer. In Figure 15–4, examples I-1 and C-1 represent zero stages because the producer sells directly to the consumer without using intermediaries. Direct mail and catalogue selling are the most common forms of zero stage distribution systems. In the case of industrial sales, zero stage systems are most frequently used in highly technical fields where the producers' sales representatives call on

TABLE 15–2: Definitions of Marketing Intermediates

SOURCE: Reprinted from *Marketing Definitions: A Glossary of Marketing Terms,* compiled by the Committee on Definitions of the American Marketing Association, Ralph S. Alexander, Chairman, published by the American Marketing Association.

Agent. A business unit which negotiates purchases or sales or both but does not take title to the goods in which it deals. The agent usually performs fewer marketing functions than does the merchant. He commonly receives his remuneration in the form of a commission or fee. He usually does not represent both buyer and seller in the same transaction. Examples are: broker, commission merchant, manufacturers agent, selling agent, and resident buyer.

Branch house (manufacturer's). An establishment maintained by a manufacturer, detached from the headquarters establishment and used primarily for the purpose of stocking, selling, delivering, and servicing his product. A branch office is similar, although it is limited to the last two functions.

Branch store. A subsidiary retailing business owned and operated at a separate location by an established store.

Broker. An agent who does not have direct physical control of the goods in which he deals but represents either buyer or seller in negotiating purchases or sales for his principal. The broker's powers as to prices and terms of sale are usually limited by his principal.

Commission house (sometimes called *Commission merchant*). An agent who usually exercises physical control over and negotiates the sale of the goods he handles. The commission house usually enjoys broader powers as to prices, methods, and terms of sale than does the broker, although it must obey instructions issued by the principal. It generally arranges delivery, extends necessary credit, collects, deducts its fees, and remits the balance to the principal.

Consumers' cooperative. A retail business owned and operated by ultimate consumers to purchase and distribute goods and services primarily to the membership; sometimes called *purchasing cooperatives.*

Dealer. A firm that buys and resells merchandise at either retail or wholesale.

Discount house. A retailing business unit featuring consumer durable items, competing on a basis of price appeal, and operating on a relatively low markup and with a minimum of customer service.

Distributor. In its general usage this term is synonymous with *wholesaler.*

Facilitating agencies in marketing. Those agencies which perform or assist in the performance of one or a number of the marketing functions, but which neither take title to goods nor negotiate purchases or sales. Common types are banks, railroads, storage warehouses, commodity exchanges, stock yards, insurance companies, graders and inspectors, advertising agencies, firms engaged in marketing research, cattle loan companies, furniture marts, and packers and shippers.

Industrial store. A retail store owned and operated by a company or governmental unit to sell primarily to its employees. Nongovernmental establishments of this type are often referred to as *company stores* or *commissary stores.* In certain trades the term *company store* is applied to a store through which a firm sells its own products, often together with those of other manufacturers, to the consumer market.

Jobber. This term is widely used as a synonym of *wholesaler* or *distributor.* The term is sometimes used in certain trades and localities to designate special types of wholesalers.

Mail-order house (retail). A retailing business that receives its orders primarily by mail or telephone, and generally offers its goods and services for sale from a catalog or other printed material.

Manufacturer's agent. An agent who generally operates on an extended contractual basis; often sells within an exclusive territory; handles noncompeting but related lines of goods; and possesses limited authority with regard to prices and terms of sale. He may be authorized to sell a definite portion of his principal's output.

Merchant. A business unit that buys, takes title to, and resells merchandise. The distinctive feature of this middleman lies in the fact that he takes title to the goods he handles. Wholesalers and retailers are the chief types of merchants.

Middleman. A business concern that specializes in performing operations or rendering services directly involved in the purchase and/or sale of goods in the process of their flow from producer to consumer. Middlemen are of the two types, merchants and agents. The essence of the middleman's operation lies in the fact that he plays an active and prominent part in the negotiations leading up to transactions of purchase and sale. This is what distinguishes him from a marketing facilitating agent who, while he performs certain marketing functions, participates only incidentally in negotiations of purchase and sale.

Rack jobber. A wholesaling business unit that markets specialized lines of merchandise to certain types of retail stores and also provides the special services of selective brand and item merchandising and arrangement, maintenance,

Table 15-2: Definitions of Marketing Intermediaries

and stocking of display racks. The rack jobber usually, but not always, puts his merchandise in the store of the retailer on consignment. Rack jobbers are most prevalent in the food business.

Resident buyer. An agent who specializes in buying on a fee or commission basis, chiefly for retailers.

Retailer. A merchant, or occasionally an agent, whose main business is selling directly to the ultimate consumer.

Selling agent. An agent who operates on an extended contractual basis, sells all of a specified line of merchandise or the entire output of his principal, and usually has full authority with regard to prices, terms, and other conditions of sale. He occasionally renders financial aid to his principal. This functionary is often called a *sales agent.*

Voluntary group. A group of retailers, each of whom owns and operates his own store and is associated with a wholesale organization or manufacturer to carry on joint merchandising activities, and who are characterized by some degree of group identity and uniformity of operation. Such joint activities have been largely of two kinds: cooperative advertising and group control of store operation.

Wholesaler. A business unit which buys and resells merchandise to retailers and other merchants and/or to industrial, institutional, and commercial users, but which does not sell in significant amounts to ultimate consumer. In the basic materials, semifinished-goods, and tool and machinery trades merchants of this type are commonly known as *distributors* or *supply houses.* Generally these merchants render a wide variety of services to their customers. Those who render all the services normally expected in the wholesale trade are known as *service wholesalers;* those who render only a few of the wholesale services are known as *limited-function wholesalers.* The latter group is composed mainly of cash-and-carry wholesalers who do not render the credit or delivery service; drop-shipment wholesalers, who sell for delivery by the producer direct to the buyer; truck wholesalers, who combine selling, delivery, and collection in one operation; and mail-order wholesalers, who perform the selling service entirely by mail.

their customers. By way of contrast, C-4 is a long distribution chain with four stages or intermediaries between the producer and consumer.

Multiple Channels of Distribution

Thus far, we have discussed distribution channels as though a particular producer would employ only one channel. This is, of course, unrealistic. In many product fields, making products available to consumers requires a variety of outlets. Consider cigarettes as an example. Cigarettes are sold through grocery stores, drugstores, filling stations, newstands, cigarette machines, motels, and other outlets too numerous to mention. Although this is an extreme example, other product fields also require different types of outlets to reach their potential consumers effectively. Expensive chocolates, for example, are sold through retail candy stores, drugstores, department stores, and airport gift shops. Tires are sold through auto supply stores, garages, service stations, tire dealers, department stores, discount houses, and general merchandise stores. Similar observations can be made about magazines, phonograph records, and many other consumer and industrial products. No single distribution channel is capable of reaching all of the retail outlets requiring these products. As a consequence, producers often use multiple channels in their distribution systems.

FIGURE 15–4: Channels of Distribution for Industrial and Consumer Products

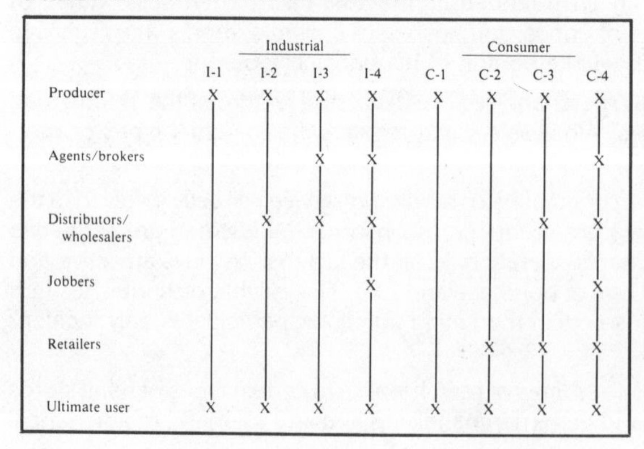

Figures 15–5 and 15–6 show the channel systems used for magazines, paperback books, and phonograph records, and Figure 15–7 the channel system used by a manufacturer of electrical wire and cable. The channel systems for these products illustrate that: (1) each is fairly complex, although some are more complex than others; (2) each product requires a variety of channel intermediaries to reach the ultimate cus-

tomers of the products involved; and (3) each system is different. Even producers in the same product field often use different channel intermediaries in their channel systems. For example, in the cosmetics field, Avon sells through individual representatives who call on customers in their homes; Merle Norman sells through its own specialty shops; and Revlon distributes widely through drug and grocery outlets. Differences such as these raise the question of channel design.

DESIGNING CHANNELS AND OBTAINING DISTRIBUTION

Often, when we speak of distribution, we think solely of product availability. However, availability is only one dimension of the distribution system. Practically, the distribution system serves four distinct functions in marketing.

- As a mechanism for making a product available to those consumers for whom it is intended.
- As a symbolic communication of product worth.
- As a guarantor of satisfaction and customer service.
- As an invaluable sales tool for those products where the need for product demonstration and personal selling repudiate the possibility of self service.[4]

When planning distribution, these four strategic functions must be kept in mind. Only the first of these functions deals solely with product availability; the other three are concerned with the type of retail outlets employed for consumer goods. These same strategic considerations apply to industrial products, and determine whether one uses an industrial distributor or a corporate sales force for contacting customers, as well as the qualification and training of the sales force itself.

The type of distribution is more important for some products than for others because the amount of service and personal selling required varies by product. For example, the first function of distribution (product availability) is often the only essential requirement for low—priced, mass-distributed packaged goods such as cigarettes and soft drinks. By contrast, all four functions of distribution are important for a variety of high-priced, luxury goods, ranging from automobiles to carpeting. Similar considerations also apply to industrial goods.

Major Considerations in Designing Systems

Avon distributes its line of cosmetics through individual representatives who call on customers in their homes while Revlon distributes through drug and grocery stores. Exxon sells gasoline through its own service stations. Procter & Gamble uses company salespeople to call on grocery chains and wholesalers. Ralston Purina employs food brokers for this purpose. Why these differences? Because a number of considerations influence the selection of distribution channels. Let's identify and examine some of these considerations.

CONSUMER CONSIDERATIONS. The overriding consideration in choosing a particular channel system is its ability to reach the product's target market. If the number of potential customers is large, and they are widely dispersed geographically, many channel intermediaries are usually required. Cigarettes, gum, and candy bars are examples of this requirement. Similarly, if users typically purchase in small quantities, a variety of intermediaries is usually necessary. Conversely, if the number of potential customers is relatively small, direct marketing may be more efficient. For example, many marketers of hobby and craft products rely wholly upon catalogues which are distributed by mail to potential customers on selective mailing lists.

PRODUCT CONSIDERATIONS. Product characteristics are another major variable influencing

4. Generally, when marketing texts talk about the *functions* of distribution, they speak of specific marketing activities such as buying, selling, warehousing, transportation, advertising, and so forth. Although I recognize the essentiality of all of these activities, and the complexities involved in properly coordinating them throughout the channel system, thinking of the *true* functions of distribution in a broader, more strategic sense is more helpful. For this reason I have taken the point of view that I have in the text.

FIGURE 15–5: Marketing Channels for Magazines and Paperback Books
SOURCE: Edwin H. Lewis, "Description and Comparison of Channels of Distribution," in *Handbook of Modern Marketing,* ed. Victor P. Buell (New York: McGraw-Hill Book Company, 1970), pp. 4–6.

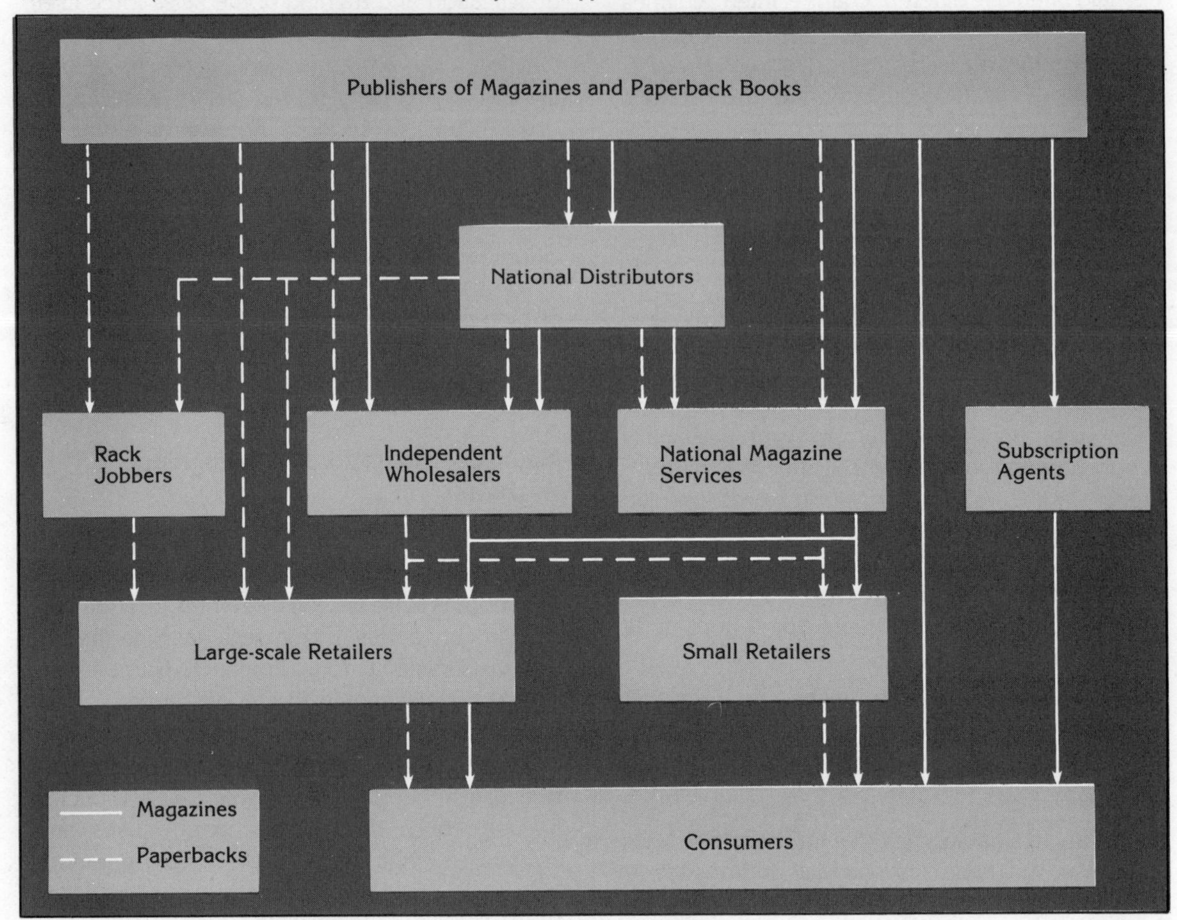

channel design. Frozen foods, for example, must use channel systems that have refrigerated facilities. Highly perishable products, such as milk, require short channels and frequent delivery. Coors beer is a product which requires a different channel system than competitive beers. Unlike most beers, Coors is not pasteurized and, therefore, has a shorter shelf life. As a consequence, Coors requires refrigerated warehousing and transportation facilities, and a closer control of inventories than competitive products.

Products positioned as high-style or exclusive generally avoid mass distribution outlets and concentrate their retail distribution in retail stores whose images are compatible with those projected by the brands in question.

CONTROL CONSIDERATIONS. Some products and services require greater control by the producer at the point of sale than do others. For example, motel chains such as Holiday Inn and fast-foods operations such as McDonald's demand rigid controls at the point of sale to guarantee the integrity of the products or services being offered. Since control is easier with short channels of distribution than with long ones, these organizations have opted for franchise arrangements, or outright corporate ownership of their outlets.

FINANCIAL CONSIDERATIONS. Regardless of other considerations, the channel system must be affordable. Generally, the greater the financial resources of the producing firms, the more options they have in establishing their channel systems. A

FIGURE 15–6: *Marketing Channels for Phonograph Records*
SOURCE: Edwin H. Lewis, "Description and Comparison of Channels of Distribution," in *Handbook of Modern Marketing*, ed. Victor P. Buell (New York: McGraw-Hill Book Company, 1970), pp. 4–7.

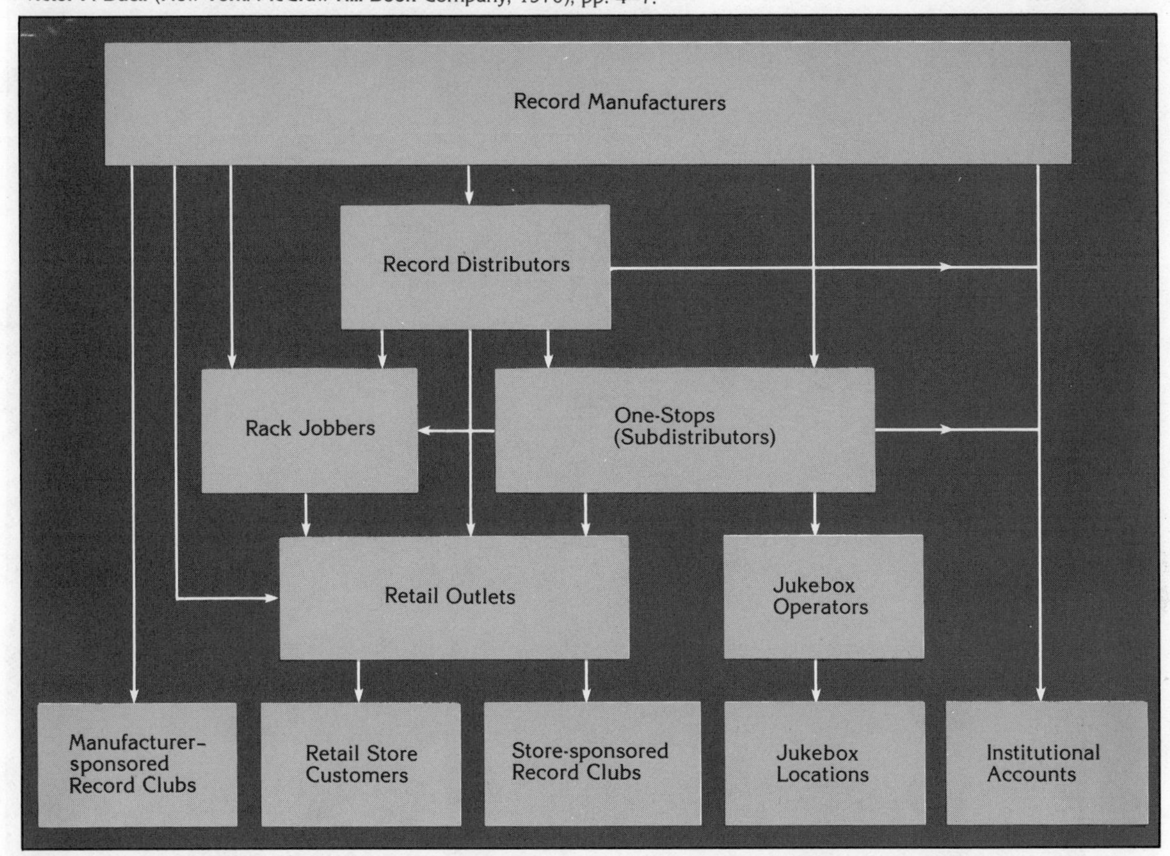

firm with few resources may be limited to using existing distribution structures, whereas a firm with substantial financial assets may bypass some established channel functionaries to gain greater control or efficiency. Thus, as noted earlier, some producers establish corporate-owned retail stores, while competitors with fewer resources must use independent channels. Some producers employ sizable sales forces, while others must rely on agents or brokers who serve their product fields.

ENVIRONMENTAL CONSIDERATIONS. In many well established fields limited options are available to producers. The producers of most grocery items, for example, must use chain grocery stores and voluntary and cooperative retail groups if they expect to generate substantial sales. Any other course of action will limit potential sales significantly. In some instances, particularly in intensely competitive fields, producers are unable to persuade established retailers to carry their products. Sometimes, these producers bypass established channels by developing other outlet types. For example, Russell Stover overcame problems in obtaining drugstore distribution for its fancy chocolates by using retail candy stores and leased sales areas in department stores. Other producers sell directly to consumers through direct mail or company sales agents. In still other cases, producers simply go out of business.

The foregoing variables are only some of the factors that influence channel design. Others are the need for credit, for demonstration, for follow-up service, and for personal selling. The point is that companies are not totally free in designing their distribution systems. They are surrounded by constraints. Often, companies are

FIGURE 15–7: *Marketing Channels of a Manufacturer of Electrical Wire and Cable*
SOURCE: From *Marketing Electrical Apparatus and Supplies* by Edwin H. Lewis, p. 215. ©1961 by McGraw-Hill, Inc. **Used with** permission of McGraw-Hill Book Company.

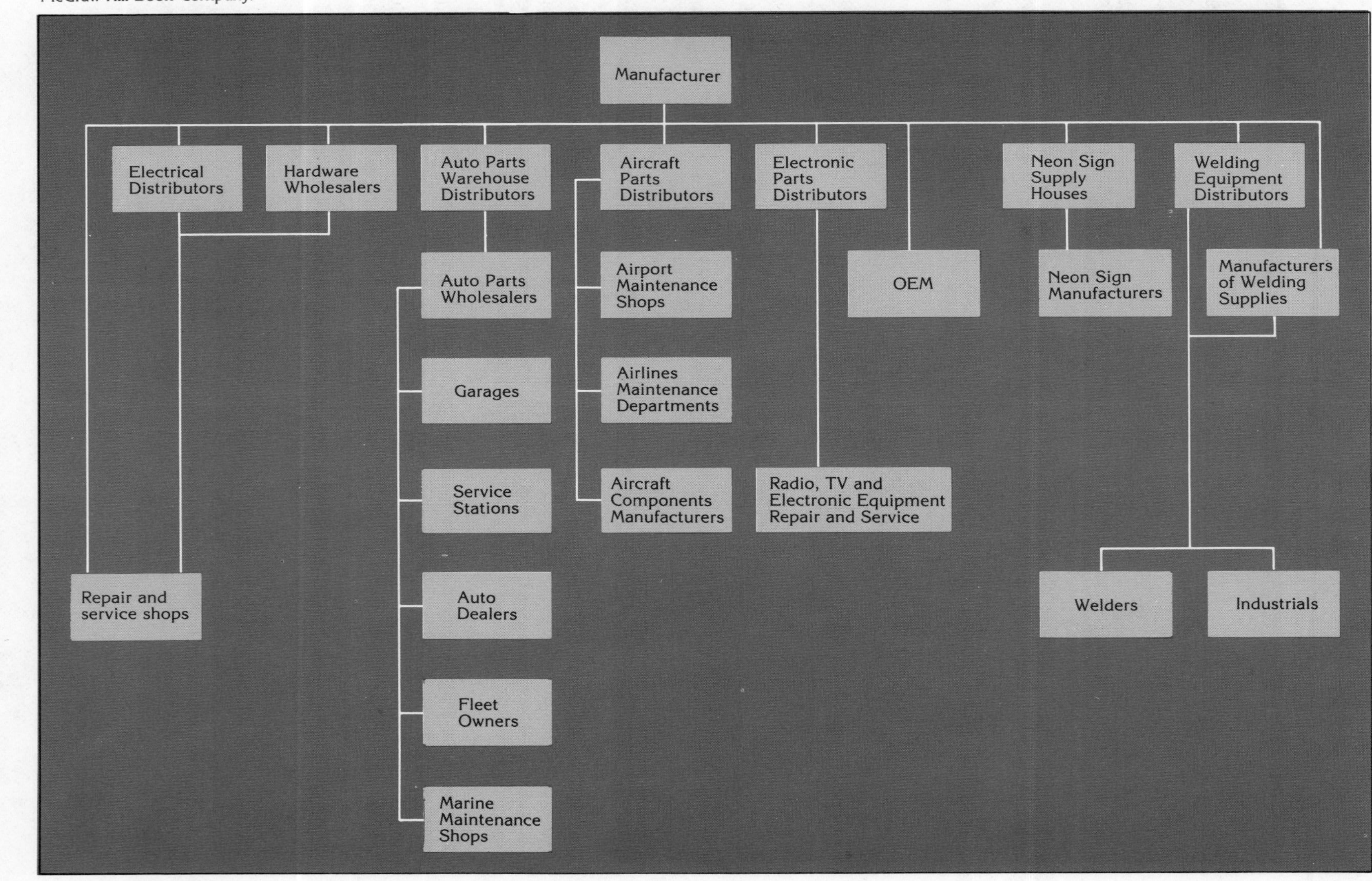

Door to door selling—for some products it pays well. (Photo courtesy of Avon Products, Inc.)

unable to do what they would prefer to do, and trade-offs have to be made. Designing distribution channels is often a complex task, and one that is not always completed successfully.

Obtaining Distribution

Designing a distribution system and obtaining distribution are two different problems. Designing a channel system is often a piece of cake compared to obtaining and keeping the distribution process together. This is true because the decision to stock a brand in established outlets is made, not by the producer, but by retail management. Further, shelf space is limited, and retail management is often reluctant to take on new products which increase its inventory and complicate its billing. In the grocery field, for example, a major supermarket may carry fourteen thousand different items, including different package sizes, brands, and flavors. Each week, store management will be offered as many as one hundred new items—five thousand a year. Since shelf space is not elastic, the addition of a new product requires some adjustment in existing stocks. Either the shelf facings on existing products must be reduced, or items must be discontinued. Reduction in the shelf facings is often uneconomical from the retailers's point of view because it increases stocking costs and the danger of out-of-stock. Consequently, when a new brand is added, an existing brand often must be dropped from inventory. A similar situation exists in other retail fields such as drugstores, hardware stores, department stores, variety stores and clothing stores. The difficulty of obtaining distribution often causes producers to opt for an independent distribution system, bypassing conventional channels. For most marketers of consumer products, however, producer controlled outlets are not feasible because the costs are high and the distribution they afford is too limited. As a consequence, the retail outlet ultimately determines what brands are and are not available to consumers.

The primary responsibility for obtaining and servicing distribution lies with the sales force. As a consequence, good trade relations are a priceless asset in sales effectiveness. In addition, sales presentations are designed to magnify the profit potential for the retailer stocking the brand, and advertising schedules are carefully explained (merchandised) to buyers. For maximum effectiveness, these activities are also supplemented by other marketing activities, such as trade magazine advertising, stocking allowances (price discounts for all initial purchases), display allowances, and advertising allowances. Heavy consumer advertising, consumer coupons, and other consumer promotions are often scheduled to pressure retailers into stocking a particular brand. A classic use of consumer pressure was related to me several years ago by a buyer for a major grocery chain in Chicago. According to this buyer:

> One day this nondescript little guy came in and wanted me to stock a new liquid cleaner called Lestoil. I hadn't heard of the brand nor the company, and wasn't very interested be-

cause we had shelves full of cleaning products of every size, shape, and description. When he finished his sales call, he left me his calling card which I casually tossed in my desk drawer only because I didn't want to hurt his feelings by throwing it in the wastebasket.

About three weeks later, Lestoil hit Chicago. And I do mean *hit.* It was a blitz! I think they used every newspaper, TV, and radio station in the market with heavy schedules. My telephone went wild with calls from our store managers saying that consumers were demanding the stuff. I tore my desk apart trying to find that damn calling card.

Although massive efforts like that of Lestoil are common in the food and drug trade, more modest efforts may also be successful. Pet-Ritz, for example, was having trouble getting distribution of its frozen pies in A&P stores in key markets where A&P was an important factor. A marketing strategy was designed to bring selective pressure against A&P. Pet-Ritz advertising, containing a coupon, was scheduled in *Woman's Day,* a women's service magazine sold only through A&P stores. Consumer coupons were also mailed to selected residential areas surrounding A&P outlets. This activity was merchandised or "sold" by Pet-Ritz food brokers in their calls upon A&P regional buying offices. The program accomplished its purpose in a number of key markets.

The point is that, since distribution is often difficult to obtain, marketing activities sometimes must be coordinated to achieve distribution goals. And, the marketing plan is the instrument of this coordination.

MANAGING DISTRIBUTION SYSTEMS

The problems of a producer do not end when a channel system is designed and distribution obtained. Instead, they often just begin. This is true because channel member performance must be managed carefully if the system is to operate effectively. Three aspects of channel management will be discussed in this section: conflicts in channel relationships, evaluating channel members, and modifying channel structures.

Conflicts in Channel Relationships

Cooperation is the dominant theme in channel systems because channel members join forces to foster their mutual interests in increasing sales and enhancing profits. However, few channel systems do not also manifest elements of conflict. Two types of conflict that often crop up in the channel system are vertical and horizontal conflict.

VERTICAL CONFLICT. Vertical conflict occurs between two channel members at different levels in the distribution system; for example, between producers and retailers. One reason that such conflicts are almost inevitable is that producers and retailers have different goals. For example:

Producers are interested in:	Retailers are interested in:
Multiple distribution	Exclusive distribution
Sales of their brands	Sales in their stores
Producers' profits	Retail profits
Display of their brands	Display of the most profitable items
Consumer loyalty to their brands	Consumer loyalty to their stores

Often, producers must display flexibility and imagination to resolve vertical conflicts amicably. For example, franchised dealers in one sales region refused to cooperate with the advertising and sales promotion programs developed by a farm equipment producer. The dealers did not believe these programs were effective, and felt the programs required too much effort on their part. The equipment producer could have insisted upon compliance by threatening to cancel the franchises of dealers who refused to cooperate. At best, however, this approach would have evoked half-hearted cooperation and encouraged a variety of subtle forms of sabotage. Instead, the producer established an Advertising and Promotion Advisory Board consisting of leading dealers in the region. This board was encouraged to suggest advertising and promotion ideas, and given authority to approve or disapprove suggestions of the manufacturer. The board was so successful that the producer extended the idea to other regions.

HORIZONTAL CONFLICT. Horizontal conflicts occur between members on the same level of the distribution chain. For example, department stores were threatening to discontinue a line of vacuum sweepers because the same sweepers were also sold through discount stores at lower prices. The producer resolved the conflict by producing a separate line of sweepers for the discount outlets. The major difference between the department store line and the discount store line was a cosmetic one—the department store line carried a strip of chrome across the face of the sweeper head and was given a different model number. This insignificant change enabled department store salespeople to justify their higher prices by pointing out to consumers that they carried the "top of the line" model. Since channel conflicts are inevitable, the burden is often on the producer to establish and enforce clear and equitable policies for all channel members, and to be sensitive to incipient problems, resolving them before they get out of hand.

Evaluating Channel Members

Evaluation of channel member performance is a continuing task for producers. When performance falls short of expectations, a producer should identify the cause for channel failure, and determine appropriate remedial action. Evaluation always involves three steps: (1) definition of performance standards; (2) measurement of performance against these standards; and (3) determination of the action to be taken.

Without clear standards of performance, evaluation is not possible. Further, performance standards must be understood and agreed upon by all parties to avoid future conflicts. The kinds of standards defined will depend upon the level of distribution involved. For example, when dealing with wholesalers or industrial distributors, standards may include quotas, frequency and depth of customer coverage, inventory levels, delivery time, treatment of damaged and lost goods, methods of billing, geographic areas of operation, participation in training programs, specific services to customers, and inventory adjustments for price and model changes. Some of the foregoing standards—such as geographic areas of coverage, billing procedures, average inventory levels, treatment of damaged goods and so forth—are long-term and will be spelled out in the initial producer–distributor agreement. Others, such as sales goals, frequency and depth of coverage, and special customer services may vary by marketing period, and often must be renegotiated annually.

In dealing with retailers, the standards of performance are usually less comprehensive, and may involve little more than agreement by retailers to carry the producer's product; agreements on damaged or lost goods and billing procedures; and protection for price or model changes. Of course, standards of performance must be realistic in terms of the nature of the relationship.

The third step in the evaluation process is to determine the action to be taken when performance falls below standards in one or more areas. Here, the producer should identify the underlying cause of the problem and take appropriate remedial action. In some cases, the producer–middleman relationship may be terminated, although this is usually an action of last resort. In other instances, negative sanctions short of termination may be used. Sometimes, depending upon the situation, more effective ways of motivating inadequate performers may be sought.

Most producers prefer to continue middlemen relationships unless they have reasonable alternatives. The reason for this is that good middlemen are hard to find, and instituting a search for replacements and developing an effective new relationship is often time consuming and expensive. In addition to purely economic reasons, producers often develop close, personal relationships with members of their channel systems, and will strive to preserve these relationships.

For example, an appliance dealer with whom General Electric had enjoyed a long-term, successful relationship began falling far short of past performance. Investigation by General Electric revealed that the owner of the dealership was seriously ill, and uncertain if he would ever be able to resume active management of his firm. General Electric could have discontinued the dealership. Instead, GE gave one of their key appliance salesmen an indefinite leave of absence, and guaranteed his income, while he managed the dealership during the owner's illness. In this particular instance, the owner recovered his health in about a year, the dealership was returned to his management, and the General Electric salesman returned to GE.

Modifying Channel Structures

Although channel systems are generally thought of as relatively long-term relationships, marketing conditions change. New uses are found for existing products, consumers change their buying practices, producers add products to their lines that require new channel structures, and new outlets come into existence. The growth of food chains, for example, changed the complexion of food wholesaling in the United States. As chain stores grew in size and importance, they started bypassing wholesalers and buying directly from producers. Many traditional food wholesalers were unable to compete, and went out of business. Other, more innovative independent wholesalers, broadened their services and established voluntary wholesaler-retailer chains. In still other instances, independent grocery stores formed wholesaler-retailer cooperatives.

Changes in retailing have been even more dramatic than changes in wholesaling. The history of retailing is a history of change. Department stores came into existence in the mid–1880s. They have been followed by mail-order houses; chain store organizations; supermarkets; variety stores; suburban shopping centers; discount houses; automatic vending; fast-food outlets; neighborhood convenience stores; specialty stores and boutiques; door-to-door selling; catalogue stores; and warehouse outlets for carpeting, appliances, clothing, food, electronic equipment, and other products.

In the face of such changes, channel systems must constantly be monitored to make sure that they are still serving the target markets which they were established to serve. Often, they are not. A case in point is the channel system for wood flush doors.[5] Traditionally, the market had been served by wholesalers who accounted for some 95 percent of the wood flush door business, and who distributed to retailers, contractors, and industrial component and home builders. Figure 15–8 depicts the traditional channel system. This system emerged when only wholesalers were large enough to order carload lots, the normal lot size shipped by building supply manufacturers.

Over a period of time, the market changed. The appearance of major industrialized home builders, major component builders, and large chain retail lumberyards forced changes in the structure of distribution. These changes are reflected in Figure 15–9. Building supply manufacturers who failed to recognize these changes in the structure of distribution, and to modify their channel systems accordingly, would be courting financial disaster.

5. William G. Brown and E. D. Reiten, "Auditing Distribution Channels," *Journal of Marketing* (July, 1978): 38–42.

DISTRIBUTION STRATEGY

The particular distribution system used by a firm depends on the nature of the markets being served, the types of products involved, and the resources of the producer. Generally, three distribution strategies are available in the consumer field: intensive, selective, and independent distribution.

Intensive Distribution

In intensive distribution, the marketer seeks widespread availability of the brand, often using multiple channels. Intensive distribution is generally appropriate for *convenience* goods. Cigarettes, candy, and soft drinks are commonplace examples of an intensive distribution strategy; these products are found in grocery stores, drugstores, eating and drinking establishments, and in vending machines—a modern American art form that graces most public and many private establishments.

Many, if not most, of the products sold through food and drug outlets fall within the convenience goods classification. For these brands, the type of distribution is relatively less important than widespread availability. Even in these instances, however, intensity is sometimes sacri-

FIGURE 15–8: *Historical Channel Arrangement: Wood Flush Door Suppliers*
SOURCE: William G. Brown and E. D. Reiten, "Auditing Distribution Channels," *Journal of Marketing* (July, 1978): 41.

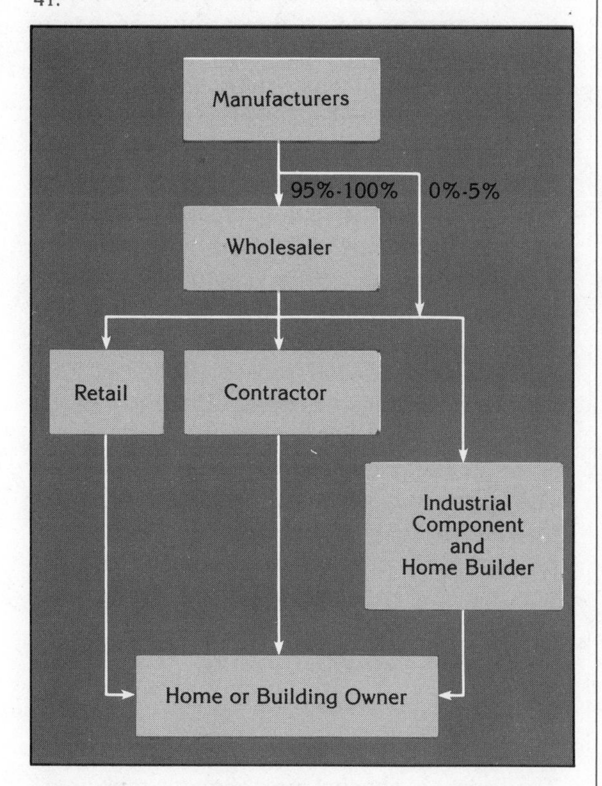

FIGURE 15–9: *Current Channel Arrangement: Wood Flush Door Suppliers*
SOURCE: William G. Brown and E. D. Reiten, "Auditing Distribution Channels," *Journal of Marketing* (July, 1978): 41.

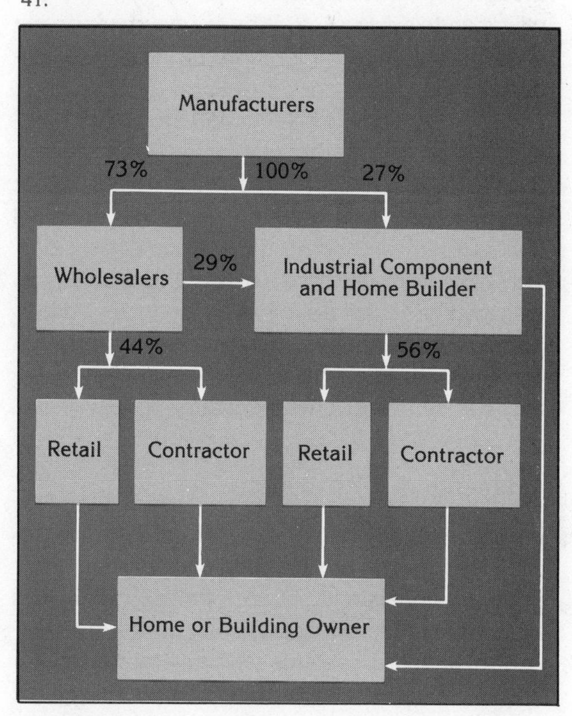

ficed for other considerations. For example, a product which has a relatively short shelf life may be distributed only in outlets that have high volume turnover to protect product freshness. Or, a particular brand that is attempting to project a "clinical" or "prescription" image may adopt a strategy of restricting distribution to drugstores and use this strategy as a device for enlisting the support of registered pharmacists and medical doctors. This strategy, in fact, was followed by Coricidin for years. It was also the initial distribution strategy of Contac.

Multiple channels of distribution are often necessary to reach different segments of the same market. Fancy chocolates are a case in point. Fancy chocolates are generally sold through specialty candy shops, department stores, and drugstores. However, many consumers reject "drugstore" candy as inferior or stale and insist on buying candy elsewhere. So, for market coverage, drugstores need to be supplemented with other forms of distribution. Interestingly enough, attempts to sell fancy chocolates in food stores have been unsuccessful, even though many food store customers also buy fancy chocolates. Apparently, consumers believe food stores symbolize "window box" or inexpensive candies and are an inappropriate source for expensive chocolates.

Selective Distribution

In a selective distribution strategy, the producer does not seek intensive distribution but elects instead to distribute through a limited number of outlets that complement the brand image and/or provide personal selling and customer service. This distribution strategy is often critical for *shopping* and *specialty* goods where the images of the retail outlets themselves may have a profound effect on the consumer's perception of the brand. For example, a television set that has a marketing emphasis on stylish design, quality performance, and prompt customer service will probably not be sold in an automobile accessories store, even though such a store may be appropriate for more utilitarian television sets. Why? Consumers do not shop for stylish furniture in automobile accessories stores.

Similarly, clothing and household furnishings producers that rely on high style, expensiveness, and snob appeal as selling points cannot afford to have their products distributed by retail outlets that do not reflect these same dimensions. The consumer does not expect to find a flawless diamond at K-Mart or Yellow Front and is likely to be suspicious if these outlets purport to carry such items. On the other hand, one does not go to Tiffany's in search of cheap costume jewelry.

Independent Distribution

Independent distribution is a form of selective distribution in which producers bypass existing distribution channels and set up a private distribution system that meets their particular needs. Independent distribution systems take several forms.

Direct mail and catalogue selling are particularly appropriate for infrequently purchased specialty items with buyers widely but thinly dispersed throughout the general population. A great deal of hobby equipment and supplies is sold in this way, although this approach has also been used by clothing manufacturers, producers of gift cheeses, and book publishers to avoid the cost and difficulty of obtaining distribution through conventional channels. A relatively recent development in catalogue sales is the offering of a wide variety of nationally advertised brands of durable and semidurable goods at substantial price reductions.

Direct sales agents are used by firms to sell directly to consumers on a door-to-door basis. Avon has successfully used this approach for cosmetics; the Fuller Brush Company was a pioneer in this field; and Tupperware has developed in–home selling into an art.

Company owned stores often sell a particular manufacturer's brands exclusively, although they may also distribute noncompetitive items for other manufacturers. The Delmar Corporation, the retail division of International Shoe, uses this strategy, as do the tire industry and major oil companies.

Franchise distribution uses independent entrepreneurs to make products or services available to consumers. Under the franchise system, the parent company executes an exclusive agreement with independent business people. The parent company generally provides a protected geographic area, technical service, and managerial help in return for compliance with company standards and capital to establish the local outlet. Long used by automobile manufacturers, in recent years this strategy has found favor in the tourism industry (Holiday Inns, Travelodge, Motel-6), and in food service (Kentucky Fried Chicken, McDonald's, Baskin-Robbins, Burger Chef) as well as other industries.

The primary advantages of independent distribution are: guaranteed maximum control by the manufacturer at the sacrifice of widespread product availability; and an alternative for products that have been rejected, or are unsuitable for established channel systems.

SUMMARY

The variety of channel arrangements make it difficult to formulate a simple generalization about distribution channels. Some producers distribute their products directly to their ultimate consumers while others employ intermediaries. Not all producers use the same types of channel arrangements. Four channel arrangements are commonly used in contemporary marketing: corporate, contractual, independent, and mixed channels. In recognition of the variety of forms that channel arrangements can take, a channel of distribution may be defined as a sequential arrangement of producer-owned and/or independent organizations established by producers to facilitate the sales of their products and services to the ultimate consumer.

Although many of us think of channel intermediaries as being an unnecessary expense, channels exist because they are economically efficient. The economies of channels of distribution manifest themselves in four ways: economy of

Distribution is getting the product to consumers where they want it and when they want it. (Photo by Freda Leinwand)

contacts, economies of specialization, economy and speed in obtaining marketing information, and economy and convenience for consumers.

Many different intermediary organizations may make up a channel system, each performs somewhat different tasks. Channel systems differ in length, or the intermediaries between the producer and the ultimate consumer, and in their complexity—that is, the number of different channels required. Many producers use multiple channel systems to cover the diversity of retail outlets required to make their products available to consumers.

A channel of distribution serves four basic functions: as a mechanism for making products available to consumers; as a symbolic communication of product worth; as a guarantor of satisfaction and consumer service; and as a sales tool for those products that require personal selling at the retail level. Not all of these functions are necessary for all products; channel systems should be designed to provide only those functions necessary for the specific product. Major considerations in designing channel systems include: consumer needs; product requirements; the need for producer control; and environmental factors.

Designing channel systems and obtaining distribution are two different problems because producers must persuade channel intermediaries to distribute their products. After a channel system has been established, the producer faces the problem of managing it. Management of a channel system often involves channel conflict, channel evaluation, and channel modification.

Generally, producers may follow three channel strategies: intensive, selective, and independent distribution.

REVIEW QUESTIONS

1. Identify and explain the four activity flows in channel systems.
2. Explain facilitating agencies, and why they are important to channels of distribution.
3. Explain the distinction between corporate channels, contractual channels, and independent channels.
4. Identify and explain the differences between the three contractual channels discussed in the text.
5. Explain product assortments, and how this concept relates to channel systems.
6. Explain how channels are economically efficient.
7. Identify the four basic functions of distribution.
8. What are the major considerations in designing a channel system?
9. Identify the differences in interests between producers and retailers that lead to conflict in the channel system.
10. Identify and explain the basic channel strategies available to producers, identifying a product type for which each strategy might be most appropriate.

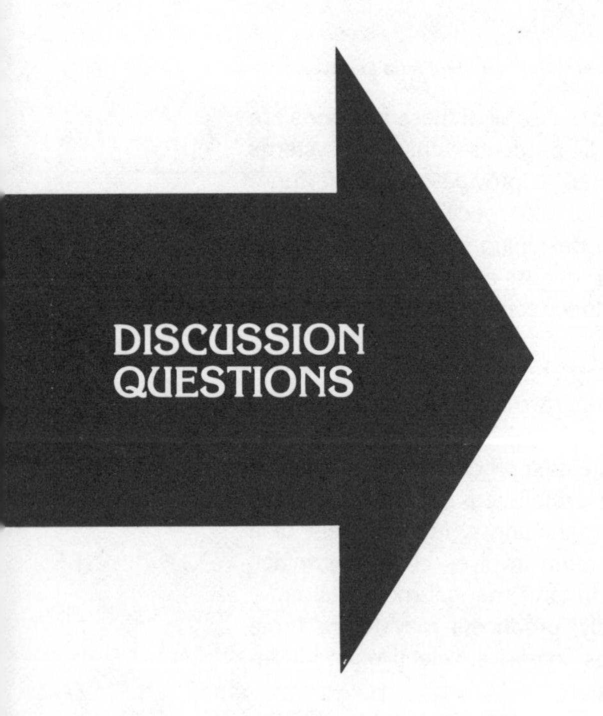

DISCUSSION QUESTIONS

1. According to the text, middlemen exist because they provide distribution economies. Yet, many people believe that middlemen unnecessarily increase the costs of goods. Which of these two points of view do you most agree with? Why?
2. Can you think of some alternative ways of distributing: (A) automobiles? (B) lumber? (C) beer? What would be the advantages and disadvantages of the alternatives you suggest?
3. It has been suggested that house-to-house selling is the most efficient form of retail selling because it eliminates wholesalers and retailers. Do you agree with this statement? Why or why not?
4. The average gross margin for department stores is about 40 percent. Many people think this is exhorbitant. Can you make any suggestions for ways of reducing the costs for its middlemen?
5. Assume that you work for a farm machinery company that has developed a new and revolutionary lawn and garden tractor. The manufacturer is not sure about the kind of a distribution system that should be established for this new product. You have been asked to develop some alternative distribution systems, and explain the advantages and disadvantages of each. What do you suggest?

CHAPTER PROBLEM

CHANNELS OF DISTRIBUTION

The Warwick Drug Company produces a line of beauty products which are sold through beauty shops. The company has an outstanding reputation in its field, and its products are premium priced.

In 1979 the company developed a line of color shampoos which were easy and safe to apply, and which gave excellent results. Because of the line's ease of application and safety, company management was considering retail distribution in drugstores and department stores. These markets were substantially larger than the market served by beauty parlors.

The total market for color shampoo was estimated at $20.5 million at manufacturers' prices. Of this total, $3.5 million were sold through beauty shops and $17 million were sold through drugstores, and department and grocery stores.

Warwick's research department had estimated the company could attain a share of market through beauty shops of 30 percent, plus or minus 10 percent. An advertising and promotion expenditure of $45,000 would be required for introducing the product into beauty shops where the company had an established reputation and good trade relations.

Since the company had no experience in the drugstore, department and food store fields, the research department estimated a market share of 10 percent, plus or minus 30 percent. Further, it believed that an advertising and promotion expenditure of $300,000 would be required to introduce the product.

The cost of goods, including the packaging, was estimated at 56 percent of sales. Administration and other expenses were estimated at $45,000, regardless of the channel used, and variable sales costs were estimated at 16⅔ percent of sales for each channel.

Cynthia Holmes, the president, felt that the company should distribute the product through beauty shops because "This is the business we know. We have a good reputation with both wholesalers and retail outlets, and there is less risk in going the beauty shop route."

Max Steiger, the sales manager, wasn't so sure. He argued that sales of beauty aids were growing rapidly in self-service outlets. Further, Steiger believed that the new color shampoo would be well accepted in these outlets; if the line was successful, it could serve as an entry for other company products, and substantially increase sales and profits.

Assignment

Which channel of distribution do you recommend and why?

16

Physical Distribution

- *The nature and scope of physical distribution.*
- *Major components of the physical distribution system.*
- *The total cost approach to physical distribution.*
- *Planning distribution strategy.*
- *Managing the physical distribution system.*

MARKETING EXAMPLES

WHERE ARE THE TRUCKS WHEN YOU NEED THEM?

McLean Trucking Company is a $320 million trucking firm that handles a wide range of freight—anything from air conditioners to tires and almost everything in between. McLean operates a fleet of over ten thousand tractors, trailers, and delivery trucks in thirty-three states. A major problem of the company can be stated in eight words: "Where are the trucks when you need them?"

For example, a company representative in Providence had a one-shot crack at some new business, but he needed an open-top trailer immediately to haul a load of washing machines to Baton Rouge. A call to the dispatcher and an inquiry check into the company's computer located the equipment where it was needed—in Providence.

> **That's a sale the nation's fourth largest trucker probably would not have made without its computerized message-switching and equipment control systems. Using some 175 IBM 3767 Communication terminals linked to a System/370 Model 145 and IBM's Freight and Equipment Reporting System for Transportation (FERST/VS), the system keeps track of McLean's 10,158 tractors, trailers, and city delivery trucks operation in 33 states.[1]**

---

1. "Computers in Distribution," *Distribution* (Chilton Publishing) (February, 1977): 31.
2. "Distribution-Marketing Interface," *Distribution* (Chilton Publishing) (June, 1977): 33–34.

WHY INSTAMATIC GETS TO THE STORES ON TIME

According to Roger Koeling, Eastman Kodak's manager of estimating and distribution in the late 1970s, timely deliveries are made because of the coordination of marketing and physical distribution activities.

> **At Kodak, distribution is charged by management with total product involvement. It isn't merely a matter of the physical aspect of storing and "delivering" the product. We're deeply involved in everything from new product planning to the actual sales of finished goods. With the setting of sales estimates. With inventory objectives. With the production schedules for factories. We're involved with a product from the planning stage until the product is discontinued.[2]**

HOW ABOUT SOME ATTENTION TO THE NUTS AND BOLTS?

According to market researchers Douglas Lambert and James Stock, business is placing too much emphasis on demand-creation activities, such as advertising and promotion, and too little emphasis on the supply aspect of demand. Physical distribution, they argue, has been too often neglected even though it offers the unique advantage of being able to increase efficiency and profits without substantial expenditures. Areas in which improvements are needed include stock levels, accuracy of order filling, installation, complaint handling, transportation, tracing and expediting shipments, order processing, warehousing, and inventory handling. In short, almost everywhere.

The three foregoing examples have been chosen among the many available to make three telling points about physical distribution:

- Physical distribution is an extremely complex activity that has increasingly turned to computerization in order to improve its efficiency.
- Physical distribution cannot be isolated from other marketing activities.
- Despite many improvements that have been made in our physical distribution systems, many improvements are still needed—in virtually every phase of its operation.

AN OVERVIEW OF PHYSICAL DISTRIBUTION

Most laymen never think of physical distribution when they think of marketing. Physical distribution, which has been referred to as the "other half of marketing,"[3] seems to exist as the invisible dimension of the marketing process. Even people who devote their lives to marketing products seem oblivious to physical distribution until a problem arises—until a store is out-of-stock, or until a shipment is lost, or a deadline missed—and then it becomes an object of frustration and calumny. Yet, physical distribution is one of the most complex and dynamic areas of marketing. It is also one of the most expensive.

> Physical distribution accounts for approximately one-fourth of the retail dollar and for more than one-sixth of the U.S. gross national product. In many firms, physical distribution costs are more than 50 percent of all operating expenses. Transportation alone accounts for approximately 20 percent of the operating expenses of the pulp and paper industry. In food manufacturing, PDM (physical distribution management) costs are more than 30 percent of sales. For all U.S. corporations, costs of physical distribution are double net profits, and two writers estimate that almost 50 cents of each dollar the American consumer spends for material items falls within the scope of distribution. In most firms, however, procurement of raw materials, manufacture, legal, accounting, and other activities greatly overshadow physical distribution as a responsibility of management. Some company executives either disregard the fact that physical distribution is an essential step between production and consumption or regard distribution as a twilight zone between raw material and ultimate consumer.[4]

In most firms, physical distribution is a neglected source of additional profits. In the retail grocery business, for example, profits run about one percent of retail sales. So a savings of one dollar in physical distribution costs would have the same effect on profits as a sales increase of $100. Or, $10,000 saved in physical distribution would have the same effect on profits as a sales increase of $1 million. And, savings of $10,000 or more are not unusual when systematic controls in inventory and materials management, transportation, warehousing procedures, and warehouse location are installed.

One problem is that top management is often poorly informed about distribution costs. An extreme example, uncovered in a survey of distribution economics and distribution management, is a major food processor with sales of over $1.5 billion a year.

> In this company, as in the industry generally, distribution represented a large part of the cost of doing business. Yet management had only fragmentary information on distribution costs. When asked about the company's total dollar outlay for transportation, key executives could only give off-the-cuff estimates ranging from $65 million to $120 million. Deeper probing revealed that effective control over this high-cost operation really stopped at the level of the traffic department, which simply secured the best rate and route for each shipment—a graphic illustration of the piecemeal attack on distribution not un-

3. Paul D. Converse, "The Other Half of Marketing," in Alfred L. Seelye (ed.), *Marketing in Transition* (New York: Harper, 1958).

4. William H. Joubert, *Profit Potentials in Physical Distribution* (New York: American Management Association, Inc., 1972) pp. 1–2.

common even among profitable companies.[5]

It should be apparent from the foregoing observations that physical distribution deserves closer examination as a marketing function. Let's begin with a definition of the field.

Definition of Physical Distribution

Physical distribution, sometimes referred to as *logistics, marketing logistics,* and *business logistics,* has been defined in a variety of ways by various writers. The National Council of Physical Distribution Management has stated:

> Physical distribution is the term employed in manufacturing and commerce to describe the broad range of activities concerned with efficient movement of finished products from the end of the production line to the consumer, and in some cases includes the movements of raw materials from the source of supply to the beginning of the production line. These activities include freight transportation, warehousing, material handling, protective packaging, inventory control, plant and warehouse site selection, order processing, market forecasting and customer service.[6]

From this statement, we can abstract the following, somewhat abbreviated definition. *Physical distribution is a marketing subsystem which consists of all activities, including planning and control, involved in the physical movement of raw materials and finished goods from producers to consumers.* From this definition, and the statement upon which it is based, the following points should be noted.

- Physical distribution is a subsystem of marketing, not an independent activity. This means that it is an integral part of the marketing program and has strategic and profit implications.
- It is a system, not an aggregate of independent activities. Thus, a change in any individual activity will have implications for, and effects on other activities in the system.
- Finally, a physical distribution system does not just happen. It requires both planning and control to insure efficient and effective operation.

The Scope of Physical Distribution

Figure 16–1 illustrates the scope of physical distribution. Beginning with distribution planning and accounting, this figure identifies some fourteen major tasks to be completed before the distribution system fulfills its function. Some of these tasks, in turn, may be subdivided into still other tasks which also require planning and control. For example, inventory management at the plant level can be subdivided into management and control of raw material inventory, goods-in-process inventory, and finished goods inventory—all of which must be coordinated with consumer demand. The cogs used in Figure 16–1 emphasize the point that each task must be meshed with every other task in order to provide a smoothly operating system. Malfunction at any point in the process either disrupts the system or brings it to a grinding halt. Inefficient performance of any task not only increases the costs of that task, but may also generate inefficiencies in other portions of the system.

Objectives of the Physical Distribution System

The objectives of the physical distribution system are easier to define than to achieve. An idealized statement of physical distribution objectives is to *maximize customer service while minimizing costs.* Unfortunately, this idealized statement contains an inherent contradiction. The very concept of maximizing customer service is incompatible with the concept of minimizing costs because customer service is expensive. Further, the interrelationships between the costs of the various facets of the physical distribution system are so complex that they defy simple analysis.

5. Robert P. Neuschel, "Physical Distribution—Forgotten Frontier," *Harvard Business Review* (March–April, 1967): 127–28.

6. D. J. Bowersox, *Logistical Management* (New York: Macmillan Publishing Co., Inc.: 1974), p. 1.

FIGURE 16–1: *Physical Distribution*
SOURCE: Wendell M. Stewart, "Physical Distribution: Key to Improved Volume and Profit," *Journal of Marketing* (January, 1965), p. 66.

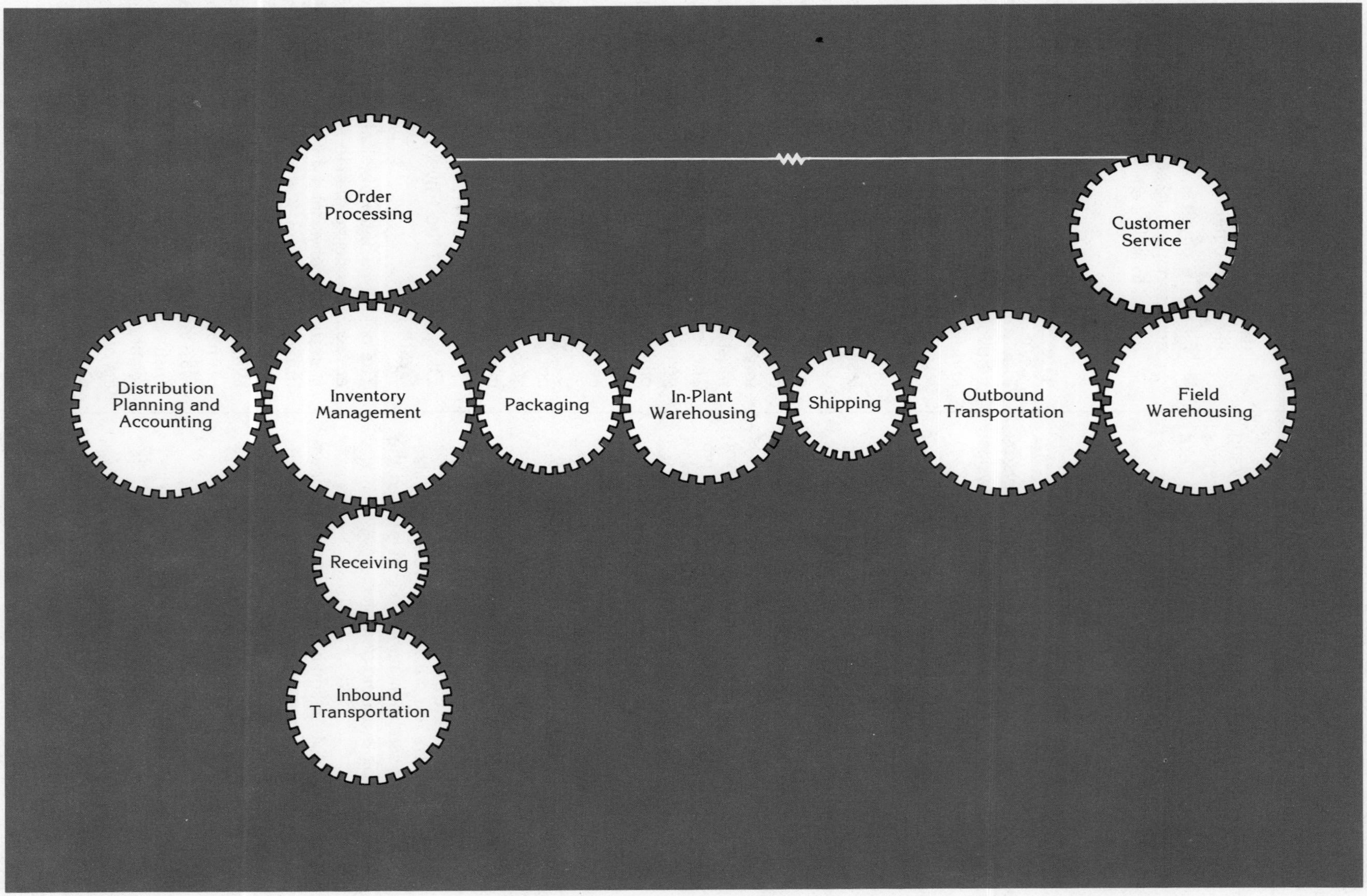

Order Processing
Customer Service
Distribution Planning and Accounting
Inventory Management
Packaging
In-Plant Warehousing
Shipping
Outbound Transportation
Field Warehousing
Receiving
Inbound Transportation

FIGURE 16–2: *Interrelationship of Cost Factors of Physical Distribution*
SOURCE: Ramond LeKashman and John F. Stolle, "The Total Cost of Distribution," *Business Horizons* (Winter, 1965), p. 34.

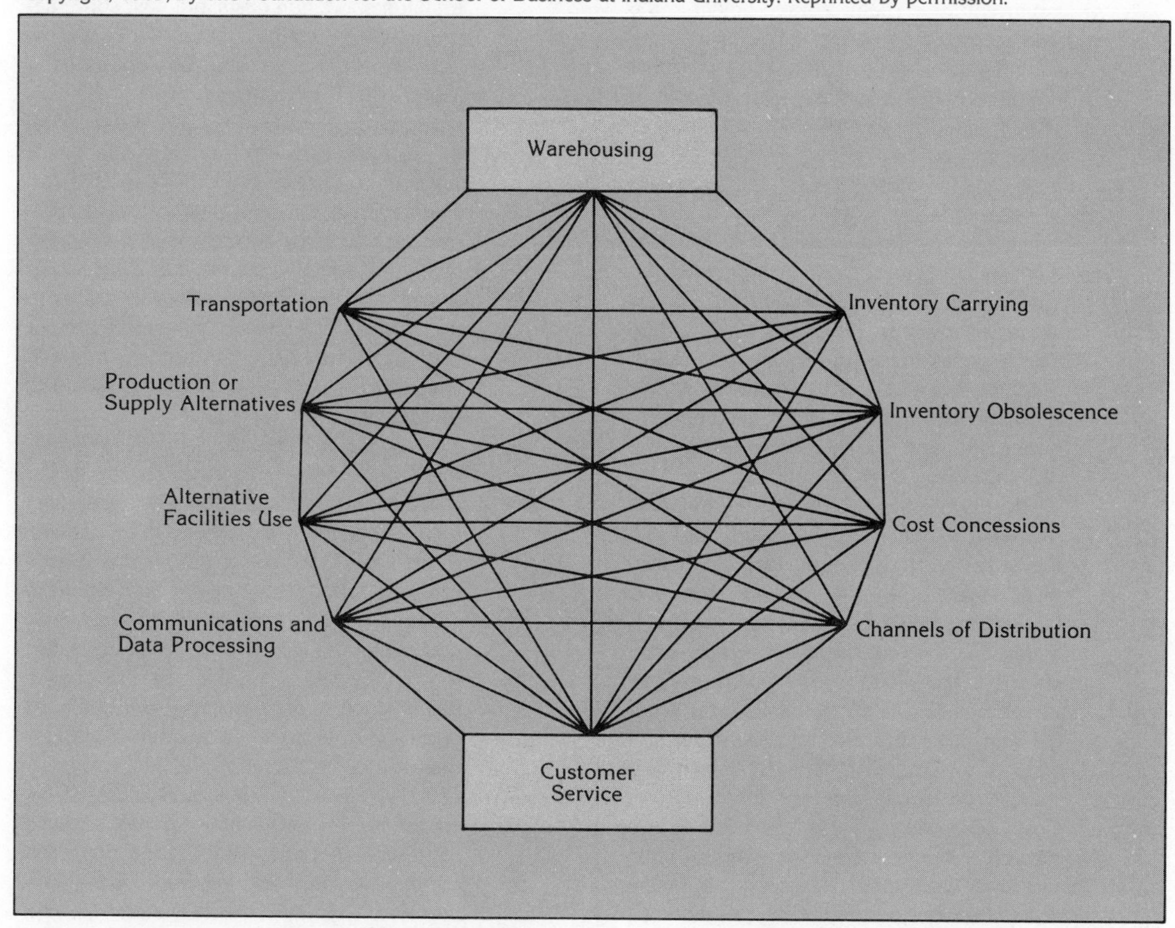

This point is dramatized by the illustration in Figure 16–2 and the following description of the interrelationships depicted in this extract:

> The real cost of distribution includes much more than what most companies consider when they attempt to deal with distribution costs. In a sense, any major distribution decision can affect every cost in the business, and each cost is related to all the others. Our experience indicates that the following ten cost elements and interrelationships are the ones that are most likely to prove critical in evaluating the impact of alternative distribution approaches on total costs and total profits.
>
> *Warehousing.* To provide service through the company's chosen channels of distribution, some warehousing is required, involving from one in-plant warehouse to a multiple-unit network dispersed across the country. Service usually becomes better as the number of warehouses is increased, at least up to a point. However, as the number of warehouses increases, their average size decreases; this will begin to reduce the efficiency to customers. Also, costs increase. Thus any change in the three variables—number, type, or location of warehouses—will affect both service and costs.
>
> *Inventory Carrying.* The ownership of inventory gives rise to costs for money, insurance, occupancy, pilferage losses, and custodial services, and sometimes inventory taxes. Depending on the business involved, this group of costs may range from 10 percent to 30

percent of average annual inventory value. Customer service will be improved by keeping inventory at many storage points in the field near to customers, but this will increase total inventory and the cost for carrying that inventory. Thus inventory carrying cost is closely linked to warehousing cost and customer service.

Inventory Obsolescence. If (at a given level of sales) total inventory is increased to provide better customer service, then inventory turnover is decreased. Also, the greater the "pipeline fill" in the distribution system, the slower the inventory turnover. This automatically exposes the owner to greater risks of obsolescence and inventory write-down. This is a particularly important cost for companies having frequent model changeovers, style changes, or product perishability.

Production or Supply Alternatives. Production costs vary among plants and vary with the volume produced at each individual plant. Plants have different fixed costs and different unit variable costs as volume is increased. The decision of which plant should serve which customers must give weight not only to transportation and warehousing costs, but also to production and supply costs; these will vary significantly with the volume allocated to each plant.

Cost Concessions. A special aspect of production or supply alternatives arises from the fact that distribution decisions can affect costs otherwise incurred by suppliers or customers. For example, when a retailer creates his own warehouses, this may free suppliers from packing and shipping small quantities or from maintaining small local warehouses in the field. A retailer who establishes his own warehouse network may be able to recoup some of these costs by negotiation with the supplier.

Channels of Distribution. The choice of distribution channels profoundly affects the nature of costs of a company's sales organization, its selling price, and gross margin structure, its commitment to physical distribution facilities. These in turn will affect production and supply costs.

Transportation. Changing the number or location of warehouses changes transportation costs, sometimes in unanticipated and complex ways. For example, an increase in the number of warehouses may initially reduce total transportation costs; but past some determinable point, the cost trend may reverse because of the decreasing ratio of carload to less-than-carload tonnage.

Communications and Data Processing. These costs vary with the complexity of the distribution system and with the level of service provided, including costs for order processing, inventory control, payables, receivables, and shipping documents. These costs rise as more distribution points are added to the system. Additionally, as the cycle time or response time of the communications and data processing system is shortened, costs of this service are increased.

Alternative Facilities Use. Changes in inventory requirements or in other aspects of the distribution operation will change space requirements and utilization in a plant–warehouse facility or a retail store. Space used for distribution may be convertible to selling space which yields incremental sales and profits. In the case of retail business, this is actually a variation of the customer service factor since it increases the availability of goods with which to fill customer requirements.

Customer Service. Stock-outs, excess delivery time or excess variability of delivery time all result in lost sales. Any change in the distribution system will influence these elements of customer service, and therefore must either gain or lose sales for the company. These effects, while difficult to measure, must be considered part of the real distribution costs.[7]

Because of the complex interrelationships existing between the various aspects of physical distribution, it is widely recognized—but infrequently practiced—that a *total-cost* approach to physical distribution is necessary to realize meaningful distribution economies. Before examining the total cost approach to distribution, however, let's examine some of the major components of the physical distribution system.

7. Raymond LeKashman and John F. Stolle, "The Total Cost of Distribution," *Business Horizons* (Winter, 1965): 34–35.

MAJOR COMPONENTS OF PHYSICAL DISTRIBUTION

Figure 16–3 shows a breakdown of physical distribution costs for consumer products and for equipment and machinery in the industrial field. Note that three of these component costs—transportation, inventory carrying costs, and warehousing—account for 90 percent of the physical distribution costs for consumer goods, and 81 percent for the industrial products represented.

Let's examine each of these three major cost components to see what they entail.

Transportation

Transportation represents a major cost in physical distribution. Yet, costs per se are not the only consideration in selecting a particular transportation mode. In addition to costs—usually defined as costs per ton mile—variability in delivery time and compatibility with the product being shipped are also key considerations.

For example, a major manufacturer of expensive chocolates on the east coast used refrigerated rail cars to transport its products to California. For most of its products, this mode of transportation worked well. However, for one of its product lines—whipped creams—it was a disaster. The whipped creams differed from the other chocolates in that air was stirred into the chocolate centers in order to give them a smooth, light texture. The problem was that, when these creams were transported over the mountains, the rarified atmosphere at 7,000 feet caused them to explode.

The Chevrolet Division of General Motors is another case in point. In 1975 General Motors introduced the Chevette. The car was significantly smaller than most other American cars, which proved to be a marketer's dream and a physical distribution manager's nightmare. The car was thoroughly tested in every respect except for its ride on rail cars to dealers. The trains had been designed to hold larger cars securely. The smaller Chevette was jostled around and often arrived at dealers damaged. Replacement proved extremely costly. If more thought had been given to the means of getting the car to the market, the problem could have been avoided.[8]

MODES OF TRANSPORTATION. Five modes of transportation link producers to consumers—trains, trucks, ships, planes, and pipelines. Figure 16–4 shows the relative importance of these transportation forms in ton miles from 1950 to 1977. In this figure, note that rail and water modes have decreased in importance during the period shown, while motor, pipeline, and air forms have increased in importance. No form of transportation is best for all purposes; each has advantages and disadvantages. For this reason, each serves a unique role in the nation's transportation system.

Railroads. Railroads remain our most important form of transportation in terms of ton miles. Although they have diminished in importance during the past thirty years, trains still transport approximately 38 percent of all ton miles shipped.

All railroads in the United States are classified as common carriers, and have no restraints imposed on the types of commodities they can carry. As a consequence, they can be used by anyone and for shipping all types of products. Railroads vary in size. In 1973, sixty-five railroads were classified as Class I carriers because they had annual gross operating incomes of $5 million or more. Another 265 railroads, with gross revenues of less than $5 million, were classified as Class II carriers.

The major advantage of railroads as a form of freight transportation is their ability to move large volume long distances at relatively low rates. For this reason, they are widely used for products from forestry, mines, and agriculture. Since these products are characterized by high density and low value, and since transportation accounts for a substantial portion of their selling price, railroads provide an excellent form of transportation.

On the negative side, railroads offer limited accessibility and are relatively slow. Accessibility is the ability of a transportation mode to provide service between specific points. Once tracks

8. "Distribution-Marketing Interface," p. 32.

FIGURE 16–3: Breakdown of Physical Distribution Dollar for Consumer and Industrial Goods.
SOURCE: Herbert W. Davis and Co., "Breakdown of Physical Distribution Dollar," *Sales and Marketing Management 1976 Survey of Selling Costs,* pp. 106–107.

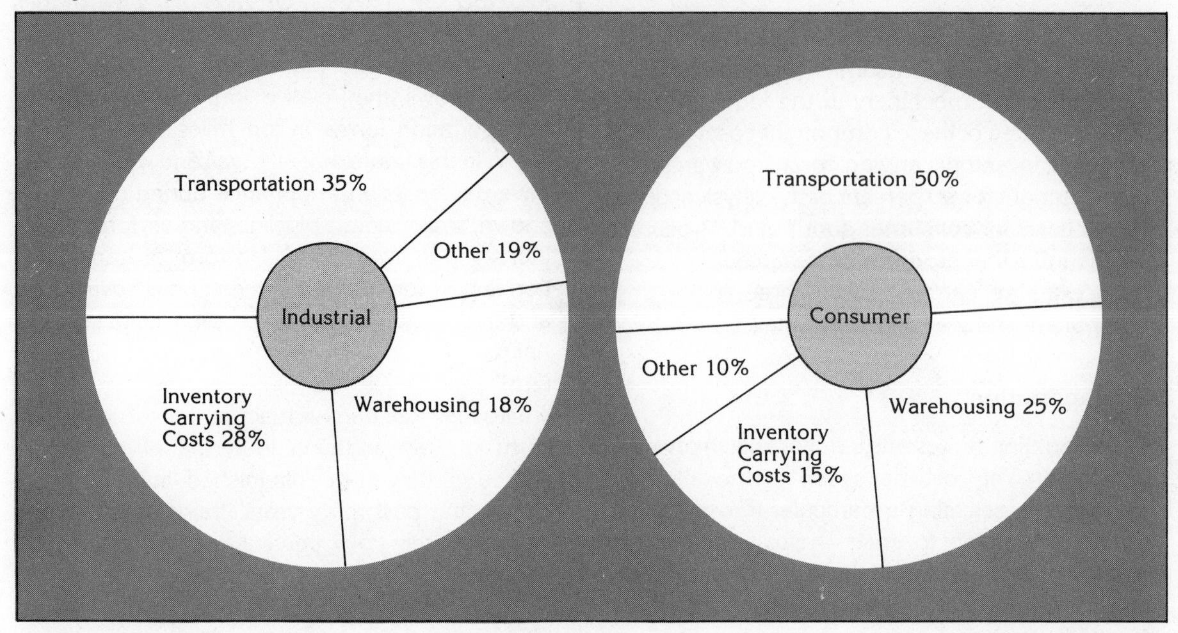

are laid, trains cannot deviate from these routes, so shippers not on the right-of-way do not have easy access to rail transportation and must use other forms of transportation to reach shipping points.

FIGURE 16–4: Major Transportation Modes in Ton Miles, 1950–1977.
SOURCE: *Statistical Abstracts of United States: 1979,* p. 635.

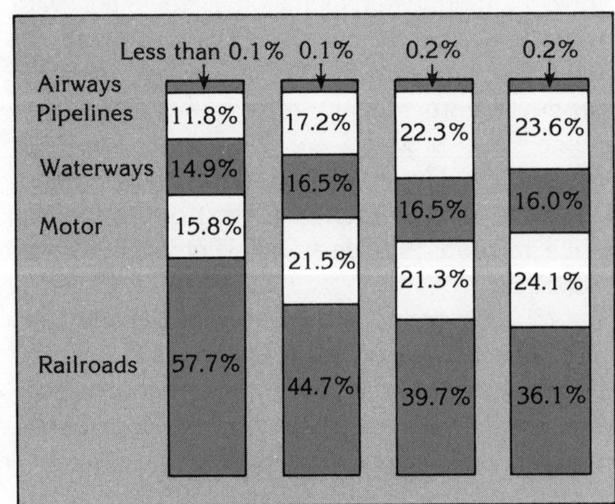

The average speed of a boxcar is about 20 miles per hour. Although speeds of 60 to 70 miles per hour are attained in the open country, the average speed is significantly reduced by the tremendous task of separating-out boxcars in railroad yards in order to route them to their proper destinations. And, as one might expect, cars are sometimes temporarily lost in the process. I recall one situation in which chocolate syrup shipped from St. Louis to Boston was delayed for over a week. When we put a tracer on the shipment, it was finally located three days later on a siding in Pittsburgh. In the meantime, serious out-of-stock problems were occurring in Boston, with a subsequent loss of sales.

Motor Carriers. Motor carriers are an integral part of any firm's logistic system. Some form of motor transporation—be it a pick-up truck or an eighteen-wheeler—is used in almost every logistics operation. Because of the development of an extensive highway network during the past thirty years, and technological improvements in motor vehicles, motor transportation has more than doubled its share of the nation's shipping since

Railroads—the workhorse of the transportation system. (Photo courtesy of Union Pacific Railroad Company)

1940 and made deep inroads into the share formerly held by railroads.

Unlike railroads, motor carriers are a low-fixed-cost, high-variable-cost mode of transportation. Motor carriers do not require extensive investments in terminals and equipment, as railroads do, and do not have to build their own right-of-way. Instead, they use highways constructed with public funds. Highway-use taxes and license fees are high, but these are a part of the variable cost of operations. Since it is relatively inexpensive to enter business as a motor carrier, there are some 15,000 motor carrier operations in the United States. Of these, approximately 1,700 have operating revenues of $1 million or more, over 2,000 have operating revenues of $300,000 to $1 million, and over 11,000 have operating revenues of under $300,000.

Unlike railroads, which are classified as common carriers and, as such, are available to anyone, motor carriers may be common, contract, exempt, or private carriers. The technical differences between these types of carriers are beyond the scope of this text, being a hodgepodge of administrative regulations, exemptions, and sometimes ambiguous differences. Essentially, however, they differ in economic regulation, service regulation, and availability for public use. Common carriers are available to the general public and are the most regulated. Private carriers are owned by individual firms for their own use, are not available for public use, and are not sub-

Motor transport—fast and flexible. (Photo courtesy of American Trucking Associations, Inc.)

ject to economic or service regulation. Contract carriers and exempt carriers fall between these two extremes.[9]

The primary advantage of motor carriers is their flexibility—the ability to provide service to any location. Motor vehicles are not restricted by tracks, waterways, or airport facilities. The available network of streets and highways provides access to all shipping and receiving points. Thus, the motor carrier is the most accessible mode of transportation available today. In addition, motor transport offers relatively low transit times, is fairly reliable, and amenable to small shipments. These characteristics—low transit times, small shipments, and reasonable reliability—often enable motor transport users to reduce inventory carrying costs while maintaining customer service standards.

9. For a summary discussion of the major differences between the various types of motor carriers, see John J. Coyle and Edward J. Bardi, *The Management of Business Logistics* (St. Paul: West Publishing Company, 1976), pp. 154–59.

The major disadvantage of motor transportation is its relative high cost—about five times as much as railroads and about twenty-five times as much as water transportation per ton mile. For this reason, motor carriers are particularly appropriate for relatively short hauls, and for high value items which can more easily absorb higher transportation costs than can low value commodities.

Water Carriers. Water transportation was a major factor in the development of the nation's commerce. Before the advent of railroads, the availability of coastal shipping and major waterways, such as the Great Lakes and the Mississippi and Ohio rivers, determined the location of major shipping and receiving centers, and shaped the patterns of distribution. Although water transportation has suffered with the development of modern modes of transportation, it still accounts for about 16 percent of freight transportation.

Like motor carriers, water transport is a relatively low-fixed-cost, high-variable-cost mode of transportation. This is so because no investment is required for right-of-way. The waterways are provided by nature and maintained by public funds. One consequence is that water transportation is dominated by exempt and private carriers which account for over 90 percent of its ton miles. Common and contract carriers make up the remainder.

The principal advantage of water transportation is its low cost. Its average revenue per ton mile is substantially below those of rail, motor, or air. As a consequence, water transportation is most appropriate for large volume shipments with low value that can be loaded and unloaded with mechanical devices. Thus, waterways are primarily used for transporting forestry, mining, and agriculture products.

The principal disadvantages of water transportation are its relatively slow transit time and its lack of accessibility. Not only is the transit time slow, but it may be disrupted by weather conditions—ice or low water. Its lack of accessibility is evident since large sections of the country have no immediate access to water transportation.

Air Carriers. The primary business of air carriers is passenger service. Air transport of freight is still in its infancy, accounting for only about two-tenths

Water transportation—slow but cheap. (Photo by Rohn Engh)

of one percent of domestic ton miles. The air carrier industry is made up of a relatively small number of firms, all regulated by the Civil Aeronautics Board (CAB) as common carriers.

Although air carrier equipment is relatively expensive, the cost structure of the industry is still one of relatively low fixed costs and high variable costs because the skyways are free and air terminals are built with public moneys. However, lease payments and landing fees add to the variable costs of the industry.

Air freight started as an off-shoot of the passenger business by utilizing the unused belly of the plane for cargo shipments. Subsequently, airlines have developed equipment specifically designed for freight movement, and cargo air lines are becoming more common.

The primary advantage of air carriers is speed. Air carriers provide a distinct advantage in moving relatively small shipments long distances with short transit times. Air freight is particularly appropriate for emergency shipments and for perishable products, particularly if the products have a high value and are able to absorb the high costs of air transportation in their cost structure.

The primary disadvantages of air carriers are high cost, lack of accessibility, and possible disruption of service. The average cost per ton mile for air carriers is approximately twenty times that of railroads and three times that of motor carriers. Lack of accessibility requires shippers to use other forms of transportation to and from airports. And, weather is always a problem since adverse weather conditions, particularly during the winter, often delay flights or prevent landings.

Pipelines. The final mode of transportation is the pipeline. Although pipelines account for over 22 percent of the nation's freight in ton miles, the types of commodities that can be transported by this mode are extremely limited since the commodity must be in liquid or gaseous form. Historically, pipelines for intercity transport have been

Air transportation—fast but expensive. (Photo courtesy of Emery Air Freight)

restricted to liquid petroleum products and natural gas. More recently, however, pipelines have been used to transport coal which has been pulverized and mixed with water to form a slurry. In 1980 the only company in the United States transporting coal slurry through pipeline was the Black Mesa Pipeline Company. The company's pipeline ran 278 miles from North Eastern Arizona to Bullhead City on the Arizona-Nevada border. Two other pipelines for transporting coal have been considered—one from Utah to Nevada and the other from Montana to Arkansas. However, these two projects have been effectively blocked by environmental protection groups.

Pipelines, like railroads, are a high-fixed-cost, low-variable-cost mode of transportation. The Alaskan pipeline, for example, cost almost $8 billion to construct, and was financed by a consortium of major companies.

Related to the pipeline, although not normally considered a basic mode of transportation, are power lines used for transporting electrical power. Like pipelines, power lines are expensive to construct and have limited use.

The advantages of pipeline transportation are its low variable cost, its ability to move a large volume of product, its dependability, and its ability to protect the product from damage during transport. Because of these advantages, consideration is being given to the construction of two petroleum pipelines, one across the northern states to the midwest, and a second across the south to the east coast.[10]

The primary disadvantages of pipelines, of course, are their high construction costs and

10. "Deciding on Alaskan Oil Line to Midwest," *New York Times* (January 12, 1978): D1.

FIGURE 16–5: Ranking of Basic Transportation Modes on Selected Criteria

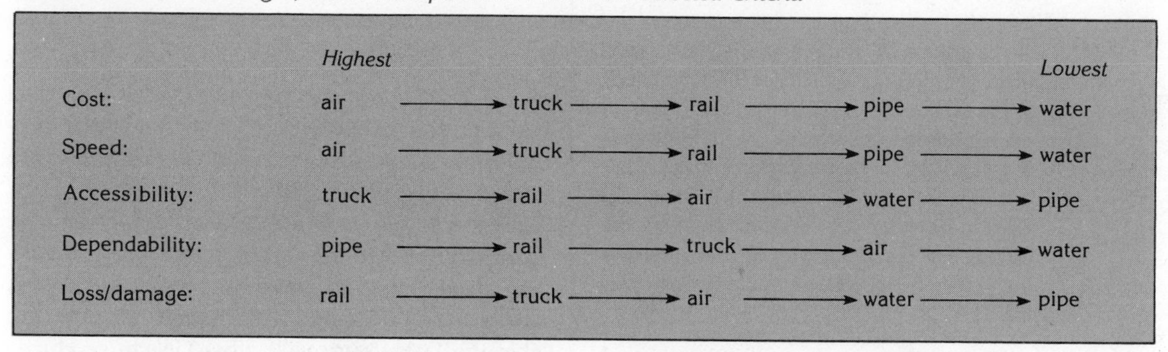

	Highest				Lowest
Cost:	air	truck	rail	pipe	water
Speed:	air	truck	rail	pipe	water
Accessibility:	truck	rail	air	water	pipe
Dependability:	pipe	rail	truck	air	water
Loss/damage:	rail	truck	air	water	pipe

the limits they impose on the commodities that can be transported. Figure 16–5 compares the characteristics of the major modes of transportation.

COORDINATED TRANSPORT. To achieve transportation economies, shippers often use a variety of transportation modes. One problem with this approach is the requirement for loading and unloading at transfer points. This not only substantially increases distribution costs, but also—because of corruption and organized theft at transfer points—often leads to severe losses. One successful solution to these problems that has grown into a major industry is *containerization.* A container is simply a big, sealed box. It may be a truck trailer, or a box car, or a large, sealed container. The commodities being shipped are loaded in the container and sealed. At transfer points, the entire container is shifted from one mode of transportation to another without its contents having to be handled individually. A variety of descriptive names such as piggyback, birdyback, and fishyback have been applied to these operations which are shown in diagramatic form in Figure 16–6.

RATES AND REGULATION. One of the most controversial aspects of transportation is the subject of rates and the effects of government regulation. Federal regulation of transportation began with the *Act to Regulate Commerce* in 1887. This legislation was passed because inland transportation was dominated by railroads, and the rate practices of these carriers were rapacious and discriminatory. From these modest beginnings, federal regulation of freight and tariffs has grown into what many consider to be a monstrous boondoggle that handcuffs competition and defrauds consumers. The tariff or rate system has become immensely complex, and has led to the following observation.

FIGURE 16–6: Coordinated Transport.
SOURCE: Reproduced by permission from *The Management of Business Logistics* by John J. Coyle and Edward J. Bardi, copyright © 1976 by West Publishing Company. All rights reserved.

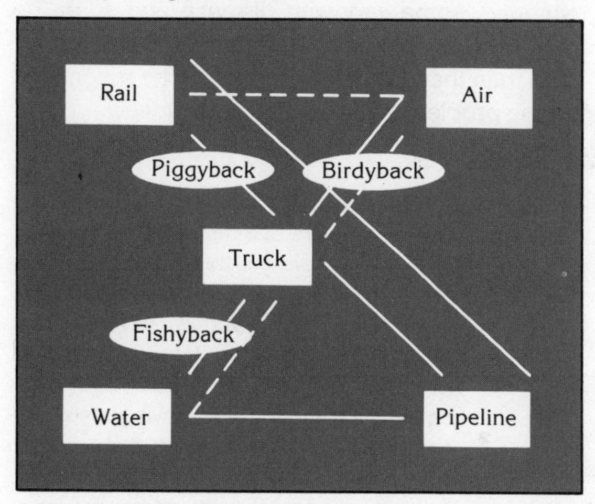

> "There are certain things," said a general attorney for one of the western railroads, "spiritual and material, in the presence of which ordinary mortals stand dumb. When I stood at the tomb of Napoleon, first viewed the Washington Monument, gazed into the Grand Canyon, words were superfluous.
>
> "Feelings akin to this arise within me when I contemplate a freight tariff, with its exceptions, items, notes, commodities, distances, proportionals, disproportionals, gateways, basing points, arbitraries, and God knows what. If the thing itself amazes, what must be

the feeling when one views from afar the mind that conceived it.

"I can approach a Superintendent, a General Manager, a General Solicitor, or a President, if you will, with a certain amount of assurance, and composure; but when I approach the portals of a Traffic Expert's office, I not only remove my hat, but also my shoes, and like the devout Moslem, chant as I near the throne: 'Great is Muhammad,' but greater is the man who understands freight tariffs.'"[11]

This problem arises because of the various bases upon which rates are assessed. Some are assessed on the basis of cost of service, some are assessed on the value of the commodity being shipped, some vary with distance and some do not, most are based on volume but some are not, and then there are the exceptions. The magnitude of the problem is pointed up in the following quotation:

> For an appreciation of the problem let's examine the nature of a transportation service. It would be simple if all transportation service were sold on the basis of ton-miles, that is, we would have to pay X dollars to move one ton, one mile. But, in fact, transportation services are not sold in ton miles. Transportation services are sold for moving a specific commodity, pickles, between two specific points, Toledo and New York City. This fact gives some insight into the enormous magnitude of the transportation pricing problem. There are over 33,000 important shipping and receiving points in the United States. Theoretically, the number of different possible routes would be all the permutations of the 33,000 points. The result is in the trillions of trillions. In addition, it is necessary to consider the thousands and thousands of different commodities and products which might be shipped over any of these routes. On top of that there are the different modes to consider and different companies within each mode. It also may be necessary to give consideration to the specific supply and demand situation for each commodity over each route.[12]

Although the problem for the individual shipper may not be quite as complex as the foregoing quotation suggests, it is complex enough to cause costly miscalculations. For example, when Gillette introduced its Daisy razor for women, the company packed the razors in a display stand to get dealer support. However, because of this method of packaging, the company could not ship the Daisy razor with other Gillette products. Because government regulations assign freight to classes according to weight and volume, the Daisy packaging placed the product in a more expensive class. As a consequence, the company was required to pay higher freight costs for months, until they were able to correct the problem.[13]

Aside from the complexity of rates, the Interstate Commerce Commission (ICC) and the Civil Aeronautics Board (CAB) have promulgated regulations which require new carriers to justify their entry into the field by demonstrating a need for their services. Many feel that these regulations protect established systems, reduce competition, and increase the costs of freight service.

These criticisms came to a head in the late 1970s, and resulted in legislation designed to reduce or eliminate government regulation of the transportation industry. In 1976 the *Railroad Revitalization and Regulatory Reform Act* was passed. This act allows much greater rate freedom for the nation's railroads. In 1978 the *Airline Deregulation Act* brought Adam Smith's invisible hand of competition to the airline industry, with the promise that the CAB would close shop for good by 1985. Currently, similar deregulation of the trucking industry is under consideration.

The ultimate consequence of this legislation is still unclear. When industries that have never really had to compete are told to compete, almost anything can happen, and the effects on

11. Paul T. McOlhiney and Charles L. Hilton, *Introduction to Logistics and Traffic Management* (Dubuque, IA: William C. Brown Company, 1968), p. 229.

12. John J. Coyle and Edward J. Bardi, *The Management of Business Logistics,* p. 179.

13. "Distribution-Marketing Interface," p. 35–36.

the nation's transportation systems are uncertain. In the airline industry, deregulation has initially resulted in a senseless and devastating price war that drained resources away from replacing an aging fleet of carriers. By late 1981, a semblance of sanity was returning to the industry, but major airlines were still fumbling for effective marketing strategies to deal with the new competitive climate, and passenger rates were still a nightmare of confusion.[14]

Inventory Costs

A second major component of physical distribution is inventory costs. The magnitude of this distribution cost becomes apparent when one considers the effects of skyrocketing interest rates in 1981. In the spring of 1980, major retailers were paying 20 percent interest to finance their costs of inventory. This interest charge squeezed profits, raised retail prices, and catapulted inventory control systems into a top management priority.

Inventory costs actually involve interrelated cost variables that can be grouped into three categories.

- *Carrying Costs. Inventory carrying costs include all of those costs necessary to hold an item in inventory.* Normally, these costs include such things as the cost of the material being inventoried (or interest on its value), material handling, storage, insurance, taxes, depreciation, and obsolescence costs. These costs may vary widely from product to product. One thing that should be noted about inventory carrying costs is that they vary directly with the size of the inventory. That is, as the size of the inventory increases, the carrying costs also increase.
- *Procurement Costs. Procurement costs include those costs involved in obtaining the goods to be inventoried.* Procurement costs for manufacturers and distributors are somewhat different. For manufacturers, they involve costs associated with change-over time for machinery as well as accounting time, materials, and labor used when an order is placed, received, or inspected. For distributors, procurement costs generally include order processing, checking the material received, and preparing and processing payments. These costs vary, not with the size of the inventory, but with the frequency of orders. Thus, if one carries small inventories, one must order frequently; by contrast, large inventories decrease order frequency with a correspondent decrease in procurement costs.
- *Stock-out Costs. Stock-out costs are the costs of lost sales because the product wanted by consumers is not available on the premises.* Stock–out costs are generally avoided, or minimized, by carrying safety stocks. That is, by carrying inventories above the level of anticipated sales during a particular period. However, the size of safety stocks to be carried is a management decision. Note that as the level of customer service increases, the cost of inventory rises disproportionally. For example, an increase of customer service from 95 to 98 percent may double the size of the inventory required.

INVENTORY DECISIONS AND ECONOMIC ORDER QUANTITY (EOQ). The inventory decision boils down to two basic considerations: the size of the order; and frequency of ordering. These two considerations always involve a trade-off between carrying costs and procurement costs because large inventories increase carrying costs, and frequent orders increase procurement costs.

One resolution of this problem is the use of the Economic Order Quantity (EOQ) model for inventory decisions. The purpose of this model is to find the optimal order size and frequency that will minimize annual inventory costs. The relationship between total cost of inventory and each of its components (carrying costs and procurement costs) is shown in Figure 16–7. The minimum

14. For an interesting article on the airlines response to deregulation, see: "The Airlines Are Flying in a Fog," *Fortune* (Oct. 20, 1980): 50–56.

FIGURE 16–7: *Relationship between Total Inventory Cost and Each Component*

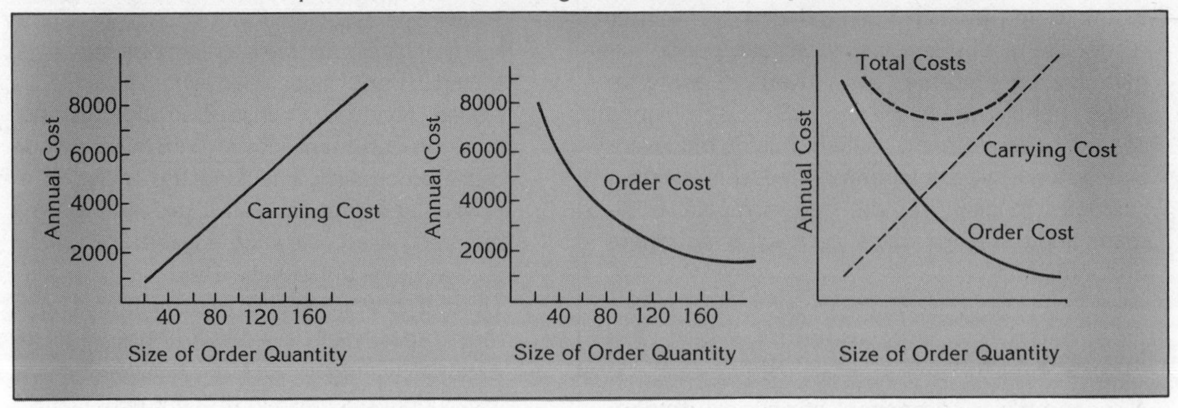

point on the total cost curve occurs at the intersection of the two component cost curves.[15]

LIMITATIONS OF THE EOQ MODEL. Although the basic EOQ model provides a way of determining optimal order size and frequency, the model makes a number of simplifying assumptions:[16]

- A continuous, constant and known rate of demand.
- A constant and known replenishment or lead time.
- The satisfaction of all demand.
- Constant price or cost which is independent of the order quantity or time, e.g., purchase price, transport, cost, etc.
- No inventory in-transit.
- One item of inventory or no interaction between items.
- Infinite planning horizon.
- No limit on capital availability.

In addition, the model assumes that all costs involved in the inventory system are known. Unfortunately, the world isn't that simple. Many companies do not have a firm fix on the costs involved in using the EOQ model. Beyond this, the preceding assumptions do not always hold true. As a consequence, adjustments must be made in the model and, in some cases, these adjustments are complex and uncertain. Nonetheless, the EOQ model represents a starting point for inventory control, and emphasizes the need for specific kinds of information. Further, with the development of computer technology and the use of statistics to handle uncertainty in relevant variables, reasonably effective inventory control systems can be developed for highly complex inventory requirements—provided, of course, that inventory costs justify a sophisticated inventory model. Sometimes they do, and sometimes they don't.

Warehousing

The third major component of physical distribution is warehousing. Key considerations in warehousing decisions are the type of warehousing to be used, and the number and location of warehousing facilities. As in other areas of physical distribution, decisions in these areas always involve trade-offs in which the basic objective is to find an optimal answer from the opposing perspectives of costs and customer service.

The warehousing or storage function occurs at various levels in the distribution chain.

---

15. A simple formula for computing the economic order quantity is: $EOQ = \sqrt{\frac{2RS}{CI}}$, where R = demand for the time period; S = the cost for each order; C = cost per unit of the product in question; and I = the inventory carrying cost as a percent of inventory value. As an example, assume that R = 12,000; S = $15.00; C = $3.00; and 1 = 15%. Then $\sqrt{\frac{(2)\,(12{,}000)\,(15)}{(3)\,(.15)}} = 894.4$

16. John J. Coyle and Edward J. Bardi, *The Management of Business Logistics,* p. 68.

Plant warehousing is essential for incoming raw materials and finished goods prior to shipment. Normally, producers accumulate a certain quantity of finished product on the plant site to take advantage of economies of volume shipping. In extreme cases, the nature of the product requires major storage facilities within or near the plant. A case in point is the distilled spirits industry. Consider the marketer of a five-year old bourbon who sells 2 million cases a year. At any given time, 10 million cases will be stored on or near the plant site in charred, oak barrels prior to bottling. Or consider a highly seasonal product such as fancy chocolates. Eighty percent of the sales occur between Thanksgiving and Mothers Day. Yet, for production efficiency, the plant runs twelve months a year, requiring refrigerated warehousing facilities until shipments start.

In addition to plant storage, most products require field warehousing near their points of distribution so that products can be delivered to retailers quickly to avoid stock-outs.

Finally, distributors and retailers maintain minimum stocks of products, and national retail chains maintain extensive field warehousing facilities in each region to service their stores.

In the following material, we will confine ourselves to field warehousing since many warehousing problems arise in connection with this form of storage. The two basic issues that must be dealt with when planning warehouse facilities are the type of warehousing that will be employed and the number and location of warehouse facilities.

TYPE OF WAREHOUSING. The first question to be answered here is whether one will use public or private warehousing. Public warehousing may be appropriate if the quantity of goods to be stored is relatively small, if products are highly seasonal, and/or if maximum flexibility is needed. If one opts for public warehousing, some 15,000 public warehouses in the United States offer a variety of services:

- *Conventional warehousing.* In conventional warehouses, the primary emphasis is on storage, with a minimum of services.
- *Office and display space.* Some warehouses provide office and display space which may be used by company representatives to show merchandise to prospective buyers.
- *Distribution centers.* As distinguished from conventional warehouses, the emphasis in distribution centers is on processing and moving goods, rather than simple storage. These centers offer a variety of services, including data processing equipment, inventory control maintenance, local delivery, unpacking, assembling, price marking, breaking up shipments into smaller packaging units, and so forth.
- *Bonded warehouses.* Bonded warehouses do not release goods until federal taxes, duties, or other fees are paid. These warehouses are appropriate for distilled spirits or tobacco where it is desirable to postpone the payment of government levies as long as possible in order to reduce investments in inventory.
- *Specialty warehouses.* These facilities exist for the storage of commodities that require unique storage conditions. For example, refrigerated warehousing for frozen foods, silos for grain storage, tanks for oil storage, and special facilities for perishables such as butter, produce, or furs.

Although there is a demand for the entire range of facilities described above, the trend seems to be toward distribution centers because of the value of the services they offer.

A second decision relates to the number and dispersion of warehouse facilities. One may employ a centralized system with one or few warehouses serving the entire distribution area, or one may use many widely dispersed warehouses. This decision depends upon the size of the firm, the size of the distribution area, the level of customer service to be provided, the need for centralized control, and economic factors involving the cost of storage and transportation.

As an alternative to public warehousing, one may choose private facilities operated by the company and acquired through leasing arrangements or outright ownership. Leasing, while more expensive than ownership, avoids major capital investments and is more flexible since the firm is not saddled with unused capacity should storage needs decrease significantly over a period of time. In either case, however, greater control is gained over the warehouse operation. Many large companies, whose product lines are stable, diversified, and sufficient to keep warehouse facilities filled, find private warehousing economical. Some firms require a combination of private and public warehousing. If private warehousing is chosen, key questions are how many and where.

NUMBER OF WAREHOUSES. Determining the number and location of warehouses is a complex question that involves trade-offs between many variables. One problem in making warehouse decisions is that many companies do not know their real costs of warehousing, nor do they have the accounting records necessary to make this determination. This point is dramatized by the following quotation from LeKashman and Stolle:

> 1. The impact of distribution costs is more difficult to unravel than is the effect of other business decisions. All functions of a business are somewhat interrelated, but distribution is more complexly intertwined with each. And it is these interrelationships—rather than the costs of the distribution function per se—that are the cause of high distribution costs and the key to understanding and reducing these costs.
> 2. Because corporate accounting has historically been oriented to finance and production, rather than to marketing and distribution, the operating reports that guide managerial action do not tot up in any one place the full impact of distribution on costs. The real cost of distribution never stares management in the face.
> 3. Even where managements have become aware of these costs and their impacts on profits, there was until recently very little that anyone could do about the pervasive effects of distribution. Even a relatively simple problem in distribution system design can involve hundreds of bits of information that interact in thousands of ways. So there was no way of dealing with the distribution cost complex until techniques were developed to manipulate this mass of material as a single integrated entity.[17]

Figure 16–8 illustrates the complexity of making a decision on the optimal number of warehouses for a hypothetical company. In this illustration, ten variables influence the number of warehouses the company should have. Each variable has its own cost curve based upon the number of warehouses that are established. For example, warehousing costs are minimized when the company has no warehouses. Transportation costs are minimized when the company has ten warehouses. The cost of production and supply alternatives are minimized when the company has thirty warehouses, and so forth. The optimal number of warehouses is a combination of all of the individual cost curves. In this illustration, the optimal number of warehouses shown in the "Total Cost Curve" is five.

PHYSICAL DISTRIBUTION STRATEGY—THE TOTAL COST APPROACH

The starting point of physical distribution strategy planning is a decision about the level of customer service to be provided. All other determinations flow from this decision, so it is critical. The customer service level is defined as the percentage of orders that will be shipped within a specified time. For example, a customer service level of 95 percent means that the firm will ship 95 percent of its orders within twenty-four hours (or any other specified time period). As pointed out earlier, the higher the level of customer service, the higher the distribution costs. One major company, for example, found that reducing its customer service level from 95 percent to 90 percent would cut its distribution costs by $8 million. The question then becomes whether this reduction in customer service level would do more harm than good in terms of customer dissatisfaction and lost sales. This determination is not easy to make, and

17. Raymond LeKashman and John F. Stolle, "The Total Cost Approach to Distribution," p. 37

FIGURE 16–8: Total Cost Approach

SOURCE: Ramond LeKashman and John F. Stolle, "The Total Cost of Distribution," *Business Horizons* (Winter, 1965), p. 39. Copyright, 1965, by the Foundation for the School of Business at Indiana University. Reprinted by permission.

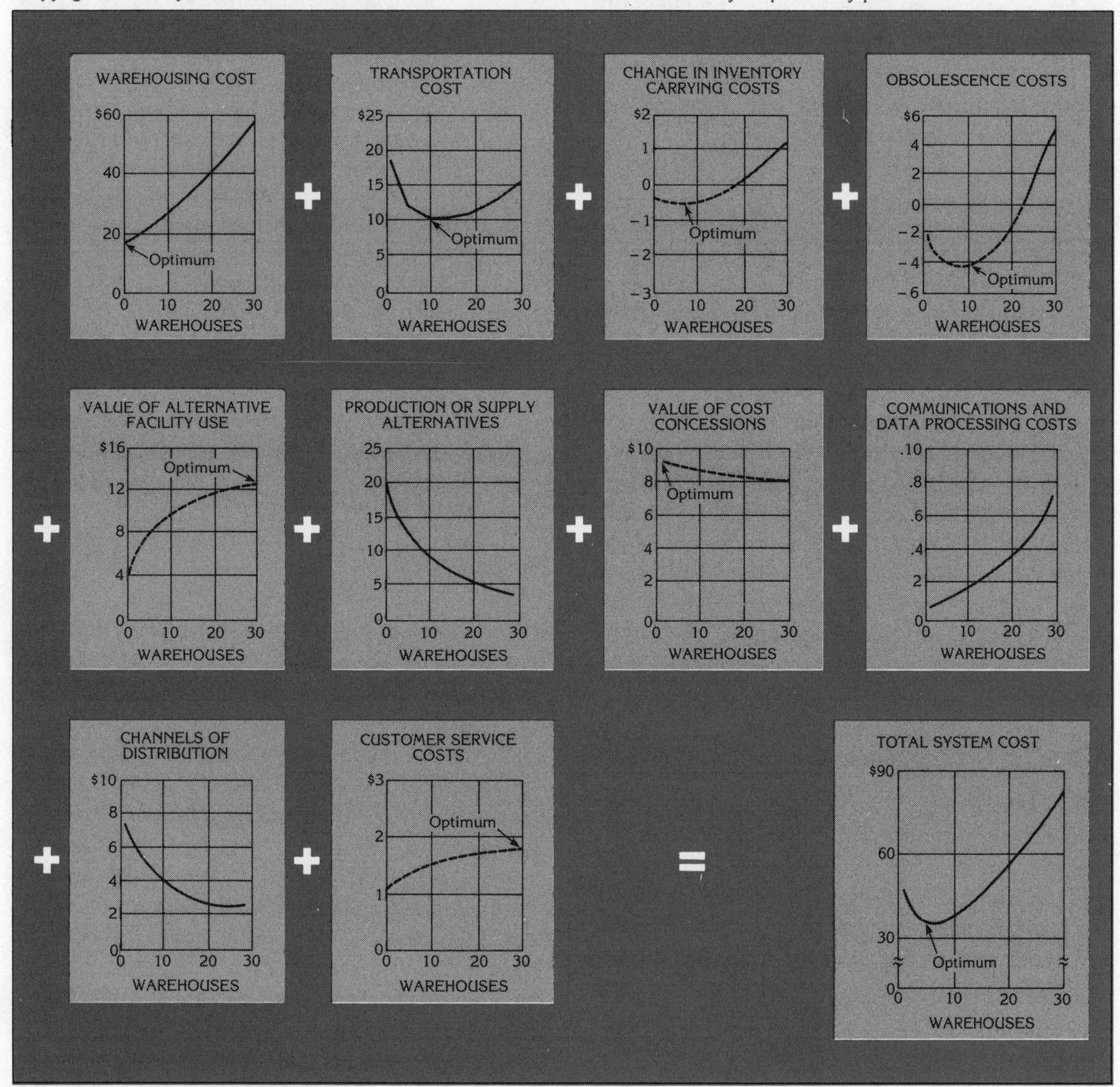

must be approached cautiously. Much depends upon the nature of the business, the level of service acceptable to major customers, and competitive practices. Marketing research can be used to gather information on customer expectations and competitive practices. But the decision itself is a responsibility of top management.

Planning Distribution Strategy

In broad strokes, planning physical distribution strategy requires the following steps:

- Ascertain the level of customer service required. As noted above, marketing research can be helpful in determining customer expectations and needs, in identifying competitive practices, and in estimating the effect on sales of different service levels.

- Identify the major cost variables affecting physical distribution costs. This may require an operations research approach.
- Develop an internal records system that will pull relevant costs together.
- Determine optimal facilities and methods for each cost variable.
- Develop an optimal total cost plan for physical distribution.

Do most companies follow this approach? No. In many cases planning never occurs to them. In other cases, it appears too complex, cumbersome, and expensive. In addition, many companies probably feel that future developments in the field of physical distribution will result in such an approach becoming obsolete by the time it is developed. Do some leading companies follow this approach? Yes, oh yes. That's why they are leaders.

Managing the Physical Distribution System

Once established, a physical distribution system must be implemented and managed. It won't implement and manage itself. Further, a complex physical distribution system cannot be managed on a piece-meal, fragmented basis with each functional area being handled independently—with traffic focusing only on transportation, with the sales department concentrating on field warehousing, with production being only concerned with in-plant storage.

Effective physical distribution management requires an integrated logistics department, staffed by specialists, and managed by someone within the organization high enough in the management hierarchy to have some clout, and reporting to the chief executive officer. Further, this manager should be a part of top management, and intimately involved in corporate marketing decisions. Otherwise, the firm may find itself in the position described in the following quotation:

> The president of an Ohio-based $350-million business, on finding that his company's distribution bill had reached a new high of $35.8 million, or $8 million more than the company's profit, called his director of traffic severely to task. A little historical analysis showed, however, that the sharpest increase in total distribution costs had followed a series of top management policy decisions in which the traffic man had had no part. During the previous four years, management had authorized product line additions that nearly doubled the number of items. And only six months before calling the traffic manager to task, the president had announced that all orders to Mountain State customers would be serviced within 48 hours of receipt—a decision that necessitated shifting, at substantial expense, from rail to truck.[18]

SUMMARY

Physical distribution is one of the most complex and dynamic areas of marketing. It represents a major cost factor, accounting for approximately one-fourth of the retail dollar and more than one-sixth of the gross national product. Too often, however, distribution is a neglected area because management is often poorly informed about its costs.

Physical distribution may be defined as a marketing subsystem which consists of all activities, including planning and control, involved in the physical movement of raw material and finished goods from producers to consumers. Three components of physical distribution—transportation, inventory costs, and warehousing—account for some 80 to 90 percent of physical distribution costs.

Each of the five major modes of transportation has unique advantages and disadvantages. They are railroads, motor transport, water carriers, air carriers, and pipelines. Railroads are our most important form of freight transportation in terms of ton-miles, although motor transport,

18. Robert P. Neuschel, "Physical Distribution—Forgotten Frontier," p. 131

because of its flexibility, is the most rapidly growing form of transportation. In order to achieve transportation economies, shippers often use a variety of transportation forms for a single shipment. Containerization, the packaging of goods in sealed shipping containers which may be easily moved from one transportation mode to another, has encouraged the use of multiple transportation forms.

Two of the most controversial aspects of transportation are the subject of rates and the effects of government regulation. Rates and regulations have become so complex that many feel they stifle competition and increase transportation costs. As a consequence, a major movement to deregulate transportation emerged in the late 1970s.

A second major component of physical distribution is inventory. Inventory costs involve carrying costs, procurement costs, and stock-out costs. The basic inventory decision consists of two prime considerations: the size of orders and the frequency of orders. Large orders increase carrying costs, but reduce procurement costs; small orders reduce carrying costs, but increase procurement costs. One tool for optimizing these opposing variables is the EOQ (Economic Order Quantity). The simple EOQ equation must be modified for application to complex situations.

The third major component of physical distribution is warehousing. Key considerations in warehouse decisions are the type of warehousing to use and the number of warehouses to employ.

The starting point of physical distribution planning is the decision about the level of customer service to be provided. All other determinations flow from this decision. An effective physical distribution system must be carefully managed. Effective management requires an integrated logistics department, staffed by specialists, and headed by a member of top management who is intimately involved in corporate marketing decisions.

REVIEW QUESTIONS

1. Explain physical distribution and identify the key thoughts in this definition.
2. Identify and explain the major components in the physical distribution system.
3. What are the advantages and disadvantages of the major modes of transportation?
4. Explain some of the reasons for the complexity of transportation rates.
5. What are the major components of inventory, and how do they interrelate?
6. Given the following information, compute the EOQ: Demand for time period = 14,000 units; Cost of each order = $14.00; Cost of each unit = $4.00; Inventory carrying costs as a percent of inventory value = 16%. Are there any other considerations involved in determining order size?
7. What are the key considerations in warehouse decisions? What are the advantages of public rather than private warehouses?
8. If private warehousing is employed, why are warehouse decisions particularly difficult?
9. Identify the steps in planning physical distribution strategy.
10. Identify the essential requirement for effective management of a physical distribution system.

1. The purpose of a physical distribution system should be to operate at the lowest possible cost. Do you agree or disagree with this statement?
2. Identify the departments of a company that might be involved in some aspect of physical distribution. Explain their involvement. Based on your answer, how do you think the physical distribution function should be organized in the company?
3. Do you agree or disagree that a company with warehouses in all sections of the country should be able to eliminate wholesalers in their distribution chain?
4. Many people believe that the provision of a high level of customer service will inevitably result in high distribution costs. Do you agree or disagree?
5. Explain which mode(s) of transportation would probably be most suitable for: (A) shipping 200,000 board feet of lumber from Washington to a lumber wholesaler in Chicago; (B) 200 pounds of Rocky Mountain trout from a fishery in Colorado to a restaurant in New York; (C) 600 automobiles from a factory in Japan to Phoenix, Arizona; (D) A carload of appliances from Louisville, Kentucky, to Denver, Colorado; (E) 200 high-fashion dresses from New York to San Francisco.

PHYSICAL DISTRIBUTION

Coutra-Appliance is a major manufacturer of small household appliances distributed through department, hardware, appliance, and general merchandise stores in the United States. Total sales are approximately $700 million annually. The company operates five warehouse distribution centers which are supplied from manufacturing facilities in the East and Northeast. The distribution centers are in large population centers like Newark, Orlando, Chicago, Houston, and Los Angeles to minimize transportation costs. The company's policy was to price competitively, and to maintain a complete stock of appliances and replacement parts in all distribution centers.

Although Coutra-Appliance has been highly successful, high interest rates and price competition have eroded profits during the past three years. A new company president has been appointed recently and given the task of finding ways to increase the company's profitability. One of the new president's first steps was to instigate cost analyses of major company activities.

One area of cost analysis was that of physical distribution, where costs totaled over $17 million. Physical distribution costs had increased rapidly in recent years, and currently totaled 12.2 percent of sales, well above the industry average of 10 percent. In addition, a recent research study had estimated that the company lost approximately $40 million a year in sales because retail stores were out-of-stock of the particular item sought by consumers. This same study suggested that sales losses from out-of-stock conditions might be expected to increase in the future because many retailers were reducing their inventories in an effort to reduce operating costs. As a consequence, rapid processing of orders and quick delivery from company warehouses was becoming increasingly important in the appliance business.

Since profit before taxes was 5 percent, a sales loss from out-of-stock conditions cost the company about $2 million in pretax profits. Further, as the company had added products to its line, inventorying of parts had become increasingly complex. This problem was made particularly difficult since individual appliances had been designed "from the ground up," with little concern for standardization and interchangeable components.

A task force established to study the company's physical distribution system developed three alternatives to reduce costs:

- *The installation of a computerized inventory control system at each of the distribution centers. The initial cost of each installation would be $2 million. The primary value of this alternative is improved processing speed and increased storage efficiency. This alternative was estimated to reduce out-of-stock losses by 20 percent, reduce storage costs by 6 percent, and decrease handling costs by 10 percent. At the same time, however, administrative costs would increase by 15 percent.*
- *The second alternative was to improve the existing manual inventory control system. The initial outlay for this alternative was $150,000 for each distribution center. This alternative was estimated to improve the out-of-stock situation by 5 percent, storage and handling by 2 percent and 3 percent respectively, and increase administration costs by 20 percent.*

- *Alternative three involved purchasing new material handling equipment. Initial costs were $500,000 per warehouse. This alternative was estimated to reduce handling costs by 10 percent and breakage costs by 5 percent.*

The task force emphasized that these anticipated savings were only estimates, but that a great deal of care had gone into preparing them. The task force ended its report with the note: "A primary problem of physical distribution is the number of company products, some of which have low sales, and the lack of standardization of component parts."

The costs of the basic components of the company's present warehouse distribution centers were:

Average Costs per Warehouse Center	
Annual product volume	*$140,000,000*
Inventory turnover	*12 times*
Storage space	*750,000 sq. ft.*
Storage costs	*$ 5,000,000*
Transportation costs	*$ 6,500,000*
Handling costs	*$ 3,000,000*
Breakage/obsolescence costs	*$ 1,900,000*
Administrative costs	*700,000*
Total costs	*$ 17,100,000*

Assignment

1. *Identify the key factors that have given rise to the company's relatively high physical distribution costs.*
2. *How does the design of the system meet current problems in serving retail customers?*
3. *On what basis should the three alternatives presented be evaluated?*
4. *What decisions do you believe management should make? Why?*

Personal Selling

- *The importance of personal selling in the marketing effort.*
- *The variety of selling jobs that exist.*
- *Ways of organizing the sales force.*
- *Managing the company sales force.*

MARKETING EXAMPLES

SELLING STARTS WHEN THE CUSTOMER SAYS "NO!"

One of my favorite stories about selling is one told by Red Motley, a great salesman, when he was president of *Parade* magazine. It seems that a salesman and a physicist were neighbors. One Saturday morning the physicist knocked on the salesman's door and said, "I have a problem. Maybe you can help me."

"What is it?" the salesman asked. "I can try."

"Well," the physicist said, "it's my five-year-old son, Johnny. Last week we were out hiking and we found a turtle that we brought home. Johnny has never had a pet before, and he really loved that turtle. This morning when we came downstairs, we found the turtle lying on its back, dead. Johnny is hysterical. There's nothing we can do to quiet him down. I've offered to get him another turtle, but he won't listen. You know more about persuading people than I do, so I thought maybe you could help."

"Let's go talk to Johnny," the salesman said.

Sure enough, when they entered the physicist's house, there was Johnny lying on the floor beside the turtle, crying his heart out. The salesman looked at the turtle and then at Johnny, and said, "Johnny, that was a real fine turtle. He was probably the best turtle that ever lived and we ought to do something special for him. Maybe we ought to have a big funeral with music and flags, and everything."

When Johnny heard this, he started sniffling instead of wailing, and began to listen.

"Yes, sir," the salesman said, "we ought to have a big funeral. We could take your wagon and drape some cloth around it. And, we could hitch my dog up to the wagon to pull it. Your mother plays the flute and I play the drums. She could get her flute and I could get my drums and we could have a parade. You could lead the parade and your father could bring up the rear, carrying an American flag, and we could bury that good old turtle out in the corner of the yard under the willow tree."

By this time, Johnny was really interested. He had stopped crying, and his eyes were getting as big as saucers.

"The only trouble is," said the salesman, "we need a casket."

The mother interrupted to say, "I have an old jewelry box upstairs that we can use. Johnny, it's on the bottom shelf in the closet. Why don't you go get it?" Well, Johnny was off like a shot.

While Johnny was upstairs, the silly turtle started to show some signs of life. It poked out its legs and neck, arched its neck and turned itself right side up. When Johnny came running downstairs with the jewelry box for a casket, his mother called to him excitedly, "Johnny! It's all right! We don't have to have a funeral! Your turtle is alive!"

Johnny stopped dead in his tracks. His face turned white, he clinched his fists, and screamed "KILL HIM! KILL HIM! KILL HIM!"

THE MORE THINGS CHANGE, THE MORE THEY STAY THE SAME

The musical play, *Music Man,* opens with a railway coach scene. A group of turn-of-the-century drummers (salesmen) sing a number in which the refrain is "but you gotta know the territory." By "knowing the territory" they meant that to be good salespersons, they had to know who the customers were, what they were like, what their politics were, the names of their wives and their children, what subjects to avoid, how to get along with them, and how to sell them on an individual basis.

Well, things have changed since the turn-of-the-century—even in the past ten years. *Fortune,* in an article on Louis Manara (a salesman for American Cyanamid), points out:

> . . . in the past decade the salesman's job has become vastly more complex—so much so that a number of executives believe that a

new job title is required. "Salesman is just too narrow a word," says one marketing manager. Gordon Sterling, Manara's division president, pinpoints the basic change. "Ten years ago, it was sales, sales, sales," he says. "Now we tell our salesmen: Don't just sell—we need information. What do our customers need? What is the competition doing? What sort of financial package do we need to win the order?

That probing for market intelligence is not the only new duty. Manara also is expected to mediate disputes between Cyanamid's credit department, newly vigilant in these times of costly money, and slow paying customers. He has to sort out customer complaints concerning Cyanamid products. He must keep abreast of fast changes in both government regulations and world chemical markets. . . . Managers are particularly anxious for salesmen to develop a grasp of finance. "We want them to know about the cost of money and be able to relate that to the customer's inventory and accounts receivable situations, so they have an idea of what financial package might swing the sale," says one marketing manager.[1]

Yes, selling has changed. But the fundamentals are still there. Management's concern with the sales effort has given rise to a number of selling systems.

One system, CALLPLAN, cranks all relevant information into a computer—right down to the personality traits of each buyer and

1. Hugh D. Menzies, "The New Life of a Salesman," *Fortune Magazine* © 1980 Time, Inc. All rights reserved.

seller. The computer then advises which salesman will be most successful with which customers and which accounts to concentrate on.[2]

So, you see, in the 1980s, just as at the turn of the century, you've still "gotta know the territory."

TECHNICALLY UP AND BRED TO ACHIEVE

Sales recruiting isn't what it used to be either. In an article on recruiting and hiring of salespeople, *Sales and Marketing Management* reports:

> Each time Jack Neff, vice-president, North American Marketing, a part of Dana Corp.'s Industrial Group . . . sets out to recruit a new salesperson, the odds are about 30 to 1 against him. But he's not complaining. That's because Neff needs technically competent, applications-minded people—what he calls technical types—who *appear* to be able to sell. Accordingly, Dana recruits on college campuses.
>
> Each prospect is subjected to a long morning's or afternoon's interview. If he or she is technically "up," and only then, the interview turns to personal goals and family background, for Neff believes that candidates whose families are studded with achievers tend to belong to that mold, too. The candidates who survive their campus interviews are invited to do it all over again with Dana's sales and marketing management, at company headquarters in Warren, Michigan, where the actual selection is made.[3]

2. Ibid, p. 174.
3. Arthur J. Bragg, "Higher Stakes—but Better Odds," *Sales and Marketing Management* (August 18, 1980): 46.

These three examples have been selected to emphasize three key points about personal selling: First, to highlight a traditional view of sales jobs—personal persuasion. Second, to point out that, in today's competitive climate, salespeople are expected to do much more than just persuade, although persuasion and "knowing the territory" are still important aspects of the job. And, finally, to acknowledge that more and more companies are becoming increasingly sophisticated and demanding in their selection of salespeople. It is no longer a catch-as-catch-can process. They are seeking people how are technically trained and who have a desire to succeed.

AN OVERVIEW OF PERSONAL SELLING

"Hewers of wood and haulers of water," is the phrase used by a major management consulting firm to describe the sales force's indispensable contribution. It is not meant as a denigrating phrase. Rather, it is a complimentary acknowledgement of the critical role that personal selling plays in the marketing of products. "Nothing happens until a sale is made" is another phrase that emphasizes the importance of personal selling in the current marketing scene. Whether one is speaking of industrial marketing or consumer products, in most cases the sales force forms the crucial link between producers and their customers.[4]

There is no such thing as the typical salesperson. Sales jobs vary widely in the skill and training they require. For example, the technical knowledge and training required by a sales clerk in a department or variety store is vastly different than that required for a computer sales representative for IBM. For this reason, we will restrict our discussion of salespeople, and their management, in this chapter to producers' sales forces. That is, the sales representatives of producer organizations who call on industrial, wholesale, and retail firms. Even in this more restricted sense, there is no such thing as a typical salesperson.

Sales and Marketing Management, in their annual survey of selling, describe five different categories of salespeople:

- *Account representative.* A salesperson who calls on a large number of already established customers in, for example, the food, textiles, apparel, and wholesale industries. Much of this selling is low key and there is minimal pressure to develop new business.
- *Detail salesperson.* A salesperson who, instead of directly soliciting an order, concentrates on performing promotional activities and introducing products. The medical detail man, for example, seeks to persuade doctors, the indirect customers, to specify the pharmaceutical company's trade name product for prescriptions. The firm's actual sale is ultimately made through a wholesaler or direct to pharmacists who fill prescriptions.
- *Sales engineer.* A salesperson who sells products for which technical know-how and the ability to discuss technical aspects of the product are extremely important. The salesperson's expertise in identifying, analyzing, and solving customer problems is another critical factor. This type of selling is common in the chemical, machinery, and heavy equipment industries.
- *Industrial-products salesperson, nontechnical.* This salesperson sells a tangible product to industrial or commercial purchasers; no high degree of technical knowledge is required. Industries such as packaging materials or standard office equipment use this type.
- *Service salesperson.* A salesperson who sells intangibles such as insurance and advertising. Unlike the four preceding types, those who sell services must be able to sell the benefits of intangibles.[5]

Many companies employ more than one of the categories described above because their selling job is complex and there are many selling tasks that have to be done.

4. I have used the term *in most cases* because of the growth of direct marketing and catalogue sales in which contact with consumers is made through the mail. Even in these instances, however, the development of persuasive letters, the writing of catalogue copy, the processing of orders, and the handling of customer complaints requires people whose functions are quite similar to the functions provided by salespersons in other industries.

5. Thayer C. Taylor, "A Letup in the Rise of Sales Call Costs," *Sales and Marketing Management* (February 25, 1980): 24.

TABLE 17–1: Costs of Personal Selling as a Percent of Industry Sales and of Total Industry Promotion.
SOURCE: Reprinted, by permission of the publisher, from EXECUTIVE COMPENSATION SERVICE, *Sales Personnel Report*, 25th Edition, 1980–1981

	Promotion as a Percent of Industry Sales	*Personal Selling as a Percent of:*	
		Industry Sales	*Industry Promotion*
Consumer Goods			
Apparel	11.2%	3.3%	29.4%
Durable goods	5.1	1.1	21.6
Ethical pharmaceuticals	13.5	3.6	26.7
Food	5.4	1.7	31.5
Major household durables	2.8	2.2	78.5
Proprietary drugs and toiletries	16.1	1.8	11.2
Industrial Goods			
Automotive parts and accessories	4.0	2.5	62.5
Building materials	2.8	1.2	42.8
Chemicals	4.2	2.1	50.0
Container and packaging materials	2.7	1.8	66.6
Electrical materials	5.6	2.2	39.3
Electronics	4.4	1.7	38.6
Fabrics	4.0	1.3	32.5
Fabricated metals (heavy)	3.4	1.6	47.0
Fabricated metals (light)	4.0	1.8	45.0
Instruments	7.3	2.0	27.3
Iron and steel	1.4	0.8	57.1
Machinery (heavy)	4.3	1.9	44.2
Machinery (light)	5.5	2.1	36.4
Paper	2.1	1.1	52.4
Printing and Publishing	10.4	6.1	58.6
Rubber, plastics, leather	1.7	1.0	58.8
Tools and hardware	5.6	2.3	41.1

Promotion includes sales force expenses (including compensation, travel, lodging, meals, and entertainment), advertising, and sales promotion.
Sales force expense includes compensation, travel, lodging, meals, and entertainment.
One problem with the data shown is that companies differ in the ways they define sales expense, and the costs included in the definition. Thus, these figures should only be used as a general guide to costs.

The Cost of Personal Selling

The cost of personal selling is high, and getting higher. These costs have not been helped much by the inflation that has ravaged the U.S. economy during the late 1970s and early 1980s. In 1980 personal selling costs for American industry were approximately $150 billion and, for many companies, represent the largest single element of marketing costs. But, this figure is too large to be easily grasped. Another way of understanding the costs of personal selling is to examine them as a percent of total sales and as a percent of total promotion, where promotion is defined as personal

TABLE 17–2: Cost of Salesperson's Call.
SOURCE: *Sales and Marketing Management* (February 25, 1980), p. 28.

	Metropolitan area		*Rural area*	
	Range	*Median*	*Range*	*Median*
Account representative	\$23–\$45	\$32	\$46–\$90	\$63
Detail salesperson	\$13–\$25	\$17	\$21–\$38	\$28
Sales engineer	\$24–\$62	\$37	\$41–\$82	\$59
Industrial product salesperson	\$16–\$29	\$21	\$25–\$58	\$37
Service salesperson	\$13–\$23	\$17	\$22–\$45	\$31

Costs are based on direct compensation, automobile costs, travel, and entertainment.

selling, advertising, and sales promotion. This has been done in Table 17–1 for a variety of product groups. Examination of this table shows:

- Although there are wide variations in sales force expenditures, sales force expenses are a major cost component, exceeding 50 percent of total promotion costs in a number of instances
- Generally, the proportion of promotion costs accounted for by sales force expenditures are higher for industrial products than for consumer goods.

Still another way of looking at the cost of personal selling is to examine the cost per call. That is, how much does it cost to have a salesperson make one call on one customer? Costs vary, of course, depending upon levels of compensation, the category of salesperson, and the average number of calls that a salesperson is able to make in a year. For example, in a metropolitan area where many customers are concentrated, a salesperson can make many more calls than is possible in a rural area in which customers are widely dispersed and a large portion of the salesperson's time is spent traveling. Nonetheless, *Sales and Marketing Management* has made estimates of the cost-per-call, based on the American Management Associations' annual *Sales Personnel Report*, supplemented by telephone calls to companies for verification. These estimates are shown in Table 17–2.

Table 17–2 should be read in the following way: The average cost of a single call by an account representative in a metropolitan area ranges from a low of \$23 to a high of \$45, with a median average cost of \$32. In a rural area, the range for an account representative is from \$46 to \$90, with a median average of \$63. The following conclusions can be drawn from this table:

- Sales calls are expensive even under the best conditions.
- The cost per call varies widely, both within salesperson categories and between categories.
- The cost of sales calls in rural areas is substantially higher than in metropolitan areas.
- It is difficult to draw a simple conclusion about the cost of the average sales call.

Because of the high cost of personal selling, the efficient management of sales representatives' time, and the effective deployment of a firm's sales force are major concerns of management. This is also why many managements despair over poor preparation by the company's salespersons when they call on customers.

For example, I spent two years as a space buyer for magazines in an advertising agency. My job was to recommend which magazines our clients should purchase advertising from and, upon acceptance of the recommendation, to issue contracts to those magazines. I was called upon by magazine representatives hired to persuade me that I should recommend their magazines to the agency's clients. Many of the magazine representatives were excellent. Some were pretty poor. The poor ones were ill-prepared for their sales calls. Sometimes, they just dropped in to pass the time of day, or because they were in the area. Or, they would open up the conversation with a general question such as "Do you have any clients that would be interested in using my magazine?" I didn't like to see the poor ones because they wasted my time. The good ones were another matter. I was always delighted to see them because they knew what products they were interested in, they provided me with specific information about why their magazines would be effective advertising mediums for these products, they brought me information on competitive activity and, often, they brought me relevant information about my agency's clients that I needed to know. In short, they were prepared for the sales call, and used their time and my time well.

Similar situations exist in other fields. Some salespeople are well prepared. Others are not. Those who are not well prepared for their sales calls are wasting their companies' resources and wasting their customers' time.

The Changing Nature of Sales

The complexion of selling is changing. Increasing sales costs, increased competition, the need for marketing information, and increasing demands for customers have transformed salespeople from their traditional roles as drummers, to essential links between company management and its markets.

Another change in selling should be noted. Throughout the preceding material, I have carefully used the terms *salesperson, salespeople,* and *sales representative* in place of the more traditional *salesman.* This has been done because the company sales force is no longer the unique domain of men. More and more women are entering sales work and finding it professionally rewarding. Most of the major companies today recruit men and women for their sales staffs; there is little question that this trend will become more pronounced in the future.

The demands made on salespeople today are extremely broad. In addition to selling, providing customer service, explaining management policies, and serving as a source of marketing information, they are also often expected to be knowledgeable about finance, economics, engineering, and other technical matters. Not long ago I visited the sales training director of a major division of a national electronics company. During our discussion, he asked me if I could set up an economics seminar for the company's industrial salespeople. "More and more," he said, "customers expect our sales representatives to have a basic understanding of the balance of payments, foreign exchange, and international markets." There is reason to believe that this trend will continue. Professionalism among sales representatives is the picture of the future.

Relationship of the Sales Force to the Company

The relationship of the sales force to the company employing it varies widely. Many companies employ their own sales representatives and compensate them primarily through an annual salary, although commissions and bonuses may also be used as a special incentive. Some companies employ their own sales force, but compensate them wholly through commissions on the sales they make, often offering a drawing account or advance payments if their commissions fall below a certain level during a particular sales period—that is, weekly or monthly. Advances made through drawing accounts must be paid back to the company from future commissions.

Some companies use agents or brokers who are independent business people working strictly on a commission basis. Still other companies share sales forces which call on the same types of customers, with noncompetitive firms. For example, a manufacturer of a limited line of consumer carpeting, with sales too small to support an independent sales force, may contract with another carpeting producer to distribute its product. Still other companies use some combination of the foregoing alternatives.

No universal rule defines the nature of the relationship between a company and its sales representatives. The type of representation that a company employs depends upon such variables as the size of the company and its resources, the breadth of the product line, the nature of the customers to which the product is sold, competitive practices, and market structure. The ultimate decision on this question is basically a financial one, and always involves trade-offs. Thus, a company that cannot afford to employ its own sales force, may forego the greater control that a company sales force affords for the coverage offered by some alternative method of sales representation. For example, at one point, Ralston-Purina concluded that its sales force was too small to compete effectively with the sales forces of its major competitors, so it converted to a system of independent food brokers, retaining only a supervisory sales force employed by the company to oversee broker activities.

Regardless of the type of sales representation used, the task of organizing and managing sales personnel is a major management function. In the following material, we will discuss these two aspects of the sales function.

Since the particular type of sales representation employed will influence the freedom that a producer enjoys in structuring, deploying, and managing its sales representatives to some extent, we will confine our discussion to those firms that employ their own sales personnel. To do otherwise would lead to a highly complex exposition that is better left to texts dealing solely with the sales function.

ORGANIZING THE SALES FORCE

Among the many questions that must be asked in setting up a sales organization are three that merit special consideration:

- How many sales representatives should be employed?
- How should they be assigned geographically to assure efficient and effective coverage of customers?
- How should the sales organization be structured to provide effective supervision of sales activities?

These questions have no easy and universal answers. Rather, each must be answered on an individual company basis. Sometimes the ideal answers to these questions are not affordable and companies have to make compromises. For example, a firm might conclude that 1,000 sales representatives are required for adequate customer coverage, yet the current level of company sales and resources may permit a sales force of only 300. At this point, management must decide whether to establish its own sales force, or pursue some other alternative. Assuming that management decides that it is still desirable to establish and gradually build up its sales force as increased sales warrant, it is generally better to develop a planned organizational structure and territorial design for the entire complement of 1,000 representatives. Initially, the company may combine territories as well as jobs on the organizational chart. Temporarily, it may be necessary to leave some territories uncovered, or cover them by using independent agents or brokers.

The advantages of developing a complete plan at the beginning, however, are two-fold. *First,* management can assess the magnitude of the enterprise upon which it is embarking. *Second,* additions to the sales staff may be made in an orderly and systematic manner, with a well defined goal in mind.

Determining the Size of the Sales Force

At the simplest level, the size of the sales force depends upon the nature of the sales task, the number of customers to be contacted, and the frequency of contact required. These relationships can be expressed in the following algebraic formula:

$N = CF/K$, where

N = the size of the sales force;

C = the number of customers to be contacted;

TABLE 17–3: Average Annual Sales Calls.
SOURCE: *Sales and Marketing Management* (February 25, 1980), p. 28.

	Metropolitan Area	*Rural Area*	*Difference*
Account representative	1,195	598	597
Detail salesperson	1,912	1,195	717
Sales engineer	1,045	665	380
Industrial products salesperson	1,673	956	717
Sales service person	2,151	1,151	1,000

F = the number of contacts to be made in a year; and

K = the average number of contacts that can be made in a year by a single salesperson.

Thus, if a firm has 20,000 customers who must be contacted six times a year, and the average number of contacts that can be made by one salesperson in a year is 1,000, then

N = (20,000) (6)/1,000 = 120.

Practically, however, size determination is not quite that simple for two reasons. *First,* customers vary in size and importance; it is generally desirable to call on large customers more frequently than on those who offer lesser opportunities for sales. *Second,* the average number of sales contacts that can be made in a year varies dramatically between metropolitan and rural areas, and by the type of sales representative required. For example, Table 17–3 shows the average number of sales contacts that can be made by various types of sales representatives in metropolitan and rural areas. Note that, depending upon the type of sales representation required, those working in metropolitan areas can make from 380 to 1,000 more sales contacts than their counterparts working in rural areas. Note also, that the average number of sales contacts that can be made varies in terms of the different types of salespeople.

As a consequence of these two reasons, management should use the following procedure:

- Classify customers into size-classes according to their annual sales. One might, for example, set up three classes of customers. "A" accounts might include all customers whose annual sales volume exceeded $10 million; "B" accounts might be those with annual sales volumes between $5 million and $10 million; "C" accounts would be customers with annual sales volumes of less than $5 million.
- Determine the optimal number of sales contacts to be made on accounts in each class size. For example, "A" accounts might be contacted twenty-four times a year; "B" accounts, twelve times; and "C" accounts, six times.
- Determine the number of accounts in each size class in metropolitan and rural areas.
- Determine the type of sales representation that will be required.
- Ascertain the average sales contacts that can be made in a year by the type of sales representatives that is appropriate.

Once these determinations have been made, the original algebraic formula can be modified in the following way:

$$N = \sum_{i=1}^{3} \frac{C_{mi}F}{K_m} + \sum_{i=1}^{3} \frac{C_{ri}F}{K_r}$$

Where:

N = the number of sales representatives required.

C_i = the number of customers in each size group.

F = the desired call frequency.

K = the average number of calls that can be made by a representative in a year.

m = metropolitan areas.

r = rural areas

By substituting the appropriate numbers, one can compute the total number of sales representatives required to meet the desired coverage criteria.

Note, however, that this approach will only provide a rough gauge, or ballpark figure. In practice, adjustments will have to be made because of specific customer locations, and because this approach is only concerned with coverage and not with costs. Nonetheless, it represents a systematic starting point that can be adapted to real world exigencies.

Criteria for Geographic Assignment of the Sales Force

Sales representatives are usually assigned to relatively confined geographic areas to minimize travel costs. When this is not done, strange patterns of coverage can emerge and high travel costs are incurred. For example, one time I was working with a client who marketed a line of high-fashion women's shoes, and used selective distribution in exclusive women's shoe stores. One concern of the company management was its high travel costs; in discussions with management, I learned that they had never established sales territories. Instead, they had hired a small number of experienced sales representatives who had established followings among retail outlets, and let each representative exploit their personal contacts with these stores. At my request, management provided a list of these sales representatives and their customers. I had our research department plot this data on a United States map, using different color codes for each sales representative. The results would have been funny had they not been so wasteful. Representative "A", for example, might call on outlets in San Francisco, Los Angeles, Dallas, Chicago, New York, Boston, Philadelphia, Washington D.C., Miami, and a half a dozen cities in between. At the same time, representative "B" was calling on stores in Seattle, San Francisco, San Diego, Detroit, Cleveland, Houston, St. Louis, Pittsburgh, New York, and Miami. Similar patterns existed for other representatives. In short, every representative was traveling from coast to coast and from border to border. When I showed the map to company management, I said "Surely, you must have known this." The answer was, "Well, we suspected it, but we didn't know it was this bad."

Most companies establish sales territories consisting of contiguous geographic areas. Small territories are sometimes referred to as *sales areas,* although the designations used by different companies are often idiosyncratic. For purposes of administration and supervision, several contiguous sales areas are combined into larger units that may be referred to as *sales districts,* and contiguous sales districts are combined into even larger units, often referred to as *sales regions.* Thus, a company that markets its products nationally might have six sales regions, thirty sales districts, and 120 or more sales areas.

A great deal of thought must go into the design of sales territories and, once designed they should be thought of as relatively permanent. The reason for this is that sales potentials as well as historic sales data are compiled on the basis of sales territories. If the boundaries of the sales territories are changed significantly, historical data becomes garbage until it has been reworked to conform to the new territorial definitions. One major packaged goods manufacturer with whom I worked found it desirable, for a variety of reasons, to redefine its sales territories as part of their major reorganization plan. From the standpoint of sales analysis, it created chaos. Reworking historical data in terms of the new territory definitions took almost two years, and during that time we were flying blind as far as sensible sales analysis was concerned.

Another key consideration in designing sales territories is to follow county and state lines insofar as possible. The reason for this is that population, income, and consumption statistics compiled by the government and other sources are generally compiled on a county-by-county, state-by-state basis. To make maximum use of this data, which can be exceedingly useful in determining sales potentials and in making demographic analyses, it is helpful to follow the same conventions as the government in defining sales territories.

In establishing the size of sales territories, companies generally seek the following objectives insofar as possible:

- Ease of administration and supervision.
- Ease in estimating territory sales potential.
- Reduction of travel costs to a minimum.
- Equalization of work load.
- Equalization of sales potential.

If one could achieve all of these objectives, administration and supervision would be simplified because interterritory comparisons of both staffing and performance would be facilitated. Unfortunately, this ideal is seldom attained. The major obstacle to its attainment is differences in the concentrations of customers in various parts of the country. For example, a territory consisting of Manhattan Island in New York might contain more customers and a higher sales potential than the Mountain States of Montana, Wyoming, Idaho, Utah, Nevada, Arizona, and New Mexico combined. Further, any customer in Manhattan could be reached quickly by subway or bus, whereas in the Mountain States, customers could be separated by hundreds of miles and transportation connections between customers both scarce and uncertain.

Since most companies try to establish reasonably comparable income opportunities for their sales representatives, the cost of sales (basic compensation and travel expenses) are much higher in sparsely populated areas than in territories that are primarily metropolitan. It also means that it is difficult to compare the performance of individual sales representatives because comparable skill and effort will generally generate more sales in metropolitan areas than in sparsely populated areas. Often, there is no good answer to this problem although companies attempt to compensate for these inherent differences in sales potentials by establishing objectives for individual sales representatives that take these factors into consideration.

Bases for Organizing the Sales Force

The way in which a sales force is organized often determines its effectiveness. In Chapter 1, when discussing the organization of the firm, I noted that a number of organizational principles can be used, and that the most appropriate form of organization depended upon the nature of the firm in question, and the tasks to be done. These same observations apply to the sales force. Among the most common ways of organizing the sales force are by territory, by product, and by industry served.

ORGANIZATION BY TERRITORY. Perhaps the most common way of organizing the sales force is to structure it in terms of territorial lines. Indeed, this form of organizaiton is so common that it is often used in combination with the other organizational bases that we will discuss. The primary advantages of organizing by territory are:

- Travel costs are lower because travel is limited to a localized geographic area.
- Responsibilities are easily defined. The sales representative is solely responsible for all customers in a territory.
- Assignment to local territories increases the salesperson's incentive to cultivate personal, long-term relationships and to develop individual accounts.
- By restricting sales activities to a relatively small geographic area, sales representatives have a greater opportunity to become familiar with local market conditions, and become a dependable source of marketing intelligence.

Figure 17–1 shows a typical organization chart for a territory-based organization.

The territory-based organization is most appropriate when the product line is relatively sim-

FIGURE 17–1: *Typical Organization Chart for a Territory-based Sales Organization.*

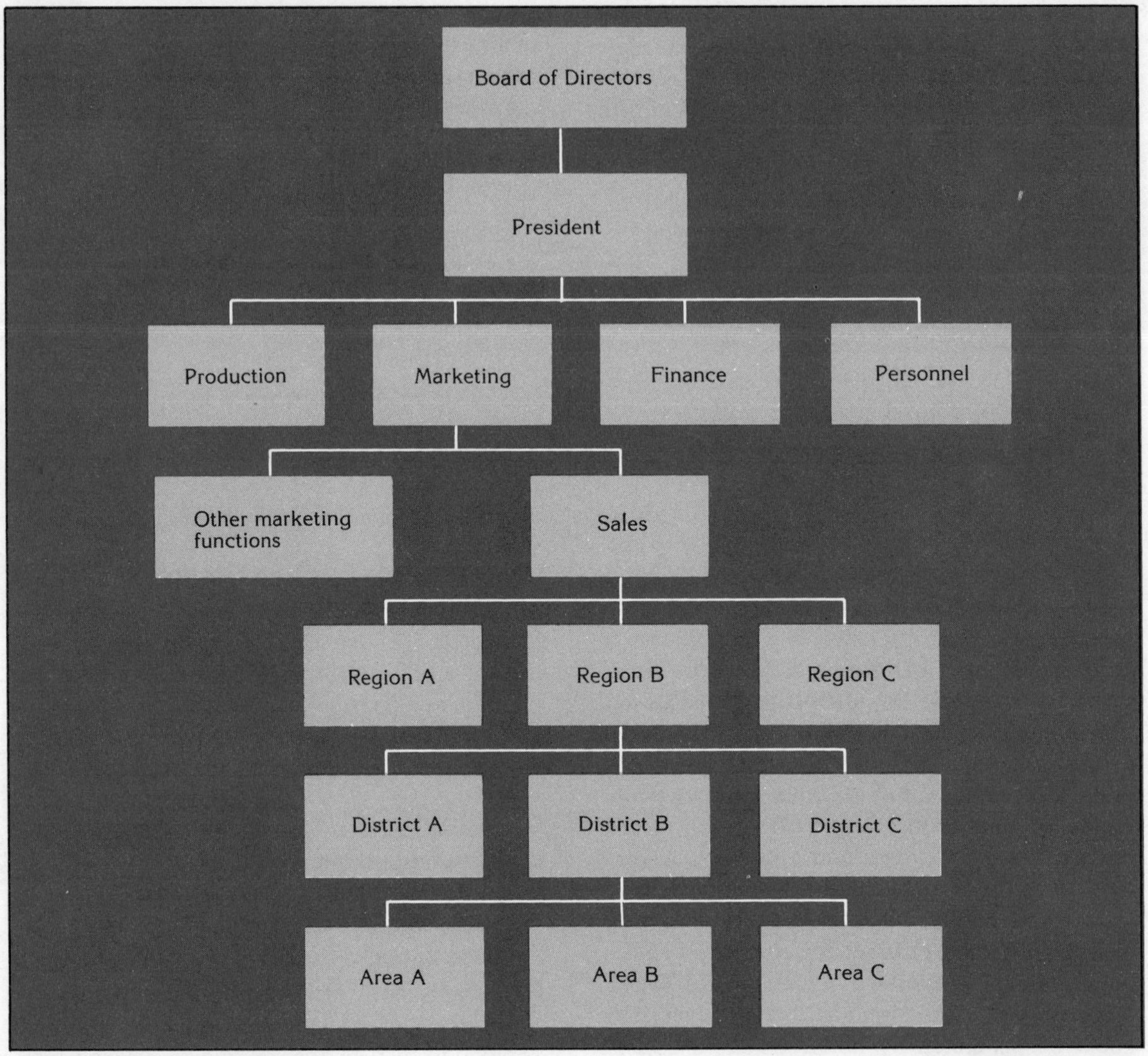

Board of Directors
President
Production
Marketing
Finance
Personnel
Other marketing functions
Sales
Region A
Region B
Region C
District A
District B
District C
Area A
Area B
Area C

ple, and different products produced by the company are purchased by the same buyers. As product lines become more complex, organization by product may be desirable.

ORGANIZATION BY PRODUCT. Organization by product may be desirable when:

- The product line is broad and diverse.
- Products are technically complex and unrelated.
- Different buyers within the same buying organizations are involved.

When sales forces are organized along product lines, usually more than one company representative will be working in each sales area, often calling on the same customer organizations. Such dual representation increases travel costs, and can only be justified if the product line is so diverse and specialized that a single sales representative cannot handle it effectively. A fairly simple case in point occurred early in the history of the frozen food industry.

As the frozen foods industry began to grow, producers of diversified grocery products,

FIGURE 17–2: Typical Organization Chart for Product-based Sales Organization.

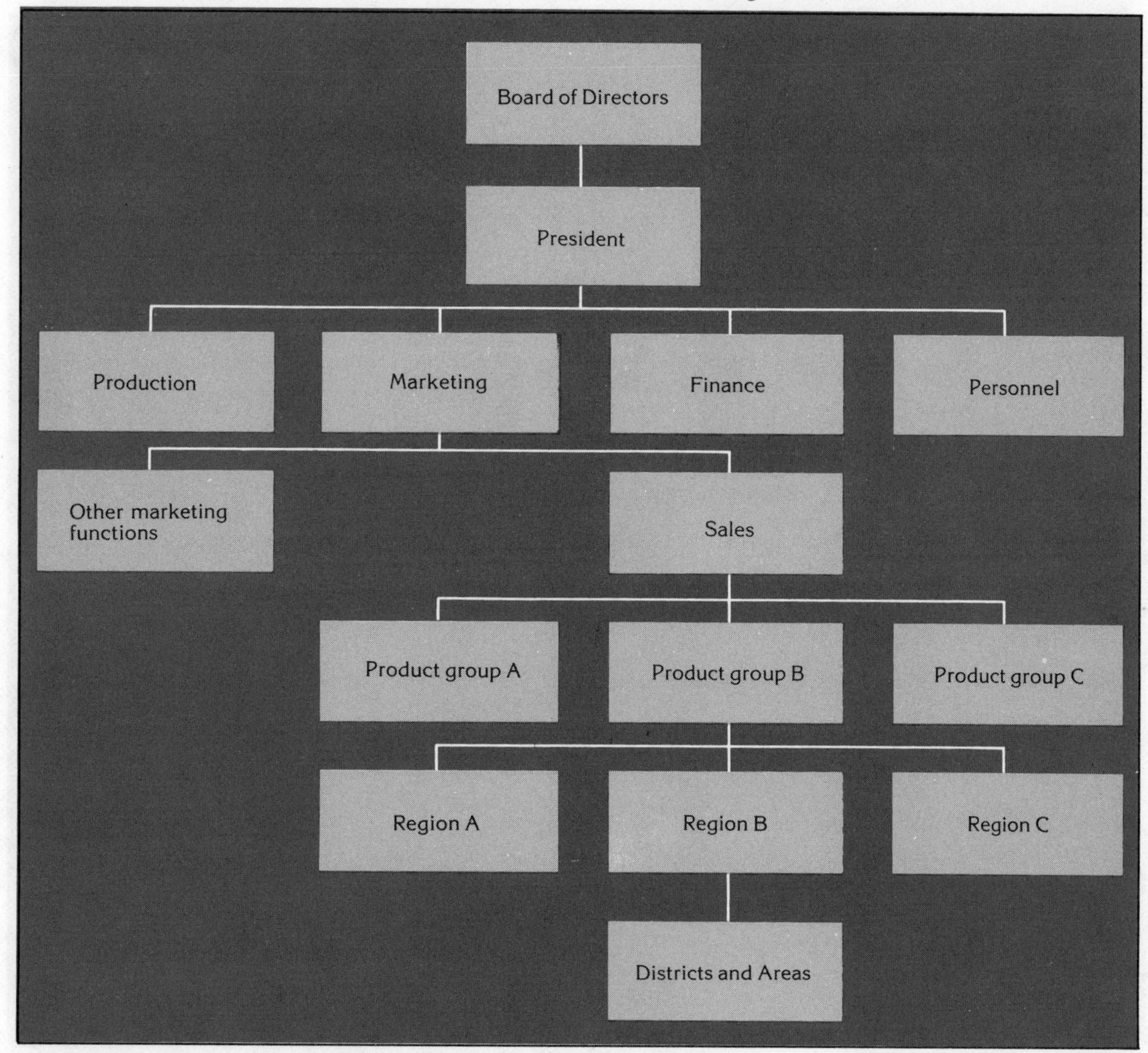

such as Pet and Carnation, entered the field with a line of frozen products. In each case, these companies initially turned their frozen food lines over to their regular sales forces which were already calling on dry-grocery buyers in the food field. This decision proved to be an unhappy one for two reasons: (1) Frozen foods were bought by frozen food buyers, not dry-grocery buyers and the time spent in the waiting rooms and in the offices of frozen food buyers severely reduced the time available to call on dry-grocery buyers. (2) The frozen foods business was a dynamic, promotion and price oriented business that required a disproportionate amount of the sales representatives' time. This resulted in the neglect of dry–grocery items and high sales force costs for the frozen food divisions of Pet and Carnation. As a consequence, both companies withdrew their frozen food items from their regular sales forces and turned them over to frozen food brokers.

Figure 17–2 shows a typical sales organization based on product lines. Note that, in this particular case, organization by territory is superimposed over organization by product.

FIGURE 17–3: *Typical Organization Chart for Industry-based Sales Organization.*

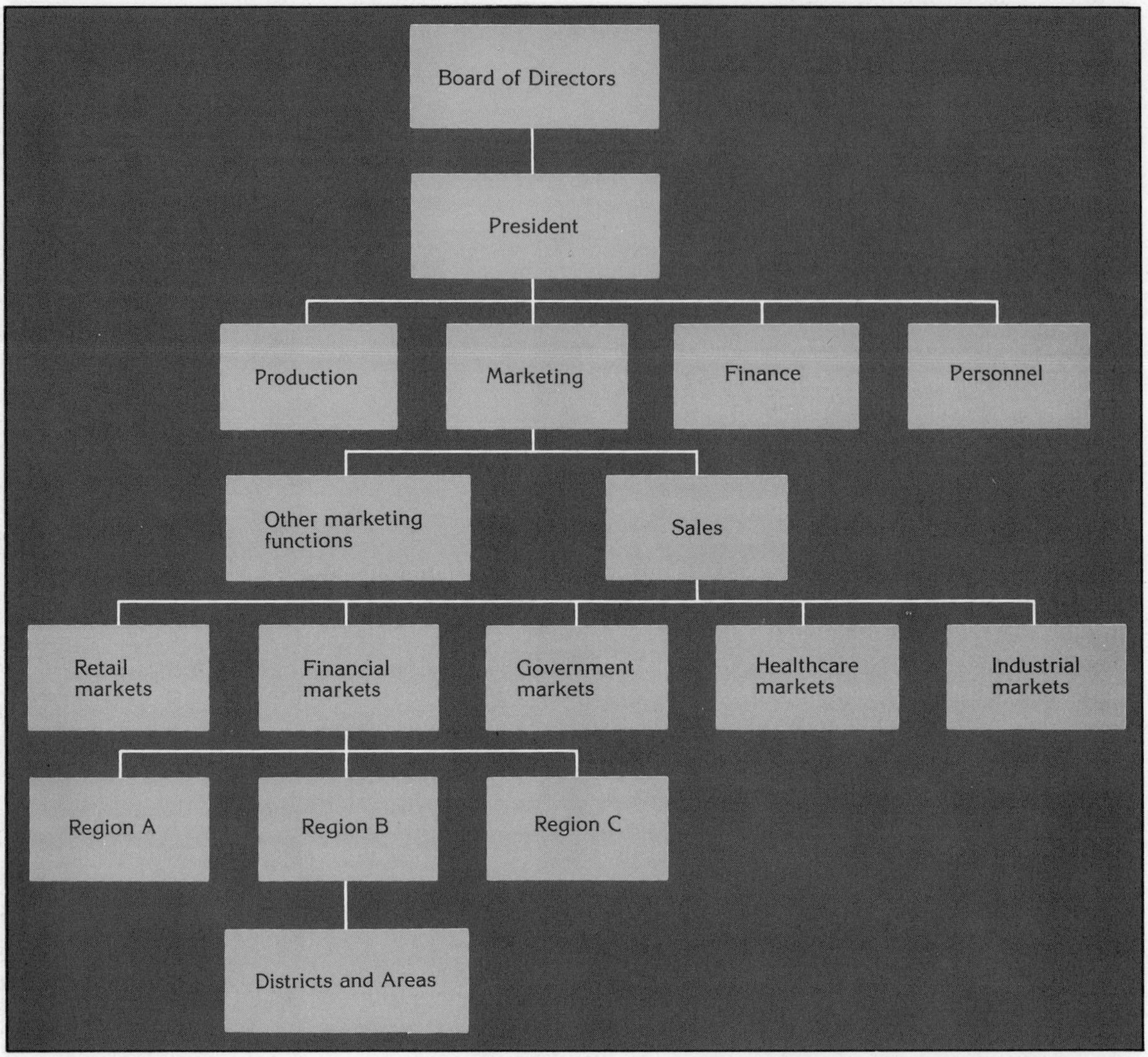

Still a third form of organization is often used when companies serve diverse and well–defined markets.

ORGANIZATION BY INDUSTRY. In some cases, a firm may sell a product or line of products to different industries. Each industry represents a coherent market segment with unique needs and specialized services. In such cases, producers need sales representatives familiar with the specialized problems of each industry served, whose time can best be spent in developing business in the industries with which they are most familiar.

A case in point would be a firm that sells accounting machines, data entry terminals, and copying machines to such diverse markets as retailers, financial institutions, government markets, health care centers, and industrial customers. The sales organization most appropriate for such a firm might take the form shown in Figure 17–3. Again, note that territorial organization has been superimposed over an organization by market. This is not always necessary, but it is often both convenient and economical.

OTHER FORMS OF ORGANIZATION. Other

FIGURE 17–4: Simplified Organization Chart following General Foods' Reorganization.

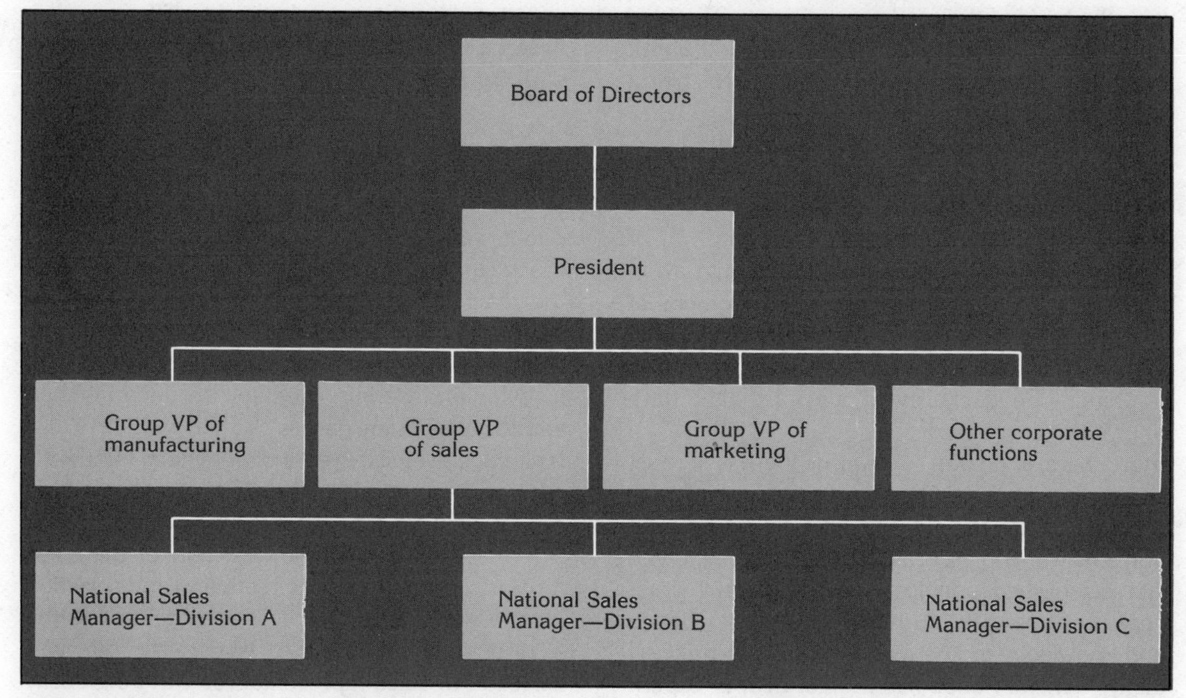

more complex forms of organization might be used, depending upon the needs of the company in question. One interesting development in sales organization has recently surfaced at General Foods.

In Chapter 1, I noted that marketing coordination is enhanced when marketing functions are brought together under a marketing director. And, for several years, the prevailing trend in business has been to have the sales manager report to the director of marketing. In addition, the relatively recent move to organize complex businesses in Strategic Business Units (SBUs) has tended to reinforce this trend.[6] In recent years, General Foods was organized in SBUs, with a separate sales force integrated into the marketing department of the SBU of which it was a part. Then, in 1980:

> With a stroke of the corporate pen, General Foods has dismantled the much-heralded "strategic business units" (SBUs) that controlled the destiny of its packaged foods products and replaced them with a more traditional organization designed to deliver greater sales and marketing clout.[7]

At the heart of General Foods' reorganization was the separation of marketing and sales. General Foods established six marketing divisions for related products, with the head of each marketing division reporting to a group vice-president. Each marketing division was responsible for marketing and research. In addition, General Foods established separate sales and manufacturing divisions which will service the marketing divisions. The sales operation under the new structure consisted of three separate sales divisions, each headed by a national sales manager who reported to a group vice-president. As I understand the General Foods reorganization, it looks something like the simplified diagram in Figure 17–4.

To coordinate the sales divisions with the marketing divisions, "each of the three field sales organizations will have 'division sales managers' with dual reporting responsibility. These people will be under the national sales manager,

6. See Chapter 21 for a brief review of the SBU concept.

7. "GF splits marketing and sales," *Sales and Marketing Management* (May 19, 1980): 10.

but each will also have a dotted line relationship with the head of the marketing division. The idea is to keep the division manager informed about how his particular product lines are being sold."[8]

To the organization and marketing purist, what General Foods has done may appear to border on blasphemy because it has violated a number of hallowed principles such as *unity of command* (which means that one should avoid dual reporting relationships) and the integration of marketing functions into a single operational unit. But, when a company is as large and as complex as General Foods, hallowed principles often have to give way to practical considerations. If there is a moral here, and I don't know that there is, it must consist of two parts: (1) regardless of established principles and traditional practices, if the organization isn't working, fix it; and (2) but, when you violate established principles and traditional practices, be sure that you have enough experience and knowledge to know what you are doing. Certainly, General Foods has a great deal of experience and knowledge.

MANAGING THE SALES FORCE

Organizing the sales force is only part of the job—the easy part. Managing the sales force is the hard part. Sales force management can be subdivided into at least six separate but interrelated tasks: recruiting and selecting personnel, training, setting sales force objectives, supervising the activities of sales representatives, compensating and motivating sales personnel, and evaluating performance. Each of these areas will be discussed briefly.

Recruiting and Selecting Personnel

As in all other areas of human endeavor, the key to an effective sales force lies in the selection of sales representatives. This point is dramatized by a story that is told about Amos Alonzo Stagg, widely recognized as one of the all-time-great football coaches. On his 80th birthday, Stagg, who was still active as a football coach, was asked by a reporter: "Mr. Stagg, what's the difference between a team that ends up on top and one that ends up in the cellar?"

"Well," Stagg is reputed to have answered, "when I first started coaching some sixty years ago, I thought it was the coach. So, I set out to become the best coach in the business. After about twenty years, I found that I had lost about as many games as I had won, so I concluded it wasn't the coach. The real secret to the game, I decided, was strategy. So, I set out to be the finest strategist in the field. Again, after about twenty years of studying and planning strategy, I found that I had lost about as many games as I had won. Now, as I look back over sixty years of coaching, I know it's not the coach, and it's not the strategy. It's the kind of material you get to work with."

This is why the selection of the sales force is so important. The recruiting and selection procedures that a company uses determine the kind of material it has to work with. Improper selection of sales representatives can be a costly mistake. There are no good, current figures on the rate of sales force turnover that should be expected in the typical company—primarily because there is no such thing as a typical company. Too much depends upon the type of sales representative being recruited, and the nature of the sales job. Surveys of sales personnel turnover range from 4 to 68 percent.[9]

The turnover rate for new people just entering the field of selling is undoubtedly higher than that for established representatives who are more mature, who have worked at the job longer, and who have decided upon selling as a career. Although no one knows for sure, a reasonable turnover rate of new salespeople could easily be as high as 30 percent during the first year. Even one percent is too high from the standpoint of

8. Ibid, p. 10.

9. A 1966 study of 665 large manufacturers indicated the median rate of resignations plus discharges totaled 4 percent of the sales force. See David A. Weeks, "Turnover Rates for Salesmen," *Conference Board Record* (April, 1966): 18–22. A 1964 study of 500 companies made by the Sales Executive Club of New York indicated that of the 16,000 sales representatives hired by reporting companies, 31.5 percent left or were discharged by the end of the first year. See *Business Week* (February 1, 1964): 52.

TABLE 17–4: Average Cost of Training a Salesperson.
SOURCE: *Sales and Marketing Management* (February 25, 1980), p. 68.

Type of Company	*Training Cost* Including Salary 1979*	*1978*	*% Increase 1978–79*	*Median Training Period (Weeks) 1979*	*1978*
Industrial products	$19,025	$15,479	22.9%	26	24
Consumer products	13,173	11,338	16.2	16	16
Services**	9,918	8,828	12.3	9	8

*In addition to salary, covers such items as instructional materials prepared, purchased, and rented for training program; transportation and living expenses incurred during training course; instructional staff; outside seminars and courses; and management time spent with salesperson when it is a part of the training budget.
**Includes insurance, financial, utilities, transportation, retail stores, etc.

costs to the company. Table 17–4 shows the average cost of training a salesperson in the industrial products, consumer, and services fields based on *Sales and Marketing Management's 1980 Survey of Selling Costs.*

The costs shown in Table 17–4 are only training costs and do not include costs for recruitment, which may also be sizable. This table demonstrates that it is expensive to recruit salespeople who do not stay with the company. What is sometimes less apparent is the cost to the company of recruiting incompetent sales personnel who do stay with the company.

Recruiting sales representatives would not be so troublesome if one knew what to look for. A technical background, when relevant to the sales job in question, is not too difficult to assess. Beyond this, the personal attributes that make an effective sales representative are pretty much up for grabs. Some effective salespeople are socially outgoing; some are not. Some are highly articulate; some are not. Some are diplomatic; some are not. Any number of lists of character traits are supposed to predict selling effectiveness. Some of these lists are quite elaborate, and most are about as useful as flipping a coin. One of the shortest lists was suggested by Mayer and Greenberg who, after several years of work, concluded that an effective salesperson has at least two characteristics: *empathy,* or the ability to experience a customer's feelings; and *ego drive,* or a strong personal need to succeed in making a sale.[10] This two-item list is matched in brevity by the example given at the beginning of the chapter. Jack Neff, vice-president of North American Marketing, indicated that *technical training* and *being reared in a family that was "studded with achievers"* are key criteria for sales effectiveness for the products sold by his company.

One of the problems is that different sales jobs require various kinds of talents and make particular demands upon their holders. Most companies devise a list of attributes they are seeking based upon the particular job requirements involved. If the job requires a great deal of travel, the candidates should have no objection to travel. If the job requires a great deal of detail work, the candidate should enjoy detail work. If the job requires a great deal of written communication, the candidate should be proficient in writing. If the job requires a high degree of intelligence, an intelligence test for candidates may be appropriate.

An increasing number of companies are giving formal batteries of tests to sales applicants. In addition, they often rely heavily on personal interviews and the reactions of interviewers to the behavior of candidates in the interviewing situation. The point is that the recruiting and selection of good candidates is not a routine task. But, it is also true that this is not purely a random selection process either. And the best evidence is that some companies do a better job of picking winners than do others.

Sales Training

There was a time when sales training was a cliché, and considered an unnecessary expense. Sales

10. David Mayer and Herbert M. Greenberg, "What Makes a Good Salesman?" *Harvard Business Review* (July–August, 1964): 119–25.

TABLE 17–5: Length of Training for New Salespeople.
SOURCE: *Sales and Marketing Management* (February 25, 1980), p. 68.

	Type of Company					
	Industrial Products		Consumer Products		Services*	
Time Period	1979	1978	1979	1978	1979	1978
0 to 6 wk.	14%	16%	27%	25%	31%	36%
Over 6 wk. to 3 mo.	7	9	24	16	33	28
Over 3 mo. to 6 mo.	30	42	39	42	25	27
Over 6 mo. to 12 mo.	49	33	7	9	9	9
Over 12 mo.	0	0	3	8	2	0
Total	100%	100%	100%	100%	100%	100%
Median Training Period (wk.)	26	24	16	16	9	8

*Includes insurance, financial, utilities, transportation, retail stores, etc.

representatives were hired, given an order book and a list of the company's products, assigned to a sales territory, and told to sink or swim. Today, most companies have formal training programs designed to:

- Familiarize new sales people with the company, its policies, and its products.
- Acquaint them with the types of customers they will encounter, customer buying motivations, and purchasing patterns.
- Make them knowledgable about competitive products and competitive selling practices.
- Teach them how to make effective sales presentations, to deal with customer questions and complaints, to use the selling aids and tools with which they will be provided, and to gather marketing information for the home office.
- Indoctrinate them in field procedures and responsibilities, including such routine procedures as preparing expense accounts and call reports.
- Give them an understanding of what will be expected of them and how they will be evaluated.

The content, nature, and the intensity of the training varies by product field. With highly technical products, for example, training periods are often lengthy and demanding. For less complex products, less so. Table 17–5 shows the median length of the training periods for industrial products, consumer products, and for services as revealed by *Sales and Marketing Management's 1980 Survey of Selling Costs.*

Much of the sales training that takes place occurs in the field under the direction of a sales supervisor. Training also takes place at other sites as well, however. Table 17–6 shows the sites, other than the field, where training is done along with the median length of training at each of these locations.

In addition to training for new salespeople, many companies require refresher courses for their representatives, and maintain sales training departments which keep abreast of new developments in selling techniques, and hold seminars and other training activities on a periodic basis.

The point is that, in a competitive economy, the sales function is considered so important that major company resources are devoted to sales training activities.

Sales Force Objectives and Marketing Strategies

Recruiting good sales representatives, training them well, assigning them to sales territories, and expecting them to do their jobs well is not enough.

TABLE 17–6: *Most Frequent Sales Training Sites.*
SOURCE: *Sales and Marketing Management* (February 25, 1980), p. 68.

Location	% Of Companies Conducting Training At This Location			Median Length Of Training Time At This Location		
	Industrial Products	*Consumer Products*	*Services**	*Industrial Products*	*Consumer Products*	*Services**
Home office	80%	78%	96%	2 wk.	2 wk.	3 wk.
Field office	74	56	83	24 wk.	12 wk.	4 wk.
Regional office	53	34	52	3 wk.	5 wk.	1 wk.
Plant locations	46	4	0	4.5 wk.	1 wk.	0 wk.
Central training facility (away from home office)	13	7	17	3 wk.	2 wk.	3 wk.
Noncompany site (hotel, restaurant, club)	7	0	23	1 wk.	0	1 wk.

*Includes insurance, financial, utilities, transportation, retail stores, etc.
Note: Length of time should not necessarily be considered cumulative because not all training programs include all locations.

They must be given objectives. A sales force without objectives is like a ship without a rudder—it sails aimlessly, getting nowhere, and often going off in directions diametrically opposed to the destination that the captain has in mind.

It may be argued that the objective of the sales department is to make sales. But, this is an over-simplification. The real objective of a sales force is to increase the effectiveness of the total marketing effort by undertaking those sales tasks that best contribute to this goal. This means that the activities of the sales force must be coordinated with other marketing activities through the strictures of the marketing plan.

Since marketing objectives and strategies may change from year to year, dependent upon the problems and opportunities defined in the marketing plan, the objectives of the sales force must be adapted to marketing plan requirements. For example, a major grocery products company sold one of its products in two package sizes. The small package size, which contributed 80 percent of the total product's sales volume, had about 85 percent all commodity distribution. The larger size, on the other hand, had only 50 percent all commodity distribution, and contributed only 20 percent of the brand's sales. On the basis of sales per point of distribution, the small package size was by far the most important. As a consequence, marketing strategy and sales force time were devoted primarily to the small package size, with the sales force trying to increase its distribution, improve its shelf facings, and seeking in-store promotions and price features in retail outlets.

A special analysis of A. C. Nielsen data revealed that, in those stores in which both package sizes were carried, brand share was 30 percent higher than in those stores which carried only one package size. In other words, the presence of both package sizes in the store increased sales disproportionately to the contribution of each package size by itself. As a result of this analysis, a key marketing strategy became increasing the distribution of the large package size through special sales promotion activities.

This meant that sales force objectives had to be changed. In practice, virtually all sales force time spent on the brand had to be shifted from promoting the sales of the small package size to obtaining distribution on the larger package.

The particular objectives assigned to a sales force will, as emphasized above, depend upon marketing plan requirements. Some of the areas in which sales force objectives may be defined are:

- *Achieving sales and profit goals.* In multiple product companies, different products often carry different profit margins. Left to their own devices, sales personnel may devote their time to selling the products easiest to sell, rather than to those that are most profitable. As a consequence, management often gives sales representatives specific sales goals for the individual products they produce.

- *Increasing distribution.* Sometimes, marketing strategy is best served by increasing distribution on one or more products that are selling poorly because of inadequate exposure.
- *Increasing shelf facings or improving shelf position.* In self-service outlets, market share is often influenced by the number of shelf facings, or by shelf position. Marketing strategy may require that sales representatives devote a significant portion of their time to these activities.
- *Checking product freshness.* Many products deteriorate with age, and are dated by a company code printed on the label. Marketing strategy may require rigorous control of product freshness, and sales representatives are charged with checking product codes and replacing aging products with fresh stock.
- *Training retail sales personnel.* In many product fields, such as home appliances, furniture, carpeting, cosmetics, photographic equipment, and so forth, the influence of retail sales personnel is often critical in influencing consumer buying decisions. In such cases, marketing strategy may require sales representatives to devote a significant amount of their time to retail sales training.
- *Identifying opportunities for new products.* Often, particularly in the industrial field, technically trained sales representatives may devote a significant portion of their time to identifying new product opportunities.
- *Obtaining dealer cooperation for major promotions.* Marketing strategy often calls for retail promotions. Sales representatives must not only obtain retail cooperation, but also build and stock special displays.
- *Introducing new products.* While often crucial to marketing strategy, introducing new products can be a frustrating and, initially, an unprofitable activity for the sales representative. Yet, the sales force is often required to neglect products that yield immediate profits in order to introduce new ones.
- *Gathering marketing intelligence.* Since sales representatives are a primary source of local marketing intelligence, a significant portion of their time may be directed to this activity.
- *Preparing reports.* Preparing call reports for their immediate supervisors and for the home office is often one of the less popular demands made upon salespeople. Yet, reports are an essential part of their job.

These are only some of the activities assigned to sales representatives. Others, undoubtedly, can be identified. Since the emphasis given to these activities may change as marketing strategies change, the objectives of the sales force will change as well.

In summing up the importance of sales objectives, recognize that sales objectives serve two important functions: *First,* they give direction to sales force activities, coordinating them with the total marketing program. *Second,* they provide an objective basis for evaluating sales force performance.

Supervising Sales Activities

Supervision is an ever present problem in sales management. One of the reasons is that salespeople work alone most of the time, with only periodic, and sometimes infrequent, personal contact with the home office or with regional and district headquarters. Thus, they are responsible for organizing their time, establishing their call patterns, and determining how time with customers will be spent.

Since the salesperson's most valuable commodity is time, *time management* is a crucial aspect of the sales position. Companies often aid sales representatives in this task by establishing the frequency of call patterns on accounts of various sizes, preparing routing lists which reduce the travel time spent between calls, and developing call norms which specify the average calls a sales representative should be able to complete in an average day.[11]

Such company aids are only guides, however, and should be superseded by the judgment of the salesperson when situations warrant it. For example, let us assume that the call norm for a certain sales job is ten per day. Let us now assume that, toward the end of a sales representative's eighth call, (made in the middle of the afternoon), she presents something to a buyer that arouses his interest and generates a flood of questions. The salesperson realizes that if she responds to all of the buyer's questions, the rest of the afternoon will be shot, and she will fall two calls short of making the day's quota. It would be sheer nonsense for the salesperson to break off a meeting with an interested customer simply to meet the daily quota of calls. Yet, it happens.

Or, to take an example I recently encountered. A few days ago, I dropped by the student book store for some supplies. As I left the store, I encountered a book representative from one of the major publishing companies. "Hi, John," I greeted him. "What are you doing on campus? I saw you less than two weeks ago." His response was, "I'm supposed to call on this campus four times a year. I've only been here three times this year. Also, company policy requires that I complete all of my out-of-town calls by November 1. So, I either come up this week, lie in my call report, or have a hassle with management." "John," I said, "that sounds like a lot of nonsense to me. You're too good of a salesman to be hamstrung by arbitrary policies." "Well," he answered, "there's a lot of nonsense in this business."

There is a lot of nonsense in all businesses. And, the nonsense is compounded when companies lose sight of their objectives, and focus on controlling behavior rather than results. Controlling behavior and controlling results is not the same thing. The problem is not a simple one, however. Sometimes behavior control is necessary. For example, one major food company required that its regional and district sales offices be open by 8:00 a.m., ready to take customer calls and provide company service. The sales manager of the company received complaints from customers that sales offices were often not open for business until 8:30, 9:00, or even later in the morning. He handled the problem in two very simple ways. First, he instructed his secretary to send notices of all complaints to the offending offices, with a carbon copy to him. Secondly, in his visits to regional and district offices, he made a point of showing up unannounced at the offices of the worst offenders at 8:00 in the morning and waiting outside until the office opened. He never said a word about lateness. He didn't have to. Word quickly got around, and behavior improved dramatically.

The amount of supervision and behavior control required is inversely proportional to the visibility of the results of the salesperson's job. If the results are highly visible, little direct supervision is required. If, for example, the salesperson's objectives are to achieve sales quotas, the results are readily apparent, and a minimum of supervision is required. If, on the other hand, salespeople have many tasks, the results of any one of which are not highly visible, then close supervision is often required to make sure that the tasks are done.

This means that sales management should devote considerable thought to determining the sales objectives of its representatives, using highly visible objectives whenever possible, and devising methods for measuring performance that are objective. For example, if one of the objectives of the sales force is to obtain special display, sales management often requires a photograph of each display built. If objectives call for increasing shelf facings, management often requires before-and-after photographs. Detailed call reports are often required in which salespeople specify whom they called on, how much time was spent in the call, and what was discussed. In addi-

11. In addition to route lists developed by company management, newspapers in major markets often develop local route lists for major forms of retail trade, such as grocery stores, drugstores, hardware stores, and so forth. Often, when calling on stores in unfamiliar markets to check on clients' products, I have first gone to the local newspaper to obtain city maps and routing lists that would enable me to cover the market thoroughly with a minimum amount of driving time.

TABLE 17–7: Sales Compensation and Incentive Plans.
SOURCE: Reprinted, by permission of the publisher, from EXECUTIVE COMPENSATION SERVICE, Sales Personnel Report, 25th Edition, 1980–1981,

Compensation methods	Companies using plan in 1979 Consumer products	Industrial products	Other	All industries
Straight salary	12.1%	21.0%	34.2%	21.4%
Draw against commissions	8.8	6.7	1.3	6.3
Salary plus commissions	15.4	30.6	29.0	27.8
Salary plus individual bonus	49.4	26.3	19.7	29.3
Salary plus group bonus	6.6	4.6	4.0	4.8
Salary plus commission plus individual or group bonus	7.7	10.8	11.8	10.4
	100.0%	100.0%	100.0%	100.0%

tion, sales supervisors often call on sales representatives unannounced, ask to see their daily work plan, and spend the day making calls with them.

Compensation and Motivation of Sales Personnel

Compensation and motivation are closely linked in the sales organization, and the performances of sales representatives are strongly influenced by the method of compensation and by less tangible "organizational climate" considerations.

METHOD OF COMPENSATION. A variety of methods is used to compensate salespeople: salaries, commissions, drawing accounts against future commissions, bonuses, and various combinations of these forms. Table 17–7 shows the use of alternative compensation and incentive systems as revealed by a recent survey.

All sales compensation systems are a compromise between the desire for company control over sales costs and the activities of sales representatives; and the need for the company to meet salespersons' financial requirements, and to motivate them. These two objectives are often in conflict because the needs of the company and the needs of salespeople aren't necessarily the same. For example:

Management wants

- Easy to administer compensation plans.
- Plans based on sales.
- Control over sales activity.
- Low sales costs.

Salespersons want

- Recognition of individual effort.
- Dependability of income.
- Freedom to plan their own activities.
- High incomes.

Each of the methods of sales compensation identified in Table 17–7 has advantages and disadvantages. Let's examine each of these methods briefly.

Straight Salary. Under this plan, sales representatives receive a fixed salary, paid at regular intervals. Generally, but not always, sales representatives also receive a payment for out-of-pocket expenses incurred for travel, meals, lodging, entertaining customers, and other incidental expenses.

From the standpoint of management, a straight salary system has certain clear advantages. Easy to administer and easy to project into the future, a straight salary system is easy to justify, and gives management greater freedom in directing the activities of its salespeople without incurring resentment from the sales force. On the negative side, a straight salary method of compensation does not give sales representatives any incentive for doing more than an average job and, when sales decline, the company faces high sales costs and reduced profits—usually at a time when high profits per unit of sales are needed to support other company activities.

From the standpoint of the sales representatives, the primary advantage of straight salary compensation is that they have a dependable source of income with which to meet day-to-day living expenses. On the negative side, it does not recognize extraordinary effort nor superior sales performance. Further, straight salary compensation seldom keeps pace with costs of living during periods of rapid inflation, and salespeople sometimes feel that their freedom of action is restricted by management demands on salaried personnel.

Straight Commission. Under this method of compensation, sales representatives are paid a fixed or sliding percentage on the sales they make. If they make no sales, they have no income.

From the standpoint of the company, the primary advantages of this system are that it relates compensation directly to performance, serves as an incentive for extra effort, is easy to administer, and easy to justify. In terms of disadvantages, management loses a great deal of control over sales activities since sales representatives will actively resent the assignment of objectives that interfere with their selling time, or keep them from calling on the most profitable customers and selling the most profitable items.

From the standpoint of the sales representatives, a straight commission system recognizes differences in effort and ability. It also gives them maximum freedom to determine their own activities. A disadvantage is that it provides no security, and the morale of the sales force may plummet when sales decline because of economic conditions or other factors over which the sales representatives have no control.

Mixed Systems of Compensation. Since the straight salary and the straight commission systems have strengths and weaknesses, most companies devise compensation systems incorporating the best features of each. Base compensation is often a salary, or drawing account, which guarantees regular income. Then, commissions or bonuses are used to reward extraordinary effort and sales performance that exceeds assigned quotas. Companies also use bonuses to reward important, nonselling activities. For example, sales representatives may receive special bonuses for each product display of a certain size built in a retail store. Or, they may get bonuses for increasing shelf facings, for identifying new product opportunities, or for other activities that yield long-term, rather than short-term benefits. These bonuses are often paid in cash. Sometimes, however, they are given in the form of prizes, such as vacation trips or merchandise.

ORGANIZATIONAL CLIMATE. A second factor that influences sales performance is organizational climate. Organizational climate is an ambiguous term for a company's internal method of operation. It involves such variables as fairness, integrity, concern for employees, trust, openness, encouraging employee participation in decision making and problem solving, delegation of responsibility, and so forth.[12]

Management philosophy and practices determine the organizational climate of a firm. If the organizational climate is healthy, employee loyalty and motivation tend to be high. Under an unfavorable organizational climate, morale, motivation, job satisfaction, and cooperation tend to be low. Under such conditions, job turnover is high, efficiency is reduced, and employees often thwart management's goals.

The development of a favorable organizational climate within the firm should be a basic concern of management; various management theorists have different prescriptions for accomplishing this.[13] For specific discussions of management practices that facilitate the development

---

12. For a discussion of the concept of organizational climate, see Richard W. Woodman and Donald C. King, "Organizational Climate: Science or Folklore," *The Academy of Management Review,* (October, 1978): 816–26.

13. In 1961 Harold Koontz, a professor of management at the University of California, wrote an article titled "The Management Theory Jungle" in which he identified six different schools of management thought. In 1980 Professor Koontz wrote another article titled "The Management Theory Jungle Revisited." The situation hasn't improved. In the 1980 article, Professor Koontz identifies eleven different schools of management—an increase of five in less than two decades. See Harold Koontz, "The Management Theory Jungle Revisited," *The Academy of Management Review* (April, 1980): 175–87.

of a favorable organizational climate for sales personnel, students should turn to some of the basic texts on sales management or on organizational behavior.

Evaluating Sales Performance

A final, major function in managing the sales force is evaluating sales performance. The whole question of evaluation is as complex as it is necessary. Evaluation is complex because its methods vary with the tasks assigned to sales representatives. It is necessary because, only through a systematic evaluation procedure can problems of sales performance be identified and remedial action be taken.

Initially, remedial action should help poor sales representatives improve their performance. This help can take the form of counseling, additional training, and/or closer supervision. If these methods fail, the offending representative should be replaced for the good of the firm and for the morale of the remainder of the sales organization.

Key aspects of an equitable evaluation system require that sales representatives *know* what is expected of them, how they will be evaluated, when they will be evaluated, and that they will be able to appeal evaluations they believe unfair without fear of prejudice. This means that evaluation procedures should consist of the following steps.

- *Define the objectives of the sales position.* These objectives should be clearly communicated to the sales representatives, who should both *understand* and *accept* them.
- *Define the methods to be used in measuring the objectives.* No objective should be set without defining specifically how its accomplishment will be measured. Further, sales representatives should be consulted at this stage to make sure that they are willing to accept the measurements that have been defined.
- *Set aside specific times for formal evaluations.* A sales supervisor should set aside a specific time for formal evaluations. Sales representatives should know when evaluations are going to be made; such discussions should be conducted in quiet surroundings, removed from interruptions. This does not mean that performance should not be praised or criticized at other times. On the contrary, both praise and criticism of performance should be made as warranted. Such informal evaluations should not replace a periodic, thorough review of performance, however.
- *Formal appeal procedures should be established.* No sales representative should ever feel that an evaluation by an immediate supervisor is final and not subject to appeal. Sometimes, mistakes are made. Sometimes a supervisor is unfair, or thought to be unfair. When these situations arise, sales representatives should have a way of appealing such evaluations without prejudice.

SUMMARY

"Nothing happens until a sale is made" is an acknowledgment of the importance of personal selling in the marketing program. Whether one is speaking of industrial marketing or consumer products, the sales force forms the crucial link between producers and consumers.

There is no such thing as a typical salesperson. Sales jobs vary widely in the skill and training they require. The complexion of selling is changing as sales representatives are required to do more things—selling, providing customer service, explaining management policies, and serving as sources of marketing information. The relationship of the sales force to the company employing it varies widely. Some companies employ their own sales forces; others use agents or brokers, or share the sales forces of other firms.

In establishing a sales organization, three questions merit special consideration: how many sales representatives should be employed; how should they be assigned geographically; and how should they be organized to provide effective service.

The size of the sales force depends upon the nature of the sales task, the customers to be contacted, and the frequency of contact required. From the standpoint of travel costs, assigning sales representatives to relatively confined geographic areas is usually economical. In establishing the size of sales territories, companies generally attempt to achieve an optimal balance between ease of administration and supervision, ease of estimating territory potentials, minimum travel costs, equalization of work load, and equalization of sales potential. Sales forces may be organized on a number of bases, with the most common forms of organization being by territory, by product, and by industry served.

One of the more difficult tasks is that of managing the sales operation. Sales force management may be subdivided into six separate, but interrelated tasks: (1) recruiting and personnel selection; (2) training; (3) setting sales force objectives; (4) supervising sales activities; (5) compensating and motivating sales personnel; and (6) evaluating salespersons.

Sales personnel must be assigned objectives to direct their activity productively. And, sales objectives should be derived from the marketing plan so that personal selling will be coordinated with other marketing activities.

REVIEW QUESTIONS

1. Explain the statement "There is no such thing as a typical salesperson."
2. Explain the statement "There is no universal rule that defines the nature of the relationship between a company and its sales representatives." Why is this so?
3. Identify the key questions that must be addressed in setting up a sales organization.
4. Given the following information, compute the number of sales representatives required. (1) Customers by class size—Class A = 10,000; Class B = 15,000; Class C = 25,000. (2) Optimum number of calls by customer class—Class A = 12; Class B = 6; Class C = 3. (3) Average number of calls that can be made in a year by a single salesperson = 1,000.
5. Outline the steps that should be followed in determining the number of sales representatives a firm will require.
6. What are the primary advantages of organizing a sales force by geographic territory?
7. Identify the points of conflict between management and sales representatives in regard to methods of compensation.
8. What are the advantages and disadvantages of a straight salary system of compensation?
9. What are the advantages and disadvantages of a straight commission system of compensation?
10. Identify and explain the steps that should be involved in an evaluation procedure for sales representatives.

1. What do you think are some of the advantages and disadvantages of a career in sales?
2. What personal characteristics do you think would be important in selecting sales representatives to sell: (A) computer installations to major companies? (B) securities? (C) grocery products? (D) cosmetics door-to-door?
3. The sales manager of a food product sold through grocery stores complained: "A 30-second television commercial costs about $75,000. A salesperson costs about $35,000 a year. We could make a lot more sales if we cancelled a few commercials and hired two or three more sales representatives." Evaluate this argument.
4. Develop a sales compensation system that would provide incentives for experienced salespeople and yet be satisfactory for new salespeople who are in the process of learning their jobs.
5. There is considerable evidence that salespeople are poor at gathering and reporting marketing information. Why do you think this is so? What do you think could be done to improve this situation?

PERSONAL SELLING

Cotter-Reese manufactures small cutting and grinding tools and supplies which are sold to machine shops and metal fabricating plants throughout the United States. Total company sales in 1981 were $108 million.

Founded in 1953, the company has grown steadily, primarily because of quality products, emphasis on prompt delivery and service, and safety innovations engineered into the tools. About 75 percent of the company's sales involved standard equipment and supplies, and 25 percent special tools designed for specific tasks.

The company sales force consists of thirty salaried sales representatives and twenty-five manufacturer's representatives. Initially, the company used only manufacturer's representatives on commission; recently Cotter-Reese has been replacing these reps with salaried sales personnel. In addition to selling the firm's line of products to established customers, sales representatives are also expected to develop new customers, gather information on competitive products, and introduce new products.

Competitive activity increased significantly in the 1970's, and Cotter-Reese sales growth began to falter. An analysis of sales performance by product, by sales territory, and by type of representation indicated that: (1) sales in the territories served by manufacturer's representatives were only 80 percent of those served by salaried personnel. Management attributed this difference to the fact that manufacturer's representatives also represented other noncompetitive products and were not spending enough time on the Cotter-Reese line; (2) the rate of new customer acquisition had decreased in all areas; and (3) sales of speciality products, which provided higher margins but were also harder to sell, were decreasing, as the proportion of standard products increased.

Based on these findings, management decided to accelerate their replacement of manufacturer's representatives with salaried salespeople. Since Cotter-Reese still faced the problem of how to gain new customers and to increase the sales of speciality items, a management consultant was retained to analyze sales costs, and to identify potential customers for the company's products. Among the findings of this analysis were the following points:

- *Approximately 18,000 establishments represented 80 percent of the potential market for Cotter-Reese products. The consulting firm classified these customers by size into three groups and recommended an optimum call frequency for each group:*

Class of customer	*Establishments*	*Optimal call frequency*
A	*2,000*	*12*
B	*6,000*	*6*
C	*10,000*	*3*

- *The average number of calls that could be made by a company sales representative in a year was approximately 12,000.*
- *The industry median cost per call was $29.*
- *The average cost of personal selling for the industry was 1.7 percent of sales.*

The sales manager was asked to determine how many sales representatives would be needed to call on the eighteen thousand potential customers on an optimal call frequency. He was also asked to estimate the total company sales that would be required to implement the plan while keeping personal selling costs at the industry average. Finally, he was asked for his thoughts on how sales of speciality products and new customer acquisition could be increased.

Assignment

1. *Cotter-Reese management attributed the relative poor performance of manufacturer's representatives to the fact that they handled the products of other companies and consequently devoted less time to Cotter-Reese products. Can you think of any other reason or reasons for their relatively poor performance?*
2. *Given the information provided, how many sales representatives will the company require to call on potential customers on an optimal call basis?*
3. *What level of company sales would be required to afford a sales force of this size?*
4. *What suggestions do you have for increasing the sales of speciality products and for gaining new customers?*

18

Advertising

- *The dimensions and structure of advertising in the United States economy.*
- *The role of advertising agencies.*
- *The client-agency relationship.*
- *The organization and functions of advertising agencies.*
- *The uses of advertising.*
- *Advertising objectives and strategies.*

MARKETING EXAMPLES

$11.7 BILLION

The national debt? No, this is merely the combined expenditure of the nation's one hundred largest advertisers in 1979. The top ten spent over $3.2 billion, with Procter & Gamble leading the list with an expenditure of $614.9 million. Expenditures for the top ten are shown below.

	Million
Procter & Gamble	$ 614.9
General Foods Corp.	393.0
Sears, Roebuck & Co.	379.3
General Motors Corp.	323.4
Phillip Morris, Inc.	291.2
K Mart Corp.	287.1
R. J. Reynolds Industries	258.1
Warner Lambert Co.	220.2
American Telephone and Telegraph	219.8
Ford Motor Co.	215.0
Total	$3,202.0[1]

Does it pay? It must because these companies are among the most successful marketers in the business.

30 BILLION BARS OF SOAP

This is the number of bars of Ivory soap that have been sold since Procter & Gamble recorded its first sales of Ivory soap in 1879. From its initial expenditure of $11,000 in advertising in 1882, Ivory soap

1. Marion Elmquist, "100 Top Advertisers Spent $11.7 Billion," *Advertising Age* (Sept. 11, 1980): 1.

has been consistently advertised. Over the life of the product, an estimated $250 million have been spent in its support, an expenditure of less than a cent a bar. And, Ivory soap has been the leading seller among bar soaps for 99 of its first 100 years of existence.[2] Ivory Soap—99 and 44/100 percent pure. So pure it floats. A good product + a good price + good advertising = an American tradition.

THE BOSS AS PITCHMAN

Strange things are happening in television studios these days. Imagine the following hypothetical scene as described by *Fortune:*

> *Okay, here's what I want you to do. When you get to this part of the script, turn a little to your left. Will you be comfortable saying that line? Fine . . . We have maybe seven seconds for it. Remember to keep looking at the camera, and check the teleprompter. And look at me for timing cues. But whatever you do, don't look like you're looking at me or at the teleprompter . . . Be serious, but not too serious . . . You need just a little more powder on your forehead. Remember to keep your chin down. It'll be terrific. Trust me. Quiet! Take one! Action!*

Nodding obedience to this kind of singsong, a lot of chief executives these days are launching careers in show business by appearing in their own television commercials. They are not out to win Clios—advertising's Oscars—for their stirring recitations of ad copy pitching cars or wines or chickens. They are out to win customers, corporate or consumer, by the force of their all-too-human personalities—under the glare of hot lights and the cold eyes of perhaps as many as twenty production people. Picture your average, late-fiftyish company chairman, buttoned-down, pin-striped, and accustomed to command, taking orders from a mid–

2. Nancy F. Millman, "The Saga of P&G's Ivory Soap: Keeping a Brand after 100 Years," *Advertising Age* (April 30, 1980): 50–53.

thirtyish commercial director in silk shirt and jeans, chattering an argot the executive can barely understand. Cut! Print![3]

This is a part of the changing face of advertising. Only a few year ago, David Ogilvy, one of the great advertising practitioners of this century, wrote "Only in the gravest cases should you show clients' faces."[4] Yet, today, it is being done more and more as the presidents of major corporations pursue sales and customer credibility by personal appearances in their company's advertising. The old adage, "Pride goeth before a fall," may have a modern counterpart in "Corporate dignity goeth before falling profits."

---

3. Ann M. Morrison, "The Boss as Pitchman," *Fortune Magazine* ©1980 Time, Inc. All rights reserved.
4. David Ogilvy, *Confessions of an Advertising Man* (New York: Athenium, 1962), p. 121.

The foregoing examples are only some of the dimensions of advertising which is, perhaps, the most fascinating, complex, and controversial part of the marketing mix. In order to gain some perspective on this strange phenomenon—and its role in the marketing program—let's turn our attention to advertising, a subject about which much has been written but about which little has been said.

AN OVERVIEW OF ADVERTISING

Few aspects of marketing are as widely discussed and as little understood as advertising. Almost everyone, it seems, has a strong opinion about advertising, but few agree if it is a hero or villain in the nation's economic affairs. Rance Crain, Editor-in Chief of *Advertising Age* in 1980, said:

> One of the great anomalies of our time is that advertising, which had had such a profound effect on our society and on our economy for the past fifty years, is today as little understood by not only academicians and economists but also by business people and even admen and women themselves . . . advertising is often blamed for things it doesn't do and is not given adequate credit for things it does do.
>
> Advertising, of course, is a handy instrument to blame for the ills (or perceived ills) of society, because advertising is pretty much a mirror of how we view ourselves. For the most part, I've observed critics who attack advertising are really railing against our affluent way of life or a product or service they don't approve of. For instance the FTC's interest in children's television advertising, many people believe, was really focused on children's television programming and the staff's predilections against presweetened cereals.
>
> I've always felt that advertising is one of the greatest democratizers our society has ever known, for it brings to the masses information on new products and services formerly reserved for the elite. What some critics object to, I've discovered, is not advertising itself but the fact that it enables everyone to have access to the same information, thereby breaking down one more barrier between the great unwashed and the self-proclaimed chosen few . . . for decades economists generally ignored advertising and its influence on the economy. Even today . . . while they are at

least becoming aware of advertising, they still contend that admen have not yet proved their claim that advertising stimulates competition and lowers costs by increasing demand and therefore production.[5]

Even at the work-a-day level of marketing, advertising professionals cannot agree about what constitutes good advertising, and agree even less about how advertising effectiveness should be measured. Yet, hard-headed, cost-conscious business executives, who wouldn't approve a $10,000 expenditure for a new piece of equipment without a complete study of its proposed value, replete with cost and performance documentation, will blithely approve $20 million for an advertising campaign based on a slick presentation and confidence in the presenter. Rosser Reeves quotes a company president as saying:

> Advertising, to me, is really one of the mysteries of American business. I can inventory my stock. I can calculate the cost of my factories. I can figure my taxes, estimate my depreciation, determine my sales cost, derive my return per share. Yet, there are times when I spend as much as $18 million a year on advertising—and have no idea what I am really getting for my money.[6]

Advertising has been defined by the American Marketing Association's Committee on Definitions as *any paid form of nonpersonal presentation and promotion of ideas, goods, or services by an identified sponsor.*[7] A similar definition has been made by the International Chamber of Commerce in its *Dictionary of Marketing Terms.*

Although these definitions are useful in helping us distinguish what is and what is not advertising, they fail to capture the spirit of what advertising really is. Sidney R. Bernstein, former editor and publisher of *Advertising Age,* captures the spirit of what advertising is in the following observation:

> . . . in essence, advertising is a substitute for the human salesman talking personally to an individual prospect or customer across a store counter or a desk or an open door. And, as a substitute for the human salesman, advertising has pretty much the same functions, abilities, and attributes as the human salesman.
>
> It is less effective than personal selling, however, principally because it must be designed to appeal to a mass audience, in contrast with the personal salesman's ability to tailor his sales message to each individual prospect, and because, again unlike the personal salesman, it has no opportunity to "talk back," explain or refute objections.
>
> This is advertising, no more and no less—a mechanical substitute for the personal salesman.[8]

Advertising and Marketing

If advertising is simply a substitute for personal selling, and I believe that it is, then advertising's role in marketing immediately becomes apparent: a marketing tool—no more, no less—and, as a marketing tool, its value must be assessed in financial terms. If, for a particular marketer, advertising is not an efficient and effective way of promoting products, it should not be used because it has no inherent value in and of itself. Sidney R. Bernstein, long a defender of advertising, recognizes this truism in the following statement:

> If and when any advertiser discovers some quicker, more effective, more economical method of promoting his business, he will abandon advertising with no hesitation and no regrets. Those who pay for advertising consider it only as a selling tool, and measure its value carefully under that criterion.

5. Rance Crain, "Advertising: The Brick and Mortar of Our Economy," Reprinted with permission from April 30, 1980, *Advertising Age.* Copyright 1980 by Crain Communications, Inc.

6. Rosser Reeves, *Reality in Advertising.* Copyright by Alfred A. Knopf, 1961, p. 11.

7. *Marketing Definitions: A Glossary of Marketing Terms,* compiled by Ralph S. Alexander and the Committee on Definitions of the American Marketing Association, (Chicago: American Marketing Association, 1960), p. 9.

8. Sidney R. Bernstein, "What Is Advertising," Reprinted with permission from April 30, 1980, issue of *Advertising Age.* Copyright 1980 by Crain Communications, Inc. As a historical note, this is an elaboration of a definition of advertising given by John Kennedy about 75 years ago. For a delightful account of how this definition came about, see: Alfred D. Lasker, *The Lasker Story, As He Told It* (Chicago: Advertising Publications, 1963).

TABLE 18–1: *Estimated Advertising Expenditures by Media (Expenditures in millions of dollars)*
Reprinted with permission from the April 30, 1980, issue of *Advertising Age.* Copyright 1980 by Crain Communications, Inc.

	1940	*1950*	*1960*	*1970*	*1979*
Newspapers	$ 815	$2,070	$ 3,681	$ 5,704	$14,585
Magazines	186	478	909	1,292	2,930
Farm publications	19	58	66	62	120
Television	—	171	1,627	3,596	10,195
Radio	215	605	693	1,308	3,265
Direct mail	334	803	1,830	2,766	6,650
Business papers	76	251	609	740	1,595
Outdoor	45	142	203	234	535
Miscellaneous	420	1,122	2,342	3,848	9,815
Total	$2,110	$5,700	$11,960	$19,550	$49,690
Increase over previous period	—	170%	110%	63%	149%

The only people and organizations who have a vested interest in advertising as such are the *sellers* and *producers* of advertising, not the buyers—the various media, the advertising agencies, the panoply of individuals and organizations involved in producing today's television and radio commercials, and so on.[9]

The Dimensions of Advertising

If advertising is a mystery to many, it is a big one, and growing bigger all of the time. Since 1940, advertising expenditures in current dollars have grown from $2.1 billion to $54.6 billion. By the year 2000, advertising expenditures are expected to reach $305 billion. Somewhat over half of the 1980 total ($30.3 billion) was spent by national advertisers, with the remaining $24.3 billion being spent by local and regional advertisers. A summary of advertising's growth, by media, is shown in Table 18–1.

Nor do the figures in Table 18–1 reflect the entire dimension of advertising. For example, the $535 million shown for outdoor advertising in 1979 only reflects the expenditures of what is referred to as the "organized" outdoor advertising industry. The organized outdoor advertising industry represents only an estimated 5 percent of the total funds spent for outdoor advertising. In addition, the expenditures in Figure 18–1 only represent media expenditures, and do not include the costs of producing the advertisements and commercials which appear in the media shown.

In general, the growth of advertising has paralleled the growth of the national economy. For the past fifty years, advertising as a percent of gross national product has hovered around 2 percent.

9. *The Lasker Story,* p. 28.

The Structure of Advertising

Only about 40 percent of the $54.6 billion spent in advertising is handled by the nation's eight thousand advertising agencies. The remainder is developed by corporate advertising departments, or by smaller companies and retail outlets which are not large enough, or do not think they are large enough, to afford advertising agency service.

The advertising industry consists of four classes of participants: client organizations, advertising agencies, media, and collateral services.

Client Organizations. Client organizations are business firms that produce products or services. They include producers of consumer and industrial goods as well as retail and other service organizations. Client organizations range from giant retail organizations, such as Sears, Roebuck, and Company, to small, family-owned and operated delicatessens. From multibillion

TABLE 18–2: *Distribution of 628 U.S. Advertising Agencies*
Reprinted with permission from March 14, 1979, issue of *Advertising Age.* Copyright 1979 by Crain Communications, Inc.

Gross Income of Size group	*Advertising Agencies* *Number*	*% of total*	*Gross Income* *Millions of $*	*% of total*
over $15 million	29	4.6%	$2,446.3	70.7%
$5 to $15 million	46	7.3	390.2	11.3
$1 to 4.9 million	205	32.6	462.5	13.4
Under $1 million	348	55.5	161.0	4.6
Totals	628	100.0%	$3,460.0	100.0%

dollar corporations, such as Exxon, to small producers of specialty and custom items which operate out of a home workshop. Client organizations are highly concentrated, with less than 2 percent of the total business organizations accounting for almost 80 percent of business revenues.

Although any business can benefit from a systematic, professional approach to its advertising tasks, few of them bother. Only a minute proportion of them employ an advertising agency, and only a fraction of these develop a systematic marketing plan. Yet, it is this tiny group that we are primarily concerned with because this miniscule is the dominant force in the U.S. economy.

Advertising Agencies. The nation's eight thousand advertising agencies range in size from J. Walter Thompson, with billings approaching $1.5 billion and a gross income of almost a quarter of a billion dollars, to small, one and two person shops whose gross incomes barely cover the living expenses of their principals.

Table 18–2 summarizes *Advertising Age's* report on agency operations in 1979. This report covers 629 advertising agencies which had a combined gross income of $3.45 billion, and an estimated billing of $23.3 billion. Table 18–2, illustrates that less than 5 percent of the advertising agencies account for over 70 percent of the gross income, pointing up the concentration of business that exists in the industry.

Aside from size, advertising agencies differ in a variety of ways. For example, some agencies specialize in industrial products, in consumer products, and in fashion products. There are agencies, generally the smaller ones, that specialize in retail accounts, or in real estate, or in financial advertising. In short, advertising agencies, by tradition or plan, sometimes carve out highly specialized niches for themselves. Most of the larger agencies, however, handle a variety of accounts, cutting across the specialty spectrum.

Media Organizations. The major media organizations in the advertising industry are newspapers, magazines, radio, and television stations. In addition, minor media include outdoor advertising (billboards), transit advertising (cards in subways, buses, and taxicabs), movie theater films, programs for entertainment events (plays, baseball games, musical performances, and so forth), as well as a variety of miscellaneous media (baskarts in grocery stores, match covers, and almost anything else upon which an advertising message can be printed or from which it can be broadcast). Along with advertisers (clients) and advertising agencies, media organizations dominate marketing and advertising in the United States.

Collateral Businesses. Dozens of collateral businesses are supported by client organizations, advertising agencies, and the media. These collateral businesses make up the fourth component of the advertising industry. They include package design houses, sales promotion firms, premium shops, media buying services, research organizations, printing companies, production studios, program producers, consulting firms, free-lance artists and copywriters, photographers, recording studios, mailing list houses, coupon redemption centers, and dozens of others. Each provides a highly specialized service which advertisers and their agencies use as the need arises. The advertising industry is a highly complex one. As the need for a particular service arises, companies emerge to meet this need. As needs are eclipsed, so are the companies that provide them.

TABLE 18–3: Advertising Agencies Used by Procter & Gamble in 1980.

Agency	*Products assigned*
Benton & Bowles	Bounce, Charmin, Crest, Dawn, Ivory Snow, Pampers, Rely, Scope, Wondra, Zest, and Attend.
Leo Burnette Co.	Cheer, Era, Camay, Lava, Lilt, Secret, and Gleem.
Compton Advertising	Tide, Cascade, Crisco, Top Job, Comet, Ivory bar and liquid soap, High Point coffee, Duncan Hines cake mixes, and Pert.
Cunningham & Walsh	Folger's instant, flaked, and vacuum–packed coffee; Certain cleansing bathroom tissue; Crush, Hires, and Sun Drop soft drinks.
Dancer, Fitzgerald, Sample	Bounty, White Cloud, Oxydol, Dreft, Luvs, and Solo.
Doyle Dane Bernbach	Coast deodorant soap, Gain, and Puritan oil.
Grey Advertising	Downey fabric softner, Joy dishwashing liquid, Bold 3, Jif, Puffs facial tissue, Duz, Duncan Hines Moist & Easy cake mixes, Duncan Hines cookie mix.
Tatham–Laird & Kudner	Biz, Head & Shoulders, and Mr. Clean.
Wells, Rich & Greene	Pringles, Safeguard, Sure, Liquid Prell, and Prell Concentrate.
Young & Rubicam	Dash, Spic & Span, and Procter & Gamble Productions.

The entire industry is a microcosm of the marketing economy.

The client organization's most extensive contacts and closest working relationships are generally with advertising agencies. For this reason, we should examine the advertising agency field to gain a better understanding of the client agency relationship, and the ways in which advertising agencies are generally organized.

THE ADVERTISING AGENCY

For most marketers of consumer goods and services where advertising is a major consideration in their marketing programs, advertising agencies play a major role in the development and implementation of marketing plans. Procter & Gamble, the nation's largest advertiser, funneled its advertising expenditures through ten major advertising agencies in 1980. Table 18–3 lists these agencies and the P&G business handled by each. The number of advertising agencies used by a particular client organization depends upon the number of products marketed and the predilection of its management.

Advertising agencies serve a variety of functions for the clients they serve. In many cases, they participate extensively in all areas of market planning, sometimes writing the product marketing plans, as well as in the development and production of advertising and sales promotion materials. In other instances, agency participation and influence are largely restricted to the planning and development of advertising.

The extent to which the advertising agency is used depends upon the desires of the client as well as the capabilities of the agency. Many advertising agencies, particularly the larger ones, are eminently qualified to develop an entire marketing program because their staffs include highly qualified market planners as well as specialists in the fields of marketing research, pricing, distribution, packaging, sales promotion, public relations, and advertising. For example, when Duncan Hines cake mixes were first introduced by Nebraska Consolidated Mills, a regional producer of flour and other milling products, its advertising agency was charged with the primary responsibility for establishing a network of food brokers to represent the company. When Jack Daniel's was forced to allocate its product because of excessive demand, its advertising agency was asked to recommend an equitable plan for allocation. And, it is commonplace for advertising agencies to work closely with their client organizations in defining product positions, identifying viable product concepts for new products, and in developing sales presentations for both retail and industrial accounts.

Those client organizations that rely extensively upon their advertising agencies for marketing counsel do so because they respect their agencies' competence, and because they value the outside, independent judgment that an agency can bring to marketing decisions. Most organizations badly need an outside, independent point of view because, caught up in internal problems and conflicts, they too often view their marketing activities, not from the standpoint of the consumer, but from the perspective of their internal preoccupations.

At the same time, most agencies are eager to become involved in basic marketing decisions that are, of course, the ultimate responsibility of the client organization. The reason for this is that advertising agencies are judged by the success or lack of success of the products they represent. And, advertising agencies are acutely aware that product success depends upon the entire marketing effort—not on advertising alone. A faulty market forecast, a weak product concept, an inadequate product, ineffective packaging, poor distribution, noncompetitive consumer pricing, insufficient distributor margins, ambiguous packaging instructions, and beggarly allocations of advertising and sales promotion funds can mortgage the future of a product to the extent that no amount of advertising creativity can salvage the program.

The Client-Agency Relationship

The client-agency relationship is, at best, a tenuous one based on mutual respect and confidence. Unfortunately, confidence is a fragile commodity that is difficult to build and easy to destroy. In 1970 Lennon and Newell was the sixteenth largest advertising agency in the world and the thirteenth largest in the United States. With billings of $160 million, Lennon and Newell employed over a thousand people, represented a galaxy of blue-chip accounts, and appeared to have a brilliant future. In 1971 Lennon and Newell billed less than $90 million, and street rumors had it that, by year's end, its current billings would be less than $25 million. In February 1972 Lennon and Newell filed a petition for bankruptcy, and soon thereafter ceased to exist. In less than a year and a half, a major advertising agency became a suite of empty rooms.

Crises of confidence precipitated the bankruptcy of Lennon and Newell. Poor management weakened the agency financially and led to the loss of one or two major clients. Other clients became concerned about the agency's stability. Clients started panicking, and Lennon and Newell went down the tubes.

Every issue of *Advertising Age* reports a number of account changes. Each year, usually in March, this publication devotes an issue to advertising agencies. This issue gives brief profiles of some 600 United States advertising agencies, listing among other things the clients that each has gained and lost. These profiles read like a game of musical chairs; the reasons behind many agency switches are often arbitrary, political, or merely capricious.

Not all client-agency relationships are unstable. Some have endured for fifty to sixty years, or even longer. But, these are the exceptions. The problem is, of course, that advertising is a highly competitive business. Large sums of money are at stake. The field is filled with bright, ambitious people. Personal reputations are on the line, and there are no sure answers. The reasons that products succeed or fail are sometimes obscure, and the role of advertising in their success or failure is not always clear. Most client organizations are looking for miracles. When a miracle is not forthcoming, they sometimes seek a scapegoat. That scapegoat is often the advertising agency.

Types of Advertising Agencies

In the beginning, advertising agencies were sellers or brokers of space. That is, they either sold space for newspapers or magazines, collecting a commission for their efforts, or they contracted for space on a wholesale basis and retailed it to individual advertisers. After a while, advertising agencies began to take on their present character as they added services—copy, art, market research, marketing counsel, and so forth—as they competed for the business of advertisers. Today's advertising agency is a far cry from the sellers of space that inaugurated the industry.

Even today, however, advertising agencies come in different shapes and forms. There are four types of advertising agencies that account for the bulk of the advertising industry: the full service agency, the modular agency, in-house agencies, and creative boutiques.

FULL-SERVICE AGENCIES. A full service advertising agency is one that provides a broad, if not totally complete, range of marketing services. Generally it is staffed to handle the entire gamut of marketing counsel for its clients with the exception of personal selling and public relations, although some full-service agencies also undertake public relations functions. In addition to the necessary internal functions of any business organization, such as management, finance, accounting, personnel, new business acquisition, and so forth, full service agencies generally provide all or most of the following functions:

- *Account Service.* Account service or account management is the liaison between the advertising agency and its clients. The function of an account manager, usually referred to as an account executive or an account supervisor is to: 1) work with agency clients on a day-to-day basis, and to interpret client needs to agency personnel; and 2) work with agency personnel in developing plans and recommendations for clients' products.
- *Creative Services.* The creative services department of an advertising agency is responsible for the creation of advertisements, commercials, and often for package designs, point-of-sale material, and other forms of promotion. Creative services generally include four functional areas: copy, art, print production, and radio and television production.
- *Traffic.* As agencies become larger, and more complex, coordination becomes a major problem. To insure coordination, a traffic department is established and given the responsibility for meeting schedules and closing dates.
- *Media.* The job of the media department is to analyze, plan, select, and contract for the media that will be used in clients' marketing programs. The activities of the media department must be closely coordinated with the activities of the creative department and with the budget constaints of the client. Often, media considerations—the ability of a medium to create a particular mood, or portray some aspect of the product—have a major influence on the creative effort.
- *Marketing Research.* The role of the marketing research department is to gather, analyze, and report information that will be helpful in preparing the marketing plan and developing advertising. Although most major clients have their own marketing research departments, the agency research department is an invaluable asset to the advertising agency and its management.
- *Other functions.* Although the foregoing functions are the central activities of full–service agencies, many large agencies are also organized to perform other marketing functions, depending upon the needs of their clients. For example, some agencies have sales-promotion departments, home economics departments, public relations, and product publicity departments.

The 1960s saw a rebellion on the part of advertisers who, in an effort to cut costs and improve service, wanted to dispense with some of these services and to shop around for others. For example, an advertiser might want to buy the creative service of one agency, the media expertise of another, the research capability of a third, and so forth. A number of major agencies refused to participate in this process, and lost clients as a result. Other agencies yielded to these pressures. This resulted in the modular advertising agency.

MODULAR ADVERTISING AGENCIES. A modular or *a la carte* advertising agency is, essentially, a full-service agency that sells its services on a piecemeal basis. Thus, an advertiser, for a fee, may commission the agency's creative department to develop an advertising campaign, while obtaining other agency services elsewhere. Or, an advertiser may hire the media department of an agency to plan and execute a media program for advertising that another agency has developed. In each case, a fee is charged for the service provided, with the size of the fee being negotiated on the basis of work done.

IN-HOUSE AGENCIES. The in-house agency is owned by the advertiser and operated under the advertiser's direct supervision and control. Generally an in-house agency provides all of the media and creative functions of a full-service agency, but does so at a lesser cost because the profit normally retained by an independent advertising agency is pocketed by the advertiser.

Critics of the in-house agency (and there are many) argue that the advertiser loses the benefit of the experience and "outside" point of view that an independent agency can bring to bear on marketing problems, that creative groups grow stale working on the same product lines, and that in-house agencies are unable to attract the same quality creative personnel as the independent advertising agency. There is merit to these arguments, particularly in the loss of an independent, outside point of view. Anyone who works in or with an advertiser controlled organization tends to become narrow in their thinking, and to focus attention inward on internal problems and concerns, rather than outward toward the consumer. Nonetheless, in-house agencies appear to be growing in popularity and are utilized by a number of advertisers, including J.B. Williams, Norton Simon, General Electric, Ralston Purina, and others. Some advertisers that have in-house agencies also retain outside agencies for some of their product lines.

CREATIVE BOUTIQUES. During the 1960s, increasing competition led to a renewed interest in advertising creativity. Some advertisers felt that full-service agencies were emphasizing other marketing services at the expense of creativity. Simultaneously, many members of agency creative departments felt that their creativity was being hampered by the management structure of the agency, and that some of their best ideas were not being presented to clients because of excess caution on the part of account management. As a result, some of the "star" copywriters and art directors (often with covert arrangements with leading clients) left full-service agencies to set up their own shops which became known as *creative boutiques.* The creative boutique performs only the *creative* function, usually for a fee and/or an agreed upon percentage of the media expenditure.

Creative boutiques reached the peak of their popularity in the late 1960s, and appeared to be on the wane by the mid-1970s. A major reason for their decline was that clients who were originally intrigued by the idea of a purely creative shop, found that they still wanted traditional agency services. As a consequence, many of the original boutiques became full-service agencies as they found that a creative service alone was not sufficient to retain clients.

Advertising Agency Organization

Advertising agencies may be organized in different ways, although there is a basic organizational structure that underlies most large agencies. Figure 18–1 shows the typical functional organization for a large or medium agency.

The organizational structure shown in Figure 18–1, however, represents the *formal* organization for purposes of staffing and salary administration. The actual working arrangements within an advertising agency consist of a series of informal groups organized around clients' products. For example, let us assume that account group A represents a detergent advertiser. Depending upon the size and importance of the account, the account group may consist of a single account executive or of an account supervisor with a number of account executives. The account executive or supervisor will serve as the coordinator of an informal group which will have one or more representatives assigned to it from each of the agency's functional departments. The resulting work group is diagrammed in Figure 18–2.

Thus, the advertising agency work group is a loose organization of experts, all doing their own jobs, tied together by a personal sense of responsibility for their own contributions, and

FIGURE 18–1: *Typical Advertising Agency Structured along Functional Lines*

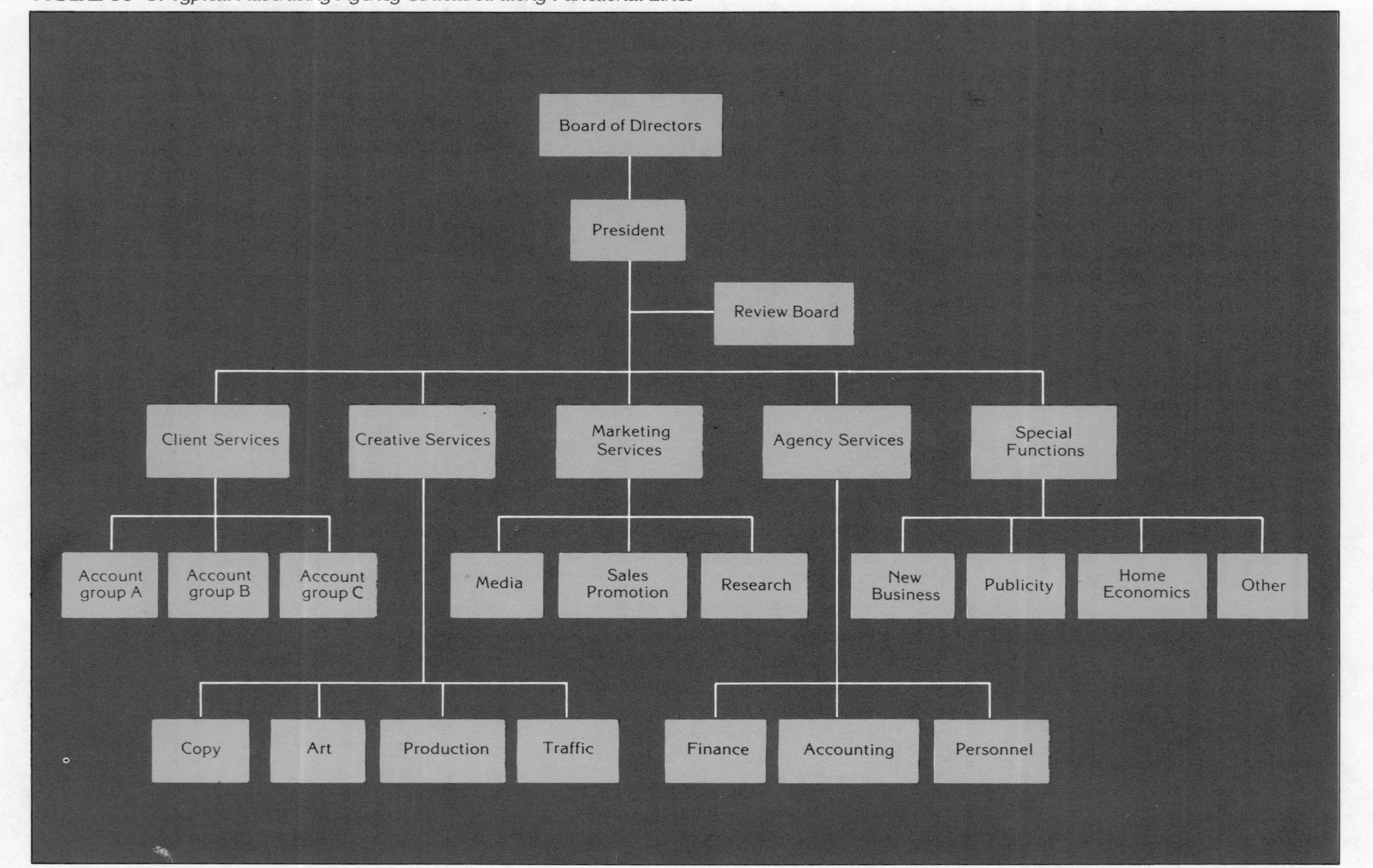

FIGURE 18–2: *Typical Advertising Agency Work Group*

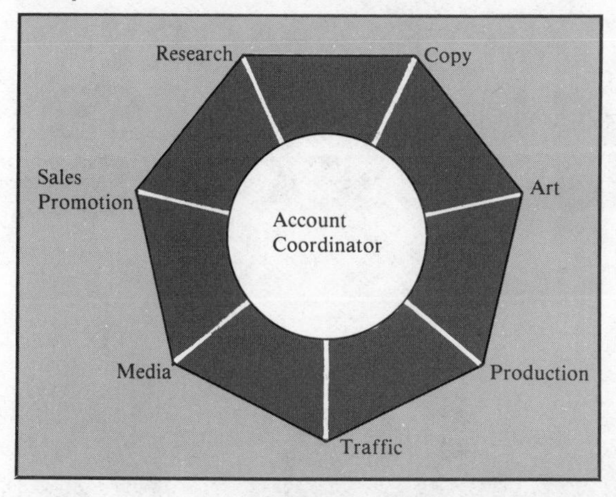

coordinated by the account manager and the strictures of the marketing plan. The group's work sounds casual, but it is not. It is demanding, backbreaking work, governed by performance and accountability.

Advertising Agency Compensation

Traditionally, advertising agencies have been paid a percentage of the gross billing charged by media and other suppliers. Also, traditionally, this commission has been 15 percent of gross billing, although there is some variation in the percentage paid by specialized media such as outdoor and trade publications.

Over a period of time, many advertisers and advertising agencies began to feel that the commission system was inherently wrong because there was no necessary relationship between the amount of work done by an advertising agency and the compensation it received. For example, two advertising campaigns might require the same amount of agency work to create and produce. Yet, one of the campaigns would have $100,000 spent behind it, generating $15,000 in agency commissions, while the second campaign might have $3 million spent behind it, thereby generating $450,000 in agency commissions.

As a consequence, advertising agency compensation methods have undergone significant changes in recent years. Although many clients still use the traditional commission system in compensating their agencies, others negotiate a fee for agency services, or work on a cost-plus basis. Often, depending upon the amount and type of work done, the agency compensation structure may be a combination of commissions and fees.

THE USES OF ADVERTISING

Different kinds of advertising can serve a variety of advertising objectives. The effectiveness of a given advertising campaign is directly dependent upon how clearly the objectives are stated. If the objectives are obscure or ill-defined, little productive advertising will result. Before examining the statement of advertising objectives further, let's identify the kinds of advertising businesses use because the objectives of advertising are directly related to the general purpose of the advertising itself.

Kinds of Advertising

Broadly speaking, six kinds of advertising are widely used by business firms: product, sales promotion, trade, corporate, classified, and retail.

PRODUCT ADVERTISING. Product or brand advertising is that advertising designed to provide consumers with information about the product or service and to translate the product concept into an appealing consumer benefit. Product advertising is sometimes referred to as *display* advertising because it displays the product for everyone to see, or as *image* advertising because it attempts to create a favorable image of the product being advertised. Its general purpose is to affect consumer beliefs and attitudes about a product or service over a period of time, and through repeated exposures. Most of the advertising that appears on television and in magazines is product or display advertising. Plate 18–1 is an excellent example of product advertising for the Singer *Touch-Tronic* Sewing Machine. Note that it shows the product, features economy and ease of use, and the body copy provides a summary statement of the product's outstanding features.

PLATE 18–1: Singer ad in Family Circle *(February 1, 1980) reprinted with permission.*

OUR TOUCH-TRONIC* MEMORY MACHINES ACTUALLY COST LESS THAN LESS MEMORABLE ONES.

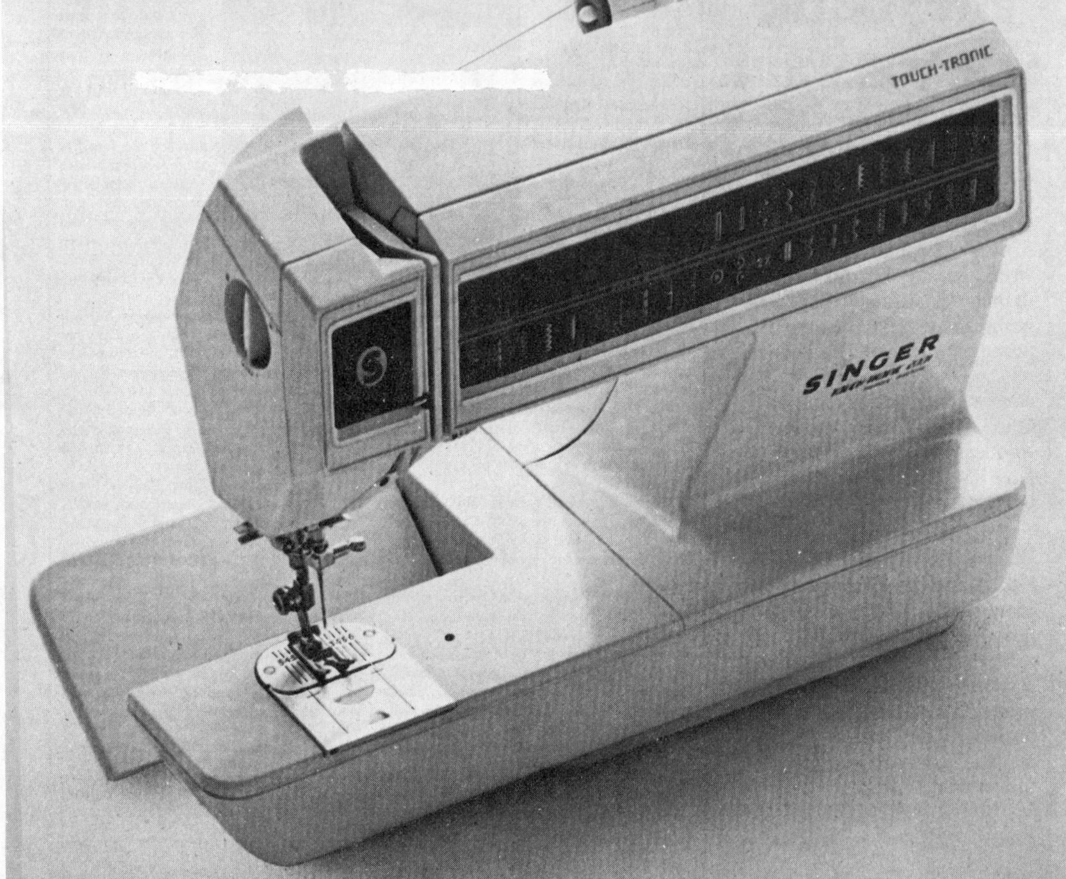

Only Singer makes *Touch-Tronic** memory machines.

Just touch. The memory remembers your stitch pattern with the right width, length and balance. Instantly. No dials to set, no cams to change, no adjustments to make.

ONE-STEP BUTTONHOLER

The *Touch-Tronic* 2000 machine has 25 stitches. The 2001 has even more.

Our memory machines also have bobbins that wind themselves. Buttonholers that measure your button and make a buttonhole to fit, all in one step. And *Flip & Sew** free-arms that let you sew in cuffs and pant legs just by dropping a panel.

SELF-WINDING BOBBIN

In fact, a *Touch-Tronic* memory machine is so easy to use, you can forget about your sewing machine and concentrate on sewing.

You can't buy a machine with features like these anywhere but Singer.

Yet they actually cost less than some other sewing machines that can't do what they do.

If you've already got a sewing machine, we'll give you a trade-in allowance for it that means your new machine costs even less.

"SINGER, THANKS FOR THE MEMORY." —POLLY BERGEN.

Come in to Singer and touch a *Touch-Tronic* memory machine.

It's an experience you'll never forget.

SINGER

100 MILLION PEOPLE SEW EASIER WITH SINGER.

*A Trademark of The Singer Company. © 1980 The Singer Company. Trade-ins optional at participating dealers. Polly Bergen is a member of the Singer Board of Directors.

PLATE 18–2: *Duncan Hines ad in* Woman's Day *(February 1, 1980) reprinted courtesy of the Procter & Gamble Company.*

THE BOOK:

It's *packed* with 242 deliciously moist dessert and snack ideas you make with Duncan Hines mixes. It's *illustrated* with dozens of photos. It's *indexed* with new ideas for each month. It's bound in a handy loose-leaf folder. It truly is a *Bake Shop in a Book*. Look for Duncan Hines mixes on display at your store.

THE OFFER: Get the Duncan Hines Bake Shop in a Book Cookbook by mail: For **$4.95** when you buy (2) boxes of any of the participating Duncan Hines mixes—Duncan Hines Deluxe II Cake Mix (any flavor); Duncan Hines Pudding Recipe (any flavor); Duncan Hines Moist & Easy Snack Cake Mix (any flavor).

Enclosed is:
$4.95* and 2 weight statements from any of the participating Duncan Hines mixes.
*Check or money order payable to Duncan Hines Bake Shop in a Book Cookbook Offer.

Please send my Duncan Hines Bake Shop in a Book Cookbook (shipping charges paid) by mail to:

NAME ____________

ADDRESS ____________
(print clearly, proper delivery depends on a complete and correct address)

CITY ____________

STATE ________ ZIPCODE ______

AREACODE ______ TEL. ________
(used only if more delivery information is needed)

Place in stamped envelope and mail to: Duncan Hines Bake Shop in a Book Cookbook Offer, P.O. Box 260A, Maple Plain, Minnesota 55348.

Please note these additional terms: 1) Offer good only in U.S. 2) THE ATTACHED CERTIFICATE MAY NOT BE MECHANICALLY REPRODUCED AND MUST ACCOMPANY YOUR REQUEST. 3) Your offer rights may not be assigned or transferred. 4) Limit three Duncan Hines Bake Shop in a Book Cookbooks per name or address. 5) Offer good from December 1, 1979 to December 31, 1980. 6) Please allow 6-8 weeks for delivery. Duncan Hines Cookbook Offer certificate (Cash redemption value 1/20 of 1¢).

***PLATE 18–4:** Sunkist ad in* Progressive Grocer *(June 1980) reprinted with permission.*

Announcing the Sunkist "Squeeze the Best Out of Summer" promotion.

This summer, Sunkist has put together an exciting promotion that will help you sell more Sunkist® citrus. We're calling it the "Squeeze the Best Out of Summer" promotion and it's bound to squeeze out extra profits for you.

How can I get in on it?

All you have to do to participate is promote Sunkist citrus during the "Squeeze the Best Out of Summer" promotional period as specified by your local Sunkist District Sales Office.

What kind of support will I get?

That depends on your specific region. You could receive cash incentives, outdoor billboards, radio or newspaper advertising with consumer premium offers, or a combination of the above.

What else?

Point-Of-Sale materials. Including:

- Four beautifully photographed 4-color posters featuring delicious citrus beverages and sherbets. They're real eye-openers and they include Sunkist summer citrus as well as other popular summer fruit.
- Recipe booklets.
- Price cards.

Plus, you'll get ad slicks featuring the four summer beverages, sherbets, all our summer citrus, and the "Squeeze the Best Out of Summer" copy line.

Of course, all our regular Point-Of-Sale materials and our summer ad slicks will be available to everyone.

So I should call my Sunkist Sales Office, right?

Yep. Call today to find out about the "Squeeze the Best Out of Summer" promotion in your area. You'll see that it's a hot idea for you and your produce section. You have our word on it.™

SALES PROMOTION ADVERTISING. Whereas display advertising is generally designed to affect consumer beliefs and attitudes over a period of time and through repeated exposures, *sales promotion advertising* is intended to create immediate action. Thus, it generally carries an urgent message, such as an announcement of a sale, a contest, a coupon, or some other offer. Major sales promotion activities (which will be discussed in Chapter 19) are frequently supported by advertising, and the specific objectives of this advertising are determined by the nature of the promotion being used. Advertising in support of a consumer contest or sweepstakes, for example, is designed to describe the prize structure, the rules of the contest, and what consumers must do to enter. If the promotion features a premium, the primary objective of the advertising should be to describe the premium clearly, and tell consumers how they can obtain it.

Plate 18–2 is an example of a sales promotion advertisement for Duncan Hines cake mixes. In this instance, the sales promotion is built around a cookbook that can be obtained for $4.98. Note that the entire ad is built around the cookbook, and says virtually nothing about Duncan Hines mixes.

TRADE ADVERTISING. Trade advertising for consumer products is generally directed to the retail trade and designed either to help gain distribution or to enlist retail cooperation in a product promotion. In the first instance, such advertising usually emphasizes the profit that the retailer can realize by stocking the brand, and often offers a *stocking allowance* for all initial purchases. In the second instance, the trade advertising generally describes the promotion, specifies its dates, indicates the extent of consumer advertising support that it will have, and often offers a *promotion allowance* for in-store displays during the promotion period. Both of these goals—gaining distribution and announcing promotions—are supported by the activities of the sales force. The advertising is used to provide broad coverage of the retail trade, and to pave the way for personal sales presentations. Plates 18–3 (opposite page 468) and 18–4 are examples of trade advertising. The Rust Craft ad is an excellent example of an advertisement designed to gain distribution. The Sunkist ad announces a promotion, describes it briefly, and tells retailers how they can get further information.

CORPORATE ADVERTISING. A clear distinction needs to be made between *product* advertising on the one hand and *corporate* advertising on the other. The difference is one of *primary focus.* Whereas product advertising is undertaken in support of a particular brand or brands, corporate or *institutional* advertising is undertaken in support of objectives of the company at large. Its purpose is to provide information and influence attitudes concerning the company itself. True, favorable attitudes toward a company may help the sales of its brands, but the focus of corporate advertising is on some aspect of the company itself—not on individual company brands.

Corporate advertising may be undertaken for a variety of reasons and directed toward diverse publics. The purpose of such advertising may be financial, political, public relations, and so forth. A survey conducted by the Association of National Advertisers provides a summary of some general objectives of corporate advertising as viewed by corporate advertisers. These objectives include:

- Enhance or maintain the company's reputation or goodwill among specific public or business audiences.
- Establish or maintain a level of awareness of the company's name and nature of business.
- Provide a unified and supportive marketing approach (umbrella) for a combination of present and future products and services.
- Educate the audience on subjects of importance to the company's future (for example, profits, free enterprise, economics).
- Establish the company's concern for environmental or social issues.
- Bring about a change in specific attitudes of the audience toward the company or its products.[10]

Although corporate advertising can have value, the truth is that many corporate ads are

---

10. Harry L. Darling, *Current Company Objectives and Practices in the Use of Corporate Advertising* (New York: Association of National Advertisers, Inc., 1975), pp. 6–7.

PLATE 18–5: *Young and Rubicam ad in* Fortune *(Nov. 3, 1980) reprinted with permission.*

"All
that is necessary
for the forces of evil
to win in the world
is for enough good men
to do nothing."

EDMUND BURKE

VOTE
TUESDAY, NOV. 4
YOUNG & RUBICAM INC.

poorly conceived, badly executed, and largely a waste of company resources. Historically, corporate advertising has been considered by many in the advertising industry as a bad joke. Too frequently, such advertising has been used, not because there was an objective need for it, but because it was an ego trip for the chairman of the board, the president, and the board of directors of the company—it didn't do much damage, and it made them feel important.

Judging the value of corporate advertising is often difficult because, in order to judge its value, one must know: 1) what the advertisement was expected to accomplish; and 2) how well it accomplished it. Often, this information is not available.

Plate 18–5 is an excellent example of a corporate advertisement run by Young and Rubicam, a major advertising agency, in *Fortune* magazine. The advertisement deals with a serious issue of social responsibility. It is clear, direct, and well written. It expresses a concern by the company for the state of representative democracy in the United States. Clearly socially responsible, the ad is nonpartisan in a political sense. Whether this use of corporate funds is a better use, from the standpoint of the company's welfare, than the use of these same funds in promoting the advertising and marketing excellence of Young and Rubicam is an open question, however.

CLASSIFIED ADVERTISING. A fifth kind of advertising is classified advertising. Classified advertising, as it is used by major corporations, generally has as its primary purpose the recruitment of employees for specific job openings.[11] Classified advertising, sometimes referred to as *nondisplay* advertising, is usually segregated in the back pages, or a special section, of publications. It consists of small, *reader* ads (closely set type in an inch or so of space), or somewhat larger ads using different type faces and/or simple illustrations. Plate 18–6 shows several classified ads clipped from the classified section of *Advertising Age.*

RETAIL ADVERTISING. Retail advertising isn't a separate type of advertising as such. Rather, it is a term reserved for the advertising done by retail stores in local media. Retail advertising generally appears in two forms—as *display* (image) advertising which focuses on the store as a product, or as *sales promotion* advertising which features prices and sales. Most retail advertising is of the sales promotion variety, and the pages of local newspapers are filled with it. Very few retail stores use display or image advertising, although some of the more successful do. Plate 18–7 shows an image advertisement that is generally considered a classic in the advertising industry. The ad is for Ohrbach's, a New York department store positioned as a high style-low cost retail outlet.

11. Direct mail companies, as well as individuals, often use classified advertising to sell specific products and services. Local, retail businesses (particularly automobile dealers) also use the classified sections of local newpapers for the same purpose. For most major corporations, however, employee recruitment is the primary purpose for which classified advertising is used.

PLATE 18–6: Employment ads.
Reprinted with permission from the September 8, 1980, issue of *Advertising Age.*

ART DIRECTOR

Energetic, highly creative art director with diverse publications experience being sought by expanding national farm magazine with offices in southeastern Pennsylvania. Position entails full responsibility for designing and executing new format, including all freelance assignments and production coordination. Exceptional opportunity to use your talents to their fullest, with support of quality editorial staff and growing, multi-publication company. Send resume and salary requirements to:

Personnel Department
RODALE PRESS, INC.
33 E. Minor Street
Emmaus, PA 18049
E. O. E.

Specialists for Personnel in
ADVERTISING • MARKETING
PUBLIC RELATIONS

WILLIAM BOLTON ASSOCIATES
1700 Walnut St., Phila., Pa. 19103
(215) 546-1330
Service nationally since 1948

BEST $18M+ ACCOUNT EXECUTIVE IN CHICAGO

Good present, great future: young sales promotion agency with "heavy" creative credits will give you the back-up to build your future—fast!

Must have fast-track mind: quick, people-sensitive and capable of ramrodding jobs through, start to finish. Previous big consumer account experience a must!

Great North Shore location!

Box 8905, ADVERTISING AGE
740 Rush St., Chicago, Ill. 60611

ADVERTISING AND PROMOTION MANAGER FOR PRESTIGIOUS MERCHANDISING INSTITUTION

Extensive experience in all phases of advertising; Retailing emphasis most desirable.
Creative individual to plan continuous promotions for national and international markets.
Must have ability to develop and manage budgets.
Seeking mature executive with proven record of success.
Salary negotiable.
Responses will be handled in confidence.
Equal opportunity employer.
Send resume to:

M. B. Gregory
Suite 1190
Chicago, IL 60654

Top draw-er opening.

We need a good agency art director. Experienced. Proven. Award winning. Variety of responsibilities from TV to paste-ups. Fringe benefits. Salary commensurate with experience and abilities. Send resumé, best samples and salary range to:

Lewis Advertising, Inc.
P.O. Drawer L, Rocky Mount, NC 27801

ADVERTISING OBJECTIVES AND STRATEGIES

In Chapter 4 (The Marketing Plan), I noted that the advertising objectives section of the marketing plan is an extension of general marketing strategy. Further, since advertising is only one of the controllable marketing variables that affect sales results, advertising objectives should not be defined in terms of sales. Rather, advertising objectives should be defined in terms of what advertising does—namely to provide information and to influence attitudes. Since advertising objectives are supported by separate copy and media strategies, they should cover only those decisions which affect both copy and media. Normally, advertising objectives should do two things:

- Define the target audience groups in terms of *who* they are and *where* they are.
- Provide specific, measurable communication goals such as awareness of the product, knowledge of product attributes, or attitudes toward the product.

The advertising appeals that will be used, and the types of media that will be used, are not derived from advertising objectives, but from the copy and media strategies.

Copy Strategy

The copy strategy lies at the heart of the creative advertising effort, and provides the basis for development of specific advertisements and commercials. The purpose of the copy strategy is to translate a product concept into an appealing product benefit, and to provide general direction about how this benefit will be presented.

As a result, a well-written copy strategy will always have four elements.

- A statement of the *principal benefit(s)* offered by the product.
- A statement of the principal characteristics of the product that cause these benefit(s) to exist. This statement is often referred to as the "reason why."
- A statement of the *character* or *personality* of the product that will be reflected in the mood, tone, and overall atmosphere of the advertising.
- A statement of *what the product is* and *what the product is used for.*

PLATE 18–7: *Ohrbach's ad reprinted with permission.*

The way she talks, you'd think she was in Who's Who. Well! I found out what's what with *her*. Her husband own a bank? Sweetie, not even a bank *account*. Why that palace of theirs has wall-to-wall *mortgages!* And that car? Darling, that's horsepower, *not* earning power. They won it in a fifty-cent raffle! Can you imagine? And those clothes! Of course she *does* dress divinely. But really…a mink stole, and Paris suits, and all those dresses…on *his* income? Well darling, I found out about that too. I just happened to be going her way and *I saw Joan come out of Ohrbach's!*

Ohrbach's

34TH ST. OPP. EMPIRE STATE BLDG. · **NEWARK** MARKET & HALSEY · "A BUSINESS IN MILLIONS, A PROFIT IN PENNIES"®

Precisely *how* these four dimensions of strategy are reflected in a particular advertisement or advertising campaign is a question of execution and style which lie within the province of the skill and expertise of the copy and art people who create the advertisement.

Media Strategy

The media strategy provides guidance in the selection and scheduling of media. Closely related to copy strategy, media strategy is generally developed in discussion with copy people. For example, if large space units are needed to execute the copy strategy, this information must be communicated to the media planner. If a particular type of media is essential for creative presentation, this information also must be communicated to the media planner. A case in point is the advertising of stylish furniture. Research has shown that potential buyers of stylish furniture want to see the furniture in home settings, to be able to study it, and to imagine how it would appear in their homes. This means that magazines are required for effective presentation. Television presentations are inadequate because they do not give consumers the opportunity to study and visualize the product in its setting. Similarly, if "action" is needed to present a particular product to its best advantage, then television—not a magazine—is the ideal medium.

A well-written media strategy generally contains the following four elements:

- Decisions concerning the general kinds of media to be used, along with a rationale for these decisions.
- Decisions concerning types of media within broad media classifications, and the rationale for these decisions.
- Decisions concerning space and time units, and the reasons for these decisions.
- Decisions concerning the ways in which other marketing factors will influence media timing.

Within the framework of such strategy statements, specific media may be selected and justified, schedules may be assembled, and costs estimated.

In a complex media schedule, where a number of media combinations are being considered, thousands of comparisons must be made in arriving at the most efficient combination of media for the schedule in question. Joseph St. George points up the magnitude of this problem with the following comment:

> As an example of the potential complexity of the media decision . . . in the simplest circumstances, a media buyer selecting three media from a group of six has twenty potential different choices. The same media buyer selecting ten media from a group of 100, has 17.31 trillion different alternatives available to him. If he could analyze 1 alternative per second, 24 hours a day, 7 days a week, he could cover all of his choices (in) one-half million years.[12]

Obviously, such comparisons require a computer. As a consequence, the development of high speed computers and sophisticated computer programs for evaluating media have been a boon to the problem of media selection. I do not want to give the impression that satisfactory media programs can be selected wholly by computer. They can't. Judgment is still required for media selection. In recent years, computers have, however, made major contributions to both the effectiveness and efficiency of the media task.

SUMMARY

Few areas of marketing are as widely discussed and as little understood as advertising. Even marketing professionals cannot agree about what constitutes good advertising; and they agree even less about how advertising should be measured.

Advertising can be defined as any paid form of nonpersonal presentation and promotion of ideas, goods, or services by an identified spon-

12. Joseph St. George, "How Practical Is the Media Mode," *Journal of Marketing* (July, 1963): 31–32.

sor. In essence, advertising is a substitute for personal selling. Less effective than personal selling, advertising does not have the opportunity to answer questions and clarify misunderstandings on a one-to-one basis.

The advertising industry consists of four classes of participants: client organizations, advertising agencies, media, and collateral businesses. In consumer goods companies that employ advertising agencies, these agencies often play a key role in developing marketing plans, although the extent of the participation by agencies in client marketing programs varies widely.

Advertising agencies began as brokers of space, and added marketing services as devices to attract clients. Today, four types of agencies, differ in the breadth of the services they offer and their independence of the client organizations which they serve: full-service agencies, modular agencies, in-house (client owned) agencies, and creative boutiques. Traditionally, advertising agencies have been compensated by commissions on the funds they spent with media and suppliers. More recently, this form of compensation has often been replaced or supplemented by fee arrangements between agencies and their clients.

Broadly speaking, six kinds of advertising are used by business organizations: product, sales promotion, trade, corporate, classified, and retail. Each has a somewhat different purpose, and the type of advertising used will depend upon the objectives of the advertiser.

Advertising objectives are an extension of marketing objectives in the marketing plan. Normally, objectives should define the target market, and provide specific, measurable communication goals. Advertising objectives are supported by copy and media strategies that specify the appeals to be used and the kinds of media to be employed.

In a complex media schedule, where a number of media combinations are being considered, thousands of comparisons must be made. The development of high-speed computers has simplified this task, although it has not eliminated the need for personal judgment in media selection.

1. Explain what advertising is in terms of: A) a formal definition; and B) the function it performs.
2. Identify and characterize the four types of participants in the advertising industry.
3. Identify and characterize the four types of advertising agencies described in the text.
4. Identify and characterize the major functional areas in a full-service advertising agency.
5. Explain and distinguish between the formal organization of an advertising agency and the way in which it works.
6. Distinguish between product, sales promotion, trade, corporate, classified, and retail advertising.
7. Normally, what should be contained in the statement of advertising objectives?
8. What are the four basic elements in the copy strategy?
9. What are the four basic elements in the media strategy?
10. Why have computers proved to be a boon to media planners?

1. According to Rance Crain, Editor-in-Chief of *Advertising Age*, critics who attack advertising are really railing against our affluent way of life or a product or service they don't approve of. Do you agree or disagree with this statement?
2. Do you agree that advertising is "pretty much of a mirror of how we view ourselves?"
3. How do you think marketing would be affected if all media advertising were prohibited? Would the cost of marketing be reduced?
4. In the late 1970s, the staff of the Federal Trade Commission proposed that advertising on television programs directed to children under the age of eight be banned because children of this age were unable to understand it, and were, therefore, "unfairly influenced." Do you agree with this proposal? Why or why not? What do you think would be the effects of such a ban?
5. Select a brand of some product with which you are familiar. Using the guidelines for an copy strategy given in the text, write a copy strategy for this product.

ADVERTISING

A good advertisement should always start with a clear statement of its copy strategy. If the strategy is carefully adhered to, it can be inferred from the advertisement. In addition, as pointed out in the chapter on consumer behavior, similar products may use different appeals. This means that often several copy strategies could be used by the same product.

Assignment
Select a magazine advertisement for a consumer product with which you are familiar. Make sure that the ad contains body copy which discusses the product and its benefits.

Analyze the advertisement to discover the four basic elements of copy strategy that are discussed in the chapter and write a copy strategy for the advertisement.

Now, on the basis of the information contained in the advertisement, write a different copy strategy for the product. In what ways do you think your strategy is stronger or weaker than the one that has been used?

Plate 8-5: *Mellow Roast ad reproduced courtesy of General Foods Corporation, owner of the registered trademark MELLOW ROAST.*

The Rust Craft Turn-Key Profit Program

It's less work and more pay.

To turn bigger profits, call Al Vickowski at (617) 329-6000.

RUST CRAFT
. . . for all the best reasons

Boston, Chicago, Atlanta, Phoenix

Plate 18-3: *Rust Craft ad created by Giardini/Russell, Inc. of Boston, Massachusetts.*

Sales Promotion and Product Publicity

- *The nature and uses of sales promotion.*
- *The kinds of sales promotion used to stimulate the sales force, the trade, and consumers.*
- *The nature and uses of product publicity.*
- *The basic ingredient of product publicity.*

MARKETING EXAMPLES

THE $100 MILLION PROMOTION

In 1980 Brown and Williamson Tobacco Company unfolded plans to introduce Barclay cigarettes as their entry into the ultra-low tar market with what was rumored to be the most massive introduction ever accorded a new brand of cigarettes. Although the company had released few details of its plans, industry estimates put the price as high as $150 million—$50 million for advertising and $100 million for sales promotion.

A brochure sent to the trade indicated that Brown and Williamson would give away free cartons—not packs, but cartons—to consumers who would use a toll-free number to call the company and ask for a free carton coupon. In addition, Barclay planned to distribute 21 million free packs and coupons—many of them on street corners.[1]

Apparently, the philosophy behind giving away free cartons is that, by the time recipients work their way through a carton, they will have become accustomed to the new brand and will cease to long for the taste of their former cigarettes.

WHAT EVER HAPPENED TO PERSONAL INTEGRITY?

One problem with cents-off coupons is their misredemption by petty theft and organized fraud. Misredemption has been increasing, and current estimates place it as high as $200 million a year.[2] With the number of coupons being distributed running over 80 billion a year, opportunities for misredemption are rampant.

Coupon misredemption may be classifed as *systematic* or *casual.* In systematic misredemption, one or more retailers, along

1. John J. O'Connor, "Barclay Launch Largest Ever," reprinted with permission from September 8, 1980, issue of *Advertising Age.* Copyright 1980 by Crain Communications, Inc. Also see Arthur M. Louis, "The $150-million Cigarette," *Fortune* (November 17, 1980): 3.

2. Louis J. Haugh, "Who Pays for Coupon Savings?" reprinted with permission from September 8, 1980, issue of *Advertising Age.* Copyright 1980 by Crain Communications, Inc.

with fellow conspirators, devise a wholesale method for defrauding manufacturers. One such conspiracy in Sioux City, Iowa, was prosecuted in 1977; the defendents were found guilty of bilking national advertisers of at least $350,000, and given fines and jail sentences.

Probably, most misredemptions are of the *casual* sort. Individual retailers, valuing convenience more than integrity, rebate the face value of the coupon to customers without requiring them to purchase the product for which the coupon was issued. Or, some employees at the nation's checkout stands collect coupons and surreptitiously slip them into the cash drawer, while pocketing their value in cash. If one assumes that the average value of a coupon is 15 to 20 cents, and that misredemption runs as high as $200 million, this represents over a billion acts of petty thievery each year. It makes one wonder whatever happened to the old-fashioned concept of personal integrity.

$40 BILLION FOR SALES PROMOTION

According to an article in *Advertising Age*, the estimated expenditure for sales promotion is $40 billion a year, and growing. One reason for the growth of sales promotion as a marketing tool may be related to the growth of the brand management system. According to Louis J. Haugh, a leading promotion expert:

> The growth of the brand manager system has had a profound and expansionary effect on the promotion category . . . A brand manager can often easily change a promotion tactic but can't change the advertising or sales distribution portion of his or her marketing strategy without major consequences.[3]

3. Louis J. Haugh, "Sales Promotion Grows to $40 Billion Status," reprinted with permission from April 30, 1980, issue of *Advertising Age*. Copyright 1980 by Crain Communications, Inc.

Another reason, of course, is that sales promotion is often a source of quick and easy short-term sales gains, although it may not contribute as much to the long-term health of the brand as advertising, market research, business building tests, and other slower but surer marketing activities. Since brand managers often see brand management as a stepping stone to higher corporate positions, they may be tempted to opt for short-term gains and the immediate recognition that it brings.

But, whatever the cause, sales promotion is a big business in contemporary marketing. As sales promotion has grown, it has also become more sophisticated, and both client organizations and advertising agencies have developed cadres of sales promotion specialists to design and implement their sales promotion activities.

The foregoing examples have been selected to emphasize the importance of sales promotion as a marketing tool. Although sales promotion may not seem as dramatic as advertising, it is a big, growing, and exciting field.

AN OVERVIEW OF SALES PROMOTION

Sales promotion includes so many diverse activities that it is hard to get a handle on it. The $40 billion estimate for sales promotion expenditures given earlier may be high or it may be low. No one knows for sure. The reason no one really knows is because of the variety of activities—many of which are unmeasured—that fall within the definition of sales promotion. Sales promotion includes such activities as advertising specialities, premiums, incentives, trade shows, sales meetings, point-of-purchase signs, special displays, coupons, price-off offers, in-store demonstrations, cash refunds, sampling, contests, sweepstakes, and what have you.

The field is so varied that it is hard to find people who are experts in all aspects of sales promotion. Instead, one finds people who have carved out a small segment of the field as their domain of expertise. This observation is supported in the following quotation.

> Although there may be some who will disagree, the concept of a "full service" sales promotion agency, which appeared ready to flower a decade ago, has failed to blossom into a full-fledged partner in the advertising and marketing community.
>
> The advent of a service company that could provide savvy sales promotion ideas and implement services for national advertisers, particularly consumer package goods companies is still not here. There are a few exceptions, but they are just that, exceptions . . .
>
> There are any number of reasons to explain why the era of sales promotion or marketing services agencies has eluded the hardy brand of practitioners who wanted it to happen. Not the least of these reasons is that there are few, if any, companies which possess or have developed the breadth of knowledge and experience to provide demanding clients with widespread sales promotion counsel and implementation.
>
> Sales promotion is too diversified and, as a result, suppliers have not been in a position to build competent staffs. Consider, if you will, some of the various promotion areas

that would be required for a "full service" sales promotion agency: sampling, cents-off coupons, packaging, direct mail, premiums and incentives, point of purchase materials, sales literature, meetings and conventions, trade shows and exhibits. In fact, there are competent suppliers in each and every one of the categories.[4]

Many sales promotion activities are applicable to both consumer and industrial products. Some—such as retail displays—are more applicable to consumer items; others—such as exhibits—are primarily used for industrial, wholesale, and retail trade shows. In this chapter, we will direct our attention to sales promotion used in support of retail distributed consumer products. In doing so, remember that many of the points made and some of the activities described are equally applicable to industrial products and to products that are sold directly to consumers, bypassing retail channels. This restriction of our focus on sales promotion is necessary because the field is so diverse that a complete description of it is well beyond the scope of this text. For example, the *Sales Promotion Handbook,*[5] issued by the Dartnell Corporation, contains over 1,200 pages devoted to the subject—somewhat more than can be encompassed in an introductory book on marketing.

Definition of Sales Promotion

Sales promotion may be defined as *special incentives or other activities directed toward consumers, the trade, or the sales force designed to stimulate action by one of these groups—excluding advertising, packaging, product publicity, and normal pricing.* The trouble with this definition, as well as with others that have been given, is that it fails to capture the essential nature of sales promotion, and it tends to define sales promotion in terms of what it is not. Thus, it is not advertising, although advertising may be used in its support. It is not product publicity, although publicity is often a part of a sales promotion program. It is not normal sales activity, although sales promotion is an indispensible tool of the sales force. And, it is not packaging, although packaging may have a major role in a particular sales promotion program.

One way of gaining insight into the nature of sales promotion is to identify some of its salient characteristics. Sales promotion is:

- A relatively short-term activity.
- Directed toward the sales force, distribution channels, or consumers, or some combination of these groups.
- Used in order to stimulate some specific action.

Two key thoughts in this definition are *short-term in duration* and designed to *stimulate some specific action.*

An analogy that I found useful in distinguishing between *advertising* and *sales promotion* is borrowed from the field of armaments: Advertising is like a shotgun. Sales promotion is like a rifle. Advertising is a shotgun in that it scatters its charge against the broad objective of reaching target audiences with a message about the product. Normally, it is not expected to generate immediate action, but to disseminate information, persuade, influence attitudes, and, ultimately, to contribute to sales. In fact, advertising that is designed to generate *immediate* action—such as advertising featuring a price reduction or sale—is referred to as *sales promotion* advertising.

By contrast, sales promotion is a rifle because it zeroes in on a specific objective, and is designed to provoke immediate action. To sample consumers, to induce trial, to deplete inventories, to increase distribution, to gain retail support, to provoke the sales force to focus on a particular activity—these are typical of the objectives of sales promotion.

It follows from this distinction that sales promotion is more *precise* that advertising; both in its target objective and the time span over which it operates. It also follows that, unless a particular

4. Louis J. Haugh, " 'Full-service' Sales Promotion Agency Still Just a Good Idea," pp. 71–72. Reprinted by permission from the May 13, 1977, issue of *Advertising Age.* Copyright 1977 by Crain Communications, Inc.

5. David Riso, (ed.), *Sales Promotion Handbook* (Chicago: The Dartnell Corporation, 1979).

sales promotion is aimed at a specific and relatively narrow objective, it will probably be ineffective. This, in fact, is a major cause of failure among sales promotions. Some promotions try to do so many things that they do nothing well.

Sales promotion is *always* a *supplementary* activity that does not, and cannot, replace advertising. Without a solid advertising base to build product recognition and acceptance, promotions tend to fizzle. A brand that is well conceived and carefully positioned may decline in sales because of inadequate advertising support. If it does, an increase in advertising expenditures, supported by strong copy, can reverse the decline and lead to a continuing pattern of growth in market share. This growth can be accelerated by supplementing the advertising with periodic sales promotion activity.

Without an infusion of advertising, the same brand can seldom achieve a permanent reversal of a share decline by sales promotion alone. Instead, it only achieves temporary arrests on its journey to oblivion. This point has been demonstrated over and over again through studies of consumer products by companies such as A.C. Nielsen which measure product movement at the retail level. Figure 19–1 shows the typical share of market patterns for the two situations described above. Example 1 demonstrates the effect of advertising *and* consumer promotion on a well-positioned product. Example 2 demonstrates the typical effect of sales promotion alone. The reason for these two patterns is that sales promotion works best on products for which advertising is generating recognition and acceptance. A coupon on a well-known brand is an incentive to buy. The same coupon on an unknown brand is no bargain. To express it another way, the history of a successful brand is characterized by three phenomena:

- Advertising, *which creates* value.
- *Sales promotion,* which induces *trial.*
- The *product itself,* which provides *satisfaction.*

The purpose of the foregoing example is not to discredit promotion as a marketing tool. In

FIGURE 19–1: *Typical sales patterns of brand 1 supported by advertising and sales promotion, and brand 2 supported by sales promotion alone.*

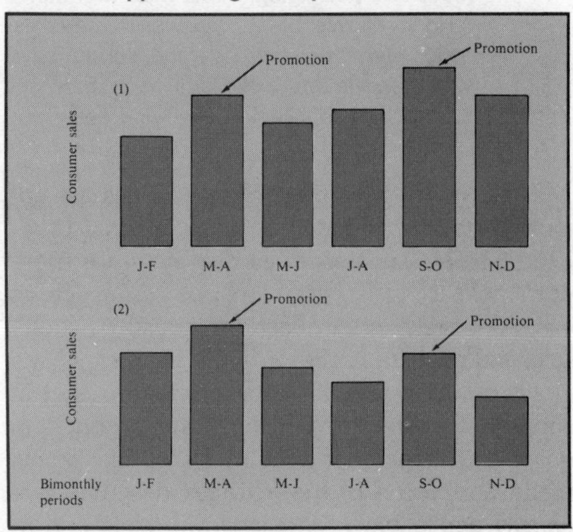

some fields, and at certain periods of time, it is exceedingly important. Sales promotion generally plays a larger role in the marketing mix in fields with similar products than fields in which product differentiation is clear. It generally plays a larger role in the *mature* and *decline* stages of the product life cycle than in the *introductory* and *growth* stages; and it plays a larger role in times of economic recession than in times of affluence.

Types of Sales Promotions

One way of classifying sales promotion devices is by their audiences. In the following material, we will examine typical sales promotion activities designed for the sales force, for the trade, and for consumers. However, a combination of devices directed against two or more of these groups is often used. For example, a stocking allowance to encourage retail distribution of a new brand or package size will be accompanied by a consumer coupon to stimulate consumer purchases and thereby consolidate the new distribution gained. At the same time, a sales contest may be used with the sales force; the salespersons who obtain the most new distribution receive prizes or bonuses. Or, a consumer price-off label allowance may be coordinated with a display allowance to the trade in order to make the consumer offer more effective. The selection of a particular sales promotion technique, however, must always be made in terms of the specific problem to be solved.

SALES FORCE PROMOTIONS

Sales promotions directed to the sales force are often considered an integral part of the sales force compensation system and, as a consequence, are charged to the sales budget and do not appear in the marketing plan, per se, but in the companion sales plan. Nonetheless, sales force activities must be coordinated with marketing objectives and strategies to obtain optimal results from the marketing program. Sales promotions directed toward the sales force is one way of assuring this coordination.

Many companies use some form of a commission system—either straight commissions on sales, or salary plus commissions—as a basic device for motivating salespeople. When such systems are normal or standard practice, they are *not* considered sales promotion. On the other hand, a special, short-term sales force incentive in support of a particular marketing activity—such as gaining distribution on a new product or new package size, increasing shelf facings, obtaining displays, or gaining retail advertising support—is properly considered sales promotion. Often, some sort of sales contest will be used in these instances, and salespeople will be awarded points for performance. For example, let us assume that the sales promotion section of the marketing plan calls for a major consumer promotion supported by media advertising and in-store displays. To assure sales support for the promotion, a separate contest might be structured for the sales force. Under the conditions of this contest, members of the sales force might be awarded points for obtaining in-store displays—say, 100 points for a 50 case display, 50 points for a 25 case display, 10 points for a 10 case display, and so forth. Prizes would be awarded to those sales people in each region who accumulated the most points.

The point is that sales promotions directed to members of the sales force should not be neglected if it is considered crucial to the success of a consumer or trade promotion. In fact, it can be argued that the well conceived sales promotion should contain something for every one—for the sales force, for the trade, and for consumers—in order to assure its success.

TRADE PROMOTIONS

The ultimate fate of a retail distributed product is in the hands of the retailer because, with the exception of company-owned stores and franchised distribution, which together account for an infinitesimal part of retail sales, the retailer determines whether or not a particular brand will be stocked, where it will be stocked, how many shelf facings it will receive, and whether or not it will be given special displays, price features, and retail advertising support.

It has long been recognized that in-store treatment can have a profound effect on the sales of retail distributed brands. In the case of products requiring personal sales support (such as appliances, home furnishings, clothing, cameras, hi-fi equipment), support by retail sales personnel is critical. A retail salesperson only has to say, "Our customers have been extremely pleased with brand X, but have had nothing but trouble with brand Y," to relegate brand Y to the list of unwanted merchandise. Nor, need the behavior of the retail salesperson be that blatant. By subtly directing the customer's attention to a particular brand, and extolling that brand's merits, the prospect's choice of brands may be swayed.

In the case of self-service stores (grocery, drug, and variety stores), in-store treatment is a less obvious, but significant, factor in influencing sales. If a particular brand is not stocked or is temporarily out of stock, it cannot be bought, and a substitute may be chosen. A.C. Nielsen, in a survey of 1,173 grocery shoppers, found that, on the average, 58 percent will accept a substitute brand if the one they want is not available.[6]

Aside from brand availability, in-store treatment may also spell the difference between

6. James O. Peckham, Sr., *The Wheel of Marketing* (Chicago: A. C. Nielsen Company, 1973), p. 10.

success and failure. *Progressive Grocer* introduces its book, *Display Ideas for Supermarkets,* with the observation:

> As any veteran of the food and grocery business knows, the so-called "self-service revolution" owes much of its success to the selling power of displays. For display almost single-handedly has assumed the function of countless sales clerks. Its historic mission has been to uphold the high-volume, low-unit profit principle of mass retailing—to cut operating costs, increase productivity, decrease prices for consumers.... The modern grocer builds his sales dramatically with the help of four merchandising tools—namely, special displays, promotional pricing, departmentalization, and storewide promotions.[7]

A variety of sources testify to the value of displays, feature pricing, shelf position, and so forth in generating sales.[8] In the face of heavy advertising competition, some authorities believe that in-store treatment may be the single most important variable in determining brand sales and market share.[9]

A number of devices may be used to elicit retail cooperation. Most can be classified in terms of their primary purpose, although each may also have desirable side effects. Thus, a sales promotion designed to obtain special displays may also result in price features or retail advertising support. Major purposes of retail promotions are: (1) to obtain distribution or increase inventories, (2) to gain support of retail sales personnel, (3) to gain special displays and/or price features, and (4) to gain retailer advertising support. Often, these devices are used in combination with one another or in combination with consumer promotions. In any event, the sales promotion plan should specify the primary purpose of the device used and what it is expected to accomplish.

Trade Promotions to Gain Distribution or Increase Inventories

Primarily, two promotional devices are used to gain distribution or increase inventories. One, *stocking allowances,* clearly falls within the realm of sales promotion. The second, *consignment selling,* is borderline. In some fields, consignment selling is a standard operating procedure; in other fields, it is infrequently used and so qualifies as a sales promotion technique.

STOCKING ALLOWANCES. Stocking allowances are the most frequently used sales promotion device to gain distribution. Under a stocking allowance, a retailer will be given an allowance for each case on initial orders or on all orders for a specified period of time, such as one month. The ethical justification for a stocking allowance for new distribution is that it compensates the retailer for the expenses incurred in adding a new item to inventories. Practically speaking, it is a legal bribe that has become hallowed by use and thoroughly institutionalized as an acceptable and ethical practice. The use of stocking allowances to increase the inventories of brands already stocked is called *loading.* Loading may be used by manufacturers to increase dealer inventories because of out-of-stock problems (retailers' normal orders are insufficient to keep up with consumer demand) or to increase inventories prior to a consumer deal of some kind that is expected to accelerate sales. Stocking allowances are widely used in package goods marketing, particularly in the food and drug fields.

Several modifications of stocking allowances are often used. The most common is the "one free with" offer. That is, one package free for each six bought; or, for larger retailers, one case free with the purchase of six cases. This approach is widely used in drugstores, particularly for items that are carried only seasonally. Each year, prior to the season, it is customary to make a "one free with" offer to encourage early ordering.

---

7. M. Alexander, (ed.), *Display Ideas for Supermarkets* (New York: *Progressive Grocer,* 1958), pp. 2–3.

8. Ibid; "The Dillon Study," *Progressive Grocer* (Oct., 1960): D-81; "Improving Sale Item Display: The Display and Merchandising Workshop," *Chain Store Age* (January, 1965): 64; *Awareness, Decision, Purchases,* (New York: Point-of-Purchase Advertising Institute, 1961), p. 14; *Drugstore Brand Switching and Impulse Buying* (New York: Point-of-Purchase Advertising Institute, 1963), p. 11; "Shelf Merchandising Strategy: A Key to Increased Sales," *Progressive Grocer,* (March, 1964): 126.

9. H. S. Gorschman, "New Dimensions in Unhidden Persuasion," *Journal of the Academy of Marketing Science* (Fall, 1973): 110–18.

A second modification that is sometimes used is *leasing* store space. This approach is most likely to be used when trying to expand product distribution into nontraditional outlets. For example, a manufacturer of fancy chocolates might lease space in a supermarket for a display stand carrying its brand. This tactic relieves the supermarket of the risk of stocking a new product and guarantees an income from the venture. If the venture proves successful, fancy chocolates may ultimately be incorporated as a normal food store item, and the leasing arrangement will be terminated. *Leased departments,* an expansion of the "lease" idea, have been used in department stores, notably by Russell Stover candies.

CONSIGNMENT SELLING. In consignment selling, the manufacturer retains ownership of the product while giving possession of it to retailers so that they can sell it to consumers. Thus, the manufacturer absorbs the full cost of carrying the inventory, and the dealer pays for the goods as they are sold. The Hanes Corporation used consignment selling to induce supermarkets and drugstores to handle its L'eggs pantyhose.[10] A single display rack of Leggs can generate $1,300 a year in profits to the retailer since stocking and inventory control are performed by the manufacturer. Consignment selling is also used as a standard selling practice for some big ticket items, particularly to industrial distributors. When it is used as a device to obtain new distribution, however, it may be considered as a sales promotion tactic.

Trade Promotions to Gain Support of Retail Sales Personnel

Retail sales personnel have a minimal role in the selling of self-service products. However, in many other fields (cars, appliances, furniture, carpeting, electronics, clothing, fabrics, proprietary drugs, and so on) retail salespeople are extremely important in consummating the final sale. Four broad sales promotion devices are sometimes used to enlist retail sales personnel support: retail training, contests, push money, and merchandising the advertising.

10. *Business Week* (March 25, 1972): 96–100.

"May I help you?" (Photo by Freda Leinwand)

RETAIL TRAINING. In this approach, sales seminars are held for retail salespeople. In these seminars, technical information about the product is given, as well as suggestions on how to approach customers, how to sell related items, how to close a sale, and so forth. Since retail salespeople like to sell merchandise they are knowledgeable about, and since they are often appreciative of the sales training they have been given, such efforts may pay off handsomely.

CONTESTS. Contests designed for retail store owners and/or their employees are often used to gain retail support. Such contests may take a variety of forms. For example, the Frigidaire Division of General Motors undertook a major promotional effort to regain a major share of the appliance industry after a slump of several years. Prominent in its plans were dealer-support programs (dealer incentives, volume rebates, sales literature, and even a minitheater for in-store movies). Among the dealer incentives were a series of minivacations for retail dealers and their spouses. About one hundred people in each region (fifty dealer couples) would be eligible for trips earned through points from Frigidaire's on-going "Sell 'n' Share" promotion. In addition to the minivacations, dealers could earn points redeemable in merchandise, including General Motors cars.[11] Admiral Corporation, in 1952, sent fifty dealers and their wives to witness the coronation of the Queen of England as part of a dealer incentive program. The promotion was considered so successful in enlisting dealer support for Admiral's products that it became a key factor in the company's marketing program. During the past twenty years, over 20,000 dealers and their wives have traveled to virtually every major tourist attraction and world capital on the globe. Themes used to attract dealer attention and enlist their participation in the travel-incentive program have included "London Getaway," "Rendezvous in Rome," "Holiday in Mallorca," "Fiesta in Mexico," and "Tour de Paris."[12]

PUSH MONEY. Push money (PM) involves paying retail salespeople commissions to "push" a particular brand. PMs are sometimes used in selling cosmetics and other personal care items, proprietary medicines, as well as other products where consumer knowledge is weak and recommendations are welcome.

MERCHANDISING THE ADVERTISING. To "merchandise the advertising" is to sell the advertising and sales promotion program to channel intermediaries, particularly the retail trade, to generate enthusiasm and gain support. Annual sales meetings scheduled by a manufacturer for its sales force usually devote a significant portion of the meeting to outlining the advertising and promotion plans for the forthcoming year. At the conclusion of these meetings, salespeople are often provided with *merchandising kits* (a summary of planned activities) to show to channel members to engender enthusiasm for the firm's advertising

11. S. Ayling, "Merchandising Helps Turn Frigidaire Around," *Promotion* (April 29, 1974): 22.

12. R. Gransee, "Admiral Finds Travel Motivates, Builds Goodwill, and Has Glamour," *Promotion* (March 4, 1974), Section 2, Business Meetings Selector, p. 2.

Special display = sales. (Photo courtesy of Safeway Stores, Inc.)

and promotion activities. Merchandising kits often include media schedules, copies of advertisements and television storyboards, and descriptions of future promotions.

Trade Promotions to Gain Special Displays and/or Price Features

One of the most effective devices for influencing product movement, particularly in self-service stores, is the special display. The term *special display* refers to any visual device, other than normal shelf stocking, used in the store to call attention to a particular product or group of products. A special display may or may not include a price inducement; it may range from a simple shelf talker (a small sign attached to a grocery shelf giving the product name and information) to elaborate gondolas.

The effectiveness of special displays in moving merchandising is well supported by research. One study, carried out in Super Value stores over twelve weeks, tested the effects of approximately 1,500 separate displays. The study found that, on the average, an item given special display will sell five and one-half times as much as it will from the normal shelf position.[13] These findings have been confirmed by the Dillon study,

13. M. Alexander, (ed.), *Display Ideas,* p. 35.

which found that the average display boosted sales by 536 percent over normal shelf movement.[14] Still another study reports that 5 percent of all supermarket sales are the results of displays.[15] If this figure is projected to total grocery volume, it would indicate that over $4 billion worth of merchandise is sold from grocery displays each year.

However, products differ widely in their responsiveness to special displays. The Super Value study, for example, found increases as high as 3,453 percent for candy and as low as 36 percent for paper towels. Display effectiveness for a particular product will depend upon: (1) the product field, (2) the type and size of display used, (3) whether the display includes a price inducement, and (4) the point of purchase material used with the product display. For example, point–of–purchase material tied in with the advertising is generally thought to be more effective than that which is unrelated to advertising.

There is no shortage of studies testifying to the effectiveness of special displays in moving merchandise. It is little wonder, then, that sales promotions designed to obtain displays is a major preoccupation of consumer goods marketers.

The primary methods used in obtaining special displays of the product, particularly in self-service stores, are display allowances, display cards and stands, and nonbranded promotions.

DISPLAY ALLOWANCES. A manufacturer using a display allowance offers retailers a payment (perhaps 25¢ or 50¢ a case) for each case placed on special display. For simplicity in administration, display allowances are often based on fixed quantities. For example: $2.50 for a 10 case display; $6.25 for a 25 case display; $12.50 for a 50 case display; $25 for a 100 case display. Manufacturers usually provide free point-of-purchase material for use on the display; this material may range from posters and banners to easily assembled structures made of metal or wood and cardboard. Display allowances and display structures are frequently used in conjunction with major consumer promotions, such as coupons and contests.

DISPLAY CARDS OR STANDS. Another device for obtaining in-store displays is a brand-identified display card or stand for stocking merchandise. A display card of key rings, for example, might take the form of a *counter card* that can be mounted near the cash register and would have a number of key rings affixed to it; the customer would make a selection by removing a key ring from the card. The L'eggs display stand (Figure 19–2) is an example of a display stand used in drugstores and groceries.

NONBRANDED PROMOTIONS. Nonbranded promotions, sometimes called *storewide promotions,* consist of a wide variety of nonidentified promotional material offered by an advertiser to enable the retailers to decorate their stores. The material usually consists of window signs, store banners, display cards, shelf-talkers, price stickers, and other decorative material associated with a theme such as Thanksgiving, Christmas, Valen-

FIGURE 19–2: *L'eggs Display Stand. Used with permission.*

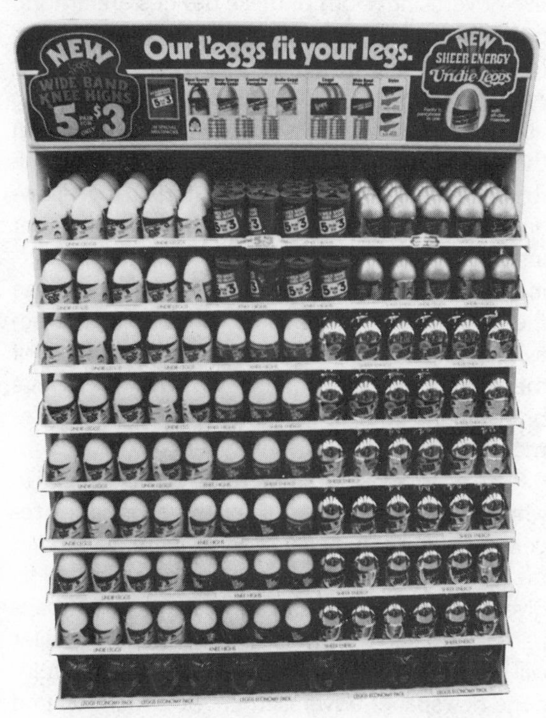

14. "The Dillon Study," *Progressive Grocer* (October, 1960): D-81.

15. "Improving Sale Item Display: The Display and Merchandising Workshop," *Chain Store Age* (January, 1965): 64.

tine's Day, back-to-school, new store openings, and so forth. Included with the nonbranded material will be brand identified point-of-purchase pieces for the brand or brands of the advertiser offering the material. The basic philosophy underlying the use of nonbranded promotions is reciprocity. The advertiser provides the material free; as an expression of appreciation, the retailer gives special displays to the advertiser's brands.

Trade Promotions to Gain Advertising Support

Retail advertising support of a national brand appears to be an excellent way to extend national advertising dollars and to localize a brand's advertising. It extends advertising dollars because the rates for retail advertising are generally significantly lower than national rates and because the cost of the ad is sometimes shared by the retailer. Advertising is localized because it appears in the local media and is identified with the store or stores carrying the brand. Two basic devices are used by national advertisers to gain retail advertising support: advertising allowances and cooperative advertising. Both of these devices are among the most widely used and most severely abused forms of sales promotion.

ADVERTISING ALLOWANCES. An advertising allowance is similar to a display allowance in that the retail organization is given a case allowance for advertising purposes. Sometimes the allowance is offered on a continuing basis; in other instances, it is offered only on orders placed during a specified period. The retailer agrees to use the allowance for advertising; she verifies her activity by sending the advertiser (1) tear sheets of the retail advertising containing the advertiser's brand along with (2) an apportioned cost statement indicating the amount spent.

Advertising allowances can be effective when the retailer accumulates the allowances received so that significant space can be devoted to the brand *and* when the sponsoring brand is given a price feature. Usually, that's not what happens. What happens most often is that the retailer will give the brand a column inch or less in a full-page newspaper advertisement or a mention in a radio or television spot *without* a price feature. In the advertising industry, these casual mentions in newspaper ads are referred to as *obituaries* as a reflection of the low esteem in which they are held.

Particularly in the food and drug trade, advertising allowances are often more trouble than they are worth and represent, at best, a form of legal blackmail by retailers. *If* they are carefully policed by the advertiser, and *if* advertising mats of a minimum size are supplied with the requirement that the mat be used to qualify for the allowance, and *if* a price feature is given or required, *then* advertising allowances can be worthwhile.

The absolute worst form of advertising allowance is the *continuing allowance.* It is almost impossible to keep the advertising support given under this arrangement from becoming casual, and if the advertiser withdraws the allowance, he runs the risk of offending the retail organization and, perhaps, losing distribution. The moral in regard to advertising allowances is that, if they are used, (1) they should be used only on orders received during a specified period of time, (2) minimum criteria for the ads should be agreed upon, (3) and the effort should be carefully policed.

COOPERATIVE ADVERTISING. Cooperative advertising is most generally used on big ticket items. Often, it represents the major advertising effort of the manufacturer. Used properly, and carefully policed, it can be extremely effective. Used carelessly, it is a waste of company resources.

Under a cooperative advertising agreement, the manufacturer agrees to pay a portion of the cost (typically 50 percent) of the advertising for its brand run in local media under the name of the cooperating retailer. The annual obligation of the manufacturer is specified, usually based on an estimate of sales that will be made through the retailer organization, and payment is made upon receipt of a tear sheet and a copy of the invoice from the media. For example, a retailer runs a full-page ad in the local newspaper on the manufacturer's brand; the cost of the advertisement is $1,800. Upon receipt of a tear sheet and copy of the invoice, the manufacturer rebates half of the total cost ($900) to the retailer in the form of a check or credit memorandum. Also, the manufacturer usually provides the mats or other advertising material required by the medium used.

This arrangement has advantages for both the manufacturer and the retail store. The manufacturer obtains local advertising that is identified with a local retailer, gains the advantage of local rates, is only obligated for half of the advertising space costs, and regains control over what is said in the advertisement. The retail organization, on the other hand, obtains advertising at half its normal cost, is provided with professionally prepared advertising copy, and is identified with a prestigious national brand. The advantages of cooperative advertising are acknowledged by estimates that over $3 billion annually is spent in this fashion.[16]

One disadvantage to cooperative advertising is the great deal of paper work necessary to implement and police the program. Because of lethargy or doubts about the values of advertising retailers must be carefully supervised to assure their participation, and tear sheets must be checked to see that advertising is run according to specifications. When broadcast advertising is used, the checking problem is even more difficult since verification requires that station logs be checked or the actual broadcast monitored. Since these procedures are expensive, a more common practice is to obtain an affidavit from an executive of the broadcast station certifying that the commercial actually ran. Such affidavits are widely used but subject to error or fraud. A retailer may conspire with the media to submit an invoice that reflects a higher rate than was actually paid, or fail to follow up with in-store support in accordance with the cooperative agreement. And then there is the problem of waste circulation. As pointed out earlier, local newspapers and television are basically mass media and provide little selectivity for the advertiser.

Cooperative advertising does have value for the manufacturer who uses selective or exclusive distribution. It has less value for the brand that is widely distributed. When cooperative advertising is used for convenience products such as detergents or other grocery store items, it is usually simply a device to give the retailer a price discount, with no expectation that the advertising itself will contribute any appreciable value.

16. John S. Wright, Daniel S. Warner, Willis L. Winger, Jr., Sherilyn K. Ziegler, *Advertising Age* (New York: McGraw–Hill Book Company, 1977), p. 621.

CONSUMER PROMOTIONS

Consumer promotions are generally used for two primary purposes: to attract new customers, and to increase the purchases of existing customers. Inherent in these purposes, however, are two functions that consumer promotions often serve. First, they create an aura of *excitement* around the brand, calling attention to it in fresh and unusual ways. Second, they may serve to *deplete inventories* that have become excessive and stimulate retailers to reorder or to order in larger than usual quantities. Further, in the case of new product introductions, consumer promotions are widely used as a forcing device to get retailers to stock the product. The assumption is that if customers start demanding the product, retailers will be forced to stock it to maintain customer good will and patronage.

Consumer promotions are often used in conjunction with related trade promotions. For example, a consumer contest or coupon distribution will often be backed up by display material, display allowances, stocking allowances, or even cooperative advertising.

Consumer Promotions to Sample New Customers

No attempt will be made to identify all of the consumer promotions or combinations of promotions that may be used to attract new customers. The type of promotion used is limited only by the budget and imagination of the marketer. Time–worn promotions are constantly being refurbished by the addition of new wrinkles, and I doubt that any promotional device is really new. Underneath its cosmetics, one will generally find a tried and true promotional technique. At the heart of most effective consumer promotions designed to attract new customers are five basic approaches:

coupons and price-off label offers, sampling, demonstrations, premiums, and contests and sweepstakes.

COUPONS AND PRICE-OFF OFFERS. One of the most popular devices for attracting new customers is coupons. Earlier, it was pointed out that 80 billion coupons a year are distributed in the United States. If price-off label offers are added to the coupons, the number of consumer deals represented by these two devices defies imagination.

Basically, coupons designed to attract new customers differ in face value, breadth of distribution, method of delivery, and method of redemption. When New Purina Dog Chow was test marketed in Little Rock, Arkansas, a coupon redeemable for a two-pound box of the product was mailed to every other household in the Little Rock metropolitan area.

Generally, a coupon should be for at least 10 to 15 percent of the normal product price to attract consumer attention, and coupons of less than ten cents are generally unattractive. Table 5–15 shows the estimated costs for delivering 25 million coupons by a variety of delivery methods. The average face value of the coupons used in these calculations was fourteen cents; in addition, five cents per coupon was paid to retailers for handling, and a one-cent charge has been included for internal processing. No allowance was made for misredemption, although it was estimated at 20 percent. If misredemption is as high as 33 percent, as some recent industry sources contend, the effectiveness of the programs would be reduced even further. The cost per coupon redeemed ranges from a low of 23.3 to a high of 75.5 cents.

Other methods of delivering coupons include the in-package coupon, redeemable on the next purchase. This method of delivery is not particularly good for attracting new users because a coupon good on the next purchase may have little incentive value for the consumer who has doubts about how well she will like the first purchase. As a sales promotion device, this approach is more effective in generating additional purchases by current users. A variation of the in-package coupon that is used by marketers who have multiple products is *cross-couponing.* For example, a coupon in a package of Betty Crocker Hamburger Helper is redeemable on a box of Betty Crocker cake mix.

There are also variations in the way in which coupons are redeemed. Normally, coupons are redeemable at the checkout counter of the retailer. An alternative requires that the consumer mail the coupon along with a label from the product directly to the manufacturer. The manufacturer then rebates the face value of the coupon to the consumer. This technique may decrease misredemption somewhat, but it is an extremely weak promotional device because few consumers will bother to mail the coupon in unless its value is exceedingly high. And, if the coupon value is high enough to overcome consumer inertia, the cost of the couponing effort may become exorbitant, and imaginative methods of misredemption will be invented.

The price-off label is a substitute device for couponing that eliminates some handling problems associated with coupon redemption and reduces, but does not eliminate, cheating. Price-off label offers are generally limited to a certain production quantity, such as a one month supply at retail. The manufacturer either prints the price-off offer directly on the package or prints it on a removable "sleeve" or band that encircles the package. In either case, additional packaging costs are incurred. The deal merchandise is then sold to retailers at a reduced cost to maintain retailer margins. When the offer is printed on a removable sleeve or band, cheating occurs because unscrupulous retailers will remove the band and sell the packages at the normal shelf price. Greed is a powerful motivator.

Price-off label offers are usually more expensive than coupons because the manufacturer loses income on the face value of the price reduction on all packages carrying the offer, whereas average coupon redemption generally runs less than 10 percent, depending, of course, on the face value of the coupon and its method of delivery. In addition, marketers are often reluctant to use a price-off label offer during a *new product introduction* because the retail value of the product has not yet been established. As a conse-

"Try it—you'll like it." (Photo courtesy of The Kroger Company)

quence, coupons, rather than price-off label offers are the preferred incentive for new product introductions.

SAMPLING. Consumer sampling is a direct device for reaching new customers. In this method, a sample of the product (usually a miniature package) is distributed to consumers at home, in retail stores, on shopping center parking lots, or in other high traffic locations. Sampling is expensive, and costs are dependent upon the size of the sample, the number distributed, and the method of distribution. Sampling can be a highly effective device *if* the product being sampled is discernibly superior to competitive brands on some relevant dimension. Because of the costs involved, sampling is generally restricted to new product introductions and major consumer promotions.

DEMONSTRATION. Demonstration is a form of sampling that is widely used on a variety of products ranging from food items to automobiles. Although product demonstrations may be made at the home or at the place of purchase, they are most frequently made at the place of purchase because of the economy of having a central demonstration point. In the case of automobiles, a demonstration ride is a conventional selling technique. Most department stores will from time to time have in-store demonstrations of carpet sweepers, microwave ovens, sewing machines, and so forth. Both department stores and drugstores will often have in-store demonstrators dabbing new fragrances on passers-by. Food stores often have demonstrators handing out samples of food.

Demonstrations are expensive since they require the salary of a demonstrator in each store as well as the cost of the product involved. For this reason, demonstrations are usually restricted to high volume outlets and peak shopping periods.

PREMIUMS. Premiums of all kinds attract new customers. In-pack premiums, near-pack premiums (where the premium is stocked in the store *near* the product), mail-in premiums, trading stamps, combination offers (buy a package of razor blades and get a razor free or at a reduced price), and premiums for opening a new bank account are only a few of the methods used as incentives for new customers.

Many marketers feel that premiums are often unimaginative and over used. For example, Louis J. Haugh, a promotion authority, observes:

> Why so many banks and other financial institutions persist in turning their quarterly quest for new savings deposits into bug eye advertising featuring multiple premiums defies common sense.
>
> Some members of this financial community use such unimaginative advertising with its panoply of electronic appliances and other gimcracks that even the defense that such ads are successful in pulling in new savings and new accounts can hardly hold water.
>
> All too often, banks festoon their lobbies with displays of the products used in the premium offer, running the very real risk, it would seem, of confusing someone who may think he or she has walked into a department store rather than a bank.[17]

---

17. Louis J. Haugh, "Banks Going Premium Crazy, but Promos Lack Imagination," reprinted with permission from the December 19, 1977, issue of *Advertising Age*. Copyright 1977 by Crain Communications, Inc.

Despite abuses (and everything that works for one marketer is abused by another), premiums remain a major incentive, both for attracting new customers and rewarding loyal ones.

CONTESTS AND SWEEPSTAKES. Contests differ from sweepstakes in that the consumer is required to do something that is judged, and prizes are awarded to the winners. Consumers may be asked to name a product, compose or complete a limerick, write an essay, think up a slogan, guess how many beans are in a jar, or almost anything else. Another form of contest is to have participants prepare something from the manufacturer's product and submit it for judging. An outstanding example of this approach is the Pillsbury Bake-Off that has been run annually since 1949. Heavily supported by advertising, the contest attracts some 250,000 women a year who submit their favorite recipes made from Pillsbury flour. Each year, one hundred winners are flown to New York where the final judging is done at the Waldorf Astoria. This particular contest has had some outstanding payoffs for Pillsbury. For example, Bundt Cake, a prepared cake mix that has earned Pillsbury several millions of dollars in profit since its introduction in the early 1970s, was the winning recipe in one of the bake-offs.

The attractiveness of a contest depends both on the magnitude of the prize structure and the complexity of the task. Often consumers avoid contests because the requirements are too great, or the rules too exacting. Professional contest entrants sometimes make up a sizable (but unknown) proportion of the entrants; some consumers avoid contests because they believe that these professional contenders win most of the prizes.

Sweepstakes avoid the skill element of contests by awarding prizes on the basis of chance. Entrants' names are pooled, and the winners are selected at random. More people are likely to enter a sweepstakes than contests because it requires less effort. On the negative side, of course, it also requires less personal involvement.

Participation in a sweepstakes sometimes requires that the consumer purchase one unit of the sponsor's product and send a label with the entry. However, lottery laws in some states prohibit this requirement because it involves a payment (purchase of the product) and is therefore interpreted as gambling. To circumvent lottery laws, many sweepstakes either require no qualification for entry or permit entrants to submit a facsimile of the label or to print the brand name on the entry blank.

The success of a sweepstake depends upon the prize structure, the number of winners, and the amount of advertising weight devoted to it. Publishers' Clearing House, for example, in its annual drive for magazine subscriptions, offers a $100,000 house as first prize, plus a vacation home, cars, and a galaxy of other consolation prizes. On the other hand, Pepsi-Cola ran a sweepstakes in the mid-1970s which offered 65,000 prizes, ranging from $1 to $50 worth of groceries.

While the foregoing consumer promotions have as their primary purpose the acquisition of new customers, few of them pay for themselves on this basis alone. Important collateral values include the retention of existing customers, the combatting of competitive promotions, the creation of excitement around the brand, and the stimulation of both the sales force and trade.

Consumer Promotions Designed to Increase Purchases of Current Customers

While some of the sales promotion techniques used to gain new customers are also used to increase the purchases of existing patrons, they are usually modified when the latter objective is the primary purpose of the promotion. For example, a blanket mailing of coupons or the use of magazine distribution will have as its primary purpose the acquisition of new customers. On the other hand, an in-pack coupon good on the next purchase is more appropriate for generating loyalty and repeat purchase by current customers. Similarly, a one-time premium offer may be effective for attracting new customers, while a continuing premium offer (a set of dishes or silverware, one piece with each purchase) is intended, primarily, to retain the loyalty of existing buyers.

Some brands are known as *premium*

brands because continuing premiums constitute their major promotional effort. For example, Bonus, a Procter & Gamble detergent, contains a premium in every box (a dish towel, a piece of dinnerware, or some other premium) and is positioned to appeal to those consumers for whom premiums are a primary motivation for purchase. Similarly, Raleigh cigarettes contain a coupon in every package; these coupons are saved and exchanged for a variety of merchandise—bridge tables, lawn chairs, small appliances, household furnishings, sports equipment, and personal items—selected from a premium catalogue.

In addition to these devices, two other sales promotion techniques are commonly used to increase purchase among present customers: two-for-one offers and multiple packs. In the two-for-one offer, two packages will be banded together and sold for the price of one or at a substantial discount from the normal price. In multiple-packs, products are sold in special packaged multiples of 3, 4, 6, etc. as well as in individual packages. Soft drinks, beer, fruit juices, antacid tablets as well as other products are sold in this way. A standard brewing industry sales promotion is the "Pick a pair of six-packs" promotion, widely used in the height of the beer-drinking season.

While these approaches may also attract new customers, their primary intent is for people who have already tried the brand and are familiar with it. Customers unfamiliar with the brand are less likely to commit themselves to multiple purchases on their first trial.

SALES PROMOTION AND THE MARKETING PLAN

In our discussion of sales promotion, sales promotion methods have been classified and discussed in terms of their *primary* objectives. This has been done to emphasize that sales promotions are relatively short-term, limited-objective marketing devices. The primary functions of sales promotions are to solve particular marketing problems or take advantage of specific marketing opportunities, such as to deplete inventories, to encourage stocking, to sample consumers, and so forth. These tasks require activities above and beyond the normal advertising program or routine selling activities. And, although sales promotions are an essential part of marketing, care must be taken that they are not used too frequently because to do so dulls their effectiveness, diminishes their excitement, and (in the case of price-off promotions) depreciates the value of the brand in consumers' minds. Sales promotions are, after all, *supplementary marketing activities,* not the heart of the marketing program.

The need for sales promotion activity should be established in the problem and opportunities section of the marketing plan. The general marketing strategies section should define how funds will be divided between advertising and sales promotion. The sales promotion strategy itself should be founded on one or more points of marketing strategy, and will typically contain statements on:

- The promotional techniques that offer the most effective and efficient means of meeting marketing strategy requirements.
- How total promotion weight will be allocated by package size, by marketing area, by season, and so forth.

Generally, specific sales promotion techniques to accomplish a particular strategy requirement are selected on the basis of company experience, traditional practices in a given industry, and the results of past sales promotion tests.

PRODUCT PUBLICITY

Product publicity is probably the most controversial and the least used marketing tool. Perhaps one reason is that it is often handled badly. Thus, an article in the *Public Relations Journal* makes the following comment about product publicity releases: "Far too many new product releases are targeted for the wrong publications, and a depressing number are poorly written, not clear or do not contain enough information."[18]

In view of this comment, it is little wonder that product publicity is sometimes considered the stepchild of marketing. Let's look at this step-child more carefully in order to see why it is treated so badly. *Publicity* is a somewhat ambiguous term that is used in a variety of ways. For example, Norman A. Hart, in a book titled *Industrial Publicity,* said:

> The term *publicity* here is used in an all-embracing sense of publicizing anything for any purpose. It thus includes activities which contribute to selling and are known as sales promotion. . . .
> Under the heading *sales promotion* are included all the various 'channels of persuasion' such as advertising, direct mail, exhibitions, and so on.[19]

In contrast, Rolf Gompertz in *Promotion and Publicity Handbook for Broadcasters* has said:

> But whatever publicity is, it is *not* advertising and it is *not* promotion. It is important to make this distinction and to keep it in mind.
> Much confusion arises among the general public—not to mention among some clients—over this difference and the failure to make that distinction. The difference between advertising and publicity is quite simple: advertising is *paid for* space (or air time), while publicity is *free* space (or air time).
> You can *control* what goes into an ad (or a commercial). You *cannot control* editorial content or editorial space. (You can influence it by the information you make available and the professional service you render, but you *cannot* control the way this information is used. You cannot even guarantee that it will be used.)[20]

18. "Why New Product Releases Don't Get Published," *Public Relations Journal,* (January, 1980): 43.

19. Norman A. Hart, *Industrial Publicity* (New York: John Wiley & Sons, 1971), p. 3

20. Rolf Gompertz, *Promotional and Publicity Handbook for Broadcasters* (Blue Ridge Summit, PA: Tab Books, 1977), p. 13.

This latter definition is the one that is generally accepted by the advertising industry and the one that is used in this text. In Chapter 4, publicity was defined in the following way:

> Publicity is a form of promotion. It differs from advertising in that it is not paid for at standard rates, and the sponsor is not identified. Usually, publicity appears—unidentified as such—in the editorial or news columns of printed media, or in the noncommercial portion of radio or television programs.[21]

Two key points are implied by this definition and made explicit in the quotation from Gompertz that precedes it: (1) publicity is *free,* and (2) the advertiser does not *control* it. Both of these points deserve further comment.

The fact that media do not charge for publicity does not mean that it involves no cost. On the contrary, plans have to be made and coordinated, personnel have to be assigned to the activity, press releases have to be prepared, and press conferences are often elaborately staged. Further, when a press conference is given in behalf of a product, product samples as well as product literature are often distributed to those attending. As a consequence, a budget must be established for a well-organized publicity program; the budget should be a part of the marketing plan because it does represent a *cost* for promoting the product.

The second point is that the advertiser has *no control* over the way publicity will be used or whether it will be used at all. At best, the advertiser can try to influence what will be said by releasing favorable information. But sometimes even the best of publicity programs backfire. For example, I was involved with a publicity disaster for a consumer product of a major client. As a part of a product publicity program, a series of press conferences was scheduled for newspaper writers in the cities where the product was being introduced. The press conferences were well staged and included a free dinner and a brief presentation by company executives on the product and its

21. S. W. Dunn and A. M. Barban, *Advertising: Its Role in Modern Marketing* (Hinsdale, IL: The Dryden Press, 1974), p. 9.

values. One popular columnist of a major metropolitan newspaper, either because of an antibusiness bent or because it was his day to be offended, took exception to the press conference and wrote a satirical column that ridiculed the client company, its executives, and the product. While I personally regretted the incident, I thought the column was humorous. Client executives, however, were deeply offended and vacillated between suing for slander and having the columnist tarred and feathered. Ultimately, after some heated and interminable meetings, discretion won out, and it was decided to ignore the incident. Although this example does not represent a common occurrence, such things do happen. Normally, the worst outcome of a publicity program is that press releases are ignored and the effort is largely wasted.

In view of these limitations of publicity, the question naturally arises. "Why bother with it?" Many companies do not bother. They prefer to devote their efforts to advertising and sales promotion activities over which they have greater control. Other companies, however, use product publicity extensively, primarily for the following reasons:

- *Publicity Is Free.* The greatest value of product publicity derives from the fact that it is not paid for in the normal sense of payment. As a consequence, its appearance implies independent editorial validity of product claims. Generally, the public trusts media (certainly more than it trusts advertising) and the product benefits from this trust.
- *Advertising Is Expensive.* Few clients could afford to pay for the media space and time that results from a successful product publicity campaign. And, in the competitive world of marketing, products need all of the support they can get.
- *The Demand by Media for Information on Products.* As one of the services they provide their readers or viewers, newspapers and magazines often have a "product corner," a column devoted to consumer products. It is desirable for an advertiser to take advantage of this demand. If he doesn't there is the strong possibility that his competitor will.

The Basic Ingredient of Publicity

The basic ingredient of successful publicity is *news.* Publicity releases that are truly newsworthy have a high incidence of use. The major problem with publicity releases that are not used is that they are not newsworthy. It's almost as simple as that. This suggests that product publicity is generally more effective for a new product than for an established one, and this is generally true. On the other hand, there are news opportunities for established products. The fact that a particular brand of reconstituted citrus drink is used by astronauts in their extraterrestrial perambulations because of its high nutritional content is news. The selection of a particular brand of trucks for construction work on the Alaskan pipeline because of its ruggedness and starting dependability is news. Preference for a particular brand of tires or sparkplugs by the winner of the Indianapolis 500 because of its performance under trying conditions is news. The manufacturers of outboard motors spend fortunes entering boats powered by their motors in national and international outboard races because the fact that the winning boat was powered by a Mercury motor or an Evinrude motor is news (it is widely believed in the outboard motor industry that share of market is related to share of wins).

The facts surrounding many established products contain elements of news. And, while news is only one of the techniques of advertising, it is *the* technique of product publicity.

Staffing for Product Publicity

Some companies maintain their own public relations departments, which are responsible for product publicity and which work closely with the marketing department. Seldom is product publicity a direct function of the marketing department itself, although in some instances it may be. Similarly, some advertising agencies have a public relations department staffed with experts, which can serve the publicity needs of their clients; this is not a common practice.

Often, both advertisers and advertising agencies rely on specialized public relations agencies, which charge for their counsel and time on a fee basis, with the size of the fee depending on the scope and duration of the services required.

Planning Product Publicity

Not all product publicity releases are preplanned. Sometimes they arise spontaneously and erratically, depending on the environment. An unanticipated opportunity for product publicity will arise, and the company will take advantage of it on an ad hoc basis.

Our primary concern, however, is the systematic use of product publicity as a part of the marketing plan. When used in this way, references to product publicity will appear in various parts of the marketing plan.

PROBLEMS AND OPPORTUNITIES. The problems and opportunities section of the marketing plan for a particular product might carry the following statement: "The development of a new circuitry and display mechanism for our model 3062 pocket computer, which extends the life of the battery from 30 to 2,000 hours, appears to be a newsworthy technological advance that should be featured in our advertising and promotion during the forthcoming fiscal period."

MARKETING STRATEGY. The marketing strategy section of the plan might state: "Because of the newsworthyness of the extended battery life of model 3062, product publicity will be used to capitalize on this development. Particular attention should be devoted to: retail buyers of pocket computers in major department stores; technical journals, product columns in newspapers and magazines, and general newswriters."

OBJECTIVES AND STRATEGY. An objectives and strategy section for product publicity would be prepared by appropriate specialists. This section would include:

1. A brief statement of the purpose and rationale for the publicity program.
2. An identification of the specific audiences to be reached.
3. A description of the publicity activities that will be undertaken and the timing of each.
4. A statement of how product publicity will be coordinated with the advertising and sales promotion programs.
5. An estimate of the costs of the publicity program.
6. Finally, and this point is highly desirable, although it is not essential and is sometimes neglected, there should be a statement of how the effectiveness of the publicity program will be evaluated.

SUMMARY

Sales promotion is a $40 billion business that involves a variety of diverse activities. It includes such things as advertising specialties, premiums, incentives, trade shows, point-of-purchase signs, special displays, coupons, price-off offers, in-store demonstrations, case allowances, sampling, contests, sweepstakes, and so forth. The field is so varied that it is hard to find people who are experts in all aspects of sales promotion. Instead people have carved out small segments of the field as their domain of expertise.

Sales promotion may be defined as special incentives or other activities directed toward consumers, the trade, or the sales force and designed to stimulate action by one of these groups. Generally, it is helpful to think of sales promotion as a relatively short-term activity, used to stimulate some specific form of action. Sales promotion is always a supplemental activity, and does not replace advertising as a marketing tool.

Sales promotions directed against the sales force are used as incentives to enlist sales effort in support of particular marketing strategies such as gaining distribution, obtaining displays, improving shelf facings and introducing new products. Sales promotions for the trade are used for a variety of purposes, and include such activities as stocking allowances, retail training, contests, push money, display allowances, display cards, point-of-sale material, and advertising allowances. Consumer promotions typically are used for two reasons: to attract new customers and to increase the purchases of existing customers. Activities include coupons and price-off offers, sampling, demonstrations, premiums, and contests and sweepstakes.

Product publicity refers to editorial or news support of a product that is given by media without charge, generally in response to publicity releases prepared and distributed by producers of goods and services. Product publicity is one of the most controversial and least used of the marketing tools available because it is difficult to control, and its effectiveness is difficult to document.

The basic ingredient of successful publicity is *news.* Publicity releases that are high in news value have a high incidence of use, whereas those that are not newsworthy are generally a waste of effort.

Both sales promotion and product publicity, to be effective, should be planned carefully. They should be a part of the marketing plan, rooted in specific marketing strategies, and with clearly defined objectives and strategies.

1. Explain why the growth of the brand manager system has had an expansionary effect on the use of sales promotion.
2. Explain sales promotion. What are its essential characteristics?
3. Explain why sales promotion is considered as a supplementary activity.
4. How is sales promotion used against the sales force? Give an example of such use.
5. Explain why sales promotion directed to the retail trade is particularly important.
6. What are the four basic purposes of sales promotion directed against the retail trade? Give an example of each.
7. What are the two primary purposes of sales promotion directed to consumers?
8. Identify the basic sales promotion devices designed to attract new customers.
9. What is meant by product publicity? What does it mean to say that product publicity is not really free?
10. What points should be included in the objective and strategies section for product publicity in the marketing plan?

1. A local bank has decided to use sales promotion to attract new customers and to increase the use of the bank's services (saving accounts, checking accounts, safety deposit boxes, loans, and so forth) among existing customers. How would you approach this problem? Consider the groups against which promotions should be directed, and the types of promotions that would be appropriate.
2. Visit a supermarket, a drugstore, and a department store. Make a list of all of the sales promotion devices that you are able to identify. Indicate which of these you believe would be most effective, along with the reasons for your choice.
3. Select a product of your choice and indicate which sales promotion tools you think would be most effective.
4. A major league baseball team has suffered a decline in game attendance during the past two seasons. A decision has been made to employ sales promotion to increase attendance. Suggest how this problem might be approached, and some promotion ideas that might be useful.
5. What characteristics should a product have to receive generous publicity support from general media? Can you identify any such products?

SALES PROMOTION AND PRODUCT PUBLICITY

You are a member of the sales promotion department of a grocery products firm. Your company has recently developed a new convenience package for a widely–used, prepared mix product. Since consumer tests have shown that consumers strongly prefer the new convenience package to the conventional packages used by competitive products, management has decided to use a coupon to sample consumers with the new package. The sales promotion strategy for the forthcoming year states:

- *In view of the need to sample consumers with the new convenience package, primary promotional emphasis will be placed on a consumer coupon promotion, coupled with a display allowance.*
- *A twenty-cent consumer coupon will be used since company experience has shown this coupon value to be the most efficient in generating redemption in this product field.*

- *Part of the strategy shall be to sample 2.4 million households with the improved package.*
- *The coupon effort shall not cost more than sixty cents per sampled household. A second part of the strategy is to minimize duplication among coupon recipients.*
- *The couponing effort will be supported by a display allowance to encourage store displays, with emphasis given to displays of twenty-five cases or more.*
- *The promotion period will extend from September 1 through October 31 to avoid the characteristic decrease in the effectiveness of summer promotions for prepared mix products, and to avoid conflict with the Thanksgiving-Christmas holiday season.*

You have been asked to recommend a specific sales promotion plan and to prepare a budget for the sales promotion effort.

You have past figures on cost-per-thousand for printing and delivering various types of coupons, as well as redemption rates for each method of coupon distribution. (Use the figures from Table 15-5 for these two variables.)

You estimate that to sample 2.4 million households, you will have to make an allowance for misredemption of 25 percent. Coupon costs will include a $0.20 coupon plus $0.09 for handling by retailers and $0.02 for internal handling.

In estimating display costs, you include 50,000 class A stores. If you offer $15 for a twenty-five case display, you estimate on the basis of past experience, that 20 percent of these stores will cooperate. There are also 200,000 class B stores. Here you estimate that an offer of $5 for a ten case display will obtain cooperation from about 10 percent of these stores.

Assignment

Prepare your recommendation and budget.

Franchise operation. When you've seen one McDonald's, you've seen them all. (Photo courtesy of McDonald's Corporation)

PART 4

SPECIAL TOPICS IN MARKETING

Thus far, in the text, we have dealt with product marketing in the United States. In this section, we will turn our attention to three special topics of marketing that have attracted increasing attention in recent years: International Marketing, Corporate Planning, and Business and Society.

Chapter 20 is devoted to international marketing. Although international marketing is not new, active pursuit of foreign markets grew rapidly in the 1960s as U.S. firms turned to international markets in search of expanded sales and to compensate for the loss of domestic sales to foreign competitors. Since the nations of the world are becoming increasingly interdependent for raw materials and manufactured goods, it is probable that international marketing will become even more important in the future.

Chapter 21 deals with corporate planning, a topic that moved to the forefront of marketing thought in the 1960s. Interest in corporate planning emerged with the growth of conglomerates and multiproduct organizations, and with increases in the cost of money that required these companies to turn their attention to internal sources of funds to finance corporate growth.

Finally, Chapter 22 is concerned with the relationship between the business enterprise and the society within which it operates. Since the 1950s, the rise of consumerism has led to widespread criticisms of business in general, and of marketing activities in particular. In this chapter, we will examine some of these criticisms in an attempt to assess their validity.

20

International Markets

- *The size and scope of international marketing.*
- *Why many companies do not market internationally.*
- *The international marketing environment.*
- *Investigating international markets.*
- *Methods of entering international markets.*
- *The international marketing mix.*

MARKETING EXAMPLES

THE MULTINATIONAL PROMISE THAT TURNED SOUR

A multinational company can be defined as a business firm that has direct investments in two or more countries. The 1950s and 1960s witnessed an unparalleled upsurge in the growth of U.S.-based multinationals as business firm after business firm turned to direct investments in foreign countries as a source of growth and profits. Many U.S. firms thought multinational operations were the promise of the future. But, by the 1970s, the promise was turning sour and, according to *Fortune* magazine, the multinational boom showed incipient signs of decay.

> An unpublished study by Brent Wilson, an assistant professor of business at the University of Virginia, shows that American companies are selling off their foreign subsidiaries at what amounts to a breakneck pace. From 1971 through 1975, they sold off a total of 1,359, which was close to 10 percent of all American overseas subsidiaries. . . .
>
> Not surprisingly, the rise in the number of divestments coincided with a decline in the number of new foreign subsidiaries being formed. In 1971 there were 3.3 new investments for each disinvestment; by 1975 that ratio had shrunk to 1.4 to one. It is obvious that American business is losing its taste for foreign adventure.
>
> The disenchantment of the Seventies represents a sharp reversal of the attitudes prevailing in the Fifties and Sixties. In those halcyon years, nothing seemed more seductive to U.S. business than a foreign climate. American manufacturing companies of all types trekked abroad in prodigious numbers. And wherever they migrated, their banks, advertising agencies, and accounting firms went with them. The book value of U.S. foreign direct investment swelled from about $12 billion to more than $50 billion in 1966. It is now estimated at between $140 billion and $150 billion.[1]

1. Sanford Rose, "Why the Multinational Tide is Ebbing," *Fortune* Magazine © 1977 Time, Inc. All rights reserved.

Why the second thoughts about foreign investments? Many reasons. Some investments were ill-considered and poorly planned; some generated losses instead of profits. Increased competition from other multinationals and from local foreign firms reduced the attractiveness of foreign markets. Legal restrictions by foreign governments fettered business operations, and unfavorable tax treatments of foreign profits by the U.S. government discouraged investment. In short, multinational operations were much more complex than they appeared at first blush.

JAPAN'S CHANGE IN EXPORT STRATEGY

Japan is widely envied by the western world for its export success. In automobiles, steel, and consumer electronics, Japanese products have flooded western markets and wreaked havoc with their economies. Yet, in looking to the future, the Japanese government and its business leaders see storm clouds on the horizon.

The storm clouds arise from the low cost of labor in developing countries where labor costs may be as much as one-tenth or one-twentieth of those in industrialized nations such as Japan, the United States, and western Europe. In labor intensive industries, this wage differential is too great to be offset by technology and automation. As a consequence, Japan sees its future, not in exporting domestic production, but in multinational operations with manufacturing plants located in undeveloped countries such as Taiwan, Sri Lanka, China, and South America.

According to the chief economist of one of Japan's leading trading companies:

> China . . . will by the year 2000 have attained no more than one-fourth or one-fifth the output per manufacturing man-hour of any of the developed countries today—and that's optimistic. But it is also irrelevant when you consider that the real wage will be around one–

twentieth of that of the developed countries. China will have to find work for 70 million to 100 million additional urban dwellers or risk social explosion. The only work they could possibly do is in labor-intensive manufacturing for export. Brazil or Mexico—and with a decent government, Indonesia—are likely to have cost advantages in comparable ranges.[2]

Thus, in the future, instead of exporting domestically produced manufactured goods, Japan sees itself exporting capital, technology, technically-educated young people, and management know-how. Will this change in export strategy work? Who knows? In an unstable world, multinational operations are a source of high opportunity and great risks.

INTERNATIONAL POLITICS AND SOFT DRINKS

An exclusive agreement with the Soviet Union to distribute Coca-Cola at the Moscow Olympic Games gave rise to rosy visions of increased sales as millions of Russians queued up for a taste of the "real thing." Then came the invasion of Afghanistan and the U.S. boycott of the Moscow games, and the Coca-Cola Company discovered that it's not enough to have a good product to crack international markets. One must also have good political relationships.

2. Peter Drucker, "Japan Gets Ready for Tougher Times," *Fortune* Magazine © Time, Inc. All rights reserved.

These three examples have been selected to emphasize both the opportunities and risks that exist in international marketing. In an increasingly complex world in which international interdependence is a fact of life, international marketing has become a major concern of many U.S. businesses. The American Assembly of Collegiate Schools of Business, the accrediting organization for business schools in the United States, has urged its members to institute courses in international business, and to introduce the topic in all relevant courses. Certainly, it is relevant in marketing. So, let's examine some of the major dimensions of international marketing.

THE SCOPE OF INTERNATIONAL MARKETING

International trade is important to individual business firms as a source of growth and profits and to nations as a means of economic well-being and survival. Industrialized nations are dependent upon imports of raw materials to fuel their industrial base while undeveloped countries must import technology, consumer and industrial goods, and capital to feed and clothe their growing populations, and to develop their economies.

In 1977 foreign trade amounted to 14.5 percent of the gross national product of the

FIGURE 20–1: *U.S. Exports and Imports, excluding Military.*
SOURCE: *Statistical Abstracts of the United States: 1979,* p. 866.

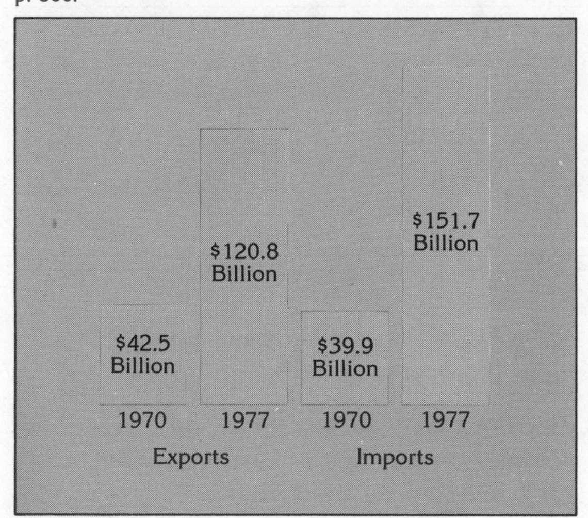

FIGURE 20–2: *1978 U.S. Imports and Exports in Billions of Dollars.*
SOURCE: *Statistical Abstracts of the United States: 1979,* p. 862.

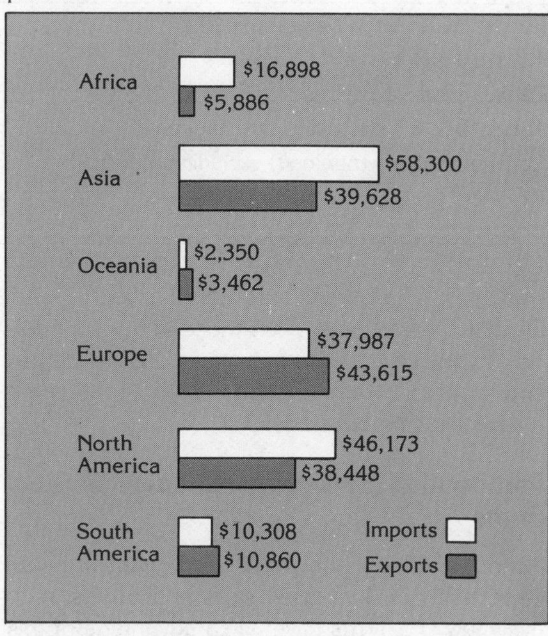

United States, up from only 8 percent in 1970. Figure 20–1 shows the growth in U.S. imports and exports from 1970 to 1977. In 1970 the United States enjoyed a balance of payments surplus (imports minus exports) of $2.6 billion. In 1977, the U.S. had a balance of payments deficit of $30.9 billion, a factor contributing to the weakness of the dollar and domestic economic woes.

The worldwide dimensions of the international trade of the United States is shown in Figure 20–2 which shows the magnitude of import–export activity by continent. It is apparent from this figure that the United States' major trading partners are Asia, Europe, and North America, and that its major trade deficit lies with Asia.

Finally, Table 20–1 shows the total value of foreign trade by end-use class from 1970 to 1978. All areas have grown substantially, with the greatest absolute growth occurring in industrial supplies and material, and in capital goods.

The foregoing information emphasizes that foreign trade represents a large and growing market for those firms willing to make the investments required and to take the risks entailed. If foreign marketing has been a disappointment to some U.S. firms, it has been a bonanza for others.

For some companies, such as Boeing Aircraft, the export market is a major source of sales and revenue. In 1979 Boeing exported almost $4 billion worth of products, and exports accounted for almost 49 percent of its total sales. Table 20–2 lists the fifty largest United States based exporters, showing their total sales, total exports, and exports as a percent of total sales. Although these fifty companies accounted for almost $32 billion in exports, this figure is deceptively small. This is true because the figures shown in Table 20–2 do not include returns from investment abroad since such investments are not "exports" in the everyday sense of the word, even though they are an integral part of international marketing.

Note that the U.S. companies that have been most successful in their international enterprises tend to be those in high technology and capital goods industries, and those (such as IBM, Xerox, and Texas Instruments) which provide a highly integrated package of production and marketing services that cannot be easily matched by local competitors or other multinationals. The

TABLE 20–1: *Growth in United States Import-Export Trade by End-use Class: 1970–1978.*
SOURCE: *Statistical Abstracts of the United States: 1979,* p. 866.

	1970	*1978**	*Difference*	*Increase*
Foods, feeds, and beverages	$ 5.9	$25.2	$19.3	327%
Industrial supplies and materials	13.9	30.3	25.4	183
Capital goods, except automobiles	14.6	46.5	31.9	218
Automobile vehicles, parts, and engines	3.9	15.3	11.4	292
Consumer goods (nonfood) excluding automotive	2.8	10.4	7.6	271
All other	1.5	5.2	3.7	247

*1978 figures are preliminary.

least successful have been those in low-technology, highly competitive industries such as textiles and apparel, leather goods, tires, agricultural chemicals, and beverages.

Participation in International Trade by U.S. Firms

Although international trade offers many firms an opportunity for increased sales and profits, relatively few U.S. firms have taken advantage of this opportunity. Thus, in terms of manufactured products, only 250 U.S. firms account for 85 percent of U.S. exports.[3]

Participation in foreign trade is least frequent among small firms. Many of these firms, of course, do not produce products that lend themselves to export markets. For example, producers of bulky, hard-to-ship items, and those who manufacture component parts designed for domestic manufacturers are at a disadvantage. Similarly, differences in standards between countries create trade barriers. For example, export of lumber to Japan is hampered because of substantial capital investments required by U.S. firms to convert sawmills to process lumber in the dimensions required by the Japanese.[4] Aside from these restrictions, however, some twenty thousand U.S. firms capable of participation in the export market fail to do so.

3. S. Tamer Cavusgil and Richard A. Yanzito, "Consulting Services and Trade Co-ops Can Assist Small Firms in Exporting," *Marketing News* (October 17, 1980): section 2, p. 3.
4. Russell M. Moore, "Conflicting Political, Socioeconomic Issues Can Discourage U.S. Exports," *Marketing News* (October 17, 1980): Section 2, p. 8.

Reasons for Failing to Participate in International Trade

U.S. firms fail to exploit the export opportunities for many reasons. Most of them, however, can be attributed to three major factors:

- *Negative attitudes.* Many firms are reluctant to consider export prospects and voluntarily exclude themselves from entering new markets because they feel exporting is too risky, complicated or unprofitable. Others are not export minded, or are simply indifferent to exporting. Thus, they are unwilling to invest management time and money.
  Interest and commitment at the top management level appears to be a critical determinant of export involvement. But there is a tendency among American managers to avoid the burden of long–term decisions and risks necessary for developing export markets.
  After all, success in export marketing is the result of patient and meticulous preparations, with a long period of market development before the rewards are available.
- *Operations/Resource Limitations.* This is a significant barrier because many activities related to exporting are new to management and require commitment of physical and financial resources as well as close managerial attention.
  Small firms, however, are especially constrained in this respect. Management is typically preoccupied with daily activities, other staff cannot be spared, marketing skills may be scarce, and sufficient distribution channels and a business image may yet need to be developed.
- *Lack of Assistance Programs.* Many private sector sources as well as the U.S. Department of Commerce offer a variety of motivational, informational,

TABLE 20–2: The Fifty Leading U.S. Exporters.
SOURCE: "The 50 Leading Exporters," (Sept. 22, 1980) *Fortune* Magazine

Company	Products	Sales ($000)	Exports ($000)	Exports as percentage of sales
1. Boeing	Aircraft	$ 8,131,000	$3,967,900	48.80%
2. General Electric	Generating equipment, aircraft engines	22,450,600	2,772,100	12.34
3. Caterpillar Tractor	Construction equipment, engines	7,613,200	2,499,900	32.84
4. McDonnel Douglas	Aircraft	5,278,531	1,788,425	33.88
5. E.I. du Pont de Nemours	Chemicals, fibers, plastics	12,571,800	1,764,000	14.03
6. United Technologies	Aircraft engines, helicopters	9,053,358	1,417,257	15.65
7. Weyerhaeuser	Pulp, logs, lumber, wood products	4,422,653	978,000	22.11
8. Lockheed	Aircraft and related support services	4,069,800	956,000	23.49
9. Westinghouse Electric	Generating equipment, defense systems	7,332,000	979,840	12.00
10. Raytheon	Electronic equipment	3,727,930	734,000	19.69
11. Northrop	Aircraft and related support service	1,582,477	701,577	44.33
12. Union Carbide	Chemicals, plastics	9,176,500	602,000	6.56
13. Archer-Daniels-Midland	Soybean meal and oil, wheat, corn	2,297,838	546,808	24.58
14. Signal Companies	Trucks, engines, chemicals	4,241,200	544,700	12.84
15. Rockwell International	Electronic, automotive, and industrial equipment	6,466,100	536,000	8.29
16. Phillip Morris	Tobacco products	6,144,091	521,235	8.48
17. Occidental Petroleum	Agricultural and chemiproducts, coal	9,554,795	499,000	5.22
18. Kaiser Aluminum & Chemical Company	Aluminum	2,926,500	496,800	16.98
19. Textron	Helicopters, chain saws, metal products	3,392,974	489,000	14.41
20. John Deere Company	Farm equipment	4,933,104	480,000	9.73
21. R.J. Reynolds Industries	Tobacco products	7,133,100	476,000	6.67
22. FMC	Industrial and farm equipment	3,307,484	462,398	13.98
23. International Harvester	Farm equipment, trucks	8,392,042	447,000	5.33
24. Dresser Industries	Oil field and industrial equipment	3,457,400	435,500	12.60
25. Monsanto	Herbicides, textile fibers, specialty chemicals	6,192,600	406,400	6.56

TABLE 20–2: *Fifty Leading U.S. Exporters—continued.*

	Company	Products	Sales ($000)	Exports ($000)	Exports as percentage of sales
26.	American Motors	Automotive vehicles and parts	$ 3,117,049	$ 343,288	11.01%
27.	Universal Leaf Tobacco	Tobacco	978,174	302,788	30.95
28.	Williams Companies	Phosphate products, fertilizer	1,850,013	296,000	16.00
29.	Allied Chemical	Fibers, plastic, chemicals	4,538,835	294,000	6.48
30.	Dana	Motor vehicle components	2,761,135	290,996	10.54
31.	International Paper	Pulp and paper products	4,605,000	283,000	6.15
32.	Kennecott Copper	Nonferrous metals, abrasives, resistant materials	2,433,637	279,500	11.48
33.	Celanese	Fibers, chemicals	3,146,000	278,000	8.84
34.	Borg-Warner	Cooling systems, automotive parts	2,717,400	268,000	9.86
35.	Combustion Engineering	Oil field and industrial equipment	2,757,504	258,901	9.39
36.	Warner Communications	Movies, records, video games	1,648,027	253,368	15.37
37.	TRW	Truck, auto, and aircraft parts, oil field equipment	4,560,303	251,700	5.52
38.	Harris	Communications equipment	982,111	247,900	25.24
39.	Bendix	Automotive parts, aerospace products	3,828,700	245,200	6.40
40.	Cummins Engine	Engines and engine components	1,770,834	244,000	13.78
41.	St. Joe Minerals	Coal, lead	1,148,105	242,495	21.12
42.	Louisiana-Pacific	Pulp, lumber, wood products	1,301,910	236,000	18.13
43.	International Minerals & Chemical	Potash, phosphate, industrial minerals	1,474,700	235,900	16.00
44.	Cessna Aircraft	Aircraft	939,311	233,000	24.81
45.	Teledyne	Industrial and electronic equipment	2,705,600	229,629	8.49
46.	White Consolidated Industries	Home appliances, steel mill machinery	2,010,114	225,900	11.24
47.	Emerson Electric	Electronic components	2,614,110	219,917	8.41
48.	Gold Kist	Peanuts, soybean products, poultry	1,639,809	215,577	13.15
49.	Motorola	Electronic components	2,713,795	211,531	7.79
50.	Walter Kidde	Hydraulic cranes, fire protection systems	2,284,146	210,141	9.20

and operational programs designed to assist firms in their international marketing.

However, these programs do not generally take account of the attitudes and capabilities of smaller firms. Most programs are primarily suited to the needs of large corporations.

One president of a small firm, for example, suggested that President Carter's Export Council was deliberately constituted in the big business mold on the assumption that small companies are not, and need not be involved in international markets. The head of the small firm went on to question the usefulness of the Domestic International Sales Corp. and the Export-Import Bank for small business.[5]

These reasons add up to parochialism and shortsightedness on the part of individual firms and the U.S. government. Regardless of these factors, the 1980s most likely will bring increasing pressure on U.S. firms to turn their attention to foreign markets. This pressure will become even more acute as foreign companies succeed in capturing significant shares of U.S. domestic markets.

THE INTERNATIONAL MARKETING ENVIRONMENT

United States based marketers contemplating foreign ventures should recognize at the outset that the marketing environment in foreign countries often differs dramatically from that which exists in the United States. Firms that fail to recognize these differences, or to analyze their impact on international marketing ventures, risk failure in their foreign endeavors. In this section, we will briefly review three variables—political, economic, and social-cultural—that differ widely among nations.

Political-Legal Variables

International marketers often find themselves adrift in a sea of political-legal considerations. For example, United States marketers are subject to three sets of laws when they enter foreign markets:

- First, are the laws of this country. These laws not only define the foreign countries with which one may trade, but also impose restrictive taxes on profits earned abroad, and may involve antitrust actions if a foreign subsidiary of a U.S. firm exports to the United States.
- Second, are the laws of the foreign countries in which firms attempt to do business. Few countries are as economically free as the United States, and government bureaucracies often ensnare apparently simple transactions in mountains of red tape. Often, they prohibit marketing activities that are taken for granted in the United States. Italy, for example, forbids the advertising of cigarettes; France prohibits door-to-door selling; and Australia requires justification of price increases. Tariffs may be levied either on the physical quantity of goods sold or on the value of shipments, quotas often set limits on the amounts and types of goods that will be accepted, and, in some countries, local facilities must be managed by nationals of the host country. One recurrent problem is transferring foreign profits back to the United States. When nations face shortages of foreign exchange, controls may be levied over the movement of capital in and out of the country. This may require the foreign investor to reinvest profits in the country of their origin, or they may take their profits in the form of locally produced goods which may be virtually worthless in the world market.

  In many countries, labor unions have strong government support, and have exacted special concessions from business. Layoffs may be forbidden, profits may have to be shared, and innumerable special services may have to be provided.
- Third, international laws cross national borders. Both the United Nations and the European Economic Community have established commissions to develop commercial codes applicable to all participating nations.

As a consequence, large multinational companies have established international legal departments to keep abreast of legal develop-

5. S. Tamer Cavusgil and Richard A. Yanzito, "Consulting Services and Trade Co-ops Can Assist Small Firms in Exporting," p. 3.

International marketing. (Photo courtesy of Matson Navigation Company)

ments. Small companies which lack these facilities may unknowingly find themselves in conflict with domestic, foreign, or international legal restrictions.

Aside from the legal complexities that may plague the international marketer, governmental instability—particularly in undeveloped countries—exists as a constant threat. A friendly government may be overturned overnight by violent revolution or by a more peaceable coup d'etat. Production may be disrupted by nationwide strikes, transportation brought to a standstill, factories seized or destroyed, or corporate executives kidnapped or murdered. Expropriation of foreign investments by beleaguered governments is always another possibility.

None of this means that foreign investments should not be made, or foreign trade avoided. However, foreign involvements should be undertaken cautiously, and with a realistic analysis of the risks and problems.

Economic Variables

The nations of the world vary widely in their economic purchasing power. Unfortunately, nations representing much of the world's population have very little economic clout. At the present time, as much as half of the world's population is economically unattractive to marketers. Per capita disposable income ranges from as high as $12,000 in Nauru to as low as $70 in Bhutan.[6] Table 20–3 shows the average per capita income for major geographic areas of the world in the mid-1970s. For North America, the average per capita income was in excess of $7,000. For Africa, it was only $430. And, although the average per capita income for Asia was $1,560, it was less than $200 for some countries in this geographic area.

As a generalization, those countries with a low per capita income represent poor markets

6. *United Nations Statistical Yearbook*, 1978.

TABLE 20–3: *Per Capita Income by Geographic Areas of the World.*
SOURCE: Compiled from Table 193 of the United Nations *1977 Statistical Yearbook* and the *Statistical Abstracts of the United States, 1978.*

Geographic Area	*Per capita income*	*Population (in millions)*	*Percent of population*
North America	$7,150	240.2	6.0%
Oceania	5,190	21.9	0.5
Europe	4,950	478.1	12.0
Asia	1,560	2,485.9	62.2
Caribbean and Latin America	1,150	341.6	8.5
Africa	430	430.7	10.8
Total		3,998.4	100.0%

*Data does not include per capita income nor population from centrally planned economies.

for manufactured goods, whereas those with high per capita incomes represent good markets for such products. Such a generalization is an oversimplification, however, because the *rate* of economic development, as well as *governmental emphasis on consumer versus industrial goods,* influence the demand schedules for various products. Further, wide variations in income distributions within individual countries mean that many countries must be analyzed on a region–by–region basis. Morocco, is a case in point. With a per capita income of $540, a strong agricultural and mineral base, and a growing industrial community, Morocco has all the earmarks of a developing country. Yet, illiteracy is high, its population growth exceeds that of its gross national product, unemployment is widespread, and poverty and affluence exist side by side. Casablanca, Tangiers, and other tourist and industrial centers are modern cities with department stores, attractive shops, and an abundance of consumer goods. Yet, in its small villages and countryside, Morocco is almost prebiblical in its economic development. It is a nation of contrasts: wooden ploughs exist side–by-side with modern combines; motorized forms of transportation share the roads—which are pretty bad—with donkeys. And, government currency restrictions introduce a note of caution in those foreign investors who contemplate investments in the country.

A number of classifications have been devised to distinguish the stages of market development of the world's economies, and to serve as a guide to their marketing potential. For example:

- *Preindustrial societies.* These countries are characterized by low per capita incomes, low literacy rates, a low degree of urbanization, linguistic heterogeneity, and an undeveloped industrial base. They are dependent upon foreign sources for most manufactured goods—for which these countries have little ability to pay.
- *Underdeveloped societies.* These countries are characterized by rising literacy rates, small factories developed to supply the domestic market with essential goods, increasing gross national products, and growing urbanization.
- *Semideveloped societies.* In these economies, some 30 percent of the population is urban, literacy approaches 50 percent, industrial sectors are well developed, and market opportunities exist for both capital goods and consumer products.
- *Developed societies.* Literacy is high, urbanization is well advanced, wage levels increase sharply, ownership of consumer durables is high, new industries are being created rapidly, and there is a strong demand for labor-saving devices.
- *Affluent societies.* These societies are represented by countries such as the United States, Canada, and western Europe. Literacy is almost universal, urbanization dominates living patterns, saturation levels for consumer durables is high, and market opportunities are heavily dependent upon new products and innovations.[7]

7. Warren J. Keegan, *Multinational Marketing Management* (Englewood Cliffs, NJ: Prentice-Hall, Inc., 1974), pp. 51–56.

TABLE 20–4: Obstacles to Standardization in International Marketing Strategies.
SOURCE: Robert D. Buzzell, "Can You Standardize Multinational Marketing," *Harvard Business Review* (November-December, 1968), pp. 108–109

Factors Limiting Standardization	*Product Design*	*Elements of Pricing*	*Marketing Program Distribution*	*Sales Force*	*Advertising & Promotion Branding & Packaging*
Market characteristics					
Physical environment	Climate Product use conditions		Customer mobility	Dispersion of customers	Access to media Climate
Stage of economic and industrial development	Income levels Labor costs in relation to capital costs	Income levels	Consumer shopping patterns	Wage levels, availability of manpower	Needs for convenience rather than economy Purchase quantities
Cultural factors	"Custom and tradition" Attitudes toward foreign goods	Attitudes toward bargaining	Consumer shopping patterns	Attitudes toward selling	Language, literacy Symbolism
Industry conditions					
Stage of product life cycle in each market	Extent of product differentiation	Elasticity of demand	Availability of outlets Desirablility of private brands	Need for missionary sales effort	Awareness, experience with products
Competition	Quality levels	Local costs Prices of substitutes	Competitors' control of outlets	Competitors' sales forces	Competitive expenditures, messages
Marketing institutions					
Distributive system	Availability of outlets	Prevailing margins	Number and variety of outlets available	Number, size, dispersion of outlets	Extent of self-service
Advertising media and agencies			Ability to "force" distribution	Effectiveness of advertising, need for substitutes	Media availability, costs, overlaps
Legal restrictions	Product standards Patent laws Tariffs & taxes	Tariffs & taxes Antitrust laws Resale price maintenance	Restrictions on product lines Resale price maintenance	General employment restrictions Specific restrictions on selling	Specific restrictions on messages, costs Trademark laws

Although such classifications may be useful as a rough gauge of marketing opportunity, they are seldom precise enough to serve as an accurate guide for individual marketers considering foreign expansion. Instead, foreign countries need to be examined on an individual basis—and often on a region-by-region basis within countries. Further, political stability, governmental policies in regard to imports, currency restrictions, and investment risks may convert an attractive marketing oportunity into one that should be avoided.

Cultural Variables

A third source of differences between countries is cultural variables. The major error U.S. marketers may make in foreign countries is to assume that these countries hold the same values, use the same symbols, exhibit the same behaviors, and use the same decision processes as those to which they are accustomed in the United States. Usually, they do not. Difference, not similarity, is the prevailing rule between countries.

Ethnocentrism (the assumption that one's own cultural values and conventions are superior to those of other cultures), combined with the obvious cost advantages of using the same marketing strategies everywhere, often leads to crucial marketing mistakes. The opportunity for possible errors is emphasized in Table 20–4.

Many examples of marketing failures have arisen through failure to understand the values, decision patterns, symbols, and language of other cultures. General Motors was embarrassed a few years ago when its European Division developed a sales promotion piece that was inadvertently macabre. The Flemish translation of the famous slogan "Body by Fisher," came out "Corpse by Fisher," an expression that was deadly to sales.

Pepsi Cola's slogan, "Come alive with Pepsi," ran into trouble in the Chinese and German editions of *Reader's Digest.* In Chinese, it came out "Pepsi brings your ancestors back from the grave." In German, it translated "Come alive out of the grave." Obviously, neither of these promises were intended.

When General Mills first introduced its cereals in the United Kingdom, it misread British attitudes toward children. In its introduction, General Mills used a typical American kids' cereal package that showed a freckle-faced, red-haired, crew-cut, smiling boy saying, "Gee Kids, It's Great." Unfortunately, the British family is not as child-centered as its American counterpart. Britishers held to the admonition that children should be seen and not heard. As a consequence, the British housewife rejected both the package and the product.

One of the more humorous examples of using the wrong phrase occurred when a manufacturer of laundry soap sought to introduce its product in the French-speaking province of Quebec. "The ad campaign promised a 'really clean wash' especially for *les partes de sale.* The product just wasn't achieving the expected market share. When the advertising was analyzed, it was discovered that *les partes de sales* was the wrong idiom; the ads promised squeaky clean 'genitals.' The ad was changed and turned the tide."[8]

Communication errors can also be made without using language. A water recreation company operating in Malaysia used a green corporate symbol that was affixed to everything the company made. Unfortunately, in Malaysia green symbolizes the danger of death and disease found in the jungle; green effectively sabotaged the company's promotion efforts. White indicates mourning in China and some Near-East countries; blue connotes femininity in Holland and masculinity in Sweden.

Most companies and their advertising agencies are learning to avoid these kinds of problems by employing "nationals" as copy editors and giving them discretion to change copy, slogans, and even product concepts. Nonetheless, mistakes will probably continue to occur because of carelessness, thoughtlessness, and ignorance.

Although these marketing mistakes are the most humorous, less dramatic errors can be equally damaging. Taking the variable of distribution as an example, let us look at the role of wholesalers in the distribution system. The importance of wholesalers and the functions they perform differ radically in various societies. In relatively undeveloped countries, the role of the wholesaler is critical because retail distribution is dominated by small retailers who are not credit-worthy. At the same time, wholesalers' funds are limited, so that they carry limited stocks and often do not employ salespeople to call on retailers. Thus, manufacturers often have a difficult time forcing their products through the distribution channels.

In such instances, manufacturers may find it necessary to sell to wholesalers on consignment, that is, providing wholesalers with merchandise without charge until after it has been sold to retailers or even consumers. After the sale is completed, the wholesaler deducts its charge for the services performed (minimal as they may be) and

8. Kevin Lynch, "Adplomacy Faux Pas Can Ruin Sales," Reprinted with permission from January 15, 1979, issue of *Advertising Age.* Copyright 1979 by Crain Communications, Inc.

forwards the balance to the manufacturer. This, in fact is the procedure adopted by a division of Lever Brothers operating in India.[9]

Generally, the importance of wholesalers decreases as countries become more industrialized. Japan, however, is an exception. In Japan wholesalers are active in most merchandise lines, and often many levels of wholesalers occur in a single channel of distribution. The naive marketer could easily go astray in seeking distribution if unaware of Japan's complex system of distribution.

The point is that sociocultural differences are filled with traps for the unwary. Marketers who hope to avoid costly errors should familiarize themselves with the cultures in which they plan to market their products or services. Through marketing research or other knowledgeable sources, they should:

- Ascertain the central values of the target cultural group.
- Investigate the buying practices and decision patterns characteristic of the group.
- Identify the marketing institutions and channels applicable to the product.
- Familiarize themselves with the appropriate symbols for communicating with the target cultural groups.

INVESTIGATING INTERNATIONAL MARKETS

The decision to market internationally is an important one for most companies because it often entails great opportunities and serious risks. As a consequence, it should be approached systematically, in a step-by-step fashion.

Stages of Analysis

The basic questions that must be answered in international marketing are the same as those for domestic markets. Essentially, the marketer must determine *where* marketing shall take place, *what* should be marketed, and *how* the marketing operation should be conducted.

David Leighton has suggested a five–stage approach for answering these questions.[10] This approach is diagrammed in Figure 20–3, and each stage in the approach is described briefly:

- *Stage 1: Environmental Analysis.* This stage is a preliminary analysis in which the marketer examines the political, economic, and social conditions of the foreign countries being considered. At this stage, emphasis is on political stability, legal restrictions, economic development, purchasing power, and rate of social change.
- *Stage 2: Market Potential.* At this stage, the analysis becomes more specific and is directed toward the size of the market for the particular product or products to be sold. The number of users, frequency of purchase, rate of market growth, the structure of distribution, pricing practices, and the nature of competition must be assessed. Often this data is not readily available, and data must be developed through tailor-made marketing research studies.
- *Stage 3: Future Company Sales.* Here, the company must attempt to assess the share of market that it can gain initially, and in the future. This requires an analysis of the competitive structure, an assessment of the intentions and financial strengths of competitors, and an evaluation of company strengths and weaknesses. At this point, forecasts of market development must be made.
- *Stage 4: Prospective Profitability.* The purpose of this stage is to weigh the costs of entering the market—capital facilities, personnel, marketing expenditures—against the returns that may be realized. At this point, alternative methods of market entry—export,

9. David Carson, *International Maketing: A Comparative Systems Approach* (New York: John Wiley & Sons, 1967), p. 301.

10. David S. R. Leighton, *International Marketing: Text and Cases* (New York: McGraw-Hill, 1966), pp. 22–27.

FIGURE 20–3: Stages for Evaluating International Marketing Opportunities.
SOURCE: Based on: David S. R. Leighton, *International Marketing: Text and Cases* (New York: McGraw-Hill, 1960), pp. 22–27.

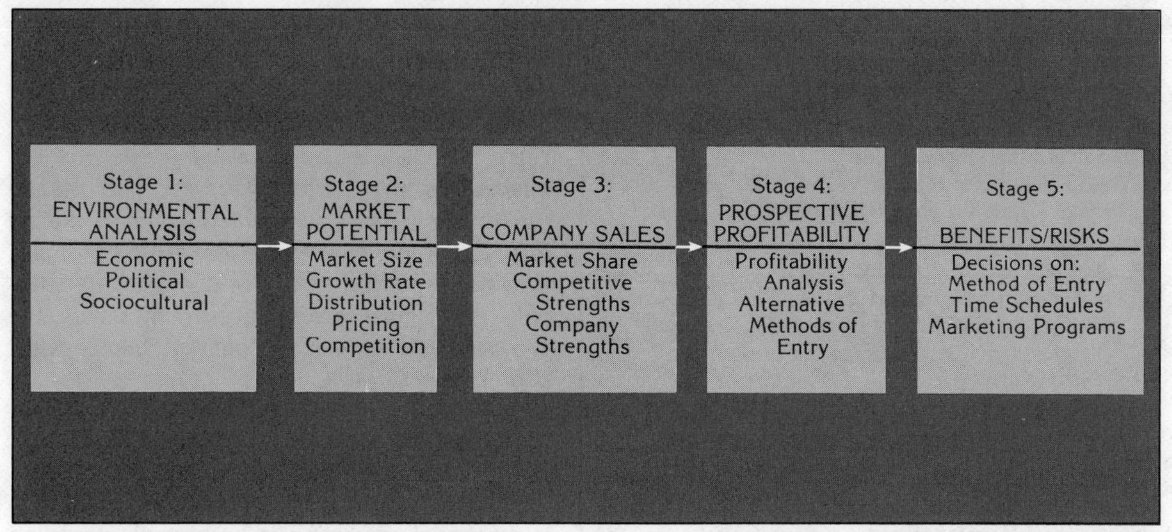

licensing, joint ventures, direct investment, and so forth—must be evaluated.

- *Stage 5: Benefit versus Risks.* This is the stage of the "go, no go" decision, actually the most difficult because there are no sure ways of estimating the outcome of the venture. In this stage, time horizons and the method of entry must be determined, and marketing programs developed.

Data for Analysis

In order to make sound decisions at each stage of the analysis, one must have reliable information—and reliable information on international markets is often hard to come by. Few governments provide the wealth of public data on income and consumer demographics comparable to that provided in the United States. This is particularly true of undeveloped countries and those governed by authoritarian administrations. A cursory review of statistical data developed by international organizations such as the United Nations and the World Bank indicates that much of this data is incomplete and, sometimes, contradictory. To complicate matters further, comparing data about countries is often difficult because different bases are used for collecting, ordering, and reporting the findings that are available.

Nonetheless, a number of organizations compile international statistics that serve as at least a starting point for international marketing investigations. Table 20–5 lists a number of such "starting points."

In many instances, however, companies find that more specific and detailed information is required, and are forced to turn to specially designed marketing research projects. Even marketing research is hampered to a greater or lesser extent in most foreign countries. For example, low telephone ownership, even in many of the industrialized countries, limits the value of this research approach. Low literacy rates limit the use of mail surveys in undeveloped countries. In many societies, the variety of linguistic groups and distrust of interviewers complicate the gathering of data through personal interviews with consumers. From the standpoint of distribution research, poorly developed channel structures and a multiplicity of small, specialty shops make the gathering of reliable data difficult.

Private research organizations in industrialized and semiindustrialized countries provide a valuable service for firms considering expansion in these areas. Many companies, however, choose to develop their own sources. For example, a major producer of grocery store products, having determined on the basis of public statistics that it

TABLE 20–5: Sources of International Marketing Data.
SOURCE: R. J. Dickensheets, "Basic and Economical Approaches to International Marketing Research *1963 Proceedings of the American Marketing Association* (Chicago: American Marketing Association, 1963), p. 364.

For Major Producing & Exporting Countries
Official Government Statistics
- Production
- Foreign Trade (Imports & Exports)
- Statistical Abstract

Foreign Industry Associations
- Production, Consumption, In Use, Saturation
- Industry Directory (List of member firms, product scope, etc.)
- Industry Magazines

Foreign Periodicals
- Magazines directed to wholesale and retail trade

International Marketing Indicators
United Nations
International Monetary Fund
U.S. Department of Commerce
Regional Organizations, e.g.,
- Organization for Economic Cooperation & Development (OECD)

General Background Information
Complementary or Served Industry Publications, e.g.,
- Frozen foods, coffee, steel, shipbuilding

International Press & Newsletters, e.g.,
- "Business International"

Research Organizations, e.g.,
- Ford Foundation

International Banking Publications

U.S. Sources of Industry Information
U.S. Industry Associations' International Publications, e.g., E.I.A. "International News"

U.S. Department of Commerce
U.S. Import & Export Statistics
Overseas Business Reports
BDSA Short Market Surveys & Trade Reports
Foreign Service Dispatch Loan Service
"International Commerce"

Competition
Annual Reports of Major Competitors, U.S. & Foreign

was interested in Spain, sent a company marketing executive to spend a year in this country with the assignment of familiarizing himself with the culture, learning the language, establishing business contacts, and identifying areas of opportunity.

METHODS OF ENTRY

Having selected one or more countries for marketing investment, a decision must be made concerning the method of entry. Major alternatives include exporting, joint ventures, and direct investment. The key issues in selecting one of these alternatives are the *extent of the risk involved* and the *amount of control required* by the marketing firm. Exporting involves the *least risk,* but it also provides the *least control* over marketing activities. In contrast, direct investment incurs the *greatest risk* as well as offering the *greatest degree of control.*

Exporting

The simplest way for a firm to become involved in international marketing is by exporting existing products. Manufacturing facilities remain in the home country, few if any modifications of the product are required, and minimal financial investments must be made. In 1978 United States exports exceeded $143 billion. Leading exports are agricultural products, machinery, industrial supplies and materials, chemicals, and automotive vehicles, parts and engines. Nonfood consumer goods (excluding automobiles and parts) accounted for less than 7 percent of the total. Almost 60 percent of U.S. exports were sold in developed countries—Canada, Western Europe, and Japan.

Firms that choose the export route have two options open to them: *indirect export* through the use of middlemen; or *direct export* wherein they sell directly to foreign buyers, thereby avoiding the payment of service charges to international intermediaries. *Indirect exporting* is the most frequently used method for firms entering the international trade arena for the first time. It is the easiest, requires the least knowledge, and involves the least risk since the middlemen employed are usually knowledgeable about the foreign markets they serve.

Direct export is often employed by firms whose international sales have grown substantially, and who, through experience, have gained confidence in their ability to handle international sales directly with foreign buyers. This approach is also often used by inexperienced firms who have been approached by foreign buyers desirous of handling their products. Just as the risk is somewhat greater in direct export operations, the potential returns are also higher since fees to middlemen are eliminated.

Joint Ventures

Joint ventures are intermediate to exporting and direct investment in terms of risk and control. Actually, the term "joint venture" is a broad designation that has been applied to a variety of shared arrangements between two or more firms from different countries. The most common forms of joint ventures are licensing, contract manufacturing, contract management, and shared investment.

LICENSING. Licensing is the simplest form of joint venture. Under this arrangement, a seller *(the licensor)* grants a foreign firm *(the licensee)* the rights to a process, patents, or trademarks in exchange for a license fee or royalty. Under this method, the licensee assumes the financial risks for production and marketing activities in the foreign country. However, licensors also incur risks because they are dependent upon the competence of the licensee to maintain product quality and to insure the success of the venture. A number of companies, including Gerber, RCA, Pepsi–Cola, Westinghouse, and Continental Can, have used this approach where it appeared to be beneficial to do so. Franchising, which is a form of licensing, has been used throughout Europe and North Africa by fast food operations such as McDonalds, as well as by hotel and motel chains.

CONTRACT MANUFACTURING. Sometimes a firm prefers to retain control of the marketing activities for its products in foreign countries, but is unprepared to make investments in foreign production facilities. Under these conditions, they may contract with a foreign producer to manufacture their products. Sears, Roebuck and Company has used this approach in Latin America and Spain, and Procter & Gamble contracted with local producers when it introduced its soap products in Italy. One danger of this approach is the loss of quality control over the manufacturing process, but this risk may be justified by the savings in capital investment that accrue to this method of operation.

CONTRACT MANAGEMENT. Under contract management, the seller provides management skills while the investment required by the enterprise is provided by nationals in the host country. Some extractive ventures such as oil, gas, and mining are conducted on this basis. Contract management has also been employed by hotel and motel chains such as Hilton and Holiday Inn.

Contract management is a low cost, minimum investment approach to international marketing that has advantages and disadvantages. On the positive side, the firm exporting management skills makes no investment in facilities, runs no danger of expropriation and, in the event of insurrection, simply pulls its management personnel out of the country. On the negative side, however, local investors may feel that they can dispense with the management services once they have learned the business, and terminate the management contract at the earliest opportunity. This is precisely what happened to a major U.S. motel chain in Marrakech, Morocco.

SHARED INVESTMENT. Under a shared investment arrangement, foreign investors join with local investors to establish a local enterprise in which they share ownership and control in proportion to the amount each has invested.

From the standpoint of the foreign investor, shared investment arrangements may be desirable for economic, management, and political reasons. Economically, the foreign firm may lack the financial resources to undertake the venture alone. From a management standpoint, the local firm often possesses valuable business experience and marketing skills in the host country. Politically, some governments require joint ownership with nationals as a condition of entry.

One disadvantage of the shared investment approach is that the foreign and local investors may have different philosophies of business that lead to policy and operational conflicts. If one investor owns a majority share of the joint enter-

Export markets. (Photo by Peggy Lentz)

prise, the other investor is faced with a loss of control over key business decisions. Some U.S. companies attempt to solve this problem by insisting on at least 51 percent ownership in all of their joint ventures. Still others prefer a fifty-fifty ownership arrangement, so that each partner has an equal voice in policy decisions. When Ralston Purina first embarked on joint ventures, its management insisted on equal ownership. The company's philosophy was that, unless they and their partners could reach a consensus on major decisions, there was little likelihood that the enterprise would function well.

Direct Investment

Under this approach, the investing firm acquires sole ownership of foreign facilities which it operates as a totally owned subsidiary. Since direct investment incurs the most risk, it represents the ultimate commitment to international marketing. Since it also provides complete control, direct investment offers greater freedom of operation than the other methods discussed.

During the 1960s, U.S. firms invested heavily in foreign countries because such investments enabled them to avoid tariffs enacted against U.S. imports, and because cheap labor reduced production costs. In many instances, the lower costs of foreign production enabled U.S. firms to maintain profits by producing abroad and exporting to the United States.

Today these advantages no longer exist to the extent that they did. Tariffs have been negotiated downward, and increasing labor costs in industrialized countries—combined with a weakened dollar in international exchange—have offset many of the production economies formerly available. As a consequence, many U.S. companies have liquidated their foreign holdings.

A number of problems have also arisen in the management of foreign subsidiaries. Chief among them are: (1) a 1978 revision of the U.S.

tax laws that makes it prohibitively expensive for U.S. based companies to send executives overseas; and (2) difficulties in hiring competent international executives and conflicts between home lffices and foreign subsidiaries.[11]

The tax law revision requires U.S. citizens working in foreign countries to pay taxes on earnings abroad (in addition to tax payments to foreign countries) as well as on additional cost-of-living expenses paid to them by their companies. As a consequence, a $40,000 executive can end up paying taxes on $95,000 of gross income, with the extra tax bite amounting to about $30,000. This has forced many U.S. firms to either abandon overseas investments or to staff them with less expensive executives from the host countries.

In terms of the second problem, a recent survey published in the *Harvard Business Review* identified these areas of conflict between home offices and foreign subsidiaries.

Home offices complain about:

- Shortage of qualified personnel to staff international operations.
- Subsidiary managers' deficiencies in planning and marketing know-how.
- Shortcomings in the communications and control processes of the multinational enterprise.

Subsidiary managers complain about:

- Too many constraints imposed by headquarters.
- Too little attention given by headquarters to local differences.
- Inadequate information from headquarters.[12]

Although these complaints are similar to those found in any complex organization that involves subsidiary operations, they are undoubtedly more critical in far flung international operations were distances are greater and local marketing differences more diverse.

11. "Johnny Comes Marching Home," *Time* (Sept 29, 1980): 60.

12. Ulrich E. Wiechmann and Lewis G. Pringle, "Problems that Plague Multinational Marketers," *Harvard Business Review* (July-August, 1979): 118–124.

A Summary Note on Method of Entry

The particular method of entry that individual companies choose in launching international enterprises will depend upon the opportunities, experience, resources, and confidence of the company's management personnel. No one way is best in all situations, although the inexperienced company might be well advised to gain experience in exporting or licensing before leaping headlong into direct investments.

THE INTERNATIONAL MARKETING MIX

Companies contemplating international marketing must decide to what extent they will modify their existing products and marketing programs to capitalize on foreign markets. Some products have universal appeals while, in other cases, tastes vary across national borders. For example, Pepsi-Cola and Coca-Cola sell the same product in their domestic and international operations. Oil of Olay, a skin moisterizer, uses the same formulation wherever it operates. On the other hand, Nestlé has found it necessary to blend many varieties of coffee to meet local taste preferences; the British prefer a different style of cake than that produced from American cake mixes; the voltage of office equipment has to be adapted to the electrical systems of the countries in which such products are marketed; and Exxon reformulates its gasoline to meet varied climatic conditions.

The extent to which products must be modified varies by product and by country, so that there is no single product strategy that applies in all cases. The same is true of the advertising appeals that are used. Warren J. Keegan has identified five different strategies involving either the adaptation of the product, adaptation of communications about the product, or both. These five strategies are discussed briefly and shown in matrix form in Figure 20–4.[13]

13. Warren J. Keegan, "Multinational Product Planning: Strategic Alternatives," *Journal of Marketing* (January, 1969): p. 59.

FIGURE 20–4: *Product and Communication Strategies in International Marketing.*
SOURCE: Adapted from Warren J. Keegan, "Multinational Product Planning: Strategic Alternatives," *Journal of Marketing* (Jan., 1969), pp. 58–62.

	Same Product	Adapt Product	
Same Communications	*Same Product Same Communications*	*Adapt Product Same Communications*	
Adapt Communications	*Same Product Adapt Communications*	*Adapt Product Adapt Communications*	New Product
		New Communications	*Innovation*

- *Same Product—Same Communication.* This is the easiest and most economical approach for the marketer. It requires no expenditures for research and development, no changes in manufacturing procedures, and no major changes in communication appeals. It has been used by soft drink manufacturers, for many food and clothing items, and for industrial and farm equipment.
- *Same Product—Adapt Communications.* This approach is applicable when the same product form serves different needs in different countries. For example, bicycles and mopeds are used mainly for recreation in the United States, but as basic transportation in other countries. Or a food product that may be used as an entreé in one country, but as an appetizer in another.
- *Adapt Product—Same Communication.* In this approach, minor adaptations in the product may have to be made to meet local conditions, but the basic product function remains unchanged. Detergents and soaps, for example, may be reformulated to meet local water conditions; agricultural chemicals may be modified for local soil conditions; household appliances may have their voltage adapted to local electrical systems; or the steering wheel and driving controls of an automobile may be moved from the left side of the car to the right side because of local driving customs.
- *Adapt Product—Adapt Communications.* In this approach, both the product and the communications about it must be altered. Cosmetics providing the "natural look" in the United States need to be reformulated and appeals changed in countries in which cosmetics are used lavishly and ostentatiously. Low-cost, nonmechanized agricultural equipment can be sold in underdeveloped countries whereas higher-priced, more fully mechanized equipment would be required in the United States. Similarly, hand-powered washing machines and hand wringers—largely obsolete in the United States—may be in demand in underdeveloped countries.
- *New Product—New Communication.* Differing from the other four, this strategy requires the identification of specific needs and the

development of new products and communication approaches to serve them. This approach is the same as new product development in the United States. This strategy is appropriate both in developed countries where product innovation may be required for market entry and in undeveloped countries with unique and unfulfilled product requirements. This strategy is the most expensive of those identified, and carries the highest risk.

In choosing which of the foregoing strategies is the best, companies must remember the truism that the best strategy is the one that optimizes growth and profits. Each company must analyze its particular products and the relationships of these products to the needs of international markets.

Other Elements of the Marketing Mix

Thus far, we have discussed product and communication strategies for international marketing. Other variables in the marketing mix also may require modification to adapt the marketing program to foreign environments. Packaging, pricing, sales promotion, distribution, and even the product name need to be carefully examined. In Sweden, for example, Helene Curtis changed the name of its Every Night Shampoo to Every Day Shampoo because Swedes wash their hair in the morning. And, as pointed out earlier, the Chevrolet Division of General Motors changed the name of its Nova to Caribe to avoid negative connotations in Puerto Rico.

The development of a marketing mix in international marketing requires the same kinds of analysis and planning that is required in a successful domestic marketing venture. It is somewhat more complex, however, because separate marketing plans must be prepared for each country in which a product is sold.

ORGANIZING FOR INTERNATIONAL MARKETING

The type of organization required for international marketing is heavily dependent upon the depth of a company's involvement. In a simple export operation, a firm may identify an individual or a relatively small department to handle negotiations and supervise shipping and billing. As international involvement becomes more intense—possibly including a number of products and countries—more complex organizational arrangements may be required. For the truly multinational company, with widespread foreign holdings, an international division may be required.

International marketing will grow in importance during the 1980s, and organizational structures will grow apace. Some companies will enter foreign markets to offset gains made by foreign competitors in their domestic markets. Others, simply because the profit potential of foreign markets will become too attractive to ignore. The form that international marketing will take, and the organizational structures that will be required are more uncertain.

At the beginning of the chapter I note that Japan envisions a future in which it will export technology and skilled managerial and technical talent, using relatively inexpensive labor in developing countries for labor-intensive manufacturing facilities. Such a strategy will require truly multinational organizations in which top management will be intimately involved in international planning, financial analysis and investment, and logistical systems. No other country, to my knowledge, has articulated a long-range, international marketing strategy. Certainly not the United States.

The predominant form or forms that international marketing will take for United States firms depends heavily upon policies formulated by the U.S. government. Historically, the United States government has not formed the kind of partnership with business that has characterized the international ventures of Japan, West Germany, and other highly developed nations.

Whatever transpires in U.S. policies and incentives for U.S. firms, it seems apparent that—from a worldwide standpoint—international marketing will assume even larger proportions in the next decade. Interdependence among nations is increasing, the aspirations and ambitions of undeveloped countries will have to be recognized, and mutually beneficial economic arrangements among the nations of the world will have to be developed.

SUMMARY

International trade is important to individual business firms as a source of growth and profits and to nations as a means of economic well being and survival. Industrialized nations are dependent upon the imports of raw materials to fuel their industrial bases, while undeveloped countries must import technology, consumer and industrial goods, and capital to feed and clothe their growing populations, and to develop their economies.

Foreign trade represents a large and growing market for those firms willing to make the investments and take the risks entailed.

International marketing has been a boon for some U.S. firms and a disappointment to others. Those U.S. companies that have been the most successful in their international ventures tend to be those in high technology and capital goods industries, and those which have a highly integrated package of production and marketing services that cannot be easily matched by local competitors or other multinationals.

Essentially, firms become involved in international trade in order to achieve growth and increase profits. Yet, many U.S. firms that could profit from international marketing fail to do so because of lack of interest, reluctance to make the required investments, and lack of encouragement on the part of the U.S. government.

Domestic firms contemplating foreign ventures should recognize that foreign environments often differ dramatically from that which exists in the United States. Among the differences that should be noted and analyzed are political–legal differences, economic differences, and sociocultural differences.

The investigation of international marketing opportunities requires a systematic, step–by-step analysis of the opportunities and risks that exist. Such analysis is often made difficult by the absence of reliable, public data and by the fact that much of the data available is not directly comparable between countries.

Major alternatives for entering foreign markets include exporting, joint ventures, and direct investment. The key issues in selecting one of these alternatives are the extent of risk involved and the amount of control required by the marketing firm in question.

The marketing mix usually must be varied for international operations. These variations often require product and communication modifications, as well as adaptations of other marketing variables.

Firms employ a variety of organizational arrangements for their international operations, with the complexity of the particular arrangement being dependent upon the degree of international involvement. Organizational arrangements range from small export departments to truly multinational structures in which top management is intimately involved in international planning, financial analysis and investment, and logistical systems.

1. Why is international trade important to both individual firms and to governments?
2. Many firms capable of participating in international trade fail to do so. What major reasons for this are given in the text?
3. Identify and briefly explain the three major environmental variables which differentiate countries.
4. Why are generalizations about foreign markets based on per capita incomes or market classifications sometimes misleading?
5. What steps should marketers take to minimize mistakes in marketing in foreign countries?
6. Identify and briefly characterize the five stages involved in investigating international markets.
7. Explain why it is often difficult to obtain reliable data on foreign markets.
8. Identify the major methods of entry into foreign markets and characterize each in terms of the issues of risk and control.
9. Identify and describe the various forms of joint ventures discussed in the text.
10. Identify the conflicts which often characterize the relationships between home offices and foreign subsidiaries. Why are these differences more critical than those existing in a wholly domestic organization?

1. Prepare a list of U.S. products that might be well-received in Mexico. Select one of these products and discuss the major problems you would anticipate in introducing it to the Mexican market.
2. Select a foreign country. Using library sources or personal knowledge, identify some of the political-legal, economic, and sociocultural differences between this country and the United States.
3. Discuss some of the problems that Japan may encounter in its strategy to export technology and skilled managerial and technical talent to undeveloped countries.
4. Discuss some of the things that the U.S. government might do to encourage international investment.
5. In the past few years, U.S. firms have been prosecuted for using bribery in foreign countries to secure business, even though such bribes are common practice and used by firms of other countries. Discuss the ethics of this practice.

CHAPTER PROBLEM

INTERNATIONAL MARKETING

Buy Mart, a major chain of discount department stores in the United States, had been extremely successful by following a strategy of:

- *Locating its outlets on relatively low-cost, commercial property in suburbs of major cities, and providing ample parking facilities.*
- *Including large drug and grocery departments in their department stores in order to provide one-stop shopping.*
- *Stocking a wide line of private label packaged goods formulated and packaged to duplicate leading U.S. brands as closely as possible, but sold at a substantial discount.*
- *Providing minimum store service in order to reduce operating costs, and in order to keep prices down.*

Stuart Holbein, president of Buy Mart, had recently read an article in a leading business magazine on the "Americanization" of Europe. The article had pointed out that self-service stores—particularly in the drug and grocery fields—were finally beginning to meet with success in Europe, and there appeared to be a trend away from shopping at small, neighborhood stores for household needs. As a consequence, he felt that the time was right for a mass merchandise, one-stop discount store such as Buy Mart operated in the United States.

He was also aware that some U.S. brands had been successfully introduced into Europe, and believed that Buy Mart's policy of copying major, advertised products and pricing the copy well below the advertised brand would be successful in European markets.

After a preliminary investigation of European markets, Holbein concluded that England represented a logical point of entry. He based this conclusion primarily on three considerations: (1) similar traditions and a common language in the United States and England created fewer entry barriers than in other European countries; (2) many U.S. packaged goods were selling successfully in England; and (3) the relatively high inflation rate in England should provide a receptive climate for a discount store such as Buy Mart.

In order to gain additional information on the English market, Holbein made an appointment with Marie Fortner, an employee of the U.S. Department of Commerce who specialized in counseling U.S. firms considering overseas investments. Fortner was somewhat doubtful of Holbein's proposed venture. "I don't want to throw cold water on your project," she began, "but, despite our common traditions and language, the English people are quite different from Americans. In the first place, they tend to be much more traditional in their shopping habits than Americans, and accept new ideas much less easily. Also, they are still inclined to shop at small, specialty stores, and make many more shopping trips than Americans. In addition, gasoline prices are much higher in England, and shoppers are less inclined to travel to a central shopping area, depending much more on neighborhood stores. You know, of course, that, because of the size of the country, land prices are relatively high, and their central cities more fully integrated with the suburban areas through mass transportation. Finally, the exchange rate is uncertain. Although American products are still relatively inexpensive in England, the dollar appears to be strengthening throughout Europe, and any initial price advantage you might enjoy could easily be lost within a fairly short period of time."

"I'm not so sure," Holbein answered. "It still looks like a good investment to me."

Assignment

What do you think Stuart Holbein should do?

21

Corporate Planning

- *The importance of growth to the business firm.*
- *Strategies for corporate growth.*
- *The nature of strategic planning in a corporation.*
- *Formal planning methods used in strategic planning.*
- *The results of strategic planning.*

MARKETING EXAMPLES

DAVID AND GOLIATH

Société Bic has worldwide sales of about $600 million; sales of Gillette are about $2 billion. Yet, Société Bic has taken aim with its slingshot and hit Gillette where the giant is most vulnerable—its price.

In the early 1960s, Bic challenged Gillette's 98-cent Papermate with a 19-cent throwaway pen and gained a foothold in the U.S. market. Ten years later, Société Bic "flicked its Bic" at Gillette's disposable cigarette lighter, Cricket, and again came out on top by underpricing the Gillette product. Gillette retaliated by cutting its price to undersell Bic by about 10 percent, but the damage was done and Gillette's counterattack had no appreciable effect on Bic's share of market.

In the late 1970s, Société Bic again challenged Gillette in the razor and blade market. Bic's disposable razor, at 20 cents, was priced well under Gillette's more expensive shaving systems which retailed for about 36 cents a blade. And, this time it hurt because the razor and blade market accounts for 30 percent of Gillette's sales and 70 percent of its pretax profits.

Gillette struck back with its own disposable razor, priced at about 25 cents, but featuring a double blade whereas the Bic product has a single blade. The results? From 1977 to 1980, Société Bic, caught between modest margins and heavy promotional expenditures, lost about $25 million on its disposable razor, while Gillette has shown a consistent profit.[1]

1. For a discussion of the marketing battle between Société Bic and Gillette, see: Linda Snyder Hayes, "Gillette Takes the Wraps Off," *Fortune* (February 25, 1980): 148–50.

EFFICIENCY VERSUS EFFECTIVENESS

Texas Instruments and Hewlett-Packard have employed quite different corporate strategies in their pursuit of the calculator market. Texas Instruments has pursued an "efficiency" strategy in which it has concentrated on production economies and low prices in order to obtain market penetration and a dominant market share. Hewlett–Packard, by contrast, has taken an "effectiveness" route, maintaining its prices while concentrating on developing advanced-technology products for which customers are willing to pay premium prices. Thus far, although using widely different corporate strategies, both companies have been successful.

ONE CAR—MANY MODELS; ONE MODEL—MANY CARS

Japanese automobile builders and their American competitors have adopted different strategies in seeking dominance of the automobile field. In addition to one obvious difference—fuel-efficient cars versus large, fuel-inefficient cars—the Japanese initially entered the market with a limited number of models whereas U.S. automobile manufacturers have traditionally produced a model for every conceivable consumer need. One advantage of the Japanese strategy is that, by concentrating on fewer models, they could become more proficient in production—thereby lowering production costs, improving quality control, and competing for market share on the basis of price.

Thus, when U.S. car manufacturers finally responded to the threat of fuel-efficient cars by producing their own small cars, they found themselves operating at a price disadvantage vis-a-vis Japanese imports.

These three examples represent two fundamentally different strategies for corporate success. Gillette, Hewlett-Packard, and U. S. automobile manufacturers have followed a premium price strategy by concentrating on products that have design, style, or technological advantages. Société Bic, Texas Instruments, and Japanese car marketers have concentrated on production economies and low prices as their dominant corporate strategy. Each of these strategies has had demonstrated successes and demonstrated failures.

Behind these different corporate strategies, however, is the need for growth—increased sales and increased profits—by the companies involved. Before turning our attention to corporate growth strategies, let us briefly examine the concept of growth in the business field and see why it is a business community preoccupation that borders on being a mania.

GROWTH AND THE FIRM

Growth in the U.S. economy is intimately bound up with the success of a firm. "Small" may be beautiful, but it is seldom as profitable as "large." Business firms often seem preoccupied with growth for several reasons:

- *Economies of scale.* Most firms find that their unit costs decline with volume, at least up to a certain point. This holds true because fixed and semifixed costs can be written off over a larger number of units and because costs decrease with experience. One problem Chrysler has always had in competing with General Motors and Ford is that the company's substantial smaller unit sales volume results in higher unit costs, squeezing profits when it tries to price competitively.
- *More efficient utilization of resources.* Most salespeople spend only about 40 percent of their time in direct selling. The remainder of the time is spent in traveling, setting up appointments, waiting for buyers to be free, writing call-reports, and so forth. Many firms find that a salesperson can often handle two or three products as easily as one, provided the products are purchased by the same buyers. Thus, compatible products, added to a firm's product line, can increase sales and improve selling efficiency substantially.

  Similar opportunities exist in other areas of company activity. For example, highly seasonal products, such as skis or swimming suits, may require production facilities and selling effort only during a part of the year. Compatible products, which have different seasonal patterns, may result in a more efficient use of company resources and corresponding increases in profits. Also, there may be economies in purchasing raw materials, in shipping finished products, and in warehousing.
- *Economic stability.* Firms that are dependent upon a single product are often vulnerable to competitive inroads or to other uncontrollable environmental variables. As a consequence, income and profits can often be stabilized by diversifying into additional product lines.
- *Opportunities for young executives.* Most young executives, particularly competent ones, are ambitious, desiring economic gains and increased responsibility. Few are willing to wait for senior executives to leave or retire before they can be promoted. Inability to offer advancement within the company leads to high executive turnover, and executive turnover is expensive. For example, in the company in which I worked, the personnel director and I figured out that the company required a 10 to 15 percent real growth rate each year to meet the expectations of our young executives. If we failed to meet these expectations, some of our most competent talent would leave us and join competitive firms where opportunities were greater. We also estimated that it cost the company between $40,000 and $50,000 to hire and train a college graduate to the point where he or she was a valuable employee.
- *Owner requirements.* In many instances, the expectations of stockholders force growth on a company. By requiring corporate managers to reinvest profits in growth opportunities,

rather than paying them out in dividends, stockholders stand to reap capital gains which are taxed at a lower rate than dividends.

- *Ego demands.* Prestige, personal challenge, and power are strong ego stimulants. Corporate executives, like most of us, have strong ego needs. Company growth often provides ego gratification by making jobs more challenging, by increasing economic and social power, and by inspiring recognition and praise from peers.

For these reasons, and possibly others, growth often ranks high among corporate objectives.

STRATEGIES FOR GROWTH

Broadly speaking, the three strategies for corporate growth are integrative growth, increased sales from existing products, and expanding the product line. Let's examine each of these strategies briefly in order to understand them more clearly, and to assess their benefits and their risks.

Integrative Growth

In integrative growth, a company moves backward, forward, or horizontally within the industry which it serves.

BACKWARD INTEGRATION. In backward integration, a company gains control over its source of supply. This form of expansion is particularly appropriate where it either reduces the cost of materials, thereby increasing profits; or guarantees a source of supply in an industry in which supply is uncertain.

The evaporated milk industry, for example, integrated backwards by setting up their own can manufacturing plants because it was much cheaper to manufacture the cans they required than to buy them from existing can companies. The plan's disadvantage was that it tied up company resources in production facilities that were only useful for the production of a single consumer product—evaporated milk. When consumer demand for evaporated milk started to decline, the industry's excess can manufacturing facilities became a white elephant, and had to be closed down or sold off at a loss. All in all, however, over the lifetime of the product, the decision to integrate backward was a wise one because the increased profits over the entire time more than offset the losses incurred in closing down the plants.

A more tragic example of backward integration occurred in the case of the Curtis Publishing Company, long the leading publisher of several consumer magazines in the United States. Two of Curtis's magazines—*The Saturday Evening Post* and the *Ladies' Home Journal*—dominated the rest and required extensive, high-speed printing facilities. In order to reduce printing costs and gain greater control over printing quality, Curtis invested in one of the finest, high-speed printing plants in the world.

But, the printing plant required huge amounts of paper. In order to gain a dependable source of supply of paper, Curtis acquired paper pulp mills. Paper pulp mills require huge amounts of wood fiber for their product, so Curtis acquired thousands of acres of timberlands. Figure 21–1 shows the structure of the Curtis Publishing Company after it had completed its strategy of integrating backward. Note that the entire corporate structure is supported by the sales of two magazines—*The Saturday Evening Post* and the *Ladies' Home Journal.* Curtis did publish other magazines—*American Home, Holiday, Jack & Jill,* and others—but these magazines did not have large enough circulations to make a difference.

Over a period of time, consumer tastes in magazines began to change. Picture magazines, such as *Life* and *Look,* were introduced by competitive companies. News magazines, such as *Time* and *Newsweek,* became a source of consumer satisfaction. Special interest magazines began to siphon reader interest and advertising revenues away from the two mass circulation publications upon which Curtis was dependent. The management of Curtis was slow to recognize these competitive threats. Eventually, *The Saturday Evening Post* and the *Ladies' Home Journal* had to close down because of a lack of advertising

FIGURE 21–1: The Structure of the Curtis Corporation Before and After The Saturday Evening Post *and* Ladies' Home Journal *went bankrupt.*

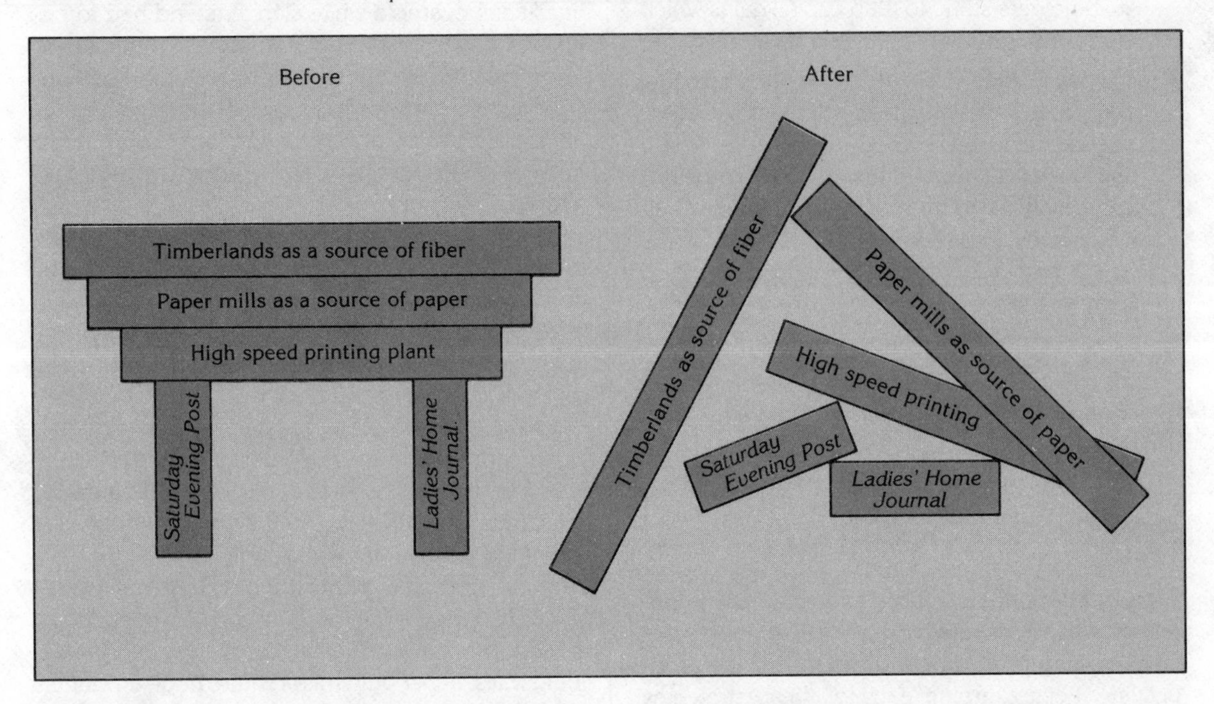

revenues and increasing circulation costs. Figure 21–1 shows what happened. The whole Curtis Corporate structure came tumbling down.

This does not imply that backward integration is always a disaster. Often, it is a sound growth strategy. Unfortunately, no strategy is without risk.

FORWARD INTEGRATION. In forward integration, a company gains control over its distribution systems. This is an appropriate strategy if it increases profits, or provides more effective service to ultimate consumers.

The shoe industry has always been a highly competitive business, and distributor margins on shoes are relatively high. In addition, the historical practice of exclusive distribution for major department stores often made obtaining adequate distribution in many major markets difficult. One response to this problem is for the shoe manufacturer to integrate forward by setting up its own retail outlets. This is the strategy followed by the International Shoe Company when it formed the Delmar Corporation as a retail division to handle some of its leading brands, such as Florsheim.

Oil companies have integrated forward by building company-owned service stations, rather than relying wholly on independent station owners. One of their reasons for adopting this strategy is that, since all brands of gasoline are pretty much alike, major companies try to build brand loyalty through attractive service stations, clean restrooms, and courteous service. Unfortunately, many independent stations are characterized by unattractive stations, dirty restrooms, and slovenly service.

Fast-food chains, such as McDonald's, and motel chains, such as Holiday Inn, have gained control over their outlets through carefully written and rigorously-policed franchise agreements. The parent company provides the service concept, recipes, menus, service standards, management supervision, national promotion, and so forth. Individual entrepreneurs provide the capital for building the outlets, and local management to run them. The relationship is governed by a franchise agreement that may be revoked if the local operators fail to meet the company's standards. In these instances, the parent company integrates

FIGURE 21–2: Diagram of Backward, Foreward, and Horizontal Integration.

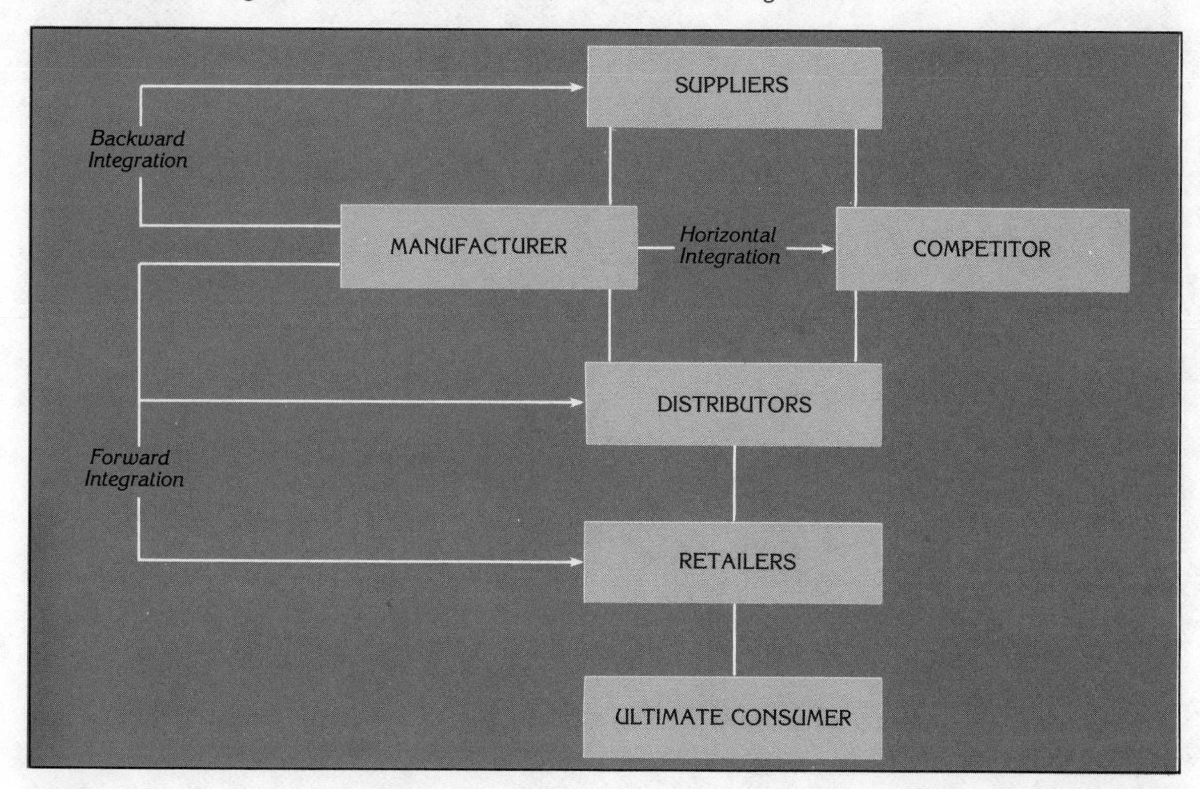

forward, not by physically owning the outlets, but by franchising them under a performance agreement.

HORIZONTAL INTEGRATION. In horizontal integration, a company gains control over competition, usually through acquisition. This form of integration is appropriate when a company is able to increase sales and profits by acquiring the assets, products, technological expertise, or management talent of a competitor.

Lever Brothers employed a strategy of horizontal integration when it acquired All detergent from Monsanto. The Falstaff Brewing Company, throughout the 1950s and 1960s, expanded sales and profits by acquiring local breweries in various parts of the country. And retail businesses, particularly grocery chains, often expand the scope of their operations by buying out competitors.

Figure 21–2 diagrammatically depicts backward, forward, and horizontal integration at the manufacturer's level, although an integrative strategy can be used at any level of the distributive chain. A wholesaler, for example, may integrate backward into manufacturing to obtain a private brand, or forward to control retail outlets for the products it distributes. Much of the efficiency of major retail grocery chains has resulted from backward integration to take over wholesaling functions. In some cases—with A&P and Safeway being outstanding examples—chains set up their own manufacturing plants to produce their private label brands.

Increased Sales from Existing Products

Companies obtain significant sales increases from existing products in essentially three ways: (1) maintaining or increasing share of markets that are growing rapidly; (2) increasing share in markets in which their current share is relatively low; and (3) discovering new uses or new markets for products already being marketed.

"How can we think small when we have 3 million cars to sell?" (Photo courtesy of Volkswagen of America, Inc.)

Since the bulk of this text has been devoted to the marketing of existing products, we only need to note that these activities are a major preoccupation of marketing companies. Existing products are the bread and butter of business firms; they generate the cash flows that produce profits and provide resources for future investments.

As we have noted, increasing sales from existing products is not an easy task and, eventually, a growth ceiling is reached or existing products are made obsolete by technology. When this occurs, companies must turn to other sources of growth—to integrative strategies or to the development or acquisition of additional products for their lines.

Expanding the Product Line

Expanding the product line is a viable growth strategy when: (1) the opportunities for an integrative strategy are limited; (2) the existing products are approaching their growth ceilings; and (3) the growth and profit opportunities inherent in new products exceed other growth and profit opportunities available to the company.

Companies may follow many strategies in developing new products. They may expand a product line, as Campbell has done in developing some sixty separate varieties of soup, and as Sara Lee has done in developing a wide variety of frozen desserts. They may expand into technologically related fields as did Procter & Gamble—a leading authority on edible oils—when it entered the peanut butter market with Jif, a product with a high oil content. Or, as Eli Lilly did when it expanded from pharmaceuticals to related products in the animal and agricultural fields. Companies may expand into products related by their end use, as General Foods has done by developing a large and diverse stable of food products. Or, Carnation which expanded into products distributed through a particular outlet type with products as diverse as Friskies dry dog food and Instant Breakfast.

In order to make wise decisions concerning the direction of corporate growth, we need to turn to the subject of strategic planning.

STRATEGIC PLANNING

Strategic planning differs from the product marketing plan in two respects:

- It is a long-range plan [typically for five years or longer] whereas the product marketing plan is essentially a short-term document [one to three years].
- It is concerned with the allocation of company resources among divisions and products, whereas the product marketing plan is concerned with the marketing mix for individual products.

Strategic planning is a relatively recent development in marketing, having arisen in the 1970s. To understand the need for strategic planning and the reasons for its emergence, it is helpful to trace the development of market planning through three stages: traditional planning, product planning, and strategic planning.

Traditional Planning

Traditional planning can best be described as long-range forecasting and budgeting. Typically, it consisted of the following steps:

- Each year, corporate management issued planning instructions and general economic guidelines for each of its divisions. Planning instructions generally included guidelines for growth and profit. They also required division managers to fill out a variety of forms providing sales forecasts and specific plans for marketing, manufacturing, research and development, and so forth.
- Controllers of each division—working with managers of the various functional departments—compiled a five-year plan. The completed plan usually contained pro forma balance sheets and income statements, often broken down by product, for the five-year planning period.
- Plans were reviewed by corporate management, modifications were made, and the plans accepted. The first year of each five-year plan became the budget for the following year.

Traditional planning procedures had these shortcomings:

- Management guidelines on growth and profitability were sometimes unrealistic, reflecting management's aspirations rather than market conditions.
- Divisional managers found that planning for a five-year period was largely a waste of time since they always operated on the basis of the first year of each plan, and largely ignored subsequent years.
- Preparation of divisional plans was largely under the direction of divisional controllers who were often more concerned with overall financial data than with the health of individual products in the marketplace.

During the 1950s and 1960s, the nature of marketing changed, bringing changes to the planning process. As markets became more competitive, product managers were appointed to develop and supervise programs for individual products and product lines. The locus of planning shifted from divisional controllers to product managers.

Product Planning

Along with the shift of planning responsibility from controllers to product managers, was a corresponding shift in planning horizons. The time frame of the planning period was shortened, and the product marketing plan became the basic building block for corporate planning. Under this approach:

- Product managers prepared detailed marketing plans for their individual products. Although the formats for product marketing plans differed somewhat from company to company, they were generally similar to the product marketing plan presented in Chapter 4 of this text.
- Divisional plans became the aggregation of each division's individual product marketing plans, and corporate plans were a simple aggregation of divisional plans.

While strengthening marketing plans at the product level, this approach often resulted in the misuse of corporate resources for the following reasons:

- Product managers tended to protect their own products, and often overspent on products which had little chance of becoming long–range corporate successes.
- Since each product and division was expected to generate its own funds, products with high long-range potential but low current sales were often undersupported. Thus, growth opportunities were missed while funds were dissipated on marginal or declining products.
- Sometimes product managers in different divisions were engaged in related activities. However, since these product managers operated largely on an autonomous basis, there was little coordination of their activities. This led to wasteful duplication of effort and failure to develop markets effectively.

These shortcomings led to the inefficient use of corporate resources. As profit margins shrank during the 1960s, and as inflation increased the difficulty and cost of borrowing, many companies found themselves strapped for funds to invest for future growth.

A basic question that many companies faced was how to discriminate between those divisions and products which required funding for future growth and those which could provide this funding. A second question was how to coordinate the activities of different divisions that were working in related areas. These problems gave rise to strategic planning.

Strategic Planning

Strategic planning differs from earlier forms of marketing planning in four ways:

- Complex businesses are broken down into *Strategic Business Units* (SBUs). A Strategic Business Unit may be considered as an autonomous profit center, generally with these characteristics:
  It is a single product or a collection of related products.
  It serves an identifiable market that is served by the same competitors.
  It has an identifiable strategy.
  It is generally managed by an individual who has responsibility for its overall operation.

  A SBU may be a single product or a combination of divisions. The SBU may cut across traditional divisional lines and be based on a technology, or on a market to be served. For example, separate divisions may be marketing different products for pollution control. The pollution control activities of both divisions could be combined into a SBU. Or, two or more divisions could be serving the automotive industry through some of the products they produce. These activities relating to the automotive market could be combined into a single SBU.
- SBUs are recognized to have different objectives and to contribute to company objectives in quite different ways. The term *portfolio* is commonly used to describe the group of SBUs that make up a company.
- Planning is preceded by an exhaustive analysis of each SBU's market, its market position, its competitors, its technology, its potential for growth, environmental trends, and whether it represents a source of cash for the company or will require investment.
- SBUs are classified by their present performance and future potential, and funds are

Our strategy is to keep from going broke. (Photo courtesy of Nationwide Insurance Company)

allocated to optimize future growth and profits of the company as a whole. Thus, some SBUs may be earmarked for liquidation, some for strategies designed to maintain market position, and some for investment.

Not all business firms are capable of serving all markets because business firms' resources differ. Strategic planning explicitly recognizes the need to match a firm's resources with the markets it is best equipped to serve, and to direct the firm's efforts to those areas which offer the greatest opportunities for success.

Although matching company resources with marketing opportunities is seldom an easy job, it is not an impossible one. Further, along with the development of the concept of strategic planning, certain formal planning methods have emerged that enable companies to approach this problem systematically.

FORMAL PLANNING METHODS

In the following material, we will look briefly at three methods that are often used in strategic planning. Note that there is nothing really new about these approaches, as such. What is relatively new is: (1) the emergence of high-speed computers that facilitate complex analyses and sometimes permit simulation of alternative courses of action; (2) better educated and more sophisticated managements than have existed in the past; and (3) private management consulting firms which, in seeking devices to facilitate their own growth, have directed their entrepreneural

FIGURE 21–3: General Electric's Business Screen and Multifactor Assessment.
SOURCE: David S. Hopkins, "Business Strategies for Problem Products," Report No. 714 (New York: The Conference Board, 1977), p. 48.

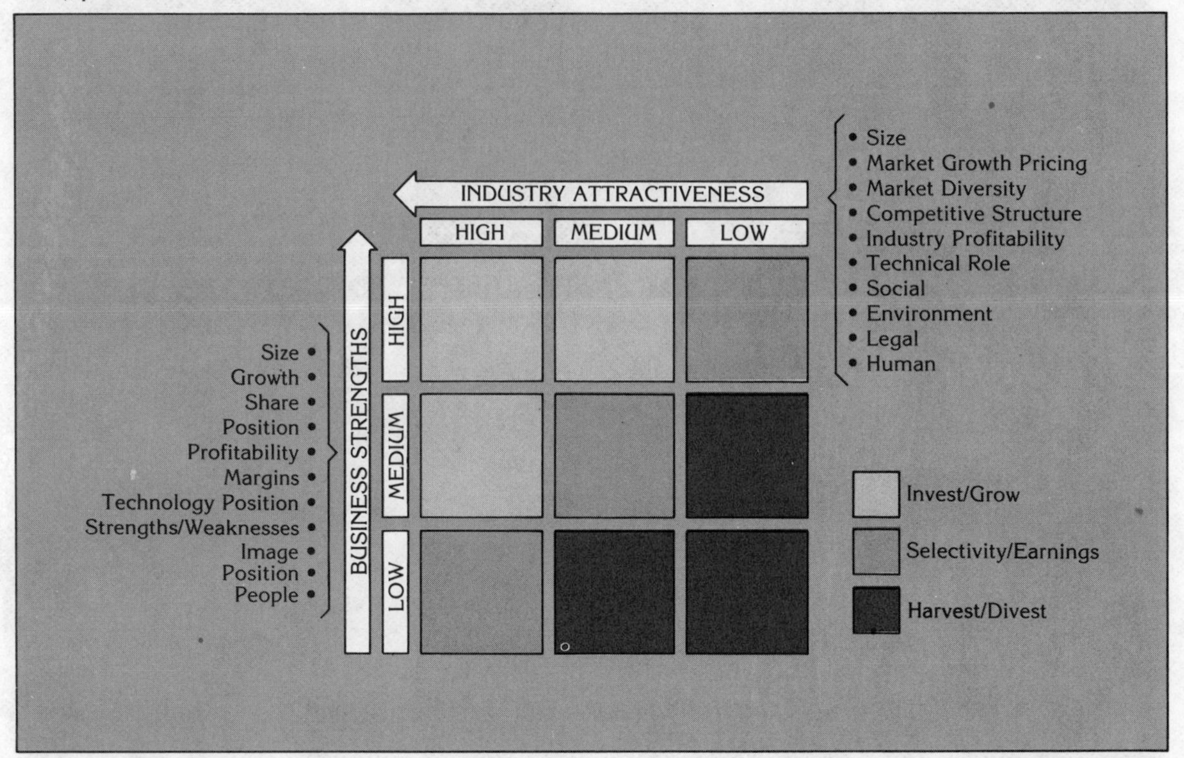

talents to innovative applications of existing knowledge.

The three analytical approaches that we will examine are the General Electric Business Screen, the growth-share matrix, and the PIMS (Profit Impact of Marketing Strategies) program.

The General Electric Business Screen

The General Electric Business Screen is particularly appropriate for large, diversified companies, such as General Electric, which have many divisions, many products, many resources, and many investment alternatives.

Aided by McKinsey & Company (a management consultant firm), General Electric devised the notion that a multiproduct company could be divided up into SBUs based on the different products it made and the different markets it serves.

Through the use of the General Electric Business Screen, the investment opportunities for each of a company's SBUs are evaluated with the help of a nine cell matrix in which the two dimensions of the matrix are *business strengths* and *industry attractiveness* (see Figure 21–3).

The cells of the matrix are divided into three categories:

- *Invest/grow*
  SBUs falling in this category enjoy a medium to strong position in an attractive industry and are candidates for investment and growth.
- *Harvest/divest*
  SBUs falling into this category are those that are medium to weak in the less attractive industries. Suggested strategy here is either to divest the company of these SBUs, or harvest them. To harvest means to reduce marketing expenditures to increase earnings, and to maintain the SBUs only so long as they are profitable.
- *Selectivity/earnings*
  SBUs in these cells are borderline. They range

from weak SBUs in attractive industries to strong SBUs in unattractive industries. These SBUs should be carefully examined on an individual basis to determine how each should be handled in the future—whether they should be candidates for investment and growth, or candidates for divesture or harvesting.

A primary purpose of the business screen is to force executives to face outward (toward the market) as well as inward (toward the business) in making strategic decisions. In order to classify SBUs within this matrix, an extensive analysis of the SBU's strengths and weaknesses and the industry's attractiveness must be made. Typical dimensions of these analyses—size, growth, share, position, profitability, margins, technological position, and so forth—are shown in Figure 21–3.

The manager of a SBU that has been identified for divesture or harvesting may appeal the decision by providing information that indicates the SBU has a greater potential than it has been judged to have. If this appeal is rejected, however, he must accept the corporate decision. This means that the marketing task is not always to build market share. If a SBU has been identified for harvesting, the task of the marketer is to develop plans for harvesting the SBU as profitably as possible. This means reducing marketing expenditures, eliminating research and development, reducing services, cutting back plant and equipment investments and, possibly, raising the price.

The Growth-Share Matrix

Another approach to strategic analysis is the growth-share matrix (also referred to as the business portfolio matrix) developed by the Boston Consulting Group.[2] The growth-share matrix is based on the concept of cash flows in a business firm—some products generate cash flows and some products require cash to support growth and generate future profits. The two dimensions of the growth-share matrix are *market share position* and *industry growth rate.* Figure 21–4 shows a simplified growth-share matrix.

FIGURE 21–4: *Growth-share Matrix.*
SOURCE: Adapted from "The Product Portfolio" (Boston: The Boston Consulting Group, 1970), Perspectives No. 66.

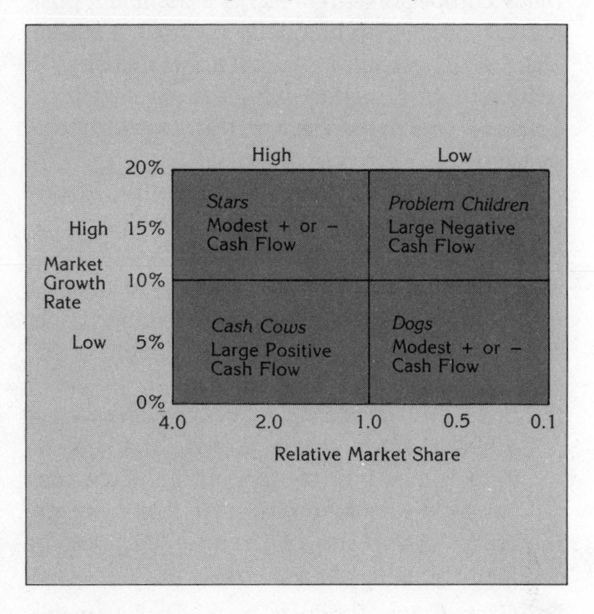

The vertical axis represents the annualized growth rate of the industry in which a particular product is marketed. This axis is arbitrarily divided into two parts. High growth industries are generally considered to be those that have an annual growth rate of over 10 percent. Low growth industries are those with a growth rate of less than 10 percent.

The horizontal axis represents the market position of the product being examined *relative* to the market position of the leading competitor. For example, if a product's market share is half that of the market leader, its relative position would be .5. If the product being examined *is* the market leader, with a market share half again as large as its nearest competitor, its *relative* market position would be 1.5. Relative market share is considered a better measure of market dominance than absolute market share because markets differ significantly in the number of competitors and the size of the absolute market share that

2. Walter Kiechel III, "Playing by the Rules of the Corporate Strategy Game," *Fortune* Magazine © 1979 Time, Inc. All rights reserved.

is feasible. For example, a market share of 5 percent in the cereal industry—a large industry with many competitors—represents a dominant position for a particular brand. By contrast, a market share of 20 percent in the cake mix industry—a moderate-sized market with relatively few competitors—would represent a fairly weak market position.

Based on these two criteria—market growth and market dominance—products are then placed in one of the four cells in the matrix. The four cells of the matrix have been labeled descriptively as: Stars, Cash Cows, Problem Children, and Dogs.

- *Stars.* Products falling in this cell typically have a high share in rapidly growing markets. Although they may or may not generate cash flows sufficient for their growth, they represent areas for investment because they will be future sources of cash flows.
- *Cash Cows.* Products in this cell generally have a dominant share in a slowly growing market. They generate more cash than they can profitably invest, and are the primary source of corporate funds.
- *Problem Children.* This cell represents products that have a small share of a rapidly growing market. Because of their relatively weak positions and high demands for cash to maintain market share, they generally produce little or no cash for profits. At the same time, they will require even higher investments—and risks—to make them important contributors to the company's stable of products.
- *Dogs.* Products in this cell have a low share in stable markets that show little promise of significant future growth. They may or may not contribute cash to the company operation, but there is a little possibility that they will ever be a source of significant cash.

By analyzing current products of a growth-share matrix, management can identify the firm's current position and project its future position based on current products. For example, a firm whose portfolio of products consists only of Cash Cows and Dogs is badly in need of Stars (new products in growth industries) if it is to avoid future problems. A firm with a number of Stars but no Cash Cows, may need to generate a source of funds—through loans, capital stock, or acquisition—in order to exploit the potentials of its products and generate future cash flows. The point is that, through a growth-share matrix analysis, a firm can better identify its present and future needs.

PIMS (Profit Impact of Marketing Strategy)

The Strategic Planning Institute, a nonprofit organization based in Cambridge, Massachusetts, was founded on the lofty goal of discovering the "laws of the marketplace" through an analysis of major variables influencing return on investment (ROI).

Basing its analysis on data provided on a confidential basis by 240 corporations with 1,800 separate SBUs,[3] the Strategic Planning Institute has found that profit performance is related to at least 37 factors, including such variables as:

- *The quality of the products or services offered.* Those products deemed to have superior quality tended to have a higher ROI, even to the point that good quality would partly offset the disadvantage of having a small market share.
- *Investment intensity.* On the average, the higher the ratio of total investment to sales, the lower the ROI tended to be.
- *The level of marketing expenditures.* Generally, ROI tended to be reduced by a high level of marketing expenditure. This was particularly true with products of lower quality.
- *The level of research and development (R&D) expenditures.* A high level of spending in R&D seems to be related to a high ROI when market share is also high. However, when market share is low, a high level of R&D spending causes ROI to plummet.
- *Corporate size and diversity.* Very large companies—those with over $1.5 billion in sales—seem to benefit in terms of ROI from having a strong market position, and also from having a diversity of SBUs. For small companies, however the findings are mixed.[4]

---

3. Ibid, p. 112.
4. David S. Hopkins, "Business Strategies for Problem Products," Report 714 (New York: The Conference Board, 1977), p. 48.

TABLE 21–1: Relationship between Market Share and Profitability.
SOURCE: "Business Strategies for Problem Products," (New York: The Conference Board, 1977), p. 41.

Market share	*Return on Investment*
Under 7%	9.6%
7–14	12.0
14–22	13.5
22–36	17.9
Over 36	30.2

One of the PIMS's findings that has attracted the most attention is that market share is one of the main determinants of business profitability.[5] Table 21–1 shows the alleged relationship between market share and profitability.

This finding, along with work done by the Boston Consulting Group for a General Instruments plant in 1966, focused attention on the "learning curve" phenomenon, also called the "experience curve." There is nothing new about the concept of the learning curve. *Fortune* has pointed out that:

> The learning curve, which has been around for at least thirty years, represents a quantification of the happy fact that people repetitively doing a fairly mechanical task get better at it. In more technical terms, man-hours per unit of production, and hence labor costs per unit, decrease in a predictable manner over time.
>
> Planners in the aircraft factories of World War II found that they could use a simple two-dimensional graph to help schedule production. The vertical axis indicated man-hours per plane; the horizontal, some measure of output. As the work progressed, they observed, each plane took fewer man-hours to produce—the point standing for it on the graph was below and slightly to the right of the point for the last plane. By extrapolating the trend the planners could predict how long it would take to build a plane at some point in the future.[6]

The logic linking the learning curve, market share, and return on investment together as a corporate marketing strategy is deceptively simple:

- A high market share requires a high level of production.
- A high level of production reduces production costs because of the experience curve.
- Reduced production costs result in higher unit profit margins.
- Higher unit margins result in higher ROI; therefore,
- One should maximize market share to maximize ROI.

This logic has been applied effectively by the Japanese in many of their marketing ventures.

> . . . the typical Japanese manufacturing company makes dedicated efforts to increase its market share. If the company can only achieve this goal by cutting prices, it will normally do so, despite the possible short-term penalties. By sacrificing short-term profits, the company may succeed in growing fast enough to reduce unit costs significantly within a few years. In these circumstances, foregone profits will shortly be recouped. What's more, the company will have simultaneously weakened its competitors by undermining their market positions. It will thus guarantee itself a proportionally larger share of the future growth in demand, setting the stage for even greater reductions in unit costs and, perhaps, also in prices.[7]

A number of U.S. companies have followed a similar strategy. For example, Bristol–Meyers adopted such a strategy in introducing Datril in competition with Johnson & Johnson's leading brand, Tylenol.[8] Texas Instruments has traditionally followed this strategy in transistors, hand calculators, and the low-priced digital watch

5. Robert D. Buzzell, Bradley T. Gale, and Ralph G. M. Sultan, "Market Share—A Key to Profitability," *Harvard Business Review* (January-February, 1975): 97–105.

6. Walter Kiechel III, "Playing by the Rules of the Corporate Strategy Game," p. 112.

7. Sanford Ross, "The Secret of Japan's Export Prowness," *Fortune* Magazine

8. "A Painful Headache for Bristol-Meyers?" *Business Week* (October 6, 1975): 78–80.

market.[9] Bic used this strategy against Gillette—first with its throwaway pen, then with its throwaway lighter, and finally in the throwaway razor market.[10]

Sometimes it works and sometimes it doesn't. The Japanese have been successful with this strategy. Johnson & Johnson countered the attack from Datril by lowering its price on Tylenol, so that Datril never achieved its expected market share. Texas Instruments has started encountering problems with its dealers and distributors by following this strategy. Thus, one of its dealers observed: "T.I. is so bent on getting the price down that when it comes to customers, they squeeze quality out."[11] And, the president of one of Texas Instruments' customers, a large business products company, complained: "Coming from an engineering background, T.I. knows only about selling on the basis of price. But I have to give prompt service to my customers—and I just can't get that from the manufacturer."[12] Finally, Gillette fought back against Bic with its own price reductions in the throwaway lighter and throwaway razor fields. In the throwaway razor field, it has been particularly successful since it has continued to be profitable while Bic has suffered significant financial losses.

The strategy of seeking a dominant market share by reducing prices to gain production experience and lower costs has come to be known as an *efficiency* strategy. Not an easy strategy to employ, this strategy requires a complex study and projection of the behavior of manufacturing costs over a period of time to ascertain whether future cost savings will be sufficient to offset the sacrifice of current profits. Further, an efficiency strategy seems to work best in these situations:

- The market is growing rapidly.
- Experience effects are significant.
- Customers are more interested in low prices than in service or special product features.
- Major competition is complacent, and does not react by slashing its own prices.
- The company launching an efficiency strategy has the resources—financial, technological, and manufacturing—to carry it out.

9. "The Great Digital Watch Shake-out," *Business Week* (May 2, 1977): 78–80.

10. Linda Snyder Hayes, "Gillette Takes the Wraps Off," pp. 148–50.

11. Bro Uttal, "Texas Instruments Wrestles with the Consumer Market," *Fortune* Magazine © 1979 Time, Inc. All rights reserved.

12. Ibid, p. 52.

RESULTS OF STRATEGIC PLANNING

To date, the results of strategic planning are mixed. Some companies have enjoyed outstanding success. Some have been bitterly disappointed. Reasons for the success or failure of strategic planning in individual companies are not always clear. One author, however, has suggested four possible reasons for the mixed results that have been obtained.

- *It is risky.* Strategic market planning requires firm decisions on the future course that a company will take. Often, it requires a complete restructuring of the company, and the investment of significant corporate funds. Projections of the future always involve risk, and chief corporate executives often must stake their reputations on the outcomes of the strategic decisions they make. The decisions required in strategic planning require a great deal of entrepreneural courage and many, if not most, chief executives prefer to play it safe. As a consequence, although they go through the motions of strategic planning, they never make the hard decisions that are necessary.
- *It is difficult.* Strategic planning deals with complex questions. Simply gathering, evaluating, and synthesizing the data required for strategic decisions is complex, arduous, and time consuming. Many executives are uncomfortable with this process, which is largely creative and unstructured, and lack both the patience and tolerance of uncertainty required to do it well.
- *It requires leadership.* Since most strategic decisions are controversial, the chief executive must take a position of strong leadership, often pushing through decisions that may be unpopular with some of the company's key managers. Too often, chief executive officers prefer consensus among their key subordinates. Yet, the controversial nature

of strategic decisions often makes consensus impossible.

- *The value system works against it.* By definition, strategic planning is long-range rather than short-range. Good managers are often promoted so quickly that they never have to face the consequences of their long-range plans. In addition, executive compensation is usually tied to short-range profit performance which may suffer under a long-term strategic plan.[13]

Despite these problems, strategic planning has emerged as a major consideration in responsible corporate management. And, as markets become more competitive, as technology changes the face of industry, and as uncontrollable environmental variables shape the conditions under which business firms must operate, strategic planning will probably become even more important in the future.[14] As a consequence, the student of marketing should be aware of its existence and of its general purpose.

SUMMARY

Corporate growth is a major concern of most United States companies. Growth is important—it provides more efficient use of resources, greater economic stability, and opportunities for corporate employees. Growth is often required by stockholders and is a source of ego gratification for corporate executives.

Three broad strategies for growth are integrative growth, increased sales from existing products, and expanding the product line. Companies may employ these strategies in many ways and strategic planning has emerged as a device to enable the management of complex companies to make wise corporate decisions.

Strategic planning differs from the product marketing plan in two major respects: (1) it is a long-range plan (typically five years or more) whereas the product marketing plan is essentially a short-term document (one to three years); and (2) it is concerned with the allocation of company resources among divisions and products, whereas the product marketing plan is concerned with the marketing mix for individual products.

A key concept in strategic planning is the Strategic Business Unit (SBU). A SBU is an autonomous profit center managed by an individual who has sole responsibility for its operation, consisting of one or more products or divisions that have the same competitors. The purpose of planning is to match a firm's resources with selected markets to optimize success.

A number of formal planning methods—the General Electric Business Screen, the growth-share matrix, and PIMS (Profit Impact of Marketing Strategy)—have been developed to facilitate strategic planning.

To date, the success of strategic planning has been mixed. Often it fails because of the refusal of chief executives to make hard decisions about a firm's future direction, and to incur risk. As markets become more competitive, however, strategic planning will probably grow in importance.

---

13. Lewis V. Gerstner, Jr., "Can Strategic Planning Pay Off?" *Business Horizons* (December, 1972): 5–16.

14. Two excellent references on strategic planning are: Derek F. Abell and John S. Hammond, *Strategic Market Planning* (Englewood Clifffs, NJ: Prentice-Hall, Inc., 1979); and Roger A. Kerin and Robert A. Peterson, *Perspectives on Strategic Marketing Management* (Boston, MA: Allyn and Bacon, Inc., 1980).

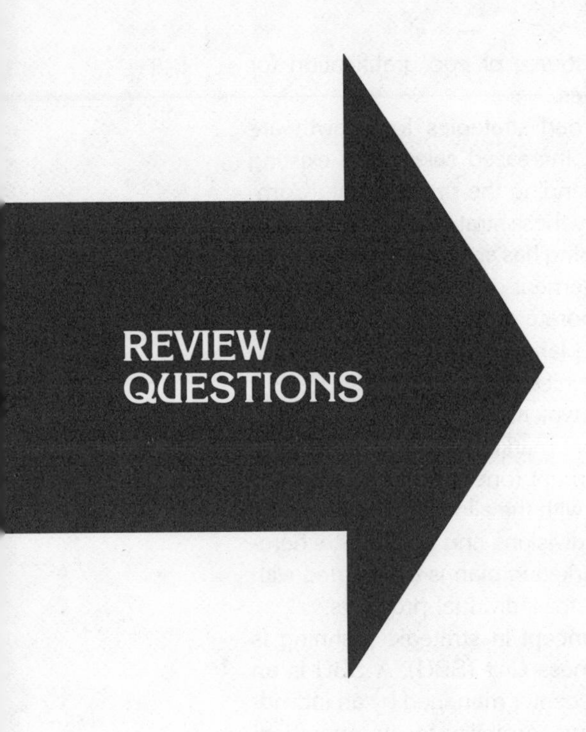

REVIEW QUESTIONS

1. Identify and explain the reasons that growth is an important concern of corporate management.
2. Distinguish between backward, forward, and horizontal integration, giving an example of each.
3. How does strategic planning differ from the typical product marketing plan?
4. Explain what is meant by a strategic business unit.
5. What are the four ways strategic market planning differs from earlier forms of market planning?
6. Explain the general structure of the General Electric Business Screen, and identify its primary purpose.
7. Explain the general structure of a growth-share matrix, and identify its primary purpose.
8. Explain the logic linking the learning curve, market share, and return on investment as a corporate marketing strategy.
9. Identify the optimal conditions for an efficiency strategy.
10. Identify the reasons for the mixed results that have been obtained through strategic planning.

DISCUSSION QUESTIONS

1. Discuss some of the growth strategies that might be employed by McDonald's or Burger Chef. Classify these strategies as integrative, increasing sales of existing products, and expanding the product line. Under what conditions might each of the strategies you have identified be appropriate?
2. How do you explain the fact that Société Bic was successful with throwaway pens and throwaway lighters, but unsuccessful with the throwaway razor?
3. Discuss ways in which an efficiency strategy might be applied to the market for housing.
4. The way in which a company defines its business largely determines its growth strategies. The Curtis Publishing Company apparently defined its business as a quality printer of general interest magazines. How else might the company have defined its business, consistent with its resources? What would be some of the strategic implications of this definition?
5. How do you think Procter & Gamble defines its business?

CHAPTER PROBLEM

CORPORATE PLANNING

A growth-share matrix visually represents the products of a company and their growth opportunity, their market share, and their ability to produce cash for investment purposes. This growth share matrix has four products:

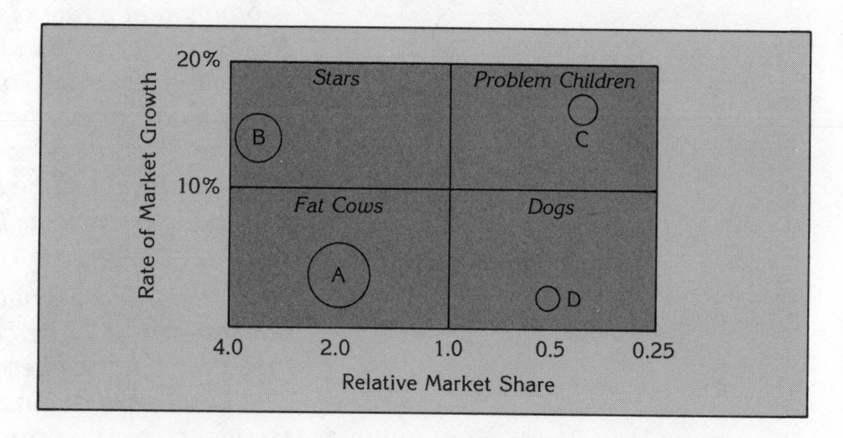

The sizes of the circles representing products A, B, C, and D, reflect the dollar sales of these products. For example, if a product with sales of $10 million is represented by a circle with an 1/8 inch diameter, then a product with sales of $15 million would be represented by a circle with a 3/16 inch diameter, a product with sales of $20 million by a circle with a 1/4 inch diameter, and so forth. In the matrix shown above, each of the four products shown may be characterized in the following ways:

- *Product A. The size of the circle for Product A indicates that its sales are relatively large in relation to the other products shown. Its relative share of market is 2.0 (note its position on the horizontal axis). Product A's share of market is twice as large as its nearest competitor. But, Product A is in a slowly growing market—its vertical axis position shows that its market is growing at a rate of about 3 percent a year.*
  Thus, Product A is a Cash Cow—a profitable product not going anywhere because it has a large share of a mature market. Increasing its share of market significantly would be very expensive. Thus, wise corporate policy would be simply to spend enough in marketing to maintain Product A's market share, and to

invest the profit it generates in products with greater growth potential.

- *Product B. Although the sales of Product B are not as great as those of Product A (note size of the circle representing Product B), its share of market is almost four times that of its nearest competitor, and the market is growing at a rate of 14 percent a year. However, Product B needs cash to continue its growth. If marketing funds are invested, it will eventually become a "Fat Cow" when the market growth levels off and become a source of cash for the company. If funds are not invested, it will be bypassed by competition, and eventually become a "Dog."*
- *Product C. Product C is a "Problem Child" with relatively small sales and a small relative share of a fast growing market—about 17 percent). With a lot of marketing investment, it may become a "Star" and eventually a "Fat Cow." Without investment, it will become a "Dog."*
- *Product D. Product D is a "Dog" with relatively small sales (note the size of its circle). It has a relative share of market of 0.5—only half the share of its leading competitor, and its market is growing slowly. Corporate strategy would call for either divesting the product or milking it and then divesting it.*

A healthy company is one that has: (1) several "Fat Cows" to generate cash for investment and profit; (2) some "Stars" which, with proper care and investment, will become the "Fat Cows" of tomorrow; (3) some "Problem Children" which, with major investment, will become the "Stars" of tomorrow and the "Fat Cows" sometime in the future; and (4) few if any "Dogs." A sick company is one with lots of "Dogs" and "Problem Children" and few if any "Stars" or "Fat Cows."

In the following table, you are given information that will enable you to prepare a growth-share matrix for two industrial companies.

Product	Sales (in millions)	Relative market share	Market growth rate
Company 1			
A	$30	3.6	5%
B	$50	1.8	3%
C	$20	2.8	16%
D	$15	1.5	12%
E	$ 5	0.5	12%
F	$ 3	0.7	15%
G	$ 6	0.3	17%
H	$ 5	0.5	19%
I	$ 4	0.5	4%
J	$ 8	0.3	2%

Product	Sales (in millions)	Relative market share	Market growth rate
Company 2			
A	$15	2.0	7%
B	$10	3.0	16%
C	$ 5	0.8	14%
D	$ 4	1.0	15%
E	$ 6	0.3	18%
F	$ 3	0.8	4%
G	$ 3	0.5	6%
H	$ 2	0.3	3%
I	$ 4	0.2	1%
J	$ 4	0.8	2%
K	$ 3	0.5	2%

Assignment

1. *Construct a growth-share matrix for each company.*
2. *Diagnose the health of each company.*
3. *Outline a strategy for maintenance, divestment, and investment for each company.*
4. *What problems might you encounter in carrying out your suggested strategy?*

22

Business and Society

- *The nature and scope of contemporary criticisms of marketing.*
- *Criticisms of the economic system, and how to respond to them.*
- *Criticisms of specific marketing activities and how to respond to them.*
- *The concept of social responsibility in marketing.*
- *Challenges for marketing.*

MARKETING EXAMPLES

Increasingly during the past twenty years, the role of business in society has been questioned. At the same time, marketing, as an instrument of business, has come under attack for social irresponsibility. Consider the following examples:

THE MARKETING CONCEPT

In Chapter 1, the marketing concept was identified as the central theory for success in an enterprise system. Briefly stated, the marketing concept suggests that to succeed in a competitive environment, a firm must offer products that consumers want at prices they are willing to pay, backed up by an integrated marketing effort designed to insure a profit for the firm as a necessary condition for continued existence.

In recent years, the marketing concept has been attacked from essentially two points of view: (1) consumers often want things that aren't good for them. For example, alcoholic beverages, cars without seatbelts, cigarettes, and so forth; (2) many things that individual groups of consumers want are harmful to society as a whole because these products create pollution, waste scarce resources, or give rise to other social costs. For example, disposable cans and bottles, nonbiodegradable chemicals and packaging materials, and convenience and labor saving devices such as electric toothbrushes, electric can openers, and a host of other products that consume energy and other scarce resources.

The presumption is that responsible marketers, not the consumers themselves, should be the final arbiters of what is good for consumers and what is beneficial to society. Further, if marketers refuse to assume this responsibility, then it should be assumed by the federal government, and enforced through restrictive legislation.

PRIVATE VERSUS PUBLIC CONSUMPTION

John Kenneth Galbraith, a noted economist, castigates the marketing system which promotes private consumption at the expense of public consumption. The consequence of this system is an imbalance between these two types of consumption. Thus, wealth in private goods—cars, homes, appliances, airplane travel, jewelery, and other personal consumption items—far exceeds our wealth in public goods such as education, public transportation, police protection, public health, public parks, and so forth. Private opulence often exists side by side with public squalor. A corollary of this point of view is that much of the $50 billion plus that is spent on advertising might better be spent on child care, public health, improved nutrition, or other public services.

MARKETING CREATES MATERIALISM

Critics believe that marketing, with its emphasis on products, profits, and self-gratification, promotes materialistic values; they do not find these values valid societal goals or useful criteria of social progress. There is little doubt that marketing, for the most part, deals with material values. Whether it creates them, or simply recognizes their existence and provides the products and services that these preexistent values demand is quite another issue. For example, early observers of the American society, notably Alexis de Tocqueville (1805–1859) and Charles Dickens (1812–1870), commented on the materialistic character of America over a hundred years before the emergence of modern marketing.

Whether or not these criticisms are valid, partly valid, or wholly invalid, they exist and must be recognized as a part of the social environment within which marketing operates. Further if these criticisms become dominant in the U.S. society, marketing as we know it will be abandoned or severely modified as a system for allocating goods and services.

Criticisms of marketing are so diverse that it is sometimes hard to sort them out and evaluate them in terms of their own merits. Critics of marketing are equally hard to classify. Some, obviously, have personal axes to grind. Others are moved by compassion for the underprivileged of society; still others are motivated by environmental concerns.

The solutions proposed for the problems that are perceived are equally diverse. Some propose that the marketing system be abandoned and replaced by a planned economy. Others urge far-reaching enactment of restrictive legislation on marketing practices. Still others believe that business firms should respond by becoming more socially responsible. And, unfortunately, the solutions urged by some groups are in conflict with the goals of others. For example, the restrictions urged by many environmentalists have a disproportionate impact on the poor by increasing production costs and raising consumer prices. Federal programs to help the poor often have the effect of increasing their discomfort. For example, urban renewal was adopted in an effort to eliminate slums, and to create improved housing for the poor. According to Martin Anderson, who has made a study of the results, urban renewal destroyed four homes for every home it built. Further, most of the new construction was occupied by middle and upper income families, while the original occupants were driven to other slum areas.[1]

1. Martin Anderson, *Welfare* (Stanford, CA: Hoover Institution, Stanford University, 1978), p. 91.

This chapter examines the relationship between the practice of marketing and the society within which it operates. In the process: (1) we will examine more closely some of the criticisms that are directed toward the practice of marketing; (2) we will consider the concept of the "social responsibility" of the business firm; (3) finally, we will examine some of the challenges that marketing will face in the future.

CRITICISMS OF MARKETING

Criticisms of marketing arise from many sources—the marketing literature itself; public statements by politicians, consumerists, environmentalists, and government agencies; special testimony before congressional committees; and social commentaries in the public press and intellectual journals.

An examination of these criticisms indicates that, generally, they are criticisms of the economic system, and criticisms of specific marketing practices. We will examine those criticisms that surface most frequently, and attempt to assess their validity.

Criticisms of the Economic System

Some of the criticisms directed at marketing are really criticisms of the free enterprise economic system of which marketing is a part. Most often, these criticisms take the following forms:

- The marketing system has failed to eradicate poverty.
- Disadvantaged consumers pay more.
- Catering to personal need satisfaction often conflicts with the general welfare of society.
- The proliferation of trivial products and services wastes scarce production resources.
- The pursuit of profit endangers the environment.

Let's look at each of these charges more carefully.

THE MARKETING SYSTEM HAS FAILED TO ERADICATE POVERTY. Although this charge is true, it neglects to mention that no other economic system has succeeded in eradicating poverty, either. The reason for this unfortunate state is probably fourfold: First, in some undeveloped societies, the lack of natural resources and productive capacity, coupled with exploding populations and high illiteracy rates, make poverty inevitable. The gross national products of these nations are simply inadequate to meet even minimal standards of sustenance. Second, in other societies, authoritarian governments supported by affluent minorities perpetuate a social system that is inequitable and repressive. Third, in highly-developed societies, the definition of poverty is constantly changing. As a result, what is considered poverty in the United States and much of western Europe would be perceived as luxury in many undeveloped countries. And finally, in highly developed societies, poverty is often a state of mind—a poverty of the spirit of individuals that prevents them from taking advantage of the economic opportunities that exist.

If we shift the emphasis from *elimination* of poverty to the *alleviation* of poverty, then we find that free economies perform exceedingly well. In the United States and western Europe, widespread welfare programs have been made possible by the remarkable productive capacity of free economic systems. Problems arise in these nations not because of poverty, as such, but due to the largesse of welfare programs that threaten the success of the economies themselves. Such programs are supported by exorbitant taxation that stifles incentive and reduces industry's ability to continue to produce; and engenders a dependency on the part of welfare recipients that discourages enterprise and willingness to work.[2]

The wealth of a nation depends upon its productive capacity; even the most severe critics of free economies concede their capacity to generate wealth in unparalleled abundance.[3] Finally, free economies, more than any other economic system, enable individuals to improve their own economic conditions. Prior to the emergence of free economies, one's role in life was largely shaped by the conditions of one's birth. To be born a peasant, or a herdsman, or the child of a guildsman, or the scion of a nobleman, or simply as a female child rigidly defined the horizons of one's aspirations. Social roles were rooted in traditional relationships, and traditional relationships were unsympathetic to immoderate ambitions. In fact, in 14th century France, fines and even prison sentences were given to members of the lower classes who so forgot their place in society that they emulated their betters in dress.

The marketing economy ushered in a new social order in which people—through diligence, hard work, and ambition—could channel their activities toward bettering their condition. And it worked.[4]

DISADVANTAGED CONSUMERS PAY MORE. Critics often charge that the poor pay more for comparable goods and services than do the more affluent. In the 1960s, a controversy arose over this issue, with some empirical studies purporting to show that they do, and others purporting to

2. For a report on the impact of extensive welfare programs on national economies, see: "Reassessing the Welfare State," *Time* (Jan. 12, 1981): 32–33.

3. Perhaps the greatest tribute to free economies' power to generate wealth appears in the most antifree economy treatise ever written—*The Communist Manifesto.* See Karl Marx and Friedrich Engels, *The Communist Manifesto,* edited, with an introduction, explanatory notes, and apprendices, by D. Ryazanoff (New York: Russell & Russell, Inc., 1930).

4. For a further discussion of this point, see: Irving Kristol, *Two Cheers for Capitalism* (New York: Basic Books, Inc., Publishers, 1978), p. X.

show that they don't.[5] On balance, the poor probably do pay more.

The reason that the poor often pay more is *not* because they are deliberately exploited by businesses—although they sometimes are. Rather, the reason they pay more arises from three interrelated factors:[6] First, the economically disadvantaged are often less mobile than their more affluent counterparts, not having access to a car or public transportation. Thus, they have less opportunity for comparative shopping. Second, retailers who serve disadvantaged consumers tend to have higher operating costs because of high rents, losses due to pilferage, higher insurance costs, higher credit losses, and smaller average volumes. For example, fewer supermarkets are located in central cities than in suburban areas. Thus, residents of central cities more often buy from small stores in which prices are, by necessity, higher. Third, the economically disadvantaged often must use installment credit for their purchases, particularly for consumer durables. The credit costs are often included in the price of the merchandise purchased. So, it is probable that the economically disadvantaged do pay more.

However, precisely the same situation exists in highly planned societies, such as Soviet Russia, where social inequalities are not supposed to exist. The Soviet government maintains special state stores for state officials, professional people, and members of the Communist party. The privileged persons who shop in these stores are charged prices far below those available to the general public; they also have access to merchandise not available to the average Soviet citizen. The point is that inequities in price between the economically disadvantaged and the more affluent are universal. In free economies, price discrepancies arise because of differences in the cost of operating a business, whereas in planned economies they are deliberately fostered by the government itself. Or, to express it another way, the governments of planned economies tax the poor to provide lower prices for the well-to-do.

THE CATERING TO PERSONAL NEED SATISFACTION OFTEN CONFLICTS WITH THE GENERAL WELFARE OF SOCIETY. Of course it does. But the converse is also true: Catering to the needs of society often conflicts with personal need satisfaction. The age-old problem is who should determine what the needs of society should be. Should the needs of society be determined by a government agency or planning board? Or, should they be determined by the individuals of society exercising freedom of choice in the marketplace?

One problem with those who believe that society's needs should be determined by a government commission is that they cannot agree among themselves on the priorities that should be given to society's needs. Unfortunately, they tend to have little respect for those whose priorities are different from their own.

THE PROLIFERATION OF TRIVIAL PRODUCTS AND SERVICES WASTES SCARCE RESOURCES. The difficulty with this criticism lies in two words—trivial and waste. What is trivial to one member of society is not trivial to another. And, whether or not production resources are wasted depends upon one's perception of the value of what is produced.

Again, the alternative to the marketing system is an awkward one: Some government agency or group, using its own criteria, decides what is trivial and what is waste—what will be produced and what will not be produced. In the process, consumers are deprived of freedom of choice. Note, of course, that the progress of product development often proceeds in small, incremental steps, any one of which may be trivial in and of itself. In the aggregate, however, and over a period of time, the sum of trivial product changes often leads to significant improvements in product performance.

THE PURSUIT OF PROFIT ENDANGERS THE ENVIRONMENT. Again, this criticism is often true. Many industries and individual companies contaminate the environment with industrial wastes in an effort to reduce costs. This problem is not unique to marketing societies, however.

5. For a discussion of this issue, see David Caplovits, *The Poor Pay More* (New York: The Free Press, 1964); and Phyllis Groom, "Prices in Poor Neighborhoods," *Monthly Labor Review* (Oct., 1966): 1085–90.

6. Frederick E. Webster, Jr., *Social Aspects of Marketing* (Englewood Cliffs, NJ: Prentice-Hall, Inc., 1974), pp. 23–24.

Industrialized societies throughout the world, regardless of their economic systems, pollute the environment. The Volga in Russia, the longest river in Europe, is a cesspool.

This does not mean, of course, that the problem of pollution is any less real. Nor, that it should be ignored. On the contrary, this is an area in which public concern, coupled with government help, should take positive steps—as has been done in the United States and many free economies. One problem in this area, however, involves the cost-benefit equation of pollution control. That is, the costs involved in eliminating a particular form of pollution may possibly far exceed the benefits gained. This simply means that judgment must be exercised in these areas, and the cost-benefit equation carefully evaluated. Too often, unfortunately, dedicated environmentalists seem oblivious to the cost side of the equation.

Further, the actions that many environmentalists urge to control pollution often seem more punitive than corrective. For example, positive incentives might be more effective than urging exorbitant fines and prison sentences for offenders. Thus, firms might be charged a price for the privilege of polluting the environment. The greater the pollution, the higher the price. As the level of pollution is reduced, the price goes down accordingly. Under such a system, profits would be increased, not by pollution, but by eliminating pollution, and the pursuit of profits could be turned into a social gain.

SUMMARY COMMENT ON CRITICISMS OF THE ECONOMIC SYSTEM. In the foregoing material, we have noted that criticisms of the marketing system, while sometimes true, are often shortsighted and naive. Generally, this naiveté is reflected in three ways:

- Rather than acknowledging the positive contributions of free economies—the creation of national wealth, the alleviation of poverty, the provision of opportunity to better one's economic condition, and freedom of choice—critics focus on the failure of free economies to solve the historic problems of mankind. Problems that no other economic systems have succeeded in solving half so well.
- Critics seem to imply that their charges are unique to free economies—which they are not—rather than applicable to all economic systems—which they are.
- Many critics seem to have little regard for freedom of choice, and are far too eager to impose their own order of preferences on others.

Criticisms of Specific Marketing Practices

Most of the criticisms of specific marketing practices focus on advertising, primarily I suppose, because it is the most visible. Note that in the following list of nine common criticisms, the first six involve advertising at least to some extent.

- Advertising creates materialistic values.
- Advertising makes people buy things they do not need.
- Advertising is deceptive.
- Advertising is often annoying and in poor taste.
- Advertising is a barrier to competition.
- Commercial sponsorship of mass media has resulted in blandness and, generally, poor program content.
- Consumers are unable to make intelligent decisions because: (A) products are unnecessarily complex; and (B) marketers provide inadequate information.
- Product quality is often inadequate, especially with respect to safety, durability, and ease of use.
- Retailers are often incompetent to install and repair the products they sell, and the consumer usually has no recourse to the manufacturer.

Again, let us examine each of these criticisms more closely.

ADVERTISING CREATES MATERIALISTIC VALUES. When referring to this criticism at the beginning of the chapter, we noted that there is no question of whether marketing does or does not focus on material values. It does. The real questions are: does marketing *create* these values or merely serve them? and is materialism a desirable value for society and for individuals?

In answer to the first of these two questions, materialism has been preeminent as an American value since the country was founded. Advertising didn't create materialism; it was always there. At the same time, however, advertising helps to perpetuate materialism with its emphasis on products and material satisfactions, even though it is not a primary cause of materialism itself. Thus, in the process of reflecting the social value of materialism, advertising undoubtedly reinforces it.

The second question is more relevant: Is materialism a desirable value for society and for individuals? Insofar as material values represent a free choice of society's members, saying that it is not a desirable social value is difficult without repudiating the basic concepts of democracy and of a free economy.

As the American society has become more affluent, a growing number of consumers have been questioning materialism as a desirable social goal; they recognize that materialism—like everything else—has a cost. The costs include dissipation of resources, environmental pollution, and diminution of other social values, as well as the quality of life.

Unfortunately, the issue of materialism is not absolute, but relative. Not a question of whether materialism is desirable, but *how much* materialism is acceptable, and how great a cost we are willing to pay. Probably the question of how much materialism we can afford will not be answered on philosophical grounds, but on pragmatic ones. As irreplaceable resources are exhausted, as energy costs increase, and as pollution becomes excessive, the limits of materialism will be defined, not by philosophical predilections, but by external, environmental considerations.

ADVERTISING MAKES PEOPLE BUY THINGS THEY DO NOT NEED. The obvious answer to this question is that advertising can't make anyone do anything. There is, for example, no way that General Motors can make me buy a General Motors car if I do not choose to do so. Advertising can make a product or service appealing, but the decision to purchase or not to purchase is always a personal one.

At a more subtle level, this criticism implies that advertising directs the attention of consumers away from things they truly *need* and toward things they merely *want*. Such a distinction between needs and wants is a terribly subjective judgment on the part of those who make it. In short, critics who adopt this point of view are saying that some purchases are more desirable than others according to their criteria which, incidentally, are seldom made explicit. And, while they can make such judgments for themselves, they cannot make such judgments for others without depriving others of freedom of choice.

ADVERTISING IS DECEPTIVE. This criticism, like many others, is much more ambiguous than it appears on the surface. Advertising is intended to persuade, but the question "When does persuasion become deception?" is difficult to answer.

Cunningham and Miller have pointed out four dimensions to deception: (1) the intent to deceive; (2) the capacity of the message to deceive; (3) whether the recipient of the message is deceived; and (4) the standard of judgment to be used in determining the extent of deception.[7]

Intent to deceive is difficult to evaluate because it is subjective. Undoubtedly, some advertisers are dishonest and do attempt to deceive. But, some dishonest people are in all areas of our society—doctors, ministers, public officials, consumers, students, professors, and so forth. However, they are in the minority. Business firms that intend to stay in business generally have unequivocal policies against deliberate deception.

The capacity of the message to deceive is again difficult to evaluate. Deceive whom? The judgment on the capacity of an advertisement to deceive is heavily dependent upon the nature of the recipient. An advertisement that is not deceptive to the audience to which it is directed may be deceptive to a lesser educated audience, or to a small child. Further, the distinction between infor-

7. M. Pearce, S. M. Cunningham, and A. Miller, *Appraising the Economic and Social Effects of Advertising,* Marketing Science Institute Staff Report (Oct., 1971): 423.

mation, persuasion, and deception is ambiguous, as has been pointed out by the National Goals Research Staff of the U.S. Government.[8] Frederick Webster has pointed out that the standards used by regulatory agencies have not been particularly flattering to the average consumer who has been described at various times as gullible, ignorant, easily persuaded, uneducated, and incapable of making sound judgments.[9]

Undoubtedly, some people are deceived by advertising, although the extent to which they are deceived is highly ambiguous and judgmental. Further, even a rudimentary knowledge of psychology indicates that some people want to be deceived, and will go out of their way to attain this result. W. C. Fields once observed, "You can't cheat an honest man." His point was that most people who are cheated have a bit of larceny in their own hearts and become victims because they are trying to cheat the cheater. Probably there is some element of truth in this assertion, and this element of truth is present in many charges that advertising is deceptive.

In summary, it is probably true that some advertising is deceptive. However, suggesting that most advertising is deceptive is irresponsible and deceptive.

ADVERTISING IS OFTEN ANNOYING AND IN POOR TASTE. This charge against advertising probably has more substance than any of the others. Some advertising is clearly in poor taste. The intentional use of poor taste in advertising is inexcusable, and is widely criticised within the industry itself. *Advertising Age,* in the following editorial, echoes this point of view.

> Shock: A Creative Shortcut
>
> The double entendre is a perennial industry problem, one that will from time to time belch forth its bad taste and blanket the industry. We see evidence of this each week as our readers send us what are called "Ads we can do without," usually ads that play off anatomical features or sexual activities.
>
> We recall the commotion that greeted National Airlines "Fly me!" campaign a few years ago, and the eyebrow lifting that occurred when the "My men wear English Leather or they wear nothing at all" campaign broke. More recently, we've had the "Flick your Bic" campaign. Such efforts, obviously in questionable taste, nevertheless managed to link product or service to a fresh slogan and thereby earned grudging recognition in some quarters as hard-working creative solutions to marketing problems.
>
> How, then, does one justify the tv commercial for Speidel's new digital watches? Speidel has a prospective groom telling his bride-to-be, "Honey, this is the day. Today, I'm going all the way." The future bride registers shock, unaware that he's only talking about the Speidel watch and watchstrap he has bought. The theme then becomes "Speidel goes all the way," thus linking Speidel to a phrase that already draws snickers from every boastful adolescent. By attaching its brand name to that expression, Speidel hopes to gain instant recognition and identification for the new entry. Where the budget is weak, the competition strong, and time short, the temptation is to treat the creative shortcut as a creative solution; too bad creative people can't make their talents transcend such temptation.[10]

When an industry is guilty as charged, what else can one say?

ADVERTISING IS A BARRIER TO COMPETITION. The charge that advertising acts as a barrier to competition is based on the assertion that the cost of advertising a new product is prohibitive for any but the giants of an industry. Thus, the advertising superiority of entrenched firms enables them to block new competitors from entering the market, thereby fostering monopolies, high prices, and excessive profits.

If this charge were valid, one would expect to find: (1) little brand switching from well–established brands to newly introduced ones; (2) a positive correlation between advertising intensity

8. National Goals Research Staff, *Toward Balanced Growth: Quantity and Quality* (Washington DC: Superintendent of Documents, U.S. Government Printing Office, 1970), p. 139.

9. Frederick E. Webster, Jr , p. 34.

10. "Shock: A Creative Shortcut," reprinted with permission from the November 28, 1977, issue of *Advertising Age.* Copyright 1977 by Crain Communications, Inc.

and the concentration of sales for consumer product industries; that is, advertising expenditures would be high in those industries dominated by a few major companies and correspondingly lower in fields characterized by many competitors; and (3) little evidence of new brands encroaching on the sales of the brands of entrenched companies. Yet, one does not find any of these things.

Testimony before the U.S. Congress Subcommittee on Monopoly, as well as everyday experience, indicates that brand switching is rampant.[11] In the detergent industry, as well as personal care, cereals, automobiles, fashions, household appliances, proprietary drugs, and many others, brand switching is a way of life. A study of the correlation between advertising intensity and concentration of sales by economist Lester G. Telser indicated no relationship between the amount of advertising and the number of new products introduced into the field.[12] And, finally, evidence of new brands making competitive inroads on well established leaders in the field is widespread. For example, import automobiles have driven major U.S. car manufacturers to the edge of bankruptcy; Timex has literally taken the watch market away from Bolova; Sony became a major factor in the television market against entrenched competition such as General Electric, Philco, RCA, and Motorola. Miller's displaced Schlitz as the number two brewery; Polaroid has had an outstanding success in Kodak's domain; Société Bic has had outstanding success against Gillette; dozens of other examples could be given.

Economist Jules Backman, in a book titled *Advertising and Competition,* concludes that entry into new markets is easier when advertising can be used[13] and, according to *Fortune* magazine, Harold Demsetz and others have "pretty well disposed of the myth that advertising is a source of monopoly power."[14]

In summary, the weight of systematic research indicates that advertising is not a barrier to entry into new fields. Rather, as Backman so succinctly suggests, it makes entry possible.

COMMERCIAL SPONSORSHIP OF MASS MEDIA HAS RESULTED IN BLANDNESS AND POOR PROGRAM CONTENT. Critics who make this charge probably have never traveled in foreign countries where television programming is controlled by the government. If they had, they would recognize that most of the decent television in these countries consists of reruns of American programs.

Nonetheless, even the most vociferous defenders of commercial television would probably concede that the average run of U.S. television shows contributes little of cultural consequence, aesthetic value, or dramatic excellence. As one observer of the American scene commented, "No one has ever gone broke underestimating the taste of the mass market."

Defense of television programming rests on essentially two significant arguments: First, television stations, for the most part, give the American people what they want to see. When a program fails to achieve an adequate rating, it is replaced. Of course, this means that if one's tastes are somewhat different from the tastes of the mass market, one indeed may find commercial television to be an intellectual wasteland. However, the market system itself is taking care of this problem. As significant numbers of consumers have become bored with standard television programs, cable television has emerged as an attractive alternative. Second, commercial television provides a forum for the exercise of free expression, virtually uncontaminated by government control. This is a remarkable blessing since the entire history of government control of communications systems is one of abuse and repression.

CONSUMERS ARE UNABLE TO MAKE INTELLIGENT DECISIONS BECAUSE PRODUCTS

11. U.S. Congress Subcommittee on Monopoly of the Senate Select Committee on Small Business, *Role of the Giant Corporations,* Part 1-A, July, 1969, p. 923.

12. Lester G. Telser, "Some Aspects of the Economics of Advertising," *Journal of Business* (April, 1968), as reproduced in *Advertising's Role in Society,* John S. Wright and John E. Mertes, eds. (St. Paul, Minnesota: West Publishing Company, 1974), pp. 38–39.

13. Jules Backman, *Advertising and Competition* (New York: New York University Press, 1967), p. 177.

14. A. F. Ehrbar, "Martin Fieldstein's Electric Blue Economic Prescriptions," *Fortune* Magazine © 1978 Time, Inc. All rights reserved.

He: "Television programming is really terrible."
She: "You can always turn it off." (Photo by Larry Hamill)

ARE UNNECESSARILY COMPLEX AND BECAUSE INSUFFICIENT INFORMATION IS PROVIDED. The contention that many products are complex is unquestionably true. Complexity is often an outgrowth of technology and consumer preferences. Whether or not they are *too* complex, is a judgment that is not easy to validate.

Undoubtedly, many products are not engineered with consumer convenience in mind. Often, product designers seem oblivious to the problems of repair. What is technically satisfying and aesthetically pleasing to the design engineer may be a nightmare to the consumer or repairperson faced with the task of fixing a product when it breaks down—as it undoubtedly will at some point. Further, difficulty of repair adds substantially to maintenance costs.

Although this is, indeed, a problem, the marketing system itself offers the best opportunity for a solution. Producers who recognize this problem can gain a competitive advantage in the marketplace by solving it in innovative ways. And, it is difficult to imagine a more powerful incentive for the business firm than that of gaining a competitive advantage in the marketplace. Certainly, this problem is not going to be solved by regulation, nor can it be solved by the government taking over production. This latter alternative, in fact, would only exacerbate the problem because, with the government as the producer, there is no recourse for dissatisfaction with what is produced. The experience of the Soviet Union, a classical example of a government controlled economy, offers dramatic testimony on this point.

The criticism that inadequate information is available for consumers to make intelligent buying decisions is highly suspect. A rash of government labeling legislation has compelled producers to provide a wide range of product information to consumers. Further, complex products are customarily accompanied by information-packed brochures containing exhaustive data about the product.

In actuality, consumers use only a fraction of the information available to them in making buying decisions. Unfortunately, protecting consumers from themselves is extremely difficult since good judgment cannot be legislated.

PRODUCT QUALITY IS OFTEN INADEQUATE, ESPECIALLY WITH RESPECT TO SAFETY, DURABILITY, AND EASE OF USE. Particularly during the 1960s and 1970s, Americans became increasingly concerned about product quality. Firms whose products became suspect are paying a high price in terms of loss of market share and a decline in profits. This is the way the marketing system works, and many American companies have been displaced in product excellence by foreign imports.

What is less clear, however, is what really happened to product quality. Did it really go down as many critics contend? The following quotation from *Fortune* throws some light on this question.

> Why are we suddenly so worried about the quality of American products? Boeing makes the best commercial aircraft in the world. International Harvester and Deere & Co. produce the most reliable tractors—equipped, if farmers want, with stereos, air conditioning, orthopedic seats, and adjustable steering wheels. European tourists carry off American-made permanent-press sheets because they're cheap, long-wearing, and dazzlingly patterned. Our plastics are stronger, our chemicals purer, and our machine tools built to finer tolerances than ever. This is all true enough—yet, unhappily, it is also largely beside the point.
>
> America's leadership in quality has been almost imperceptibly eroding for years. In the last few months, more and more U.S. executives have awakened to the fact that they are caught in a fateful struggle. They are turning their companies upside down to give quality specialists more clout. Vendors are being told to supply better parts or lose the business. In hundreds of factories, small groups of workers are sitting down periodically to search for ways of improving quality and productivity. Executive offices and factory floors ring with slogans. Says John A. Manoogian, executive director of product assurance at Ford Motor Co.: "If it's not right, we won't ship it, and we mean that." Intones a General Electric spokesman: "Quality is our No. 1 focus."
>
> While U.S. companies have steadily improved quality, they are coming under pressure largely because the Japanese have advanced by leaps. Building assiduously for thirty years on a foundation of theories developed in the U.S., the Japanese have made quality the weapon that wins the world's markets.[15]

Thus, it is not a lapse in quality that has given rise to criticisms. Rather, the sudden spurt in quality by Japanese imports has made quality the basis of competition—one of the desirable by-products of a marketing economy.

Product safety is a somewhat more complex issue. The question is not safety, per se, but how much safety can be built into products at a cost the consumer is willing to pay. Undoubtedly, some products are patently unsafe. Unfortunately, few products can be designed so that some consumers cannot injure or kill themselves through misuse. A case in point: in one of the southeastern states, a drunken driver drove his car at 105 miles per hour, had a wreck, and was killed. His family brought legal action against the automobile manufacturer under the National Traffic Safety Act of 1966. Sometimes protecting consumers against themselves is difficult.

The 1960s saw a spate of safety regulations designed to protect consumers against dangerous ingredients and faulty product design. In some instances, this legislation has undoubtedly been beneficial. For example, Deere and Com-

15. Jeremy Main, "The Battle for Quality Begins," *Fortune* Magazine © 1978 Time, Inc. All rights reserved.

pany redesigned its riding lawnmowers by equipping them with a longer discharge chute, an improved motor brake, and relocating the controls.

In other instances, federal legislation has led to unanticipated consequences. For example, the government banned the use of phosphates (a water pollutant) in detergents and approved NTA (nitrilotriacetic) as a substitute. Subsequently, when it was found that NTA had carcinogenic (cancer producing) properties, phosphates were reinstituted as acceptable. Under the Flammable Fabrics Act, standards were enforced in 1973 that led manufacturers to impregnate cloth used in children's sleepwear with Tris, a flame retardant chemical. Within a short time, 99 percent of all children's sleepwear produced and sold in the United States was treated with Tris. Later, discovered to be a powerful carcinogen, Tris was banned in 1978. Yet, for five years, under government imposed standards, millions of children were exposed to this hazard. When Tris was banned the manufacturers, not the government, bore the brunt of the adverse publicity.

The objective of consumer protection legislation is obviously good. The consequences not always so. The wording of the legislation is designed to protect consumers from *unreasonable risk*. Yet, what constitutes unreasonable risk is judgmental, and the standards employed are subject to debate.

In some instances, companies have suffered significant financial losses because of questionable federal rulings, or because of rulings that have later been revoked. In some instances, consumers are the victims, even though they are intended to be the beneficiaries. For example, in Chapter 2 I noted that regulations imposed by the Food and Drug Administration have sharply reduced the research done by the pharmaceutical industry, and that unnecessary suffering and deaths occur in the United States because effective drugs used in Europe are banned in this country.

The point is, of course, that criticisms concerning product quality and product safety are not as simple as the critics imply; sometimes corrective action leads to undesirable results.

RETAILERS ARE OFTEN INCOMPETENT TO INSTALL AND REPAIR THE PRODUCTS THEY SELL. True. But, there is no law that says one must deal with such retailers. Were incompetence a crime, a good part of the human race would be serving prison sentences. As a point of fact, however, no one is as distressed about retailer incompetence as the manufacturers whose products they handle, and no one has done more to try to correct this situation than these same manufacturers.

Because of the problem of retail service, many manufacturers—such as General Electric and Maytag—install their own repair depots in major cities. Some manufacturers establish company-owned outlets to sell and service their products. Whirlpool has a toll free "hot line" and encourages customers who have trouble with their appliances to call the company. If Whirlpool cannot diagnose and solve the problem over the telephone, they will send a repairperson to the customer's home the next day—sometimes the same day. And examination of the yellow pages of the telephone directory indicates that many nationwide companies provide a toll free number that customers can call if they have trouble with the company's products.

IMPLICATIONS OF CONSUMERS' CRITICISMS. Some consumer criticisms are justified; some are not. Some are self-serving; some are inspired by genuine concern. But, regardless of the motivation behind them, they should not be ignored by companies that have adopted the marketing concept as a philosophy of business.

Unfortunately, business firms often do not respond well to consumer criticisms or to the threat of government regulations. According to an article in *Business Week,* the response of many business firms follows a predictable pattern.

- Deny everything.
- Blame wrongdoing on small marginal firms in the industry.
- Discredit the critics.
- Hire a public relations person.
- Attempt to defang the legislation through lobbying.

- Launch a fact-finding committee to see if improvement is necessary.
- Actually do something.[16]

Only the last two represent constructive behavior. When firms fail to take either of the last two steps, they, like many of us, prove to be their own worst enemy.

In many instances, there may be little that firms can do about consumer criticisms, particularly those directed at the economic system as such, or those that are so vague that they cannot be acted upon. In other cases—particularly when criticisms are directed toward products, or services, or specific marketing practices—the criticisms can sometimes be turned into marketing opportunities.

The key to corporate success in a marketing economy is to be sensitive to consumer concerns and, when possible, to do something about them.

THE CONCEPT OF SOCIAL RESPONSIBILITY

In recent years, the concept of "social responsibility" has crept into the marketing literature as an *alternative* to the marketing concept. The concept of social responsibility has, of course, been inspired by concerns for the environment, and by the observation that consumers often want things that are neither good for them nor conducive to the ultimate well-being of society. Examples are commonplace. Many snack items, while well beloved by consumers, are not particularly nutritious and possibly harmful to health. Fast food operations serve hamburgers, french fries, and french fried onion rings with a high fat content (which may be deleterious to health) and waste an unconscionable amount of paper (a resource) in wrapping these products. Nonreturnable bottles are socially harmful both because they contribute to pollution and because they consume far more resources than returnable bottles. Fuel inefficient cars, as well as dozens of labor saving devices—ranging from electric toothbrushes to automatic dryers—consume scarce energy when these same functions could be performed manually much more economically. Dozens of throwaway products—pens, cigarette lighters, razors, paper towels, disposable diapers, and so forth—waste resources. Finally, a case can be made that alcoholic beverages, cigarettes, and other products whose threat to public health has been well documented could be included in the list of socially harmful products.

The implication of socially responsible marketing is that business firms should take the lead in eliminating these products, or modifying them in such a way that they are no longer deleterious to the well-being of society as a whole.

Unfortunately, the doctrine of social responsibility, while well-intentioned, raises some difficult problems. *First,* it places business firms in the role of being the final arbiter of consumers' needs. That is, the business firm should decide what is good for consumers and for society, rather than leaving this decision to consumers themselves. *Second,* it ignores, or at least minimizes, the impact of such actions on the profits, and, therefore, on the survival of business firms.

Business firms do indeed have responsibilities. Figure 22–1, for example, diagrammatically portrays the business firm and some of the publics to which it is responsible.

The question becomes one of determining how the business firm can best serve these many publics, including society itself. The basic doctrine of free economies is that business firms best serve these diverse publics when they serve their own interests—within the constraints of the legal system within which they operate. The basic doctrine of planned economies is that business firms best serve these diverse publics when they serve and are controlled by the government. Take your choice, but recognize the implications of this choice.

Quite often, firms do serve their own interests by serving the ultimate well-being of society—but *only when consumers perceive the ultimate well-being of society as being coextensive with their own.* The case of fuel-efficient

16. "Special Report: Business Responds to Consumerism," *Business Week* (Sept. 6, 1969): 94ff.

FIGURE 22–1: The Business Firm and Some of its Publics.

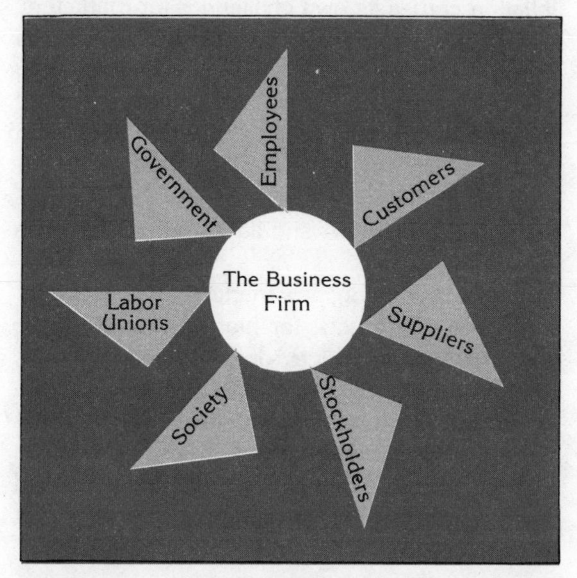

cars is a case in point. In other instances, unilateral decisions by business, while serving the ultimate well-being of society, will displease consumers and lead to the demise of the firm. In this event, a disservice will have been done to employees, suppliers, stockholders, labor unions, the government, and even to society itself since it will create unemployment.

This does not mean that buisness firms should not constantly seek to improve the quality of their products and services. On the contrary, the constant improvement of products and services is the *essence* of the marketing concept—the basic function of competition. Being sensitive to consumers, being sensitive to the environment, and being sensitive to social needs are requirements for successful implementation of the marketing concept. It is hard to see how the "social responsibility" concept improves on this.

Some critics of the marketing concept reject it, and urge a "concept of social responsibility" because many business firms have not adopted the marketing concept, or do not execute it well. Is there any reason to believe that these firms will execute a strategy of "social responsibility" any better? Such critics, I suspect, would do away with parenthood because many people are poor parents.

Perhaps, the concept of "social responsibility" in business is best summed up by the following comment from *Fortune* magazine.

> In the newspaper stories about the latest comings and goings at RCA, we kept reading that its new chairman and chief executive, Thornton Bradshaw, was a leading advocate of "corporate social responsibility." . . . We have always had a certain amount of difficulty getting our hands on this doctrine. It seems slippery in part because it doesn't have an agreed upon opposite; at least, there don't seem to be any leading advocates of corporate irresponsibility. And in part because its proponents engage in a dreadful amount of double-talk, at the end of which it's always unclear whether corporate social responsibility does or doesn't reduce profits. . . . In the introduction to his new book, Bradshaw accepts the view that "the purpose of the corporation is more than simply producing a healthy return on investment." He says that he believes "in the intrinsic value of the decentralized market system" but couples this affirmation with the statement that we "must act now to develop a more humanistic, responsible, and innovative form of capitalism to meet society's demands." Someone who is really committed to market economics could read this passage and conclude that there must be a market for double-talk.[17]

CHALLENGES FOR MARKETING

Marketing in the future will, as it has in the past, face many challenges. From a current perspective, these challenges may appear more difficult and, perhaps, more insurmountable than those of the past. In part, this seems true because each generation tends to be overwhelmed by its own problems, and lacks a historical perspective on what has gone before. Anyone who did not experience the depression of 1929, the bank holiday of 1933, the spectacle of 25 percent of the labor

17. "On Slippery Ground," *Fortune* Magazine © 1981 Time, Inc. All rights reserved.

force being unemployed, soup kitchens, and bread lines cannot appreciate the despair with which marketers of that day faced the future.

In part, the future challenge of marketing seems more threatening because of the relatively recent realization that we are running out of energy, because of the high rates of inflation that have plagued the late 1970s and early 1980s, because of international competition for markets, and the oppressive weight of government regulation.

Although it is unfeasible to deal with each of these problems in depth, perhaps a few summary comments will help put them in perspective.

Energy

The worldwide energy crisis is, indeed, forbidding. *National Geographic,* in a special issue on energy, notes that, at our present rate of consumption, we will exhaust the world's known oil resources in thirty years, and the likelihood of major, new oil discoveries is remote. Alternative sources of energy—tar sands, oil shale, coal, geothermal heat, uranium, solar, synfuels, and so forth—are still several years in the future, may require capital investments beyond our capacity, may place unsupportable demands on our water supply, and (particularly in the case of coal) create horrendous pollution problems.[18]

Yet the future of marketing is not all that bleak. The development of major new energy sources will create a large demand for technology, for equipment, and for services. Further, a number of *cogeneration* devices, which make electricity and heat together, are being applied to garbage, agricultural wastes, human wastes (all of which are renewable resources) and to increase the efficiency of natural gas by a factor of three.

In many product fields, marketing will be faced with the challenge of developing fuel–efficient products, reducing marketing costs through strategic planning, and developing more efficient methods of promotion to offset the higher costs of manufacturing.

18. "Energy: Facing Up to the Problems and Getting Down to the Solutions," a special report in the public interest, *National Geographic* (Feb., 1981).

Inflation

Inflation carries its own challenges for marketers. Not only do company operating costs increase during periods of inflation, but consumers also become more cost conscious, and must spread their purchases thinner. The reduction of costs in every area of marketing—product design, maintenance and service, logistics, promotion, packaging, and so forth—should be targets for marketing innovation.

In addition, new markets will open up for inexpensive products, for high quality products, easy to repair products, do-it-yourself products, and home entertainment. Every change in the environment creates opportunities for the alert marketer. The problem is one of keeping in touch with consumers, identifying their concerns and needs, and providing products and services that serve these needs effectively.

Competition

Competition always becomes more acute during times of economic stress. The next decade should see an increase in competitive activity, not only from domestic producers, but also from foreign imports. Further, international marketing is still in its infancy as far as most U.S. marketers are concerned. Opportunities in this area are relatively unexploited.

Competition, however, is the essence of marketing in a free economy. Competition stimulates new products, encourages efficiency and, in the last analysis, makes the marketing system work. Anyone who does not enjoy competition should not enter marketing.

Government Regulation

The 1960s and 1970s saw an unsurpassed growth in regulation of business and society. Legislative acts and administrative decisions imposed crippling restrictions on business activity and significantly increased its cost of operation. Lack of a consistent policy by the Federal Reserve System and irresponsible federal deficits contributed to a debilitating inflation that penalized business and consumers alike. By the late 1970s, the U.S. public had become dismayed by the excesses of government and called for a reexamination of its economic policies in the election of 1980.

Probably the next decade will produce a political climate that is more conducive to business and to marketing than that which has existed for the past twenty years. If this comes to pass, the next few years could offer exciting and challenging opportunities for marketers. If it does not, the future of both a free economy and representative democracy may well become a question mark.[19]

Summary Comment

The 1950s and early 1960s represented an exciting period in the field of marketing. Economic vitality and the commercialization of technologies developed during World War II created marketing opportunities and increased the wealth of the nation and of the world. The late 1960s and 1970s became a period of relative stagnation as innovation in the marketplace faltered, as product differences became increasingly trivial, and as government control of the economy became more restrictive.

The 1980s, despite its problems, hold the promise of renewed challenges. How well these challenges are met will largely depend upon the ability of business firms to seize opportunities. For those students who are contemplating a career in the marketing field, I wish you good luck, sound judgment, and smooth sailing.

SUMMARY

Increasingly, during the past twenty years, the role of business in society has been questioned. At the same time, as an instrument of business, marketing, has come under attack for social irresponsibility. Criticisms of marketing tend to be of two kinds: criticisms of the economic system and criticisms of specific marketing practices.

Criticisms of the economic system generally take the following forms: (1) the marketing system has failed to eradicate poverty; (2) disadvantaged consumers pay more; (3) catering to personal need satisfaction often conflicts with the general welfare of society; (4) the proliferation of trivial products and services wastes scarce production resources; and (5) the pursuit of profit endangers the environment. Examination of these criticisms indicates that, while well intentioned, they are often short-sighted and naive.

Criticisms of marketing practices tend to focus on advertising, primarily because of its high visibility. These criticisms most generally take the forms: (1) advertising creates materialistic values; (2) advertising makes people buy things they do not need; (3) advertising is deceptive; (4) advertising is often annoying and in poor taste; (5) advertising is a barrier to competition; (6) commercial sponsorship of mass media has resulted in poor quality in program content; (7) product quality is often inadequate; (8) retailers are often incompetent. Some of these criticisms are justified, and some are not. Too often, however, business firms are insensitive to them and thereby do themselves and consumers a disservice.

The concept of "social responsibility" on the part of business firms has emerged as an alternative to the marketing concept. Although well-intentioned, this concept is ambiguous and does not represent an improvement over the marketing concept.

Marketing, during the next decade, will face some difficult challenges. Among them are energy shortages, inflation, increased competition, and government regulation. While these areas represent problems, they also represent opportunities for marketing firms that are alert to them.

19. For a discussion of this problem, see: Robert Lubar, "Making Democracy Less Inflation Prone," *Fortune* (Sept. 22, 1980): 78–86; and Everett Carll Ladd, "How to Tame the Special-Interest Groups," *Fortune* (Oct. 20, 1980): 66–80.

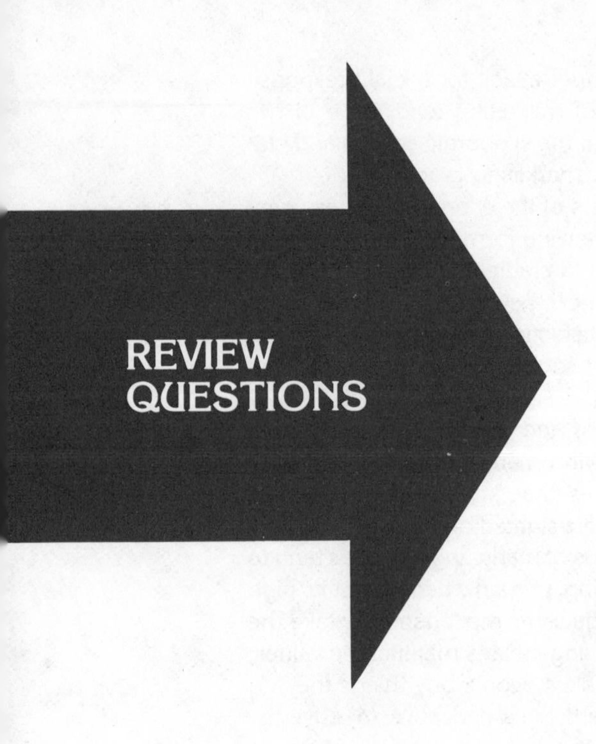

REVIEW QUESTIONS

1. What are the reasons given in the text for the fact that no economic system has been able to eradicate poverty?
2. For what reasons does the text claim that free economies, more than any other economic system, enable individuals to improve their own economic conditions?
3. For what reasons does the text state that criticisms of the marketing system are often short-sighted and naive?
4. In what way does advertising contribute to the value of materialism?
5. The text states that the charge that advertising is a barrier to competition has three implications. What are these implications and what arguments are given to support or refute them?
6. How does the text defend the charge that advertising has resulted in poor program content in television?
7. What, according to the text, is responsible for the charge that product quality is inadequate?
8. What, according to the text, has often been the response of business firms to consumer criticisms?
9. What are the two basic problems with the concept of "social responsibility" of business?
10. What does the text identify as major problems facing marketing in the next ten years? Give at least one example in each area of how marketers can turn these problems into opportunities.

DISCUSSION QUESTIONS

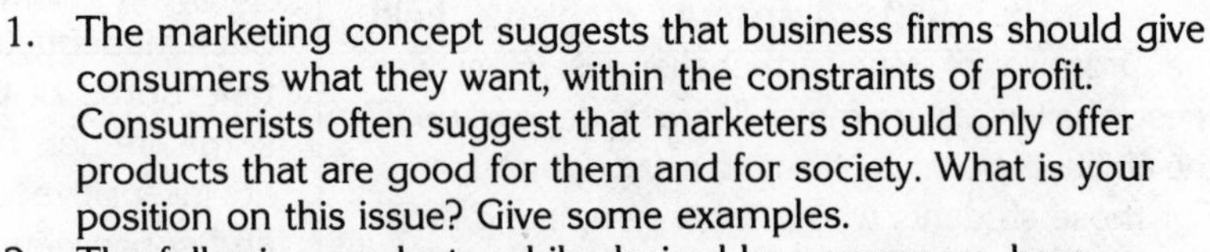

1. The marketing concept suggests that business firms should give consumers what they want, within the constraints of profit. Consumerists often suggest that marketers should only offer products that are good for them and for society. What is your position on this issue? Give some examples.
2. The following products, while desired by consumers, have disadvantageous social consequences: (A) disposable diapers; (B) cigarettes; (C) alcoholic beverages; (D) fuel-inefficient automobiles. What do you think should be done about these products?
3. Many critics of business believe that business firms should help alleviate societal problems by actions such as: (A) instigating programs to hire and train unskilled workers; (B) contributing corporate funds to social charities; (C) supporting educational television with corporate funds. Some companies do so. Opponents argue that corporate officers are simply agents of stockholders, and have no right to use stockholders' profits for such activities. What is your opinion?
4. Many consumers believe that excess business profits should be taxed to carry out socially desirable programs. What is your opinion?
5. John Kenneth Galbraith, the economist, argues that the marketing system promotes private consumption at the expense of public consumption. What do you believe should be done about this problem?

BUSINESS AND SOCIETY

During the 1970s, various consumer groups became concerned about advertising to children. Their basic argument was that because children are unable to distinguish between fact and fancy, between truth and exaggeration, they must be protected from the irresponsible persuasiveness of commercials. They further argued that, when parents refused children's requests for products seen in advertising, the child-parent relationship was injured. Many critics were particularly concerned over the advertising of sugary foods on programs directed to children.

In 1978, the FTC proposed a major restriction on children's television advertising. Specifically, the proposal included the following specifications:

- *Ban all advertising from TV shows seen by substantial audiences of children under 8 years of age because they are too young to understand the selling intent of the message.*
- *Ban advertising of sugary foods that pose a dental health risk from TV shows seen by significant numbers of children between the ages of 8 and 11.*
- *Allow continued TV advertising of less hazardous sugared foods to the 8 to 11 year old group, but only if individual food advertisers found "balancing" nutritional and/or health benefits.*

Needless to say, this proposal stirred up a great deal of controversy, and was both supported and opposed by highly vocal groups.

Assignment
Take a firm point of view on the FTC proposals and develop arguments in support of your position.

APPENDIX 1

A Sample Marketing Plan

The following marketing plan is for Golden Grain Grits, a fictitious product which has been devised to illustrate the way in which a marketing plan should be written, and the subject areas with which it typically deals.

Throughout the plan, references are made to exhibits that are not a part of the main body of the plan but which represent detailed analyses which provided data abstracted and summarized in the plan. These detailed exhibits have not been reproduced in this appendix. They serve to emphasize the kinds of backup data to which the reader of a marketing plan may refer for a more detailed understanding of the data presented.

The plan itself is a summarization of relevant findings that have been developed from extensive analyses of all data that might have a bearing on marketing objectives and strategies.

MARKET REVIEW

The following section summarizes key trends and developments in the canned grits market during the past twelve months. Data on retail distribution and sales is drawn from the A. C. Nielsen Food Index, unless otherwise noted.

- *Market Growth:* Total industry retail sales of canned grits products through grocery outlets reached 9.9 million cases during the year ending March 31, 1981, up 5.3 percent from the previous year. Based on the relatively uniform rate of growth during the past five years, it is estimated that the total market during Fiscal 1981–82 will reach 10.4 million cases.

Fiscal	Industry Retail Sales (1000's Cases)	Increase over previous year
1977–78	8,523.4	5.0%
1978–79	8,975.1	5.3%
1979–80	9,396.9	4.7%
1980–81	9,894.9	5.3%
1981–82 (est.)	10,399.5	5.1%

- *Regional Variations in Market Development:* Growth of the market continued to be uniform in all regions (Exhibit 1) with the result that two regions (S.E. & S.W.) continue to account for over 60 percent of all sales.

Regions	1000's Cases Fiscal 1980–81	% of Cases	% of Population	Consumer Index U.S. Average = 100
N.E.	791.6	8%	22%	36
S.W.	3,166.3	32	20	160
S.E.	2,968.5	30	18	167
N.C.	1,979.0	20	28	71
PAC.	989.5	10	12	83
U.S. Total	9,894.9	100%	100%	100

- *Shipments:* Golden Grain sales for Fiscal 1980–81 are currently estimated at 2,632,000 cases. While this represents an increase of 29,000 cases over last year, it is almost 100,000 cases below our 1980–81 objective of 2,730,000 cases. Failure to meet the case objective is attributed primarily to two factors: (a) trade loading during the final quarter of last year which adversely affected first quarter sales and (b) failure to achieve projected market share of 27.6 (estimated performance, 26.6 percent).

	Quarters 1st	2nd	3rd	4th	Total
Est. 1980–81 (1000's cs.)	695.0	663.0	681.0	691.0	2,730.0
Actual (1000's cs.)	645.0	651.5	660.0	675.5	2,632.0
Difference (1000's. cs)	−50.0	−11.5	−21.0	−15.5	−98.0

- *Competitive Shares:*

National. Examination of national share data for Fiscal 1980–81 compared to last year reveals three significant points: (1) Golden Grain's market share has decreased over one share point; (2) Chef's Choice exhibited a significant increase in market share; and (3) the long-term share growth of the All Other group appears to have been arrested.

	Brand Share—Total U.S. 1978–79	1979–80	1980–81*	1980–81 Percent Point Change
Golden Grain	27.2%	27.7%	26.6%	−1.1
Chef's Choice	35.0	32.5	35.0	+2.5
Martin's	14.3	15.3	14.5	−0.8
All Other	23.5	24.5	24.0	−0.5
Total	100.0%	100.0%	100.0%	

*Based on 8 months Nielsen data.

Regional. Golden Grain's national share loss can be traced entirely to the Southeastern Region where it experienced a share decline of 4.0 percentage points. This loss is the result of a sharp gain made by Chef's Choice at the expense of all brands.

Regional Share Comparisons for Golden Grain and Chef's Choice

Regions	1980–81 Golden Grain	1980–81 Chef's Choice	Share Change vs. Previous Year Golden Grain	Share Change vs. Previous Year Chef's Choice
N.E.	21.0%	32.5%	+0.2	—
S.W.	23.4	34.3	+0.5	−0.2
S.E.	30.2	38.1	−4.0	+5.3
N.C.	24.5	35.1	+0.9	+0.1
PAC.	28.7	37.6	+1.0	−0.4
Total	27.6%	35.0%	−1.2	+2.5

See Exhibit 4 for detailed analysis of regional brand share trends for all brands.

Chain versus Independent. Golden Grain's market share continues to lag behind Chef's Choice in chain stores to a greater extent than it does in independent outlets. This difference in performance is attributable to two factors: (1) distribution weaknesses in chains compared to Chef's Choice and (2) lower sales per store stocking than Chef's Choice in chains compared to independents.

	Chain Outlets Golden Grain	Chain Outlets Chef's Choice	Indep. Outlets Golden Grain	Indep. Outlets Chef's Choice
Brand Share	24.0%	37.1%	29.0%	32.9%
All Commodity Distribution	75%	85%	76%	78%
Sales Per Month Per Store Stocking	125	175	73	72

- *Distribution:* Regional examination of distribution for Golden Grain and competitive brands indicates:

(1) no major changes during the past year and (2) relatively uniform distribution by region. See Exhibit 5 for detailed distribution analysis.

- *Competitive Advertising and Promotion:* Expenditures. Chef's Choice and Martin's continue to outspend Golden Grain on a per case basis, and Chef's Choice consumer advertising remains the dominant force in the market. Significant competitive developments during the year have included:

  Chef's Choice's return to the use of daytime network television in September and increased advertising and promotion activity in the Southeastern Region directed primarily to black persons.

  Martin's shift in media emphasis from national magazines to local spot television concentrated in the top fifty U.S. markets.

  Estimated competitive expenditures in comparison to Golden Grain:

Estimated Direct Expenditures
January-December 1981 ($1,000's)

	Media	Promotion	Total	Est. expenditures per case (retail)
Golden Grain	$1,520	$380	$1,900	$0.72
Chef's Choice	2,200	500	2,700	0.80
Martin's	1,000	400	1,400	1.04

  Copy Evaluation. Two measurements of Golden Grain's 1980–81 advertising were employed during the past year.

  Theater tests of one of a pool of three commercials resulted in a competitive preference score of 14.8. This is significantly higher than our previous theater average (9.7) and the average of all competitive commercials tested (8.2).

  Although portfolio tests of our current magazine campaign indicated that it was on a par with last year's effort, subsequent Starch ratings have shown that it is significantly below the current Chef's Choice campaign in terms of both Noted and Seen-Associated scores.

  Promotional Activities. Promotion activity in the market continued to be characterized by periodic advertising allowances and intensive use of unbranded display material.

  The only significant developments were (1) the appearance of price-packs employed by Martin's nationally during the fall (results not yet available), (2) the use by Chef's Choice of heavily advertised mystery shopper promotions in black areas of the Southeastern Region.

- *Product Evaluation and Development.* Competitive Product Tests. A blind product test conducted by Golden Grain's Marketing Research Department in October indicated that Chef's Choice has improved its product texture and flavor.

  The present Chef's Choice product has apparently overcome disadvantages that it has had in these areas and is fully competitive with Golden Grain in terms of consumer preference.

  Product Research. R&D personnel have reported a temporary setback in their development of an improved product containing vitamin additives. Six-month storage tests of several alternative formulas are now being initiated in an attempt to improve product stability.

  Even if current storage tests are successful, manufacturing considerations will preclude introduction of an improved product before 1986.

- *Special Activities.* Product Usage. A special research study undertaken by the Clay Andrews Co. reveals that: (1) black per capita consumption of grits is substantially greater than was previously estimated (almost double the grits consumption of white families), and (2) there has been a sharp increase in multiple unit purchases since the previous study.

% of Total Transactions:	1978 Study	1980 Study
1 can	50%	36%
2 cans	35	32
3 or more cans	15	32
All Transactions	100%	100%
% of Total Unit Volume (All Brands):		
1 can	27%	21%
2 cans	45	27
3 or more cans	28	52
Total Units	100%	100%

  Advertising Research. An advertising penetration study conducted in September to establish a benchmark for advertising awareness revealed:

	Housewives Using Grits	
Brand	Claimed Aware of Advertising	Recalled 1 or More Sales Points
Golden Grain	30.4%	15.3%
Chef's Choice	40.3	17.2
Martin's	15.0	3.1

CONCLUSIONS—PROBLEMS AND OPPORTUNITIES

Based on the foregoing marketing review, the brand group has drawn the following conclusions pertinent to 1981–82 advertising:

- *Market Growth.* The continued strength of the grits market reaffirms our belief that the company should continue its aggressive advertising and promotion activity in order to achieve the long-range goal of brand leadership.
- *Media Strategy.* Our 1980–81 media strategy involving national magazines and spot television in selected markets appears to have been successful in achieving effective message penetration.
- *Advertising Copy.* The encouraging performance of our television commercials reaffirms our confidence in our copy strategy. However, the disappointing Starch performance of our print advertising indicates a need to strengthen the execution of the print effort.
- *Black market.* Two factors contribute to the conclusion that special emphasis should be given to the black consumer market: (1) new research data showing high per capita consumption of grits by blacks, and (2) share gains by Chef's Choice in the Southeast Region apparently achieved through stepped-up advertising and promotion activity directed to black consumers.
- *Chain Outlets.* There is a continued need to find effective devices for increasing our distribution and sales per store stocking in chain outlets.
- *Rate of Expenditure.* The elimination of Golden Grain's product advantage resulting from Chef's Choice's recent product improvement increases the burden that will have to be borne by advertising and promotion and decreases our confidence that we can continue to make share gains if we continue to be outspent by competition on both a total and cost-per-case basis.
- *Packaging.* Research findings that indicate an increase in multiple unit purchases by consumers suggest an opportunity for increasing our market share through the introduction of a multiple-pack or a larger package size.

GENERAL MARKETING OBJECTIVES

Proposed strategies and plans for Fiscal 1981–82 are based on the following basic marketing objectives:

- To attain the following case volume and market share, with a total expenditure of $2,580,000 for advertising and sales promotion:

	Est. Actual Fiscal 1980–81	Proposed Fiscal 1981–82	Change: 1981–82 vs. 1980–81
Industry Sales (cases)	9,894,900	10,399,500	+5.1%
Golden Grain Sales	2,632,000	2,870,000	+5.0%
Golden Grain Market Share	26.6%	27.6%	+1.0 points
Expenditures (adv./pro)	$1,900,000	$2,580,000	+36%
Expenditures per case	$.72	$0.90	+25%
Golden Grain Expenditures as % of Chef's Choice Estimated Expenditures	70%	90%*	

(Note: Sales and share figures may not correspond exactly due to inventory changes and minor errors in Nielsen volume estimates.)

*Assumes Chef's Choice will increase expenditures 5 percent, holding case rate constant and yielding a budget of approximately $2,830,000.

- To develop and test market both a multiple unit package and a large package size in order to ascertain the relative effectiveness of these two approaches in increasing market share—with the long range objective of adding to the product line during Fiscal 1982–83.

GENERAL MARKETING STRATEGY

Recommended activities designed to achieve the foregoing objectives are based on these major points of general marketing strategy:

- *Total planned expenditures* for advertising and promotion during Fiscal 1981–82 will be increased substantially versus this year in recognition of: (a) the competitive threat posed by Chef's Choice product improvement and dominant advertising weight, and (b) the objective of reversing Golden Grain's recent competitive setback by achieving volume and market share gains during 1981–82.
- *The augmented total marketing budget* for 1981–82 will be allocated generally as follows:

  Five percent of the total budget ($130,000) will be held in unallocated general reserve against the possibility that the volume objective cannot be met. A special recommendation for the disposition of this reserve will be submitted to management before November 1, 1981.

  An additional sum, not to exceed 5 percent of the

total budget ($130,000), will be set aside to defray the costs of test marketing and researching consumer acceptance of the multiple-unit and larger packages.

The remaining budget will be allocated between advertising and sales promotion in the ratio of approximately 80 percent/20 percent, implying that

Primary emphasis will continue to be placed on consumer advertising as a basic selling technique designed to influence brand preference among currrent users as well as contribute to further growth in the grits market.

Secondary emphasis will be given to sales promotion techniques capable of achieving temporary, periodic competitive advantages within the existing market.

- *Consistent with recent practice,* total marketing support will be distributed to

  Provide effective minimum sustaining advertising and promotion support in *all* areas of the country.

  Concentrate media weight in the Southeast and Southwest Sales Regions, where per capita brand and total industry sales are heavily concentrated. In view of the heavy inroads made by Chef's Choice in the Southeast Region, 1981–82 plans will place increased emphasis in this area.

  Concentrate promotion support insofar as practical (1) against chain outlets and (2) so as to capitalize seasonally on the October-March peak in consumer movement and the established trade pattern of "loading" during September.

- *In recognition of new information* bearing on the importance and responsiveness of the black market, increased emphasis will be placed during 1981–82 on special supplementary advertising and promotion activities directed specifically to the black consumer.

- *In view of the apparent success* of our current media and copy strategies, these basic strategies will be followed in 1981–82, with the recognition that

  Increased advertising funds will permit both an increase in our broad national effort as well as a concentration of pressure in key markets.

  New print copy must be developed and tested to strengthen execution of the current copy strategy.

ADVERTISING OBJECTIVES

- *To direct advertising to housewives* as the primary purchase group and place primary emphasis on

  Current users of grits, estimated to be 25 percent of total U.S. households, heavily concentrated in the two Southern Regions where breadth of usage reaches 50 percent of all families.

  Those socioeconomic groups that include the bulk of heavy users. That is, blacks; families in which the head of the household is under 40 years of age; larger, urban families; and families with average to slightly below average incomes.

- *To increase advertising* penetration levels as shown below and as measured by a new penetration study to be conducted approximately January 1982 (16 months after the previous study).

	Awareness Level	% Recalling One or More Sales Points
From (September 1980)	30.4%	15.3%
To (January 1982)	33.0%	16.5%

The objectives which appear above are based solely on judgment, since data is lacking that would provide a reliable basis for forecasting annual rates of change in advertising penetration.

- *To encourage retail grocery trade cooperation*—especially within chain outlets—by communicating Golden Grain brand strength to dealer personnel in buying, merchandising, and store management roles.

ADVERTISING STRATEGY

Key strategic considerations governing the use of advertising:

- *Advertising support* will be sustained throughout the year, but will

  Be reduced during June through August in recognition of reduced retail sales and media efficiency.

  Provide peak support during two periods of major promotional activity (September-October and February-March).

- *Advertising expenditures* in support of the two major promotions will not exceed $400,000 (20 percent of total media budget).

- *The basic copy unit* for print advertising will be a full-color page. This conclusion reflects both
  - Media requirements for continuity and brand reach, and
  - Creative requirements for dominant space and appealing product-use illustrations.
- Recognizing the need to achieve maximum consumer pressure in view of aggressive competitive activity, advertising production expense will be limited to a maximum of 3 percent of the total advertising budget through the reuse of existing television commercials and the production of not more than four new print ads.

COPY STRATEGY

- *Consumer Copy*
  - Golden Grain will be sold primarily on the basis of its superior creaminess and flavor.
  - Copy presentation will identify the product with appealing southern traditions and institutions (Detailed rationale for the foregoing conclusions is provided in Appendix 7).
  - The mood of the copy will be dignified but friendly, emphasizing the gracious traditions that are associated with southern living.
  - Copy will recognize that grits are a staple food that may properly be served at any meal or on any occasion.
- *Trade Copy*
  - Golden Grain will be presented to the trade in terms of its high dollar volume and its superior opportunity for profits.
  - This representation is possible because of Golden Grain's strong market position, its growing consumer franchise, its relatively high unit profit, and its responsiveness to display.
  - The copy tone will be responsible, straightforward, and businesslike.
  - Golden Grain Grits is a food staple which, because of its compatibility with a wide variety of foods, offers ample opportunity for tie-in promotions.

COPY PLAN

- *Television copy.* TV copy, executed last year in the form of a pool of three 30-second commercials is characterized chiefly by the following:
  - Both creaminess and flavor claims are employed. Emphasis is given to the creaminess claim, which is supported by a video comparison of the particle sizes of Golden Grain (extra fine) and an unidentified "leading brand" (coarse).
  - Important use is made of extreme close-up shots of the product in usage situations in association with appetizing southern specialties such as ham, yams, and black-eyed peas.
  - The introduction and concluding 10-seconds of each commercial employ the grits jingle sung by an off-camera chorus.
  - Product usage situations include family dining occasions characterized by graciousness and family participation.
  - User families are depicted as younger families with children in the 6 to 12 age group.
  - All package close-ups open with a view of the product itself and pull back to reveal the entire front panel.
- *Consumer print copy.* New print copy is currently under development. A revised print copy plan will be submitted on or about February 1, 1981.
- *Trade print copy.* Trade print copy represents an extension of the 1980–81 campaign and is characterized by
  - Pictorial emphasis on the product selling from mass display.
  - Statistics from the Dillon Study demonstrating the profit importance of grits.
  - The use of various headlines that dramatize the sales increases obtained by actual retailers when they displayed Golden Grain Grits.

MEDIA STRATEGY

Recommended media plans were developed within the framework of these basic points of media strategy:

- *National consumer magazines* will be employed as the product's basic medium primarily on the basis of: (a) their national coverage, (b) their ability to concentrate messages among younger housewives, and (c) their unique strength as a vehicle for both the dissemination of recipes and the appetizing portrayal of the product.
- *Local spot television* will be employed on a regional basis as an important supplementary medium designed to (a) complement the coverage achieved with consumer magazines, and (b) permit the brand to apply increased media weight in sales regions where potential is greatest. Spot television is selected in preference to other local and regional media primarily on the basis of its cost efficiency, broad reach, ability to extend message reach into

middle and lower-middle income groups, and its strength as a fully-dimensional copy vehicle.

- *Black radio* will be employed in selected markets to provide selective, supplemental coverage of black consumers in recognition that the basic consumer magazine program will not achieve broad reach among this high-potential group.
- *The relative emphasis* to be placed on each of the three consumer media will be determined primarily on the following two points of strategy:

  Total media expenditures per case of Golden Grain retail sales will be approximately the same in each region, except that additional weight will be applied in the Southeast Region to counter Chef's Choice's aggressive effort there.

  Total media expenditures per case will be relatively greater in markets that include substantial concentrations of black consumers.
- *Significant strategic conclusions* regarding the use of each recommended medium include:

  Consumer Magazines:

  A minimum of six insertions will be run in each magazine used to insure adequate frequency of impressions and provide continuity of support throughout the year.

  Preferred position space (basic unit: one page, four colors) will be used where available at attractive rates to increase readership of each ad.

  Spot Television:

  Thirty-second daytime and late evening commercials will be purchased in order to reach housewives with the greatest possible efficiency.

  Spot television will be purchased in separate waves of support during the year in order to maintain competitively effective short-term levels of reach and frequency and to concentrate support during the peak months of consumer sales.

MEDIA PLAN

The principal features of the media plan (see budget summary) are

- The use of eight consumer magazines. Five of these publications have been employed during the past two years and are considered the primary coverage group (nine insertions each). *True Story* and *Modern Romances* have been added to the list this year to extend coverage of blue-collar housewives (see Exhibit 8 for analysis of magazine coverage by income and occupational subgroup). *Ebony* has also been added this year to increase coverage of black consumers. The three new publications are scheduled to receive only six insertions each (all insertions are full-page, four-color units).
- The plan also provides for the use of spot television in 30 markets. The proposed market list (Exhibit 9) includes all major markets in the Southeast and Southwest regions. These 30 markets will provide coverage of an estimated 80 percent of all households in the Southeast and Southwest regions.
- Each spot television market will receive 60 to 100 gross rating points weekly for a total of twenty-six weeks, which will be divided into four waves of spot activity:

Wave No.	No. Weeks	Weekly GRP	Period
1	6	60	4/1–5/15
2	8	100	9/1–10/30
3	4	60	11/1–12/1
4	8	100	2/1–3/30

The proposed levels of spot television weight will develop an estimated reach and frequency during each four-week period of activity:

	60 GRP	100 GRP
Reach (% TV homes covered)	40%	60%
Average Frequency	6.0	6.6

- *The plan also provides* for 30 weeks of spot radio activity on 26 black stations in 21 markets (Exhibit 10 provides market list, estimated costs and a brief rationale for the market selection.) These 21 markets together provide coverage of an estimated 64 percent of total U.S. black population.

SALES PROMOTION STRATEGY

Within the broad framework of its role in providing strong, periodic sales stimulus, it is proposed that the specific objectives of Golden Grain's 1981–82 promotion program continue to be to stimulate product trial and repurchase by (1) gaining trade support in the forms of in-store display and price features by retailers, and (b) communicating appealing new product usage ideas to consumers via both point-of-purchase materials and general consumer advertising integrated with the promotion effort. Basic strategy for achieving these objectives will provide that:

- *Primary emphasis* will continue to be placed on direct trade incentives in the form of merchandising allowances. This recommendation is in keeping with the generally favorable results achieved by similar promotions during the past two years.
- *Departing from recent practice,* merchandising allowance support will take the form of contractual payments to retailers for in-store displays complying with substantial, but reasonable minimum quantities of product (that is, $5 payment for a ten–case display; $15 for a twenty-five-case display). The specific purpose of this approach will be to stimulate cooperation on the part of chain and large independent outlets.
- *All major promotions* involving merchandising allowances will be designed to capitalize on the special opportunities to tie in with other manufacturers in order to (a) reduce investment requirements for point-of-purchase materials, and (b) extend sales force coverage by utilizing personnel of the cooperating manufacturer, and (c) extend consumer advertising support.
- *Total basic national promotional* weight will be concentrated in two tie in merchandising allowance efforts during the year. These major efforts will be timed to capitalize on the seasonal peak in consumer movement and the established pattern of trade loading during September-October and February-March.
- *In recognition of the special opportunity* for promoting the product among black consumers in the Southeast Region, a supplementary effort will be initiated regionally during the year on a trial basis. Strategy governing this effort will provide for:

  Adoption of the proven "pay day" promotion format based on cash payments to black families who have the product on hand when called upon by a representative of the company.

  The use of aggressive local media advertising to support this promotion. Local spot radio will be devoted entirely to this program during the promotion period.

SALES PROMOTION PLAN

The basic sales promotion plan (see budget summary) provides for:

- Two major, tie-in promotions, one during September-October, and the other during February-March. (See Exhibit 12 for basis of allowance cost estimates.)
- A regional (Southeast Region) promotion for black consumers to be initiated in September (the earliest possible date for the availability of materials) and to continue throughout the fiscal year. (See Exhibit 13 for assumptions and estimated costs.)

SPECIAL ACTIVITIES—NEW PACKAGE TESTING

General marketing objectives and strategy provide that test marketing will be employed during 1981–82 to evaluate two new packaging concepts: (1) a larger size can, and (2) a multican package. Basic points of strategy affecting the development and testing of these new packages are as follows:

- The two package concepts will be developed and test marketed independently. Although it may subsequently prove desirable to gain market experience with both new packages in a single area, testing during the 1981–82 period will be conducted independently to (a) allow each project to progress at its own rate and (b) limit the number of variables to be evaluated under controlled conditions.
- Basic strategy provides that each package will be introduced in limited test areas representing 1 to 3 percent of total U.S. population for at least six months. Further, the program(s) of introductory support for each new package will be developed on the basis of a national effort, which will then be translated to the test areas.
- The basic technique for evaluating test market results will be the measurement of brand market share by means of retail store panel audits. Field checks and sales reports will be employed as secondary measurements of distribution, pricing, and trade attitude.
- Study of various alternatives for executing the two packaging concepts leads to these conclusions:

  That the large can should be 16-ounces because:

  - a 16-ounce can will meet the needs of larger families (16 ounces will provide 5 to 7 servings).
  - a 16-ounce can could probably be priced to retail in the favorable 43 to 45¢ range and permit special promotional pricing of 39¢ with trade cooperation.

  The multican package should contain three 8–ounce cans banded together to retail at 59¢ versus an average of 63¢ for three 8-ounce cans purchase separately.

- It will be a basic point of marketing strategy to limit the investment involved in introducing one or both of the new packages to not more than $70,000 during one fiscal year and to conduct all special activities in behalf of the new packages on the basis of a one-year theoretical payout. This implies that new funds may be requested if a volume increase can be projected.
- Basic strategy will also provide that national expansion will be executed in a series of two to four steps covering a period of not more than 18 months and not less than 9 months. A minimum of 9 months is recommended to insure adequate time for appraisal of results in the first expansion area.
- Label design work for the new packages will proceed on the assumption that it is strategically sound to relate the new labels very closely to the existing label for the 8-ounce can. However, an important objective in the final test plan will be to use marketing research to make sure that the recommended label designs are free from confusing elements.

Specific objectives and plans and estimated expenditures will be submitted separately (by June 15, 1981) when complete data is available regarding (a) delivery schedules for the new packages, (b) costs and margins, and (c) consumer acceptance of the new packages in panel placement tests.

GOLDEN GRAIN: SUMMARY OF PROPOSED ADVERTISING AND SALES PROMOTION ADVERTISING

Consumer Magazines	
6 to 9 4-color pages in 8 magazines; total exposure of 84.5 million. Estimated net unduplicated coverage of 56% of U.S. households:	$ 940,000
9 Pages 4C — *LH Journal*, *Good Housekeeping*, *Redbook*, *Family Circle*	
6 Pages 4C — *Ebony*, *True Story*, *Modern Romances* (exhibit 11 provides detail)	
Spot Television	
60 to 100 Gross Rating Points weekly for 26 weeks in 30 markets in the SE and SW Regions (exhibit 19).	710,000
Spot Radio	
15 to 20 60-second commercials weekly for 30 weeks on estimated 26 radio stations in 21 markets (exhibit 10).	173,000
Production, Preparation, Use	
Magazines: Prepare 4-color pages	$ 15,000
TV: Est. talent fees & misc.	8,000
Radio: Production and est. talent fees for pool of 6 commercials	4,000
Total Advertising	$1,860,000
Major tie-in promotion based on 50¢/case display allowance; national magazine support.	200,000
February-March: Repeat Fall tie-in promotion:	200,000
"Pay Day" Black consumers promotion—SE Region	40,000
Promotion materials	30,000
Total Promotion	$ 470,000
RESERVES	
For test marketing 2 new packages	130,000
General reserves (5% of budget)	130,000
Total Reserves	260,000
Grand Total	$2,580,000

APPENDIX 2

MARKETING ARITHMETIC

Marketing has sometimes been referred to as a "numbers game." This reference is valid in the sense that marketing results are ultimately evaluated in quantitative terms. In earlier chapters, we have used various arithmetic devices as marketing tools. In Chapter 4 (The Marketing Plan), for example, we emphasized the need to express marketing objectives in quantitative terms. In Chapter 5 (Some Useful Methods of Analysis), we introduced the concepts of per capita consumption, index numbers, market potential, market saturation, market share, and all commodity distribution—all quantitative concepts. And, in a number of the chapter problems, we have dealt with simple quantitative concepts.

Anyone who works on the business side of marketing must be comfortable working with numbers. One need not be a sophisticated mathematician to work in marketing because, for the most part, marketing deals with simple arithmetic concepts—with ratios, percentages, index numbers, and so forth. But, one needs to be comfortable with numbers.

In this appendix, we will explore five areas of marketing arithmetic with which marketers constantly deal. These five areas are: (1) the operating statement; (2) operating ratios; (3) stockturn ratios; (4) markups; and (5) markdowns.

THE OPERATING STATEMENT

The operating statement, also referred to as the income statement, the profit and loss statement, and the P&L, is the most frequently used source of internal cost and performance data. In short, it is a succinct summary of five elements:

TABLE 1: Operating Statements

XYZ Manufacturing Company for the period ending Dec. 31, 1981

Sales		
Gross sales	$350,000	
Less returns and allowances	15,000	
Net sales		$335,000
Cost of goods		
Finished inventory (beginning)	$ 30,000	
Cost of goods manufactured	196,000	
Cost of goods available for sale	$226,000	
Less ending inventory	25,000	
Cost of goods		$201,000
Gross margin		
Gross margin		$134,000
Expenses		
Administrative expense	$ 20,000	
Marketing expense	80,000	
Other expense	10,000	
		$110,000
Profit		
Net profit before taxes		$ 24,000

ABC Retail Company for period ending Dec. 31, 1981

Sales			
Gross sales	$812,000		
Less returns and allowances	28,000		
Net sales			$784,000
Cost of goods			
Beginning inventory at cost		$140,000	
Purchases at billed cost	$430,000		
Less purchase discounts	20,000		
Purchases at net cost	$410,000		
Plus freight-in	3,000		
Net cost of delivered purchases		413,000	
Cost of goods available for sale		$553,000	
Less ending inventory		105,000	
Cost of goods			$448,000
Gross margin			
Gross margin			$336,000
Expenses			
Administrative expense		$133,000	
Marketing expense		110,000	
Other expense		23,000	
			$266,000
Profit			
Net profit before taxes			$ 70,000

(1) sales; (2) cost of goods; (3) gross margin, also referred to as gross profit and manufacturing profit (in a manufacturing firm); (4) expenses; and (5) net profit before taxes. All operating statements contain these five elements, although they may be expressed in somewhat different terms, depending upon the nature of the business. Table 1, for example, shows a summary operating statement for a manufacturing firm and for a retail business. In these two statements, each of the elements of the operating statement is shown in a separate block, so that the elements may be readily separated and identified.

The periods of time covered by operating statements vary. Generally, operating statements are prepared monthly (for the past month), quarterly (for the past quarter) and yearly (for the past year). The amount of detail shown in each of the elements of the operating statement will vary, depending upon the detail required for the analysis that is to be made. The two operating statements shown in Table 1 are *summary* statements. Details of the various elements of the statement are available in separate schedules. For example, a separate schedule for cost of goods manufactured would contain entries on wages, maintenance and repairs, heat, light, and power, and so forth in order to show all of the costs that make up the cost of goods. Marketing expenses might be broken down further into sales expense, advertising expense, sales promotion expense, transportation expense, warehouse expense, and so forth. Companies may allocate certain expenses in somewhat different ways and to different categories depending upon individual company and industry practices. However, legal restrictions and "accepted accounting procedure" statements issued by professional accounting organizations such as the Financial Accounting Standards Board (FASB) provide guidelines and rulings governing such allocations.

With this background, let's look at each of the elements of the operating statement more carefully.

Sales

The sales portion of the operating statement begins with the firm's *gross sales*, or the total sales revenue received by the firm during a designated operating period. Gross sales, however, do not provide a true picture of income because some goods are returned, some are damaged resulting in a partial credit to purchasers, or discounts may be given for quantity purchases. Thus, in order to obtain an accurate picture of the actual revenue retained by a firm, *returns and allowances* must be subtracted from gross sales to obtain *net sales*. Net sales represent the actual income that a firm receives.

Cost of Goods

The cost of goods section of the operating statement contains several items. It begins with a statement of the inventory on hand at the beginning of the operating period. This is referred to as *beginning inventory*. To this beginning inventory must be added the additional *goods acquired* during the operating period. In the case of a manufacturing firm, these additional goods are those manufactured by the company. For a retail business, the additional goods acquired are those purchased during the operating period. The combination of the beginning inventory plus the goods acquired during the operating period make up the total *goods available for sale*.

Firms seldom sell all of the goods they have available for sale during a particular operating period. In order to determine what is actually sold, one must subtract the *ending inventory*. So, the *cost of goods sold* is obtained by subtracting the *ending inventory* from the *cost of goods available for sale*.

Gross Margin

Also referred to as gross profit and (in a manufacturing firm) manufacturing profit, gross margin is obtained by subtracting the *cost of goods sold* from *net sales*. Gross margin represents the total funds derived from operations during the operating period that the firm has to cover expenses and net profit.

Expenses

Expenses cover all expenses, other than cost of goods, incurred by a firm during the operating period. They include various *administrative expenses* such as accounting, personnel, executive salaries, and so forth. Expenses also include *marketing expenses*, such as salaries and commissions for sales and other marketing personnel, advertising, sales promotion, marketing research, etc. The final category in the expense section of the operating statement is *other expenses*, such as interest, depreciation, utilities, insurance, office supplies, travel and entertainment, and so forth. All expenses must be subtracted from the gross margin in order to obtain *net profit before taxes*.

Net Profit Before Taxes

Net profit before taxes is sometimes referred to as "the bottom line." Representing the net profit that a company earns during a particular operating period, the net profit for a year-end operating statement will be further modified by taxes, tax credits, unusual gains and losses, and so forth, However, the performance of a firm is gauged on the basis of net profit.

Since the operating statement is a key control document, marketing personnel need to be intimately familiar with it, its component parts, and their interrelationships.

OPERATING RATIOS

The operating statement shows in dollars how well a firm performs during a given operating period. Management, however, is also interested in how well a firm performs in comparison to budgets and in comparison to past periods of operation. *Operating ratios* are a useful tool for making such comparisons.

TABLE 2: Comparative analysis of selected operating statement items using operating ratios.

	1977		1978		1979		1980		1981	
	Dollars (000s)	%	Dollars (000s)	%	Dollars (000s)	%	Dollars (000s)	%	Dollars (000s)	%
Net Sales	$6,890.0	100.0%	$7,560.5	100.0%	$9,680.7	100.0%	$10,690.0	100.0%	$12,990.3	100.0%
Cost of goods sold										
Materials	2,790.5	40.5	3,069.6	40.6	3,882.0	40.1	4,255.0	39.8	5,118.1	39.4
Labor	399.6	5.8	430.9	5.7	580.8	6.0	652.1	6.1	805.4	6.2
Overhead	206.7	3.0	241.9	3.2	300.1	3.1	352.8	3.3	441.7	3.4
Freight	709.7	10.3	786.3	10.4	1,006.8	10.4	1,122.5	10.5	1,377.0	10.6
Total	$4,106.5	59.6%	$4,528.7	59.9%	$5,769.7	59.6%	$ 6,382.4	59.7%	$ 7,742.2	59.6%
Selling costs										
Salaries and expenses	723.5	10.5	824.1	10.9	1,093.9	11.3	1,304.3	12.2	1,623.8	12.5
Advertising and promotion	613.2	8.9	688.0	9.1	1,190.7	12.3	1,443.2	13.5	1,857.6	14.3
Miscellaneous sales exp.	68.9	1.0	83.2	1.1	106.5	1.1	139.0	1.3	155.9	1.2
Total	$1,405.6	20.4%	$1,595.3	21.1%	$2,391.1	24.7%	$ 2,886.5	27.0%	$ 3,637.3	28.0%
Administrative Costs	675.2	9.8	748.5	9.9	977.8	10.1	1,090.5	10.2	1,299.0	10.0
Other expenses	34.4	0.5	45.4	0.6	58.1	0.6	64.1	0.6	78.0	0.6
Total expense	6,221.7	90.3	6,917.9	91.5	9,196.7	95.0	10,423.5	97.5	12,756.5	98.2
Net Profits	$ 688.3	9.7%	$ 642.6	8.5%	$ 484.0	5.0%	$ 267.3	2.5%	$ 233.8	1.8%

Operating ratios are obtained by dividing each item on the operating statement by net sales. The particular operating items converted to operating ratios are those which the analyst considers relevant. Table 2 shows a comparison of selected items from a detailed operating statement for a five-year period.

An examination of the dollar figures in Table 2 indicates that, although net sales have increased from $6,840,000 to $12,990,000, profits have declined from $668,300 to $233,800. Since all dollar costs and expenses have also risen substantially during the five–year period, the source of the profit erosion is not readily apparent. However, when operating ratios are computed, the nature of the problem becomes clear.

An examination of the gross margin ratios indicates that they have hovered around 40 percent, indicating that cost of goods is not the problem. Therefore, the problem lies in the expense area. Examination of various expense ratios quickly identifies *selling costs* as the culprit. The operating ratios for advertising and promotion have increased from 8.9 percent in 1977 to 12.5 percent in 1981. The salaries and expenses portion has increased from 10.5 percent of net sales in 1977 to 12.5 percent in 1981. Clearly, these two expense areas have gotten out of hand and are responsible for the company's poor profit performance. Although increases in net sales are generally desirable, such increases are unjustified when they are made by a long-term sacrifice of profit.

STOCKTURN RATE

The stockturn rate is an important measure of performance because it reflects the speed with which a firm's inventories are moving. Management is keenly interested in stockturn rate because: (1) a reduction in stockturn rate may indicate the accumulation of unpopular items in the firm's inventory assortment; and (2) a reduction in stockturn rate means that more working capital invested in inventory is required to obtain the same volume of sales.

Stockturn rate may be computed for any operating period, although it is generally more useful when computed on the basis of a year's operations, so that it is not distorted by seasonal factors or other temporary variations in sales velocity. Stockturn rate may be computed on three bases, all of which produce the same result. It may be computed: (1) on the basis of costs; (2) on the basis of selling price; and (3) on the basis of units. The three formulas for these computations are:

Cost basis: $\dfrac{\text{Cost of goods sold}}{\text{Average inventory at cost}}$

Selling price basis: $\dfrac{\text{Net sales}}{\text{Average inventory at selling price}}$

Unit basis: $\dfrac{\text{Sales in units}}{\text{Average inventory in units}}$

Generally computing stockturn rate on the basis of cost is more convenient because the figures for these computations are readily available in the operating statement. Cost of goods sold may be taken directly from the operating statement. Average inventory is obtained by adding beginning inventory and ending inventory and dividing by two.

Using the operating statement for a retail store shown in Table 1 as an example, the computation of stockturn rate would be:

$$\frac{\text{Cost of goods sold}}{\text{Average inventory}} =$$

$$\frac{448{,}000}{(140{,}000 + 105{,}000) \div 2} = \frac{448{,}000}{122{,}500} = 3.6$$

In other words, the retail store in the example is turning over its inventory an average of 3.6 times a year.

MARKUPS

A markup is the amount added to the cost of goods in order to obtain a selling price. A markup is similar to the concept of gross margin, since it is the amount a firm has to cover its expenses and profit. An example of a markup is:

Cost of item	$6.00
Markup	3.00
Selling price	$9.00

Markups are generally expressed as percentages, and may be computed on the basis of *selling price* or *cost. Generally, however, markup is computed on the basis of selling price unless it is specifically stated that it is computed on the basis of cost.*

This distinction is important because a markup based on selling price and a markup based on cost yield different percentages. Thus, using the previous example:

$$\text{Markup on selling price} = \frac{\$3.00}{\$9.00} = 33\tfrac{1}{3} \text{ percent}$$

$$\text{Markup on cost} = \frac{\$3.00}{\$6.00} = 50 \text{ percent}$$

One can convert a percentage markup based on cost to a percentage markup based on selling price and vice versa with the following formulas:

$$\%\text{ markup on selling price} = \frac{\%\text{ markup on cost}}{100\% + \%\text{ markup on cost}}$$

$$\%\text{ markup on cost} = \frac{\%\text{ markup on selling price}}{100\% - \%\text{ markup on selling price}}$$

MARKDOWNS

Thus far, the operating ratios which we have discussed can all be derived from the operating statement. Another ratio that is widely used by retail stores is the markdown. *The markdown cannot be obtained directly from the operating statement.* Instead, it requires a special computation.

A markdown is a retail price reduction that is often necessary because customers will not buy a product at its original price. To dispose of such merchandise, the retailer must markdown or reduce the selling price. Markdowns may occur for a variety of reasons—damaged or soiled goods, a sales promotion to attract customers to the store, or because the buyer for the store made a bad buy. That is, the buyer bought some merchandise that simply does not sell at the price for which it is originally offered.

Most often, markdowns are necessary in retail operations because of errors in buying. As a consequence, markdowns are generally considered as business errors.

Markdowns are similar to allowances because in both cases a price concession is made in order to obtain sales. As a consequence, markdown ratios are computed by combining markdowns and allowances and dividing by net sales.

$$\text{Markdown} = \frac{\$\text{ markdown} + \$\text{ allowance}}{\$\text{ net sales}}$$

The operating statement for a retail store generally combines *returns and allowances* as a single entry. In order to compute a markdown ratio, however, returns and allowances must be separated because returns are not included in computing the markdown ratio. Returns are not included because returns are considered as *customers' errors,* whereas markdowns are considered as a *business error.*

Store managers compute markdown ratios as a measure of the efficiency of their buyers. Buyers whose markdown ratios consistently exceed the average are doing a poor job. Again, markdowns *cannot* be computed from the operating statement because markdowns take place *before* goods are sold, and are already reflected in the gross sales figure.

SUMMARY COMMENT ON MARKETING ARITHMETIC

The purpose of this appendix has been to describe some of the analytical ratios that are useful to marketers, and to emphasize the importance of the operating statement as a source of performance data. Other ratios that can be derived from a firm's operating statement and balance sheet are also useful, but are beyond the scope of this text.

The point is that anyone who expects to work in the business side of marketing must be intimately familiar with the operating statement and the uses that can be made of this document.

REVIEW QUESTIONS

1. Distinguish between the following terms: operating statement, P&L, and income statement; gross sales and net sales; gross margin and gross profit; cost of goods and expenses.
2. Given the following data, prepare a summary operating statement:

Gross sales	$530,000
Net sales	510,000
Purchases at billed cost	300,000
Purchases at net cost	290,000
Net cost of delivered purchases	292,000
Cost of goods available for sale	460,000
Cost of goods sold	320,000
Net profit before taxes	40,000

3. Based on the operating statement in problem 2, compute each of the following operating ratios: cost of goods sold, gross margin, net profit before taxes, stockturn rate.
4. Given the following information, compute markup: Cost = $12.00; Selling price = $18.00.
5. Given the following markups on cost, compute markup on selling price: 20%, 25%, 33⅓%, 40%, 50%.
6. Given the following markups on selling price, compute the markup on cost: 15%, 20%, 25%, 30%, 33⅓%.
7. Given the following information, compute the markdown ratio.

Gross sales	$615,000
Returns	10,000
Allowances	15,000
Net sales	597,000
Markdowns	30,000

8. Why cannot markdown ratios be computed from the operating statement?
9. What are the three ways in which stockturn rate can be computed? Why is it usually more convenient to compute the stockturn rate on the basis of costs?
10. Why are operating ratios useful for analysis of the operating statement?

APPENDIX 3

CAREER OPPORTUNITIES IN MARKETING

Most students, at some point in their college programs, wrestle with the problem of choosing a career, and worry about their ability to find jobs after they have completed their college educations. For a few, this experience is traumatic and filled with anxiety. For these students, the underlying concern seems to be summed up in the question: "Is there really a place in the business world for me?"

The answer to this question is "Yes!" In a nation of over 14 million business firms, there is a never ceasing demand for people with a wide diversity of skills, interests, and temperaments. Opportunities abound in all of the functional areas of study represented in business schools—accounting, data processing, economics, finance, management, marketing, and production. Further, career opportunities exist in all kinds of organizations—manufacturing, retailing, service industries, and in government. Opportunities also exist in large organizations, in small ones, and in starting independent businesses.

The real problem is not finding a job, but choosing a career that will provide a high level of satisfaction, and an opportunity for growth and advancement.

This appendix identifies some of the career opportunities in marketing, and offers some broad guidelines in choosing a career and obtaining an entry level job.

CAREERS IN MARKETING

Most students, when considering marketing as a professional field, have three basic questions: (1) what salary levels can one expect in entry level positions; (2) what are the opportunities for advancement; and (3) what careers are available. Let's look at each of these questions separately.

Entry Level Salaries

Many students are concerned about entry level salaries. This concern is natural, but perhaps overemphasized. When choosing lifetime careers, beginning salaries are less important than opportunities for growth and advancement. Yet, the concern is there.

During a period of inflation such as we are currently experiencing, entry level salaries change on a year-by-year basis, and a specific salary figure based on 1981 will be out of date by 1982, and even further out of date by 1983. However, according to the Endicott Report, an annual report issued by the Northwestern University Placement Center, the average entry level salary for sales and marketing positions in 1981 was $17,200, up 8 percent from 1980. By comparison, the average entry level salary for all business administration graduates in 1981 was $16,200.

Note that these salary figures are averages. Obviously, some students receive entry level salaries that are less than this amount and others receive more. Also note that salary levels for different functional areas—accounting, data processing, finance, marketing, and so forth—vary year by year depending upon demand. However, sales and marketing entry level salaries are consistently average or above when compared with other business school disciplines.

Opportunities for Advancement

Opportunities for advancement within the field of marketing are virtually unlimited. Key determinants are the individual's competencies, willingness to work, ability to express oneself well in both written and oral communications, ability to work effectively with others and, of course, the growth rate and promotion policies of the firm for which one works.

There is no question that chance—random factors—plays a role in personal progress. Being in the right place at the right time with the appropriate skills and experience is always a consideration. Yet, random factors tend to average out over the long run, and the field of marketing is filled with opportunity.

Each year, *Sales and Marketing Management* publishes a survey of the highest salaries being paid to sales and marketing executives. These salaries consistently run over a quarter of a million dollars. In 1976 *Fortune* magazine published profiles of the chief executive officers of the 500 largest U.S. corporations. Almost 28 percent of these chief executive officers had career backgrounds in marketing and distribution—a higher percentage than any other business discipline.

Not everyone will become a chief executive officer of one of the Fortune 500 companies. But, that's not the point. The point is that the opportunity is there, and a career in marketing can be highly rewarding from a financial point of view.

What Careers Are Available?

Peter Drucker has said that the purpose of a business is to create a customer, and that the two basic functions of a business are marketing and innovation. It follows from this that all business firms—regardless of their fields of operation—engage in marketing. The total number of marketing related jobs is enormous—some 40 percent of the U.S. work force is engaged in marketing-related activities. Some of these jobs are routine—working at a checkout counter in a grocery store, for example—but many are challenging. Marketing jobs exist at the entry level, in middle management, and at the top of the management hierarchy. There are too many marketing-related jobs to talk about each of them separately. So, instead of identifying specific jobs, I will briefly discuss major areas of opportunity for those who choose marketing careers.

In most of these career areas, the entry level job for a college graduate is that of a trainee or assistant. Few college graduates begin their business careers as managers. Rather, management positions are earned by performance, dedication, hard work, and loyalty.

Sales. By far, the most common of all marketing positions is in the area of sales. But, as pointed out in Chapter 17 (Personal Selling), there are many different kinds of sales positions. Some require technical degrees in engineering or the sciences, but most do not. Most large companies recruit their sales personnel from the ranks of college graduates.

Although, sales managers from different companies employ different criteria in selecting sales personnel, they often look for people who are outgoing, articulate, comfortable in meeting and working with others, and capable of assuming responsibility for scheduling their own work.

Most generally, sales recruits are enrolled in a company training program and provided with field supervision before they are assigned to a sales territory. From that point on, personal progress is largely the responsibility of the individual who, on the basis of performance and demonstrated ability, is moved up through the ranks to district, regional, and general sales manager.

Many companies also provide opportunities for lateral transfers. That is, after individuals have demonstrated their competencies, they are given opportunities to transfer to other areas of the organization.

Marketing Research. Marketing research, although small in relation to sales, represents a challenging career area. Marketing research personnel are hired by consumer and industrial firms, by advertising agencies, and by marketing research organizations.

To be successful in marketing research, one should have an inquisitive bent; enjoy analysis; have a basic background in quantitative methods, research methodology, and data processing; and be well organized and good at planning.

Product Management. Product managers are employed by both consumer and industrial firms. Their primary tasks are to analyze marketing performance, to develop marketing plans and supervise their execution, and to work with other departments of the company, as well as with the firm's advertising agency.

To be successful as a product manager, one needs to be analytical, imaginative, and capable of supervising and working well with others. Since product managers seldom have direct authority over those with whom they work, they need to be good in developing productive interpersonal relations and at enlisting cooperation. Also, product managers should be able to express their ideas orally and in writing.

Purchasing Agent/Buyer. The purchasing agent or buyer may work for a manufacturing company, for the government, or for a retail operation. The particular responsibilities required of purchasing agents and buyers vary widely depending upon the individual firm and its business.

At lower levels of the company, the position of buyer may be largely routine. At the highest level, buyers participate in setting standards, and in negotiating with sellers.

In the retail field—particularly in department stores—buyers have a great deal of discretion. Generally, they are in charge of departments and are responsible not only for selecting and buying merchandise, but also for its sale to the final customers.

Successful buyers need to be analytical, to have good judgment, to be evaluative, and capable of assuming the responsibility for important decisions. They work closely with data on costs and, in the retail field, must be intimately involved in inventory control, advertising and promotion, and thoroughly familiar with the uses of operating statements.

Packaging Specialists. Packaging manufacturers recruit interested people from a variety of fields because there is little formal academic training in packaging. Positions in this field range from simple selling of routine packages and packaging materials to package design and helping customers solve their packaging problems.

To be successful in this area, one needs to be a problem solver, to have a thorough knowledge of packaging materials, packaging handling equipment, and costs. The knowledge and training required in this area are, essentially, gained from experience in the field.

Distribution Channel Management. Careers in distribution management range all of the way from "channel relations," which is essentially a public relations-selling position, to traffic management and logistics. In this latter area, a knowledge of data processing, systems, finance, accounting, and quantitative methods is often important.

Advertising. Advertising careers exist in advertising agencies and client organizations that produce products and services. In client organizations, the importance of the advertising department varies widely. In some companies, the position of advertising manager is a high-ranking, high-paying, executive position. In others, a middle management position.

In client companies, the role of the advertising department is to administer advertising budgets, to develop advertising materials, and to buy advertising media. Many companies, however, do not develop or place their own advertising. Instead, this work is done by advertising agencies which, in turn, are supervised by the company's advertising department.

Of the many market-related career opportunities in advertising agencies, those most appropriate for a marketing education are in account management, media, and marketing research.

Account management positions are a combination of personal selling and marketing management. Account managers are responsible for servicing the advertising and marketing needs of the agency's clients—a position that requires a high degree of competence in interpersonal relations and personal selling. At the same time, successful account managers are usually competent marketing analysts and planners who work closely with their clients and with the agency's departments in developing marketing, advertising, and sales promotion programs.

Media specialists are those who analyze, recommend, and often negotiate media purchases for agency clients. Marketing research in an advertising agency is similar to marketing research in a client organization, and demands similar knowledge and skills. Broadly speaking, successful people in advertising are imaginative, analytical, well organized, and exceedingly competent in interpersonal relations.

Because of the dynamic nature of advertising agencies, individuals often follow a variety of career paths. For example, I began as a media assistant in an advertising agency and subsequently became a media buyer, director of marketing research, marketing director and chairman of the plans board, account supervisor and, finally, director of account management.

Sales Promotion Specialist. As pointed out in Chapter 19 (Sales Promotion and Product Publicity), sales promotion is an exceedingly broad field involving almost everything, except media advertising, that helps promote sales. It involves the planning, development, and execution of sales promotion programs involving point-of-sale material, premiums, coupons, contests, price-off offers, trade shows, and so forth.

Sales promotion specialists are employed by client organizations, advertising agencies, and sales promotion consultants. There is little formal, academic training for the field of sales promotion. In order to be successful in the field, one should have a sound grasp of marketing, a background in the graphic arts, and skill in oral and written communications.

Public Relations and Product Publicity. Public relations and product publicity draw many of their recruits from schools of communications and journalism, although a knowledge of marketing, finance, and accounting is a distinct asset in these fields.

Career opportunities in public relations and product publicity exist in public relations consulting firms, in public relations departments in client organizations and advertising agencies, and in nonprofit organizations.

Public relations and product publicity personnel deal directly with news and entertainment media—with editors and reporters. They are responsible for interpreting marketing developments and company policies into common, everyday language, so that the media can convey stories on corporate and product events to the public. Both imagination and ability to communicate well are prerequisite for a successful public relations practitioner.

CHOOSING A CAREER AND GAINING AN ENTRY LEVEL JOB

Choosing a career and gaining an entry level job are areas unto themselves. Your university library should have a number of books on *career planning* or *career development.* Practically, these are simply how to market yourself books involving the basic principles that you have studied in this course.

Although these books differ in minor ways, they all suggest that you:

- Identify your personal strengths and interests. In other words, identify what your product is, and what you have to sell.
- Select a career field compatible with these interests. Or, in terms of marketing, identify your market.
- Identify potential companies for which you would like to work. This is comparable to selecting your target customers.
- Develop relevant information on these companies. In this step, you gather relevant information that will help you communicate with target customers.
- Develop a resumé and cover letter. This is your advertising effort. Its purpose is to obtain a personal interview.
- Participate in job interviews and establish a followup procedure with the companies where you interview. This is personal selling.

When you put all of these steps together, you have a personal marketing plan.

Many of the books which are available in the library provide sources of information about companies and career fields. They also give examples of cover letters and resumés, and suggest systematic procedures for each step in the process.

I recommend that students obtain some of these books from their university libraries and develop personal career planning programs. In addition, most universities have career counselling and placement offices that have been established to help students choose careers and find entry level positions. These services are a part of your resources. Use them.

Like marketing, choosing a career and finding an entry level position is a systematic process that requires time, effort, and imagination. As a consequence, it is a task that one should begin at least by the junior year in college. It is also a task in which the results are generally proportional to the effort expended. Good luck!

GLOSSARY

Account representative—a salesperson who calls on a large number of established customers.

A. C. Nielsen Co.—a commerical marketing research organization that offers a variety of marketing services including store audits in drug and food stores, surveys of television viewing, coupon handling, and so forth.

Advertised brands—see producer controlled brands.

Advertising—any paid form of promotion appearing in media, including direct mail.

Advertising allowance—a special payment by producers to get retailers or wholesalers to advertise the producer's products in local media.

Affect—a psychological term meaning "feelings" or "emotions."

Affordable method—a method of setting marketing budgets based on what a firm can afford to spend.

All commodity distribution—a method of measuring distribution based on dollar volume. A grocery product having 90 percent all commodity distribution would be distributed in those stores doing 90 percent of the grocery dollar volume.

American Marketing Association (AMA)—a national professional organization for those engaged in the practice and teaching of marketing.

Analytical research—a form of marketing research that focuses on "why" consumers purchase the products they buy.

Available funds—the funds available for the marketing program within a given time period, usually a year.

Backward integration—a form of business expansion in which a firm acquires the assets of a supplier in order to reduce costs and obtain a dependable source of supply.

Bait pricing—a retail strategy in which a product is offered at an unusually low price to attract customers to the store in order to trade them up to a higher-priced model with more features.

Bonded warehouses—warehouses which hold goods upon which government taxes or fees must be paid, and which will not release the goods until the taxes or fees are paid.

Brand—a name, term, sign, symbol, or design, or a combination of these elements that is intended to identify the goods or services of one seller or group of sellers and to differentiate them from competition.

Brand manager—see product manager.

Brand mark—that part of a brand that can be recognized but cannot be vocalized.

Brand name—that part of a brand that can be vocalized.

Brand share—see market share.

Break-even analysis—a method of analysis that determines the quantity of sales required so that costs equal revenues.

Break-even pricing—pricing at a level that will enable a firm to break even.

Build-up method—a method of arriving at national forecasts by preparing forecasts for individual regions and then aggregating the regional forecasts.

Buyer's market—a market condition in which surpluses give the buyer control over the conditions of sale.

Calendar of events—a chart showing the timing of various activities that make up the marketing program.

Can cutting—a term used in the grocery trade to refer to opening cans of a product so that potential buyers may view and sample the contents.

Capital—resources, such as plant and equipment, that can be used to produce goods and services.

Caveat emptor—a Latin term meaning "let the buyer beware."

Celler-Kefauver Antimerger Act—enacted in 1950, prevents the acquisition of the assets of competitive firms if the result is to lessen competition.

Central needs—psychological needs that are closely related to our sense of identity and survival.

Channel of distribution—any series of firms involved in distributing a product from the producer to the consumer.

Clayton Act—enacted in 1914 to strengthen the Sherman Antitrust Act by defining practices unlawful where the effect is to substantially lessen competition or to create monopoly.

Client organization—a business firm that produces products and/or services and retains advertising agencies and other suppliers for special services.

Club of Rome—an international, volunteer organization of political, academic, and business people concerned about the utilization of world resources.

Cogeneration—a process for producing both heat and electricity together.

Collateral businesses—support businesses in the advertising industry such as package design houses, sales promotion firms, premium shops, media buying services, marketing research organizations, printing companies, and so forth.

Common law—an ambiguous body of doctrine that governed commercial activities prior to the passage of the Sherman Antitrust Act and subsequent marketing legislation.

Complementary products—two different products are complementary when a change in the price of one will affect the demand for the other.

Concentrated marketing—a form of marketing segmentation in which the marketer concentrates on a single segment of a larger market.

Connotative meaning—a sign-object relationship that is contaminated by the attitudes of the perceiver.

Consignment selling—a form of selling in which the buyer does not have to pay the supplier until after the buyer has sold the product.

Consolidated Metropolitan Areas—adjacent Statistical Metropolitan County Areas that are growing into one another.

Conspicuous consumption—a term coined by economist Thorstein Veblen to describe the purchase of products where the purpose of the purchase is to enhance the social prestige of the purchaser.

Consumerism—an informal, but widespread social movement demanding government legislation to protect consumers from harmful products and fraudulent business practices.

Contextual meaning—meaning is taken from the particular situation in which a word, thought, or event occurs.

Contiguity—a learning principle which holds that learning occurs by associating a product with a pleasant or attractive situation through spatial or temporal proximity.

Contractual channels—a channel system based on a contractual agreement between a producer and other members of the channel of distribution.

Controllable marketing activities—those marketing activities over which a firm has control, such as the product itself, the product name, packaging, advertising, pricing, sales promotion, and method of distribution.

Convenience goods—goods which consumers purchase frequently and with minimal effort in comparison with alternatives.

Conventional warehousing—warehousing in which the primary emphasis is on storage with a minimum of service.

Cooperative organizations—a type of contractual channel arrangement in which a wholesale firm is cooperatively owned by a group of independent retailers.

Copy strategy—a brief statement that guides the preparation of advertising copy.

Corporate channels—a channel arrangement in which the producer controls the channel by virtue of ownership.

Creative boutiques—advertising agencies that specialize in developing advertising and provide no other marketing services.

Cultural pluralism—the existence within a culture of a variety of subcultures that hold beliefs and values differing in significant ways from those of the dominant culture.

Culture—the particular patterns of beliefs, values, and expectations that characterize a society and differentiate it from other societies.

Decomposition method—a method of forecasting for regions in which a national forecast is broken down or decomposed into regional forecasts based on population or some other relevant variable or variables.

Defensive technology—technology concerned with toxicology, pollution control, work safety, and quality control.

Delphi method—a method of reconciling subjective forecasts by using a sequential series of estimates derived from a panel of experts. Often used in forecasting technological change.

Demand—an economic term referring to the willingness of customers to buy. More specifically, the amount of a given product that will be bought at a particular price.

Demographics—structural dimensions of a population, such as age distribution, income distribution, family composition, occupational characteristics, and so forth.

Denotative meaning—a relatively simple sign-object relationship.

Dependency ratio—the ratio between the number of workers in a society and the number of people who are retired.

Detail salesperson—a salesperson who concentrates on performing promotional activities.

Differentiated marketing—a form of market segmentation in which the marketer employs different products and/or different marketing programs to reach two or more market segments.

Direct selling—a process in which a producer sells directly to consumers, bypassing channel intermediaries such as wholesalers and retailers.

Discretionary income—disposable income minus expenditures for necessities such as food, clothing, housing, etc.

Display allowance—a special payment by a producer to get retailers to set up special displays of the producer's product in their stores.

Disposable income—total income minus legally required deductions such as taxes, Social Security, and other legal fees.

Distribution centers—a warehouse in which the emphasis is on processing and moving goods rather than on simple storage.

Distributive justice—a study of the ways in which an organized society distributes its benefits and burdens among its members.

Distributive research—a form of marketing research focusing on the outcomes of consumer behavior; essentially concerned with who bought what.

Distributor controlled brands—brands owned or controlled by firms that are primarily in the business of distribution. Also called private labels.

Economic order quantity (EOQ)—an order quantity that strikes a balance between the size and frequency of orders that will optimize annual inventory costs.

Economic profit—the profit that a firm makes over and above its minimal profit requirements.

Economies of scale—reductions in cost that result from producing large quantities of a particular product.

Economy pricing—pricing a product at the lower end of the pricing range in order to create an impression of economy.

Engel's Laws—a series of economic propositions stating that as income rises, the proportion of income spent for different categories of goods and services will change in predictable ways.

Experience curves—a phenomenon in which costs of production decrease arithmetically as experience increases geometrically. Also referred to as the learning curve effect.

Experimental method—a marketing research technique that structures experiments to test marketing hypotheses.

Expressive performance—product performance that embodies psychological attributes such as style and expression of the self-concept.

Facilitating agencies—support organizations such as banks and other lending institutions, transportation systems, and communication specialists that facilitate the distribution process.

Feasibility analysis—determining the financial and technological feasibility of a project, specifically a new product.

Federal Trade Commission (FTC)—the federal government agency which polices antitrust activity.

Federal Trade Commission Act—enacted in 1914, this act established the Federal Trade Commission to investigate matters involving antitrust proceedings and to serve as a "friend of the court" on technical and economic issues.

Field work—the actual conducting of a marketing research survey.

Fixed and semifixed expenses—expenditures that remain relatively fixed from year to year and do not vary with level of production.

Food and Drug Adminstration (FDA)—a federal government agency charged with responsibility for protecting consumers from harmful food and drug products.

Forward integration—a form of expansion in which a firm acquires the assets of customers. For example, a producer acquires a wholesaling operation.

Franchise—a form of contractual arrangement in which the franchisor—who has developed a pattern or format for a particular business—extends to franchisees the right to conduct such a business provided they follow the established pattern.

Free economies—economies which operate on the basis of supply and demand, with price acting as the control mechanism. There is no central authority to allocate resources as in the case of a planned economy. Also referred to as marketing economies and capitalism.

Full-service advertising agencies—advertising agencies that provide a full range of marketing services.

Functional obsolescence—a product strategy in which an existing product is made to appear obsolete by adding new and attractive features to new models.

General Electric Business Screen—a display matrix which shows market attractiveness on the vertical axis and business strengths on the horizontal axis. Used in evaluating the desirability of serving a particular market or markets.

Generic brands—unadvertised, "plain label" grocery items that often sell for 30 to 40 percent less than advertised brands.

Generic product—a basic product type.

Golden circle—a marketing term for a group of brands in a particular product field, all of which are equally acceptable to consumers.

Government markets—federal, state, and local government groups and agencies that are the target of marketing activity.

Gross National Product (GNP)—the value of all goods and services produced by a nation.

Growth-share matrix—a display matrix showing market growth on the vertical axis and relative market share on the horizontal axis. Used in analyzing the cash flow and investment requirements of a firm's products.

Hierarchy of effects models—models of advertising communications which conceptualize communications as proceeding through a succession of stages from awareness to purchase.

Horizontal integration—a strategy for expansion in which a firm acquires the assets of a competitor.

Income statement—see operating statement.

Independent channels—a loose affiliation of producers, wholesalers, and retail organizations that are independently owned and operate on the basis of short–term, minimal–condition agreements.

Industrial markets—a broad term for organizations which buy goods and services used in the production of other goods and services. Generally includes producer, reseller, and government markets.

Industrial products salesperson, nontechnical—a person who sells tangible industrial products for which no high degree of technical training is required.

Information flows—the path followed by marketing information in the channel of distribution.

In-house advertising agencies—advertising agencies that are owned and controlled by client organizations.

Input-output analysis—an analysis of interindustry purchases prepared by the U.S. government.

Instrumental needs—see peripheral needs.

Instrumental performance—the performance of the physical product, per se.

Integrative growth—expansion of a firm's operation by acquiring the assets of suppliers, customers, or competitors.

Intensive distribution—widespread distribution using many retail outlets.

Inventive research—research and development activity that emphasizes the application of existing technology.

Inventory carrying costs—all costs involved in holding an item in inventory.

Invisible hand—a concept introduced by Adam Smith to explain the mechanism that enables a free economy to meet the needs of both society and individuals. The invisible hand is competition between individual buyers and sellers.

Leading indicators—a variable or series of variables that change in the same direction but *ahead* of the variable being forecast.

Learning curve effect—see experience curve.

Legislative veto—a provision enacted by Congress which gives the Congress of the United States the right of veto over rulings of administrative agencies of the government.

Line pricing—a pricing strategy in which all products in a multiple-product line are priced at the same level.

Logistics—see physical distribution.

Macromarketing—a study of the economic exchange process of a total economy.

Marginal analysis—a method of analysis which determines the optimal relationship between revenues and costs.

Marginal cost—the change in total cost that results from the production of one extra unit.

Marginal revenue—the change in total revenue that results from the sale of one extra unit.

Market—a group of people with purchasing power who are willing to spend money to satisfy their needs.

Market instability—a market condition in which a great deal of brand switching takes place.

Market potential—the upper limit of demand approached as the industry effort moves toward infinity in a given marketing environment.

Market Research Corporation of America (MRCA)—a commerical market research firm that maintains a consumer panel of persons who record all of their purchases in diaries.

Market segmentation—a marketing strategy that subdivides a total market into relatively homogeneous segments and directs marketing activity toward one or more of these segments.

Market share—that proportion of a total product market held by a particular brand. Also referred to as brand share.

Market skimming—an introductory pricing strategy of charging a high price in order to recover investment quickly.

Marketing—the performance of business activities that direct the flow of goods and services from producers to consumers.

Marketing concept—a theory of business that assumes three criteria for success: (1) meeting consumer needs; (2) making a profit; and (3) organizing the firm to serve consumers.

Marketing economies—see free economies.

Marketing information system—the entire system employed by a firm to gather, analyze, store, and disseminate relevant marketing information to those who require this data.

Marketing intelligence—that part of the marketing information system that includes those procedures a company routinely uses to keep abreast of developments in the external environment.

Marketing mix—the particular mixture of controllable marketing activities used in a specific marketing program.

Marketing plan—a basic document that develops and details the objectives, strategies, and activities for marketing a product.

Marketing research—the collection and analysis of data to help marketing managers make decisions.

Material obsolescence—a product is made of inferior materials so that it will require early replacement.

Media—vehicles that carry advertising messages, such as radio, television, magazines, newspapers, billboards, and so forth.

Merchandising—technically, merchandising refers to the activities of retail stores in selecting, pricing, displaying, and promoting the merchandise offered for sale. Marketers and advertising agencies use the term *merchandising* as a synonym for sales promotion.

Merchandising the advertising—a term which refers to "selling" the advertising and sales promotion program to channel intermediaries in order to generate enthusiasm and gain support.

Micromarketing—study of the economic exchange process of individual firms.

Middle majority—a combination of the lower-middle and upper-lower social classes. The middle majority constitutes 60 to 70 percent of the population and represents the primary market for mass produced products.

Mixed channels—the use of a variety of channel arrangements in a single distribution system.

Modular advertising agencies—full service advertising agencies that sell their services to clients on a piece-meal basis. Also referred to as *a la carte* agencies.

Monopolistic competition—a form of competition in which the product of each competitor in a particular field differs from other competitors' in some way so that an exact duplicate cannot be obtained from another source. Most competition in the United States is monopolistic competition.

Morphological research—a form of marketing research that focuses on how decisions are made.

Multiple pricing—a price reduction is offered if more than one unit is purchased.

National brands—see producer brands.

Negative elasticity—demand moves in the same direction as price.

Negotiation flow—the path that negotiations follow in the channel of distribution.

Noise—anything that interferes with the communications process.

Nonprofit marketing—the application of marketing concepts and activities to nonprofit organizations.

Nonprofit organizations—organizations such as public schools, churches, and charities, which provide a service that does not depend upon profit.

Objective and task method—a method of setting the marketing budget based on the objectives to be accomplished.

Observational technique—a research method that entails observing consumer behavior.

Odd pricing—pricing at odd amounts. For example $0.99 instead of a dollar. Also referred to as psychological pricing.

Off-brand—a brand not considered acceptable to a consumer.

Operating statement—a routine production of the accounting department that summarizes the financial results of a company's operations for a defined period. Also referred to as income statement and profit and loss (P&L) statement.

Organizational structure—the way in which a firm organizes its people and functions.

Payout plan—a projection into the future that shows funds available, funds spent, and the resulting economic profit for a proposed marketing program.

Penetration pricing—an introductory pricing strategy designed to obtain a large share of the market and thereby discourage competition from entering the field.

Percentage of sales method—a method of setting the marketing budget based on a forecast of sales.

Peripheral needs—preferences one has for alternative means of satisfying central needs. Sometimes referred to as "instrumental needs."

Physical distribution—a broad range of activities concerned with efficient movement of finished products from the producer to the consumer. Also referred to as logistics.

Physical product—the actual, physical entity or service that is offered to consumers.

Planned economies—economies in which the government owns or controls the factors of production. Allocation of resources is determined by a central authority rather than by the operation of supply and demand.

Point of equilibrium—that point at which supply equals demand.

Prestige pricing—pricing at the upper end of a price range to create an impression of prestige for the brand.

Price elastic—a change in price will yield a disproportionately large change in demand.

Price elasticity of demand—the effect that a change in price has on demand and total income.

Price inelastic—a change in price will yield a disproportionately small change in demand.

Primary demand—demand for a product type.

Primary research—marketing research that originates data to fill a specific need.

Private labels—see distributor controlled brands.

Procurement costs—all costs involved in obtaining the goods to be inventoried by a firm.

Producer controlled brands—brands owned or controlled by firms primarily in the manufacturing business. Also referred to as national brands and advertised brands.

Producer markets—firms and individuals who buy products and services used in the production of other products and services.

Product assortment—an array of products required by consumers in order to live a reasonably comfortable existence and to engage in normal human activities.

Product differentiation—a marketing strategy in which the marketer directs marketing activities toward the total market and attempts to differentiate the product from competitive products through advertising and/or trivial product differences.

Product flows—the path of the physical product through channels of distribution.

Product manager—an individual within a firm who is charged with the responsibility for marketing a particular brand. Also referred to as a brand manager.

Product market—a group of people willing to spend their money for a particular product.

Product portfolio—a group of products marketed by the same company.

Product positioning—the way in which a product is characterized to attract consumer interest and purchase. A product may be positioned in a variety of ways, such as economic, durable, stylish, safe, convenient, and so forth.

Profit—the basic measure of performance in business. Profit has only three functions in the business enterprise: (1) to reward investors; (2) as a source of future capital; and (3) as a measure of operational efficiency and effectiveness.

Profit and loss (P&L) statement—see operating statement.

Profit Impact of Marketing Strategy (PIMS)—a model for analyzing the effects of 37 variables on cash flow and return on investment for firm's operation.

Profit maximization—an economic concept that assumes the function of a business is to make the highest possible profit. The term is meaningful only in a closed system with well–defined constraints.

Promotion—a broad term that traditionally has included advertising, sales promotion, personal selling, and product publicity.

Psychographics—a loosely defined concept which differentiates groups of consumers by their activities, interests, and opinions.

Psychological pricing—see odd pricing.

Psychological product—the physical product along with its warranties, services, and psychological overtones.

Public relations—a broad term referring to a variety of practices designed to build good relations between a company and the various publics with which it deals.

Publicity—a form of promotion. In contrast to advertising, publicity is not paid for at standard rates, and the sponsor is not identified. Publicity usually appears in the editorial sections of media.

Reciprocity—a practice whereby firms buy products from companies that buy from them. It is a widespread practice in industrial marketing.

Reference group—a group with which an individual wants to be associated and whose beliefs, attitudes, values and behaviors the individual will seek to emulate. Reference groups are widely used in consumer marketing as a persuasion device.

Reference person—an individual who serves as an ideal or model and generally embodies salient group characteristics that are admired. Celebrities are used in advertising as reference persons.

Regression analysis—a statistical technique used to extrapolate past data for forecasting purposes.

Reinforcement—a learning principle which states that rewards increase learning.

Repetition—a learning principle which states that learning occurs through repeated exposures to the material to be learned.

Research and development (R&D)—that division or department of a firm engaged in research designed to develop new products, materials, or processes; and to lower production costs.

Reseller markets—firms and individuals who buy products in order to resell them to others.

Return on investment (ROI)—a profit criterion frequently used by companies to evaluate a possible investment. ROI is a ratio between the capital required for an investment and the annual profit the investment will produce.

Rights of consumers—a doctrine enunciated by President John F. Kennedy stating that consumers have the right to safety, to be informed, to choose, and to be heard.

Robinson-Patman Act—enacted in 1936, the act makes price discrimination illegal, subject to certain defenses.

Sales engineer—a person who sells products which require technical knowledge and training.

Sales plan—usually a separate document from the marketing plan. The sales plan details the activities of the sales force and coordinates them with other aspects of the marketing program.

Sales promotion—special incentives or other activities—excluding advertising, packaging, publicity, and normal pricing—directed toward consumers, the trade, or the sales force, designed to stimulate action by one of these groups.

Saturation level—the proportion of a defined group of consumers who have already purchased one or more units of a product known to have a long use life, such as a refrigerator.

Scatter diagram—a two dimensional graph upon which sales may be plotted. Time is generally represented on the horizontal axis and sales volume on the vertical axis. Also referred to as a scattergram.

Schedule—a marketing research term for the questionnaire used in making a survey.

Secondary research—marketing research data derived from published sources.

Segmentation research—a form of marketing research which uncovers new bases for market segmentation.

Selective demand—demand for a particular brand.

Selective distribution—distribution through a limited number of outlets. Also referred to as limited distribution.

Self-concept—refers to the way in which we regard ourselves. We often buy products to project our self–images to others.

Seller's market—a market condition in which scarcity gives the seller control over the conditions of sale.

Service salesperson—a person who sells intangibles such as insurance and advertising.

Share of advertising method—a method of setting the advertising budget based on a share of the total advertising being spent in a specific field.

Sherman-Antitrust Act—enacted in 1890, this legislation made monopolies or efforts to monopolize illegal.

Shopping goods—goods the consumer characteristically compares with alternative selections on the bases of price, quality, style, etc.

Sign—a term used in communications theory to refer to a stimulus that represents an object or an idea. For example, the word "apple" is a sign for a particular fruit.

Situational analysis—an assessment of the marketing environment. A key part of the marketing plan often referred to as the market review.

Social responsibility in marketing—a nebulous concept that marketers should be socially responsible regardless of the costs or effects on the profitability of the firm.

Speciality goods—goods with unique characteristics and or brand identification for which a buyer will make a special purchasing effort.

Standard Industrial Classification (SIC) Codes—numerical codes used by the U.S. government to classify industries into 496 separate categories.

Statistical Abstracts—an annual publication of the U.S. government that provides current statistics on population, production, consumption, and other economic activities.

Statistical Metropolitan County Area (SMCA)—a single city or cluster of cities of 50,000 or more population plus the county of such a central city or cities and all adjacent counties that are found to be metropolitan in character and economically and socially integrated with the central city or cities.

Stock levels—the inventory carried by a business firm.

Stocking allowance—a special allowance by a manufacturer to encourage distributor organizations to carry a particular product.

Stock-out costs—costs of lost sales because the product wanted by consumers is not available on the premises.

Store count distribution—a measure of distribution based on the number of stores. A product sold in 90 percent of all grocery stores would have 90 percent store count distribution.

Strategic Business Units (SBUs)—an autonomous profit center that serves an identifiable market, has identifiable competitors and is managed by an individual who has responsibility for its overall operation.

Strategic planning—a form of market planning that is relatively long-term in nature and is primarily concerned with the allocation of company resources among divisions and/or products.

Structural meaning—grammar and syntax wherein meaning is gained from the logical arrangement of words.

Style obsolescence—an existing product is made obsolete by changing the style of new models.

Subjective methods—a forecasting method based on the subjective opinions of people knowledgeable about the field for which the forecast is being made.

Substitute products—products that can be used as substitutes for one another. For example, beef can be used as a substitute for pork as a source of protein.

Supply—an economic term referring to the amount of a particular product or product type available for sale.

Surface changes—shifts in consumer preferences and interests that direct spending patterns from one activity to another without signaling a basic change in fundamental cultural values.

Survey method—the most common form of marketing research. The survey method entails asking people questions.

Survey of Buying Power—an annual issue of *Sales and Marketing Management* that provides basic demographic data by city, state, region, and metropolitan county areas. One volume of the survey is published in July and the other in October.

Survey of Industrial Purchasing Power—an annual issue of *Sales and Marketing Management* that reports on the industrial market by Standard Industrial Classification (SIC) Codes.

Survey of Selling Costs—an annual issue of *Sales and Marketing Management* that provides current data on selling costs.

Surveys of buyer intentions—a survey that forecasts

purchases by asking consumers what they expect to buy within the next three to six months.

Symbolic pricing—using price to create an impression about a product or brand in the minds of consumers.

Target marketing—see "market segmentation."

Test market—the use of an actual market to find out how a new product, or some change in the marketing mix, will perform under normal, competitive marketing conditions.

Title flows—the path of the title or ownership of products as they flow through channels of distribution.

Total income—all of the income received by a family or individual in the form of wages, interest, dividends, profits, pensions, Social Security payments, and so forth.

Trade name—the name under which a company conducts its business. For example, General Motors.

Trademark—a brand or part of a brand that is given legal protection because it is capable of appropriation.

Trend extensions—a group of forecasting techniques that extrapolate historic records.

Uncontrollable variables—marketing variables over which the individual firm has no control: consumers, economic conditions, technology, competition, resource availability, government regulation, and so forth.

Unitary elasticity—a change in price will be compensated for by a corresponding change in demand so that total income will remain the same.

Variable expenses—expenses that vary with the level of production.

Variable marketing expenses—marketing expenses that vary from year to year.

Venture teams—groups of experts brought together and charged with the responsibility for developing a specific product from conception to commercialization.

Voluntary organization—a type of contractual distribution arrangement in which a wholesaler contracts with independent retailers to provide specific services in return for a certain portion of the retailers' business.

Zero-sum game—a competitive activity in which the potential rewards are fixed so that, if someone wins, someone has to lose.

NAME
INDEX

SUBJECT INDEX